FINITE AND INFINITE GOODS

FINITE AND INFINITE GOODS

A Framework for Ethics

Robert Merrihew Adams

New York   Oxford

Oxford University Press

1999

Oxford University Press

Oxford   New York

Athens   Auckland   Bangkok   Bogotá   Buenos Aires   Calcutta
Cape Town   Chennai   Dar es Salaam   Delhi   Florence   Hong Kong   Istanbul
Karachi   Kuala Lumpur   Madrid   Melbourne   Mexico City   Mumbai
Nairobi   Paris   São Paulo   Singapore   Taipei   Tokyo   Toronto   Warsaw

and associated companies in
Berlin   Ibadan

Copyright © 1999 by Robert Merrihew Adams

Published by Oxford University Press, Inc.
198 Madison Avenue, New York, New York 10016

Oxford is a registered trademark of Oxford University Press

Library of Congress Cataloging-in-Publication Data
Adams, Robert Merrihew.
Finite and infinite goods : a framework for ethics /
Robert Merrihew Adams.
p.   cm.
Includes bibliographical references and index.
ISBN 0-19-512848-6
1. Religion and ethics.   I. Title.
BJ47.A33   1998
291.5—dc21   98-29122

1 3 5 7 9 8 6 4 2

Printed in the United States of America
on acid-free paper

In memory of my father,
Arthur Merrihew Adams

(1908–1979)

ACKNOWLEDGMENTS

I have taught and written about the topics of this book for approximately thirty years, accumulating far more intellectual debts than I can now remember. The book began to take shape as a series of eight Wilde Lectures in Natural Religion given in Oxford in 1989. I am grateful to Oxford University's faculties of philosophy and theology for inviting me to give the Wilde Lectures, and to Richard Swinburne, my principal host there, and Basil Mitchell for the warmness of their welcome and the helpfulness of their comments and questions.

Though they draw in various ways on older work of mine, both published and unpublished, all of the chapters were written with this book in mind. That is true even of the three that have already been published in slightly different form.

Chapter 4 (sections 2–4 and 6–7) appeared as "Moral Horror and the Sacred" in *Journal of Religious Ethics*, vol. 23, no. 2 (Fall 1995): 201–24, which is reprinted here by permission of Journal of Religious Ethics, Inc. Copyright 1995 by Journal of Religious Ethics, Inc., all rights reserved.

Chapter 9 was published as "Symbolic Value," *Midwest Studies in Philosophy* 21 (1997): 1–15, and is reprinted here with their permission.

Chapter 16 appeared as "Moral Faith" in *The Journal of Philosophy* 92 (1995): 75–95, and is reprinted here with the permission of the journal.

Fragments of other published papers of mine, often heavily revised, have been used in various chapters, as follows:

In chapter 5 some of "Pure Love" is reprinted by permission of Journal of Religious Ethics, Inc. from *Journal of Religious Ethics*, vol. 8, no. 1 (Spring 1980): 83–99. Copyright 1980 by Journal of Religious Ethics, Inc., all rights reserved.

In chapter 5 some of "Self-Love and the Vices of Self-Preference," *Faith and Philosophy*, 15 (1998): 500–13, is reprinted by permission of the editor.

In chapters 5 and 7 some of "Saints," *Journal of Philosophy* 81 (1984): 392–401, is reprinted by permission of the journal.

Chapters 7 and 8 include material from "The Problem of Total Devotion" in Robert Audi and William J. Wainwright, eds., *Rationality, Religious Belief, and Moral Commitment* (Ithaca, N.Y.: Cornell University Press, 1986), pp. 169–94.

In chapter 8 some of "The Knight of Faith," *Faith and Philosophy* 7 (1990): 383–95, is reprinted by permission of the editor.

In chapter 8 some of "Idolatry and the Invisibility of God," in Shlomo Biderman and Ben Ami Scharfstein, eds., *Interpretation in Religion* (Leiden: E. J. Brill, 1992), pp. 39–52, is reprinted by permission of the publisher.

In chapter 9 some of my review of James Wm. McClendon, Jr., *Systematic Theology*, vol. 1, *Ethics* (Nashville: Abingdon Press, 1986), which appeared in *Faith and Philosophy* 7 (1990), 117–23, is reprinted by permission of the editor.

In chapters 10 and 11 some of "Divine Commands and the Social Nature of Obligation," *Faith and Philosophy* 4 (1987): 262–75, is reprinted by permission of the editor.

In chapter 10 some of "Should Ethics Be More Impersonal? A Critical Notice of Derek Parfit, *Reasons and Persons*," *Philosophical Review* 98 (1989): 439–84, copyright 1989 Cornell University, is reprinted by permission of the publishers.

In chapter 11 some of "The Concept of a Divine Command," in D. Z. Phillips, ed., *Religion and Morality*, pp. 59–80 (published in 1996 in the United Kingdom by Macmillan and in the United States by St. Martin's Press), is reprinted by permission of the publishers.

In chapter 11 some of "Autonomy and Theological Ethics," *Religious Studies* 15 (1979): pp. 191-94. Copyright 1979 Cambridge University Press, is reprinted with permission of Cambridge University Press.

In chapter 11 some of "A Modified Divine Command Theory of Ethical Wrongness," first published in Gene Outka and John P. Reeder, Jr., eds., *Religion and Morality: A Collection of Essays* (Garden City, N.Y.: Doubleday Anchor, 1973), pp. 318–347, copyright by Gene Outka and John P. Reeder, Jr., is reprinted by permission of Professors Outka and Reeder.

In chapter 13 some of "Vocation," *Faith and Philosophy* 4 (1987): 448–62, is reprinted by permission of the editor.

In chapter 14 some of "Religious Ethics in a Pluralistic Society," first published in pp. 93–113 of Gene Outka and John P. Reeder, Jr., eds., *Prospects for a Common Morality*, Copyright 1992 by Princeton University Press, is reprinted by permission of Princeton University Press.

In chapter 15 some of "Platonism and Naturalism: Options for a Theocentric Ethics," first published in Joseph Runzo, ed., *Ethics, Religion, and the Good Society: New Directions in a Pluralistic World* (Louisville: Westminster/John Knox Press, 1992), pp. 22–42, is reprinted by permission of the publishers.

I am grateful to the publishers for granting permission to reprint the material here.

I have taught a number of courses on topics of the book, and most of the material has been presented to various philosophical audiences. I am indebted to many students and colleagues for their questions and comments, including Rogers Albritton, William P. Alston, Timothy Bays, Todd Buras, Andrew Chignell, Cheryl Clark, Mary Clark, Philip Clark, Scott Davis, John Deigh, Keith DeRose, James Doyle, Timothy Erdel, John Exdell, Arthur Fine, William FitzPatrick, Philippa Foot, Bruce Glymour, Kent Greenawalt, Daniel Guevara, Lisa Halko, James Hanink, John Hare, John Hick, Thomas E. Hill, Jr., Arthur Holmes, Frances Howard-Snyder, Janine Marie Idziak, Timothy Jackson, Asa Kasher, Gregory Kavka, Carroll Kearley, Marc Lange, Gavin Lawrence, Brian Lee, Gary Mar, George Mavrodes, James McClendon, Owen McLeod, Wesley Morriston, Dana Nelkin, Michael Otsuka, Gene Outka, Derek Parfit, Derk Pereboom, Laurie Pieper, Alvin Plantinga, Philip Quinn, Warren Quinn, John Rawls, Michael Rea, James Read, John P. Reeder, Jr., Robert C. Roberts, Maura Ryan, Ansgar Simon, Houston Smit, Rogers Smith, Jeffrey Stout, Holly Thomas, Thomas F. Tracy, Philip Turner, Carol Voeller, Virginia Warren, Paul Weithman, Dallas Willard, Nicholas Wolterstorff, Lee Yearley, Linda Zagzebski, and Dean Zimmerman. Kelly Sorensen has been an exceptionally helpful and acute research assistant in the final stages of preparing the book, and has saved me from several errors. There are undoubtedly many others whom I am now unable to name but whose comments have enriched my work on this project.

Issues about the nature of ethics have gripped my mind since college days, and I cannot forget to thank my teachers in philosophical and theological ethics, Douglas Arner, David Lyons, and Charles West. Whitney Oates, whose question addressed to me about the relation of goodness and being in Plato has stuck in my mind for nearly forty years, should not go unmentioned either.

Marilyn McCord Adams has been my most constant source of inspiration, feedback, and encouragement, and deserves my richest thanks.

Most of my research leaves for the last twenty-five years have been devoted to work that has fed into this book. The National Endowment for the Humanities granted a Younger Humanist Fellowship that enabled me to spend 1974–75 in Oxford laying the foundations of most of my subsequent work in ethics. Residential fellowships at the Center of Theological Inquiry in Princeton, New Jersey, in the fall terms of 1983 and 1984 furthered my work on the ethics of love. UCLA supported my work with sabbatical leaves and a President's Faculty Research Fellowship in the Humanities, which, together with a sabbatical, enabled me to spend 1988–89 preparing and giving the Wilde Lectures. A research leave granted by Yale for the year 1997–98 has given me the time to finish the book. The earlier leaves yielded a number of papers, but it is here that I have finally produced what I really promised. I am very grateful for all the support that has made it possible.

It is a pleasure to recall and acknowledge these debts of gratitude.

CONTENTS

FINITE AND INFINITE GOODS

INTRODUCTION

Finite and infinite goods—many finite and one infinite. This book proposes a framework for ethics that is organized around a transcendent Good and its relation to the many finite goods of our experience. Two main themes contained in this idea should be emphasized at the outset: the centrality of the *good*, and the *transcendence* of the infinite Good. I begin with the latter.

On my view, the infinite or transcendent Good is God. When I began to study moral philosophy, in the late 1950s, writers in the subject were almost unanimous in holding that ethics *could not* have religious foundations—that the nature of the good and the right (or the meaning of 'good' and 'right', as analytical philosophers then preferred to say) could not be understood in terms of facts about God, even if God exists. This view was accepted even by many theists. This surprised me, because I had grown up in an atmosphere in which religion and ethics were treated as a single, supremely important aspect of life, grounded in the nature, action, and commands of God; and this treatment seemed to me, as it still does, to make living sense. At the same time it seemed to me that there were grounds for genuine puzzlement, not just about the relation between religion and ethics, but about the nature of the good and the right, which seemed to demand or strongly invite an explanation, which I hoped might be given in theistic terms.

Over the years since then, I and others have made a number of attempts at theistic explanation in this area, chiefly along the lines of development and defense of divine command theories of the nature of obligation. I think it is fair to say that many moral philosophers now agree that theism, if accepted, could provide foundations of ethics that are at least worthy of serious consideration. Yet I have not seen, to my satisfaction at any rate, a comprehensive, up-to-date philosophical account of what a theistic framework for ethics might look like. Such an account should not limit itself to the relatively abstract topics of the nature of the good and the right, but should also explore ways in which a variety of religious concepts may enrich the texture of ethical thought. This book is an attempt to give an account of that sort.

The second main theme is at least as unfashionable as the first one. The ethical framework presented here is one in which loving the excellent and doing one's moral duty have distinct roles, both of them important; but loving the excellent has the more foundational role. Here I am pushing against a pressure that I felt long before I encountered moral philosophy. The vision of Christian ethics with which I grew up was extremely personalistic, the well-being of persons and the quality of personal relationships being its primary (and it sometimes seemed only) concerns. It was hard to see room in it for intense interest in other values, such as aesthetic and intellectual excellence. On this point the prevailing climate of contemporary moral philosophy agrees with that version of Christian ethics.

Early in the twentieth century, moral philosophy was centrally occupied with axiology—that is, with questions of goodness or value ('value' having a more "scientific" ring than 'goodness' to some philosophers of the period); and theories of "intrinsic value" flourished. In recent decades, however, the right has come to dominate the good as a topic of ethical theory, at least in anglophone philosophy. Where the good is studied, it is likely to be well-being or welfare, rather than any sort of excellence. Conceptions of intrinsic value or excellence are viewed indeed with skepticism, and it is feared that the introduction of such a notion in ethics will have inegalitarian consequences, or that ethics will be corrupted by the inclusion of aesthetic values in it.

I have long felt, however, that our view of the values of human life will be distorted if we do not give full weight in our ethical thinking to intrinsic excellences, including those that may be classified as aesthetic or intellectual. To that I would add that theists have a special reason to care about loving the excellent, inasmuch as worship celebrates an excellence in God that is surely much more than narrowly moral. I will develop these points, and respond to some of the fears about excellence, in several parts of the book.

In its emphasis both on excellence and on a transcendent Good, my framework for ethics is broadly Platonic as well as theistic. In the prevailing climate of opinion in anglophone moral philosophy, Kantian, Aristotelian, and utilitarian approaches to ethics flourish, but Platonic approaches are rarely investigated as an object of any contemporary interest. I believe, and will try to show in this book, that this neglect of Platonism in ethics is unjustified. To avert misunderstanding, however, I should say at once that my approach is by no means as comprehensively Platonic as it is theistic. I borrow some main themes from Plato in the first chapter but will be found in disagreement with him at quite a number of points, especially in later chapters.

The book proposes "a framework for ethics."[1] That is meant to suggest something a bit broader than "metaethics." It does not consist purely of higher order reasoning *about* ethical reasoning but also addresses a number of first-order ethical issues—as perhaps any theory about the nature of ethics must, if it is to be credible. Much of the book is concerned with the traditional topics of metaethics: the meaning of such terms as 'good' and 'wrong', the nature of the properties or facts (if any) signified by them, and the grounds for belief about such things—the semantics, metaphysics, and epistemology of value and obligation, as I shall put it. In order to put some flesh on the bones of a theory of the nature of the good, however, I have thought it advisable to devote a good deal of attention to such substantive ethical topics as the nature of human well-being (in chapter 3) and the place of love in ethics (in chapters 5 to 9). I have not tried to avoid committing myself on controversial moral issues. Still, the book presents a framework, not a complete ethics. It is a framework within which one could come to quite various conclusions about many important ethical issues.

It may be clarifying to say something more at this point about the role of theism in the book. It has become unusual in philosophical writing to make substantive use of theistic hypotheses (as was still done routinely in the seventeenth century) in discussing topics that are of interest independently of theism. That is exactly what I have done, however, in large parts of this book. I have done it because I believe that theistic hypotheses suggest and facilitate real enrichments of our understanding of these subjects, not least by helping us to focus on categories, and phenomena, that moral philosophy has too long neglected. And I have done it without trying first to "prove" the existence of God because I believe that if theism can be commended persuasively to our modern minds, it will be in large part through the felicity of the contribution it can make to our treatment of such topics of common concern.

One could perhaps present theism's contributions to ethics by beginning in a way that is quite neutral regarding theism, developing the initial stages of all the main topics in that framework, and only then bringing in God, arguing in the second part of the book that the best solutions to the problems developed in the first part are theistic. That is not the way I thought out the book, and that is not the way I have chosen to present it. Precisely because of the moral illumination I find in theistic views, it is no ambition of mine to think through as much as possible of ethical theory in a way that is quarantined from theistic influence. I am trying to think through the whole field of ethics, especially its more structural features, from a certain point of view. It is a theistic point of view. There is no part of the work that is uninfluenced by that point of view. The choice of certain structural features for more emphatic and detailed treatment, for example, is largely determined by the point of view.

It does not follow that my arguments presuppose theism at every point. It is an important virtue in philosophical method to present arguments with the most eco-

1. 'Framework' is not a technical term here, and is not meant to suggest any of the (sometimes relativistic) theories of "conceptual frameworks" that are in the philosophical air. Most of the issues to be discussed in the book are not purely conceptual issues.

nomical assumptions (of those one actually believes) that will suffice for them. As a result, considerable parts of this work are developed and argued in a way that does not presuppose theism, or even an interest in theism. I doubt, however, that a nontheistic fragment could be extracted from the book that would cover the full range of ethical theory that the book itself does. It might be possible to adapt from parts I and II an account of the nature of the good, and loving the good, that could be included in a nontheistic Platonism, though I think the argument would be significantly weakened by abandoning the supposition that the Good itself is a lover. But if such a Platonism would have a theory of obligation at all, it would have to take quite a different line from that which I have pursued in part III. And moralists who do not believe in any sort of transcendent Good will have to reject even more of my framework, though they may find themselves in agreement with me on particular points.

The book began as a series of eight Wilde Lectures in Natural Religion delivered at Oxford University in the spring of 1989. The Wilde Lectureship belongs jointly to the faculties of philosophy and theology, and the lectures were prepared with the interests of both faculties in mind. I hope that the finished book will be of interest to both philosophers and theologians, as well as to others concerned with ethics and with religion.

It is philosophy throughout, employing philosophical methods of analysis, argument, and theory construction. If it is also theology, it is philosophical theology. It is not dogmatic theology or theology for a particular religious tradition. Its author is a Christian, but it is not a Christian book or a study of Christian ethics. It doubtless bears in various ways the impress of my own moderately liberal Protestant beliefs, but the framework presented here is intended to have room in it for other forms of theistic ethics, including forms of Jewish and Islamic as well as Christian ethics (though I make no claim to have avoided positions that may be controversial in one or more of these traditions, including my own). This is one of the ways in which it is important that the book presents a framework rather than a complete ethics. Although it does not incorporate a theology for any particular religious community, it is not opposed to such theologies, and it includes (in the last section of chapter 15) discussion of a place that "special revelations" claimed by such theologies might occupy in the framework.

The subject about which I am offering theistic hypotheses is not religious ethics as such, or any particular brand of it, but rather the nature of any valid ethics, the nature of the good and the right that I assume to concern human beings generally, of all religious convictions and of none. In this I make the controversial assumption that fundamental questions about ethics can usefully be discussed from a perspective that is not relativized to a particular historic tradition. This assumption receives only tangential discussion here (chiefly in chapter 15, section 2), but "the proof of the pudding is in the eating."

The book is therefore an essay in moral philosophy as well as the philosophy of religion. It offers a comprehensive framework for ethics, dealing with most of the main questions that any framework for ethics must address. The book's discussion of God and religion is less comprehensive; I have discussed only those issues that I think important for a framework for ethics. Two in particular that do come up, but are not discussed comprehensively, deserve mention here. One is the existence of God. Much that is asserted here certainly implies that God exists, and thus must be false if there is no God; but God's existence is not proved here. In showing advantages of a theistic theory of the nature of ethics, the book does in effect give reasons for accepting theism, but a complete case for theism would involve other considerations that fall outside the scope of a framework for ethics.

The book's most important omission is that it does not address the problem of evil. This problem is closely connected with the topic of the book, and in chapter 16 I have something to say about dealing with it (and I have said more elsewhere); but it is too large a subject in its own right to be treated with any adequacy here. The book does not in fact contain a complete enough theology to define the shape of the problem of evil. For instance, it does not imply any definite position on the nature or extent of God's power. If that reduces, it does not eliminate the book's exposure to the problem, which remains one of the background issues pertinent to our thinking about a theistic framework for ethics.

As philosophy, the present work is intended, of course, to be a *rational* treatment of the issues discussed in it, and that not in a merely procedural sense. I conceive of rationality as a sort of excellence: excellence in responding to reasons. This excellence can and should be manifested in action and emotion as well as belief. Conceiving of it in such a frankly and irreducibly evaluative sense, I cannot without circularity assign to rationality as foundational a role as many philosophers want it to have in an account of the nature of value. 'Rational' and 'irrational', therefore, have evaluative force for me, but they are not among my most fundamental evaluative terms and do not have a major structural role in my framework for ethics.

A brief outline of some of the book's main lines of argument may be helpful to the reader. The part played by God in my account of the nature of the good is similar to that of the Form of the Beautiful or the Good in Plato's *Symposium* and *Republic*. God is the supreme Good, and the goodness of other things consists in a sort of resemblance to God. How that resemblance is to be understood is a major topic of chapter 1, where I also argue that developments in the philosophy of language have made it possible to distinguish theories (such as this one) about the *nature* of the good from theories about the *meaning* of 'good'. The resemblance of other goods to the supreme Good is profoundly imperfect; in that sense it *transcends* them. This is a recurrent theme of the book and the main point of contrasting "finite and infinite goods." Chapter 2 develops the conception of a transcendent Good and tries to show some of its advantages for ethical theory, in comparison with an important contemporary naturalistic alternative. In the process, in sections 3 and 4, it introduces another recurrent theme of the book, the wisdom of relying on inferences from 'ought' to 'is', or from value to (other sorts of) fact, especially in moral theology.

The type of good principally exemplified by God, as transcendent Good, is intrinsic excellence. This type of good is widely neglected in contemporary moral philosophy in favor of well-being, but in chapter 3 I argue that well-being itself is best understood in terms of excellence. Another morally important type of value which many would contrast with excellence is the value of persons as persons. I believe it is a main form of a type of value that we may call the *sacred*, and in chapter 4 I try to develop an account of the sacred in terms of images of God, and thus in terms of excellence. I get at this concept largely by way of our horror at certain forms of evil that are plausibly viewed as violations of something sacred; and chapter 4 contains the book's main discussion of the nature of *evil*. I argue that evil is not to be understood in terms of a transcendent anti-ideal, parallel to the supreme Good. Evil does not stand on the same explanatory level as good, but the nature of evil is to be understood in terms of that of the good. Insofar as it is something more than the merely less good, evil is something that opposes the good.

If we ask what is the importance of the good in ethical theory, we may think first of *doing* good, or of the good as something to be brought into being. This is obviously important, but it must be far from the whole story in a theory organized around a transcendent Good, since no good that we can do is commensurate with the transcendent Good. Our appropriate ethical relation to the good is therefore conceived more broadly here, as being *for* the good, and first of all as *loving* the good, which is a major theme of the whole book, beginning in chapter 1, but also the special subject of part II (chapters 5 to 9). I begin with God's love, which is ideal love and plays an important part in the theory. I argue in chapter 5 that there is room in such love for an *Eros* that prizes relationships and nonmoral goods for their own sake, and in chapter 6 that a sound understanding of the roles of particularity and universality in love supports a characterization of divine and ideal love as *grace*. Chapter 7 presents a human motivational ideal of devotion to the Good as organizing one's whole motivational system. I address serious problems about the integration of loves for finite goods with each other and into love for God or the Good itself, including the danger that love for the supreme Good will swamp and annihilate other loves we should have, and the danger of undue devotion to finite goods that are indeed worth loving. The former danger is a main topic of chapter 7; the latter is discussed in chapter 8 in terms of idolatry.

One of our main problems in being for the good is that because of our finitude we can be for it only in very imperfect and fragmentary ways. We cannot attend to more than a small fraction of actual and possible good, and what we can do about what we do attend to is very limited. We can extend the reach of our love for the good in some ways by being for the good *symbolically*, though this of course must not be substituted in general for nonsymbolic doing and loving the good; the importance of this possibility for ethics is explored in chapter 9. I conceive of human love for the good as a fragmentary and imperfect participation in an inclusive and perfect divine love. This is a major theme of part II, but a main part of its development comes in the discussion of *vocation*, which is reserved for chapter 13, in part III, because the concept of vocation, as an assignment to individuals of their parts in God's love, involves the concept of obligation (the subject of part III), as well as that of goods to be loved.

The good is *worth* loving and doing; an obligation is what we *have* to do. In chapter 10 I argue that obligation, premoral or moral, should be understood in terms of social requirement, and that moral obligation should be understood also in relation to the good. In chapter 11 I argue further that the requirements constituting moral obligation are best understood as divine commands. This will raise in some minds the question 'What if God commanded something evil?' I address this fear in chapter 12.

Political philosophy is an important branch of the theory of the right. It is too large a field to be treated comprehensively here, but I cannot altogether avoid it, because my theory stands in obvious tension with currently influential versions of political liberalism that seek to insulate political thinking from religious ideas and from many ideas about the good as distinct from the right. In chapter 14 I argue that conceptions of the good have a legitimate and important role in political thought, and even in the grounding of the civil liberties most prized (and rightly so) by liberalism.

Throughout the book I rely freely on ethical and other evaluative judgments that I accept and that I hope most others will also be prepared to accept as true or correct. I was tempted to try to establish my title to these beliefs by beginning the book with a systematic treatment of the epistemology of value. Resisting this temptation, I have reserved that systematic treatment for part IV (chapters 15 and 16), at the end of the book, because I believe my treatment of the nature or metaphysics of the good and the right has more light to shed on epistemology than to receive from it. Our main title to the value judgments with which I think we must begin in any consideration of ethics is that through participation in a social practice of forming evaluative beliefs we have learned to do so, and have no attractive alternative to relying on the ability so acquired. This point is developed in chapter 15, where I also argue that my account of the nature of the good and the right warrants thinking of evaluative belief formation in terms of revelation, and argue further that vision of the Good should be given priority over causal inferences in thinking about revelation. Finally, in chapter 16, I argue that the dependence on *faith*, which I acknowledge is present in ethics, is not introduced by the religious aspects of my theory, but is intrinsic to morality.

I

THE NATURE
OF THE GOOD

1

GOD AS THE GOOD

> For whoever has been educated to this point in the things of love, beholding the beautiful things in order and rightly, coming now to the completion of the things of love, will suddenly perceive something astonishingly beautiful in its nature. All his previous labors, Socrates, were for the sake of this.
>
> (Plato, *Symposium* 210 E)

Thus Plato has Diotima introduce Socrates to the idea of a transcendent Beauty. Beautiful itself, it is the standard of all beauty, and all other beautiful things are beautiful by "participating" in it (211 B). It is eternal, unperishing, and (above all) unqualifiedly beautiful; whereas the beautiful objects of ordinary experience are beautiful at some time and place and ugly at others, beautiful in some respect or in some relation but ugly in others, beautiful for some people and ugly for others (211 A). Nevertheless, in experience and love of ordinary beauties, we can have some intimation of the transcendent Beauty.

These claims about the Beautiful embody main features of a Platonic structure for the realm of value and ethics. It is a structure organized around the Good; beauty is clearly a species of good for Plato,[1] and the role assigned to the Beautiful in the *Symposium* is recognizably a version of the role that belongs to a more general (and still transcendent) Good in the *Republic*. What sort of good is at issue here? It is not *usefulness*, or merely instrumental goodness. It is not *well-being*, or what is good for a person. It is rather the goodness of that which is worthy of love or admiration.

---

1. The word that clearly means *beautiful* in this context in Plato's Greek, καλός, can mean *good* more generally, normally with a connotation of intrinsic excellence; 'noble' is sometimes an appropriate English translation.

We have no word that in common usage signifies precisely and uniquely this kind of goodness; I shall refer to it often (though not always happily) as "excellence," and sometimes (where I see on the horizon no confusion with other sorts of goodness) simply as "goodness" or the "good." Moral virtues are excellences in this sense, but Platonic excellence is not exclusively moral; beauty is a prime example of it (the example showcased in the *Symposium*).

These features of a Platonic structure for the realm of value are also features of the framework for ethics that I will present here. It is a framework in which the transcendent Good is God. There are obvious points of affinity between Platonism and theism. Aspiration for a transcendent good is central to both, and so is the focus on excellence. Worship, after all, is the acknowledgment, not just of God's benefits to us, but of the supreme degree of intrinsic excellence. So it is not surprising that historically the most influential type of theistic theory of the good has been broadly Platonistic. Beginning with things that Plato says in his middle dialogues about the Form of the Good or the Beautiful, it follows a strategy associated with the name of Augustine of Hippo, but which probably originated with pagan and Jewish Platonists in Alexandria shortly before the birth of Jesus. The role that belongs to the Form of the Good in Plato's thought is assigned to God, and the goodness of other things is understood in terms of their standing in some relation, usually conceived as a sort of resemblance, to God. For centuries most philosophical theologians in the West made some use of this strategy. Here I will explore a version of it.[2]

It will be a theory of value, not a theory of universals. I will not expound Plato's general theory of Forms, and have no desire to defend it. My aims here, moreover, are not primarily historical. Although some of what I will say could be read as interpretation of Plato, I do not mean to discuss, except occasionally and incidentally, whether it accurately represents beliefs that Plato held.[3] It may be worth noting, however, two apparent strands that are sometimes distinguished in Plato's thought; one in which the Forms are conceived of primarily as properties or universals, and one in which they are conceived of primarily as exemplars. To the extent that I am following Plato at all, it is as an exemplar that I am conceiving of the Good itself. If God is the Good itself, then the Good is not an abstract object but a concrete (though not a physical) individual. Indeed it is a *person*, or importantly like a person.

Like Plato's, mine will be a theory of nonmoral as well as moral value. The divine greatness adored in the Bible, by the mystics, and in the traditions of theistic worship is by no means exclusively moral. God is the exemplar or standard of a goodness that includes much more than moral virtue. Among the Platonic roles inherited by God, so to speak, is that of Beauty itself.

2. A paper, then unpublished, by William P. Alston entitled "What Euthyphro Should Have Said" helped arouse my interest in this topic; see now Alston, *Divine Nature and Human Language*, pp. 267–73. (Full bibliographical information for all references is given in the Bibliography.)
3. And, if so, during what period of his career. In particular, though I will be developing a conception of the Good itself as something that is itself good and that has the sort of independence or "separateness" from other good things that is commonly ascribed to Platonic Forms, I will not enter into debate about the extent to which Plato himself conceived of it in that way.

1. The Semantics and the Metaphysics of Value

A particularly important obstacle has until recently stood in the way of Platonist views about ethics gaining the attention of analytical philosophers. Their style of philosophy is called "analytical" because it was long guided by the belief that the only way philosophy can make real progress in understanding is by analysis of the meanings of words or sentences. Philosophers were urged, accordingly, to shift from the "material mode" to the "formal mode"—from talking about the natures of things to talking about the meanings of words that signify them—for instance, from talking about the nature of the good to talking about the meaning of 'good'. The principal task of moral philosophy, on this view, was analysis of the meaning of the language of morals.

Platonist theories of the Good have not generally been intended as linguistic analysis, and are not well equipped for the transition to the "formal mode." They simply are not very plausible as accounts of what is ordinarily *meant* by 'good'. They go far beyond any such ordinary meaning. I freely grant, for example, that 'good' does not *mean* the same as 'resembles God', though I do favor the view that the goodness of finite things consists in a sort of resemblance to God. It is not the meaning of 'good' but the nature of goodness that I mean to analyze.

This need not be any longer an obstacle to entertaining and accepting Platonist theories in ethics. The time is past when moral philosophers (and I mean those still called "analytical" philosophers) made it their primary business to analyze ethical language. This change in moral philosophy is largely grounded in developments in the philosophy of language over the last half century. The point I want to emphasize about these developments is that they show ways to distinguish questions of the natures of things from questions of meaning, and to take the former seriously as metaphysical rather than semantical questions.

This approach has been developed most famously with respect to natural kinds. It is the nature of water to be H_2O, it is claimed; and the property of being water is, necessarily, identical with the property of being H_2O. But the word 'water' does not *mean* H_2O. What I must know, at least implicitly, about water in order to understand the sense of the word 'water', and so to be a competent user of the word, is that if there is a single chemical nature shared by most of the stuff that I and other English-speakers have been calling "water," then, of necessity, all and only stuff of that nature is water. The causal relations between concrete samples of water, on the one hand, and users and uses of the word 'water', on the other hand, serve to "fix the reference" of the word—that is, to determine which stuff the word names. But the nature of water is to be discovered in the water and not in our concepts.[4]

These ideas are commonly treated as if they were only about natural kinds. But there is a generalizable insight in them about the relation of natures to meanings, and hence about the relation of metaphysics to semantics. Whether or not we do

---

4. A now-classic source for this view, with water serving as example, is Putnam, *Mind, Language, and Reality*, vol. 2, pp. 196–290. I have made a similar use of it in discussing the nature of wrongness, in Adams, "Divine Command Metaethics Modified Again."

use the word 'water' as these views claim, we certainly could use a word in that way. And I am proposing that we do use ethical terms in an analogous way, which enables us to distinguish between the semantics of ethical discourse and what we may call the metaphysical part of ethical theory. Not that good, for example, is a natural kind; but the meaning of the word 'good' may be related to the nature of the good in something like the way that has been proposed for natural kinds.

In the sixth book of the *Republic* (505 D–E)[5] Plato refers to the Good as "what every soul pursues, doing everything for the sake of it, divining that it is something, but perplexed and unable to grasp adequately what it is or to have such a stable belief [about it] as about other things, and therefore missing whatever utility the other things might have." Plato speaks of people who "divine" that there is such a thing as the good, and who "pursue" it, but do not "grasp adequately what it is." Presumably they are competent users of the word 'good' (or ἀγαθός in Greek), and understand (at least roughly and implicitly) whatever is given by the sense of that word, but do not know the nature of the good. Perhaps they do not take themselves to know it, since Plato says they are "perplexed" and do not have "a stable belief" on the subject.

This is a very plausible description of the way the concept of good works in ordinary life. When we speak of "good" we do typically suppose that there is such a thing as good and that we are pursuing it. But we need not suppose that we begin our pursuit with a very adequate grasp of the nature of the good. On the contrary, a better understanding of the good is often a major part of the object of our quest. And we surely do not assume that an understanding of the nature of the good is within our grasp by virtue of our competent use of the word 'good'.

As good is not a natural kind in the way that water is, the meaning of the word 'good' does not direct us to anything like a chemical structure. And we cannot assume that causal interactions with concrete samples will fix the reference of 'good' in the same way that the reference of 'water' is fixed. What is it, then, that connects the word 'good' with things that are good, or with the property that is goodness?

It is possible, I think, to indicate a general pattern for the relation of natures to meanings where the nature is not given by the meaning. What is given by the meaning, or perhaps more broadly by the use of the words, is a role that the nature is to play. If there is a single candidate that best fills the role, that will be the nature of the thing. In the case of a natural kind, arguably, the role its nature is assigned by our language is that of accounting causally for the observable common properties of identified samples. The role that the meaning of 'good' picks out for the nature of the good will be rather different.

In speaking of a role that the meaning of the word 'good' picks out, I must relativize my claims to the meaning 'good' has *in certain contexts*. What most inter-

---

5. Plato is sketching here an ignorance from which the Guardians of his ideal state are to be delivered, though no such deliverance is offered to us as readers of the *Republic*. For my present, nonhistorical purpose, I think it is reasonable to abstract from that feature of the context.

ests me is not the word, but something we often use the word to talk about. We all know that a word is often used to talk about quite different things, and the same thing may be signified by different words. Accordingly, a theory of the nature of the good need not be an account of something that is signified by 'good' in *all* its contexts of use.

The contexts that primarily concern me here are those in which 'good' or 'goodness' is naturally interpreted as meaning *excellence*. There are undoubtedly contexts in which it means some other sort of value, such as well-being (a person's good) or instrumental good. What is required of a candidate for the role of the excellent is different from what is demanded by the roles of other sorts of goodness. This applies even to something so fundamental as the ontological categories of things that can possess the different sorts of value.

States of affairs, for example, can certainly have instrumental value, and can arguably be desirable for their own sake. In much recent ethical theory, indeed, states of affairs are taken as the primary subjects of goodness, perhaps because of the widespread (not exclusively utilitarian) interest in calculating the values of outcomes, which are of course states of affairs. Excellence is not a property of states of affairs, however. Consider beauty, the sort of excellence with which I began this chapter. What types of thing can be beautiful? Persons, of course; physical objects; some kinds of abstraction (such as poems and mathematical proofs); qualities (such as a beautiful shade of blue); deeds; lives—but not in general states of affairs. States of affairs do not typically have the sort of unity that is required for beauty. I believe that excellence in general is like beauty in this respect; and I think that is something we can learn by reflection on the meaning or the grammar (in a broad sense) of the language we use to speak about excellence, including 'good' in contexts where it signifies the excellent. A good candidate for the role of goodness in the sense of excellence, therefore, will not be a property of states of affairs.

For this reason an ethical framework in which excellence is the central type of goodness will not have the globalizing structure that is characteristic of consequentialist theories. It is mainly particular objects that are excellent, and that are to be respected and cherished by one who loves the excellent. Maximization of the sum of excellence in the world (if such a sum can be computed), or of the degree of excellence attained somewhere in the world, may not itself be excellent.

There is an even more fundamental issue that calls for a discrimination of contexts. Insisting on a theory that fits the meaning of 'good' in *all* contexts would probably stack the deck in favor of noncognitivist, emotivist theories. For there are few contexts in which saying that something "is good" does not express (sincerely or otherwise) a favorable attitude toward it; and there are prominent contexts in which it seems to express nothing else. Consider a Mets fan who says "Good!" when she hears that the Mets have beaten the Dodgers. She is certainly expressing a favorable attitude toward the event; but she probably supposes that Dodgers fans who say "That's too bad" at the same news are not disagreeing with her about a matter of objective fact, but simply expressing contrary feelings. But this does not show there are not other contexts in which 'good' is used to assert a supposed objective fact, and not solely to express a favorable attitude. It is a legitimate project for ethi-

the nature of the good as consisting in some fact about our desires. The role of our desires, on my view, is only to help fix the signification of our value terminology to a property or object that has its own nature independent of our desires.

Not that I can allow unbounded scope for error here. Though we are often misguided in Eros, I think we cannot always or even usually be totally mistaken about goodness. For the role that our use of evaluative language assigns to goodness is partly determined also by the things that we regard as good. It must be, to some significant extent, a property that we do see in those things. If there is indeed a single best candidate for the role of the Good itself, or the property of goodness, there may certainly be *some* things that do not agree with it, and therefore fail to be good, though virtually all of us think they are good. But a property that belonged mainly to things that almost all of us have always thought were bad would surely not be filling the role picked out by our talk of "goodness."

Goodness is therefore an object not only of admiration and desire, but also of *recognition*, at least commonly and to some degree. That is part of the role it must fill. Something's seeming good to us is not what makes it good on my view, not what its goodness consists in. But if we do not place some trust in our own recognition of the good, we will lose our grip on the concept of good, and our cognitive contact with the Good itself. And I think the most relevant sort of recognition of the good, like the most relevant sort of admiration and desire, is to be found in Eros. One can doubtless regard something as beautiful or good without loving it, and perhaps without really admiring it. But I think that is a secondary sort of recognition of beauty or goodness, parasitic on that which takes place in love and admiration. Once our admiring Eros has been awakened by some objects, we can recognize others as relevantly similar to them without actually loving the new objects. But if we had never loved beauty, we would never have a concept of it.

Nevertheless, we certainly do make mistakes about the good, and our Eros is sometimes misguided. My claim must therefore not be that the good is always in fact, and in the most straightforward sense, the object of our Eros. It must be something subtler than that. The thesis in this vicinity that seems to me most clearly correct is that to the extent that anything is good, in the sense of 'excellent', it is *good* for us to love it, admire it, and want to be related to it, whether we do in fact or not.

This exemplifies an important and more general point about the roles that are built into the meanings of evaluative and normative terms. They relate the values to other values,[11] as well as to nonevaluative features of life and the world. They involve a position, so to speak, in a structured system of values. In particular, there is a logical connection between the values of things and the norms they satisfy, on the one hand, and how it is *good* to value them or respond to them evaluatively, on the

---

11. Here is another relation of this sort that may be involved in my theory, though I don't propose to pursue it here. Admiration, as involved in Eros, plays a part in my account of the role of the good, and it may be an essential feature of admiration that the admired object is regarded as good. Belief in the goodness of the object may be incorporated in admiration, and hence in Eros. Any suspicion of circularity to which this gives rise may be dealt with along the same lines I will follow in dealing with related suspicions in the text.

other hand. To say that an act is unjust is to imply that it is good (other things being equal) to be indignant at it (or remorseful, if one was the perpetrator). Similarly, to say that an object is beautiful is to imply that it is good to admire it.

How much can this point help us in "fixing the reference" of 'goodness' or 'excellence' to a nature that things may be thought to have or lack objectively? Can I claim, for example, that if it is good to admire or love *x*, that is because *x* resembles God in a certain way? I do mean to claim that, but will the claim help me to ground a realism about values? In particular, can I reasonably be a realist about the claim itself, so as to establish a realism at the metaethical level?

A look at a somewhat similar contemporary project may help us here. Elizabeth Anderson proposes that "to judge that something is good is to judge that it is properly valued" and "that the judgment that *x* is intrinsically valuable entails that (under normal conditions) *x* is properly intrinsically valued, independent of the propriety of valuing any other particular thing."[12] Anderson and I are in agreement about the logical relation between 'good' and 'good to value'. She does not seem to want to use this relation to fix the reference of value predicates to objective properties; indeed, she seems to want to avoid identifying values with such properties.[13] But she does hope to obtain a considerable measure of objectivity by identifying propriety of valuing with a certain kind of rationality of valuing.[14] She is more optimistic than I am about what rationality theories can accomplish in metaethics, or aspires to a less robust realism about value, or both; I'm not sure which.

At present, however, I am concerned with a different issue in her position. Excellence, as I conceive of it, is a form of what Anderson calls "intrinsic value," and I agree with her that what possesses such value "is properly intrinsically valued, independent of the propriety of valuing any other particular thing." That's right as far as it goes, but I don't think it provides *enough* independence.

For Anderson, the propriety of valuing one object that is excellent will be independent of the propriety of valuing other objects at the same level, reflecting the fact that excellence is not a form of instrumental value, and is thus independent of the values of the other objects; but it will not be independent of values at other levels that may be served by the valuing. Anderson holds that higher order values or "ideals," which are largely social, control the propriety of valuing. Her theory of goods

> does not concern itself exclusively with the qualities of the goods people enjoy. It also focuses on the realization of distinct ideals of the person and community, and it views goods as mediating these relations among people. Ideals require people to care about goods in particular ways. . . . Treating a good as a particular kind of good is as much a way of realizing and expressing appropriate relations among people as it is a way of properly evaluating the good itself.[15]

12. Anderson, *Value in Ethics and Economics*, p. 2f.
13. Anderson, *Value in Ethics and Economics*, pp. 90, 112.
14. Anderson, *Value in Ethics and Economics*, pp. 3, 91–97.
15. Anderson, *Value in Ethics and Economics*, p. 14.

My concern is that this opens a culturally weak type of value, such as the aesthetic, to domination by a culturally strong type, such as the political. In fact Anderson explicitly advocates reflection on political implications as an important factor in evaluating the rational propriety of aesthetic valuations, and argues that this enhances the prospects of her theory for achieving objectivity in matters of value.[16] In Anderson's main application of her view to a particular aesthetic issue, about music, she manages to weave political considerations into her discussion in such a way that the reasons she actually offers all have, arguably, a direct aesthetic relevance. It is not clear to me, however, that there is anything in her theory to keep aesthetic considerations from being dominated (though presumably not totally obliterated) by political considerations that have, intuitively, no direct aesthetic relevance. That is ironic, inasmuch as it is one of Anderson's main aims to provide for the distinctness of different kinds of value.

I believe the claim that *x* is excellent implies not only that it is good to value *x*, but also that this goodness of valuing *x* is grounded in the excellence of *x* and independent of ulterior values that may be served by the valuing. In other words, the claim that *x* is good implies that it is, in Anderson's sense, *intrinsically* good to value *x*. Indeed, I think it must be *excellent* to value what is excellent, and that raises a worry about circularity in using the logical connection between 'good' and 'good to value' to help to fix the reference of 'goodness' (in the sense of excellence) in a way that supports a robust realism at the metaethical level. The worry is not about circularity in verbal definition, since I am not attempting that sort of definition. It is rather that if we are trying to ground the objectivity of judgments of excellence, appeal to a judgment of excellence (about excellence of valuing) introduces what looks like a vicious circle in the grounding of objectivity.

Let us consider, therefore, an alternative rendering of the Platonic thought that the Good is what we are pursuing. Can it be that the actual human quest that we think of as the quest for the excellent or the intrinsically good somehow picks out an objective property and fixes the reference of 'goodness' (in the sense of excellence) to that property? Not that in pursuing the good, or in thinking about the pursuit, we necessarily know what that nature is; but that the pursuit points in a certain direction, so to speak, and goodness is the property that is uniquely found in that direction, or that reaches the farthest in that direction. Or, perhaps more accurately, excellence is to be understood in terms of an ideal that lies far beyond the observable objects we regard as excellent, but in a direction that they combine with our pursuit to point out to us.

That's too pictorial a way of putting it, of course. Here's an attempt at a more precise formulation. The character of our pursuit of excellence, including the character of the things we think are excellent, determines what sort of thing would *satisfy* the pursuit. Now suppose there is a single property or nature such that an ideally knowledgeable judge would say that it is clearly what would best satisfy the pursuit, in the sense that it would most closely fit the criteria indicated by the character of the pursuit. That property or nature will *be* excellence—and objectively so, it may be claimed.

16. Anderson, *Value in Ethics and Economics*, pp. 12–14, 95–97.

Plato seems to hold some such view about the Form of the Good: that it is in principle possible, though extraordinarily difficult, for us to develop our minds in such a way that we at last attain an adequate "view" of that Form, and that in that ideally knowledgeable condition we will recognize it as what we were really seeking under the title of "the good." Theists hold similar views about God. In one version it is possible for humans (in this life or the next) to attain a "beatific vision" of God, which is both as adequate and truthful a cognition of God as we could ever have, and one that will leave us in no doubt that God is supremely and unsurpassably the good that we (in our better moments, at any rate) were seeking. In a different but compatible version the ideally competent judge is God, who does judge that the divine nature is what maximally satisfies our pursuit of excellence, and that the excellence of other things is therefore best understood in terms of Godlikeness. Three objections to this approach may be considered.

1. It may be argued that we are still relying on value judgments in identifying the nature of value. We may seem to avoid one value judgment by explaining "best satisfy the pursuit" as "most closely fit the criteria," but that seems likely to involve us in other value judgments, as to which criteria express the *best* interpretation of the character of the pursuit, and what factors are most *important* in determining overall closeness of fit. Likewise the concept of an ideally knowledgeable judge seems to introduce an evaluation—indeed, an evaluation of cognitive *excellence*. At this point we may begin to suspect that there is no way of grounding the objectivity of value judgments, at the metaethical level, that does not rely on judgments of value, and indeed of excellence; and I think that is probably right.

My response is to suggest that our reasonable aspiration is not to get value judgments out of the foundations of objectivity, which is probably impossible, but to allow there only value judgments that are very plausibly objective. Judgments of closeness of fit can be very plausibly objective, if they are based on extensive knowledge and are not, intuitively, "close calls." And the one and only factually omniscient being, if reflectively and unselfishly sympathetic, would very plausibly be classified as an objectively ideal judge.

If this gives rise to doubts about the sort of objectivity or metaphysical realism I can claim at the metaethical level, something similar is probably true of the claims that link metaphysics with semantics on any topic. Consider the standard example of the nature of water, discussed in section 1. It is claimed that the meaning of 'water' assigns to the nature of water the role of accounting causally for the observable common properties of identified samples of water, and that science has shown that the property of being H_2O is clearly the best candidate for filling that role. Not all versions of this thesis would appeal as explicitly to value as my rendition in terms of "best candidate," but the key question, on any rendering, is what determines the correct interpretation of accounting causally for the observable properties. Suppose we find on another planet a substance that shares the observable common properties of water (colorless, odorless, tasteless, it quenches thirst, forms solid, liquid, and gaseous states at the same temperatures as water, etc.), but is not H_2O; instead it is constituted in an analogous way of two elements unknown on Earth, so that we may call it, for present purposes, $\Phi_2\Psi$. Is $\Phi_2\Psi$ water? The received answer is that it is (necessarily) not,[17] and I am prepared to agree; but what makes it the right answer?

Our seventeenth-century ancestors, who knew nothing of the periodic table of elements, let alone H_2O or $\Phi_2\Psi$, used the word 'water', very competently, in the same sense as we do. What is determined about the nature of water by the sense of 'water', as we share it with them, can hardly be more than that it accounts causally for the observable properties of water. In my example H_2O and $\Phi_2\Psi$ may be assumed to have analogous structures which are causally relevant in analogous ways to their shared observable properties. Why not say, then, that it is not being H_2O, but a structural property common to H_2O and $\Phi_2\Psi$, that accounts causally for the observed properties of water, even on planet Earth? The answer, I think, must be that the explanation of the observed properties in terms of H_2O is a *better* explanation than that in terms of the more abstract and complex structural property common to the two chemical compositions, not because its premises are truer, but because something about the structure of the explanation, or its connection with a larger theoretical background, is better. And I remain to be convinced that the value in question here is not a sort of excellence (perhaps an aesthetic excellence) of the explanation. If that does not undermine the claim to objectivity of the identification of the nature of water with being H_2O, as I think it probably does not, that is because the superiority of the explanation in terms of H_2O seems sufficiently obvious to us.

2. What best fills the role of the nature of excellence is surely not that obvious, and that may be thought an objection to my approach. I do not count it so myself. We are not as favorably situated for knowing the nature or ideal of excellence as for knowing the nature of water. I will argue in chapter 2 that it is actually a strength of Platonistic and theistic theories, in accounting for the ideal character of value judgments, that they severely limit our cognitive access to facts of value. The key question for present purposes is not whether we can now know the value judgments involved in our metaethical judgments to be objective, which I grant we cannot, but whether it is plausible to suppose that one who knew enough would find them very plausibly objective, which is all I maintain.

3. Finally, I anticipate another version of the circularity objection—namely, that if unreduced value judgments are involved in the link between the metaphysical and the semantical in every case, this is particularly damaging where it is value that we are seeking to understand, since we will be left relying on unreduced values whose nature cannot without circularity be explained by our theory, since we rely on them in expounding it. Not so, I reply, since the explanation I am offering is not a definition intended to *introduce* excellence as something previously unknown. A theory of the nature of something will generally purport to explain something otherwise unknown about it, but it can and usually will presuppose a good deal of prior knowledge of the subject and a fairly developed competence in making some sorts

---

17. This is Hilary Putnam's answer; see his *Mind, Language, and Reality*, pp. 196–290. My indebtedness to him in the construction of the example will be obvious to students of the literature on natural kinds, though I have adapted it to my argument.

of judgments about it. A chemical theory of the nature of water, for example, is apt to presuppose a fairly developed ability to recognize samples of water. My theory of the nature of excellence presupposes an ability to make fairly competent assessments of the excellence of some things; it purports to explain something about what excellence consists in. In fact, if excellence is in general Godlikeness, then the explanatory strategy will deal easily with the bestness of interpretations and the ideality of a judge if they are forms of excellence. For the best explanations will resemble God's thought, inasmuch as they are accepted by God; and the ideal judge will be God, and hence maximally Godlike.

We may get light on our topic from another angle by relating the views advanced here to the much-discussed objection to moral realism that is based on *internalism* about the relation of reasons or motives to moral judgments. Roughly speaking, internalism is the view that motives or reasons for action are internal to the content of judgments of value and obligation in such a way that it is impossible to assent sincerely to such a judgment without having a motive, or acknowledging a reason, to act in accordance with the judgment. This widely held view claims support from the undoubted fact that, whatever else they do, assertions of value and obligation commonly do express attitudes involving motivation. Saying that something is good or right is typically acting, at least in a small way, in favor of it, and thus expresses an attitude favorable to it. If the statement also asserts a fact, that is something else it does, not the only thing it accomplishes. Internalism is thought by many philosophers to support antirealism about value and obligation, and particularly an expressivist form of antirealism. For if the meaning of assertions about value and obligation consists merely in expressing attitudes that involve motivational states, it follows of course that those who sincerely make such assertions have some motivation to act accordingly; whereas many have found it difficult to see why values and obligations could not be acknowledged without motivating, if they are facts independent of our motivation as realists commonly suppose. (This is obviously not a tight argument as it stands; I present it simply as a line of thought to motivate discussion.)

We can distinguish as forms of internalism a thesis about motives and a thesis about reasons, if 'reasons' is not synonymous with motives but means *justifying* reasons rather than whatever considerations in fact motivate.[18] I can easily accept a form of the internalist thesis about justifying *reasons*. I have already acknowledged as a conceptual truth that if anything is good, in the sense of 'excellent', it is *good* for us to love it, admire it, and want to be related to it, whether we do in fact or not. It follows that one who asserts that *x* is excellent is committed thereby (at least implicitly) to its being *good* for her to have those attitudes and desires toward *x*; and competent speakers cannot generally be insensitive to this implication, inasmuch as conceptual truth is determined by actual understanding and linguistic practice. But its being good for us to have an attitude or desire, or to act in a certain way, surely implies our having a justifying reason for doing so. Hence it follows that one who

---

18. This distinction is rightly emphasized in Brink, *Moral Realism and the Foundations of Ethics*, chap. 3. Brink's useful discussion distinguishes a larger and more diverse array of internalist theses than I will take up here.

asserts that *x* is excellent is committed (at least implicitly) to acknowledging that she has a justifying reason for taking a certain stance toward *x*. Thus an internalism about justifying reasons is compatible with my sort of realism about the good, and indeed follows from views that I hold.

The argument of the preceding paragraph depends on the claim that its being good for us to take a certain stance implies our having a justifying reason for doing so. This may not be a very controversial claim, but its basis might be thought problematic for a realist. For if the goodness of taking the stance is rooted in having the reason, and if the latter is rooted in attitudes of the one who has the reason, the objectivity of the goodness may be called into question. But in fact I think the dependency runs in the other direction, and having a justifying reason, in a practical context, is to be explicated in terms of what stance it is good to take. Its being good for us to have an attitude or desire, or to act in a certain way, is precisely what constitutes our having a justifying reason for doing so, and that is why the one implies the other. In this I agree with Warren Quinn that "the only proper ground for claiming that a quality is rational to have or an action rational to do is that the quality or action is, on the whole, good."[19] I would further explicate being a practically rational person in terms of responding well to the reasons one has, and thus to the values of things and the norms to which one is subject (where responding well includes responding with logical coherence).

Such an explication of practical rationality in terms of values and norms is one way of not having to ground reasons in attitudes, and thus of avoiding antirealist arguments. The price of this strategy is rejection of the project, cherished by many philosophers, of explicating values and norms in terms of facts of rationality that can be understood prior to all other concepts of value and normativity. It is a price that will seem higher to those philosophers than it seems to me, as the prospects for an explication of practical rationality in terms of responsiveness to values and norms seem to me much brighter than those for an explication that runs in the opposite direction.

My views have a more complex relation to the internalist thesis about *motives*. One complication is that our present subject is the good rather than the right, value rather than obligation, and the claim that the good always motivates is even less plausible than the claim that duty always motivates, because the pursuit of most values is optional in a way that the fulfillment of obligations is not. I have long believed that golf is a good sport for persons of my age and general situation in life, bringing with it the enjoyment of various excellences and other goods; but I have never had any interest in becoming a golfer. I recognize that an interest in golf could be an excellent thing, in view of the values to be realized in the sport, and that there is a justifying reason, for me too, to take up golf. But the game just doesn't appeal to me. There is nothing odd about my lack of interest, for no human being can pursue all values. Even having *some* motivation, for each good that falls under our cognition, to pursue it, is too heavy a burden for our appetitive systems. So the most that could be necessarily involved in each individual judgment

---

19. W. Quinn, *Morality and Action*, p. 254.

that something is good is a real possibility of being motivated by it, and an openness thereto.

What I am in fact prepared to grant to internalism about motives is something less definite, and is one way of developing my point that being an object of pursuit is a main part of the semantically indicated role of the good. It can be summarized by saying that the meaning of 'good' is in large part shaped by the fact that most users of the term are in fact motivated to pursue many of those things that they judge to be good, and are sometimes so motivated *because* they judge them to be good, and that it is therefore an important part of the semantically indicated role of the good to be the object of this motivated pursuit. This is what Peter Railton has called the "normative role" of evaluative terms.[20] At the metaphysical level Railton's account of the nature of the good is a form of naturalism where mine is a form of supernaturalism, but at the semantical level I agree with him that goodness can be plausibly identified only with a "property (or complex of properties) that, to a significant extent, permits one to account for the correlations and truisms associated with 'good'—i.e., is at most tolerably revisionist—and that at the same time can plausibly serve as the basis of the normative function of this term."[21]

In my Platonic rendering of this point, the structure of the concept of good is largely determined by the fact that we are motivated to pursue ends that we do not claim to understand very fully. We want more than we now understand. We both postulate and want a true goodness. The desire plays an organizing role in our motivational system, as the postulate does in our conceptual system. It is in large part a higher order desire—that is, a desire about our other motives, a desire that they should be organized around an objective standard of value. As a desire for true goodness, it presupposes as well as structures a concept of the good. In this we may compare it with the purpose of checkmating the opponent in chess, which presupposes the concepts of the game, which in turn can hardly be understood apart from the purpose. Unlike the purpose of checkmating, however, the desire or aspiration for the good seeks something that is not a mere artifact of the pursuit that it structures.

We conceive of goodness as a property that things have independently of whether we in fact want them or not, but reasons for identifying any property as true goodness had better include reasons that could in fact motivate us to love it. Any concept of God that I can accept, inasmuch as I am interpreting the Good theologically, will be loaded with features that could motivate me and, I think, most others, to love God and Godlikeness. This is not to say that my identification of the Good with God is largely a judgment about what we will or would love in a perfect, eschatological vision of the divine nature. In the beatific vision, no doubt, we would love God; that's what makes it beatific. But that is too definitional a truth to do much work here. The motivation that shapes our concept of the good is our present actual quest for a true good; and in identifying the Good with God, I am supposing

20. Railton, "Naturalism and Prescriptivity," pp. 165, 168.
21. Railton, "Naturalism and Prescriptivity," p. 162. Another version of naturalism (Richard Boyd's) with which I largely agree at the semantical, though obviously not at the metaphysical, level is discussed in detail in chapter 2.

that the divine nature is such as to be the best candidate for satisfying that present actual quest and that, to one (God) who knows enough about the quest and the divine nature, that is sufficiently obvious to be an objective fact, in the rough sense explained earlier. That is the way in which a measure of internalism about motives and a measure of realism at the metaethical level cohabit in my theory.

3. Godlikeness

A theistic theory of the nature of excellence obviously presupposes or implies the existence of God. The argument of this book as a whole is meant to commend theism, among other things, but I will not attempt here anything I would call a "proof" of the existence of God. That God is the supreme Good, and excellent without qualification, is a view I am confident that theists, at any rate, should hold. Indeed, it seems to be part of the package of views that define theism, if there is such a package. In order to get from this view to a theory of the nature of goodness in general, however, we must identify the relation or relations in which other things that are good must stand to the supreme Good. This is difficult, and I have rather less confidence in the hypotheses I shall propose.

There is more than one relation to the supreme Good that I think can constitute goodness, and more than one will be discussed in the present section. One that will be important to my argument in other chapters is a relation of *alliance* with the supreme Good (that is, with God). This is also a relation of being *for* the Good, of loving it indeed, and thus of being in alliance with others who love the Good. The opposite of this is in my opinion the principal form of positive evil (as will be discussed in more detail in chapter 4). The structure of evil is not similar enough to that of good to make it plausible to postulate a "supreme" Evil analogous to the supreme Good. Good and evil are not equally real poles of a single scale; rather, the bad must be understood in terms of the good. There is good and less good, but positive evil is worse than mere deficiency of good. It is *enmity* toward the Good, being *against* the Good, destroying or violating what is good. Being for the Good is thus an important part of the framework I am proposing for ethics, and it is an excellence; but it is not a plausible candidate for constituting excellence in general. Many excellent things (a beautiful flower, for example) are not for or against anything, and not capable of alliance, except in a rather strained sense.

Resemblance to the Good is a more plausible candidate. Here we take up Plato's suggestion that sensible particulars are likenesses or "imitations" of the Forms under which they are classed.[22] Without concerning ourselves with the general theory of Forms, we may consider the idea that other things are excellent insofar as they re-

---

22. Whatever may have been the intent of Plato's theory of Forms, it should be remembered that I am proposing no theory of the nature of universals as such. The claims about the Good itself that are under discussion here are not meant to explain how things resemble each other or have properties. They are therefore not liable to the celebrated "Third Man" objection, which is based on a regress arising in certain attempts to use the Forms to explain the relation among things that resemble each other.

semble or imitate God. Resemblance brings several advantages to this role. Much of the intuitive appeal of broadly Platonic theories of value lies in the thought that experienced beauty or excellence points beyond itself to an ideal or transcendent Good of which it is only an imperfect suggestion or imitation. The idea of resemblance can hardly be eliminated from this model. It is important also that the excellence of anything have grounds in its own nature or condition, and resemblance satisfies that requirement by having parts of its grounds in each of the resembling things.

Other structural features of resemblance help to fit it for the role of goodness. If something resembles God, it does so in some respect and by virtue of other features that could be identified by someone sufficiently knowledgeable. Goodness likewise is a property that things have in some respect and by virtue of other features they have. The concept of imitation adds a note of asymmetry, but not an unwelcome note, if the Platonic intuition of the imperfection of experienced goods is sound. The Forms, for Plato, have a certain priority. They are the originals, the standard; and in applying such terms as 'equal', 'good', and 'beautiful' to mundane things, the question is to what extent they measure up to the standard. In the same way, theists may say that God is the standard of goodness, to which other good things must in some measure conform, but never perfectly conform.

The identification of excellence with resemblance to God can also claim some explanatory force. Much philosophical discussion of the nature of goodness is motivated by a sense many people have that, though they make judgments, sometimes confident, about the goodness of things, and though they know in a way what 'good' means, and see that it seems meant to signify a property, a feature of reality, still they do not see what sort of feature of reality it would be. Like most philosophically interesting concepts, those of resemblance and of God are attended with their own questions for understanding. Nonetheless, most of us not only use the concept of resemblance with confidence (as we do that of goodness) but also think we understand that resemblances are grounded in features of reality. And whether or not we think there is (or even could be) one, we will probably see that if there is a God, a being unsurpassable in power, knowledge, and other properties thought to be excellent, God is a (very prominent) feature of reality. To that extent the Godlikeness thesis, if accepted, helps to relate goodness to reality. There remain issues to be resolved, however, before we can conclude that the thesis solves the problem of realism about value, even at the substantive level. That is because there is not obviously less problem about the objectivity of resemblance, and especially of comparative resemblance, than about that of goodness.

Does the baby resemble its parents? Some say yes, but I can't see it. Does it resemble the mother more, or the father? The grandparents disagree about that. Should we conclude that it resembles both parents equally? Not necessarily; for surely it can be reasonable in such cases to judge that one side in the dispute is right and the other wrong. But what is it for an answer to such a question of resemblance to be objectively right? This is a question that will follow us through much of our discussion of the Godlikeness thesis.

Intertwined with it will be the even more pressing question whether it is plausible to hold that all and only those things that resemble God are excellent. Applying a common philosophical distinction, we can divide this into the questions whether resembling God is *necessary* for excellence (whether *only* things that resemble God are excellent) and whether resembling God is *sufficient* for excellence (whether *all* things that resemble God are excellent).

Can resembling God really be *necessary* for excellence? Can excellence in cooking, for example, be analyzed as resembling God with respect to one's cooking? I think it can, but this does not mean that God is a cook. Saying that A resembles B in respect of A's φ-ing does not entail that φ-ing is a property that A and B share, or that B φ's too. It is enough if A's φ-ing manifests a resemblance to some aspect of B. In this case one's cooking might manifest a resemblance to the divine creativity.

It may be objected nonetheless that some excellences are simply too humble to be understood in terms of likeness to God. Can a gourmet dinner, for instance, resemble God in its excellence? Well, why not? "Taste and see that the LORD is good," says the Psalmist (Psalm 34:8), seeming to find at least enough resemblance for a metaphor here. Sacramental meals have been thought to image God, and some religious thinkers have wanted to extend a version of that to meals in general. Perhaps on a sufficiently sacramental conception of the universe we can think that excellence is coextensive with imaging God.

Of course it is theologically controversial whether our conception of the universe ought to be that sacramental, or (as a Barthian might ask) whether God is really so indiscriminately visible. Is it not claiming altogether too much for us creatures to say that we are *like God* in whatever excellences we may possess? A concern for the transcendent holiness of God has led many theologians to say that God is "wholly other," or to claim that nothing can be truly predicated of God and creatures in exactly the same sense. But I think a reasonable accommodation can be reached between this concern and an account of excellence in general in terms of resemblance to God, if the imperfection of the resemblance is sufficiently stressed.

It may help at this point to introduce another suggestion from Plato. At least sometimes, when Plato speaks of particulars imitating the Forms, he seems to mean that they are *images* of them, as a painting or a reflection on a surface of glass or water may be an image of a horse. This relation is quite different from that of a copy or duplicate to a standard object. In particular, while the images resemble the horse in various ways, and may indeed be very "horsey," they are not horses. Though we may point to a picture of a horse and say truly, "That's a horse," it is not a horse in the same sense in which Man-o-War was a horse.[23] We could say, perhaps, that 'horse' is predicated *analogously* rather than univocally of a horse and of an image of a horse.[24] Similarly, if creatures are good insofar as they image God, we could join Aquinas in saying that 'good' is predicated analogously of God and creatures.

---

23. Though not primarily concerned at present with exegesis of Plato, I am drawing heavily here on Patterson, *Image and Reality in Plato's Metaphysics*, who presents an interesting and detailed argument for taking imaging of this sort to have been the dominant relation of sensible particulars to the Forms for Plato.

24. To explain the relation of predications in such cases Patterson, in *Image and Reality in Plato's Metaphysics*, p. 42, invokes the Aristotelian notion of πρὸς ἓν λεγόμενα (predication by virtue of relation to one thing)—precisely the Aristotelian model that Aquinas takes for his conception of analogical predication in *Summa Theologiae*, I, q. 13, a. 5. This idea will come into our discussion in section 4.

The humble degree of many of them may not be the most difficult problem in bringing all excellences under the heading of resemblance to God. Some of the most admired of human excellences, in love, artistic creativity, and moral virtue, seem to depend on our finitude, and even on some of our most painful limitations, our mortality, frailty, weakness, and liability to frustration, temptation, and error.[25] Such limitations are generally thought to be incompatible with deity, and excellences involving them may therefore be seen as contrary to the divine nature, and not merely humble or fragmentary by comparison with it.

The most important basis for a response to this objection is still the point that the imaging of God by creatures is a matter of distant and fragmentary resemblance. No excellence of creatures can be regarded as a detailed copy of something in God. It will be only in certain respects that our virtues resemble or image God. In the case of those virtues that struggle against our limitations, or nobly accommodate or mourn them, the main points of resemblance to God, I suspect, will be in what we care about, and the strength and effectiveness of our caring—perhaps also in our perception of the situation. Human limitations may be inextricably involved in the only ways that such perceptiveness and care can be manifested in human life, but it does not follow that there cannot be analogues of these excellences, without the limitations, in God.

A more daring answer might question the assumption that there cannot be analogues in God of some of the limitations of human life. One way in which God has been believed by some to take on such limits is by incarnation,[26] but even the act of creating might carry with it a liability to frustration, if sufficient independence is allowed to the creatures. As I will argue in chapter 2, the transcendence of the Good is to be conceived positively, not negatively. Bliss is not absence of pain. This should make us cautious of denying analogues of pain and frustration in God.

It may be remarked that some predicates of excellence seem inapplicable to God because they signify what we might call *impure* excellences. God is not *cute*, for example. But 'cute' signifies a sort of beauty or aesthetic attractiveness, together with an implication of smallness, weakness, or immaturity, or (more broadly) lack of dignity. The full concept cannot be applied to God, but the aesthetic excellence which is the main praiseworthiness implied in the concept can be interpreted as a sort of likeness to God.

We have still to consider whether resembling or imaging God can be *sufficient* for excellence. Disturbing counterexamples arise at this point. If we think we can describe the divine nature at all, we will surely want to characterize it in terms of properties that would not necessarily be good for other things to possess. God is powerful. God assents, no doubt, to a self-ascription of deity. According to Christian orthodoxy God is three-in-one. Possessing these properties in the way that God possesses them is not only good but truly wonderful. But it seems that creatures could possess them without being good thereby. Was political power an excellence in Hitler or Stalin? I doubt it. If I thought I was God, would that be an excellence in me?

25. A similar point is made eloquently by Nussbaum, *Love's Knowledge*, p. 376f.
26. This point is acknowledged by Nussbaum, *Love's Knowledge*, p. 376.

Surely not. And consider the clovers. There seems to be a sense in which a three-leafed clover (or some part of it) shares with a triune God the property of three-in-oneness. But it is not very plausible to suppose that a three-leafed clover is therefore better in this respect than a four-leafed clover (nor to suppose that poison ivy should be valued for the three-in-oneness of its leaf structures).

One reply to these counterexamples can be ruled out at once. It might be claimed that resemblance to God constitutes an excellence only if it is in respect of properties that are part of the divine nature, not if it is only in respect of contingent properties of God.[27] This claim is rather plausible on the assumption (to which I am attracted) that characteristics that make God a good candidate for the role of the Good follow necessarily from the divine nature. In section 5 we will take up the question whether that assumption is true. But even if it is only the divine nature that defines the standard of goodness, that provides no answer to the counterexamples I have given of resemblance to God without excellence. For they are based exclusively on properties that are thought to follow necessarily from the divine nature.

Probably the best reply we could give to these counterexamples if we want to defend the theory that excellence consists simply in resembling God is that not every sharing of a property constitutes a resemblance. Judgments of resemblance are more holistic than that. Suppose there is a squirrel that has the same number of hairs on its body that I have on mine. We would not ordinarily say that this rodent "resembles" me in that respect, nor that it is thereby more like me than its twin that has twenty-seven more hairs. Similarly, I would not become more Godlike by coming to believe I was God, even though there is a property I would thereby come to share with God. And even Trinitarian Christians may think it is stretching things to say that a three-leafed clover is "more like God" than a four-leafed clover.

As this reply suggests, the notion of resemblance is trickier than we may have thought. The way or context in which a property is shared affects whether the sharing constitutes a resemblance or makes things more similar than they would otherwise have been. And no resemblance will arise from many negative properties and relational properties, such as not being a giraffe and being born later than Harry S. Truman, though it will be both plausible, and important for my theistic theory of the good, to hold that there can be resemblance in respect of some relational properties, such as loving. The degree of importance of the property matters too, and that is particularly significant for our present discussion. The shared mathematical properties grounded in leaf structures and hair counts are not *important* enough to make the clover or the poison ivy resemble God, or the squirrel resemble me.

These judgments are largely intuitive, and questions obviously arise about what, if anything, determines whether a relation of resemblance really obtains. How much truth is there to Nelson Goodman's claim that "similarity is relative, variable, culture-dependent"?[28] Here we meet again the question of the objectivity of resemblance. Can we maintain a metaphysical realism about resemblance, as an analysis of excel-

---

27. More cautiously one might claim that if a thing can be good by imitating a contingent property of God, that is only because the divine nature is manifested in the contingent properties too. On this view the latter do not define the divine goodness.

28. Goodman, *Problems and Projects*, p. 438.

lence in terms of resemblance would seem to require if it is to be realistic at the substantive level? Resemblance turns out to depend not only on the sharing of properties but also on their importance, and judgments of importance, if not themselves value judgments, are at least close kin to value judgments. A full account of what resemblance consists in will presumably require an account of what importance consists in.

We will return to these issues about the objectivity of resemblance. There is a more pressing difficulty, however, for the thesis that Godlikeness is sufficient for excellence. More decisive counterexamples to it are possible, involving holistic resemblance rather than mere sharing of properties. Consider the phenomenon of parody or caricature. Parodies and caricatures do resemble, but do not in general share the excellences of their original or object. The caricatures of a great cartoonist may of course have an excellence of their own, but that is a different matter. It is not clear that anything can be good in such a way that it cannot be parodied, caricatured, or at any rate resembled by something that is not thereby good. Even something so abstract and free of superfluous properties as a beautiful piece of music can be parodied; and the parody will resemble the original but will not thereby share its virtues. Perhaps one could plausibly maintain that the divine goodness, uniquely, is such that it cannot be parodied or caricatured. But I would not know how to argue for that, and there seem to be counterinstances. It is natural enough to say that Hitler's power is "a caricature of the divine power"—more natural, I suspect, than to deny flatly that his power resembles God's in any way.

This suggests a modification of the analysis of excellence in terms of resembling or imaging God. We can suppose that the difference between resemblances to God that do and do not constitute virtues or excellences is analogous to the difference between good portraits (by which I mean faithful portraits) and caricatures. The excellence of other things besides God will consist, then, in the *faithfulness* of their imaging of God. This cannot be more than an analogy, of course, due to the radical imperfection of any resemblance of creatures to God.

I will not offer here a full account of what the faithfulness of a portrait amounts to, and I am not sure that I could give one. It would surely include the observation that caricatures are *distorted* in a way that faithful portraits are not. The caricature exaggerates one or more features of the original, whereas the faithful portrait represents features in a balanced way and in relation to those other features to which they are most importantly related in the original. How much, and what, must be included in a faithful image depends on what is most *important* about the way in which the original has the features shared or represented.

Applying the distinction between faithful images and caricatures seems to require something like an aesthetic judgment. In most cases of intentional caricature it is an easy judgment to make. As with the judgments of resemblance and importance that are involved in it, however, there is no formula for getting it right. What, then, is the standard of faithfulness, and is there a metaphysically objective difference between faithful images and caricatures?

Our discussion has turned up important problems about resemblance—problems in determining whether the relationship between two things constitutes a resemblance and whether an acknowledged resemblance images God "faithfully" enough to constitute an excellence. It appears that both questions may turn on how *important* the shared properties in the case are; and this adds urgency to the question whether in general there are objectively correct answers to these questions. For a theistic theory it is natural to appeal at this point to God's view of things or God's attitude toward things. I will discuss two versions of this appeal. They are not mutually exclusive, and I think there is merit in both.

1. The theist can appeal to God's view of things as the definitive standard of importance, and hence of resemblance and of faithfulness, at least where the question is about images of God—saying that considerations in these matters have the importance God sees them as having, and that they resemble, and faithfully image, God, insofar as God sees them as doing so. It is important that this identification of the standard not be taken as the whole story about the nature of faithful imaging. Here too the general principle holds, that our linguistic practice establishes a role to be filled—in this case by the best candidate for an objective standard of faithfulness in imaging. And part of the role is that the standard should set the boundaries of the extension of a concept that it is assumed we can usually apply correctly if we have a good enough view of copy and original. Most of the content of the idea of God's having a view of what images are faithful comes from a similarity or analogy between our views and God's, with regard to both what is classed together and on what basis. Among other things, I think we must assume that there is something in God's view of these matters that is analogous to the implicit rootage of our judgments of image-faithfulness in judgments of importance. Without these analogies the claim that God's view of faithfulness in images is the standard of faithfulness in images would be a vacuous circle.

One of the ways in which our judgments of importance, and of faithfulness in images, are akin to aesthetic judgments is that they have an affective ingredient. We are taking such judgments as analogous to that in God which determines which resemblances to God are faithful in such a way as to constitute excellences. I see no reason to exclude the affective component from the analogy. We may say that creatures are good insofar as God *appreciates* them as faithfully imaging God. In us, I have argued, the typical context for appreciation of goodness is Eros. By analogy, the divine appreciation of faithful imaging of God can be seen as part of the divine Eros toward creatures. This is not to say that God's regarding something as, in some measure, a faithful image is a purely affective matter. It is also cognitive, as are our analogous judgments. This bridging of the cognitive/affective distinction in God corresponds appropriately, I think, to the fact that in my account of goodness, values are recognized but are not distinguished from facts.[29]

A vicious circle might be suspected here, on the ground that the concept of appreciation may involve a conception of good, and I am using it to explain the nature of the good. I would remind any who harbor this suspicion that I am not offering a reductive analysis of the meaning of 'good', but am speculating about what

---

29. Some theologians, following Nygren, *Agape and Eros*, will object to my ascription of Eros to God. This ascription will be defended in chapter 5. Eros, properly understood, seems to me to play so essential a part in the perception of value that it is hard to see how we can deny Eros to God without denying all value to God's creatures.

is there in reality corresponding to our talk about good. And an important part of what is there, I am suggesting, is something in God analogous to what we call appreciation in ourselves. This analogy is not destroyed by the fact that God's appreciation does not involve reference to an external standard, since God *is* the standard. On my theory we can say that what God appreciates is indeed good; and that directedness toward what is good can help to place the divine appreciation on our conceptual map, even though it is not a distinct and independent determinant of the nature of the divine attitude.

2. Once we have given God's love a part to play in explaining the nature of excellence, we may wonder whether we should not bypass our worries about resemblance, and go right to the divine love to explain excellence. There is certainly a close connection between excellence and God's love. I have claimed that it is excellent to value the excellent. Indeed, I believe it is analytic, or close to analytic, that if *x* is excellent, it is excellent to value *x*. Together with the Godlikeness thesis, this seems to imply that if *x* is excellent, then it is Godlike to value *x*, which seems to imply that if *x* is excellent, God values *x*.[30] And some sort of Eros seems the most appropriate sort of valuing here.

So should we just say that excellence consists in being loved by God? If we substituted 'desired' for 'loved' here, we would get what has been called a divine desire theory of the good. That would not be an improvement, if it is excellence we are trying to understand; for it is less plausible to suppose that God would *love* things that are *not* excellent in their own nature and intrinsic properties, than that God might *desire* such things for their part in some larger scheme.

However, even the identification of excellence with being *loved* by God is not an intuitively satisfying substitute for the explanation in terms of resemblance to God. Supposing that excellent finite things are indeed loved by God, we may well think nonetheless that their excellence must consist, not in God's attitude toward them, but in something in them that grounds God's attitude, or provides God with a reason for it. For excellence should have grounds in the nature or condition of the excellent thing. Resemblance to God indicates such grounds, and the divine love theory, without further elaboration, does not. This is a reason for retaining an essential reference to Godlikeness in our explanation of the nature of excellence.

This argument directs our attention to the question whether the connection between excellence and God's love is explanatory and, if so, which way the explanation runs. Does the excellence of *x* explain God's love for *x*, or the other way around? Intuitively, as I've said, the excellence of *x* should have its grounds not simply in God's attitude, but in something in *x* itself. Among the features of the role that I think ordinary understanding assigns to excellence, moreover, are not only that it is good to value the excellent, but also that the excellence of something provides a reason for admiring or loving it, and that it is good to admire or love the excellent *for* that reason. This suggests that the excellence of *x* should provide God with a reason for

---

30. I don't in fact accept this last implication, unless 'values' is understood in a rather thin sense. What I will accept in the end is that if *x* is excellent, there is for God a *reason* to value *x*.

loving *x*, and that God should love *x* for that reason, which will presumably be grounded in whatever it is in *x* that grounds *x*'s excellence. These grounds, I have suggested thus far, are constituted by *x*'s resemblance to God, or by whatever it is in *x* by virtue of which *x* resembles God. On this account it seems to be *x*'s excellence (or its grounds in *x*) that explains (or helps explain) God's love for *x*.

It does not follow that we cannot have explanation running in the other direction too. I think we probably should, but we will have to move carefully to avoid a vicious circle. The previous paragraph gives us a clue for avoiding it in the idea that the connection between the excellence of finite things and God's loving them runs through God's *reasons* for loving them. (By 'God's reasons', in the present context, I mean simply whatever factors God *counts in favor* of loving them.)[31] God's loving is explained, at least in part, by God's reasons; and thus that in the finite things that contributes to God's reasons for loving them contributes to the explanation of God's loving them. My proposal is that it is their resemblance to God, which also constitutes their excellence, that thus helps explain God's loving them. At the same time, we can have an explanation running in the other direction, too, if we suppose that the resemblance's contributing in this way to God's reasons is part of the explanation of its constituting excellence in the finite thing. Thus we will have explanations running in both directions, but without circularity, since the terms in the two explanations are significantly different. The fact that *x* resembles God helps explain God's loving *x*; and (not God's loving *x*, but) the resemblance's contributing to God's reasons for loving *x* helps explain (not the fact of resemblance, but) the resemblance's constituting excellence.

Following this line of thought, there is something to be said for the hypothesis that *being excellent in the way that a finite thing can be consists in resembling God in a way that could serve God as a reason for loving the thing*. On this hypothesis excellence is the intersection or conjunction of two types of feature. There are features by virtue of which things resemble God, and features that could serve as reasons for God's love. It is features that have both qualifications that will constitute excellence.

We can allow that neither feature alone entails excellence. We have already seen reasons for suspecting that not every resemblance to God is an excellence. It is also not obvious that only an excellence could serve God as a reason for loving. Othello says of Desdemona, "She lov'd me for the dangers I had pass'd, and I lov'd her, that she did pity them."[32] Desdemona might love Othello for the excellence with which he met the dangers, and we may suppose she had that reason too; but the mention of pity suggests that Othello means that Desdemona's love found a reason in the dangers themselves, which were not exactly an excellence in him. Certainly human love does sometimes have such reasons, and references in religious literature to God's pity and grace suggest we should not be hasty to deny the possibility of analogous reasons for God's love.

It seems more plausible, however, to maintain that a resemblance to God that gives God a reason for loving, and a reason for God's love that is found in a resem-

---

31. The subject of reasons for love will be discussed at greater length in chapter 6, section 3.
32. Shakespeare, *Othello*, act 1, scene 3.

blance to God, must constitute an excellence. Is there a counterexample to this hypothesis? To take the example most strongly suggested by our previous discussion, could a caricature's nonexcellent resemblance to God be a reason for God to like it? If God has a sense of humor, as I think we ought to suppose, then God might like a caricature of God as such—but not simply and precisely for its resembling God as a caricature—rather for its elegance as a caricature, its funniness, its irony. These are aesthetic excellences, and correspond, I suppose, to something in God. The Bible finds irony and humor in God's projects, acts, and views;[33] it would be wooden to suppose there is nothing like that in God. Thus far, therefore, I am not convinced there is a counterexample that defeats the hypothesis.

There are important advantages in invoking God's attitude by way of reasons God could have for loving. Some of them have already been mentioned: the appeal to reasons, grounded in resemblance to God, preserves the intrinsic aspect of excellence in finite things; it also preserves nonarbitrariness of divine choice, letting excellence (or what constitutes excellence) serve God as a reason as intuitively it should. It is also important that the reasons invoked are reasons God *could* have for loving, and do not necessarily inspire *actual* love. There are presumably many things God could have created but didn't that would have been excellent if they had existed, and it seems less plausible to say that God actually loves them than that God recognizes reasons that *could* ground divine love for them.

The potentiality here is presumably grounded in the divine nature as well as in the features that finite things could have. In this way the supreme standard of excellence is constituted partly by aspects of God to be imitated or imaged by finite things, and partly by an aspect of the divine nature that can be seen as part of the divine rationality. Divine rationality is not to be understood here as conformity to an independently specifiable standard, but rather as whatever in the divine nature determines what counts as a reason for God, which is itself the ultimate standard of the relevant sort of rationality.

The line of thought we are now pursuing suggests three alternative hypotheses regarding the standard of *comparative* excellence. One is that where excellence is present its degree is proportional to the degree of resemblance to God. That is the most satisfying hypothesis intuitively. On the other hand, the resemblance of finite things to God is to be conceived as very remote and fragmentary, so that calibration of degrees of resemblance to God may be inappropriate—though perhaps the conclusion to be drawn from this point is rather that we should be very cautious in judgments of comparative excellence where the comparability and comparison are not very clear. A second hypothesis is that for one finite thing to be more excellent than another is for their features to give God reason to love the former more than the latter. This hypothesis may be in tension with God's grace and freedom in loving, and suggests that God is a value maximizer, and that value-maximizing is Godlike, which are conclusions to be avoided, as I will argue in chapter 6. The third,

---

33. See, for example, Jonah 4 (indeed, the whole book of Jonah); Psalm 2:4. Mark 12:13–17 is probably another text in which a viewpoint saturated with irony, and savoring it, is presented as God's. I am much indebted on this point to Marilyn McCord Adams.

slightly different, alternative is to say that where excellence is present its degree is proportional to the strength or weight of the reasons it gives God for loving. This may be a good alternative, but only if we can suppose that God's reasons can differ in strength or weight without the strongest compelling God's love. Otherwise we will end up with the same problems about God's grace and freedom in loving as in the second alternative.

4. Varieties of Excellence

One of the objections most commonly voiced against Platonistic accounts of the Good is that they are too unitary, making insufficient allowance for the varieties of goodness. The classic text for this objection is in the first book of Aristotle's *Nicomachean Ethics*. Aristotle acknowledges that the Platonist accounts are "not about every good," but claim only of "those that are pursued and loved for themselves" that they are called good "according to one form," while merely instrumental goods are called so "in another way" and on account of those that are good for their own sake (1096b8–13). Similarly, the account I am developing here applies in the first instance only to things that are *non*instrumentally good. Indeed, my account has a narrower primary scope than that discussed by Aristotle, leaving aside for now what is good *for* someone, as such, to focus exclusively on the excellent. This narrowing of focus is certainly not enough to escape Aristotle's objection. He is explicitly claiming that the diversity of things that are noninstrumentally good is too fundamental for their goodness to be accounted for in terms of a single Platonic Form (1096b14–26); and I will freely grant that there are deep differences between types of excellence.

I will not discuss all the arguments Aristotle offers in support of this objection. They are saturated with peculiarities of the Platonic and Aristotelian philosophies, and do not all seem relevant to our present nonhistorical inquiry. One of them, arguably the most central as well as the most famous, does deserve our attention, however. Aristotle points out that 'good' is predicated in all of his categories, "as of God and the mind in [the category of] substance, and of the virtues in that of quality, and of the moderate in that of quantity, and of the useful in that of relation, and of the opportune in that of time, and of habitat in that of place" (1096a24–27). Some of these examples are merely instrumental goods, but I think that is not crucial to the argument and will ignore it here.

Why would the goodness of items in different Aristotelian categories have to be too diverse to be understood in terms of a single Form of the Good? Aristotle's reasoning on this point is not as explicit as we might wish. It has been suggested that his point is that there are different grounds, different reasons [λόγοι] (1096b24) for predicating good in the different categories.[34] No doubt that is true. Even in the same category things can be good in different ways and for different reasons. But it is not obvious why that should be thought to show that goodness is not the

---

34. Ackrill, "Aristotle on 'Good' and the Categories," pp. 21–24.

same property in all the different cases. Consider a simpler but not altogether unrelated example. A circle is symmetrical because all the points on it are equidistant from a single point; a typical crossword puzzle is symmetrical for much more complex reasons. But it still seems plausible to say they share a single property of symmetry.

"The nerve of [Aristotle's] argument," according to a major commentary, "is evidently the assimilation of the Idea to *a univocal universal concept.*"[35] There is support in the text for this interpretation. Aristotle's list of examples of the good in different categories leads him to the conclusion "Clearly [the good] would not be something universally shared and one" (1096a27–28). If different things are good in themselves, he claims, "the ground [λόγος] of the good will have to appear the same in all of them, just as the ground of whiteness does in snow and in white lead" (1096b21–23). The ground of whiteness in snow and other white things, according to Aristotle, is a quality, an Aristotelian form as it has often been called; and it is supposed to be qualitatively identical in every case. So perhaps his point is that the things that are good in themselves are too diverse for all of them to contain such an identical form. This again can hardly be said to have been proved, but it is plausible, and I'm prepared to grant it.

It does not contradict Plato's theory or mine, however, as neither Plato (as I read him) nor I maintain it is the presence of something qualitatively identical in all good things that constitutes their goodness. In our theories things are good by virtue of a relation to some one supreme Good, but the goodness is not something qualitatively identical in all of them. The supreme Good being vastly better than all the other goods, nothing qualitatively identical to its goodness is present in them; and once we have accepted that, we might as well agree that even the lesser goods differ from each other in the type, and perhaps the degree, of their goodness.

Must not all excellent things, as such, have something in common, in a broad sense? As Aristotle himself says, the good "does not seem like those things that have the same name by chance" (1096b26–27). In the *Nicomachean Ethics* he begs off trying to solve this problem (1096b30ff.), but he offers a couple of suggestions. Could 'good' be predicated "by analogy? For as sight [is good] in the body, so intellect [is good] in the soul" (1096b28–29). To the extent that this suggestion moves away from the idea of something qualitatively identical present in all good things toward a looser resemblance among them, it is not uncongenial to the account I have been developing.

Aristotle's other suggestion is also helpful. He asks whether all goods share the same name "because they derive from one thing or all contribute to one thing" (1096b27–28). These are special cases of what G. E. L. Owen has called "focal meaning," which is important in Aristotelian semantics, or at least in some influential accounts of it. The general idea is that one term can be predicated of different things by virtue of their being related in suitable ways to one single thing. Such things are πρὸς ἓν λεγόμενα, "called [what they are called] in relation to one thing." The standard example, Aristotle's own, is health: "Everything healthy

---

35. Gauthier and Jolif, *L'Éthique à Nicomaque*, vol. 2, part 1, p. 42.

is related to health, one thing by protecting it, another by producing it, another as a symptom of it, another as a receiver of it" (1003a34–b1). In the *Metaphysics* Aristotle opts for just such a focal account of the meaning of 'being', a term he thinks is predicated in all the categories as 'good' is. "Being is said in many ways, but in relation to one thing [πρὸς ἕν] and some one nature and not ambiguously" (1003a33–34).[36]

A focal meaning account of 'good' fits my sort of Platonism very well. All other good things are good by virtue of their relation to one supremely good thing, the central relation being a sort of resemblance or imaging. But the relation might be somewhat different in different categories. Perhaps God, a substance, is resembled or imaged, strictly speaking, only by substances. Perhaps qualities do not themselves image God, but an excellent quality is one by virtue of which a substance images God. It may be no accident if this approach is congenial to Platonism; it has been argued that the focal meaning account was not invented by Aristotle but had been used in the Academy to defend a Platonic view.[37]

I have not even begun here to give an exposition of Aristotle's own account of the good, and I have not meant to assess the part the texts discussed here play in the development of that account. I have tried simply to give reasons for thinking that Aristotle's celebrated objections to Plato's account of the good pose no insuperable obstacle to the sort of Platonism I am advocating. It does not follow, however, that the diversity of excellences poses no serious problem for my theory. The most considerable difficulty I face at this point, in my opinion, is that of accounting for differences between excellences, with only one transcendent object (God) to serve as a standard.

This may not be difficult with regard to some types of excellence, particularly those most "thickly"[38] characterized by observable and describable conditions. Honesty, for example, differs from other virtues in ways we can probably describe pretty well. This is *not* to say that we can isolate a "purely descriptive" aspect of honesty about which we can reliably make judgments that are not judgments of excellence. It is only to say that we can describe pretty well the realm in which it pertains to honesty to be excellent. To be honest will be to be excellent in the describable ways; on my theory, roughly, it will be to resemble God in the corresponding respects—not that God can be literally honest in all the ways that we can, but it should not be too hard to specify respects in which the particular excellence of honesty would resemble a supreme being (for instance in prizing truth, and caring more about reality than about appearance). Perhaps the difference between honesty and other virtues will not be totally unproblematic on any view—such is the difficulty of moral philosophy; but I doubt that it will be much more problematic on my theory than on others.

---

36. The topic of this paragraph is helpfully discussed in Gauthier and Jolif, *L'Éthique à Nicomaque*, vol. 2, part 1, pp. 45–47.

37. Owen, "Logic and Metaphysics in Some Earlier Works of Aristotle," pp. 26–32.

38. For this currently influential way of speaking about concepts that combine evaluation with a richness of empirical descriptive content, see, e.g., Williams, *Ethics and the Limits of Philosophy*, p. 129f., and Anderson, *Value in Ethics and Economics*, pp. 97–103.

I face a much more difficult problem with excellences such as beauty, which are moderately "thin" but not quite as thin as excellence in general. Beauty is one type of excellence, but there are others. It is an aesthetic excellence, and as such somewhat different from moral excellence. Even within the category of aesthetic excellence something can be sublime without exactly being beautiful, and can certainly be beautiful without being sublime. What will constitute beauty, on my theory?

One who believes in distinct Platonic Forms of Beauty, Sublimity, and other sorts of excellence may say that being beautiful consists in resembling the Beautiful itself. On my theistic adaptation of Plato, however, God is the Beautiful itself and the Sublime itself, as well as the Good itself more generally; so faithful imaging of God, as such, will not distinguish a beautiful human life, as such, from a sublime or a morally virtuous human life. We can still say that creatures are beautiful by faithfully imaging God; but it must be by imaging God in a certain respect. And it will not be easy to say in what respect that is, otherwise than by saying, circularly, that it is in respect of beauty. For the features that distinguish beauty from other sorts of excellence are not describable in the same way as those that distinguish honesty from other sorts of excellence.

One might try to differentiate beauty from other sorts of excellence by the attitude that it is good to take toward it,[39] which will be at least analogous to the attitude that God finds reason to take toward it and does take toward it in some instances. But it is not clear that there is an attitude that is uniquely appropriate to beauty. Beauty is not the only excellence that may appropriately inspire Eros, and most excellences are rightly admired.

The following is the best account I can give at this point. We do make judgments of beauty, and we do distinguish beauty from sublimity and other sorts of excellence. If our judgments of beauty track something objective, as I believe they do, they presumably are tracking some way in which experienced, mundane beautiful objects resemble each other, and in which they do not resemble sublime things universally or as such. In my view this will also be a way in which beautiful objects point beyond themselves to a transcendent ideal, and in which they resemble or image God. Sublime objects will also resemble or image God, but in a different way, related to the different way in which they resemble each other. Subject to further qualifications, as indicated earlier, both these excellences will consist in resembling or imaging God, but in different ways or in different respects. What the way is in which God is resembled or imaged by beautiful things, or what it is in God that is resembled or imaged by them, we probably are not in a position to specify without using the concept of beauty, and our cognitive access to it must probably remain dependent on our ability to classify mundane objects together as beautiful. If that is so, it certainly limits our ability to explain substantively what beauty is. But the account I am giving in terms of Godlikeness (in a certain respect) may still explain what sort of property beauty is.

---

39. This is the approach to distinguishing types of value in general that is advocated, and richly developed, in a theory very different from mine, in Anderson, *Value in Ethics and Economics*.

5. The Divine Nature

This chapter concludes with discussion of four points related to the specifically theistic character of the theory I have been developing.

1. If God is the Good itself, then the Good is not an abstract object but a concrete (though not a physical) individual. Indeed, it is a *person*, or importantly like a person. Theists have sometimes tried to infer the personality of the supreme Good from the premise that persons, as such, are the most excellent things that we know, from which it is claimed to follow that the supremely excellent being must be of that sort. A more cautious line of argument begins with the premise, harder to deny, that most of the excellences that are most important to us, and of whose value we are most confident, are excellences of persons or of qualities or actions or works or lives or stories of persons. So if excellence consists in resembling or imaging a being that is the Good itself, nothing is more important to the role of the Good itself than that persons and their properties should be able to resemble or image it. That is obviously likelier to be possible if the Good itself is a person or importantly like a person.[40] In section 3, of course, I ended up with an account of the relation of the Good itself to other goods that relies in various ways on the assumption that the Good itself is a person and, indeed, a lover; and its usefulness in this context may provide an additional argument for the assumption.

This is not to exclude the applicability of impersonal as well as personal analogies to God. The Good itself, and God as the Good, must certainly be very unlike us in various ways. My account of the nature of beauty implies that beautiful objects that are not persons do resemble or image God; and theistic piety makes extensive use of models for our relationship with God that are not straightforwardly interpersonal. Speaking of God's spirit as "poured out" on human persons,[41] for example, suggests a model that is more hydraulic than personal; and mystical aspiration for union with God often strains the conceptual structures of the interpersonal. What is essential to my theory at this point is just to postulate a strong enough analogy of personality in God to sustain such claims as that God loves, commands, has reasons.

2. The Good itself is a *real* being. The most famous argument for this conclusion is Anselm's: that nonexistence, and even possible nonexistence, are imperfections, and therefore must not be ascribed to the supreme Good. This argument carries the intriguing suggestion of a being *so excellent that it could not fail to exist*. Anselm's "ontological" argument may indeed be best interpreted in a metaethical context, as an argument that the supreme Good must be understood as an existing being,

---

40. A similar but doubtless shakier line of argument might be used to support the conclusion that the Good itself is also importantly like a *society* of persons, as claimed by the Christian doctrine of the Trinity. For we confidently ascribe excellences to social systems and to interpersonal relationships, and we value those excellences highly. So if we think excellence consists in resembling or imaging the Good itself, we seem to be committed to the belief that societies and social relationships can resemble or image the Good itself. And that is likelier to be possible if the Good itself is importantly like a society.

41. The image is biblical: Joel 2:28 (3:1 in the Hebrew numbering); Acts 2:17.

and moreover as existing necessarily.[42] The argument from chapter 2 of Anselm's *Proslogion* concerned with existence (leaving necessary existence out of account) can be laid out in the following form:

(1) "Something exists in the understanding, at least, than which nothing greater can be conceived."

(2) "Suppose it exists in the understanding alone" and not in reality.

(3) "Then it can be conceived to exist [also] in reality,"

(4) "which is greater." [That is, what can be conceived according to (3) is greater than what exists in the understanding alone according to (2).]

(5) "Therefore, if that than which nothing greater can be conceived exists in the understanding alone [that is, if (2) is true], the very being than which nothing greater can be conceived is one than which a greater can be conceived."

(6) "But obviously this [which follows from (2)] is impossible."

(7) Therefore (2) is false and "a being than which nothing greater can be conceived . . . exists both in the understanding and in reality."

One influential modern objection to the argument points out, in effect, that the absurdity alleged in (5) follows from the previous steps only if (1) means that something exists, in the understanding at least, that is not merely *conceived* as unsurpassably great but *actually is* so great that nothing greater can be conceived. The objector then argues that while we might be ready to accept (1) on the weaker interpretation of it, on the ground that we understand the meaning of the phrase 'something than which nothing greater can be conceived', our understanding of a phrase could not possibly show that there actually is something of such surpassing greatness. Much more argument would be required to show that.

In a previous work Anselm actually had given an extensive argument that might in his mind have justified the strong interpretation of the first premise of his onto-logical argument, and this provides a starting point for a metaethical interpretation of the latter argument. In the first chapter of his *Monologion* he gives a Platonic argument that there must be some one thing through which all good things are good, and that it alone is good through itself and supremely good. The argument of the *Monologion* is not nearly as clearly articulated as that of the *Proslogion*, and is al-ready an argument for the *existence* of the supreme Good. But if we take *Monologion* 1 as an argument that there must be a standard of all goodness that is itself un-surpassably good, whether or not it is a really existing being, and combine it with *Proslogion* 2, we may get an argument that is more promising than can be found in either text alone. For if step (1) in the "ontological" argument appeals not merely to our understanding of a phrase (the appeal that is explicit in *Proslogion* 2) but also

---

42. A similar view of the argument is the theme of chapter 13 of Murdoch, *Metaphysics as a Guide to Morals*.

to a metaethical conviction that there must be a standard of all goodness that actually is unsurpassably good, whether it actually exists or not, and if we are persuaded that it would not be unsurpassably good if it did not exist, we will then have reason to conclude that it actually exists. If we give him this much, Anselm might argue, in support of step (3), that anything incapable of existence would be too defective to be the objective standard of goodness; and, in support of step (4), that the standard would be more impressive if it actually exists; and that the rest of the argument follows from those premises.

This is not the place for a detailed assessment of Anselm's much-debated argument. Instead I want to offer an argument analogous to the metaethical version of Anselm's that I have sketched. This will be an argument about what my theory demands, metaphysically, of the Good itself. It will not be so ambitious as to be a "proof" of the existence of God, though I do hope that, taken together with whatever advantages my theory possesses, it commends the proposition that the Good itself is an actually existing being.

Could the role of the Good itself be filled by a being that is not actual but, presumably, at most a possible being? Not as well, I think, if it is indeed an advantage for the theory to be able to draw, as I have in section 3, on the assumption that the Good is a being that actually appreciates things and has actual aims and actual causal influence on other things. Other reasons for thinking the Good should be something actual may be found in misgivings about the ontological status of the merely possible. Perhaps mere possibilities have no standing in the world except as objects of understanding, especially if they are not physical possibilities, as a transcendent Good would not be. But *we* do not understand the Good itself, in all its perfection. And if God understands it, then God is there as a real being to fill the role of the Good.

"Must it really be God who understands it?" an objector may ask. "Could there be a supreme intelligence that envisages a perfect standard of excellence that it lacks the power to exemplify in itself?" I doubt that, for I am inclined to think that the representation of anything rich enough to be a perfect standard of excellence must depend on its actual exemplification. It is relevant here that I think the perfect or transcendent good is positive and cannot be adequately conceived by negation of the imperfect (as I will emphasize in the first section of chapter 2), and thus is richer rather than poorer or more abstract than the imperfect. However, a thorough development of this way of excluding alternatives to my hypothesis would carry us deep into ontology, and far from the center of our present, ethical investigation.

Another argument is drawn from the rather determinate character (ideally a completely determinate character) that the Good itself must have in order to serve as the standard of excellence. If there is to be such a thing as the Good itself, our apprehension and pursuit of excellence must be sufficient, under actual conditions, to fix the paradigm reference of 'good' or 'excellent' to a determinate object. But on my version of the Platonic view, nothing like an adequately complete determination is implicit in our apprehension and pursuit. They can fix the reference of 'good' or 'excellent' only if some candidate for the role is salient, under actual conditions, in relation to them. God is surely the salient candidate, if God really exists. But if no suitable candidate really exists, and there are only the merely possible candidates, none of them is likely to be salient. This is not to say that other possible beings would be as good as the actual God, assuming that God does exist; it is rather to say that our semantic practice does not have the power that the nature of a real deity has to determine a standard of excellence. The possible objects that fit the fuzzy and fragmentary indications of our apprehension and pursuit of the excellent will be too many and various; and there will be no objective standard of excellence. For this reason I am inclined to say that an actually existing being is needed to fill the role of the Good itself. It might be an alternative to allow that what is good may be as indefinite as the plurality of possible ideal standards; but that would be a major concession from the point of view of the interest in finding an objective standard of value.

3. If we take the idea that the excellence of other things consists in a sort of resemblance to the Good itself, and infer from it (as I have suggested that we might or might not) that degrees of excellence must correspond to degrees of similarity to the Good itself, we can give an argument for the view that any being that is to be the Good itself must be, in Anselm's famous phrase, "a being than which nothing greater can be conceived." 'Greater' must be taken here, of course, as Anselm meant it, as signifying *better*. And whatever he may have meant by 'can be conceived', for our purposes it must mean *could possibly have been actual*. It is no more possible for a being that exceeds our powers of conception, than for one conceivable by us, to be more excellent than the Good itself is.

Here is the argument. Let X be the Good itself; and suppose that excellence therefore consists in a sort of resemblance to X. No being could be more like X than X itself is. So if excellence consists in a sort of resemblance to X, no being could be more excellent than X is.

Similar reasons might be given for thinking that X itself could not have been better than it is. Suppose (contrary to a suggestion I shall shortly make) that X could have been different in some respect intuitively relevant to its value. What would be the standard for determining which version of X, the actual or the merely possible, is better? Our hypothesis excludes any standard of goodness distinct from X. So the standard must be X itself; and surely X cannot serve as a standard except in one of its possible versions. The obvious version of X to take as the standard of goodness is the actual version. If we do not appeal to a standard distinct from X, what grounds could there be to prefer some other possible version to the actual version of X as the standard? And if the actual version is the standard, how could some other possible version be more like it than it is like itself?

It is more difficult to determine whether X could grow better if X is the Good itself—that is, whether some actual but future state of X could be better than the present state of X. It might seem natural to answer this question in the negative, on the ground that if X is to be the standard of goodness, it must be so in one of its possible states, and that if any of X's possible states is obviously salient for this purpose, it is its present actual state. On the other hand, it might be suggested that if X is changing in a direction that is already determined with certainty, it is the direction of change, rather than any of the temporary states, that should be taken as determining the nature of the good, and X could thus be regarded as continually increasing in value. I have not stated my theory in a form that allows for this, but perhaps it could be done. The question is obviously relevant to disputes between process theologians and more traditional theists.

4. These thoughts suggest a larger question: What would be true about goodness if God were different, or if God did not exist? In such a case might kindness or creativity fail to be good? If there are possible worlds in which God would be sadistic, or would love cowardice, would sadism or cowardice be good in such a world? That conclusion is too much to swallow; but at least two approaches remain open to me. I will begin with the less ambitious approach, but only after raising another question.

What *is* true about goodness if God *does* not exist, or *is* not in fact a suitable candidate for the role of the Good? This is a conditional question about the actual world, not about other possible worlds; and I am confident of my answer to it. If there is no God, or if God is in fact not a suitable candidate for the role of the Good, then my theory is false, but there may be some other salient, suitable candidate, and so some other theory of the nature of the good may be true.

Against this background I offer the less ambitious approach to the corresponding question about other possible worlds, which I asked on the assumption that God does exist, and is a suitable candidate, in the actual world. A deity would have to satisfy certain conditions (for instance, not being sadistic, and not loving cowardice) in order to be the salient candidate for filling the role indicated by our concept of the Good, though it is part of the point of my theory that such requirements do not completely determine what the deity would be like. If there is a God that satisfies these conditions imposed by our concepts, we might say, then excellence is the property of faithfully imaging such a God, or of resembling such a God in such a way as to give God a reason for loving. In worlds where no such God exists, nothing would have *that* property, and therefore nothing would be excellent. But beings like us in such a world might have a concept subjectively indistinguishable from our concept of excellence, and there might be an objective property that corresponded to it well enough, and in a sufficiently salient way, to be the property signified by it, though it would not be the property that we in fact signify by 'excellent'.

Alternatively, we could say that excellence is the property of having whatever property best fills a certain role indicated by our language, rather than being the property that itself fills such a role. Thus God could be the best candidate for an objective standard of excellence in the actual world, and something else could be the best candidate in some other possible world, and things conforming to the two standards in their respective worlds would have the same property of excellence, on this account. This trans-world property of excellence might be too artificial, and relative in too many dimensions, for the taste of some, however. Another possibility, perhaps no more satisfying, would be to say that we evaluate possibilities from our standpoint in the actual world and that excellence in any possible world is measured by conformity to the standard of excellence as it is in the actual world—so that, on my theory, what God is like in the actual world will determine the nature of excellence in all possible worlds.

The less ambitious approach may fail to satisfy, due to the strong intuitive support for the view that excellence is so tightly tied to what things are like that it should not be a contingent matter what it would be excellent to be like.[43] This is one of the considerations that incline me toward the more ambitious approach, which rejects the presupposition that God could have failed to exist or to be a good candidate for the role of the Good. It supposes that God's existence is metaphysically, or absolutely, necessary. This is a controversial view, and I know of no conclusive proof of its truth. I have argued elsewhere, however, that it is an eligible hypothesis for metaphysical speculation,[44] and I will not repeat those arguments here. What calls for more discussion here is the further supposition that those properties that fit God, so to speak, for the role of supreme Good follow necessarily from the divine nature—so that God *cannot* be sadistic, or love cowardice, for example.

This thesis has drawn objections alleging that it is inconsistent with divine omnipotence, but I am not persuaded that it limits God's power in the relevant sense. Things can have powers that they are prevented from exercising. You can have the physical power to accomplish a certain result even if for some reason it is impossible that you should choose to do so, perhaps because you are too nice to do it. A fully armed soldier may have the power to kill an enemy soldier, but be "unable to bring himself" to do it (I have read that that often happens). Something similar can be true of God. On the assumption, controversial but correct, in my opinion, that there can be truths about what would happen under impossible conditions, it can be true that a state of affairs would obtain if God chose that it should, even though for some reason it is absolutely impossible that God should make that choice. This indicates a sense in which God's metaphysical power could extend beyond God's possibility of choice, and I believe it is the sense with which the doctrine of divine omnipotence is concerned.

More disturbing is the objection that this limitation of God's possibility of choice diminishes the divine *freedom*. In response to this objection let us note first that there is no suggestion here of God's will being subject to any external constraint or any external standard. The only limits envisaged are those that are thought of as following from God's own nature. Moreover, we need not suppose that God's actions are determined in detail by the divine nature. What I would suppose follows in the first instance from the divine nature is a certain general character of God's disposition and life, from which, to be sure, God's actions spring. Certain features of God's desires and aversions, likes and dislikes are determined in this way. We may suppose it is part of the divine nature, for instance, that God is generally disposed to rejoice in the joys, and dislike the sufferings, of any actual being, and would not want or will eternal misery for the innocent. This seems consistent enough with the conception of God as a voluntary agent. Some of *our* desires are given by our natures, after all, or at any rate by something in our makeup that we do not control.

---

43. The grounds alleged here have specifically to do with *excellence*. I am not endorsing the widely held view that *none* of the most fundamental evaluative and normative standards can be contingent. In chapters 11 and 15 I will argue that the most fundamental standard of ethical right and wrong may be in some ways contingent.

44. Adams, "Has It Been Proved That All Real Existence Is Contingent?" and "Divine Necessity."

I go a step farther when I suggest that there are higher order desires that follow from the divine nature. These are desires about God's other desires and voluntary choices—for instance, a desire to live in harmony with the desires that are part of the divine nature. Here there is certainly a disanalogy between God and us, on this account. For our higher order volitions are not given as part of our nature, but acquired in the course of personal development; and our choices have a lot to do with the development. But we would not expect God to be very like us in this anyway, if (with most of the theological tradition) we do not think of God as acquiring a character by a personal development.

A crucial point is reached with the additional assumption that it is part of the divine nature that God's higher order desires are necessarily harmonious with each other and necessarily efficacious. It follows from the divine nature that God wants what God wants to want and lives as God wants to live. This is not exactly a part of divine omnipotence, but it is very much akin to omnipotence. It is also connected with freedom. Indeed, it has been suggested that freedom of the will is found precisely in the ability to have and be governed by the desires one wants to have and be governed by.[45] And even if we will not go so far as to accept that suggestion, few would consider it a bondage to be so constituted that one always wants what one wants to want, and always chooses in harmony with one's desires.

Now let us add that the desires, and especially the higher order desires, that are part of the divine nature are such as fit God for the role that our concepts indicate for the supreme Good. Higher order desires that would help to fit a being for that role would certainly be desires for a disposition and a life suited to the role. So if such higher order desires follow from the divine nature and are necessarily efficacious, God will be necessarily, not contingently, suited to the role.

We can still say that many features of God's preferences and actions, and indeed of God's loves, are contingent. God could have created quite a different world, or none at all, and could have had rather different aspirations for a world at least very similar to the actual world. Doing any of those things would have been compatible with being what the divine nature determines that God wants to be. God must appreciate all those alternatives as good possibilities, or possibilities there would have been some reason for actualizing, though without necessarily loving them in such a way as to want to actualize them.

The freedom thus ascribed to God does not include, as ours does, a possibility of desiring or choosing those ends that are rightly counted as bad. But this is not a perfection of which God is deprived, as it is not something that in us is good in itself, though it may be necessary, in a creature, for something that is good in us. It may be necessary for our autonomy in loving and choosing the good, necessary for the small measure of independence we may be thought to have in relation to God; whereas preferences following from the divine nature are perfectly compatible in God with the divine aseity, or absolute independence, which our autonomy only distantly imitates.

45. Frankfurt, "Freedom of the Will and the Concept of a Person."

I think this account of the modality of God's character has sufficient attractions, particularly from the point of a theistic theory of the Good, to be provisionally adopted in this context. But I must confess that if asked *how* certain desires, for example, would follow from God's nature, I can only plead the extreme imperfection of human insight into the divine nature.[46] That is certainly reason for hesitation about the hypothesis.

Against this background, and with that caution, I can introduce the following qualifications into my theory of the nature of the Good. It is with respect to the divine nature that God must be faithfully imaged by other good things. A thing can be good by imitating a contingent property of God; but that is because the divine nature is manifested in the contingent properties too. They do not define the divine goodness. The standard of goodness is defined by the divine nature, and thus is defined for all possible worlds (assuming that God exists necessarily).

46. I obviously cannot use an account that explains what God is like in terms of a prior standard of excellence. I admit that I am more suspicious of the appeal to our ignorance of the divine nature in this context than in a defense of belief in the necessity of God's existence, because what is supposed to be necessary here is much richer in detail.

2

THE TRANSCENDENCE
OF THE GOOD

The realm of value is organized around a transcendent Good. That is the thesis I am most concerned to commend in this book. It is opposed to all forms of subjectivism, noncognitivism, and antirealism about value, and particularly about excellence. Within the realm of realism about value, it is opposed to all forms of naturalism, which would seek the nature of value exclusively within the horizon of the physical and human world. The debate with naturalism will furnish much of the material of the present chapter.

The Good is transcendent in the sense that it vastly surpasses all other good things, and all our conceptions of the good. They are profoundly imperfect in comparison with the Good itself. This is an aspect of the opposition of the transcendence thesis to antirealism about value. If the Good so surpasses all we understand, it has properties that go beyond anything that we have any way of conceiving or any basis for believing. There must therefore be a distinction, and not merely in principle, between what is true about it and what we conceive or believe or have reason to believe about it. And that is the sort of distinction that is postulated by metaphysical realism about any subject.

Plato stresses the imperfection of all natural objects by comparison with the Good. At the same time he seems to have thought that when we correctly perceive anything as valuable or good, as worthy of love or admiration, we are apprehending, albeit imperfectly, the Good itself; this points to an experiential ground of belief

50

in a transcendent Good. Typical experiences of value can be seen as fragmentary glimpses (or, on Plato's view, reminders) of a transcendently wonderful object. In the *Symposium* Plato develops this view of the experience of beauty; and I think its plausibility with respect to aesthetic value has long been a main source of the appeal of Platonic philosophy. In the experience of beauty—the beauty of a person or a work of art or the evening light falling on leaves or mountains—is it not true that we are apt to feel that we are dimly aware of something too wonderful to be contained or carried either by our experience or by the physical or conceptual objects we are perceiving? We may also be tempted to dismiss this feeling as a romantic illusion; but I am inviting the reader to make, in good Platonic company, the experiment of regarding it as veridical.

The point is important also for the theistic adaptation of Platonism. There are points at which aesthetic and religious perceptions mingle, and the experience I am describing is at least close kin to that which leads people to speak of "seeing the glory of God" in a beautiful sunset. The glory of God here is the wonderful though fragmentary visibility of something vastly more valuable than other things, something too good for us to have more than a dim and imperfect apprehension of it. To a theism that identifies the Good itself with God, this sort of transcendence of the Good will be of the utmost importance.

1. The Holy

Theistic Platonism seeks a standard of goodness, not on a human scale, lying primarily within nature, but far above nature. The good is not exactly "at home" in human life. It is not just that human lives generally lack identifiable deeds and attitudes that ethics demands or recommends. That sort of deficiency, on which simple moralism loves to dwell, is superficial by comparison with that which is inherent in the perspectival character of human excellence. In profile, so to speak, we image the Good, but not frontally. What from one point of view, and not falsely, is a creative, courageous, public-spirited action is likely from another point of view, and again not falsely, to be a deeply questionable act of self-aggrandizement. What in one perspective is truly seen as an admirable independence of mind is as truly seen in another as a readiness to despise others. This variability of perspective is reflected in the religious sensibility that sees "all our righteousness as filthy rags." I do not mean to deny that there is real excellence, real imaging of the Good, in human life; but in such ways as I have been mentioning it is not "at home" in human life.

Conversely, we are not likely to be wholly comfortable with the Good itself; it has an alien aspect. It is not merely an extension and refinement of familiar values. How can we characterize an excellence that lies beyond our cognitive grasp? The commonest move, in both philosophy and theology, has been to the negative. It is claimed that we cannot say what God is, but only what God is not. Or we characterize God in terms of universal quantifiers, which (as every logician knows) are implicitly negative. God knows everything, can do anything; that is, there is nothing God does not know, nothing God cannot do. This is the refinement and extension of familiar values. We cannot afford to do without these negative and universal claims altogether, but this strategy has had a harmful effect on our thinking both about God and about perfection in general.

Consider the saints. We often think of the saint in essentially negative terms, as someone who never, or almost never, does a no-no; or in terms of universal quantification, as a person all, or almost all, of whose actions meet a high moral and religious standard. This conception does not meet the test of reality very well. Saints, and especially the most interesting and attractive among them, are typically rough-edged and controversial characters, liable to quite reasonable and often serious criticism from various directions. What is wonderful about them is nothing so tame as a freedom from faults, but something much more positive—and much stranger, as I will soon be arguing.[1]

Similarly, in thinking about the divine perfection, or the attributes of the being that is the standard of value, we should suppose that God's superiority exceeds our cognitive grasp in a positive direction, and is not exhausted by negative or universalizing operations on properties familiar to us. The divine knowledge, love, beauty are not just free from defects we can identify; they contain a richness we can hardly name.[2] To us this richness is bound to be alien in ways we may find uncomfortable.

Here it may be helpful to give the transcendence of the divine perfection the name that has characterized it for the Western religious traditions, and call it *holiness*. The idea of the Holy, as Rudolf Otto argued,[3] is an idea of something that is wonderful in a way that escapes both human understanding and human purposes. The Holy is fascinating, the Holy is beautiful, the Holy is bliss; the Holy is just, the Bible claims, though we may not understand its justice; the Holy is love, according to Christians; but 'nice' is definitely not the word for it. From a human point of view, the Holy has rough edges. It screams with the hawk and laughs with the hyenas. We cannot comprehend it. It is fearful to us, and in some ways dangerous. All of this, on the theistic view that I favor, is true of the Good itself. We are not the measure of all things, and have at best a very imperfect appreciation of the full dimensions of the good.

The strangeness of the Holy can be reflected in ideals of human life, or of sainthood; *holy person* is the original meaning of 'saint'. There are undoubtedly excellences of the normal and natural, and theists in the Platonic tradition have typically thought that life and health, for example, are ways of resembling God. But what theists most admire, even within human life, is not easily identified as normal and natural. The saints are occasionally flourishing specimens of humanity in all the obvious ways, but usually not. They feel compunctions, and are torn by doubts, that others do

---

1. I have written more, in a somewhat similar vein, in Adams, "Saints."

2. Similarly, though I won't give the point a full development here, I think the extreme doctrine of divine simplicity, of Neoplatonist inspiration, which grounded much medieval thought about the otherness of God, offers much too formal a conception of that otherness. Its formality is a sign of its excessive reliance on materials that are only too familiar to our intellect. Certainly, if Platonistic theism is forced to choose between extreme simplicity and the imaging of God by creatures, it is the simplicity doctrine that must be abandoned; and I think it can be given up without insult to the divine transcendence.

3. Otto, *The Idea of the Holy.*

not know. They cling to a longing for goods that lie beyond any ordinary human possibility of attainment. Their behavior seems occasionally bizarre, and often unnatural. Kissing lepers and praying for people who are torturing you definitely do not seem natural responses. Indeed, I think it is often precisely in the unnaturalness, or better the supernaturalness, of the saints' goodness that their wonderfulness is found. In them it seems that we can glimpse or touch a goodness that is more than theirs, a superhuman, a transcendent goodness that we too long for.

The sense that an acceptable standard of value must lie beyond anything that normality can help us to recognize as natural is not peculiar to theists. Nietzsche, no friend of theism, foresaw with lamentation a time "when man will no longer shoot the arrow of his longing beyond man," and declared, "One must still have chaos in oneself to be able to give birth to a dancing star."[4] The inner chaos to which Nietzsche refers is certainly a part of much human creativity; and the fracturing of the finite, as in the paintings of Van Gogh, seems to many to put us in touch with something even more wonderful than the more perfect finite things represented in, for example, the art of Raphael.[5]

The transcendence of the Good thus carries over from the divine object of adoration, the Good itself, to ideals of human life, and thus to human ethics. Not that sainthood is all there is to anyone's ethics; but if we incorporate it in our ethical thinking, as I think we should, it does imply that full development of the normal and natural is not the capstone of ethical aspiration. We cannot expect this view to be uncontroversial, and it will be worth confronting it with Martha Nussbaum's recent critique of ethical ideals of transcendence.[6]

It should be noted first of all that her claims and mine are not squarely and neatly opposed. Her main model for the transcendence she rejects is the Greek gods, and thus what she herself calls "the image of an anthropomorphic perfection" formed by refining the best of human life by "the removal of constraints that make human life a brief, chancy and in many ways miserable existence."[7] She is able to argue persuasively that the result of such refinement is not clearly better than the best of human life, because she is able to argue (echoing much theodicy) that much of the best of human life depends, not just causally but conceptually, on the very constraints to which the gods are not to be subject. I can accept what she says about the Greek gods because the superiority ascribed to them, achieved by subtracting some features of human life and magnifying other features that remain straightforwardly conceivable and essentially familiar to us, is much less than the transcendence that I mean to ascribe to the Good. The Greek gods are much less than God. A truly transcendent Good, which we image, and conceive, only in a fragmentary way, need not, and presumably cannot, have all the properties that are involved in our fragmentary imaging of it. And if we free ourselves from the devices of negation as our primary strategy for conceiving of transcendent excellence, we may be better able to think of the divine perfection as compatible with analogues of properties, such

---

4. Nietzsche, *Thus Spoke Zarathustra*, p. 129.
5. This is not to deny, of course, that religious symbolism is present in the art of Raphael.
6. "Transcending Humanity," chap. 15 in Nussbaum, *Love's Knowledge*.
7. Nussbaum, *Love's Knowledge*, p. 371.

as change and pain, that the strategy of negation has commonly denied to God. Bliss is something much more positive (and much harder to conceive, in the perfect case) than absence of pain.

As regards human ethics, Nussbaum's main thesis seems to be that we should not seek to transcend *humanity*. That is, we should not aspire to imitate the Greek gods by escaping our natural limits so as to live something other than a fully human life. This too I largely accept. Sainthood is not to be conceived as something other than a fully human life. Saints do not merely accept such human limits as physical and mental weakness, mortality, and liability to frustration and suffering; they sometimes positively revel in them. They are admired and imitated more for their perceived ability to cope with such problems than for any supposed ability to escape them.

There remains a strand in Nussbaum's critique of transcendence that seems to be more opposed to what I want to say about the manifestation of the Holy in human life. She proposes for us, as part of an Aristotelian conception, what she calls "the fully human target of complete virtue."[8] That it is a *target*, not an actual achievement, allows for what she calls an "internal" transcendence, a "transcendence of our *ordinary* humanity"[9]—that is, of our numerous actual moral deficiencies. That it is a fully human target I can accept, as I have said. My sticking point is the concept of "complete virtue." Completeness signifies a limit. There is no such thing as going beyond *complete* virtue, though there is plenty of falling short of it. This is expressed by Aristotle's statement, quoted with approval by Nussbaum, that "there are many ways of missing the target . . . and only one way of hitting it," which Aristotle explains with the comment "For evil belongs to the unlimited, as the Pythagoreans say, but good to the limited."[10] The association of good with the limited was extremely influential in ancient thought, and may lie at the root of essentially negative conceptions of perfection. It is diametrically opposed to the fundamentally positive conception of transcendent Good that I espouse, which sees the primary case of excellence in the infinite.

I am not sure that the phrase "complete virtue" and the image of scoring a bull's-eye on a target are truly representative of Nussbaum's ethical outlook. She affirms emphatically an incommensurability of values that leaves human agents often having to make tragic choices in which what must be sacrificed if another value is to be achieved is not simply less of the same value but something qualitatively different, unique, and not fully comparable.[11] The concept of "*complete* virtue" does not seem to me to fit comfortably whatever excellence can be manifested in making such tragic choices. And the idea that one may have scored a bull's-eye in deciding to sacrifice one value (or one person!) for another strikes me as downright repulsive. Whether or not the phrase "complete virtue," as I understand it, really fits Nussbaum's view,

8. Nussbaum, *Love's Knowledge*, p. 378.
9. Nussbaum, *Love's Knowledge*, p. 378.
10. Aristotle, Nicomachean Ethics, 1106b28–31. I quote the first statement in Nussbaum's felicitous translation (*Love's Knowledge*, p. 97); the second in my own translation. In relation to issues discussed later, it is worth noting that the context is one in which Aristotle is presenting his conception of virtue as a *mean*.
11. E.g., Nussbaum, *Love's Knowledge*, pp. 133, 137.

it does fit some important ethical views; and it is with them that I wish to contrast an ethics that makes room for holiness and for saints.

Two conceptions of complete virtue as a limit may be considered here. One is an Aristotelian conception of virtue as a "golden mean" between extremes. Vice is in excess or deficiency, virtue in hitting the right balance between them. There are particular virtues and vices in particular qualities or areas of life in which we may hit or fail to hit the mean; there is also a more encompassing virtue which consists in a balanced development of different virtues and different natural capacities, and a balanced pursuit of our natural motives. Apart from the elimination of flaws that are in principle identifiable and typically minor, there cannot be levels of possible human excellence above ordinary human virtue on this view. To *go beyond* the mean of virtue is to fall into the vice of excess.[12]

The golden mean is not acceptable, in my opinion, as a complete ideal of virtue. There is certainly an excellence, sometimes largely achieved, in the judiciously (perhaps even exquisitely) balanced human life. But the value of such balance is one of the often incompatible values among which we sometimes have to choose. There are also values of extravagance, and some of them are great values, and command a more astonished admiration than the values of the balanced life. What is most admired in saints is often to be found among the values of extravagance.

The other most prominent conception of complete virtue as a limit is one of deontological perfection (perfection with regard to the fulfilment of obligation). Since 'ought' implies 'can', it may be argued, it must be possible to do *everything* one is morally obliged to do; and when one does that, and is disposed to do it, there is no way to go farther in virtue, if virtue consists wholly in moral dutifulness. This is of course an essentially negative conception of moral perfection as omitting, and being disposed to omit, *nothing* of what one ought to do. Such a conception does not necessarily exclude the possibility of extravagant virtue, for the demands of duty can be extreme. If they require us to do *whatever* will have the best outcome, as utilitarians hold, they may typically be more extreme than most (or perhaps any) of us will be willing to fulfil. Even in such an extreme and rigorous form, however, the ideal of deontological perfection lacks an important open-endedness.

My point is not just that morality should allow for the possibility of supererogation—that is, of morally meritorious deeds that are not morally required. I do believe that, but I am more interested here in a qualitative than in a quantitative open-endedness.[13] The saints, to be sure, are often remarkable in quantitative ways,

12. My project is not one of exegesis of Aristotle, but I should note that it may be questioned whether the doctrine of virtue as a mean fully represents Aristotle's own view. The virtue of contemplation in Book X of the *Nicomachean Ethics* (not Nussbaum's favorite part of Aristotle's ethics, to be sure) does not appear to be a mean between extremes, and has no clear human limit. I am indebted to Owen McCleod for pressing me on this point.

13. This is related to the distinction made earlier between negative and positive conceptions of perfection. Quantitative open-endedness can be conceived negatively, as a possibility of transcending the morally ordinary by omitting less of what is obligatory or good to do. The qualitative open-endedness of the virtue of the saints, as a possibility of expanding the human repertoire, cannot be conceived in such negative terms. It can only be a possibility of transcending the morally ordinary in a positive direction.

doing and caring more about things we all recognize we should care and do something about. But that is not what is most characteristic of the saints that seem to me most interesting ethically—people like Francis of Assisi and Gandhi. They don't just do more of what we all know to do. More important, they envisage and do, and show others how to do, things that no one else had thought of doing. They don't just draw from a standard repertoire of what is natural for humans; they expand the human repertoire, and in ways that may never seem entirely natural. It seems too confining to suppose there is any definite limit on the possibilities of such expansion. Reflecting about this, we may be more inclined to reject, as insufficiently open-ended, the standard utilitarian assumptions that there is a best possible outcome, and hence a best possible way to act, in any situation.

For such reasons as these the idea of *complete human* virtue seems to me implausible. If there is to be a complete excellence, it must be one that transcends the human. Of course one could try to maintain an open-ended aspiration without believing in any complete Good, but I think it is no accident that expansions of the repertoire of human virtue have so often been associated with aspiration and devotion directed toward a superhuman, transcendent Good.

As a Christian, I may be asked, must I not think that complete human virtue is actual at least in Christ, and therefore possible in principle? I think not. Mistakes have often been made on this point in christology. The range of historic senses of 'perfect' facilitates confusion. In one of its oldest senses it is a synonym of 'complete'. When it is said, traditionally, that Christ is "perfect man and perfect God," the principal meaning is that both his human nature and his divine nature are complete—for example, that he has both the divine intellect and a human rational soul, as opposed to having the divine intellect *instead* of a human rational soul, as proposed by the Apollinarian heresy. Perfect (or complete) humanity in this context means having everything that belongs to a normal human being, and I have offered no argument against the possibility of perfect humanity in that sense.

The idea of a person having every human excellence in unsurpassable degree, on the other hand, does seem to me inconsistent with the nature of human excellence. There is not much pressure for christology to assert that much anyway. Few would be disturbed by the admission that there have been more accomplished athletes and greater musicians than Jesus. It is chiefly with regard to moral and spiritual excellence that people have been concerned to assert the unsurpassability of Christ's human nature. Even in this area, however, I think christology would be well advised to conceive of Christ's human virtue along the lines I proposed earlier for the virtue of the saints—as extraordinary indeed, and expanding the human repertoire, but as qualitative, positive, and open-ended, rather than as quantitative, negative, and a limit. There is no need for Christians to assert that the courage, love, faithfulness, and moral and spiritual insight of Jesus define a limit to the excellence that human life can exemplify in those areas. Jesus is presented indeed in the Bible as saying that those who believe in him will do greater works than he has done (John 14:12).

The doctrine of incarnation does imply the presence of a fully transcendent goodness in Christ. But if one accepts the Chalcedonian[14] conception of the one

14. So called after the council of Chalcedon, 451 C.E., which defined the doctrine in these terms.

person of Christ as having two distinct natures, one a complete divine nature and the other a complete human nature, one can attribute the fully transcendent goodness to the divine nature, and need not ascribe to the human nature a perfection that a finite nature is not fitted to bear.

According to the traditional doctrine, of course, Christ was perfectly *sinless* in his human nature. I believe the concept of a sinless person is compatible with the limitations of humanity, as the concept of a morally unsurpassable person is not. I invoke here a conception of sin that I think is consonant with much religious literature and that draws on ideas of devotion and vocation that will be developed in chapters 7 and 13. It identifies sin, not with wrongdoing or guilt as such, but with being against the good, or failing to be for the good (in some way that one ought to have been for the good), and thus failing (at least in part) to be allied with the Good. This includes failures to *love* the good, to *respect* it, *care about* it, *appreciate* it—and also failures to *do* the good.[15] This conception should be construed broadly enough also to count as sin disordered interests in good things, such as may constitute idolatry or selfishness. Sin, in this sense, is compatible with morally correct behavior—a point often stressed in religious exhortations to a rigorous examination of conscience.

Wrongdoing will in most cases constitute sin in this sense, but perhaps not in every case. Some wrongdoing arises from inadvertence, or simply from not seeing what goods are at stake; and this can happen because one was attending, perhaps rightly, to other things. Liability to this kind of error is arguably inseparable from human nature and its very limited capacity for attention. What is done in this way is still wrong; one may owe apologies and be liable to penalties for it; but it is not necessarily sin in the sense of a failure to be for the good as one ought to have been. For one may have been loving the good as one ought to have, in attending to the goods one in fact attended to, rather than others; and being for the good is primarily a matter of motivation, and paradigmatically of loving the good, and of action only as the relevant motives ground and demand the action.

The idea that there are some ways rather than others in which an individual *ought* to be for the good is obviously important to this conception of sin. It is connected with the thought that in view of our finitude a human individual can be responsible only for attending to a limited set of goods. That is part of the idea of *vocation*, especially if that idea is developed, as it will be in chapter 13, in terms of goods that are given to an individual to love. Which failures to be for the good in particular ways are sin will depend on an individual's vocation—on what the person is individually called by God to be and do. Not every imperfection, even in moral matters, is sin, but only failure to fulfill one's vocation. This includes, I think, the point that one may without failing to fulfill one's vocation, and thus without sin, fail to be for the good in ways that may draw reasonable moral criticism from some point of view, and in ways that may give one occasion to offer apologies.

---

15. Failures of love, respect, appreciation, and other moral attitudes will not always be straightforwardly voluntary, of course. I do not think that keeps them from being sins. I have argued elsewhere that bad attitudes are sometimes involuntary sins, and I will not repeat the argument here. (See Adams, "Involuntary Sins.")

Whether one is entitled to be *confident* that one is not sinning in such a case is, of course, another question.

To ascribe complete freedom from sin in this sense to the Christ is to say that he was and did everything that was required by his divinely given vocation.[16] This conception of sinlessness is compatible with the perspectival character of human excellence. There are perspectives from which some of the behavior ascribed to Christ in the Gospels is not attractive, and we get a more plausible picture of the humanity of Christ if we do not have to suppose, for example, that members of his family were wrong ever to be angry at him. Even for a humanity personally united to the divine nature and in the relevant sense sinless, rough edges may go along with an extravagant virtue that marks an irruption of transcendent goodness into human life.

2. Naturalism

Much of section 1 has focused on ways in which the difference between a conception of the Good as transcendent and a more naturalistic conception may be reflected in contrasting substantive ideals for human life. Since the publication of G. E. Moore's *Principia Ethica* in 1903, however, 'naturalism' has served anglophone moral philosophy above all as a name of a type of *meta*ethical position, a view about the meaning of ethical terms and the nature of ethical properties. It is, roughly, the view that ethical terms signify natural properties, properties that are or will be mentioned in the best development of the natural sciences, including psychology and the other social sciences.[17] Naturalism was eclipsed for half a century, first by Moore's nonnaturalist realism and later by expressivist antirealism; but a vigorous revival in the last forty years or so has made it a strong competitor in contemporary metaethics. One influential form of naturalism particularly claims our attention here, because it adopts a view in the semantics of morals that is very similar to mine while holding a position in the metaphysics of morals that is quite opposed to the transcendence of the Good as I conceive of it. I will take Richard Boyd's "How to Be a Moral Realist" as a canonical statement of this type of naturalism.

Boyd relies on the same recent developments in philosophy of language to which I appealed in chapter 1, section 1, mentioning the same standard example of water being H_2O.[18] Boyd and I agree (1) that basic ethical terms are used to signify real properties, if there are any such properties that fit the roles indicated by our use of the terms, and (2) that understanding the linguistic meaning of the terms (being a competent user of the terms) does not imply knowing with any precision what properties they signify (except trivially, that they signify goodness, rightness, etc., if they signify anything). We also agree (3) that, nevertheless, as Boyd puts it, "ordinary

---

16. That is the obvious meaning of the famous last word τετέλεσται (it is finished or completed) from the cross (John 19:30).

17. This is a variation on the definition given in Moore, *Principia Ethica*, p. 92 (§26).

18. Boyd, "How to Be a Moral Realist," p. 195f.

use of moral terms provides us with epistemic access to moral properties,"[19] so that a significant proportion of our judgments about the moral properties of things are substantially correct—if our moral terms do indeed signify real properties.

We part company in choosing the realm in which to look for the ethical properties. Boyd chooses the natural realm and I the supernatural. This affects the way in which we compare the meaning of ethical terms with that of natural kind terms such as 'water'. The widely applicable semantical thesis, in my view, is just that the sense of the terms in question (in this case ethical terms) picks out a *role* that must be filled by the properties or objects (if any) to which the terms refer. I think that ethical terms do not signify *natural* kinds, and do not pick out the same kind of role that natural kind terms do. For Boyd, on the other hand, ethical terms do signify natural kinds, and the role they pick out is a *causal* role quite similar to the role his semantics of natural kinds would assign to water. They fall, in his view, under a widely applicable, naturalistic semantical thesis that he formulates as follows: "*Roughly*, and for nondegenerate cases, a term t refers to a kind (property, relation, etc.) k just in case there exist causal mechanisms whose tendency is to bring it about, over time, that what is predicated of the term t will be approximately true of k (excuse the blurring of the use-mention distinction)."[20]

Unlike many metaethical naturalists, Boyd does not offer a *definition* of the good. This is partly because he does not claim to know enough to offer a definitive account. He thinks that there has been progress in ethical understanding, but that fuller understanding of the nature of the good remains a task for science—that is, for natural science, broadly conceived.

A further reason for not offering a definition is that he favors the hypothesis that good is a natural kind constituted by what he calls a "homeostatic property-cluster."[21] Such a kind is characterized by a cluster of natural properties which tend to occur together, not accidentally but by virtue of homeostatic mechanisms or processes which tend to produce or maintain the rest of them when enough of them are present. There will probably be cases in which some but not all of the properties belonging to the cluster occur together. Causal factors involved in scientific theory can help us to decide which of these cases of imperfect clustering belong to the kind in question, but there will probably be borderline cases for which there is no correct answer to this question, no fact of the matter as to whether they belong to the kind or not. Boyd refers to these as cases in which "bivalence" fails, in which the claim that the case belongs to the kind has neither of the two values 'true' and 'false'. As examples of homeostatic property cluster kinds in this sense Boyd suggests *health* and *biological species*.[22] The latter example, by virtue of the evolutionary character of biological speciation, illustrates the further point that the membership and underlying mechanisms of a homeostatic property cluster can change (not too abruptly) over time.[23]

19. Boyd, "How to Be a Moral Realist," p. 210. I have changed "uses" to "use" to correct a grammatical error.
    20. Boyd, "How to Be a Moral Realist," p. 195.
    21. Boyd, "How to Be a Moral Realist," pp. 196–99, 217–18.
    22. Boyd, "How to Be a Moral Realist," p. 198.
    23. Boyd, "How to Be a Moral Realist," pp. 217–18.

It is a feature of homeostatic property cluster kinds that they have "no analytic definition."[24] There is a complex story to be told about any such kind, explaining what it is; but the same possibilities that lead to failures of bivalence also preclude the development of any algorithm for determining which cases belong to the kind, and hence of any useful analytic definition. Boyd's theory is thus not reductionist at the semantical level. There is not likely ever to be a theoretically or practically valuable replacement for the concept *tiger* in thinking about the natural kind, tigers; and Boyd does not seem to suppose that there will ever be a theoretically or practically valuable replacement for the concept *good* in thinking about the natural kind, good. If we are trying to classify something that has some but not all of the properties belonging to a kind's homeostatic cluster, what we want to know is whether the thing is a tiger, or good, as the case may be; and nothing is likely to be gained by restating the question in other terms, as long as we have no algorithm for answering it.

Boyd's hypothesis is explicitly consequentialist. The good is more fundamental than the right in his view, and well-being or what is good *for* people is more fundamental than moral goodness. He treats the value of morality as merely instrumental to well-being, and I cannot see that he offers any account of what I have been calling excellence. The most fundamental facts he supposes in this whole area consist in there being "a number of important human goods, things which satisfy important human needs." In typical human circumstances these goods are clustered by homeostatic mechanisms such as institutions of justice. What these mechanisms are, and which human goods (of well-being or welfare) there are, are important questions for empirical science. "Moral goodness is defined by this cluster of goods and the homeostatic mechanisms which unify them. Actions, policies, character traits, etc. are morally good to the extent to which they tend to foster the realization of these goods or to develop and sustain the homeostatic mechanisms upon which their unity depends."[25] Boyd does not claim to know definitively or in detail what is good, but he already commits himself to consequentialism. The mention of "actions" in the passage I just quoted suggests, indeed, that he is committed to act consequentialism, the doctrine that the moral value of each act depends on how well *it* fosters the recommended consequences—though he does not explain here how he thinks the consequentialist evaluation of actions is related to that of "policies" and "character traits."[26]

The sort of naturalism represented by Boyd is one of the most discussed positions in contemporary metaethics, and interesting arguments have been made against it as well as for it. A critical appreciation and evaluation of this naturalism will be helpful in formulating and assessing my opposing case for the transcendence of the Good. In this evaluation I will first of all set aside certain disagreements. I do not agree with Boyd's consequentialism or his neglect or avoidance of excellence. These

24. Boyd, "How to Be a Moral Realist," p. 196.
25. Boyd, "How to Be a Moral Realist," p. 203.
26. For argument to the effect that consequentialist evaluation of these diverse objects might lead in incompatible directions, see Adams, "Motive Utilitarianism."

are substantive ethical issues of great importance, but addressing them at this point would probably not help us to focus on the *meta*ethical issues.

In the end I will disagree fundamentally with Boyd's naturalism, but I want to acknowledge emphatically that it is a shrewdly and subtly articulated position that has important attractions, some of which I would like to appropriate, in part, for my own position. I will discuss four advantages of Boyd's theory before going on in sections 3 and 4 to consider the objections to it that most interest me, defending him against one of them in section 3, and urging the opposite one against him in section 4.[27]

One attraction of Boyd's position, which he himself emphasizes, is its realism. If goodness is a kind constituted by a homeostatic cluster of natural properties in the way that Boyd hypothesizes, it is certainly a real property that things have or lack objectively. Objectivity may be compromised to some extent by the failures of bivalence that Boyd allows, but it will be compromised only in the cases in which bivalence fails, and Boyd generally seems to think that these will be a relatively unimportant minority of cases. I think this problem may be more important than Boyd admits, and will return to it in section 4; but he certainly has a clearly articulated approach to achieving an attractive realism. The attraction of realism, of course, will belong to other forms of naturalism as well as Boyd's.

So will a second attraction, arising from the fact that there is wide agreement that the values of natural things (including our own lives) depend in some way on their natural properties. This is often put by saying that values "supervene" on natural properties, where that is understood to mean that any things with the same natural properties would *necessarily* have the same values. Not all metaethicists would accept this thesis about necessity; indeed, Boyd would not unless "the same natural properties" is understood as including sameness of historical circumstances *very* sweepingly construed. The less precise thesis, however, that natural things have their values *by virtue of* their natural properties is relatively uncontroversial. It is a thesis that I accept, inasmuch as natural things that resemble God do so, in general, by virtue of their natural properties.[28] On any plausible view natural properties have a large role in the determination of value. It is worth trying to see how far we can get in understanding values in purely natural terms, and Boyd offers an impressively sophisticated attempt at this.

It is also true that on any plausible view empirical knowledge plays an important role in ethical thinking. It is a commonplace that ethical wisdom is associated with rich experience, and we should expect that to be true if values depend on natural properties. Without experience of the natural properties on which values depend, we will lack knowledge of the values. (I will have much more to say about this in

27. One objection that I will *not* discuss is the *internalist* charge that Boyd is unable to tie motives or justifying reasons sufficiently tightly to the properties with which he identifies the good. Boyd can probably give a response somewhat similar to the one I have given to internalist questions about my own position (at the end of section 2 of chapter 1), but it would take too long a digression to show that here.

28. A property can be a natural property, in the sense that is relevant here, even if it is supernaturally *caused* in the particular case.

chapter 15, section 4.) Boyd's position has a third and special strength in this epistemological area. He not only emphasizes the role of experience in moral knowledge but also integrates his moral philosophy into a sophisticated philosophy of science (in ways that I will not attempt to summarize here). I will not be able, in the end, to identify moral knowledge with natural science to the extent that Boyd does; but it would be fatuous to deny the deserved appeal that such an integration of ethics with our most esteemed sciences has for modern minds.

Finally, it is a strength, I believe, that distinguishes Boyd's position from some other important sorts of naturalism that, as I have noted, he avoids semantical reduction of values, rejecting analytic definitions of the good. This feature has led some to speak of the position exemplified by Boyd as "nonreductionist" or "nonreductive naturalism."[29] No naturalistic analytic definition of the good has been able during the twentieth century to command wide acceptance. I believe that is because they are all, at best, too simple to be convincing. Boyd's account is subtler, and therefore stands a better chance of being right. Whether it escapes altogether the sorts of attack that have tended to discredit more reductionistic sorts of naturalism remains a question, however, to which we will return in section 4.

3. Empirical Testing, Explanation, and Value

The type of naturalism exemplified by Boyd has been charged both with allowing too little empirical testing of ethical doctrines and with relying too much on such testing. I will ultimately endorse the "too much" objection, which will be discussed in section 4; and, as that suggests, I am opposed to the "too little" objection, which will be discussed in the present section. In many contexts I would not discuss at length an objection I reject to a view that is not mine, but in this case I must attack the objection at least as radically as Boyd and his allies; for if their naturalism allows too little empirical testing in ethics, my supernaturalism allows less.

The "too little" objection has been pressed by Gilbert Harman, the main sponsor of one of the most interesting current versions of empiricism in ethical theory. In the second quarter of the twentieth century, and into the third, analytical metaethics was powerfully shaped by a radical empiricist criterion of meaning, which held that sentences have no cognitive meaning at all except insofar as they can be empirically verified or falsified (unless they are analytic, in the sense of being true simply by virtue of their meaning). Large areas of discourse were declared cognitively meaningless on the basis of this criterion. It gave a major impetus to the development of expressivist and other antirealist or noncognitivist analyses of ethical discourse, as ethical claims were widely held not to be empirically testable. One motive for revival of interest in naturalism at midcentury, conversely, was the hope that if ethical properties are identical with natural properties, theses about them will be empirically testable.

---

29. Darwall, Gibbard, and Railton, "Toward *Fin de siècle* Ethics," pp. 168–74.

The verifiability criterion of meaning was found by its sponsors to be burdened with serious, apparently irresolvable problems, and has long since been abandoned (though we still see revivals of closely related doctrines). Harman's empiricist doctrine is not a theory of meaning. He does propose a sweeping criterion to exclude claims that are not acceptable from an empiricist point of view, but he locates the criterion in epistemology (empiricism's most obvious home) rather than in semantics. His criterion is that no claim can reasonably be accepted as a statement of fact unless it is "empirically testable in all the ways that scientific claims are empirically testable."[30]

Against this epistemological background, in 1977, Harman opened his introductory text in ethics with "a basic philosophical problem about morality, its apparent immunity from observational testing," labeling this "the problem with ethics."[31] There is a deliberately provocative strategy here to get the attention of beginning students. The word "apparent" in the statement of the problem is significant, and Harman ultimately (though cautiously) favors a metaethical view (a reductionist form of naturalism) that would make ethical claims empirically testable. His statement of the problem is serious, however, and has been very influential.

It rests on a view of his own, also influential, about the nature of empirical confirmation. Harman holds that hypotheses are empirically tested by "inference to the best explanation." A thesis is empirically confirmed if it plays a part in the best explanation of our observations; empirically disconfirmed, if it is excluded (or made less probable) by the best explanation of our observations. This is Harman's version of a point that is at least as old as Hume: that empirical evidence for what is not directly experienced depends on broadly causal, explanatory relations with what is directly experienced.

3.1 Explanation and Value

In this context "the problem of ethics" is based on the claim that "you do not seem to need to make assumptions about any moral facts to explain the occurrence of . . . observations."[32] If you see some children setting fire to a cat (Harman's example), you will doubtless make what may be called the "moral observation" that the children are doing something wrong. "In order to explain your making" this judgment, Harman says, "it would be reasonable to assume, perhaps, that the children really are pouring gasoline on a cat and you are seeing them do it." But, he suggests,

> an assumption about moral facts would seem to be totally irrelevant to the explanation of your making the judgment you make. It would seem that all we

---

30. This phrase is found in Harman, "Moral Explanations of Natural Facts," p. 60, where it (with similar phrases in the same paper) represents the operative form of his criterion. Some empiricists would restrict application of the criterion to *nonanalytic* claims, but Harman avoids commitment here to the analytic/synthetic distinction, arguing that even mathematics, for example, is subject to empirical confirmation, at least indirectly; see Harman, *The Nature of Morality*, p. 9f.

31. Harman, *The Nature of Morality*, pp. vii, xi.

32. Harman, *The Nature of Morality*, p. 6.

need assume is that you have certain more or less well articulated moral principles that are reflected in the judgments you make, based on your moral sensibility. It seems to be completely irrelevant to our explanation whether your intuitive immediate judgment is true or false.[33]

It should be noted, with emphasis, that the suspicion of explanatory irrelevance that Harman presents in this pedagogically motivated, tentative, but still serious way can be disturbing to moral realists even apart from his particular epistemology of inference to the best explanation. For it is widely held that a belief can hardly be justified unless the truth of the belief is supposed to play some part in explaining one's holding the belief. This is not a wholly uncontroversial thesis. There are well-known doubts about explanatory connections between beliefs in higher mathematics, for example, and the truth of propositions there which are nonetheless almost universally thought to be rationally believed. But what we face here is not a narrowly empiricist issue. It is among the motives of "reliabilist" epistemologies that go in quite a different direction from Harman, and also of Kant's "Copernican turn" in his *Critique of Pure Reason*. The point here is that if we have knowledge, it should not be merely accidental that we are right; and if we have justified belief, it should be likely that we are right—likely not just subjectively but in terms of the causal, or at least explanatory, connections of things. This has led to the claim that knowledge and justified true belief should be explained, at least in part, by the fact known or truly believed. So if no moral facts are relevant to the explanation of our moral beliefs, that may be reason, from quite a variety of epistemological perspectives, to doubt the factuality of moral beliefs.

Some of the liveliest debate about Harman's articulation of the problem has focused on the explanatory relevance or irrelevance of moral facts, with Nicholas Sturgeon, who favors a form of naturalism similar to Boyd's, as Harman's principal debating partner; and this issue will repay attention here. It was an important thesis of much classical philosophy that values can indeed help explain why things happen. In his *Phaedo*, for instance, Plato has Socrates introduce the Forms as causes, with the Form of the Beautiful as a prime example (100C–D); and this in a context in which Socrates is responding to his own complaint against systems of explanation that fail to include the value of what happens among its causes (97C–99C). In the *Republic*, likewise, and famously, Plato offers the Form of the Good as the source of the being [εἶναι], the essence [οὐσία],[34] and the being known of the objects of knowledge (509B), and thus as maximally explanatory. In Aristotle the explanatory force of value is connected with the doctrine of the "final cause." The explanation 'for the sake of something' [ἕνεκά του] is equated with 'because it is better' [ὅτι βέλτιον] (*Physics* 198b17). It is the supreme value of God that fits God in Aristotle's system to be the final cause of the motion of the universe and thus, by being loved, to be the unmoved mover; in this connection Aristotle remarks that "in all things

---

33. Harman, *The Nature of Morality*, p. 7.
34. These two terms are close in meaning in Plato, οὐσία not having become yet the technical term that it is for Aristotle, but I take it that in this context εἶναι at least includes existence.

the good is supremely a principle" (*Metaphysics* 1075a37), where by "principle" [ἀρχή, source] he certainly means an explanatory factor and in a broad sense a cause.

In modern thought the idea of values as causes has been one of the more un-popular parts of the classical heritage. The rejection of final causes in modern physical science has carried with it the exclusion of values as terms of "scientific" explanations. It can hardly be denied that modern physics has prospered without admitting values among the terms of its theories. One could take this as warranting only a "local" conclusion about the appropriate strategies of explanation and inference in a particular scientific domain. Among early modern thinkers that was notably the view of Leibniz, who allowed that everything in physics can be explained mechanically, but held that final causes are useful for heuristic purposes and must be employed to understand the metaphysical foundations of things.[35] As one who believes that this world was created by God *because* it is the best of all possible worlds, Leibniz is particularly insistent on the explanatory value of goodness.[36] The dominant tendency of modern thought, however, has been to universalize, rather than to localize, the explanatory and inferential strategies of physical science. As a result, the social sciences have been profoundly influenced by the idea that they too, like physics, should be "value-free," refusing to admit values as terms of their theories and explanations.

It remains surprisingly easy, even at the end of the twentieth century, to find indications that values continue to play a part in our thought as terms of explanations and of broadly causal relations. Sturgeon has proposed and defended a number of examples of explanation in evaluative terms, where the explanations seem to be such as one might very well offer in ordinary life. Adolf Hitler's moral depravity, Sturgeon argues, can rightly be viewed as an important factor in explaining "the degradation and death of millions of persons."[37] In another historical explanation he proposes that more opposition to slavery arose in certain places in the eighteenth and nineteenth centuries than in other times and places because slavery "was much *worse*" in the first-mentioned times and places than in the others.[38] On a smaller stage, "a judge's thinking that it would be wrong to sentence a particular offender to the maximum prison term the law allows . . . may be due in part to her decency and fairmindedness, which [Sturgeon takes] to be moral facts if any are."[39]

Harman grants the appeal of such explanations. They are "cases in which moral aspects of a person or action are appealed to in order to explain certain natural events." His main strategic response is that "the explanations are clearly not of a sort that would allow us to test moral claims against the world in all the ways in which scientific claims can be tested against the world";[40] but I am setting the epis-

---

35. See Leibniz, *Discourse on Metaphysics*, sections 19–22, where Leibniz quotes at length from the passage of the *Phaedo* that I cite earlier.

36. On the importance of this point to Leibniz, see Adams, *Leibniz*, p. 21.

37. Sturgeon, "Moral Explanations," pp. 232, 245f., 249.

38. Sturgeon, "Moral Explanations," p. 245.

39. Sturgeon, "Moral Explanations," p. 244.

40. Harman, "Moral Explanations of Natural Facts," p. 61f. These comments apply explicitly to the examples of Hitler and the judge.

temological issue aside for now. He also argues that in such cases the moral terms are not really needed to explain the events, because the events can be explained as well in nonmoral terms. If we think it is *because* Albert did something wrong (setting the cat on fire) that Jane believes Albert did something wrong, Harman argues, we could just as well give a merely psychological explanation of Jane's believing as she does, in terms of her moral beliefs about the treatment of animals, without committing ourselves to any evaluation of Albert's action.[41] Similarly, David Zimmerman argues, against Sturgeon, that we do not have to classify Hitler's character traits morally, as depravity, in order to explain his acts in terms of them; and that increased opposition to slavery can be explained in terms of reactions to particular features of nineteenth-century American slavery, nonmorally described. Indeed, Zimmerman argues that the nonmoral explanations might well be richer and better explanations, because more detailed, than the moral ones.[42]

So far as I can see, these responses to Sturgeon do not tend to show, and are not meant to show, that we are wrong to offer explanations in moral terms in such cases as these. An explanation is not refuted by the availability of an alternative explanation in other terms, even if the latter is in some way a better explanation. 'The fire was caused by his carelessness' and 'He started the fire by flicking a smoldering cigarette butt without thinking about it' can both be true, and both explanatory, even though the second offers far more information than the first. Perhaps, however, the alternative, nonmoral explanations show that moral explanations are not *needed* in the examples discussed thus far; and that seems to be of interest to Sturgeon's critics.

It is not always so easy to give satisfactory value-free explanations. An example that is aesthetic rather than moral is due to Michael Slote, who suggests that serious listeners tend increasingly to prefer Mozart to Bruckner *because* Mozart is aesthetically superior.[43] Slote's suggestion seems plausible to me, and I have no idea how to replace aesthetic superiority in the explanation with a value-free mechanism.

One important type of context in which it is not so easy to give an explanation in nonevaluative terms is that in which the fact to be explained is stated in evaluative terms. Adapting an example of Sturgeon's, we might say that it was *because* of someone's *cowardice* that he responded *inappropriately* to the dangers he faced.[44] Here a personal trait identified in moral terms, as a vice, is alleged as explaining a fact that is described evaluatively, in terms of inappropriateness. 'He ran away because he was afraid' is not an explanation of the same purported fact, precisely because it is nonevaluative in both its terms. The first explanation might interest us much more than the second in some contexts. For instance, if our interest is moral education, we may want to know specifically what are the effects of cowardice, and what would explain acting appropriately and inappropriately in various contexts.

The interest in moral education as inspiring reliance on moral explanations is exemplified by John Rawls. In developing an account of education in justice as part

41. Harman, "Moral Explanations of Natural Facts," pp. 62–64.
42. Zimmerman, "Moral Realism and Explanatory Necessity," p. 87.
43. Slote, "The Rationality of Aesthetic Value Judgments."
44. Sturgeon, "Moral Explanations," p. 244.

of a moral psychology to support the claim that a society organized in accordance with his principles of justice would be sustainable, he postulates "three psychological laws," governing the acquisition of successive stages of morality. He acknowledges that these laws do not respect the ideal of a value-free social science, but he argues that value-free laws and explanations will be too limited in their usefulness in the area of social theory that concerns him. Rawls's three laws all include, in their explaining condition, the *moral* proviso that certain social arrangements are "just." And in the third and culminating law the result to be achieved or explained is stated in terms of a "corresponding sense of justice," which I believe is meant as a moral term here.[45]

Of course, if our interest is the challenge of moral skepticism, simply helping ourselves to moral terms in describing the phenomena to be explained by moral facts is begging the question, as Harman may fairly point out. I have been leaving epistemological issues to one side for the moment, however, and exploring the role that explanations in moral terms play in our ordinary thinking, which is not dominated by the skeptical challenge, but by trying to make our way in life. In that endeavor, I believe, we often have occasion to state in moral or evaluative terms both facts that explain and facts to be explained. That will not of itself settle any epistemological issue, but it will be relevant when we come to consider how plausible any epistemology could be that asked us to renounce all such explanations.

Edging closer to epistemology, we may observe that moral and other evaluative terms play a central part in the ordinary, so-called folk psychology on which we rely in understanding and predicting people's behavior and interpreting their utterances. One important evaluative concept belonging to practical psychology is that of *good judgment*. The concept may be used globally, or with reference to a specific area. The concepts of good *moral* judgement and good *aesthetic* judgment (the latter being close kin to *good taste*) are doubly evaluative. The concept of good judgment implies at least a subjunctive conditional or probabilistic connection between the judgments made by a person who has it and their correctness. If *s* has good judgment about area *a*, it follows that in area *a*, *s* is likelier to judge that *p* if the judgment that *p* is correct than if it is not. If I think you have good moral judgment, I believe that (other things being equal) you would be much less likely to believe an action virtuous if it were really vicious. Similar remarks apply to closely related traits of moral psychology such as moral and aesthetic *sensitivity* and a *sense of fairness*.

Concepts of this sort have a clear relevance to issues of moral explanation in dispute between Harman and Sturgeon. Consider Mary, who "is not convinced that there is anything wrong with causing pain to animals." So long as we are operating with ordinary, unreduced value concepts, Harman argues, "it is no harder for Mary [than it is for Jane] to explain Jane's belief" that Albert is doing something wrong in setting fire to the cat.[46] Mary can explain this particular belief in the light of Jane's more general ethical beliefs. On this account the fact, if it is one, that torturing animals is wrong plays no essential role in explaining Jane's beliefs, which are there-

45. Rawls, *A Theory of Justice*, pp. 490–92.
46. Harman, "Moral Explanations of Natural Facts," p. 62.

fore no evidence for the purported moral fact. Sturgeon replies that a very possible version of the case has different implications. It may be that Mary "thinks Jane's moral judgment quite good." Sturgeon argues that in that case Mary may reasonably be led by her belief in Jane's good judgment to suspect that there is something wrong, after all, about torturing animals.[47] That seems right to me, and I believe the reason is the following. If she has good judgment, Jane is likelier to believe that torturing animals is wrong if it is indeed wrong; and that implies an explanatory connection between the wrongness and the belief such that the belief is evidence (to some degree) of the wrongness.[48]

Similarly, I may believe that Tom will judge something unfair *because* it seems clearly unfair to me and I believe Tom has a well-tuned sense of fairness. In this explanation, or reasoning, we cannot necessarily replace 'Tom has a well-tuned sense of fairness' with 'Tom tends to think like me about fairness'. I could not reach a favorable opinion of Tom's sense of fairness without often agreeing with him on the subject, but we may sometimes disagree and I may have come to hold a higher opinion of his sense of fairness than of my own. So my reason may not be that we tend to think alike, but rather that I expect him to agree with me in this case because I trust his sense of fairness in general and in *this* case (which is so obvious) I also trust my own.

This is an example of an important class of cases in which I rely on my own value judgment, and not on value-free causal reasoning, in interpreting or predicting what other people think or will think about the same thing. This type of interpretation is highly prevalent, and works well for us. Other instances of it, of great systematic importance, are those in which I rely on a "principle of charity" in interpreting the utterances of others. Virtually every linguistic utterance affords a significant diversity of at least minimally possible interpretations. Most of these alternatives will be crazy; in the least ambiguous cases perhaps all but one will be. The principle of charity tells me to ascribe to the speaker or writer the meaning that seems to me the best, the one that constitutes the most reasonable or intelligent thing to say (unless I know something specific about the speaker or the context that makes it likelier that something else was meant instead). The key point for our present purpose is that in using the principle of charity I rely on value judgments of my own, about what would be reasonable, intelligent, and in that way *good* thinking. To try to replace such value judgments with value-free causal reasoning would be to abandon the principle of charity as such, and there is little reason to think that would lead to a hermeneutics as satisfactory as our customary value-laden practice.

It is not necessary to speculate here about whether our ordinary value-laden reasoning in such matters *could* in principle be reduced to value-free terms, or replaced without grievous loss by value-free reasoning. Such speculation could fill a book or more, and would probably not reach uncontroversial conclusions. As we shall see presently, however, the issue Harman poses that concerns us here is not so

---

47. Sturgeon, "Harman on Moral Explanations of Natural Facts," p. 72.
48. This is implied by a famous (though not uncontroversial) principle of inductive reasoning, known as Bayes' theorem, which is closely related to the principle of inference to the best explanation.

much whether inferential and explanatory reasoning in evaluative terms *can* be replaced with value-free reasoning, but whether it *needs* to be.

That applies also to one further point about reliance on value judgments in our ordinary reasoning that will be important in thinking about Harman's epistemology. This point is made forcefully by Geoffrey Sayre-McCord, with reference to what he calls "the Explanatory Criterion," which requires a hypothesis to figure in the best explanation of our observations if it is to be justifiably believed.

> No argument that depends on the Explanatory Criterion will get off the ground
> unless some explanations are better than others. This poses a dilemma for those
> who suppose that the Explanatory Criterion will support the wholesale rejection
> of evaluative facts. Either there is a fact of the matter about which explanations
> are best, or there is not. If there is, then there are at least some evaluative facts
> (as to which explanations are better than others); if not, then the criterion will
> never find an application and so will support no argument against moral
> theory.[49]

The value normally ascribed in 'best explanation' is not moral, but I think it is a case of excellence, and is often plausibly thought to have a dimension of something like aesthetic value, when "simplicity" is invoked as a criterion of the value of explanations. Whether or not it could ultimately be replaced by a value-free account, the invocation of value in these contexts is at least serious and more than merely verbal. No doubt many criteria of good explanation can be stated in value-free terms; it must be logically consistent, for example. So can some criteria of justice, which must also be consistent. What is not so easily dispensed with, because we have no algorithm for weighing all the relevant considerations, is the character of the overall judgment as a judgment of the comparative *value* of the explanations.

Theologically it is intriguing to ask whether the acceptability of evaluations of theories requires that theory values contribute to causal explanations. Consider the following argument. We think that aesthetically better theories should be preferred. There is some irrationality in our position unless we also think that aesthetically better theories are likelier to be true, which implies that there is an explanatory factor here. Therefore, we ought also to believe that aesthetically good theories, when true, are true at least partly *because* of their aesthetic value. Here we are close to the design argument for theism, since the action of an intelligent, aesthetically sensitive creator may offer the best account of the explanatory factor demanded here.

Thus far I have been discussing the explanatory and inferential value of values on the basis of what we may call the "appearances" of common sense. Conclusions reached on that basis might be undermined if theories (particularly realist theories) of the nature of values suggested no way in which values could cause or explain anything. In fact some such theories support the explanatory value of values. This is obvious in the case of naturalistic theories that identify values with natural properties. For natural properties in general have causal roles, and can be appealed to

---

49. Sayre-McCord, "Moral Theory and Explanatory Impotence," p. 277; cf. ibid., p. 267f.

unproblematically for explanation in appropriate contexts. Harman recognizes this, of course. His worry with regard to naturalistic theories, as we shall see, is whether they relate evaluative terminology to natural properties in the way that epistemology requires.

The implications (for our present topic) of identifying values with theological properties are similar to those of identifying them with natural properties, though the identification will probably have to be supplemented with some theory of divine action in order to yield explanations. If excellence is identified with a sort of Godlikeness, for example, it will contribute to the explanation of the existence of some things if we can correctly suppose that God takes such Godlikeness as a reason for creating things. Even more important, if we suppose that God directly or indirectly causes human beings to regard as excellent approximately those things that are Godlike in the relevant way, it follows that there is a causal and explanatory connection between facts of excellence and beliefs that we may regard as justified about excellence, and hence that it is in general no accident that such beliefs are correct when they are.

This last is a point of wide epistemological relevance. The identification of values with either natural or theological properties suggests plausible causal and explanatory relations between real values and evaluative beliefs, so that correctness of justified evaluative beliefs need not be viewed as a mere accident. In this way realism about value seems able to satisfy the most widely accepted causal or explanatory constraint on justified belief.

3.2 Empirical Confirmation and Reflective Equilibrium

This will not satisfy Harman, however; and it is time to confront his epistemological challenge. It may be a requirement of rationality that our view of the world not be such as to imply that we ourselves are at best accidentally right in most of our beliefs, but the demand that Harman makes is a further one: that the explanatory relations among our beliefs should be such as to enable us to *test* our beliefs *empirically* "in all the ways in which scientific claims can be tested."[50] He doubts that Sturgeon's naturalism satisfies this demand; and I think the doubt must apply equally to Boyd's. Harman bases his doubt on Sturgeon's claims "(a) that it is a mistake to require of ethical naturalism that it even promise reductive definitions for moral terms, and . . . (b) that even if such definitions are to be forthcoming, it is, at the very least, no special problem for ethical naturalism that we are not *now* in confident possession of them."[51]

Harman's principal criticism of Sturgeon's position is that it does not require ethical naturalism to propose hypotheses that have the detail *now* that they must have in order to be testable *now* in the way they must be in order to be worthy of rational belief. He avoids a direct confrontation with Sturgeon on the topic of reductive definition, professing not to know enough about what Sturgeon means by "definition." But, Harman declares, "in order to show that moral claims are em-

50. Harman, "Moral Explanations of Natural Facts," p. 64.
51. Sturgeon, "Moral Explanations," p. 239.

pirically testable in the relevant sense, the naturalist must say enough about the natural facts with which the moral facts are to be identified to indicate how the moral facts can be manifested in the world in a way that allows the relevant testing. Otherwise, the naturalist has no answer to what seems to me to be the central issue in moral philosophy."[52] The key word in this formulation is "how." In Harman's view a claim that moral facts are empirically confirmed must imply that they are part of the best explanation of our experience, and this cannot be credible without a theory of *how* the moral facts help explain the experience. Here we must remember also that (as Sturgeon acknowledges)[53] the purported "moral facts" to which Harman applies this demand are not concrete events but moral principles—not, for instance, that Albert did something wrong (when he tortured the cat) but that it is in general wrong to torture animals.

I will offer on Boyd's behalf a response to this challenge; at an appropriate point in it I will cite a main part of Sturgeon's reply to Harman's demand. Boyd's account of the general moral wrongness of torturing animals will have two parts. In the first place, if torturing animals is wrong in general, that is because its tendency is contrary to that of fostering the natural properties and mechanisms making up the homeostatic cluster that ultimately constitutes moral goodness. Why, in the second place, does that cluster constitute moral goodness? Because there exist "causal mechanisms whose tendency is to bring it about, over time, that what is predicated of 'morally good' will be approximately true of" the kind that is defined (roughly, with some failures of bivalence) by that cluster.[54]

All the tendencies and mechanisms postulated in Boyd's account are *natural* causal tendencies and mechanisms relating natural properties and events. Their existence, if known, would seem to have all the naturalistic explanatory force that anyone could desire. If Harman has a complaint at this point, it must be that Boyd does not yet offer us enough information about them to make his view credible. Here Sturgeon's response is relevant.[55] He observes, first of all, that not having "anything close to a systematic theory, what Harman calls a reduction," does not leave us totally in the dark as to how moral facts contribute to the (natural) explanation of phenomena. "We all certainly have . . . views" on what some of "the salient features" are by which people identify wrong actions. In that way we have a pretty good idea, in Boyd's terms, of a good part of the mechanisms by which our use of 'wrong' tracks the homeostatic cluster of natural properties that it tracks (if that is indeed what it is doing). In this way, Sturgeon argues, in the second place, we already have enough rational basis for provisional acceptance of some moral explanations, and for using such explanations in working toward the sort of (nonreductionist) moral theory to which he aspires.

Sturgeon's response seems to me reasonable, and probably adequate, in relation to his (and Boyd's) theoretical aims. I do not see why rational acceptance of a supposedly empirical theory, subject to correction in the light of further experience

52. Harman, "Moral Explanations of Natural Facts," p. 67.
53. Sturgeon, "Moral Explanations," p. 250.
54. See Boyd, "How to Be a Moral Realist," p. 195.
55. Sturgeon, "Harman on Moral Explanations of Natural Facts," p. 73. All the quotations in the present paragraph are from that page.

and reflection, should depend on the kind of reductive definitions that Harman demands. It is true that the lack of such definitions may make it harder to achieve the kind of tight connection between particular experiences and specific theoretical claims that would allow decisive empirical refutation of a theory; but most empiricists today do not generally aspire to that tightness and decisiveness.[56]

In any event Boyd has a more radical disagreement with Harman's epistemology; and I must have one too, inasmuch as I think Boyd's view relies *too much* on empirical testing of ethical doctrines. Much recent discussion in the epistemology of morals revolves around what John Rawls has called the method of "reflective equilibrium."[57] Boyd is for it and Harman is against it.[58] In this method we begin with what we already believe about the subject matter (in this case, ethics), emphasizing our most confident judgments. These will largely (though not exclusively) be judgments about particular cases. On this basis, and with the benefit of further experience, we begin to construct a theory, making the theoretical judgments that seem most reasonable to us with a view to developing principles of some generality. Initial ethical judgments, interpretations of experience, and general principles we are developing are all tested against each other. We may abandon a principle because we cannot bring it into harmony with our strong initial beliefs, but we may also modify or abandon initial beliefs or interpretations of experience for the sake of general theoretical principles that are sufficiently strongly supported.

Harman objects to the way in which the method of reflective equilibrium relies on initial moral beliefs. He puts this objection very emphatically:

> A moral philosopher who tries to find general principles to account for judgments about particular cases, hoping eventually to get principles and cases into "reflective equilibrium," is studying commonsense ethics. The results of such a study are results in moral psychology. Just as a study of commonsense physics is not a study of physics, the study of commonsense ethics is not a study of right and wrong, *unless* what it is for something to be right and wrong can be identified with facts about moral psychology.[59]

Harman must know that this is not a correct account of what is *intended* by the partisans of reflective equilibrium. They are *relying on* their initial ethical beliefs in studying *right and wrong*. Their own believings are not the object of their study,

---

56. The reasons for not so aspiring can be traced back to Quine, "Two Dogmas of Empiricism," and are involved in the point that, as Harman says, "there are no pure observations. Observations are always 'theory laden'" (Harman, *The Nature of Morality*, p. 4).

57. Rawls, *A Theory of Justice*, pp. 20, 48–51.

58. Perhaps it would be more precise to say that Harman thinks reliance on reflective equilibrium is unjustified, and not fully rational, *in ethics*, unless and until a fuller and more satisfying account has been given than he thinks nonreductive naturalism can offer "of the place that value and obligation have in the world of facts" as revealed by science. Subject to some such qualification, he has been willing to "agree that we must begin at the beginning with our initial beliefs, both moral and nonmoral, and . . . hope to arrive [eventually] at a 'reflective equilibrium'" (Harman, "Is There a Single True Morality?" p. 29).

59. Harman, "Moral Explanations of Natural Facts," p. 61.

except at a methodological "meta" level. Harman's claim must rather be that it cannot be *rational* to rely on our initial ethical beliefs as indicators of anything beyond our own psychology unless those beliefs are furnished with empiricist credentials that reflective equilibrium does not assure. Among the credentials he demands, of course, is a fuller account than nonreductive naturalism offers of the place of our moral beliefs in best explanations.

Boyd believes, on the other hand, that even natural science cannot do without the method of reflective equilibrium and the initial tentative reliance on our existing beliefs that it involves. He states that "the dialectical interplay of observations, theory, and methodology which, according to the [scientific] realist constitutes the *discovery* procedure for scientific inquiry *just is* the method of reflective equilibrium, so that the prevalence of that method in moral reasoning cannot *by itself* dictate a nonrealist conception of morals."[60] "The epistemic reliability of scientific methodology is contingent," Boyd claims, on scientists already having a "theoretical tradition" that "contains theories which are relevantly approximately true." Similarly, his moral realism requires that "it must be possible to explain how our moral reasoning *started out* with a stock of relevantly approximately true moral beliefs."[61] Boyd's thesis about the role of reflective equilibrium in natural science is an intriguing (and, of course, controversial) thesis in the philosophy of science (a field in which he is a leading practitioner). I will not pursue it systematically here, however, as I must on my own account defend against Harman a conception of ethics that is less oriented than Boyd's to natural science.

I believe that reliance on many of the evaluative and normative beliefs with which the method of reflective equilibrium begins can claim a considerable measure of empirical support, broadly understood, but does not rationally require either decisive empirical testing or a well-articulated, well-confirmed epistemology of value. I believe also that comparison of the methods of ethics with those of the physical sciences is less important epistemologically than consideration of the relation of evaluative and normative judgments to the web of commonsense belief and judgment in which science is embedded and on which it inescapably depends. (For examples of this dependence, consider the kinds of perceptual and hermeneutical judgment that enable us to read the dials of scientific instruments and understand the reports of scientists.)

Beginning in childhood, we have all learned to make a large variety of evaluative and normative judgments. Some such judgments we make quite confidently; others, with more diffidence. This ability is in large part linguistic and, like all linguistic abilities, is acquired as part of socially transmitted practices.[62] It works for us. An enormous proportion of our judgments are couched in evaluative or normative terms of one sort or another (by no means all moral), and we are reasonably successful in making our way in life with their aid. The project of renouncing all use of evaluative judgments would be so monumentally inconvenient that few indeed are likely to undertake it. We would have to learn to think all over again—and

60. Boyd, "How to Be a Moral Realist," p. 199f.
61. Boyd, "How to Be a Moral Realist," p. 200f.
62. These points will be developed more fully in chapter 15, section 2.

it is not clear how well we would do so—if actions, apples, arguments, books, explanations, feelings, ideas, intentions, interpretations, meals, outcomes, performances, and so forth could not be classified as good or bad.

Evaluation plays a part in much of our understanding of our experience, in ways that I have described to some extent earlier. We rely on our own judgments of what is good and bad, morally and in other ways, in forming expectations of what other people will judge good and bad, and hence of what they will do. Following a principle of charity, in interpreting people's utterances, we rely on our own judgments of what would be good thinking. To the extent that our thinking conforms to a principle of inference to the best explanation, we rely on our own judgments of the comparative value of explanations. Science relies on such evaluations, inasmuch as it evaluates explanations and depends on interpretations of the utterances of scientists. The successes of science, and the frequent empirical confirmation of expectations based on interpretation of people's utterances, or on beliefs about what they will value, provide a loose empirical confirmation of the truth-tracking reliability of the practices and skills of evaluation that we use in various stages of arriving at the scientific and ordinary beliefs that are directly confirmed.

This empirical confirmation is loose in several ways. One that is important to Harman is that it does not provide decisive empirical tests for value judgments. This is partly because they mainly enter procedures of empirical thought at a structural level fairly far removed from the more or less observational predictions that are most easily verified or refuted. That is a feature that value judgments share with theoretical elements whose cognitive status is much less often questioned. There is another feature, however, that makes the empirical testing of evaluation looser. What stands here to be confirmed or disconfirmed empirically is more the reliability of evaluative practices and skills than any set of principles and judgments of value. Probably we cannot make empirical tests for the reliability of practices as precise or as tight as for many propositions, given that the practices generate an indefinite variety of beliefs; but we also cannot reasonably proceed without relying on belief-forming practices and skills that have this feature.

Another aspect of the looseness of the empirical confirmation of evaluation, on which Harman may wish to dwell, is related to the fact that it does not involve any particular well-developed epistemology of value. The ordinary and scientific belief systems that are empirically confirmed include more or less well developed, generally accepted beliefs about *how* physical and psychological facts contribute causally to the formation of our beliefs about them. The *truth* of such beliefs therefore figures directly in what we take to be the best explanation of the phenomena when the beliefs are empirically confirmed. It seems fair to say, however, that people ordinarily use practices of evaluation without any developed (let alone generally accepted) belief about *how* the *truth* of evaluations contributes causally to the phenomena (though this is easily recognized as a subject for metaethical speculation of the sort in which we are now engaged). Should this feed a skeptical reading of the situation, according to which the experienced success of cognitive enterprises in which we rely on practices of evaluation confirms only the *usefulness* of those practices, and not their reliability as indicators of *truth*?

Here a comparison with mathematics is relevant.[63] Like evaluation, mathematics is *used* by physical science without being its subject matter. It is widely doubted or denied that mathematical facts can play any causal role in the formation of our beliefs. Harman makes this point rather strongly, saying, "We do not and cannot perceive numbers, for example, since we cannot be in causal contact with them. We do not even understand what it would be like to be in causal contact with the number 12, say."[64] On the other hand, he also says, "Since an observation is evidence for what explains it, and since mathematics often figures in the explanations of scientific observations, there is indirect observational evidence for mathematics."[65] Why shouldn't we say that in the same way there is indirect observational evidence for evaluation?

Harman may reply that there is a crucial difference here. Mathematics often "figures" in scientific explanations. That is, mathematical propositions are often *part* of scientific explanations. But value judgments are not in the same way *part* of scientific explanations, even if science relies on them in communicating evidence and evaluating explanations. Therefore, Harman may argue, the reliability of evaluative practices as guides to truth is not supported by the principle of inference to the best explanation.

It is not clear that the truth of evaluations does not in fact figure in empirically confirmed explanations. Granted it does not figure in explanations in the physical sciences. But to the extent that we use concepts such as moral sensitivity and good moral judgment in forming expectations of people's behavior, it seems that we have at least an explanatory framework couched in moral terms, if not a detailed explanation, for understanding why these expectations are so often empirically confirmed.

More fundamentally, in any event, we may think it quite implausible to count only propositions directly contained in explanations as confirmed by the empirical success of the explanatory enterprise. If we rely on value judgments in interpreting scientists' reports and evaluating explanations, are we not irrational in relying on the results of the whole process, regarding it as producing empirical confirmation, if we do not think, or cannot rationally believe, that the evaluative practices involved in it are reliable? But if we can rationally believe such practices reliable, then surely it is not irrational to rely on them in the way that the method of reflective equilibrium requires.

---

63. Ethics is compared with mathematics, but not (so far as I can see) in the respect indicated in my next sentence, in Harman, *The Nature of Morality*, p. 9f. The comparison is pursued, in relation to metaethical theories much less realistic than those with which Boyd, Sturgeon, Harman, and I are concerned, in Wiggins, "Truth, Invention, and the Meaning of Life," and Lear, "Ethics, Mathematics and Relativism."

64. Harman, *The Nature of Morality*, p. 9f.

65. Harman, *The Nature of Morality*, p. 10. This view about empirical confirmation of mathematics is fairly widely held but is not uncontroversial. The most important recent statement of the opposing view that scientific *usefulness* is not grounds for believing in the *truth* of mathematics is Field, *Science without Numbers*. For responses critical of Field on this point, see Malament's review of the book and Shapiro, "Conservatism and Incompleteness."

Although I believe that the reliability of ordinary, pretheoretical practices of evaluation can claim in this way a measure of indirect empirical confirmation, I do not believe that the rational acceptability of relying on them depends wholly on this confirmation. No cognitive enterprise can get off the ground without initial reliance on many confident, pretheoretical beliefs; and a large proportion of such beliefs remain more deeply entrenched than the theoretical superstructure erected on them. It did not require any scientific theory to teach humans, for example, that stones tend to fall toward the earth; and a development of physical theory that would advise us to give that up completely would almost certainly discredit itself rather than the pretheoretical belief. Many of our largely pretheoretical evaluative and normative beliefs seem almost as confident and deeply entrenched as any beliefs that we hold. To take a fairly extreme comparison, it would surely be crazier to give up the belief that it is wicked to torture children than to think that there must be something wrong with quantum mechanics. I would not want to say that such confident pretheoretical beliefs are "self-evident," both because they are not totally exempt from possible revision and because it seems better to avoid the most epistemologically charged terminology at this point. But I do think they commend themselves strongly enough to make the sort of initial reliance on them that is involved in methods of reflective equilibrium as reasonable a procedure as any that is available to us.

Virtually all reflective people today are rightly impressed with the successes of the modern tradition in the physical sciences, and confident of the substantial correctness of the best confirmed conclusions of those sciences. This confidence has led many philosophers to try to extend the empirical methods of the physical sciences to other domains, and even to suppose that only what can be established by those methods is rationally credible. It is eminently reasonable, of course, to wish to see what might be accomplished in other areas by methods that have been so successful in one field. But it is important to distinguish between the successes of modern physical science, which are great and uncontroversial, and the successes of modern empiricist, science-inspired epistemology, which are arguably much less impressive, and certainly much more controversial.

If a pretheoretical ethical belief held confidently by all of us were irreconcilable with well-established principles of physics, that would be a severe problem for ethical theory; and if there were too many such cases, it could certainly call into question the acceptability of the method of reflective equilibrium in ethics. But if initial reliance on confident pretheoretical ethical beliefs fails to conform with an epistemology of exclusive reliance on inference to the best explanation, or with some other empiricist epistemology, that is a much less serious problem. Nor do we need an elaborate theory to justify going with pretheoretical belief rather than with empiricist epistemology, if such a choice is forced on us. I do not believe that epistemology, as a philosophical discipline, is in as flourishing a state today as substantive or "normative" ethical theory; and I take it my view on this point is not eccentric, though it may be controversial. To those who agree with me about that, the insistence that we should not base ethical theory on our considered ethical opinions without having a well-developed epistemology of morals to justify our practice must seem a counsel of despair.

Since the theistic metaphysics of morals that I advocate is not physicalistic, I should note that something very like the argument of the previous paragraph applies to the concern to place ethics in the context of an exclusively physicalistic metaphysics, a concern that inspires many ethical naturalists, including Harman.[66] This is not the place for a thorough discussion of physicalism, but only for some remarks about its intellectual status. It is not a theory in physics, nor more generally a result established by modern physical science. It is rather a metaphysical theory, inspired by enthusiasm for science. It holds, roughly, that all the facts there are can in principle be described in the vocabulary, and explained by the laws, of modern physics, in some ideal development thereof. It is obvious that such a theory is issuing large promissory notes to be paid by future developments, and hence is highly speculative. It is attended by much-debated and, I believe, grave and unresolved difficulties. Given the strength of our confidence in many pretheoretical evaluative and normative beliefs, and the pervasiveness of their role in our thinking, I believe that physicalism has much more need to be found compatible with them than they have to be found compatible with it. This is not an argument against physicalism; that's business for another occasion. It is rather an argument for not allowing physicalist worries to undermine ethical beliefs.

4. Transcendence Vindicated

In my argument thus far I have allied myself with Boyd and Sturgeon in defending nonreductive naturalism against the charge that it allows too little empirical testing. In fact I believe it invites *too much* empirical testing of ethical beliefs. It is time to argue that point, which is important for the vindication of transcendent value against ethical naturalism.

My central thesis in this part of the argument is that allowing empirical reasoning of the causal explanatory sort to have the last word is incompatible with a stance that is essential to ethical thinking and some other important types of evaluative and normative thinking.[67] Suppose Boyd's hopes for the progress of science to have been vindicated, in some future decade, in the following way. Scientific understanding of human behavior and other relevant phenomena has reached a point at which experts have identified homeostatic clusters of natural properties and mechanisms satisfying Boyd's criterion for identifying human nonmoral and moral goodness as natural kinds. Suppose also that the consequentialist part of Boyd's hunches and hopes regarding ethical theory has been vindicated—that what the relevant scientifically identified homeostatic cluster picks out as moral goodness of actions is exclusively their tendency to maximize what the relevant clusters pick out otherwise as goodness. In this situation most moral judgments of most people (or at least of

---

66. See Harman, "Is There a Single True Morality?"

67. I am indebted to broadly similar critiques of causal explanatory criteria for ethical truth in Nagel, *The View from Nowhere*, pp. 144–46; in Copp, "Explanation and Justification in Ethics"; and especially in unpublished work of Sigrún Svavarsdóttir; but I will not attempt to press their words into service in developing my line of thought.

most well-informed, reflective people) will agree with those implied by the scientific hypothesis; otherwise the hypothesis would not satisfy Boyd's criterion. A few people may well disagree on some points, however. I suspect that I would still disagree with the act-consequentialist thesis. Should I regard myself as refuted by the empirical evidence that the explanatorily best account of moral goodness as a natural property cluster tracked by our use of 'morally good' is one that implies act-consequentialism? I think not.

To take the explanatory reasoning as decisive in such a context would be to abandon a *critical stance* that is very important to ethics. Indeed, I think the critical stance is part of the general intentional framework in which we use evaluative and normative terms, at least where morality and excellence are concerned, and thus affects the semantically indicated role of such terms. The stance amounts to at least this. For any natural, empirically identifiable property or type of action that we or others may regard as good or bad, right or wrong, we are committed to leave it *always* open in principle to raise evaluative or normative questions by asking whether that property or action-type is *really* good or right, or to issue an evaluative or normative challenge by denying that it is *really* good or right.

This is my version of "the truth behind" G. E. Moore's famous "open question" argument.[68] Like most other philosophers today, I don't think that argument succeeds in its original context. The fact that the correctness of an analysis can be intelligibly questioned does not show that the analysis is not correct. In the case of evaluative and normative language, however, we have a special commitment to allow that language to be used to question or challenge the value of any human thought or action and any object of human experience. We have no other language similarly apt for evaluative and normative questions and challenges; and to treat the value of any natural object or action, or (as Boyd perhaps must) the correctness of any human consensus, as immune to such criticism is a fearful abridgment of ethical possibility. In a religious perspective it is idolatry.

The critical stance is related to the topic with which we closed section 3, the acceptance of evaluative and normative belief as a *starting point* in our thinking. Consider the question of inferential relevance between 'is' and 'ought'. Moral realists, who think moral truths express facts about reality, must acknowledge at least the *possibility* of such relevance, but here I am primarily concerned with the *direction* of inference. Inferences from 'is' to 'ought' or from "fact" to "value" have been subject to great suspicion, to say the least, in anglophone moral philosophy of the twentieth century, but inferences from 'ought' to 'is' have been even more suspect. This is of course connected with the prevalent aspiration to render the physical and even the social sciences "value-free," and it may well contribute to Harman's motivation for objecting to *beginning* with moral judgments in a context of moral realism.

It is possible, however, for a moral realist to argue in the other direction. If moral truths are facts about a reality, why shouldn't confident moral beliefs warrant conclusions about a reality? In the middle dialogues Plato, an archetypal moral realist,

---

68. Moore, *Principia Ethica*, p. 67f. (§13).

takes our apprehension of value as a clue to the nature of what is most real. At a more mundane level, my observations in section 3 about the pervasive role of value judgments in our ordinary thinking about matters of fact support the reasonableness of inferences from value to (other sorts of) fact.

Kant also famously endorses a sort of inference (practical, not theoretical) from 'ought' to 'is' in postulating immortality and the existence of God on moral grounds. His preference of this inference to any inference in the opposite direction, from 'is' to 'ought', is clearly motivated by commitment to what I am calling the critical stance in ethics. In this connection, he voices emphatic praise for Plato's *Republic*. Plato offers the notion of an *idea*, Kant says, as "something that not only can never be borrowed from the senses, but that even goes far beyond the concepts of the understanding . . . since nothing encountered in experience could ever be congruent to it."[69] In order to serve as a criterion of the moral value of experienced actions, Kant holds, the idea of virtue must not be derived from experience.[70] "Nothing," Kant concludes, "is more reprehensible than to derive the laws about what I *ought to do* from what *is done*, or to want to limit it to that."[71] Kant's point is that experienced objects are not good enough to furnish the ultimate standard, and that we must therefore not surrender the critical function of evaluation to any empirical criterion.

To what extent can Boyd accommodate the critical evaluative stance in ethics? It must be said first of all that he would not require anyone to abandon that stance right now. For he does not claim that moral science has reached the point at which a satisfactory empirical, causal explanatory criterion of moral or nonmoral goodness can be formulated. If we are to succeed *now* in predicating of the good approximately what is true of the homeostatic property cluster with which it should ultimately be identified, we can do so only by relying on our own present moral convictions, in the hope that they represent an approximately true tradition of thought which is already tracking the right property cluster. Given that our actual tradition incorporates the critical stance, Boyd offers us no reason to abandon it now.

The serious question is whether Boyd must envisage as really possible a cognitive development which would lead to a situation in which, on his principles, we would have to abandon, or seriously compromise, the critical stance. Considerations of continuity might lead him to suppose that even in such a secular moral *eschaton*, a version of the critical stance would continue to be part of the mechanism that would keep our use of 'good' tracking the relevant cluster. In this way there might be no pressure on people to give up the critical stance as long as they did not study the achievements of empirical moral science. For those of us who would know about those achievements, however, there would be a problem. Suppose I accept it as well established on empirical, explanatory grounds that a theory implying act-consequentialism best satisfies, and well satisfies, Boyd's criterion for identifying

69. Kant, *Critique of Pure Reason*, A313/B370.
70. Kant, *Critique of Pure Reason*, A315/B371f.
71. Kant, *Critique of Pure Reason*, A318f./B375.

correctly the natural kind that is the good. If I accept Boyd's criterion, it would seem that I cannot then reject act-consequentialism in my judgments about what is morally good, even if my own moral inclinations would otherwise lead me to do so. Likewise, if I accept Boyd's criterion, it is hard to see how I can take the critical stance toward the correctness of act-consequentialism, viewing it as a question in principle open for further discussion in moral terms, rather than regarding it as settled by empirical facts and explanatory considerations.

I suspect in fact Boyd does hope for progress in moral science that would leave such questions settled rather than open. In that case he faces the question what he should say about me (for example) if, in the face of such progress and with full knowledge of the theoretical situation, I would stubbornly refuse to assent to act-consequentialism (assuming it to be vindicated in Boyd's terms). He might say that I would in that case be mistaken about what is morally good; indeed, that verdict is implied by his theory. But if I am using moral vocabulary to express a critical challenge to act-utilitarianism in that situation, I will say that Boyd is mistaken about what is morally good. What account can Boyd then give of this disagreement between us?

To be precise, can Boyd give a *realistic* account of this disagreement? The issue of realism versus antirealism is topic-relative. I have already distinguished realism at the substantive ethical level from metaethical realism, but the topic relativity can cut much more finely than that. It seems possible to inquire, regarding any ethical dispute, whether that particular issue can be given a realist interpretation, taking the positions of the disputants comprehensively into account. In many contexts Boyd can certainly give a realist interpretation of his claim that precisely the actions dictated by act-consequentialism are morally good. Their moral goodness consists, on his view, in their having certain straightforwardly natural and uncontroversially real properties. It does not follow, however, that he can give a realist interpretation of his disagreement with me. In the case envisaged, I agree that the actions in question have those straightforwardly natural properties, and still I claim that they are not all morally good. So our disagreement is not about whether the actions have the (real and natural) properties that Boyd will identify with moral goodness. Is there some procedure of empirical discovery that Boyd and I would agree would settle the issue if we could carry it out? If so, Boyd might interpret us, realistically, as debating what result that procedure would have. But I don't see what procedure Boyd could think that would be, since we are considering a situation in which all the empirical procedures Boyd believes in for deciding such matters would have settled the issue in favor of act-consequentialism.

One response that would be open to Boyd in that situation would be simply to say that I am misusing the expression 'morally good', since my use of it is deliberately uncontrolled by the property cluster that constitutes moral goodness according to his theory, as I know as well as he does. In my view that would be abandoning, idolatrously, a crucial critical function of moral discourse. I suspect in fact Boyd would prefer a different response, related to the fact that his theory allows for "failures of bivalence" in moral discourse. Admitting failure of bivalence about an issue (admitting that it has neither a true nor a false answer) is a widely recognized way of being an antirealist about it. And Boyd already admits a "pessimistic" possibility of empirically irresolvable fundamental conflict between alternative comprehensive outlooks in ethics which would entail a "relativist" and "nonrealist" view of the disagreement between them. This is not exactly the same sort of conflict as I am envisaging between Boyd's empiricism and a nonempiricist view that I would hold. What Boyd envisages can be seen as a family quarrel among empiricists that would arise if "there are two (or more) stable [but mutually inconsistent] ways of achieving homeostasis between [the relevant human] goods, each capable of sustaining a morality and moral progress of sorts."[72] If Boyd is already willing to countenance this much nonrealism, is there any reason he should not give a similarly nonrealist interpretation of the dispute I envisage between him and me?

Boyd claims that the pessimistic possibility that he allows of empirically irre-soluble conflict between ethical systems is "only in a relatively uninteresting sense *nonrealistic*,"[73] because it permits a realistic interpretation (in Boyd's terms) of is-sues *within* each system. Boyd can't offer *me* the same sort of realism on his terms, if I am espousing a nonempiricist and nonnaturalist view; but his dispute with me still allows *him* his realistic interpretation of issues within his system. So perhaps this outcome would not seem to him nonrealistic in a very interesting sense.

The nonrealism in these contexts (including the one that Boyd explicitly ad-mits is possible) strikes me, however, as much more interesting and disturbing than he allows. The dispute I envisage, after all, is about act-consequentialism, and Boyd gives not the slightest reason to suppose that that could not be one of the issues in empirically irresoluble dispute between conflicting ethical systems. Act-consequen-tialism is introduced here only as an example, of course; but it is an example of an important ethical issue. A view that is forced to be nonrealist about a fundamental dispute between consequentialists and nonconsequentialists is forced to be nonrealist on an important topic, and hence in an important way, I should think. This will be an objection to virtually any naturalistic identification of ethical properties. It will allow substantive, and often practically important, ethical disputes to arise at its boundaries, in which its identification of moral properties will be questioned. Thus it will fail to maintain realism regarding some important ethical issues.

Is there an alternative to nonrealism as a way of accommodating the critical evaluative stance on fundamental issues? The main alternative, I believe, is a realist view of the Good as transcendent. Such a view accommodates the critical stance by keeping all actual substantive evaluative issues open, or at least those for which the relevant standard is the transcendent one. For human knowledge of the transcen-dent Good is always imperfect. Many theologians have held, for example, that God cannot be "comprehended" by any finite mind, even in the life to come. Given that our knowledge of the Good is necessarily imperfect and fragmentary, it can never be out of order to question or challenge any human view about the Good. Keeping evaluative questions open is indeed a way of recognizing the transcendence of the Good, and that is why I think it appropriate to regard the abandonment of the critical stance as idolatry.

72. Boyd, "How to Be a Moral Realist," p. 224f.
73. Boyd, "How to Be a Moral Realist," p. 225.

A realist view of the Good as transcendent favors a particular version of the critical stance. It is a stance that stands ready to question or challenge any human view about what the Good is, and any empirical test of value. At the same time it is not a stance of arbitrariness or mere self-expressiveness, as some existentialist versions of the critical stance must be. It reaches out toward an objective standard that is actually glimpsed, though never fully or infallibly. As Iris Murdoch has said, "Good is indefinable not for the reasons offered by Moore's successors, but because of the infinite difficulty of the task of apprehending a magnetic but inexhaustible reality."[74] I believe this to be the most intuitively satisfying version of the ethical stance. Making it possible is a major advantage of realism about a transcendent Good.

74. Murdoch, *The Sovereignty of Good*, p. 42.

3

WELL-BEING AND EXCELLENCE

We have noted some fundamental distinctions between types of goodness or value. There is *usefulness*, or merely instrumental goodness, the value that something may have as a means to something else that is good or that is valued. Usefulness has an obvious importance, and connects with significant philosophical issues about instrumentality and probability; but more fundamental issues for ethical theory are posed by the goods or ends that the useful is to serve. Within the realm of what is good for its own sake, and not just instrumentally good, most contemporary ethical thought focuses mainly on *well-being* or welfare—that is, on the nature of human flourishing or what is good *for* a person. The theory developed here, however, gives a primary place to *excellence*—the type of goodness exemplified by the beauty of a sunset, a painting, or a mathematical proof, or by the greatness of a novel, the nobility of an unselfish deed, or the quality of an athletic or a philosophical performance. It is the goodness of that which is worthy of love or admiration, honor or worship, rather than the good (for herself) that is possessed by one who is fortunate or happy, as such (though happiness may also be excellent, and worthy of admiration).

Excellence is obviously an important topic for theism, inasmuch as a god must be worthy of worship, and it lies equally at the heart of Platonic conceptions of the good. In a contemporary context, however, a focus on excellence stands in need of defense. We are all interested in well-being, but many today are reluctant to give a large place in ethical theory to conceptions of excellence. In this chapter I will try to show that our interest in well-being should lead to an interest in excellence.

1. Well-Being and the Satisfaction of Desire

It is one of the more difficult tasks of ethical theory to explain what human well-being consists in—what it is for something to be good *for* a person. A successful explanation must account for both the evaluation expressed by 'good' and the relation expressed by 'for'. The relation will be particularly important if some things are good for their own sake that would not be good *for* every person involved in them. Retributivists, for example, may think it is good, for its own sake and not just instrumentally, that the guilty be punished, without supposing that punishment is good *for* the guilty.

On some theories of the nature of the good, to be sure, the relation expressed by the beneficiary 'for' in 'good for' is obvious and uninteresting. Perhaps the most important theory of this type is hedonism. If we hold that pleasure alone is good for its own sake, it will be natural to think also that *my* pleasure alone is noninstrumentally good *for me*. But there are weighty objections to a hedonistic view of what is good for us. A life rich in achievements and friendships seems much preferable to an idle and narcissistic existence, even if the latter were to feel equally pleasant to the person who lived it. Or consider a life spent on Robert Nozick's experience machine,[1] doing nothing, but having the experiences of one's choice, artificially caused by electrodes implanted in one's brain. Most of us would not think that such a life is more enviable than a somewhat less pleasant life of fairly successful coping with reality.

Currently the most influential type of account of a person's good is in terms of the person's desires. I shall discuss an important and representative theory of this sort, formulated by Henry Sidgwick in his *Methods of Ethics*. It is controversial to what extent Sidgwick himself agrees with the theory; he clearly dissents from it on one point at least,[2] which I will shortly discuss. It is not a "straw man," however. It is a standard reference point in discussions of desire-satisfaction theories of well-being. For example, it forms the core of the theory of "goodness as rationality" that is adopted in John Rawls's *Theory of Justice*. I will not discuss most of the bells and whistles that Rawls adds to Sidgwick's account, because they do not seem to me to help with the problems that will engage our attention here, though they are importantly related in other ways to Rawls's larger project. I believe that Rawls inherits most of the difficulties that we will find in the theory articulated by Sidgwick. Indeed, I doubt that any desire-satisfaction theory has a plausible escape from them.

The first difficulty that desire-satisfaction theories of a person's good must face, as Sidgwick notes, is "the obvious objection that a man often desires what he knows

---

1. Nozick, *Anarchy, State, and Utopia*, pp. 42–45.
2. Shaver, "Sidgwick's False Friends," rightly emphasizes that the theory is not exactly Sidgwick's own, and documents the extent of the controversy.

is on the whole bad for him,"[3] or, more broadly, that people often want what is not good for them, whether they know it or not. Sidgwick's solution for this difficulty is "that if we interpret the notion 'good' in relation to 'desire', we must identify it not with the actually *desired*, but rather with the *desirable*" (110f.). He suggests a definition of 'desirable' as meaning

> [S1] what would be desired, with strength proportioned to the degree of
> desirability, if it were judged attainable by voluntary action, supposing the
> desirer to possess a perfect forecast, emotional as well as intellectual, of the
> state of attainment or fruition. (111)

Since Sidgwick has said, earlier in the context, that he "will consider only what a man desires for itself—not as a means to an ulterior result—and for himself—not benevolently for others" (109), I take it that [S1] is meant as a definition of what is desirable *for* the desirer, and is intended to yield an account of what it is for something to be more than instrumentally good for a person.

Going on to a related concept, Sidgwick frames a definition of "a man's future good on the whole" as

> [S2] what he would now desire and seek on the whole if all the consequences of
> all the different lines of conduct open to him were accurately foreseen and
> adequately realised in imagination at the present point of time. (111f.)

This formulation provides for comparative evaluations, and for the consideration of merely instrumental goods, though the fundamental judgments to which it appeals are not judgments of instrumental value, since the alternative courses of action, considered together with all their consequences, form wholes so comprehensive that they are not evaluated as means to further goods.

Sidgwick has crafted the hypothetical form of these definitions, quite explicitly, with a view to enabling them to account for some of the ways in which people commonly want what is not good for them. I may want such a thing only because I mistakenly think it is a means to something else that I want, or because its "bad effects, though fore-*seen*, are not fore-*felt*," as Sidgwick puts it. I may want something that would not be good for me, and want it for its own sake, but only because I have not adequately realized what it will be like when I get it. As Sidgwick says, "It may turn out a 'Dead Sea Apple', mere dust and ashes in the eating: more often fruition will partly correspond to expectation, but may still fall short of it in a marked degree" (110). All of these possibilities are accounted for by the provision, in [S1] and [S2], that the desires that determine what is good or desirable for one are those one would have if one possessed "a perfect forecast, emotional [and imaginative] as well as intellectual," of what the realization of the desire would be like in relevant respects.

---

3. Sidgwick, *Methods of Ethics*, p. 109f. Subsequent references to this work (and to no other) will be given, in the present section, by page numbers in parentheses in the text.

Another cause of wanting something that is not good for one on the whole is failure to consider more desirable alternatives. This is accounted for by the attention to alternatives in [S2]. And the proviso in [S1] that it is "if it were judged attainable by voluntary action" that the desirable would be desired is meant to deal with the fact that I may fail to want something because I judge it to be impossible, though it would be very good for me if I could have it (110).

This strategy has its costs, however. The hypothetical form of these definitions threatens to undo some of the apparent advantages of a desire-satisfaction theory.

1. Desire-satisfaction theories have sometimes seemed politically appealing to liberals because the idea that one's good is determined by one's own preferences seems to afford a bulwark against paternalism. But the hypothetical character of [S1] and [S2] involves a radical departure from this idea, and deeply undermines any such bulwark. Anyone who has been told that something is what she herself would want if only she knew better, knows that it was not being commended to her on the basis of her own preferences, but on the basis of supposedly superior wisdom. Perhaps, in view of our frequent desires for what is bad for us, it never was very realistic to suppose that any plausible theory of a person's good can provide a bulwark against paternalism.[4] But I think the substitution of hypothetical for actual desires is likely to undermine *any* advantage there may be in defining what is good or desirable for me in terms of *my own* desires. The acquisition of an understanding of reality that would be ideally adequate for decision making would change me quite drastically— so drastically, indeed, that I doubt that the question, what *I* would want if I had such an understanding, has a moral importance very different from that of the question, what another, better informed person would want if he were in my position, or what he would want for me if he loved me.

2. Another apparent advantage of a desire-satisfaction theory is the fact that it offers a reduction of the notion of a person's good to empirical facts about preferences. As Sidgwick puts it, it is supposed to be a notion of good that "is entirely interpretable in terms of *fact*, actual or hypothetical, and does not introduce any judgment of value fundamentally distinct from judgments relating to existence;— still less any 'dictate of Reason'" (112). This is a feature that will be attractive to many philosophers of an empiricist bent. But I see a metaphysical fly in the ointment. I am skeptical about the "hypothetical facts" to which the theory appeals. Not being a strict determinist in psychology, I see no compelling reason to believe that there are always, or even usually, objects or courses of action that I would definitely desire or prefer if I knew facts that I do not actually know.[5]

This, by the way, is the point at which Sidgwick explicitly dissents from the desire-satisfaction theory he has formulated. Not that he is skeptical, as I am, about the hypothetical facts; but it seems to him more plausible to ascribe to the notion of a person's "good on the whole" a commendatory force, a "rational dictate," as he

---

4. A similar point is made well in Griffin, *Well-Being*, p. 11.
5. I have developed this sort of skepticism much more fully in Adams, "Middle Knowledge and the Problem of Evil."

calls it, which is not captured by [S1] and [S2].[6] He does not believe in reductive definitions of ethical terms. In the end, therefore, he prefers to incorporate an un-reduced normative notion of "reason" in his definition,

> [S3] interpreting 'ultimate good on the whole for me' to mean what I should practically desire if my desires were in harmony with reason, assuming my own existence alone to be considered. (112)

One could of course think that 'good' has a commendatory force that [S1] and [S2] fail to capture, and still believe that they accurately state the conditions under which an end is good for a person. It is not clear to me whether that is Sidgwick's view, or whether he ultimately disagrees in some further way with [S1] and [S2].[7] In any event the main burden of my objections to [S1] and [S2] will be that they are not adequate as an account of the conditions under which an end is good for a person.

The gravest disadvantage of the theory articulated by Sidgwick in [S1] and [S2] is that though it accounts well enough for some of the ways in which we may desire what is not good for us, it cannot cope so well with all of them.[8] I believe this is a disadvantage that it shares with other desire-satisfaction theories of the nature of a person's good. I will discuss four problems of this sort. The first two are about the force of the beneficiary 'for' in 'good for'; they impinge on [S3] as well as [S1] and [S2]. The third and fourth problems focus rather on the value signified by 'good' in 'good for'; they specifically affect [S1] and [S2].

1. Altruistic desires might lead you to sacrifice your own good for the good of another. This seems to imply that what you would prefer, on the whole, with full knowledge, is not necessarily what is best, on the whole, *for you*. Sidgwick attempts to deal with this problem by stipulating that altruistic desires do not enter into the determination of a person's good. He states at the outset that he will consider "only

---

6. This is the only explicit objection to [S1] and [S2] that I have found in Sidgwick. Shaver ("Sidgwick's False Friends," p. 316) argues that Sidgwick thought they do not deal adequately with the possibility of weakness of will. Shaver seems to take it that when Sidgwick speaks of "a rational dictate to aim at this end [one's own good on the whole], if in any case a conflicting desire urges the will in an opposite direction," the "conflicting desire" is a desire that conflicts with one's good even though it is formed under the ideal conditions specified in [S1] and [S2]. I think it much likelier, however, that Sidgwick meant a desire, not so formed, that conflicts with the desire formed in the ideal conditions. Schneewind (*Sidgwick's Ethics and Victorian Moral Philosophy*, p. 225) thinks Sidgwick objects to the privileged role of present desire in [S2]; but Sidgwick (p. 111) seems to me rather to suppose (rightly or wrongly) that equal regard for all relevant times is adequately provided for in [S2] by the requirement of full imagination of the whole future. Parfit (*Reasons and Persons*, p. 500) suggests that Sidgwick objects to the desire-satisfaction account (as I will) on the ground that my desires, though fully informed, might still be too base to define my good; but I see no clear evidence of that in the text of Sidgwick.

7. Sidgwick grants that they supply "an intelligible and admissible interpretation of the terms 'good' (substantive) and 'desirable,' as giving philosophical precision to the vaguer meaning with which they are used in ordinary discourse" (p. 112). On the other hand, the desire-satisfaction theory does not play a clear explicit role in Sidgwick's argument when he concludes, chapters later, that pleasure alone is the ultimate good for anyone.

8. As indicated in note 6, Sidgwick does not seem to me to object to [S1] and [S2] on this ground.

what a man desires . . . for himself—not benevolently for others" (109). This is too short a way to take with the problem.

How are we to determine which of a person's desires are "for himself"? A good test case here is the desire to be of service to others. This is not the purely other-regarding desire that others be served. It is a partly self-regarding desire. For if you have it, you want yourself to be one who does the serving. Nonetheless, it is commonly an unselfish desire. It is not a desire for one's own good as such; and in fulfilling it one might be willing to sacrifice one's own good.

Sidgwick might refuse to count the desire to serve as a desire for oneself, although it seems intuitively to be a desire that is partly for oneself. The notion of a desire "for oneself" threatens thus to become a technical one, for which an explication will be needed. But what explication can be given? In some contexts we could use the criterion that if you want something because it seems to you that it would be *good for you*, then the desire is for yourself. We cannot appeal without circularity to this criterion, however, if we are using the notion of a desire for oneself to define the notion of a good for oneself.

Another approach would be to restrict desires for oneself to desires for non-relational states of oneself. This might be suggested by the phrase "assuming my own existence alone to be considered" in [S3]. This restriction may seem innocent to hedonists, if they construe pleasure as a nonrelational state of oneself; and Sidgwick was a hedonist. But he explicitly wanted his hedonism not to be presupposed in the analysis of the notion of a person's good (109). And most non-hedonists will think that some relational desires—particularly desires to be really related to other people in certain ways, and not just to believe or feel oneself so related—have as much claim as any other desires to a share in determining what is good for oneself.

Indeed, even the desire to be of service to others cannot plausibly be denied a voice in determining what would be good for the desirer, if this is to be determined by his desires. It does not seem unreasonable to count it a great blessing to be able really to help other people. A desire-satsifaction theory should therefore not exclude this desire from all influence in the definition of a person's good, but only from undue influence. This makes the discrimination all the more difficult. Perhaps Sidgwick might say that the desire to serve others is to be considered in this context *to the extent that* it is for oneself, being weighted according to the portion of its motivational force that is for oneself, ignoring the portion that is for the benefit of others. But here we are surely dancing on conceptual quicksand, as we have little reason to believe that the motivational force of the desire can be divided so neatly as this response would suppose into self-regarding and altruistic portions.

2. Something like the problem I have just been discussing arises in connection with desires that are not necessarily altruistic but may be called "idealistic." One may clearheadedly do what is worse for oneself out of regard for virtue, or for some other ideal. Love of truthfulness, or of human dignity, may lead a person to tell the truth, or to refuse to abase herself, at great cost to herself and for nobody else's benefit. It may be that Sidgwick meant the influence of such motives to be excluded by his announced intent to "consider only what a man desires . . . for himself" (109). For earlier in his book he seems to imply that an "ideal end, as Truth, or Freedom,

or Religion," would be "extra-regarding" (51f.). But this is not a very plausible classification, when it is one's own truthfulness, freedom, or dignity that is at stake; nor is it completely satisfying even with regard to one's own religious piety. Desires for these ends could plausibly be excluded from the realm of the self-regarding or the "for oneself" only if hedonism were presupposed, which Sidgwick did not want to do in the analysis we are discussing. Indeed, it is not clear under what description these motives could be excluded, if hedonism is not presupposed. To exclude desires for anything other than the desirer's own good would render the account viciously circular. To exclude desires for anything other than a state of the desirer's consciousness would edge back toward a presupposition of hedonism.

And idealistic desires probably ought not to be totally excluded anyway. A typical nonhedonist will think they should have something to say, though not too much to say, about what is good for the desirer, if any desires are allowed a voice on this subject. For she will not want to deny that it is better for me (other things being equal, and apart from the consequences) if I am truthful and free and uphold my dignity as a human being. And here we cannot even begin to apply the very questionable strategy I suggested for Sidgwick with regard to the desire to serve others, the strategy of saying that the end should count in determining one's good *to the extent that* it is an end one wants "for oneself." For we are already considering the ideal ends to the extent that one does desire them for oneself.

Of course desire-satisfaction theorists need not try to exclude in any way the influence of idealistic desires—or of altruistic desires either—if they are prepared to accept a paradox. I mean the paradox that if under the relevant conditions I would choose, all things considered, for the sake of my ideals, or for the good of others, to sacrifice my own comfort, tranquillity, physical and social pleasures, health of mind and body, and length of days, then that is what is *best for me*. Rawls says some things about happiness that suggest he might be prepared to take this line.[9] But I think it is not plausible. And Sidgwick's position was less heroic. He said that "when the sacrifice is made for some ideal end, as Truth, or Freedom, or Religion: it may be a real sacrifice of the individual's happiness" (52). He must also have thought it could be a real sacrifice of the individual's own *good*, since he was in the end a hedonist.

3. Quite a different class of motives that may lead us away from our own good are those that are characteristic of ill will or indifference toward oneself. I may want things that are bad for me *because* they are bad for me, or because they are painful, if I hate myself or despise myself or am angry at myself, or if I feel guilty and want to punish myself.[10] It is only too familiar a fact that people can and often do have it in for themselves, though many theories of human nature imply the contrary. People sometimes do themselves serious bodily harm, or even kill themselves, at least partly out of self-hatred. One may refuse something that seems likely to make one happier, because one feels one does not deserve to be happy. And even without active ill will one can be indifferent toward oneself. People sometimes, in depression, ex-

---

9. Rawls, *A Theory of Justice*, p. 550f.

10. The possibility of a desire to punish oneself is developed persuasively as a counterexample to desire-satisfaction theories of a person's good in Kraut, "Desire and the Human Good," p. 40f.

haustion, or ennui, do not care very much about their own lives; and that is another way in which one can fail to desire what is good for oneself.[11] To the extent that one is influenced by ill will or indifference toward oneself, it seems unreasonable to take what one wants, or even what one would want if one had all relevant knowledge, as definitive of one's good.

This phenomenon poses a serious problem for desire-satisfaction theories of a person's good. It is one that is not already solved by the hypothetical structure of [S1] and [S2]. For it is not plausible to suppose that ill will toward oneself would disappear if one had full realization of one's alternatives and their consequences.[12] And it still is not plausible if we also demand[13] full realization of the causal history of one's motives. A fuller understanding of our histories, capacities, and tendencies does not always make us like ourselves better.

A desire-satisfaction theorist could try to deal with this problem by adding the stipulation that one's good is determined by what one would desire *if* one were free of ill will and indifference toward oneself (in addition to satisfying the other conditions laid down by [S1] and [S2]). This will be circular, of course, saying only that one's good is what one would desire if one cared for one's own good, unless ill will and indifference toward a person can be understood independently of the conception of a person's good. But I think the gravest objection to this strategy is that it would carry the reliance on hypothetical preferences quite beyond the bounds of plausibility, even for those who are less skeptical than I am about hypothetical preferences in general.

Consider a person in the grip of self-hatred or depression, and suppose he has not recently been free of this affliction; suppose it enduring and not merely intermittent. If we ask what he would want for himself if he cared more for himself, is that an intelligent question? Is it reasonable to assume he has a motivational structure that can be projected across such a radical change in attitude toward himself so as to determine what would be good for him? Perhaps his tastes in food and music can be projected, but more important preferences regarding personal relationships and style of life are harder to project. What he would want in such matters if his attitude toward himself were changed is likely to depend on how it got changed. Do we want to know what he would desire if he were helped by psychiatric treatment? (And shall we specify Freudian, behavior modification, or chemical treatment?) Or is our question what he would want if his feelings about himself were transformed as a result of his falling in love with someone who really loved him? (And shall we specify anything about that person's interests and lifestyle?) Or is it what he would want if his spirits were lifted by involvement in something he perceived as a great cause? (And does it matter for our present purpose whether he would be raising money for AIDS research or walking a picket line at abortion clinics?) Alternatively,

11. See the persuasive treatment of this subject in Stocker, "Desiring the Bad."

12. This is noted, in a similar context, by Anderson, *Value in Ethics and Economics*, p. 131, where she also notes the interesting point that some kinds of *over*valuation of oneself, such as vanity, "can also lead one to desire things that are not good for oneself."

13. With Rawls, *A Theory of Justice*, p. 419f., and Brandt, *A Theory of the Good and the Right*.

we might wonder what he would desire if he were reconciled with himself through a religious conversion—and surely it would matter what sort of religion it was. Thus instead of a single question, 'What would he want if he cared more for himself?', we have an indefinite variety of questions of the form 'What would he want if he came to care more for himself as a result of *x*?' These questions will have quite different answers. And while some values of *x* can probably be excluded as too unlikely in view of the subject's actual circumstances and character, no one of these questions can be expected to emerge as uniquely relevant to the question, what would be good for him.

No doubt we often think we know what someone would want for herself if she cared more for herself. But I suspect that is mainly because we think we know what she believes would be good for her, and we assume that if she cared more for herself she would want what she (in fact) believes would be good for her—ignoring the effects that the process of transformation of her attitudes toward herself might have on her beliefs about her own good. Or perhaps we project into her transformed mind, not her actual beliefs, but our beliefs about human good in general. In either case we do not have a promising strategy for the desire-satisfaction theorist. For making the definition of a person's good depend on her beliefs or ours about what would be good for her would introduce a vicious-looking circle as soon as we start to ask what is being believed, by her or by us.

4. I have argued that our desires regarding our own lives may be too idealistic to define our good; they may also not be idealistic enough to define it. I may fail to prefer what is better for me because my desires are base. I may prefer money to friendship, idleness to creativity, casual commercial sex to love.

Are such preferences due only to failure of foresight and imagination, as [S1] and [S2] would require them to be if they are not to define a person's good? I doubt it. Perhaps it will be replied that one who prefers money to friendship does not *appreciate* friendship as he should, and that this is a failure of imagination. I grant that there is a failure of appreciation here, in that such a person does not value friendship as highly as he should. But that is not a failure of imagination in the relevant sense; it is rather that which is supposed to be explained by a failure of imagination. And other explanations are possible. Sadly, it sometimes happens that one who has tasted friendship comes to prefer money or some other form of power. Must he have forgotten what friendship is like, or can he just have come to like the power more than it deserves?

Here I have in mind an argument of John Stuart Mill's. He held, famously, that pleasures must be rated as to their quality as well as their quantity. One type of pleasure is of better quality than another, on his view, if a smaller quantity of the former is preferred to a greater quantity of the latter by a great majority of "those who are competently acquainted with both."[14] The crucial point in this criterion is the notion of "competent acquaintance." The effect of Mill's use of it is to stack the deck against the sensualist and in favor of intellectual, social, and moral pleasures.

14. Mill, *Utilitarianism*, chap. 2, paragraph 5.

This is manifest in the way Mill deals with the objection "that many who begin with youthful enthusiasm for everything noble, as they advance in years sink into indolence and selfishness." His reply is that

> those who undergo this very common change [do not] voluntarily choose the
> lower description of pleasures in preference to the higher. I believe [he says] that,
> before they devote themselves exclusively to the one, they have already become
> incapable of the other. . . . It may be questioned whether any one who has
> remained equally susceptible to both classes of pleasures ever knowingly and
> calmly preferred the lower.[15]

Here we must ask *how* those who have fallen have lost their capacity for the higher pleasures. Is this really a change that could have *preceded* the change in their preferences? I think not. The only way in which people can plausibly be said to have lost their capacity for social or moral pleasures in such cases is by ceasing to *care* very much about other people and about morality.

Mill's deck is stacked against the sensory pleasures precisely because we are all susceptible to them. It requires no devotion to maintain a capacity for them. Therefore even those who are devoted to higher things are still competently acquainted with sensory pleasures. But the pleasures of friendship and moral rectitude cannot be separated from devotion to their objects. If a fully operative capacity for any given pleasure is required for "competent acquaintance" with it, small wonder that those who are "competently acquainted" with the pleasures of friendship and morality prefer them! If they did not prefer them, they would lack the devotion or interest necessary for a capacity for them.

Mill's argument can be parodied. It seems that the pleasures of vengeance must be of very high quality. Vast amounts of comfort, safety, and sensory pleasure have been sacrificed for vengeance by real connoisseurs. No doubt there are some who once tasted the fierce joys of revenge but have now become merciful and prefer the milder pleasures of forgiveness. But they are no longer competently acquainted with the pleasures of vengeance, having lost the capacity for them. For they would not fully savor the sufferings of an enemy if fortune should offer them such a prize.

Similar considerations apply to the desire-satisfaction theory articulated by Sidgwick. If we are willing to accept a pushpin-is-as-good-as-poetry version of it, we will not be bothered by this problem. But if we think that people sometimes choose what is worse for them because of desires that are base, or insufficiently idealistic, we will think that the better ways of life are adequately appreciated only by people who are "into" them. But the superiority of a way of life cannot be established by the fact that it is preferred by people who are into it, for preferring a way of life is part of being into it.

In view of all these considerations, I do not think the prospects are very bright for a desire-satisfaction theory accounting for all the gaps between what we want and what would be good for us. But that is probably not my deepest reason for re-

15. Mill, *Utilitarianism*, chap. 2, paragraph 7.

jecting such a theory. Someone more favorably disposed than I am to the theory may be able to arm it with more successfully ingenious epicycles than I have found to defend it against some of the objections I have presented. Even if it could be rescued from all of them, however, I think a desire-satisfaction theory is not particularly plausible in view of the quite different roles that considerations about people's desires and about their well-being play in our lives.

We do sometimes ask, 'What would be the wisest thing for me to do, in view of all my aims?' and, 'What would she want, if she considered these facts?' But note that neither question excludes altruistic desires from consideration. In these questions we are inquiring about what is best *from the point of view of* the person whose desires are being considered, but I think we are not normally inquiring about what is best *for* that person, as such.

The question, what would be best *for* a given person, is less characteristic of that person's own point of view (the point of view defined by the whole system of his aims) than of the point of view of someone who loves him. The lover could of course be himself, but the focus of self-love is quite different from that of trying to optimize the satisfaction of all one's aims. (The former is typically narrower than the latter.) The question 'What would be best *for* him?' is particularly apt to arise (perhaps indeed most apt to arise) in situations in which some measure of paternalism is inevitable, in which we have to decide on behalf of a child or some other person whose system of preferences is undeveloped or immature, or whose capacities for choice are in some way impaired. Our interests and desires are in large part the product of our education; and though our desires are in some ways corrupted by our culture, the desires we would have had without any education or cultural influences at all would hardly constitute a fully human motivational system, let alone one adequate to define our good. In thinking about what would be good for a child for whose education we are responsible, therefore, we must think about what interests and habits of choice to encourage and foster in her, and cannot presuppose a system of preferences and volitional tendencies already in her as defining the good that we intend for her.

This is emphatically not to deny that a child's actual desires claim our attention and respect; but their claim cannot be satisfied by respecting her hypothetical desires. Respecting a child's actual desires and caring for his good are obviously distinct, and both important. Respecting his hypothetical desires is yet a third thing, and has, in its own right, no obvious moral claim on us.

2. Well-Being as Enjoyment of the Excellent

If desire-satisfaction theories of the nature of a person's good won't do, what will? Without pretending to offer here a complete theory of the nature of a person's good, I wish to explore the idea that what is good for a person is a *life* characterized by *enjoyment of the excellent*. More precisely, I shall argue that the principal thing that can be noninstrumentally good for a person is a life that is hers, and that two criteria (perhaps not the only criteria) for a life being a good one for a person are that she should enjoy it, and that what she enjoys should be, in some objective sense,[16] excellent. Its being more excellent, and her enjoying it more, will both be reasons for thinking it better for her, other things being equal—though (for reasons that will become clearer in chapter 4, section 5) I distrust judgments based on comparative evaluations of widely different types of excellence, and I do not mean to endorse any maximizing or optimizing calculus. The exposition of my view will come mainly in three parts: about the idea of a life, and about the criteria of enjoyment and of excellence.

1. It is in your life, primarily if not exclusively, that what is noninstrumentally good for you must be found.[17] I insert the qualification 'primarily if not exclusively' because it has sometimes been supposed, quite apart from any belief in life after death (which would be part of your "life," in the relevant sense), that things happening after your death could be good for you—things such as posthumous fame or the prosperity of your grandchildren or the execution of your last will and testament. Such goods seem to lie outside the bounds of your life. But even if they are, arguably, good *for you*, they could not plausibly be made a primary criterion of your happiness or good.

It is not easy to formulate a criterion for what is to count as "in" your life, and what lies outside its bounds. Your subjective experiences and your actions are certainly part of your life. So are some of your relations, but it is harder to say which ones. Most of us would count it an important feature of our lives that we have real, and not just illusory, friends. Distant and very external relations that only philosophers would think of, on the other hand, such sharing a birthday with quintuplets you have never heard of, can plausibly be excluded from your life. The effects caused by your actions are often part of your life. It can make a difference to the character of your life whether some benefit or harm to other people really was a result of what you did. But if the effect were both unknown to you and remote from your agency in such a way as to relieve you of moral responsibility, it might be thought to lie outside your life.

Difficult questions can also be raised as to what counts as a life, what you are, and which lives could be yours. It may be doubted, for instance, whether "life" on Nozick's experience machine would really be a *life* in the sense that now concerns us, even apart from doubts about its excellence. Whatever else is to be true of an existence that is a good one for me, it must be a life that I am living; and plugging into the machine seems distressingly like giving up the chance to live a real life. What is good for me depends in part on what I am. I am indeed a subject of experience; and considered purely as a subject of experience, I might have a good enough time on the experience machine. But I am more than a subject of experience. I am also an agent, and an existence without agency would not be a real life, let alone a good one, for me. Other issues, which I will leave aside here, are connected with the plau-

16. The realism of my view of excellence plays a part in my arguments here. I acknowledge, however, that it is not such a prominent part that the main arguments of the present chapter, taken in isolation from the rest of the book, could not be adapted for use in a less realist or less cognitivist theory. The main task of this chapter is not the defense of moral realism, but the vindication of the place of excellence in ethics.

17. Cf. Griffin, *Well-Being*, pp. 21–23.

sible thesis that a life, in the relevant sense, must have at least a minimal narrative unity.[18]

2. Another truth about human well-being that is intuitively evident is that a person's good is not very fully realized[19] unless she likes or enjoys her life in the long run. You may be very virtuous; you may be brilliant, beautiful, successful, rich, and famous; but if you do not enjoy your life, it cannot plausibly be called a good life *for you*. We may think of this as the kernel of truth in hedonism, or as the important truth to be found in the neighborhood of hedonism.

Satisfaction of desire regarding one's life does not entail enjoyment; that is obviously important for my argument.[20] A self-sacrificing person may be satisfying a predominant preference regarding her life in being tortured to death for her devotion to a great cause, but the event will not necessarily contribute anything to her *enjoyment* of her life. Enjoyment essentially involves an occurrent quality of life that can hardly be present when one's consciousness is wholly swallowed up by pain. (The consciousness of a martyr of extraordinary fortitude or saintliness may perhaps not be swallowed up even by extreme torture, but the self-sacrificing person I have in mind here is not that extraordinary.) In enjoyment, what one likes or values about one's life must be able to hold a dominant place in one's consciousness.

At the same time, enjoyment must be understood here as including more than what is usually meant by 'pleasure'. Enjoying life is not simply a matter of "feeling good" or having pleasant experiences. It is also, and much more, a matter of the zest or interest with which one engages in the activities of life. The jaded sensualist may have sensations that are pleasant in themselves, but fail to enjoy them because he has lost interest in them. On the other hand, the "old curmudgeon" who sincerely complains about almost everything, but who pursues a variety of projects with evident interest and energy, and with considerable success, is enjoying life in the sense that interests me—though we may grant that grouching less might be a sign of even greater enjoyment. Of course one can also enjoy a lazy day, but not if one is thoroughly uninterested in everything that is going on in and around one.

What we enjoy, likewise, is not limited to states of consciousness, but also includes actions, and objects to which we are related. Swimmers enjoy swimming by doing it. Nature lovers enjoy woods by walking in them, and birds by hearing and seeing them. We enjoy our friends by relating to them in many ways; and some people have claimed to enjoy God. None of this enjoyment is without experience, but it is not only the experiences that are enjoyed. Because we can enjoy objects distinct from ourselves, we can enjoy excellence that is not our own. No doubt the ability to enjoy what is excellent is itself an excellence, but we are not necessarily excellent in proportion to the excellence we enjoy.

18. For a particularly interesting discussion of the relation of narrative unity to a person's good (claiming more than I would be prepared to claim for the importance of this factor), see MacIntyre, *After Virtue*, p. 203f.

19. I say "not very fully realized" because I wish to allow that in tragic circumstances a life that is not enjoyable might be the best that is possible for a person.

20. I am indebted to Owen McLeod for an acute question that brought this point to my attention.

In insisting thus on what we might call the "external" aspects of enjoyment, I am not motivated by a general skepticism about feelings or inner states. Behaviorist, or even Wittgensteinian, views in the philosophy of mind might lead one to interpret enjoyment in terms of ways of acting rather than introspectible feelings; but I have never found those views plausible. I take it that feelings of pleasure are real and important, and that exemplary cases of enjoyment will be characterized by feelings of pleasure as well as by active interest.

There is yet another point, however, at which an obsession with pleasure might mislead us about the kind of enjoyment or liking of one's life that is essential to a person's good; and that is the relation of the enjoyment to time. If we think of enjoyment in terms of feelings of pleasure, it will be natural to think that what matters is that the moments of one's life should be enjoyed or liked while they are occurring. That certainly adds to one's enjoyment of life, if it happens, but it is not the only thing to be taken into account when considering to what extent someone has enjoyed her life. Suppose she has succeeded in swimming the English Channel. Perhaps the hours she spent in the water were mostly unpleasant, full of weariness, anxiety, and cold. Nonetheless, we may count her swimming the Channel as something that she enjoys in her life, if she savors her achievement.

Savoring the achievement is important. It was not so much while she was doing it as after she had done it, and knew that she had succeeded, that she liked the swim. And the value that she sets on it retrospectively seems, intuitively, quite relevant to how good it was for her that her life included this episode. But this "savoring" is not to be evaluated by counting moments of pleasure spent remembering or celebrating what she had done. It would be quite wrongheaded to try to calculate the cumulative duration of the moments of retrospective pleasure, and their intensity, and weigh them against the duration and intensity of unpleasant moments involved in the swim and in the preparations for it, in order to ascertain whether doing it really made a net contribution to her good. Suppose, for instance, that she died of some unrelated[21] cause so soon after the swim that she did not have time to accumulate moments of retrospective pleasure equivalent in duration and intensity to the unpleasantness she had endured. It would be misguided to argue that in that case she would have enjoyed her life more on the whole if she had not made the swim.

More important than the duration and intensity of the moments of retrospective pleasure, when we are considering whether she enjoyed her life more by making the swim, is "what it meant to her"—what difference her knowing that she had done it made to the value that she set on her life as a whole, or on some major part of it. The relation of this consideration to moments of consciousness is complex. On the one hand, it does matter that there be a moment, well connected to the rest of her life, in which she knows that she has accomplished the thing that means so much to her. Without such a moment of knowledge, her achievement would con-

---

21. I say 'unrelated' because I want a case in which the swim does not cause her death. Many natural or accidental causes of sudden death in this situation would not be unrelated in this sense. One that would be unrelated, though particularly gruesome, is a nuclear war so bad that it would have killed her wherever she was.

tribute nothing to her *enjoyment* of life. The loss of enjoyment would be reflected in such comments as 'What a pity she never knew that she succeeded!' (And if the moment of savoring or joy does not follow the swimming so closely as to form a single event with it, but comes some time later, we may think that what she enjoyed was not *swimming* the Channel but *having swum* it.)

On the other hand, the meaningful knowledge requires only a moment to make its chief contribution to the enjoyment of life. This is reflected in the very frequent concern that people should know certain things before they die, even if the good news arrives only at the last minute. Doubtless it is even better to have more time to savor the joy; but I think the attainment of the highly valued knowledge matters much more than its duration in assessing how much the person enjoyed her life.

We probably do not have a metric that yields a nice mathematical treatment for questions of how much a person enjoys her life. There is no perspective on one's life such that how much one likes it as a whole from that point of view settles how much one has enjoyed it, for most of the enjoyment of life is found in enjoying it as one goes along. On the other hand, as noted previously, adding up the enjoyment value (if it could be computed) of minutes and seconds of consciousness does not seem to correspond very well to what we are after in asking about the enjoyment of life; what we really and reasonably care about in life is not very amenable to mathematical treatment. The enjoyment (and the excellence) of somewhat enduring projects and relationships that tend to give meaning and unity to one's life as a whole, or to major parts of it, is important to the fully human enjoyment of one's life (and to the excellence of what is enjoyed).

3. The most controversial of my theses about a person's good (and the most important for my larger aims in ethical theory) is that it depends on the *excellence* of what she enjoys. In practice we tend to think in accordance with this thesis. I have claimed that the primary point of view from which the question about a person's good arises is that of a person who loves her. And we surely do desire for those we love the enjoyment of the excellent, in preference to the enjoyment of things of lower quality, though they might be equally enjoyed. Few parents would desire for their children a lifetime of narcotic highs, no matter how much they would be enjoyed. We do not regard such pleasures, in any amount or intensity, as an acceptable substitute for friendship, knowledge, or accomplishment. Many of us, likewise, would not wish for our children or our students a life of devotion to wealth or power or fame—not because those things cannot be enjoyed, but because we think there are better things to enjoy. Probably we also believe that the greater goods are likely in fact to yield more enjoyment; but I do not think that is the main reason we believe enjoying the greater goods would be better for people. We will not conclude that our fears for someone have proved empty if her devotion to mammon leads to a long and apparently contented life of enthusiastic moneygrubbing and conspicuous consumption.

In hoping that those we love will enjoy what is excellent in preference to what is not, we are not merely hoping that they will share our personal likes and dislikes. It is not particularly a manifestation of benevolence toward someone if I hope that he will prefer raspberries (which I love) to sea cucumber (which I detested the one time I ate it). But it may well be a manifestation of love to hope that he will prefer good art to bad. This presupposes belief that excellence is objective, at least in a way that personal likes and dislikes are not. Our hopes and aspirations for people we love give reason to think that most of us hold such a belief, at least in practice and with respect to some realms of value.

The support I have offered thus far for taking the excellence of what is enjoyed as a criterion of a person's good is little more than an appeal to intuition. It is an appeal that I think most of us cannot consistently disregard unless we are prepared to change some important attitudes and practices; but it is certainly not the strongest sort of argument. It will be worthwhile, therefore, to add an argument drawn from the internal dynamics of enjoyment.

I begin with a Butlerian point.[22] Enjoyment, of the sort characteristic of persons, as distinct from merely animal pleasure, presupposes a life somewhat structured by purposes and valuings. To enjoy life as a whole, or as an ongoing project, it is important, probably necessary, to enjoy things that one *values*. And we could hardly enjoy them as we do, if we thought that our valuing them was objectively deluded or mistaken. Indeed, we could hardly value them if we thought the valuing mistaken. And few of us think we would be fortunate to live, and like very much, a life based on mistaken values. It would therefore be very hard for us to accept, in our own case, the view that the excellence of what we enjoy is irrelevant to the question how good for us it is that we enjoy it. It is important to our good to enjoy things that we think are in some degree excellent. So if we think we would not be fortunate to be deluded in such matters, we should think it important to our good to enjoy things that really are in some degree excellent.

That is, we should think so insofar as we believe that some things are objectively more excellent than others. Could we sustain our valuing and enjoying if we regarded the valuing as purely subjective, merely a matter of our individual likes and dislikes? Perhaps, but it may be doubted. I suspect the interest in such activities as art or sport would be hard to sustain if we thought (or better, if we really felt) there was nothing more to the value of the activities and the ends we pursue in them than our liking them. It would also be hard to find meaning or interest in our lives, more broadly, if we thought that about all our activities and ends.

Some activities, such as subsistence farming, might be thought to yield direct pleasure even though they are valued only instrumentally, as means to the satisfaction of physical desires so basic as to be virtually instinctive (and independent of value beliefs). But I doubt that those who enjoy subsistence farming are likely to have that simply utilitarian an attitude toward it. I suspect that they typically experience it as an activity that puts them in touch with something felt to be objectively excellent—whether the life of plants and animals, or (more abstractly) nature, or (religiously) the gods. Here too I am inclined to think that the loss of the sense of objective excellence would undermine the valuing that supports the enjoyment of the activity. For this reason even backbreaking labor in a traditional society may not be "alienating" in the way that industrial labor is apt to be when it is valued only instrumentally. This may be true even if the traditional society is objectively

---

22. Cf. Butler, *Fifteeen Sermons*, sermon 11.

very unfair, so long as it sees the labor as meaningfully related, in a more than utilitarian way, to objects whose value transcends their being liked (and even transcends their being eaten).

Some philosophers may object to the use of excellence as a criterion for a person's good because they fear it will have elitist or paternalist consequences. I think the most obnoxious sort of *elitist* consequence cannot fairly be laid to its charge. For nothing that has been said here implies that people who have achieved greater excellence, or who have more capacity for excellence, ought to have more rights or opportunities than others. To say that the excellence of what is enjoyed is a criterion of each person's good is not to say anything about how the good of different persons should be weighed in the principles of right or justice.[23] If one holds a consequentialist theory of right according to which action ought always to maximize the total or average good of persons, then the adoption of excellence as a criterion of a person's good may lead to the conclusion that action ought to favor those persons who are capable of greater excellence. But this is no worse than concluding, as some utilitarians must, that action ought to favor those persons who have a greater capacity for pleasure. Both conclusions are objectionable, but the fault in both cases can be laid at the door of the maximizing consequentialist theory of right.

A larger fear of inegalitarian consequences concerns the application of concepts of excellence to persons themselves, and not just to what they enjoy. That may be thought to threaten the moral ideal of equal regard for persons. In order to deal with this fear we will need some account of the value that belongs to persons as persons, and that will be one of the topics of chapter 4.

As for the issue of *paternalistic* implications, a theory of the good life for human beings that emphasizes excellence will not support a fastidious reverence for all human desires or wishes as such. But such reverence is implausible anyway. We are all surely aware of having had many desires whose fulfillment was never of any importance for morality or for the quality of our lives. We have also had desires whose satisfaction would have been bad for us—and this obvious fact has led desire-satisfaction theories of the nature of a person's good to abandon exclusive reliance on actual desires and appeal to hypothetical desires. But theories that appeal to hypothetical desires do not provide much of a bulwark against paternalism, as I argued in section 1.

The excellence criterion of a person's good can support a strong respect for individual autonomy if we believe, as John Stuart Mill did,[24] that the greatest excellences in human life involve or presuppose autonomous choice. The emphasis on excellence can particularly support a respect for the individual quest that seeks something beyond the conventional or the presumptively natural. The excellence criterion may lead to a somewhat selective respect for people's preferences; but that is not an implausible result. Probably most of us believe that much stricter protec-

---

23. Indeed, it is not yet to say anything at all about the role (if any) that should be assigned to excellence in political ethics. That is the subject of chapter 14, and the issue of equality in political philosophy will be taken up in the first section of that chapter.

24. Mill, *On Liberty*, chap. 3. Cf. also Griffin, *Well-Being*, p. 71, and Hurka, *Perfectionism*, chap. 11.

tion should be given to freedom of speech, religion, and association than to economic freedoms. This belief could not be based very solidly on the assumption that people care more about the former than about the latter freedoms, which (alas!) is often false. A more plausible ground for paying more respect to the former freedoms is that they protect areas of choice that are essential to the enjoyment of more excellent goods.[25]

Having focused first on the criterion of enjoyment and then on that of excellence, it remains, in this section, to discuss how they are *related* in constituting our good. It may already have occurred to the reader that there is a parallelism between my account and an informed-desire-satisfaction account of well-being—that enjoyment and excellence in the former correspond, respectively, to the satisfaction and the well-informedness of desire in the latter. This is true, but there are also significant differences. The most important is my commitment to objective excellence. By insisting that enjoyment that constitutes my good should be enjoyment of what is excellent, rather than insisting that desires that define my good should be perfectly well informed, I substitute a frankly and irreducibly value-laden criterion for one that is ostensibly procedural. I think this is necessary if we are to deal adequately with the fact that our desires can be too base to define our good.

A further difference is that enjoyment is internal to my life, and even to my consciousness, in a way that the satisfaction of my desires need not be. Even though *what* I enjoy is often external to myself, the enjoyment itself must be an event in my experience. Because of this, the enjoyment criterion helps to assure that what we are assessing is *my* good rather than some other good that I care about.

At the same time, it may be wondered whether the enjoyment criterion does not make my good *too* independent of what is external to me, since it seems that illusory friendships and illusory accomplishments, for example, can be enjoyed as much as real ones. But the enjoyment criterion does not stand alone in dealing with this problem. The excellence criterion comes to its aid, as we can see in considering another question about the relation between the two criteria: are enjoyment and excellence constituents of our good independently of each other;[26] or is it the enjoyment only *of* excellence, and excellence only *as* enjoyed, that is good for us, as my phrasing thus far has suggested?

I doubt that enjoyment of what is not in any way or degree excellent can be a constituent of our good; surely it cannot at any rate be an important constituent of our well-being. There may be relatively little enjoyment that is not enjoyment of excellence. In particular, the enjoyment of physical pleasure as such is normally an enjoyment of healthy life, which I believe is an excellence, an imaging of the divine life.[27] Unfortunately, however, there is some enjoyment that is not enjoyment of

---

25. This point will be discussed more fully in chapter 14, section 2.

26. As may be suggested by the inclusion of enjoyment in a "list" of "the ends of life" in Griffin, *Well-Being*, p. 67.

27. Conversely, physical pain is a diminishment of that enjoyment, and as such is bad for us. On this point I disagree with Richard Kraut, whose views are in many ways similar to mine, but who doubts that pain is intrinsically bad for us, seeing "no feature of it that makes it worthy of avoidance" (Kraut, "Desire and the Human Good," p. 46). I think I have just mentioned a feature of pain that

excellence because it is enjoyment of the bad. Among the clearest cases of this are enjoyments that are malicious or vain, such as schadenfreude or the savoring of inflated fantasies of one's own importance.[28] These seem to me not to contribute noninstrumentally to our good at all; one reason that they do not may be that the enjoyments themselves are bad in a way that diminishes the excellence of our lives. This is not to deny that it may sometimes be better, instrumentally, for our mental health to indulge in such pleasures than to repress them. Some cases are more complex. It might be snobbish to deny that the enjoyment of bad art can be an innocent pleasure that enhances many people's lives; but then I suspect that "bad art" that is enjoyed typically has excellences, in some degree, which are the object of much of the enjoyment.

It is hard to maintain without qualification that excellence is a constituent of our good only *as* enjoyed. Some aspect of the relevant excellence may not be accessible to one's experience, and may therefore not affect one's enjoyment. Real friendships and real accomplishments are more excellent than illusory ones, and are therefore better for us, even if the illusions would yield as much subjective enjoyment. Thus, as I claimed earlier, the excellence criterion keeps the enjoyment criterion from making my good too independent of what is external to me.

I am not denying, of course, that real friendships and real achievements are enjoyed; so it does not follow from these examples that the excellence of what is not enjoyed *at all* can constitute part of one's well-being. Probably it can, for it is plausible to think it remains better for oneself to do what is excellent when no available course of action affords any enjoyment. But a life rich only in that sort of excellence is no life to wish on a friend. It is in the enjoyment of excellence that a person's good is primarily to be sought.[29]

---

makes it worthy of avoidance, though perhaps Kraut won't think so; he does assign enjoyment a place in the human good (ibid., p. 52 n. 13), but it is not clear to me whether he means to allow it as large a place as I do. More will be said in chapter 4, section 5, about the excellence of healthy life.

28. On schadenfreude I am disagreeing with the (to my mind, underargued) position of Griffin (*Well-Being*, pp. 24–26).

29. I hope that this treatment of the relation between enjoyment and excellence helps deal with the objection to defining well-being (purely) in terms of enjoyment in Griffin, *Well-Being*, pp. 18–20.

4

THE SACRED AND THE BAD

1. The Bad

An account of the nature of the good can hardly be complete without some attention to the nature of the bad, which is often regarded as its polar opposite. The treatment of good and bad as polar opposites can be misleading, however, inasmuch as it may lead us to expect symmetrical accounts of their natures. In relation to my theory of the nature of the good, symmetry would require that there is something supremely (or most abysmally) bad, something transcendently bad, which would be the Bad itself and the standard of all badness; and other things would be bad insofar as they resembled or all-too-faithfully imaged the Bad itself. Perhaps the Bad itself would be the Devil.

This rather Manichean theory, with its parallel realms of good and bad and something supreme in each, is not in keeping with the main traditions of Western theism. Its coherence is doubtful too. It is hard to see how a transcendent Bad could be related to bad things in ways that mirror the relation of a transcendent Good to good things without possessing a richness of power and being that resembles that of the transcendent Good and is in fact excellent, rather than purely bad. Suppose, likewise, that the reference of 'bad' is fixed to a single transcendent object in a way analogous to that in which I claim the reference of 'good' is fixed to a single transcendent object. That would presumably involve thinking of the Bad as providing

102

a single focus for our system of aversions as I think of the Good as providing a single focus for our system of aspirations. But that sets up the Bad in competition with the Good as an organizing principle for our motivational life, and thus both undermines the role of the Good and treats the Bad with a respect that does not belong to the merely bad. It therefore seems to me more plausible to try to understand the bad, not in relation to a transcendent Bad, but rather in relation to the good, in terms of relations that bad things bear to the good.

This book about the good will not contain a full account of the many types of badness. Offering the merest sketch, without any pretension to completeness, I note here two main types of badness. One is mere lack of goodness; the other attacks or opposes something good.

Historically the most important attempt to explain the nature of the bad in terms of a single relation to the good has identified badness with a *privation* of goodness— that is to say, with an absence of goodness that *ought* to be there. The qualification 'that ought to be there' may not be easy to explain, but it is not dispensable, for the absence of an excellence does not always cast a badness as its shadow. It would be odd to call it something *bad* in a rhinoceros that it cannot play the oboe; I even doubt that it is something bad in me that I cannot.

No doubt privation of goodness often does constitute badness, but that is not an apt explanation of the nature of *all* badness. The idea of privation is too negative to cover such evils as extreme pain and malevolence. In these cases the evil is not just a matter of good that fails to exist or happen. The evil is also, and perhaps mainly, a matter of things that happen that shouldn't happen. Badness of the latter sort, I believe, consists in some sort of *opposition* (very broadly understood) to something that is good.

Badness of this type can be a merely *instrumental* badness. The instrumentally bad causes loss of some good, or prevents or impedes the realization of a good, or tends to do so; its badness is constituted by its actual or likely effects. But there is also a more than instrumental badness that is opposed to the good.

The *deterioration* or *destruction* of something good, for example, has a badness that must be understood in terms of the value of the good that is lost; and its badness is noninstrumental, for I am referring here to the badness of what happens to the good thing, and not to a badness of an act or other cause of that happening. It deserves emphasis that what is bad in these cases is specifically a deterioration or destruction, and not a mere general nonexistence, of a good. For the destruction of an actual good constitutes something bad in a way that prevention of a merely possible good typically does not (if our nonutilitarian intuitions are to be trusted as I believe they are). Celibacy prevents the procreation of children who would be images of God, and great goods, if they existed; but that does not seem to be a *bad* effect of celibacy, so long as there are enough people in the world (as there are in fact), and such prevention of the procreation of many possible children certainly does not have a badness remotely comparable to that of the destruction of a single actual child. Destruction of good is typically much more and much worse than mere absence of good.

We may wonder why that should be. I believe the main reason is that the negative relations to the good that constitute badness are those that matter from the point of view of love for the good, which is thus a dominant factor in marking out the role that belongs to the bad as well as that which belongs to the good. And love for the good is for actual much more than for merely possible goods, as we shall see in subsequent chapters.

Another relation to the good that can constitute a badness that is more than merely instrumental is that of *being against* the good, in one's intention, desire, or attitude. This relation to the good can be present, and bad, without any actual external effect. This form of evil is paradigmatically present in *hatred* toward something good. This is not to say that every opposition to a particular good is unambiguously evil. Setting oneself against a particular good can be predominantly good, for it is apt to be good to prefer the right good when genuine goods are in competition or conflict with each other and one of them must be sacrificed for the sake of another. Rejecting a particular good in such a case is not necessarily hating it or opposing goodness as such. But being against something good, without a good enough reason, is among the types of evil that earn the severest moral censure.

In rejecting the idea of a transcendent Bad, it is important not to minimize the gravity that evil can have. The idea of a supreme Good, I have argued, is commended by a sense that experiences of finite goods are fragmentary glimpses of something transcendently wonderful. Is there no parallel, we may ask, in our experience of the bad? Are there no occasions on which we seem to look into a pit of evil that is quite out of the ordinary? Surely there are, and much of this chapter will be devoted to considering what evokes *moral horrror*, as I shall put it. I will indeed postulate something evaluatively transcendent in the object of an appropriate moral horror. But what I will postulate is not a transcendent Bad. It is a transcendent Good, and the sacredness of the image of the transcendent Good that is violated in a horrific evil. I will try to show that even the morally horrible can be understood in terms of its relation to the good.

The idea of the *sacred* thus introduced as the kind of good violated by the morally horrible is the other main theme, the positive pole, of this chapter. The sacred is a morally as well as religiously important type of value. In section 5 it will provide a basis for the treatment (promised in chapter 3) of the value of persons as such and the possibility of grounding equal regard for them.

2. Moral Horror

We begin with an aspect of the bad. In this I hope to do justice to a disturbing and dangerous, but morally necessary idea, the idea of the morally horrible, and to locate it in the broader framework for ethics that I am developing. This idea is rooted in an important phenomenon of moral psychology—namely, a sense of horror toward certain types of deeds, a feeling that certain things would be *horrible* to do. Among the actions that most obviously evoke such a horror are rape, murder, and maiming, torturing, or brainwashing a human being. Some might regard this as a merely subjective feeling, but, for reasons to be discussed shortly, I take it that moral horror plays a central part in marking out the role belonging to an important sort of evil, which I am calling the morally horrible. In this an analogy may be seen to the way in which I have argued that Eros plays a comparably important part in marking out the role that is to be filled by the good. If there were a transcendent Bad, moreover, I cannot think of a psychic phenomenon better suited by its intensity to point toward such a Bad than moral horror.

The role that moral horror marks out for the morally horrible, however, is more local than we would expect of a transcendent principle of all badness. Moral horror does not have the obvious systematic importance that Eros, desire, and admiration have in our affective and motivational life. This lack of obvious systematic significance may be one reason for the fact that feelings of moral horror have usually not been given as important a place in ethical theory, theological or secular, as they have in our moral life.

Moral horror does not apply to every sort of badness, and a first step in understanding its significance will be to delineate at least roughly the area of negative value to which it pertains. The first point here is that the morally horrible, as such, is a species of the bad rather than of the wrong. We may be tempted to think otherwise because moral horror is an important source of our moral response to most of those actions that are most gravely wrong; but wrongness is neither necessary nor sufficient for the appropriate evocation of moral horror.

That it is not sufficient is obvious. We do not find income tax evasion horrifying, for example, though we think it wrong. Violations of persons evoke horror in a way that violations of some of their rights do not. Even gross injustices can seem more appropriate objects of outrage than of horror. The outrageous is not necessarily horrible, in the sense that concerns me. Outrage is akin to anger, or perhaps even a species of it, in a way that horror is not; and horror has what I am tempted to call a metaphysical depth that outrage, as such, does not.

More important for excluding the classification of the morally horrible as a species of the wrong is that one can reasonably find an action morally horrible even when one does not believe it to be wrong. Even those who believe, as most people do, that there are at least a few circumstances in which it is right to kill another human being are apt to feel a metaphysical shudder, so to speak, at any prospect of doing it, and rightly so. Not only the death is a bad thing, but being an agent of it is morally horrible, even if morally justified or required. The impulse of moral purism, to eliminate ambivalent evaluations in such cases, is to be resisted. Some of the most interesting uses of the category of the morally horrible, as we shall see, are in cases in which it may not entail moral wrongness.

Moral wrongness and moral horror seem to me quite different in nature. Moral wrongness, and moral rightness and obligation, are grounded in social requirements and institutions, and ultimately in divine commands, as I shall argue in chapters 10 and 11. Without a context of social requirements, without even commands of God, murder and torture would not have the property I think *is* wrongness; but they would still be bad, and specifically horrible. Moral horror is not a consciousness of a command or requirement laid on us by anyone, nor of a rule of any sort, but a feeling about the actions themselves and their consequences. We feel it would be horrible to do certain things even if there were no authoritative rule or social pressure against them, and even if they were not forbidden by God. Our primary feelings about such deeds as murder and torture are not about violation of a rule or requirement, but about what is done to the victims. This is not to say that moral horror has nothing to do with wrongness; on the contrary, it is plausible to suppose that an important reason that something is rightly thought to be wrong, an important reason that it is divinely forbidden, is often to be sought in the moral horribleness of the deed. Chapter 10 should make clearer the difference I see between the bad and the wrong; what is essential at this point is to be clear that I am viewing moral horror as a response to the bad rather than the wrong.

Even when the bad is distinguished from the wrong, I do not mean to *identify* the morally horrible with the morally bad in actions. It is only a *species* thereof, and there are other kinds of bad action. Actions can be bad, even very bad, without horrifying. Acts of great cowardice, for example, or gross intemperance in food and drink, as such, seem shameful, perhaps even disgusting, rather than horrible. Selfish and unconscientious acts, likewise, are bad in important ways without necessarily being horrible.

A major reason for the neglect of moral horror in ethical theory is that feelings of moral revulsion vary greatly from person to person and from culture to culture, and must often be quite subjective. Even in the case of incest, which is almost universally regarded with horror, we find that different societies have had quite different ideas of which relations, apart from the very closest, fall within the scope of the incest taboo. From the standpoint of modern societies, taboo generally seems an untrustworthy moral guide. It has led to grave injustices, such as the persecution of homosexuals. We are rightly reluctant to subject behavior to moral condemnation on the ground of personal feelings of abhorrence.

In view of this consideration especially, we might doubt that the feeling of moral horror deserves any important place in our ethical thinking. But that would be going too far. The sense of moral horror is an essential ingredient of any humane response to some types of action, and it is important to the motivational power of moral concern. One of the most chilling features of the phenomenon of Nazism was the use of a facade or pretense of scientific rationality to suppress normal reactions of horror at what was being done. I shall argue, moreover, that if we do not respect such feelings, we will find it difficult to understand the gravity with which we rightly regard certain types of bad action. I wish therefore to offer an account of something true and important in ethics that we might be apprehending by way of an appropriate sense of moral horror.

It is important to the project that the feeling of horror will not be taken to constitute, in itself, the sort of moral fact (the sort of badness) I am seeking to understand. It is rather to be taken as a signpost to an objective fact that is independent of it (as Eros is a signpost to excellence). The feeling can be mistaken. We may hope that it will sometimes be reasonable to trust it; but the possibility of criticizing feelings of revulsion and setting them aside as subjective is important. I will try to develop a theory that provides some basis for such criticism.

It will be a theory about horrible deeds, about *doing* something horrible. People also have ideas about *being* something horrible; and the horror experienced by a victim may sometimes be directed at least as much toward the agent as toward the action.[1] But I will not try to determine here what it would be horrible to *be*, or even whether there is such a thing as a person being something horrible in the relevant moral sense. The question of what it would be horrible to *do* will be enough to keep us busy.

Our initial ethical hypothesis about the ethical significance of moral horror might be that it simply expresses our awareness of the great *harm* suffered by the victims, in the sense of a cost to their interests; and we may be tempted to subsume this under a general category of loss of "utility." There is reason to regard this interpretation as inadequate, however.

The fact and degree of harm, as expressed by any general measure of utility, is not all that concerns us in the case of rape, for example. Rape is virtually always harmful to the victim, of course, and typically very harmful. But individual reactions can vary, and there might be a person who would suffer as much discernible harm, in her actual life circumstances, from having her doctoral dissertation research destroyed by malicious sabotage of a university's computer (no trivial harm that!) as from being raped. Yet the computer crime, though undeniably reprehensible, is not horrifying in the same way that the sexual assault would be.

Something similar is true of killing. There is perhaps a sense in which killing a person is necessarily harming her, but there are cases in which it is very doubtful that being killed was on balance a misfortune for the victim.[2] Even in those cases the killing evokes horror. It seems natural in this connection to speak of the violation of something sacred and of "the sanctity of human life."

3. Violation

The motif of moral horror has not usually been accorded any more fundamental a role in theological than in secular ethical theory, but I think it has a natural affinity with religious feelings. It is natural, as I have just remarked, to conceptualize it in terms of the violation of something sacred. In the Western religious tradition the idea that human beings are "created in the image of God" (Genesis 1:26–27) provides an obvious basis for interpreting human life as containing something sacred whose violation could be the object of moral horror. This idea, which I broached at the end of the last chapter, provides a suitable starting point for the interpretation of moral horror in a theistic ethical theory. It also has the advantage, in my eyes, of resonating with the view of theistic Platonism that created things are good insofar as they faithfully image God, and with a corresponding conception of the value of persons as persons.

In a theory that recognizes a transcendent Good, of course, we cannot say that the value of every person as such is the highest value there is. If there is a sacredness of finite persons, it is a derivative or secondary sacredness that belongs to them as images of the transcendent Good. That we do see in them a value sufficiently pe-

---

1. See Hallie, *Horror and the Paradox of Cruelty*.
2. See Henson, "Utilitarianism and the Wrongness of Killing," and Read, *The Right Medicine*.

remptory to be called sacred, at least in such a derivative sense, is attested, however, by our reaction to violations of human persons. Conversely, our sense of the sacredness of the human person may give some support to the belief that personhood images the transcendent Good strongly enough to justify thinking of the transcendent Good as a person.

One main issue to be resolved in developing this line of thought concerns the nature of "violation." What is it that it is horrible to do to an image of God? The most obvious part of an answer to this question is that destruction and lasting damage count as violation. Killing and maiming are horrors, as is the infliction of any injury, physical or psychological, that significantly diminishes the beauty, or impairs the normal functioning, of a person for a considerable period of time. The act is the more horrible inasmuch as the destruction or damage is intended. Some horrific actions may be justified, of course, and their horror mitigated, if not entirely removed, if they are seen as necessary for the good of the person to whom they are done, as in a surgical amputation.

Destruction and lasting damage are not the only forms of violation, however. Rape and torture typically result in serious enduring damage to the victim, but they are prime objects of moral horror even if they do not. They are surely violations of a person. We need a more general account of what constitutes a violation.

I cannot offer as clear or neat a criterion of violation as I would like, but I think I can identify two necessary conditions; a violation must satisfy *both* of them. (1) An act that violates a person must *attack* the person. Its foreseeable effects must be so damaging to the person, or so contrary to her (actual or presumed) will, that fully intending them, in the absence of reason to believe them necessary for the prevention of greater harm to her, would constitute *hostility* toward the person. I do not mean that the effects must be in fact foreseen, or fully intended, by the agent, though full intention aggravates the violative character of the act. (2) A person is not violated by every act that harms her interests or crosses her will. A violation is an act that attacks the person *seriously* and *directly*. Most (but not all) violations of a person will assault her body. Acts that mainly damage a person's possessions, what she *has* as distinct from what she *is*, will typically not violate *her*, even if they are quite hostile to her interests. This second condition is the point on which I find it hardest to attain generality and precision at once. I think we must sometimes rely on our sense of moral horror to determine which acts attack a person seriously and directly enough to violate her.

The importance of these points may be illustrated in an attempt to understand the horror of rape and other unconsented incursions into a person's sexuality, a horror that is still powerful where there is no serious physical damage or impairment of the victim's faculties. On my view such sexual incursions are violations of a person, and hence of an image of God. Why are they violations? (1) Their opposition to the victim's will qualifies them as attacks, satisfying the hostility condition. (2) The claim that the person is seriously and directly attacked receives some support from the involvement of the victim's body, but it needs more support.

We may seek it in the thought that the meaning of selfhood, if not the substance of the person, is partly defined by social structures, and that certain boundaries between distinct selves are a crucial part of those structures. Prohibitions and permissions about touching and viewing other people's bodies play an important role in defining such boundaries, and sexual restrictions can contribute to this definition. By the same token, a sexual touching or viewing without full adult consent can rightly be seen as attacking something central to selfhood, and thus as a serious and direct assault on the person, and a violation of an image of God.

The horror that many people feel about sexual violations is undoubtedly intensified when the boundary that is infringed, against or without the victim's will, is one that it would be thought *wrong* for the victim to cross voluntarily, in the same situation, with the person who is the aggressor. It is morally interesting, however, that in subcultures in which horror is rarely felt at fully voluntary crossing of sexual boundaries, crossing a person's sexual boundaries without his or her full, competent consent is still widely seen as morally horrible. This suggests that in these subcultures the sexual boundary is still seen as important to the meaning of selfhood, but (at least for adults) it is one's own control of one's boundary, rather than conformity to a general rule, that contributes most importantly here to the definition of selfhood.[3]

Reasons can be given for the importance assigned to consent in these matters. Sexual boundaries are often experienced as given; these are boundaries set by societies, and their socially conditioned character is evident from the diversity of their forms in different societies. They are important for the development of children's selfhood—so important that another agent's infringement of a child's socially determined sexual boundaries, with or without the child's (noncompetent) consent, and good or bad as the prevalent social arrangement may be, will commonly be damaging enough to be a violation of the child. Even for adults the importance of such social boundaries is great enough to provide strong prima facie moral reasons for respecting them.

Some socially drawn sexual boundaries are manifestly unjust, however—such as those that would prohibit interracial marriage, or that treat women as belonging to men without treating men as belonging reciprocally to women. The consensual infringement of these boundaries by reflective adults surely is not, in general, morally horrible. But neither is the value of the boundaries generally decisive for the violative or nonviolative character of an infringement of them. An unconsented infringement of a boundary that an adult accepts although it is seriously unjust to her may still have all the horror of rape, whereas polygynous sexuality as such, in societies where it is not merely tolerated but consciously preferred by women, has surely none of the horror of rape and is not plausibly regarded as violating their persons, though we may still think it unjust to them. These considerations support the conclusion that it is authentic consent that chiefly determines what would sexually violate a competent adult.

The involvement of both the will and the body is essential to what horrifies us in sexual violation, which can be contrasted on these points with killing or maim-

---

3. That rape is seen as horrible even where consensual sex would be socially allowed is one of the points at which the ethics of moral horror resists analysis in terms of Mary Douglas's anthropological theory of purity and defilement, which will be discussed in section 7.

ing, on the one hand, and with "crimes against property," on the other hand. People are not *violated* by sexual acts to which they give uncoerced and competent consent, even if those acts are in some way bad or demeaning; whereas such consent is by no means enough to remove the aspect of violation from killing and maiming. The nature of sexual violation cannot be understood apart from the role of the will because it is largely through the voluntary control that the morally competent person exercises over his or her own sexual boundaries that those boundaries serve in defining selfhood. Moreover, if what is done sexually to a morally competent adult is not opposed to his will, then (unless it is evidently damaging to him, which is not normally the case in fully consensual sex between adults) it is not an *attack* on him, and hence does not violate him.

Where sexual violation does occur it is still relevant, however, that the person's body is involved. The sexual violation is not only an infringement of the victim's freedom and right to voluntary control over a certain sphere of influence but also something more and in some way worse. It attacks the person directly and violates her in a way that theft of her property does not. The theft is an infringement of her rightful sphere of voluntary control, but in most cases it does not infringe the interpersonal boundaries that are most important for defining selfhood. Those boundaries must therefore be seen as a tighter perimeter, defining more of an inner sanctum, than the privileged sphere of control which typically plays a part in contemporary theories of rights. Violation of a person is something that happens on a deeper and more primitive level than violation of a person's rights (except, of course, where the rights are rights against a violation of the person). This is not to say that *no* violation of my property rights could violate me personally; that might be done, for example, by a burglary that invades a sufficiently private space.

The infliction of physical pain is like sexual violation in these ways, *if* it lies within a certain range (decidedly less than torture, yet more than trivial). Consent, as in a contact sport, removes the aspect of violation. But without consent, such a physical attack is violative in a way that annoyance not involving physical coercion or contact is not, even if the latter is deliberate and causes states equally unpleasant to the victim. It is important to the violative character of the act that both the will and the body of the victim are attacked.[4]

On the other hand, if the intensity of pain is so great that we might speak of torture, then I think the consent of the sufferer (if it were ever given) would not remove the moral horror. Torture may be like maiming in this respect, even if the effects of torture are temporary. Perhaps that is because the most intense pain, even if voluntarily accepted, dominates a person's life in a way that at least threatens, if it does not destroy, all the value of that life to the sufferer. Indeed, the grip of intense pain on a person's life probably ensures that so much of the person will be

---

4. Interestingly, the *threat* of a physical assault or sexual violation is also felt to be violative, if it is sufficiently serious and alarming. I think that imprisonment, as an invasion of a person's fundamental bodily freedom, is violative, and the more so, the more physically restrictive it is. Chains and straitjackets are most violative; small, locked cells quite clearly violative; minimum-security prisons much less so. Most punishments that human beings have devised are violative. This is not to say that violative punishments are always indefensible; but there is always a weighty reason against them.

unshakably opposed to the pain, no matter what consent may be given to it, that infliction of the pain is bound to have the aspect of a serious and direct attack on the person. In this way the infliction of truly intense suffering may be violative in itself, independently of any other reason for its being so.[5]

The view that the most intense suffering necessarily threatens the value of the sufferer's life might seem difficult to reconcile with the view of some religious traditions that a person can come closer to the image of God, and thus to true value, in suffering. But that is really a problem for my whole account of good and evil. For the view about suffering is surely that one can come closer to the image of God in suffering *evils*. Perhaps we are concerned here with an imaging of God that takes place, paradoxically, precisely in the loss or degradation of an image of God. It will be important to avoid identifying the loss or degradation with the imaging, though they may be very closely connected. This problem is obviously related to the fundamental problem about the ascription of suffering to God, that of the relation of divine suffering to divine blessedness. The union, without confusion, of divine and human natures in Christ has been seen in some Christian thought as providing an alternative solution to the problem, enabling theologians to see the deity not as suffering but as most intimately united to something that suffers. On that view, suffering would not be a way of imaging God, but might be a way of coming into fellowship with God through Christ.[6]

The following views about violation of a person emerge from these reflections. Killing and maiming, or (to put it more broadly) destruction and lasting damage, are violative independently of questions of voluntary consent. Such acts directly and seriously attack the person whether or not they oppose her will. I think the same is true of torture. In these ways, presumably, one can do violence to oneself. Otherwise, however, one can be violated only against one's will, or without one's will, or at any rate without one's fully competent consent. But not everything that crosses a person's will violates the person, and our feeling of where we would be personally violated is an important clue here.

The conception of violation presented here provides a basis for critical assessment of moral claims based on feelings of revulsion. It does not resolve all ethical issues about sexual relations between consenting adults, for example, but it does imply that because of the consent, such relations do not attack, and therefore do not violate, the persons involved. Questions can be raised about the genuineness of the consent, of course, as in many cases of prostitution. But there are surely cases in which we can hardly doubt the authenticity of consent to sexual behavior that some people do regard with horror. And in such cases I think we should not accept their sense of horror as establishing that a person has been violated, or that something morally horrifying has been done. This argument is the more compelling to the extent that feelings of revulsion toward voluntary sexual practices are principally a reaction of outsiders, not generally shared by the participants. It is reasonable to sup-

---

5. The treatment of the relation between cruelty and horror in Hallie, *Horror and the Paradox of Cruelty*, esp. p. 5, has helped me get clear about the intrinsically violative character of torture, though there is much in my theory of moral horror that is no part of Hallie's account.
6. I am indebted to Marilyn McCord Adams for help with this topic.

pose that it is the person to whom something happens whose sense of violation is most authoritative (though not, to be sure, infallible). When participants find something delightful, meaningful, and expressive of loving, loyal, and respectful relationships, the negative emotional reaction of others is not to be trusted as a ground for thinking that a participant was violated, or a person attacked.

On the other hand, the sense of moral horror does in my view provide some basis for discriminating among the claims of the human will on our respect. Mere preference is not sacred. It would be neurotic in the extreme to feel that we have violated a person or done something truly horrible whenever we are responsible for someone else not getting what he wants. One of the implausibilities of the best known forms of utilitarianism is the moral importance they attach to aggregates of satisfactions and dissatisfactions that seem individually to be quite trivial. Disregard for a person's preference is sometimes amply justified, sometimes obnoxious, and sometimes morally wrong. It constitutes a violation of something sacred only where the preference is so important and so connected with selfhood that disregarding it constitutes a serious and direct attack on the person. It is not always up to us to choose what has the kind of importance that is involved in violation; intense pain, for example, has it whether we want it to or not. I have suggested that our moral feelings provide a significant clue for judging where something that is against our will impinges on us in such a way as to violate us as persons.

4. Images of God

A conception of the object of moral horror as violation of an image of God demands an account not only of violation but also of images of God. The only images of God discussed in section 3 were human persons, and it is of course with the human person that the concept of an image of God is most strongly associated historically. I would not, however, say that we are the only images of God, for I believe that everything excellent is excellent by virtue of faithfully imaging God, as was proposed in chapter 1 (though perhaps 'image' does not have exactly the same sense here as in Genesis 1:26–27). Surely not every excellence is important enough, or perhaps of the right sort, to count as sacred, but does some degree of sacredness belong to some things besides persons? Should I hold that violations of persons are not the only actions that ought to be regarded with moral horror as violations of something sacred?

I will pursue this issue in two different directions, beginning with offenses against goods that are not alive—for instance, against art. Since such goods have no will, of course, hostility to their will is not a possibility that could take the place of destruction or damage as a criterion of violation. What would make a morally horrible violation here? The trumpeter who blows a very noticeable sour note in the middle of an otherwise wonderful performance of a great symphony will doubtless feel awful about it; but this is not an occasion of even a lower degree of the same sort of horror as arises from causing, even accidentally, serious injury to a person. Why not?

It is not that no such horror arises from any offense against art. The wanton destruction of a great painting or of the only recording of Caruso's voice, if there were only one in existence, might well seem horrible in the relevant way. In these cases it matters, I think, that what is destroyed is an enduring object, already in existence. One reason this matters, I suspect, is that it is primarily enduring objects that can be violated. A musical performance, on the other hand, is typically regarded, while it is going on, as essentially repeatable, so that no enduring focus of value is damaged if the performance is spoiled in the process of production. Neither the composer's work nor the musicians' capacities are damaged by anything that happens during the performance. Likewise a painting may be regarded as relatively repeatable or repairable so long as it is in production, so that it will be less susceptible of *violation* then than after it has been finished (or left definitively incomplete) for some time.

Even the destruction of a great work of art, moreover, is not horrifying in exactly the same way as the killing or maiming of a person. It matters that the person is a *subject* of knowledge, feeling, desire, and choice, which no work of art can be. Our evaluation on this point would support the view that an image of God (and hence the sacred) is present in us in a way that it cannot be in anything that altogether lacks subjectivity.

We speak of "violations" of the moral law, but it cannot be violated in the same sense as a person can. The moral law is not destroyed or damaged, nor its "selfhood" threatened by immoral actions. Like aesthetically bad performances, morally bad performances, as such, are not violations of an image of God, but failures to image God as one should. This applies, for instance, to an immoral act of tax evasion; and the fact that it is a failure to image God should not lead us to retract our initial judgment that such an act is not horrible in the way that murder and rape are. It would be a mistake to blot out the intuitively valid and important distinction between actions that are truly horrible and other sorts of wrongdoing.

This is not to deny that there is a kinship (both as to the nature of the fact and as to our sense of it) between moral wrongdoing in general and the morally horrible. I will argue in chapters 10 and 11 that the significance of wrongdoing arises largely from seeing it as an offense against valued interpersonal relationships, including relationship with God. Personal relationships are sufficiently real and enduring things that we can speak of violating them in the relevant sense. A personal relationship with God can indeed be something sacred; and other personal relationships, when they are truly good, can image God. In this way violation of good personal relationships can be viewed with horror as violation of something sacred. It is only loosely, however, that we could speak of every offense against a good relationship as a "violation." In general a relationship in which every possible offense must be viewed with a shudder of horror is not a good relationship.[7] It is perhaps only in

---

7. This is obviously true of interhuman relationships. Its application to relationship with God is notoriously more difficult and controversial. It has commonly been felt that sin as such, in its relation to God, should be regarded with a certain horror. On the other hand, theologians have been impelled to devise theories, of venial sin, for instance, or of justification by faith, in which that general horror is limited or overcome, and believers' relation with God is enabled to withstand some offenses, so that they can be encouraged to live boldly and without excessive scrupulosity. There is a serious mistake, I think, in allowing the awesomeness of *God* to invest every one of *our* choices with awesomeness. But this is not the place for a full discussion of this much-debated theological topic.

the case of gross betrayals of deeply significant relationships that what is done to a relationship warrants real moral horror and serious talk of violation.

Another direction in which we may look for the possibility of violations of something sacred is toward living things that are not persons. Because their wills, if any, have not the same significance as persons' wills, I think the possible violations in this direction will all be pretty straightforward cases of destruction, damage, or infliction of serious suffering. We may regard all living things as having intrinsic value and as being distant imitations of the divine life. The way in which the killing of animals is surrounded with ritual in many religious traditions also suggests an apprehension of the possibility of trespassing on something sacred that is reminiscent of the horror of killing a human being. Some religions have thought it a violation of something sacred to kill animals for food at all.

This must be distinguished from the claim made by some philosophers that such killing is a violation of "animal rights." What I am discussing here is not a matter of rights but of something more primitive (though possibly less stringent morally): a "reverence for life," in Albert Schweitzer's famous phrase. Clearly there are limits to its demands. While deliberate and totally purposeless destruction of insects, for example, is offensive, it does not seem natural to most of us to feel horror over the killing of an insect. Our life in this world (a good life, on my view) depends on our consuming other living things of some sort, and even in plants there is beauty and some likeness to the divine life. Indeed, it seems as natural to recoil from the killing of a great tree as of a chicken. The image of God is no more to be identified with sentience than with rationality.

Another issue to which the consideration of reverence for life may be relevant is that of abortion. It is debated whether a human fetus is a person, but incontestably it is a living thing, with some of the characteristics of a human being—more and more of them, the more developed it is. On my view there must surely be some sort of image of God in it. And by virtue of these characteristics it is natural to see the destruction of the fetus as a violation of something sacred.[8] Here again it is not a question of a "right to life," or of rights at all, but of something that should weigh (not always decisively, I would think) in individual decision making.[9]

Reverence for life may also be engaged in respect for the continuity and survival of *species* of animals and plants. The diversity and independence of species are part of the beauty of the world, and this variety manifests the glory of God. There is something appalling about causing the extinction of a species, though there is certainly a subjective aspect to our sense of this; we are apt to feel more keenly about the disappearance of a very visible and showy species, such as the peregrine falcon, than about a spider or even a species of sparrow. The most important single case for us is that of the human species. Quite apart from harms to individual humans, it is intuitively plausible for us to suppose that there would be something appalling, an offense against something sacred, in intentionally allowing the human race to die

8. As suggested, without theological presuppositions, in Feinberg, *Offense to Others*, p. 56f.
9. How these points should affect political and legal thinking about abortion will be discussed briefly in chapter 14, section 4.

out; and such a view is naturally interpreted theologically in terms of our species being an eminent bearer of the image of God.

For most of us, at any rate, there is no point at which an offense against non-human life, or against nonliving things, evokes a horror of the same order as that with which we regard the violation of a human person. There is more than one way in which this difference in our reactions could be valid. One might argue that the fact that we are human, and related in a special way to other humans, appropriately affects the horror we feel about one human violating another. We write ethics for humans, after all, not for angels or tigers, and we have not the possibility of writing it from a point of view as comprehensive as God's. Traditionally, however, Western thought has accorded human beings a more objectively special status, viewing them as unique among the objects of our experience in the degree of their value and in their possession of the image of God.

5. The Value of Persons as Persons

Virtually all moral philosophers—even those who believe that sheep have rights and ought not to be killed for food—ascribe a much higher value to human persons than to sheep. What is the ground of this distinction in value between human persons and sheep? *Rationality* is the answer most often given, historically and today. And what is rationality? It seems to be not a single, simple feature of persons but a complex system of capacities—some that we possess in higher degree than sheep, some that we have and they don't have at all, and perhaps some that we simply share with sheep.

It is plausible to count this system of capacities as an *excellence* with respect to which we surpass sheep. Here we confront in heightened form the issue carried over from chapter 3, whether the place assigned to excellence in my framework for ethics has objectionably inegalitarian consequences. What distinguishes persons, morally, from sheep, most moralists think, should be something that grounds an *equal* regard for persons as persons. It may be doubted that excellence can play this part, since persons seem to differ in excellence from each other as well as from sheep.

It may also be doubted that rationality can play the part, whether or not it is an excellence. For the capacities constituting rationality are possessed by different persons in different degrees; some have more aptitude than others for various forms of reasoning and acting on reasons. The best solution for a rationality theory of the matter will probably lie in specifying a type of rationality that does not come in degrees but that one simply has or lacks. Rational agency may be a plausible candidate; we could say that one has enough rationality to be a rational agent, and to be as much a rational agent as anyone else (though not as rational in *every* sense), if one is able *at all* to do something *for a reason*. How precise a line we can draw between being able at all and not able to do this is a question we need not answer here. To the extent that it works, this solution seems to me quite compatible with supposing that rational agency in the indicated sense is an excellence and, indeed, a way in which we image God.

I believe, nonetheless, that identifying the value, the special sacredness, of persons as persons with their rational agency is much too simple and one-sided. One indication of this can be found in our discussion of the violation of persons, and especially of sexual violations such as rape. If our reflection of the divine glory is founded in our rationality, we may wonder, why should we feel so violated by things that are done to our sexual organs? On this point, it seems to me, the Western intellectual tradition, in its embrace of the rationality theory, has been trying to get a tighter intellectual grip on the divine image than we can reasonably hope to have.

This is one of the places at which we can learn from the emotion of moral horror. Our sense of where we would be most deeply violated is probably a better clue than the traditional speculations are to the contours of the image of God in us, and thus of what is sacred in us and what it is that constitutes the value of persons as persons. This sense is culturally variable, no doubt, but I would resist the implication that it is merely subjective. The contours of the image of God (what it objectively is in us) may vary somewhat across cultures too. As historical creatures who image God imperfectly at best, humans may image God in different ways in different cultural settings. The sense of violation clearly marks sexuality as an area intimately linked with our personhood and its value. I doubt that we can expect a thoroughly satisfying rationale on this point. To an outside view, nutrition seems as closely connected as sex with our personal being. Yet the force-feeding of a conscious adult, while certainly offensive, and perhaps an outrage, does not seem to reach the same level of horror as rape.

Certainly rational agency is not to be excluded from the image of God. Attempts to interfere with, or impair, the normal functioning of a person's rational agency, through such techniques as brainwashing or the surreptitious or coercive administration of mind-altering drugs, are horrifying and seem to violate the image of God if anything does. The will is the faculty of rational agency, and the involvement of the will as well as the body is essential (as I have argued) to what horrifies us in sexual violation. Still there is more than rational agency, and more than rationality, to the image of God in us.

What there is to the image of God in us, and thus to the special sacredness of persons as persons, I will discuss in terms of excellence, since imaging God is excellence in my scheme of things. One of the ways in which I think the excellence that all of us possess just by being persons involves more than rationality is that it begins with the simplest functions of animal and vegetative life (which are in fact less simple than much of the intricacy on which we may pride ourselves in our own achievements). It is intuitively plausible to see something excellent in the healthy performance of these natural functions. A deep breath of clean air seems, in the relevant respect, like a good meal as opposed to junk food, like a good joke as opposed to a bad one, and like good art as opposed to bad. Indeed, the healthy functioning of living things is an integral part of much of the beauty of nature, and beauty of any sort is a prime example of what I mean by 'excellence'.

In view of my position in chapter 3, it is particularly important for me to ascribe excellence to these unglamorous natural functions. Otherwise I might be unable to allow enough value to some of the most essential forms of human good, since I believe that human well-being consists mainly in enjoyment of the excellent. Surely it is a good for me (and not just an instrumental good) to "enjoy good health," or simply to enjoy my physical, animal being, or living. I must therefore avoid a snobbish sense of 'excellent' in which that would not be enjoying something excellent.

The excellence of mere life cannot be the whole value of persons as persons, however; for persons as such are of greater value than dogs and daisies, which also live. What distinguishes us from dogs and daisies is a complex system of features reasonably regarded as excellent. It includes rationality, but also emotional, social, and creative capacities related to rationality but going beyond it in various ways.

Don't human individuals differ with respect to the degree of their possession of some of these capacities? Certainly; and this raises again the threat of inegalitarian consequences of our conception of the value of persons. Intuitively, and ethically, we want to think about the value of persons as persons in such a way that we can regard it not only as greater than the value of dogs and daisies but also as more important than the comparative excellence of the talents and achievements with respect to which we may seek to outshine each other. We seek a value with respect to which we are more excellent than dogs and daisies but one person is not more excellent than another.

I believe we can in fact find that in the complex package of features that constitute the excellence of persons as such. Some of these features are excellences with respect to which human individuals can be ranked, but it does not follow that such a ranking is possible with respect to the whole package of them. One of the ways in which excellence resists incorporation in a mathematical structure of value is that it is not an intensive magnitude that can be completely and consistently ordered on a scale of value. We should not expect it to be if it is (as I hold) a matter of the distant and fragmentary resemblance of finite things to God.

Some resemblances can be ordered in degrees. We may be able to do pretty well in ranking shades of red in their resemblance to a given shade of red. But this is apt to be impossible when the resemblance is very multidimensional. Any attempt at a complete and consistent rank ordering of human beings for their degree of resemblance to a given human being would surely be quite arbitrary. What aspects of similarity should we emphasize? Intelligence? Personality? Cultural characteristics? Physical appearance? Mitochondrial DNA? All of these, and doubtless others, would be relevant, and some of them resist ranking on a scale. No doubt I am globally more like my sister than I am like the average person, but we should not expect the ranking to get much farther than that.

The absurdity of a rank ordering is even more obvious where the resemblance is more distant. Which of a group of chimpanzees is most like a human being? Any ranking we are likely to be able to make in such a case will be sentimental, based on a few features that strike us with particular vividness. Taking into account all relevant features, physiological, psychological, and behavioral, we probably could not come up with a ranking—though we can certainly agree that chimpanzees are more like human beings than opossums are.

Similarly, we may reasonably believe that human persons are globally more like God than sheep are, while resisting any attempt to rank individual persons on their global resemblance to God, since so many dimensions of comparison are relevant, and the resemblance is so distant, though still of the greatest importance. On the other hand, the very multidimensionality of this resemblance makes it a richer and more significant resemblance to God than that of particular abilities, actions, and achievements—more significant too, for our imaging God, than the excellences that add to our happiness or well-being. This grounds a qualitative superiority of the excellence of persons as such, the excellence of persons as the sort of individual beings they are, over the much narrower excellences with regard to which we can clearly excel each other. Thus it grounds egalitarian applications of the concept of the value, or sacredness, of persons as such.

Another way in which excellence resists incorporation in a mathematical structure of value is also important for our understanding of the sacred. Excellence is not additive; it is not necessarily better to have more instances of it, and this is true of the value that belongs to persons as such. The value of things, including persons, is often equated with the value of their existence. This is a step in the transformation of values of things into values of states of affairs, which is important to much quantitative treatment of value; but this transformation is often misleading. We may certainly agree that it is good that you exist; but in what way is that good? Is it that the world is better as a whole because of your existence? That is not a plausible answer, as I will try to show. The value of your existence is *not* to be understood as a contribution to a larger value.

Many philosophers have wished to treat value as an abstract analogue of money —a coin of the ethical realm or, more generally, of the whole realm of practical reason. For if we can assign to each state of affairs a numerical index of value, we can compare the desirability of alternative outcomes, and we may be able to arrive at overall values of complex states of affairs by summing the values of their parts. All would agree that we cannot hope to be more than approximately accurate in such assignments of value, but the fantasy of incorporating all our moral and political thinking into a sort of Higher Economics in this way has exercised a powerful attraction on at least the more teleological schools and departments of ethical theory. From the perspective of such a monetarization of value, if it is good that you exist, your existence should have a certain quantity v of value, and the value of "the world" as a total state of affairs should be greater by v, because of your existence, than it would otherwise be.

There is more than one way of attacking this conclusion. Perhaps it is a mistake to assign values to states of affairs as is done in such moral economics.[10] This would undercut the very idea of making the world better as a whole. Though skeptical, myself, of global evaluations of worlds, I shall take a different approach, and argue that even if states of affairs, and worlds, do have definite values, the most plausible assignments of value do not support the view that the value of persons is such as to imply that the existence of each of them makes the world as a whole better.

If we are going to evaluate worlds as wholes, it does seem plausible to say that a world with persons in it is better than one in which there are no persons at all. But if some is better than none, it does not necessarily follow that more is better than

---

10. As argued in Foot, "Utilitarianism and the Virtues." I largely agree with her thesis, though for reasons somewhat different from hers.

fewer. Given that there are at least some persons, and enough of them to sustain a richly varied social and cultural life, it does not seem in general better to have a larger number of persons. We are not obliged to say that the United States is a better country, or in a more flourishing condition, than Canada because it is so much more populous.[11] And if the vast surface of Jupiter sustains no additional persons, that is not matter for regret. If the further growth of the human population on our planet is undesirable, that is not because intrinsic advantages of continued increase are *outweighed* by economic and ecological drawbacks. It seems intuitively that beyond a certain point, long since reached, there is no advantage at all in sheer growth in numbers. Personhood is excellent, but it does not follow that more of it is better, in any way.[12]

This does not make personhood peculiar among excellences. At least in certain contexts and from certain points of view, it is good that excellences should be exemplified rather than not. But it is not in general better that they should be exemplified more times rather than fewer. Grace and Patience, for example, are (fictitious) sisters. They are extremely similar in their good qualities. In particular, they both have many fine friendships. But Patience spends a certain portion of her spare time lying on the beach,[13] idly and alone, not thinking deep thoughts but just relaxing, which she enjoys very much. Grace, not having this taste for sunbathing, has time for a few more friendships than Patience.

Fine friendships are excellent; and I think Patience's sunbathing is much less excellent. The excellence of fine friendship is exemplified more frequently in Grace's life than in Patience's, without any counterbalancing excellence in Patience's life that is absent from Grace's. Nonetheless, I think it would be an unreasonable excess of ethical earnestness to judge that for this reason Grace's life is more excellent on the whole, or better for the one who is living it, than Patience's, let alone that the total state of affairs would be better if Patience were more like Grace. This is not to deny that Patience's life would be poorer if she had no friendships. It is also not to deny that each of Grace's additional friendships is individually excellent. Trouble begins when we assume that things that are individually excellent must have quantities of excellence that can be added together to produce a greater excellence.

With regard to the value of persons, it may be said, the question that chiefly interests us is not whether the existence of *more* people makes the world better as a whole, but whether the existence of *each* person (your existence or mine, for example) does. But if the value of persons is additive in such a way that the existence of each person, as such, makes the world better than it would otherwise be, it follows that the addition of any new person who does not in fact exist would make the world better than it actually is; and hence that, whatever persons now exist, it would be

11. This example comes from Narveson, "Moral Problems of Population," p. 80.
12. I do not mean to endorse the most sweeping rejection of quantitative considerations regarding human life. I don't think it is better for more people to exist, but I do think it is worse for more people to be killed, and therefore better, other things being equal, to save more lives if one can. I thus disagree with Taurek, "Should the Numbers Count?"
13. They live in Hawaii.

better after all (economic and ecological considerations aside) for more persons to exist in addition. The implausibility of this conclusion discredits the premise that the existence of each person, as such, makes the world better. Likewise, if more of a good thing is not necessarily better, it is hard to see why a world that lacked a few of us must thereby be worse as a whole—from an impersonal, impartially detached point of view.

With difficulty one stifles the vainglorious protest 'But surely, in view of my sterling qualities and great accomplishments, the world would be worse without *me!*' This is not a claim about the value of persons as such, but since many people (to their credit) cherish the hope of "leaving the world a better place than they found it," it may be important to reflect on the frailty of this support of one's sense of personal worth. To the extent that we can make judgments at all about how good the world is, there are reasons for thinking that the world would probably have been better without some of us, and that any of us may turn out to have been in that class. While we live in this world we do not know how great an evil we may some-day cause, perhaps accidentally. Innocently in some cases, culpably in others, people sometimes cause so much evil that even if their lives are otherwise full of good works, the most plausible global judgment from an impartial standpoint would be that it would (probably) have been a better world if they had not lived in it. Such an evil can happen long after one's death as an unforeseeable consequence of things one has done. There may have been many virtuous and happy ancestors of Adolf Hitler and Josef Stalin, for example, of whom it would now be plausible to judge that the world would probably have been better if they had never existed (if we are going to make such global value judgments at all).[14]

Despite all the reasons there are to doubt that the world as a whole is improved by the existence of each one of us, I think it is appropriate for any minimally decent and happy person (indeed, I believe, for any person) to be glad of her own exist-ence, and for others who love her to be glad of it too. And I think the appropriate gladness is unconditional and unqualified—real enthusiasm, rather than "How nice *for us* (or in *this* respect)—though of course it may be too bad (!) on the whole." This shows something both about the nature of the value of persons and about the responses that are appropriate to this value.

The primary value of persons is not a value that they derive from their contri-bution to a larger whole. It is a value that is more intrinsic to persons as individuals, and that is best appreciated in focusing on them individually. It is a value of per-sons, rather than of sums of value that they help to compose. It is, I think, a sort of excellence, an imaging of God. It is wonderful that you exist, because *you* are won-derful, in the way that parents rightly perceive their infant children as wonderful. And while this sort of value of persons can indeed be a good reason for wanting to procreate and raise a child, it is not a reason for wanting there to be more persons

---

14. It is also true, but may be less relevant here, that all of us are probably such that we, indi-vidually, would not have existed had it not been for truly colossal evils. I would probably never have existed if World War I had not been fought, for instance, for my parents would probably never have met. Issues raised by this point are discussed in Adams, "Existence, Self-Interest, and the Problem of Evil."

rather than fewer. It is primarily a reason for loving persons and, more imperatively, for respecting them, given that they exist.

In these respects the value of persons as persons is typical of the value of the sacred. "The hallmark of the sacred as distinct from the incrementally valuable," as Ronald Dworkin has put it, "is that the sacred is intrinsically valuable because—and therefore only once—it exists."[15] The sacred, in other words, is not necessarily something we have reason to want more of, but something we have reason to treat and not to treat in certain ways, given that it exists. In particular (as Dworkin substantially agrees) it is something it is horrible to violate.

6. Ontology

To explicate our sense of the sanctity of certain objects, and particularly of human life, in terms of images of God is to explicate it in terms of what the objects *are*. This sort of explication has competitors that are much less ontological. One notable competitor is the account of the sacred that forms a centerpiece of Dworkin's recent book *Life's Dominion*, the largest part of which is focused on the moral and political issues of abortion. Dworkin's interest in the sacred is connected with an idea that I share with him, that the evil, if any, in abortion may be viewed as a violation of something sacred rather than an infringement of rights of the fetus.

Dworkin's conception of the sacred is not essentially theological. It allows theists to give theological explanations of sacredness but also allows nontheists to regard human life, and various other objects, as sacred. Although he sometimes uses the term 'religious' in a more conventional way, Dworkin argues in the end that the belief that human life is sacred is religious, in a broad sense, "even when it is held by people who do not believe in God" and who do not adhere to a "traditional religion" (155f.).[16] With these views, thus generally stated, I have no quarrel. It is part of my project here to offer a theistic interpretation of our sense of the sacred; but I regard the sense of the sacred as a datum for theological interpretation, not as a result of the interpretation. It is a datum of moral experience which nontheists also have reason to embrace, and for which they have reason to seek a nontheological interpretation.

In speaking of the sense of the sacred as a datum for interpretation, I do not mean to identify the sacred with the sense of it, or to imply that the sacred is constituted by interpretation. On the contrary, I believe that the most satisfying interpretations will present the sense of the sacred as an apprehension of a kind of objective moral fact. This being so, I may think that the prospects are brighter for theological than for nontheological interpretation of the sacred, but the sense of the sacred has a grip on us that is largely independent of the adequacy of our theoretical interpretation of it.

15. Dworkin, *Life's Dominion*, p. 73f.
16. Dworkin, *Life's Dominion*. Page numbers in parentheses in the text of the present section refer to this work.

Dworkin's examples of the sacred as a morally important sort of value are largely the same as mine;[17] they include great paintings, animal species, especially our own species, and, of course, individual human lives (72–84). They also include human fetuses; Dworkin's main purpose in introducing the idea of the sacred is to argue that it is as a destruction or dishonoring of something sacred that abortion seems at least prima facie objectionable to most people, rather than as a violation of a personal right to life, which he believes that fetuses are not in general sufficiently developed to possess. Dworkin is certainly not the first to see a broadly religious dimension in such public issues as these,[18] but his powerfully argued book makes a persuasive case for a sense of the sacred as a living and influential part of our moral consciousness.

Dworkin's substantive conception of the sacred, however, is quite different from that which I have offered in terms of images of God. He assigns a dominant role to considerations of *process* in determining what is sacred. He distinguishes "two processes through which something becomes sacred for a given culture or person. The first is by association or designation." An example of that is viewing a flag as "sacred because of its conventional association with the life of the nation." This ground of sacredness plays no important part in his reasoning. "The second way something may become sacred is through its history, how it came to be" (74); and this way provides the machinery of Dworkin's argument. He thinks we view great art as sacred out of respect for the process of artistic creation, and animal species as sacred out of respect for the natural process of evolution, or for God's creative activity lying behind it, depending on our religious beliefs (74–76, 79). Individual human lives, and human fetuses, he regards as sacred because of the "investment" of both divine or natural and human creativity involved in their origination and development (82–84).

Dworkin develops the idea of investment into an organizing metaphor. He speaks of offenses against the sacred in terms of a "waste" of the investment of (divine or) natural or human creativity—or often in terms of a "waste of human life," but clearly understood in terms of wasted investment (94, 84). More precise, he thinks, is a terminology of "frustration" of investment, which focuses attention on the investment that comes to nought, rather than on mere possibilities of life foreclosed (86–88). In these terms he formulates a "metric of disrespect" by which we may weigh the gravity of the alternative insults to the sacred that may be involved (as I agree) in *all* our available courses of action, possibly concluding in some cases that a greater frustration of invested creativity would be involved in carrying a fetus to term than in aborting it (84, 89–101). Likewise, he argues that the widespread view that abortion becomes more objectionable or more questionable morally as pregnancy advances and the fetus develops is best explained as a recognition of the increasing investment of creative process in the fetus (88f.).

17. This is a convergence of independent reflections. My examples were chosen in 1989 for one of my Wilde Lectures, which was an ancestor of the present essay.

18. In Greenawalt, *Religious Convictions and Political Choice*, chaps. 6–8, there is an interesting discussion of issues of "borderlines of status," including especially environmental ethics and abortion, as a particularly obvious field for reliance on religious ethical considerations. The idea of the sacred is present in Greenawalt's discussion (p. 101), but much less prominently than in Dworkin's.

The usefulness of a "metric" for resolving inescapable moral issues (if it can be made to work) is obvious, but it gives much of Dworkin's reasoning a quantitative aspect that is also disturbing. One of the attractive features of his conception of the sacred, as he introduces it, is his insistence that the value of the sacred is not "incremental" or aggregative: valuing things of a certain type as sacred does not commit you to think that "the more of them we have the better" (70). In one way he holds consistently to this view: the sacred as such is for him always something whose given actuality we are to respect, rather than something we are to try to produce. In another way, however, the quantitative aspect of much of his reasoning threatens to overwhelm the special character of the sacred. When we get down to brass tacks, what we are offered as a practical guide to respecting the sacred in personal decision making can easily be read as a restricted consequentialist calculus of a fairly familiar pattern, in which avoiding frustration of investments of creative process is a privileged type of consequence.

My most fundamental objection to Dworkin is that I believe the sense of the sacred has a "strongly object-directed character," as I will call it, that is not adequately accounted for in terms of respect for creative processes. The metaphysical shudder that abortion evokes in many people (indeed in most, on Dworkin's view) is surely not a response to the length or complexity of the human gestation process, but to what the fetus is like. Abortion seems worse in later stages of pregnancy because the fetus then has more of the characteristics of a developed human being, and specifically of a human infant. Dworkin denies this, claiming that "increasing resemblance [to human infants] alone has no moral significance" (89), but the denial is implausible. If the resemblance were superficial, merely a matter of appearances, it might have no moral significance; but the resemblance here is grounded in what the fetus really *is* in late pregnancy: not quite a person (I agree with Dworkin about that) but profoundly rather than superficially like a human infant.

Dworkin's own account of our differential evaluation here is also implausible. The duration of gestation as such is intuitively irrelevant to our moral response, and few of us have any clear notion of the complexity of the process. If human fetuses were as developed in the fourth month as they in fact are in the seventh, an abortion in the fourth month would seem about as bad to us as a seventh-month abortion does now. The converse case is more complex. If the human gestation period were eighteen months, with the fetus after nine incredibly complex months of development no more advanced than a second-month fetus is in fact, an abortion in the ninth month would surely not seem nearly as bad to most of us as a ninth-month abortion does now. Would it seem worse than a second-month abortion does now? Certainly it might be more of a human tragedy;[19] but whether it would have more of an aspect of horror would depend mainly, I think, on how strong a bond pregnant women would feel to the fetus in those circumstances—that is, on the degree to which a present reality (in this case relational) that might seem sacred would be violated, rather than on the history invested in the case.

19. Reliance on the concepts of waste and frustration leads Dworkin, I think, into a certain conflation of the questions how tragic something is and how much it infringes on the sacred; see Dworkin, *Life's Dominion*, p. 87.

Dworkin's denial of moral relevance to resemblance is obviously in conflict with the view taken here that sees the value of creatures most fundamentally in their (admittedly very imperfect) likeness to God, a likeness that can also be seen as constituting the very nature of the creatures. Dworkin (82) does mention the traditional idea of humankind being made in the image of God, but this idea plays no important role in his account of theological grounds for beliefs about the sacred, which focuses rather on the idea of God's investment of divine creativity. The neglect of the former in favor of the latter seems to me a mistake. Respect for God's creativity, and especially for God's creative *purposes*, doubtless does and should play a part in theistic views of the sacredness of human life; but I think it should not be dominant here. The consideration of God's creative purposes yields a *voluntaristic* ground, which seems appropriate where moral *requirement* is concerned. But the sense of the sacred, and the correlated sense of moral horror, seem to me to respond primarily to *ontological* rather than voluntaristic grounds. The idea of images of God gives theological form to ontological grounds.

I do not mean that historical considerations are completely irrelevant to the sacredness of an object. Human persons are sacred not as static objects but as having lives that are dynamic processes. Dworkin's process-centered view of the sacredness of the fetus connects easily with his appropriate responsiveness to feminist protests against viewing the fetus in isolation from its mother. He quotes an apt statement about the fetus by Catharine MacKinnon: "More than a body part but less than a person, where it is, is largely what it is. From the standpoint of the pregnant woman, it is both me and not me."[20] The being of the fetus, we are reminded, is not separate from that of the pregnancy as part of a woman's life. How the sacred is engaged in the fate of the fetus may therefore depend in part on how it is engaged in the human significance of the pregnancy. As Dworkin (95–97) recognizes, this helps to explain why abortion seems less objectionable to most people when it ends a pregnancy that began in rape or incest. The pregnancy that is terminated by abortion in those circumstances may be seen as possessing only a compromised sacredness, and that is certainly due to its history. Like Dworkin, I am willing to think about this in terms of the human "meaning" of the pregnancy. What I want to resist is reducing the issue of the sacred here to one of investment of valued processes. What matters most is what the fetus, and the pregnancy of which it is an inseparable constituent, *are* in the light of their history.

7. Defilement and Symbolic Violation

An approach, quite different from mine, to something like an idea of moral horror is proposed by Jeffrey Stout in his recent book *Ethics after Babel*. Stout shares with me two aims: he wants to make a sense of moral revulsion accessible as a resource for ethics, and he wants to do this in a way that permits ethical criticism of any such

---

20. Quoted in Dworkin, *Life's Dominion*, p. 54f.

sense (156).[21] But he wants to do this in a way that builds on Mary Douglas's anthropological account of purity and defilement. Her work dominates recent discussion of uncleanness, pollution, and defilement in the study of religion. Accepting Lord Chesterfield's definition of *dirt* as "matter out of place,"[22] and drawing on a wealth of anthropological evidence, Douglas argues that it is objects and actions that straddle boundaries, or otherwise resist placement in a society's customary scheme of things, that are evaluated as unclean, and are apt to be the subject of taboos. The boundaries in question here are not those between individual persons which I have argued are protected by an appropriate sexual morality, but boundaries between culturally important categories of things.

The unclean, we should note, is not necessarily an object of moral horror at all. Though "pollution beliefs are often discussed in terms of the emotions which they are thought to express," and though revulsion is sometimes felt toward what is viewed as unclean, Douglas points out that the attitudes actually observed to be connected with "primitive" religious ideas of pollution are often as matter-of-fact as those connected with our ideas of sanitation. "There is no justification," she writes, "for assuming that terror, or even mild anxiety, inspires [pollution beliefs] any more than it inspires the housewife's daily tidying up."[23]

Douglas's account doubtless taps into deep concerns about our place in the world, and I grant its plausibility as an anthropological explanation of much uncleanness talk. In contrast to Stout, however, I have not made it the basis of my reflections here. I have consciously chosen to work with the concept of violation and *not* that of pollution or defilement. One reason for this is that some of the moral horrors that most concern me, such as those of homicide and torture, cannot plausibly be understood in terms of Douglas's theory because they do not seem to involve the straddling or blurring of socially recognized boundaries—except the boundary between right and wrong, which is not to be presupposed for our present purpose. The killing of humans by humans is culturally glorified in some contexts and is only too common, much commoner than the killing of humans by other (nonmicroscopic) animals.

Some moral horrors do involve the breach of the sort of socially sanctioned boundaries to which Douglas calls attention, but even in those cases I doubt that her theory provides a basis for rationally defensible *ethical* judgments, as distinct from anthropological explanations. Social structures and conceptual schemes vary from culture to culture, so that an obvious relativity affects the question of what things straddle their boundaries. There is no reason to suppose that objects and actions that fail to fit in socially established categories are inherently bad, much less objectively horrible. Moreover, the moral stigmatization of boundary-straddlers seems dangerously likely to lead to some of the worst effects that one fears from moralities of taboo, such as the persecution of homosexuals or lepers or others who may be marginal in some society's scheme of classification.

21. Stout, *Ethics after Babel.* Page numbers in parentheses in the text of the present section refer to this work.

22. Douglas, *Implicit Meanings*, p. 50.

23. Douglas, *Implicit Meanings*, p. 59; cf. Douglas, *Purity and Danger*, p. 1f.

Stout thinks, nonetheless, that an ethically interesting conception of "abomination" can be understood in terms of the blurring of socially or culturally significant boundaries.[24] In his view the explanatory aspects of Douglas's anthropological theory are helpful in dealing with such problems as I raised in the last paragraph. He acknowledges that there are cases "where the moral data against which one group tests its theories are not even recognized by another. What we need in such instances," he claims, "is the critical leverage an explanatory theory can provide" (158). His reason, apparently, for thinking that anthropological explanation can provide ethical leverage is that he thinks the appropriate object of ethical criticism here is the social construction of the world that sets and values the boundaries. In his opinion, "What requires defense . . . is the battery of categories that gives rise to an intuition in the first place. . . . The question is not whether homosexuality is intrinsically abominable [for example] but rather what, all things considered, we should do with the relevant categories of our cosmology and social structure" (158).

The criticism made possible in this way is not to be understood in a purely relativistic sense. Stout says, "At least some of the judgments of abomination we make seem to fall roughly where judgments about evil do on the spectrum of relativity." He has identified that as the most objective end of the spectrum (87). He goes on to say, by way of illustration, "When the Nazis made lampshades out of the skins of their human victims, that was truly abominable." Since Stout would "say the same thing about members of some more distant culture if they engaged in similar practices," his judgment of abomination in this case is not relative to social arrangements. In his view, however, it does have to do with social acceptance of "categories" inasmuch as its absoluteness must rest on an objective judgment about what categories people *ought* to have, what differentiations they ought to invest with moral significance, whether they do or not. In his judgment about the Nazis, he says, he "would of course be presupposing that the line between human and nonhuman ought to have moral significance and that there are certain ways in which human beings (and their remains) shouldn't be treated" (160).

I agree with Stout's judgment that making lampshades of human skin is an objectively appropriate object of moral revulsion, but I disagree with his explanation. I think the moral horror or abomination there is not to be found in the blurring of a socially recognized boundary (between the human and nonhuman), but in what is done to images of God. Consider a society that made *all* lampshades from human skin, refusing to use anything else in place of that material. This would be a sort of observance of a boundary between the human and the nonhuman, but I think it would be no less horrible than making only a few lampshades of human skin—

---

24. Stout's choice of the term 'abomination' may be related to his use of Douglas's theory of pollution. The concept of the abominable seems broader in some ways than that of the horrible. It may express horror, but may equally well express an intensity of disgust, or perhaps simply of disapproval. The concept of the abominable may be narrower in another way, carrying something closer to an explicitly religious connotation than that of the horrible; but that does not affect the present discussion, since I am giving an explicitly theological account of moral horror. A dialogue is invited, anyway, by the number of Stout's cases of abomination that are in my opinion objects of moral horror.

unless lampshades were treated in that culture as having something more than the utilitarian and aesthetic significance that they have in ours. Of course a distinction between the human and the nonhuman is involved in our reaction here, but that follows trivially from the fact that we think it horrible to make lampshades from human remains, but quite appropriate to make them from other materials.

A similar horror, discussed at some length by Stout, is that of *cannibalism*, which I shall understand narrowly as the action of one human being in eating the flesh of another human being—abstracting here from questions about the cause of the latter's death. In keeping with his theory, Stout explains the horror of cannibalism as grounded in a confusion of categories. He argues "that the social identity of the cannibal is the basic issue at stake when a social group abominates cannibalism." The cannibal offends by adopting a role that belongs naturally not to human beings but to wolves and leopards. "Nonhuman carnivores make no bones about eating human flesh. To eat human flesh is to become like them, to straddle the line between us and them, to become anomalous" (151f.). But this is not an adequate explanation of the horror of cannibalism. Cannibalism would be no less horrifying if humans were the only creatures that ever ate humans.

Intuitively, making the condemnation of the horrible or abominable action secondary to a judgment of the value of a social patterning seems ill suited to the strongly object-directed character of moral horror or abomination.[25] To the extent that Stout validates judgments of abomination, he fits them into something like a motive-utilitarian framework. It would be a good thing to maintain social commitment to certain boundaries. For this reason it would be worth discouraging, and hence stigmatizing, certain types of action that threaten these boundaries. Or perhaps, alternatively, our abominating certain things can be judged correct on the grounds that it springs from commitment to the desirable boundaries. But this does not seem, even to Stout, a reason to believe that the actions in question are abominable *in themselves*. And without such a reason, it seems to me unjust to stigmatize them as abominable.

This can be seen as a misgiving about the political implications of Stout's approach. He suggests, for example, that moral revulsion toward homosexual behavior arises from certain ways of defining and valuing masculine and feminine roles (154). Suppose we believed (as Stout and I do not) that those social arrangements for gender roles are good and ought to be maintained. Should we then infer that homosexuality is objectively abominable since it blurs an objectively valuable social distinction? I think that would be unjust. If, as I believe, homosexual practice is not essentially violative of persons, then it would be unjust to stigmatize it as a moral horror even if (as I see no adequate reason to believe) the ideal society would object to the practice for other reasons. Talk of abomination is too powerful to be applied to something just because it breaches an importantly valuable social distinction—though it may be that it commonly has been so applied.

The horror of cannibalism, or of making lampshades of human skin, in my view, lies not in a straddling of social boundaries as such but in what is done to the deceased person. We cannot understand this horror without understanding that we

---

25. Houston Smit helped me see this point.

think of what is done to our dead bodies as in some way done to *us*. The horrible thing about cannibalism, and about the Nazi lampshades, is that what was the physical basis of a person's life is treated as something much more ordinary. This is not just classifying something in the wrong category; it is profoundly insulting to the deceased person. For that reason, and for at least one other reason, it is a symbolic violation of the deceased person. The additional reason is that acting in a way that expresses a view of the body of a living person as (potential) meat or lampshade material is apt to be in some degree violative of the person (the degree depending in part on the seriousness of the threat that the behavior might reasonably be felt to pose). To treat the body of a dead person as meat or as lampshade material is therefore an expression of a violative attitude, or an attitude inevitably associated with violation, and is thus a symbolic violation.

If I am right in this account of the matter, the objective moral horror in cannibalism has much more to do with violation than with defilement. No doubt we would feel defiled by cannibalism. But a conception of symbolic violation is more important than ideas of uncleanness for giving objective moral validity to the horror we feel here.

My account cannot escape a certain cultural relativity, perhaps especially as it concerns cannibalism. For symbolism, including symbolic violation, is culturally conditioned. As symbolism goes, the objectivity of symbolic violation in cannibalism seems very high. For a human corpse is a "natural symbol" of the person whose body it was.[26] Eating it seems inescapably to be treating it as meat. It is inescapable for us, at any rate. That is not a meaning we could change by convention. Perhaps that meaning is not utterly inevitable, however. If[27] there are cultures in which eating a human body is really honored as a way of gaining possession of some of the "power" of the deceased, they would not be eating the human body as merely "meat."

I have not enough inner understanding of what such a culture might be like to offer a confident opinion as to whether the cannibalistic eating in it would be a symbolic violation and morally horrible. One assumes, of course, that the eating would be preceded by a killing which would be more than symbolically violative, and horrible enough. Instead, I will speak about something with which I am familiar, the Christian sacrament of Communion in the body and blood of Christ. Here is a sacred rite which is regarded, at least symbolically, as something that in other contexts would amount to cannibalism—a symbolic violation. This thought raises more questions than I can try to answer here. I will only observe that the drive to communion with another being inherently involves a temptation to violation, because it involves a desire to penetrate boundaries that define the selfhood of the other. Can we see such rites as the Christian "communion" (and many sacrificial rituals) as attempts to work through this tension? This may serve as a reminder that the relation between moral horror and the sacred is not a simple one.

26. This way of putting it is due to Feinberg, *Offense to Others*, pp. 55–57, who also applies it to cannibalism (p. 70f.).

27. A big 'if'. I do not mean to enter into the controversy to what extent there have really been societies in which cannibalism was a culturally accepted practice. For a skeptical anthropological view, see Arens, *The Man-Eating Myth*.

II

LOVING THE GOOD

5

EROS

The concept of love has played an important part in my account of the nature of the good. I have taken it as a main principle for identifying the property and the standard of excellence, that the excellent is the appropriate object of Eros. By the same token the role of the good in ethics will be in large part a matter of the ways in which it is good to love the good. How it is good to love the good will be the overarching topic of chapters 5 to 9.

That God loves the good, specifically that God appreciates the excellence of finite things in a way that contributes to a form or analogue of Eros in God, and that the excellence of finite things provides God with reasons for loving them, are also theses that have played a part in my account of the good (chapter 1, section 3). If God is the Good, and the supreme standard of value, moreover, the nature of God's love (if we can say anything about it) will have a fairly direct relevance to issues about the value of human love. For these reasons I propose to begin the discussion of how it is good to love with the question of what ought to be said about God's love. That is a thematic topic of this chapter and the next. In reasoning about God's love I will rely on frankly evaluative ethical premises. This is an instance of the pattern of inference from 'ought' to 'is', or from value to (other sorts of) fact, that I have defended in chapter 2, sections 3 and 4, and that I will defend in chapter 12, section 3, and (in a more systematically epistemological context) in chapter 15, section 3.

There is of course an asymmetry between God's love for the good and ours, inasmuch as God *is* the transcendent Good and standard of goodness, and we are not. In many contexts, however, it will not be the asymmetry but the desired resemblance between our love and the divine love that will be in the foreground. In the present chapter I will focus primarily on the aims and objects of love, and in chapter 6 on the grounds of love, though it is of course impossible to keep these two topics entirely separate. Inasmuch as we are thinking of God as the standard of excellence, we will be guided primarily by considerations of excellence, rather than of merely instrumental value, in thinking about what sorts of love to ascribe to God. I will argue in chapter 7 that a similar focus is appropriate in thinking about an ideal of human motivation.

One of my main aims in the present chapter is to combat an overmoralized ideal of love as pure benevolence, which would not allow God to desire, for its own sake, a relationship with creatures, or to love beauty or other impersonal goods. Benevolence must certainly play a major part in the divine love; but I will argue that noninstrumental interests in relationships and excellences should also be part of the ideal of love for us humans, and may reasonably be ascribed to God, and that something we can characterize as Eros may therefore appropriately be seen as a part of the divine love. First, however, we must consider some fundamental objections to the whole idea of God loving finite things at all—objections that we inherit from Plato and Aristotle.

1. Can God Love Finite Things at All?

The Aristotelian objection is the more sweeping, applying not just to love but to any sort of divine interest in finite things. Aristotle seems to have thought of God as so absorbed in self-contemplation as to have no concern or thought at all for lesser beings.[1] And why shouldn't such total absorption in contemplation of God be the ideal? Would it not be best to engage always in the best activity, and to want to do so?[2] And for Aristotle, God is the best object, and contemplation of the best object is the best activity. Why shouldn't this reasoning apply to God's activity and interests—and to ours as well?

Let us grant, for the sake of argument, that contemplation of God is the best activity. Even so, the Aristotelian conclusion does not follow. For even if self-contemplation is the best activity for God, there is no reason why God cannot always engage in it while also giving full attention to each of infinitely many creatures. Omniscience is in part a capacity for just such comprehensive attention, and it does not make sense to suppose that other concerns could distract an omniscient being from a desired contemplation. This is a metaphysical reply to the argument given for the Aristotelian view.

1. This is the natural and usual interpretation of Book Lambda of his *Metaphysics* (1074b15–1075a11), but it should be noted that in Book X of his *Nicomachean Ethics* he seems more noncommittal on the question "if the gods care at all about human affairs" (1179a24–25).
2. I am indebted to Gavin Lawrence for putting this challenge to me, and for putting it in this form.

There is also a more distinctively ethical reply, which draws on my conception of grace and anticipates points that will be developed more fully in chapter 6. I do not think it is best, or an inescapable part of the ethical ideal, always to prefer what is best. This is important for theism, inasmuch as it is difficult to sustain the view that God has chosen the best of all possible worlds (if indeed there is a best among possible worlds, which I doubt). It is part of the religious idea of grace that God's love is not strictly proportioned to the merit of its object.[3]

No doubt it is often important to choose the best among available alternatives. But that, I think, presupposes a concern for a being that has limited opportunities, a being that might lose or miss out on a precious good if the best is not chosen. As God's opportunities are not limited, and as the excellence of the divine nature is already unsurpassable, optimization cannot have the same significance for God that it has for us. That being so, I do not see in the Aristotelian argument any compelling reason that God should not take an interest in merely finite goods.

Plato's argument is aimed more precisely at love—indeed, explicitly at Eros. In a famous passage of his *Symposium* Plato argues that Eros is not a god but at most a *daimon*, an intermediary between gods and mortals—an angel, as it might be put in Jewish and Christian theology.[4] In Plato's myth, Eros is the offspring of Resource [Πόρος] and Poverty, and has some characteristics from both parents, being oriented toward perfection but essentially characterized by deficiency and need (203B–204B). Plato's argument may be summarized as follows.

Eros, he holds, involves *desire* for its object. But, he argues, one desires only what one needs and does not have (200A–B). Apparent exceptions, such as the healthy person's desire for health, are explained as desires for future continuation of a present state—the future, of course, being something one does not yet have (200B–D). Plato concludes that the object of Eros must be something one lacks and needs (200D–E). He maintains, further, that Eros, especially the gods' Eros, if they have any, will have things beautiful and good as its object (201A–C); but gods cannot lack such things or be needy in respect of goodness and beauty (202D). It seems to follow that Eros is incompatible with deity.

My first reply to this argument is that neediness is not essential to Eros because the central feature of Eros is a valuing of which desire is only one alternative form. The ordinary connotations of the Greek word ἔρως may suggest identifying Eros with a form of *desire*, but there is much more than desire in the reality Plato is trying to describe under the name of Eros. Desire, we may say, is a valuing of something future as such. This way of putting it obviously suggests a related possibility. Is there not also a valuing of something present as such? There is. For instance, there is liking. One can *like* a present state or object as present, even if one cannot desire it as present.

Once we see this, it seems obvious that Eros can be found in liking something as present just as well as in desiring it as future or absent. That must surely be true where the first moment in Eros is that of admiration, as I think it normally is, since

3. These points are developed much more fully in Adams, "Must God Create the Best?" My most obvious opponent here (though not the only one) is of course Leibniz.
4. The intermediary role ascribed to *daimones* in the *Symposium* (202E) has significant overlaps with the role of angels in Jewish and Christian thought.

(at least in the case of Eros, as distinct from envy) admiring is a kind of liking. It is typically a valuing of present good and does not presuppose the absence or futurity of its object. No doubt the moment of admiration usually begets moments of desire, which are very typical of Eros; but I think admiring contemplation can in itself constitute Eros. So far as I can see, Plato's argument fails to show that a god could not have Eros constituted by appreciative contemplation or some other form of liking of present good.

Although correct as far as it goes, this will not serve as a complete response to Plato's argument, for several reasons, to which I will attempt to reply.

1. Even if liking or valuing present good can constitute Eros, Eros may still entail a desire for future continuation of the good; and Plato is surely right that future goods are, in some sense, not yet possessed. How theists respond to this point should depend on whether they think of God as living in time or outside of it. Some have argued that God's life must be conceived as timeless, precisely because having a future (desired or not) that is not yet possessed seems to them incompatible with divine perfection. If we are not persuaded by that argument, however, and are otherwise content to think of God as living in time, then I doubt that we should think that God's not *yet* possessing future goods that God *desires* constitutes a *neediness* incompatible with divinity. We do not normally think of people as needy just because some of their good still lies in the future and is not yet present or past. On the contrary, we may think it pitiable to be unable to look forward to any future good. A person is needy with regard to a future good only insofar as its futurity renders it uncertain or unlikely of attainment. The needy are those whose lack of present good leaves them lacking in resources for assuring their future good. But God will surely be conceived as rich in resources for assuring future good. The mere futurity of some goods, the fact (if it is a fact) that God does not *yet* possess them, does not show that God's attainment of the good is uncertain.

2. There might be other grounds, however, that would render divine Eros uncertain of its future goods. In particular, if God loves creatures that are so free that they can refuse to do what God wants them to do, that may result in frustration of some of God's desires. Frustration has been thought to be incompatible with deity, but I am not convinced that it is. God must certainly be sufficiently resourceful and sufficiently successful not to be, on the whole, a tragic figure. God's transcendent excellence requires that much, but it need not exclude all frustration and failure in matters of detail. Success is not always more admirable than failure, and a life is not necessarily worse for including some failure. This is surely an implication of Christian beliefs about the crucifixion of Jesus, which represents quite a spectacular failure of some of Jesus' projects, even if it thereby, and more importantly, achieves a victory. Theists who are not prepared to accept this will presumably be forced to deny (as some have) that creatures are free in the way that gives rise to the problem.

3. If God is conceived as desiring future goods at all, it is likely that some of them will not be continuations of present goods, but will be newer than that. If God created the world in time, for instance, and did so out of love, the creative love must have involved a desire for created goods that did not exist before the time of their creation. Some have thought that a perfect being could not have such a desire for new goods, on the ground that a desire for a new good must be for something that

would improve one's condition, and hence for something without which one's condition is deficient, inasmuch as it is improvable. This is not a compelling objection, for several reasons, the first of them being that, as was noted in chapter 1, section 5, it is not clear that the condition of a God that is already transcendently good cannot be improved; and it is transcendent goodness rather than unimprovability as such that pertains most surely to the concept of a God.

In the second place, the objection about improving God's condition overlooks the possibility of altruistic desires. The new goods God desires may be created goods, features of the created world rather than of the divine being itself. Even if their coming into existence improves the condition of something, we need not think of it as improving *God's* condition. This reply assumes that having new, and perhaps better, creatures is not a part of "God's condition" in the relevant sense. The assumption may be questioned, but I think it is correct. The superiority that is ascribed to God in thinking of God as a transcendent Good is intrinsic to the divine nature, and its transcendent immensity abides through variations in other things. If a change in God's relational properties is constituted merely by changes in finite things to which God is related, it does not affect the transcendent excellence that is ascribed to God. I would not rest too much on this point, however. For if God lives in time, a full-blooded divine Eros for creatures might well involve God's wanting new goods that would involve the divine life more deeply—as would, for instance, an incarnation.

For this reason it is important, in the third place, to question the assumption that a desire for a new good is necessarily a desire for an improvement of existing conditions. Goodness is not in general a quantity subject to the laws of addition, as I have argued in chapter 4, section 5. More of a good thing is not necessarily better. Beyond a certain point, for example, a larger population, or a larger family, of good and happy people is not better, or in a better condition, than a smaller one. Thus parents desiring an additional child may be desiring a good thing without desiring an improvement in present conditions. This seems to apply strongly to the case of transcendent goodness. God may be supposed to want something good that will indeed have a part in the divine life (such as an incarnation) without wanting an improvement in a condition that is already transcendently, infinitely good.

Plato's issue about the relation of love to neediness is real. A love that springs from need, and even from desperation, is certainly to be found in human life. Such love can be unselfish, and noble in its devotion to good, particularly where the need that inspires it is not primarily the lover's own. But it is a morally important fact that there is also love that overflows from a wealth of good. The love of saints is typically of the latter sort. The saint may be poor and weak in obvious ways, but does not behave like a needy person, carefully calculating small advantages for herself or others. Because of her sense of being in contact with a goodness overflowing from a boundless source, she may well do things that embody, manifest, or convey goodness in ways that are wonderful but not efficient or necessary.[5]

---

5. I have borrowed a bit here from Adams, "Saints," where I make a similar point in a slightly different context.

The type of good that is most important to us is not just something that would be good if it existed, or that is good as it merely happens to exist, but a good that is in part a power to realize itself. It is on that type of good that the real possibility of good in our lives mainly depends. Such a good may or may not have power to achieve something external; what it has first and most essentially is a power to realize *itself*. The joy and peace characteristic of sainthood may be interpreted as consciousness of being in touch with a self-realizing power of good. And in the archetypal case this power is also a love of the good that it realizes. Such a love and such a power surely belong in our conception of divine goodness.

2. Benevolence and Self-Interest

Even if Eros does not necessarily spring from deficiency or need, as Plato supposed, many may suspect that it is too selfish to be ascribed to God. Much in our ethical tradition sees the struggle between altruism and self-interest as the central issue of the moral life, and there is something right about this view, though I will argue that it is oversimple. Altruistic benevolence is an uncontroversially good motive. It can hardly be praised too highly, and surely deserves a place in the ideal of love. And self-interest is a morally dangerous motive. The domination of our concerns by self is a great source of moral evil. Much that passes for love is selfish or self-centered in such a way as to merit no praise.

Many have concluded that divine love should be identified with benevolence, with no place in it for self-interest, and have seen Eros as tainted with self-interest. In discussions of Christian love Eros is often contrasted with Agape—Eros as self-seeking and Agape as pure benevolence. This contrast owes something to Anders Nygren's brilliant and widely influential *Agape and Eros*, but it does not perfectly fit his ideas. What I want to say about Eros can be developed more clearly in counterpoint with the stark and simple contrast between benevolence and self-interest than with Nygren's subtle and sometimes elusive views.

The term 'Agape' I will not use here in my own voice. It is an English form of ἀγάπη, which I believe means *love* quite generically in biblical Greek. Whatever is distinctive about ἀγάπη in the New Testament comes from what is said about it there, rather than from the meaning of the word. As an English word, 'Agape' is a blank canvas on which one can paint whatever ideal of Christian love one favors. There is nothing wrong with that, but I think I can find words better suited to say precisely what I mean. In the present chapter I will discuss the relation of Eros to *benevolence*, though I would not in any case simply *identify* Agape with benevolence or altruism (as Nygren also does not).[6] In chapter 6 'grace' will signify more naturally and more precisely the aspect of divine love that plays the most important part in Nygren's account of Agape. However, I am not proposing a dichotomy or polarity of Eros and grace. On the contrary, God's Eros *is* grace, and I will be arguing in chapter 6 that some of the character of grace belongs to love as such, including Eros.

6. Nygren, *Agape and Eros*, pp. 65, 95.

The term 'Eros' I do use in my own voice, and not necessarily in precisely the same sense as Plato or Nygren. Certainly I am not committed to all of their views about the nature of Eros. The Greek word ἔρως, of which 'Eros' is an English form, is not a generic word for love, but has a specifically "erotic" flavor, as we might put it in English today. The paradigm of ἔρως is a passionate desiring or prizing of a personal relationship for its own sake, and taking that as the central (but not the only) case is controlling for my use of 'Eros'. I will argue in section 3 that Eros escapes the dichotomy between benevolence and self-interest.

In the present section, after a preliminary discussion of self-interest, I focus on benevolence. It must have a central place in any plausible account of divine love, but I will try to show that it is not well suited to constitute the whole of divine love.

For present purposes, we can identify self-interest with desire for one's own good on the whole, for its own sake, and benevolence with desire for the good of others (or even of a single other person), for its own sake. Both of these motives, as I understand them, involve the notion of a person's good, which was a main subject of chapter 3. Most of what I have to say about them turns on that point.

One of our best teachers on the nature and ethical significance of self-interest is Joseph Butler (Bishop Butler), who discusses it under the name of "self-love," which he identifies with "a regard to [one's] own interest, happiness, and private good,"[7] by which he means one's good in the long run, comprehensively considered. Self-love is distinct, in his view, from "particular appetites and passions," such as a desire to eat meat, or to get a more prestigious job, or to get even with so and so. The objects of such particular desires are "distinct from the pleasure arising from them." Indeed the object would give no pleasure if there were no prior "affection or appetite" for it, according to Butler.[8] Therefore, he argues, "if self-love wholly engrosses us, and leaves no room for any other principle, there can be absolutely no such thing at all as happiness, or enjoyment of any kind whatever; since happiness consists in the gratification of particular passions, which supposes the having of them."[9]

The notion of a person's good, and hence the motive of self-interest, are fairly abstract organizing principles for portions of our motivational lives. Without goods and desires of another sort, they are incomplete. In my account of a person's good, it consists largely in enjoying things (distinct from itself) that are excellent. For its completion, therefore, it requires distinct interests in such goods. Perhaps Butler's claim that pleasure presupposes prior affection or appetite is too sweeping. We might enjoy some sensory satisfactions, for instance, without a prior or persistent interest in them. But we would be setting our sights quite low if we aimed to be satisfied with such enjoyments. Human life would be pretty boring if we did not have a lively interest in a variety of particular objects.

To have the rather abstract notion of one's own good on the whole is a rational achievement; so therefore is self-interest. That is enough to show that self-interest is not the same as selfishness, and even that selfishness is not necessarily a form of

---

7. Butler, *Fifteen Sermons*, sermon 11, paragraph 8.
8. Butler, *Fifteen Sermons*, sermon 11, paragraph 6.
9. Butler, *Fifteen Sermons*, sermon 11, paragraph 9.

self-interest. For very young children are certainly capable of selfishness long before they have any conception of their own good on the whole, and hence before they have any strictly self-interested motive. Selfishness is a tendency to seek or grasp things for oneself, and to do so excessively. But self-interest is not necessarily excessive or bad. Indeed it can be commendable, and is frequently commended, especially in children, who typically acquire a conception of their own good in being taught (as they must be taught) to take care of themselves.[10]

The topic of self-interest need not detain us further here. I will not commit myself as to whether it is appropriately ascribed to God. Many philosophers and theologians have ascribed self-love to God, and it would be odd for me to deny that God prizes and in some sense loves the excellence of the divine nature, given the views I have espoused in chapter 1. We should not ascribe self-interest to God, however, unless we suppose that something could happen that would be *good for* God and would *benefit* God. That supposition might be thought to imply a need or deficiency in God, even if love in general, or even Eros, does not, and even if self-interest can be commendable in humans. I do not have to decide this issue here, because I will argue, in section 3, that Eros, which I do think it appropriate to ascribe to God, is not necessarily self-interested.

That benevolence, on the other hand, should be counted as part, and a central part, of the divine love is hardly controversial. If an interest without any tincture of benevolence can count as love for a person, it is surely not worthy of any praise. Few motives, if any, seem intuitively more excellent than benevolence; and few, if any, are more deeply embedded in the traditional concept of God. I wish to emphasize, rather than to question, this aspect of divine love. It must also be emphasized, however, that other interests are needed in addition to benevolence for a complete divine love.

They are needed for reasons similar to those for which Butler argued that we can hardly pursue our self-interest without "particular passions" whose objects are distinct from our own good. If I am an object of your benevolence, you want my good to be furthered. If your benevolence is enlightened (by my lights as explained in chapter 3), you want me to enjoy things that are excellent. If your benevolence is a mere idle wish, it can stop with these abstract desires. But if it is to be an active and effective desire, it must be informed by some conception of sorts of excellence that it might be good for me to enjoy, and you must care about such excellences at least to the extent that you think it would be good for me to enjoy them. Perhaps there is no logical incoherence in supposing that you care about these excellences only insofar as you would like me to enjoy them because you think that would be good for me; but you will not have an imaginative and creative love for me unless you *appreciate* a lot of the relevant excellences, and I do not think you can adequately appreciate them unless you have a measure of Eros toward them, or at least have a kind of interest in them that could grow naturally into Eros if you let your energy flow in their direction.

---

10. I have developed these points about self-interest much more fully, with special reference to Butler, in Adams, "Self-Love and the Vices of Self-Preference," from which I have borrowed somewhat in the present discussion of self-interest.

Similar considerations apply to God's love, which presumably is maximally creative. In desiring our good, God will have a noninstrumental desire that we should enjoy excellence. God will prize excellences of the sort that humans can enjoy; and it is hard to see why God would prize them and want us to enjoy them if God did not care about them for their own sake as well as for our sake.

3. Eros and Self-Interest

In speaking of Eros I seek to be guided by the character of the attitudes that we would normally recognize as concrete paradigms of Eros. The central feature of those paradigms is that the lover desires or prizes, for its own sake, some relationship with the beloved. What relationship this is varies from case to case, depending in part on the object and the context. The art lover may desire chiefly to see the beloved object, whereas much richer systems of relations are typically desired with a beloved person.

Some measure of such a noninstrumental relational interest seems to me to be part of anything that would be recognized as a paradigm of *love* of any sort. This is reflected in the naturalness of contrasting love with (mere) benevolence. Whether one could count as loving at all, even nonparadigmatically, with absolutely no relational interest, is a question I will not try to resolve here, as I am more concerned with ideals of love than with the outer boundaries of the concept. In any event, we can reasonably treat the noninstrumental relational interest as an essential feature of Eros.

Is this interest in relationship part of the excellence of love in such a way that it should be ascribed to God, and thus viewed as part of the standard of excellence for love? That is the pivotal question about the ascription of Eros to God in our ethical investigation. Before addressing it more generally in section 4, in the present section I will argue specifically that the relational interest of Eros is not too self-seeking to be attributed to God.

Legitimate and useful as it is, the contrast between altruistic and self-interested desires has too often been treated as an exhaustive dichotomy. That is, it is too often assumed, particularly where personal relations are in question, that what is desired is desired either for one's own good or for another person's good. The conception of love, and particularly of Eros, has suffered much from being forced into the procrustean bed of this dichotomy. For Eros need not be either self-interested or altruistic. Its desire for relationship need not be based on a belief that the relationship would be good for anyone.

This is most obvious in the case of a tragic or destructive Eros. There are doubtless instances in which a close personal relationship is strongly desired by both of the parties to it although neither of them believes it will be good for either of them. Perhaps if they love each other in the best way they will prefer on balance to break off the relationship; but that does not change the fact that they have a desire for the relationship, a desire that is neither self-interested nor altruistic, in the sense that it is not aimed at the good of either party.

Even in a more beneficial relationship, lovers prize the relationship for its own sake and not just because they believe it would be good for one or both of them.

They would rather be happy together than in some other equally flourishing way; and if they desired the relationship in such a way that they would have no interest in it at all if they did not think it would be beneficial, we might doubt that they really love. Eros is not based on calculations or judgments of utility or benefit, and must therefore at least partly escape classification as self-interested or altruistic. The mistake, in trying to force Eros into a dichotomy of self-interest and altruism, is failure to recognize a desire for relationship for its own sake as a third type of desire that is not just a combination or consequence of desire for one's own good and desire for another person's good. It is indeed this third type of desire that is most characteristic of Eros.

This distinction may not persuade everyone to abandon the charge that Eros is a self-seeking motive. After all, if I desire a relationship with another person, what I want is partly about myself. My desire in this case is *self-regarding*, as I shall call any desire for a state of affairs that essentially involves the desirer.[11] We must consider, however, what a wide range of motives are self-regarding in this sense, and how implausible it would be to classify all of them as self-seeking.

Consider, for example, the desire to be of service to others. This might be a desire to be helpful to a particular person, in which case it is a desire for a particular relationship and may well be a manifestation of Eros; or it may be a desire to be of service to people in general. We normally count such a desire both admirable and unselfish—perhaps especially in the second, more universalistic case. But in both cases it is a self-regarding desire, distinct from the strictly selfless desire that the other person or persons be benefited. For if all one has is the latter desire, one does not care who benefits them, whereas, if one wants to be of service, one wants to be one of those that do it.

The self-regarding desire to serve another person is not in general self-interested, however, in the sense of being motivated by a desire for the good or happiness of the one who desires to serve. The service may be quite burdensome; and while one may expect to find satisfaction in serving, in the typical case that is because one wants, for its own sake, to serve the other person. The expectation of benefit to oneself in such a case depends on the desire to serve, rather than the reverse. The service to which one aspires may even involve a sacrifice, on balance, of one's own good, and in that case it is particularly clear that one's motive, though self-regarding, is not self-interested.

Consider, likewise, the conscientious desire to keep one's promises. This is a praiseworthy motive, on which decently ordered life in society depends heavily. It would be paradoxical to classify it as self-seeking. It is a self-regarding motive, however, as is any (more than merely instrumental) desire to act in one way rather than another; for when I want *to act* in a certain way, it is *myself* that I want to act in that

---

11. In Adams, "Pure Love," from which I am borrowing bits in this chapter, I used 'self-concerned' in this broad sense, but I now think it has psychological connotations too specific for my purpose. 'Self-regarding' seems to me the most neutral felicitous term here, but even it has ethical connotations in ordinary use that I must ask the reader to ignore in favor of the technical sense I am giving it.

way.[12] Of course it does not follow that they are self-interested, in the sense of being aimed at the agent's own good; and a *purely* conscientious motive is not self-interested in that sense, though it is self-regarding.

Religious writers have sometimes endorsed total selflessness while still being quite committed to motives that are agent-centered and hence self-regarding in my sense.[13] Anders Nygren is a case in point. In the process of arguing that, for Martin Luther, Christian love is free from all selfish motivation, he quotes Luther as saying that such love does the good "to please God" (726f.). It is not likely that Luther thought that he could increase the (doubtless infinite) sum of God's pleasure (nor that Nygren thought so either). The motive he commends, therefore, is presumably not a general and abstract desire for the augmentation or maximization of God's pleasure as such, but rather the particular and self-regarding, agent-centered desire *to act* in a way that is pleasing to God.

Having self-regarding, agent-centered motives is closely connected with selfhood or personhood. We may be tempted to think that God should be *above* such motives—that an omniscient being, for instance, should have no personal point of view, but only the totally comprehensive, purely objective view of things and their values that Thomas Nagel calls "the view from nowhere."[14] But that would imply a quite impersonal conception of God, certainly more impersonal than most theistic piety could accept. What sense does it make, for example, to be *grateful* to someone who has no self-regarding interests, but only the view from nowhere? An omniscient being will presumably have views from everywhere, so to speak, but must also be capable of forming personal projects of its own, and of having agent-centered motives connected with them, if it is to find the kind of coherence of purpose characteristic of persons, in making such radically contingent choices as a creator must make if (as many theists will suppose) there are infinitely many possible worlds and no objectively best among them.

4. The Value of Love's Interest in Relationship

Agent-centered motives, which are self-regarding in my sense, are so important to practically all nonutilitarian ethical theories that such theories must generally acknowledge some self-regarding motives as good and praiseworthy. Even apart from utilitarian objections that may remain, it does not follow, of course, that the desire for relationship characteristic of Eros is among the praiseworthy self-regarding motives, or that it may appropriately be ascribed to God. We must therefore inquire specifically about the value of this motive.

---

12. This point is related to things that have been said in recent ethical theory about "agent-centered" ethical constraints (Scheffler, *The Rejection of Consequentialism*) and about "agent-relative" reasons for action (Parfit, *Reasons and Persons*, p. 143; Nagel, *The View from Nowhere*, pp. 152ff.).

13. Adams, "Pure Love," is largely about a historically notable (and noble) case of this.

14. Nagel, *The View from Nowhere*.

Moralists have been reluctant to ascribe moral value to interests in personal relationships for their own sake. The *moral* worth, if any, of friendship is typically found in the desire to benefit the other person—that is, in the altruistic benevolence that is involved in a good friendship.[15] The preoccupation with interests in benefits to individuals is closely connected with the influence of what we may call "the economic model" of what is involved in doing good. Being good to people is very widely understood in terms of conferring benefits on them, and that in turn is conceived on the model of giving them money. This is obviously true of utilitarian theory, in which the concept of utility is supposed to structure the distribution of benefits in general as money structures more narrowly economic transactions. It is true in a more limited way of John Rawls's theory of justice, where the "primary goods" which play a central part are benefits to be distributed to individuals and assumed to be quantitatively measurable in relation to each other.[16] In dealing with many issues of public policy, this attention to the economic model of beneficence is an appropriate recognition of the moral importance of economics and of the distribution of costs and benefits. In some areas of human life, however, and particularly where certain kinds of personal relationship are concerned, the economic model is grossly inadequate for an understanding of what is involved in being good to people.

Suppose that a friend of mine, seized (as he at least supposes) by benevolent impulse, takes it into his head one day to confer a benefit on a number of people. The means he chooses for this purpose is to give each of them twenty dollars. Making his rounds, he comes to me. He pulls a twenty-dollar bill from his pocket and holds it out to me, saying, "Here, Bob; I'd like to give you this." Perplexed, I respond, "Well . . . thank you. But why?" He replies, "I just wanted to do something nice for you."

I don't know exactly what I would do at this point, but one thing is clear: my friend has not succeeded in doing something nice for me. He has only created an awkward situation. I will feel embarrassed about it—and underneath that, perhaps a little insulted. If he wanted to do something nice for me, why didn't he pay me a compliment? Or why didn't he invite me to lunch? That might have cost him no more, but would have been a gracious rather than an awkward thing to do.

Are all his thoughts about me uncomplimentary? Does he not care for my company? Or does he think that I am more interested in twenty dollars than in his company or his good opinion of me? All of these hypotheses are somewhat wounding to me. What keeps me from believing any of them, and thus from feeling seriously insulted, is that my would-be benefactor's behavior is so bizarre that I cannot confidently make much sense of it at all.

This example suggests several reflections about the relation between considerations of benefit and considerations of relationship in our evaluation of motives.

---

15. This seems to me to be true even of Blum, *Friendship, Altruism, and Morality*, p. 67f., though Blum is an eloquent apostle of the moral value of friendship and does not have a narrowly moralistic conception of the nature of friendship (ibid., p. 82).

16. Rawls, *A Theory of Justice*, pp. 62, 90–95.

1. The reaction that I think most people would have in my situation in such an encounter points up the fact that many of the benefits we most desire, after the satisfaction of our most basic physical needs, involve relations with other persons. We want to love and be loved, and we want others to think well of us (which is a sort of relation between us and them). We desire these relations for their own sakes, and that is typically why we regard them as benefiting us. Some of these relations, moreover, such as the mutual enjoyment of a shared lunch, also involve the other person's valuing them for their own sake. We will not regard them as benefiting us in the same way if we do not think the other person values them for their own sake; and if it is right to think that the "enjoyment" of the illusion of a good relationship is not a true benefit, then we are not truly benefited by these relations unless the other person really does value them for their own sake.

2. It is also significant that we would feel insulted by the suggestion that we are more interested in twenty dollars than in our friend's company or good opinion of us. We think it would be base, ignoble to prefer such a small amount of money to a good of personal relationship. We would be ashamed not to value personal relationships, for their own sake, above economic benefits, or at least above minor economic benefits. Thus it seems we think we *ought* to value personal relationships for their own sake.

3. Perhaps my fictitious friend's motivation and behavior are so bizarre as to call for therapy rather than moral censure. But at any rate they do not have the full moral worth that we normally ascribe to beneficent actions benevolently motivated. This illustrates the fact that the moral value of actions often depends at least as much on what they express about personal relationships as on what they cause, or are meant to cause, by way of benefit or harm to individuals. In order to act in a morally worthy way toward me, it is not enough for my friend to want, and try, to confer on me some benefit or other. He must act in a way that is appropriate to the actual relationship between us (so far as that relationship is known to him), and that expresses a good friend's regard for it; and that implies acting in a way that expresses his valuing my friendship for its own sake, and at least the hope that I similarly value his.

These reflections lead to the further thought that there is a range of behavior in which benevolent motivation and an interest in a personal relationship for its own sake are inextricably intertwined. Most sincere expressions of affection belong to this class. It is probably rare that we express affection to another person without being (benevolently) moved, to some extent, by an awareness that such an expression of affection will be gratifying and supportive to the other person. At the same time, expressions of affection normally indicate an interest in our relationship with the other person, and are not sincere if we do not value the relationship for its own sake. And an insincere expression of affection, however benevolently motivated, is rarely of much moral worth.

This intertwining of motives will tempt some moralists to say that what is praiseworthy about sincere expressions of affection is only the benevolent motivation and intention, and that one's interest in the relationship for its own sake is not meritorious in itself but is merely a resource that puts one in a position to do something good (sincerely express affection) that one would otherwise be unable to do. To lack this resource would be a misfortune, but not a moral deficiency or fault, on this view. But this is implausible. If I cared nothing for personal relationships for their own sake, then unless I had managed to avoid having anyone close to me, I would be open to criticism as failing those close to me in a very serious, painful, and obnoxious way.

What is it that we rightly expect of those closest to us? What are the characteristics of a good friend, a good parent, a good spouse? Clearly some of the characteristics fall under the heading of benevolence: a good parent, spouse, or friend is considerate, kind, and generous. And some of the characteristics can be classified under conscientiousness: a good parent, spouse, or friend is trustworthy and reliable, careful to do her duty to the other person and to be kind even when her spontaneous impulses of benevolence give out; she is discreet and respects the other person's rights. Other characteristics of a good friend or spouse or parent are cognitive, such as sensitivity, and a measure of practical wisdom, which enables one to accomplish good for one's friend as well as to wish it. Appreciativeness heads yet another important family of characteristics: a good parent, spouse, or friend is particularly ready to like and enjoy the other person, to recognize and celebrate her strengths and excellences, and to be glad of her existence; a good friend is interested in his friend, and not just in the friend's well-being.

What particularly concerns us here is that there are also characteristics having to do with relational interests. A good spouse or parent or friend values the personal relationship for its own sake, wants it to continue and develop in a good way, wants to see, hear, touch the other person, share with the other person, know and be known by the other person—all within limits appropriate to the relationship. A good friend or spouse or parent is forgiving; and this pertains not only to benevolence but also to the relational interest. It is a matter of resuming not only goodwill but also the desire to share and be together, in the aftermath of a quarrel or offense. It is part of caring enough about the relationship to stick with it through difficulties.

It is praiseworthy to be a good parent, spouse, or friend; and surely it is a fault to fail to be one through failing to care appropriately about the relationshp. This is felt with special keenness in the parental relationship. There is something important for human development that a parent, however conscientious and benevolent, who is not glad to be a parent of a given child, or does not prize the parent-child relationship, cannot give the child.

The moral importance of caring about a personal relationship for its own sake is also particularly evident where one is tempted to write off the relationship as harmful to all concerned, for there the operation of the relational interest is more easily separated from that of benevolence. There are certainly circumstances in which it is right to break off a relationship that is causing more harm than good, and people are often too slow to abandon abusive relationships; but much good is also lost by being too ready to give up on a relationship. It is good to value some relationships highly enough for their own sakes to tip the scales in their favor in some situations in which it is doubtful whether their effects are beneficial. One's loyalty is to the relationship, as well as to the other person, and one is not fully loyal in some relationships unless one is willing to hazard something of the other person's happiness, as well as one's own, for the sake of the relationship.

This is a point of great practical importance. The stability of friendships, and particularly of family relationships, depends on the parties caring about the relationship, and being committed to it, in such a way as to override periodic temptations to believe that it is detrimental. Such temptations can be strong, and in the midst of them it is not always entirely clear that the other parties want the relationship. It is an important strength, and I think a virtue, to have an interest in the relationship for its own sake to throw into the scales against these temptations.

I believe these considerations support the thesis that it is often *morally* good, perhaps even morally imperative, to be interested in a personal relationship for its own sake; but that is a controversial point which I need not press here, as the excellence that I ascribe to God is not exclusively moral. What is more important for my project is to consider whether the value of caring about one's relationships for their own sake is an excellence of the sort that ought to be ascribed to God. Do such relational interests have only an instrumental value, growing out of the circumstances of human life that affect the lover as well as the beloved? If so, we must hesitate to suppose they would be part of the excellence of a divine lover, whose infinity lies far beyond the circumstances of human life.

I believe it is clear that relational interests have great instrumental value, but most plausible also to suppose that they have an excellence that goes beyond instrumental value. Especially indicative on this point is the shame we would feel if it appeared that we were less interested in friendship than in a small amount of money. We think that would be a base, unworthy motivational structure; and that is surely because we see a certain nobility, a certain excellence, in the interest in a good personal relationship for its own sake. The perceived nobility of the relational interest reflects, in turn, our sense that the relation of friendship has a noninstrumental value that is out of all proportion to the (presumably instrumental) value of a twenty-dollar bill. It is excellent to value what is excellent, as I argued in chapter 1, section 2; and some personal relationships are excellent; so it is excellent to value them. Thus far it seems perfectly appropriate for the divine excellence to desire some personal relationships for their own sake.

If we are right in regarding many personal relationships as excellent, we may reasonably infer that divine perfection includes valuing them in whatever way is necessarily involved in *appreciating* them. In view of the disparity in nobility between a transcendent Good and finite goods, it would be rash to conclude further that divine perfection *must* include an *Eros* that wants, for its own sake, *to be related* to finite beings. Since such relations would involve the transcendent Good, however, it seems that their possible excellence would give God at least as much reason to be interested in them for their own sake as in anything else about finite beings. Some may think that if creatures like us are to exist at all, what God would have most reason to care about in their regard is their well-being. But if our well-being is constituted by enjoyment of the excellent (as I argued in chapter 3), what could enhance it more than the opportunity to enjoy a relationship with God that God prizes for its own sake? That is an opportunity that can be available to us only if God does care about the relationship for its own sake, and not just for the sake of its possible contribution to our well-being.

Though I do not want to rest my argument on appeal to authority, it is worth noting that Eros and noninstrumental desires for relationship with creatures are not alien to traditional conceptions of God. God's love for humans is seen in the Bible as involving a desire for certain relationships between God and humans, for the sake of the relationships and not merely as good for the humans. The jealous husband of Israel (Jeremiah 2:1–3:5; Hosea 2), God made the whole human race so that they might seek and find God (Acts 17:26–27). God desires our worship and devotion. Why did Christ give himself up for the church? Because he loved her and wanted to present himself to her as a bride (Ephesians 5:25–27). The goal of the divine redemptive activity depicted in the New Testament is a family or society of mutual love in which God has a parental relationship with each person. The goal includes eternal life for individuals, and the wiping away of every tear from their eyes (Revelation 7:17). But it is no sum or average of individual utilities, and is described mainly in relational terms, as reconciliation of people with God and with each other (2 Corinthians 5:18–19; Colossians 1:20; Ephesians 2:13–22); and as people being children of God (Luke 15:11–32; Romans 8:14–17; Galatians 4:6–7; 1 John 3:1–2), being able to approach God (Ephesians 2:18; Hebrews 4:16), seeing and worshiping God (Revelation 4; 21:3, 22–23), and being one with God and with each other (John 14:20, 23; 17:20–24).

No doubt it would be possible to interpret all of this on the hypothesis that God desires to be related to us only because it will be good for us, but I think that is implausible. The Bible depicts a God who seems to be at least as interested in divine-human relationships as in human happiness. Even Anders Nygren, for all his emphasis on the unselfishness of Agape, presents it as one of the distinctive characteristics of Agape that it creates *fellowship* between God and human beings (80f.). If such fellowship is desired for its own sake by God, God's desire is self-regarding inasmuch as its object involves God as essentially as it involves us. And would we have it otherwise? Let him, or her, who would rather be the object of benevolence than of love cast the first stone.

5. Impersonal Objects of Love

Diotima, and Socrates following her, in Plato's *Symposium*, have their novice in Eros move on from love of particular beautiful bodies and souls to love of beautiful practices and laws and sciences (ἐπιστήμαι; 210C). The suggestion Plato may be offering that the Eros directed toward abstract impersonal objects is nobler or more advanced than that directed toward persons is one that I do not mean to endorse (though I grant it takes more developed cognitive capacities to love the abstract objects). The primary reference of the concept of Eros is certainly to a type of love of persons for persons. Nevertheless, the extension of the concept to love for impersonal excellences is natural and plausible. Among the features that carry over from the personal to the impersonal case are the centrality of the desire for relationship with the object, and the close association with beauty. Not that the object of Eros is always beautiful, or perceived as beautiful. Eros can relate to other types of excellence. But beauty, in persons or impersonal objects, seems particularly apt to inspire Eros.

I will speak freely of Eros for impersonal objects. More substantively, I will argue that such Eros can be excellent, and appropriately ascribed to God. This will be important (notably in chapter 7) in developing a humane account of the place of the good in the ethical life. Among the possible objects of an excellent Eros, besides persons, are particular animals, plants, and other natural objects; species and other natural kinds; arts and sciences (mathematics or philosophy, for example), and particular artistic creations.

Many earnest moralists, secular as well as religious, may resist my claims on this point, perhaps even more than on the value of caring about personal relationships for their own sake. At least the latter interest has a person-centered flavor that many will see as congenial to morality; and some cases of it, such as preferring friendly to hostile relations for their own sake, even have a specifically moral flavor. Aesthetic and intellectual interests have often fallen under a cloud of moral or religious suspicion. At best, it is feared, they present dangerous distractions from more urgent concerns; and at worst, they may provide an amoral focus for a morally bad life.

Such dangers and abuses certainly exist, but they also affect kinds of love whose excellence, in typical cases, is relatively uncontroversial. Even love for one's child, comprising strands of benevolence as well as Eros, can be idolatrous, a temptation to immorality, and a suffocating burden for the child. In thinking about the value, and possibly the excellence, of any type of love, in the present context, where our focus is on ideals of love, and on divine love, we must not think of the particular type of love as embedded in bad attitudes that are not essential to it. The dangers of inappropriate love for excellent objects will be the topic of chapter 8, on idolatry; here I will argue that there is an appropriate place for love for impersonal objects in ideal or divine love. I will begin with the simplest, most direct, and probably the most convincing arguments and proceed to a more indirect line of thought that I hope will illuminate the place of this type of love in the ethical life, and its possible importance in divine love. I believe that it is *morally* good in some contexts, but I will not try to show that. A broader claim of excellence suffices here, because the goodness it is humanly important to admire, and religiously important to attribute to God, goes far beyond the narrowly moral.

My simplest argument on this point is a direct appeal to intuitions about particular cases. Do we not think it a virtue (a "green" virtue, we might say) to care, for their own sake, about various natural, nonhuman features of the world around us? To many of us, at least, it seems objectionably anthropocentric to care about such things only to the extent that they serve human well-being. Do we not admire a pure love of art or sport or mathematics or philosophy? All of those objects involve persons, but what is loved in loving them is not the persons but something (a type of excellence, we may hope) that enters into the lives of persons. And if we admire human caring about such things, why shouldn't we think of God as caring (in a divine way) about them too?

It may be suspected that what we admire in these cases is not Eros, not its desire to be related, but something analogous to benevolence, something that is not self-regarding. We admire the person who works unselfishly to protect ecosystems, or who gives generously to support the arts. In reality, however, we are as unlikely to find someone who does those things in an imaginative and committed way without personally enjoying nature or the arts, as to find someone sensitively caring for the good of people to whom she cannot imagine wanting to be related personally. And in the case of activities such as art or philosophy we admire practitioners who care in a special way about their own relation to the activity, so that they are unwilling to do poor work themselves even though their doing it would add but a few insignificant drops to the ocean of poor work that exists. Whatever benefits we derive from the existence of artistic and intellectual excellence, they would pretty clearly not be available to us were it not for people who care intensely, for its own sake, about attaining such excellence; but the caring seems admirable in itself, and not just desirable for its benefits.

A second argument, still quite direct, is based on premises important to my larger project. As explained in chapter 1, section 2, I hold that the claim that *x* is excellent implies that it is noninstrumentally good (indeed excellent) to value *x*. If many natural objects and artistic and intellectual achievements are excellent, as I believe, it follows that it is excellent to value them. And if it is excellent to value them, why shouldn't divine love care about them, given that God is the standard of excellence in general, and specifically in love?

Caring about such objects does not seem less appropriate to God's situation than to ours—quite the opposite, in fact, especially with regard to natural objects. The perspective of omniscience must be less bound to the human than ours, and the creator of a universe of which humanity occupies so small a part may be presumed interested in other things in it besides us. The latter point is vividly represented in God's speech from the whirlwind in the book of Job (chapters 38–41), with its enthusiastic delight in strange and wonderful wild animals and the ways in which they do *not* serve human purposes.

A more indirect argument takes off from my conception of human well-being as largely constituted by enjoyment of the excellent. The partisans of benevolence, or more broadly of interest in the personal, as the sole admirable aspect of love must surely suppose that the ideal lover cares for a beloved person's good in an ideal way. Given that a person's good involves enjoying excellent things, caring for it in an ideal way will involve appreciating and valuing excellences that the person might enjoy (as I argued at the end of section 2). While it is not strictly necessary that any of these be excellences of impersonal objects, enjoying the excellence of such objects is a good we can hardly afford to renounce for the enrichment of human life. The ideal lover will therefore care, at least in a general way, about such excellences, and will probably be a more imaginative and effective, and thus more ideal, lover if she loves some of them in particular.

Think about the ideal parent. He is not someone who cares only about children, or even who cares only about children and the adults that children become. The ideal parent cares also about such things as nature, art, and sport, and cares about them for their own sake. Without such interests the parent will be less than ideal both in conceiving and caring for the child's good and in providing the child with a model of a desirable life. Similar reasoning applies to God's love.

Perhaps it will be objected that the ideal parent cares about excellences not for their sake but for the children's sake (and perhaps also for her own sake). She wants the children to enjoy them (and perhaps also to enjoy them herself). But that, I reply, is precisely how we typically care about excellences for their own sake: we want people to enjoy them. The object of the desire essentially involves both the person and the excellence, and involves both for their own sake. We want this person (and not just some person or other) to enjoy this excellence (and not just some excellence or other). Of course, a benevolent love for a person could involve wanting him to enjoy just some excellence or other, but full-bodied love for an individual typically goes beyond that. We want the child to enjoy music, and perhaps even more specifically to enjoy Mozart. We do not suppose this is essential to the well-being we desire for her, but we feel it would be particularly nice, and we may be at least a little disappointed if it turns out not to be among her enjoyments.

One's desire here is for a relation (of enjoyment) between a person and an excellence. If the person is oneself, we have a paradigm case of Eros, with the excellence as object of the Eros. If the person is someone else about whom one cares, we may say we have a case of vicarious Eros.

6

GRACE

Grace is an attribute of God's love in all the main theistic faiths.[1] God is merciful, compassionate. God forgives sins, not because that's God's job, as the famous cynical remark[2] would have it, and not because sinners deserve it, but out of free and gracious love. The word 'grace' has a wide variety of theological uses, and something must be said at the outset about the sense in which I use it, though the whole chapter should help to explicate my meaning.

The most important division in the uses of 'grace' is between those in which it signifies an attitude or characteristic of God, or of someone else who is gracious toward another person; and those in which it signifies something which is in a person by a particular divine gift, and not purely by her own nature or through her own efforts. My use of 'grace' will be of the former type, which I believe to be primary. I do not mean to disparage the latter type, which has also been important, especially in Catholic theology; but I will try to avoid it here, in order to give a consistent sense to a key term.

In religious discourse about grace as an attribute of God, the emphasis often falls heavily on forgiveness. I conceive of grace, however, as a fundamental attribute that characterizes all of God's love, at least toward particular creatures, with for-

1. Including the more theistic versions of Hinduism.
2 *Dieu pardonnera, c'est son métier.*

150

giveness as one manifestation of it. In a preliminary formulation, we can say that grace is love that is not completely explained by the excellence of its object. Within certain wide parameters, at any rate, it is not proportioned to the excellence of its object, nor conditioned on the degree of that excellence. To the extent that that degree can be measured, grace typically outruns it. It is commonly and plausibly thought that the love of an infinite, transcendently good being for finite beings could not be anything but grace in this sense, on the ground that no finite excellence could *deserve* the love of such a transcendent being.

In conceiving of grace as a main part of the nature of God's love, I have an important point of agreement with Anders Nygren's conception of Agape. Agape, for Nygren, *is* God's love; and I think it is fair to say that the feature of Agape that Nygren most emphasizes is its grounding, its independence from any intrinsic value of its object. Nygren pushes this independence farther, however, than seems right to me. According to Nygren, the love (Agape) that can be ascribed to God is "unmotivated" in the sense that it is not responsive at all to any excellence of creatures.[3] Nygren's view on this subject is incompatible with my account of the nature of excellence. How love can be both grace and responsive to excellence is a main topic of this chapter, especially in section 3.

Another point of agreement with Nygren is that I take God's grace as a model for human love, though I doubt that Nygren would approve of my argument for doing so. It is not only God's love that is grace. I will argue that grace is rooted in the nature of love as such, and that any attitude toward a person that is not gracious in certain ways falls short of the ideal of love, and may fail thereby to be real love at all. One of my aims in this will be polemical: to combat conceptions of ideal love as quantitative, aimed at maximizing something.

1. Love's Particularity

The chain of reasons by which the nature of love is tied to grace begins with a fundamental principle: whatever is really loved is loved for its own sake. This principle is eloquently articulated and developed by Bishop Butler:

> The very nature of affection consists in tending toward, and resting in, its objects as an end. We do indeed often in common language say, that things are loved, desired, esteemed, not for themselves, but for somewhat further, somewhat out of and beyond them: yet, in these cases, whoever will attend, will see, that these things are not in reality the objects of the affections, i.e. are not loved, desired, esteemed, but the somewhat further and beyond them.[4]

I am not sure that what Butler says here is true about *desire,* for it seems natural enough to speak of purely instrumental desires. But it seems correct to say that something is not really *loved* if it is not loved for itself.

3. Nygren, *Agape and Eros*, pp. 75–80.
4. Butler, *Fifteen Sermons*, sermon 13, paragraph 5.

A similar articulation of the principle can be found in Plato, though he carries it in a direction quite opposite to that which I (and Butler) intend. In his *Lysis* he has Socrates suggest that there is a "first object of love, for whose sake, we say, all other objects are loved" (219D). It is later hinted that this is "the good" (220B). And Socrates argues that "it is only in a manner of speaking that we say we 'love' what is loved for the sake of something else that is loved; it looks as though what is really loved is that very thing in which all of these so-called loves terminate" (220A–B).[5] The conclusion toward which Socrates is carrying the principle that what is loved is loved for its own sake is that the good as such is "the only thing that is 'truly' (ὡς ἀληθῶς) or 'really' (τῷ ὄντι) loved—or, more precisely that *should be* so loved," as Gregory Vlastos puts it.[6]

Plato even seems to have embraced this conclusion enthusiastically in his *Symposium* (with respect to the Good conceived as Beauty). In a justly famous passage to which I have already acknowledged my indebtedness in other respects, he suggests that a novice in the education of love may rightly begin with an attachment to a particular beautiful body, and in this way get hooked, as we might say, on beauty. But he ought to recognize as soon as possible that beauty is shared by many individuals. His affections should then be transferred from the beautiful particulars to Beauty itself. His interest in beautiful individuals should come to be incidental to his love of Beauty.[7]

This conclusion is outrageous. It is not only obvious that we do really love individual human beings, for example, but overwhelmingly plausible that we should really love them. It is presumably only by misunderstanding and undervaluing his own affection for Socrates, and probably for one or more other persons, that Plato could have thought otherwise.[8]

The issue that is raised here, of the relation between love and value, is pivotal for an understanding of grace, and indeed of love. It is a tricky issue, and it is not easy to say where Plato's argument goes wrong. It would not be plausible to claim that love should have no relation at all to the value of its object. It is surely better to love good art than bad art. Love for pets enriches the lives of many people, but we generally think that we ought to care more about people than about cats, and that that's because people have a higher value than cats. Despite the gulf between finite and infinite, which can lead us to see ourselves as less in comparison with God than cats in comparison with us, it is generally supposed that God too cares more about humans than about other animals, and that that has something to do with the value of persons. A biblical formulation of this belief is ascribed to Jesus: "Are not five sparrows sold for two pennies? And not one of them is forgotten before God. . . . Fear not; you are of more value than many sparrows" (Luke 12:6–7).

5. I have used, with one change, the translation of these phrases that is given in Vlastos, "The Individual as Object of Love in Plato," p. 10. Vlastos convincingly defends the use of 'love' in translating φιλία (*philia*) and its cognates (ibid., p. 3f.).

6. Vlastos, "The Individual as Object of Love in Plato," p. 10. In Vlastos's interpretation, however, the good is not yet a transcendent Form in the *Lysis*; see ibid., pp. 35–37.

7. *Symposium* (210A–212A). I am simplifying here, of course, picking out one strand from a speech, other strands of which I have discussed earlier.

8. Cf. Vlastos, "The Individual as Object of Love in Plato," p. 26.

I believe that love for individuals has its proper place within an encompassing love for the good, and can even find reasons in the excellences of its object. In section 3 of the present chapter and in chapter 7 I will try to reconcile those beliefs with love's particularity. On the other hand, it is surely good to love many particular things, and there must be something more in that love than concern for goodness as such and in general, since the particular things must be loved for their own sake if they are to be loved at all. It is that "something more" that is our immediate concern, and that is the root of grace in the very nature of love.[9]

One of the trickiest points here is the understanding of 'for the sake of' [ἕνεκα in the *Lysis*] in the thesis that what is loved must be loved for its own sake and not (or not only) for the sake of something else. There is a wide variety of types of factor for which, or for the sake of which, we can love or care about something, as we shall see in section 3. In the present context I believe we must be concerned first of all with those that define the objects or ends of love, rather than specifying love's background in some other way.

We shall focus particularly on what may be called "teleological" senses of 'for the sake of'. If one wants x for the sake of y in this sense, one wants x as a way or means of getting y. If one loves or cares about x for the sake of y in a teleological sense, one wants (a significant part of) what one wants regarding x as a way or means of getting (a significant part of) what one wants regarding y. In loving what one loves for its own sake one does not love it solely, or too much, or perhaps at all, for the sake of something else in such a teleological sense. In Butler's old-fashioned phrase, one "rests in" the loved object as an end.

One thing that might be meant in saying that Romeo cares about Juliet "for the sake of her beauty," for instance, is that he wants to have a relationship with her as a way of having a relationship with a beautiful woman, which is his ulterior end in the matter. The latter is a quite general end that does not essentially involve Juliet, since he could in principle have a relationship with some other beautiful woman instead. If that is all there is to his interest in Juliet, he does not *love* her. His interest in her starts to look more like love if he would not just as soon be related to some other beautiful woman instead, and especially if he would not prefer a relationship with an even more beautiful woman, if one were possible for him. Then he must be interested in something more individual than female beauty as such.

What is clearest in such a case is that Romeo's interest in Juliet is not love if he wants to have a relationship with her *solely* in order to have a relationship with a beautiful woman, and in that sense *solely* for the sake of a more general end. But I think it can be said, more sweepingly, that Romeo cannot love Juliet for the sake of a more general end *at all*, in the following sense: if Romeo loves Juliet, his love for her, with its individual object, is in principle distinct from (though not necessarily incompatible with) any interest in her in which she is viewed as a way or means to some more general end, not essentially involving her. I do not have a rigorous argument for this claim, but I think it is strongly suggested by the following reflection.

---

9. There is a significant literature on love's relation to the individuality of the beloved. See, e.g., Brown, "The Right Method of Boy-Loving"; Vlastos, "The Individual as Object of Love in Plato."

Romeo may want to have a date with Juliet *both* because he loves her and because he wants to have a date with a beautiful woman. But if so, the love for Juliet and the more general desire for a beautiful date are competing or concurrent motives for the desire for a date with Juliet. Insofar as the latter, proximate desire is motivated by the general desire for a beautiful date, it is not a manifestation of love for Juliet.

What we clearly want to exclude from love for an individual, at this point, is teleological motivation in which the individual is valued solely (or even, perhaps, at all) as a way or means of realizing an ulterior end. Further progress in understanding the nature and grounds of this exclusion will require us to make a further distinction among teleological senses of 'for the sake of', a distinction that I have blurred thus far with the disjunctive phrase 'way or means'. There are two very different types of relation that can obtain between a proximate end and an ulterior end, by virtue of which the former is a way or means to the latter.

One alternative is that the relation is *causal*—that the one end is causally conducive to the other. That is doubtless what we will think of first. It is what we will have in mind if we say that the one is a "means" to the other. But that is not the only possibility. It is also possible—and importantly so for our present discussion— that the proximate end is an exemplification or *instance* of the ulterior end. In this second case, the proximate end would exemplify a general value that one wants to see exemplified.

The following is a pair of examples of teleological motivation involving the two types of relation. Let's suppose that *p*, the proximate end here, is the election of a certain candidate, *x*, to public office. The example can go either of two ways. One might desire *p* because one desires a decrease in tax rates and believes that *x* will exercise effective influence for that end, if elected. In this case one's reason involves a belief in a *causal* connection, and one desires *p* as a *means* to another end that one desires. Another reason that one could have for desiring *x*'s election (*p*), however, is that one desires the election of a candidate of a certain ethnic group and believes that *x* belongs to that group. Thus one might desire the election of Jesse Jackson because one desires the election of an African-American and believes that Jackson is African-American. The belief involved in this reason is not that *p* would be a cause, but that it would be an instance, of the election of a candidate of the desired ethnicity; and in this case one desires *p*, not as a means to that end, but as a *way* in which it could be realized. Both of these reasons are properly called "teleological"; both indicate that one wants *p* to occur "in order that" some larger or further end be accomplished. And 'for the sake of' can be used to express both: one desires *x*'s election for the sake of a decrease in taxes, or for the sake of *x*'s ethnicity.

These two different ways in which the proximate and the ulterior ends can be related in teleological motivation will be treated separately in my argument, which has, at this point, two stages. I will take the easier stage first, arguing—more briefly, because I think it is pretty obvious—that love is incompatible with desiring the well-being of the beloved, or whatever relationship one desires with the beloved, only as a *means*, causally understood, to more general ends. Then I will go on and argue that love is incompatible with desiring the beloved's well-being, or a relationship with the beloved, only as a *way* of obtaining more general ends which they would *exemplify*.

First, then, as regards teleological motivations involving a belief in *causal* connection, love requires an interest in the beloved that is not merely instrumental. If someone desires my well-being only as a means to an ulterior end—if my employer, for example, wants me to be happy only because she desires greater productivity and thinks I will be more productive if happy—she does not love me, because she does not desire my well-being for its own sake. And if one desires to be related to someone only as a means to an ulterior end, that too would normally constitute one's attitude to that person as something other than love. If Pamela wants to be friends with Angela only because she believes it will further her career, then not only does she not desire friendship with her for its own sake; she also does not love Angela for Angela's own sake, and therefore does not really love her at all (and is, indeed, no friend of hers).[10] This is true even if Pamela has a decent benevolent concern for Angela's well-being for its (and Angela's) own sake—which shows, by the way, that when we say in this case that Pamela does not love Angela for Angela's own sake, 'for Angela's own sake' does not mean for Angela's benefit, but rather has to do with being interested in a relationship with Angela as an end in itself. Examples like this are easy to think of, and our judgments about them are clear. We do not think that one's desires regarding a person that one loves can be motivated solely by interests in the proximate ends of those desires as a means causally conducive to ulterior ends not essentially involving the person loved.

It would be absurd to suppose that love excludes all instrumental interest in the beloved; and I am not claiming that it does. One is interested in one's spouse's well-being in no small part because it has a substantial impact on one's own. And a child may genuinely love his parents even though he prizes his relationship with them partly for the physical sustenance that he derives from it. Relationships in which one never uses the other person as a means at all are rare indeed. What love requires with regard to teleological reasons based on causal relations is just that one's interest in the other person not be exclusively, or too predominantly, instrumental—besides which I believe, as argued earlier, that the love is in principle distinct from any such instrumentally motivated interests that may be present with it.

The other type of teleological motivation, in which the proximate end is desired as a *way* of attaining the ulterior end because it is (or would be) an *instance* of it, is less well understood. It is also more important in the present context, for it is primarily as instances, rather than causes, of goodness that Plato suggests that particular good things should be valued; and the temptation to value them merely as instances of a more general value is subtler and more enticing than the temptation to value them merely as causes. Two rather different examples will be presented here to help us think about this type of teleological motivation.

The first example is concerned with love's benevolent interest in the *good* of a beloved person. It might be thought that this interest could be accounted for by a teleological motivation in which the good of the beloved is regarded as a way to an

10. The question could be discussed (but will not be here) whether in refusing to call this friendship I am in disagreement with Aristotle's conception of friendship on account of advantage as one of the inferior types of friendship. Cf. Cooper, "Aristotle on Friendship," pp. 304f., 308–15.

ulterior end conceived as a comprehensive good consisting in the maximization of the average well-being of all people.[11] For the well-being of the beloved is an instance of well-being; so its increase will increase the average well-being of all people. It could be argued that desiring the well-being of each individual as an *instance* of well-being, and thus as contributing to average well-being, is indistinguishable for practical purposes from desiring *for its own sake* (and in proportion to its value) each possible improvement in the lot of each individual. And it might be suggested that this is the ideal of love.

This argument is mistaken, however. It can be refuted by way of a case in which the difference between desiring the well-being of an individual for its own sake and desiring it as an instance of well-being is of more than theoretical importance. Suppose you have just heard that fifty-seven people have been seriously injured in a train accident, but you do not know the names of the victims. If you have reason to believe that someone you love (or even an acquaintance for whom you have a decently friendly regard) may have been one of those injured, you will naturally hope that she was not. This hope contains a desire that she not have been among the fifty-seven victims. This desire is one that we would expect you to have if you desire her well-being for its own sake, but not if you desire it only as an instance of human well-being. For this desire that she not have been one of those injured no reason can be found in a desire for greater average well-being for all people, unless you believe that your friend would have suffered a greater loss of well-being in being injured than whoever else would have been hurt instead of her. In most cases there would be no grounds for such a belief, and it would not be the basis of your hope that your friend was not among the victims. This is evidence that love involves a desire for the beloved's well-being that is not wholly motivated by a desire for the maximization of average well-being.

The example also provides evidence of the undesirability of at least the most extreme form of impartiality. What would we think of someone so impartial in his devotion to maximum average well-being that, if he knew the number of victims in an accident, he would not hope that his friend was not among them, because, for any given diminishment of average well-being, he would not care whose individual well-being was diminished by it? Surely we would say that he did not love his "friend," and that this form of impartiality is inhuman and anything but admirable. The case would be importantly different, of course, if you had some individual knowledge of all the people who might have been hurt. Then an impartiality that refused to hope that one rather than another of them had escaped injury would have something to be said for it. But the case in which most of the potential victims are not individually known to you is more usual and suffices to show that a lover neither would nor should desire the beloved's well-being merely as an average-raising instance of human well-being. This is a case, indeed, in which we expect the lover to prefer one outcome to others that are objectively no worse, because of the way in

---

11. Since we are not comparing situations involving different numbers of people in this example, it would not matter here if *average* well-being were replaced by the *total* sum of human well-being (assuming it to be positive). I just find it easier to think of the example in terms of average well-being.

which the beloved is involved. That shows clearly the lover's interest in something individual, and not just in value more generally.

The example is less directly useful for thinking about God's love, however, for God presumably does have profound individual knowledge of all the actual and possible victims, and we might well hope that God would view the situation with a certain impartiality arising, not from lovelessness, but from love for *each* of them—a point that will be taken up in section 5. It may therefore be helpful to look at a different type of example, involving a contrast between actual and merely possible people. The example will lose somewhat in realism because of this feature, but I hope that any absurdity we may find in it will help to underline my point.

Suppose a parent said, "Diane and Daniel are great people and very happy; they've been wonderful children to me, and I love them very much; but I'd rather I'd had somewhat better and happier children instead of them," we would be puzzled, because there is a glaring contradiction between the love professed and the preference stated. (Is the parent perhaps a fanatical utilitarian stating with conscious but only superficial sincerity an "official" preference that is not compatible with the love he really has?) This example is interesting, in the first place, because it shows a point at which we think love should have some of the character of grace, inasmuch as its preferences should *not* be calibrated in accordance with objective value. For it shows that we think love for actual people (if they are at least reasonably good and happy) should shut out preferences for merely possible people who might have lived instead of them, even on the supposition that the latter would have lived *better* lives than the actual people.

This example may be more applicable to God than the previous one; for, while we may think God should be impartial among actual people, there is no reason to think God's love should be impartial between actual and merely possible people. Actual beings are appropriate objects of a fuller sort of love than merely possible beings. They are appropriate objects of individual attachment and emotional and other sorts of commitments in a way that merely possible beings are not. And I see no reason why that should not apply to God as well as to us. If the disparity between finite and infinite goods has among its consequences, as I think plausible, that there is no best possible set of creatures, so that better sets of possible creatures must have been passed up no matter what God created, then we surely should think of divine love as focused on actual creatures in such a way that God has no regrets over the better ones that were not created instead. The example may be less applicable to God if there is a best possible set of creatures and divine perfection must have led God to create that set rather than any other, as some[12] believe. I don't believe that maximizing or optimizing in that way should be seen as a characteristic of the divine love, however, even if there is a best possible set of creatures; and I hope that further discussion of the relation of love to value in this chapter will add to the plausibility of my view on this point.

12. Most famously Leibniz. I have defended my contrary opinion in Adams, "Must God Create the Best?"

2. Love for Particular Universals

Strange as it may seem to put it this way, love's particularity extends even to universals. We do and should love certain qualities, as well as individuals; and our love for them does and should include a particular attachment to them, which precludes our loving them solely for the sake of still more general sorts of value. That is, if we valued them only as instances of less differentiated values, and as ways of attaining the latter, we would not really love the more particular values as I think we ought.

I will argue the point with respect to love for *truthfulness*. By 'truthfulness' here I mean a *quality of conduct* consisting mainly in not lying, but also in such things as giving a balanced view of the truth, and being careful to keep one's facts straight. Some who use the word to signify a trait of character, and indeed a virtue, may hold that one's truthfulness depends only on telling the truth when one ought to, and is unaffected by what one does when one ought to lie.[13] It would be most implausible to impose this restriction on the scope of truthfulness as a quality of conduct. Lying is untruthful even when one ought to lie, and giving an answer that one knows to be correct is truthful even when it is wrong to give it. It is truthfulness as a quality of conduct that will concern us here, and certainly the attitudes that I propose to explain in terms of love for truthfulness cannot be explained in terms of a regard for telling the truth *when one ought to*.

Truthfulness is a good example for the point I want to make. For we might naturally expect that a type of conduct that is normally virtuous would be prized—perhaps solely—as an instance of a more general moral excellence. Consideration of a situation of moral conflict will show that there is more than that to the regard we think we should have for truthfulness.

There are rare occasions when one morally ought to lie. Our fictitious friend Ed loves truthfulness, but finds himself in such a situation. He has been entrusted with a morally important secret; we need not know anything about the secret, except that there is nothing wrong with Ed's having knowledge of it, and he has nothing to be ashamed of in knowing it. It has been necessary for him to lie repeatedly to keep the secret. The lie is quite simple. There is no danger of discovery, so long as Ed sticks to his story. The people to whom the lie is told are casual acquaintances who have a sincere but not a pressing interest in the questions they ask. They have no stake in the matter, but they are not moved by malice. They have no suspicion of the existence of the secret, and they suffer no harm in being deceived, except insofar as false belief of every sort may be a harm.

Ed finds this lying distasteful, as I think he should, although he knows he is doing the right thing. Why is he pained by it? Because he loves truthfulness.[14] If he

---

13. Cf. Wallace, "Excellences and Merit," p. 196: "Truthfulness . . . is the firm disposition to tell the truth when one should."

14. It has been suggested to me that Ed might love prima facie rightness, and therefore be pained by the prima facie wrongness of lying—that is, by the fact that lying is a sort of thing that would be wrong, other things being equal (as they are not in this case). It seems to me implausible that this would be Ed's motive, and very implausible that it ought to be. I suppose it is prima facie wrong to drive through a red traffic signal, but right on the whole for ambulance drivers to do it in many situations. They surely should not care about prima facie rightness in such a way as to be pained by what they have to do in those cases.

loved truthfulness only for the sake of its merit or its degree of moral goodness, his moral discomfort could not rationally be anything but regret that a better action was not possible in the circumstances. But the discomfort is in fact of a quite different nature. Ed rightly judges that lying to keep the secret is, on the whole, more meritorious than many actions that he performs daily without the slightest uneasiness. The former is not only obligatory but a positively good action, requiring a certain strength of will; the latter are morally insignificant. So it is not a lower degree of overall moral goodness as such that pains him.

We can sharpen the argument by shifting our attention from feelings of regret to wishes or preferences. Suppose we ask Ed whether he would prefer that people not ask the questions that give rise to the need to lie. We could point out to him that in that case he would presumably have less merit. Surely Ed would reply that he wished he had no occasion for this meritorious lying. And we should think much less well of him if he were glad of the opportunity to gain merit by lying; we should think that he did not care enough about truthfulness in that case.

We thus think love of truthfulness would lead Ed to prefer a situation in which there seems to be less good on the whole, to one in which he has to lie; and we approve of this preference. We approve of a particular attachment to truthfulness that cannot be just a general desire for value. Doubters on this point will perhaps allege that what happens in the situation in which Ed has to lie is really worse on the whole than what happens in the case in which he does not. This claim has some initial plausibility, but let us ask what would make the situation in which Ed lies worse than the other.

1. It does not seem that the people who are asking questions would be better morally if they did not. I have stipulated that they are not asking out of malice.

2. I have also stipulated that they are not harmed by the lies, except insofar as false belief as such is bad. On the whole, moreover, it would not be better if they held a true belief about the secret. Maybe Ed ought to wish that they held no beliefs at all on the subject of their questions, but that is surely not the main reason that he ought to wish he did not have to lie to them. If no lying were involved, we would not expect him to have any wishes at all about their beliefs, so long as the secret is safe. We may suppose that Ed's answers mainly confirm false opinions his interlocutors already hold, and even correct their misunderstandings on a number of unimportant points, leaving their beliefs a little closer to the truth, on balance. It still seems just as clear that Ed should wish they were not asking the questions that force him to lie.

3. Unlike the interlocutors themselves, Ed's personal relationships with them must perhaps be harmed a bit, at least by being made less honest. But this is hardly one of the most important features of the situation, given that these relationships are casual and fairly distant anyway. If Ed were glad of the occasion to lie meritoriously, we should not think that he did not care enough about his relationship to these people, but that he did not care enough about his relationship to truthfulness.

4. It seems that the most significant badness in the situation is the intrinsic badness of lying. This badness attaches to the conduct of the liar. The fact that he is telling lies is a bad-making or indeed a bad feature of Ed's conduct. In the postulated circumstances, however, it is outweighed by good features. In lying here Ed is not only doing the right thing but also exercising the virtues of loyalty, discretion,

and strength of will. Even his love of truthfulness is expressed in the fact that he finds the lying distasteful. These are positively good features of his conduct that sufficiently outweigh the intrinsic badness of lying to lift the overall value of his conduct on these occasions, not merely above the very low value it would have if he told the damaging truth, but also above the level it normally has in such morally insignificant activities as eating mashed potatoes or shaving.

5. There is clearly one way in which Ed's life is worse (for him) because of the lying, even if it is not morally worse. It pains him to lie. But the pain is at least as much a manifestation as a ground of his wishing not to have to lie. And surely it is not the uneasiness but the lying that we think he *ought* to wish to have been spared.

The conclusion, that it is good for Ed to be led by love of truthfulness to prefer a situation in which there seems to be less good on the whole to one in which he has to lie, has survived the examination to which I have just subjected it. The reason that it is good is doubtless that because of the excellence of truthfulness a particular love of truthfulness for its own sake is excellent. Being excellent, such a love of truthfulness, and of the other particular excellences, for their own sake is reasonably ascribed to God, though God can hardly be in Ed's predicament.

3. Reasons for Love

If what is loved must be loved for its own sake and not, or not just, for the sake of something else, it might be thought to follow that one cannot have reasons for love. I believe that would be a mistake, however. Seeing why it is wrong will advance our understanding of love's complex relation to value.

Intuition and common sense can be invoked on both sides of the question. Consider the following passage of dialogue from Henry James, in which the first speaker defends his claim that he loves a Miss Osmond:

> "Could anyone in the world be more lovable than Miss Osmond?"
> "No one, possibly. But love has nothing to do with good reasons."
> "I don't agree with you. I'm delighted to have good reasons."
> "Of course you are. If you were really in love you wouldn't care a straw for them."[15]

In a more moderate as well as a more philosophical vein, Max Scheler speaks of "the unusual helplessness in which we see people fall when they are called on to 'give reasons for' [*begründen*] their love and their hate. Precisely then it appears how these

15. H. James, *The Portrait of a Lady*, pp. 372f. For a much older literary representative of the same opinion, we might turn to a couplet of Catullus:

> *Odi et amo; quare id faciam, fortasse requiris:*
> *Nescio, sed fieri sentio et excrucior.*

[I hate and I love. Why I do, perhaps you'd like to hear. I don't know, but I feel it happen; it's excruciating.] (*Catulli Carmina*, LXXXV, in *Selections from Catullus*, p. 43.) See also the footnotes of Lamb, "Love and Rationality," for rich historic and contemporary documentation of this and other opinions on the subject.

'reasons' [*Gründe*] invariably are only sought after the fact, and how in their totality they never exactly cover the nature and degree of that which is supposed to have 'reasons given for it' there."[16] There is surely something right about Scheler's comments, especially the observation that the supposed reasons "never exactly cover the nature and degree" of the love. We would expect them not to, if my claims about love's particularity are correct.

Yet it does not follow that there are not even partial reasons for love. And Romeo will not be speechless if we ask him to give reasons for his love. He loves Juliet for her beauty, affection, bravery, and freedom from ancestral prejudice. Most people would say these are reasons (indeed, good reasons) that he has for loving her.

This will not silence the doubts about reasons for love. One doubt we may have is whether the good qualities that attract Romeo to Juliet really function as *reasons*. Granted, they are *causes* of his love for her. But even if we allow, for the sake of argument, that reasons for love would also be causes of love, it is clear that not all causes of love could be reasons for love. Various hormone secretions in Romeo's body (unknown to him) are among the causes of his love for Juliet, but are certainly not reasons for loving her. What more is required of reasons?

One suggestion may be that reasons (especially good reasons) must tend to establish the rationality of that for which they are reasons, and thus to justify it. This seems to be true of reasons for action and belief. Other things being equal, if you have good reasons for doing or believing something, and none for not doing or believing it, it would be rational for you to do it or believe it, and might well be irrational not to; and if the weight of the reasons is on the other side, it would indeed be irrational for you to do it or believe it, and rational not to.

Reasons for love do not seem to affect the rationality of love in the same way. We are not quick to evaluate love as to its rationality at all. Is a mother's love for her wayward child or a child's love for his battered and bedraggled teddy bear *irrational* if they do not have good enough reasons for it? We would not normally say so, nor would we say that you need a reason for *not* loving the last attractive person that you met. Not to love someone that you have plenty of reasons for loving (if "reasons" is the right thing to call them) may be coldhearted, but in most contexts it would not be considered irrational.[17]

---

16. Scheler, *Wesen und Formen der Sympathie*, p. 152. My translation differs considerably from the published English translation, *The Nature of Sympathy*, p. 149.

17. Lamb, "Love and Rationality," argues that it should be considered at least prima facie irrational. My main response to his argument will be noted later. An incompleteness appears here in my views regarding rationality and irrationality. I have suggested in chapter 1, section 2, that practical rationality consists in responding well to reasons that one has. I have not explained which, or how many, of one's reasons one must respond well to in order to be rational, or at least not irrational; nor what sort of goodness or badness of response is involved. Surely not all of one's reasons, or not every sort of goodness and badness of response. Selfishness, for example, involves responding badly, in a way, to the totality of considerations that could be taken as reasons for action, but that hardly yields a compelling proof that selfishness is irrational. (I do not mean to foreclose on all arguments that selfishness is indeed irrational, but they will need premises that I have not provided, if they are to be convincing.) 'Irrational' is not a *fundamental* evaluative term in my ethical framework, and no systematic account of irrationality will be found in this book.

We speak fairly easily of love as wise or foolish. But the wisdom or folly of which we thus speak depends primarily on the wisdom or folly of actions to which it impels the lover, rather than on the presence or absence, or weight or value, of reasons for loving the beloved. Romeo is a case in point. His excellent reasons for loving Juliet have no force to rebut the charge that his love was foolish because it impelled him to act in foolish haste. Just how beautiful Juliet was is simply irrelevant to the question whether there was folly in a love that led Romeo to suicide. On the other hand, if people are happy in love, no lack of such reasons as Romeo had—no lack of personal attractiveness in the beloved—will be likely to make us think their love is foolish.

This need not stop us from speaking of Romeo's "reasons" for loving Juliet. We need not even infer that they have nothing to do with rationality. Love is a very complex phenomenon, and questions of rationality may arise at many levels in it. At a minimum, there can be a question of the rationality of taking something as a reason for love. There would be some sort of lapse of rationality, for example, in giving as a reason for loving someone, 'Because he is a monster of immorality' or 'Because I hardly know her'; my subsequent discussion should shed some light on why that is so.

It would not be easy to show that it can be rational to love without any reason at all. That is because it probably is not rational to love anything unless it is good in some way, but then its value will provide some reason for loving it. In particular, if the value of persons as persons is as great as I argued in chapter 4, section 5, there may always be reason enough to justify love for any person. The mother will have reason enough to love her wayward son; she just doesn't need any *special* reason to love him.

We need, of course, to take into account the varieties of love, and the varieties of relationship to which love may aspire. The mother who has reason enough, in his personhood, to love her wayward son may not have reason enough to want him to live in her home, and it may not be rational for her to want that. Reason enough to care deeply about someone as a person, and to be glad of her existence, is not necessarily reason enough to want a romantic relationship with her. Narrower excellences of the beloved, besides her personhood, may be important for the rationality of these particular relational desires—though if one thinks hard about justification of such relational interests, one is likely to be led also to prudential and moral considerations that are not what we most often think of as "reasons for love." It is not obvious, however, that relational desires are always irrational if one lacks reasons for them.

If the value of personhood always gives us reason enough to love any person we meet, should we conclude that we are being irrational whenever we don't love one of them? Whether this paradoxical conclusion is correct may depend on how we understand 'love' in it. If a minimally decent concern for another person's well-being counts as love in this context, then the conclusion may be correct. We are certainly failing to respond appropriately to the reasons available to us, when we pass a homeless stranger without the slightest concern for his or her destitution. Perhaps we should classify this failure as "irrationality," though I think we usually don't. On the other hand, if love, in this context, must be an interest that at least approaches in intensity Romeo's interest in Juliet or the interest of typical parents in their children, then it really is absurd to suppose that rationality demands we love each person we meet. For one thing, we *can't* do that, because of the limits of our emotional and other resources.

Even before we reach the limits of our capacities, moreover, we may think it rational enough to pass up possible loves that would have advantages very similar to those of some of our present loves, if our life is rich enough already in that type of relationship. More of a good thing is not necessarily better. And even where more would be better, it is not obvious that it is always irrational to choose not to go for more; enough may be enough.[18]

It is a prejudice to be avoided here that reasons that tend to justify a belief or action or attitude, in the sense of vindicating its rationality, must also tend to compel it, in the sense of rendering it irrational to abstain from it.[19] This is perhaps most plausible in the case of belief, though even there I think there are cases in which one could rationally believe something that one could without irrationality not believe. With regard to actions the prejudice is quite implausible. It is essential to the possibility of *play*, for example, that there are actions that we have adequate reason to do, but no obligation of any sort, and therefore no "rational obligation," to do. There is also play in attitudes, and it is not necessarily irrational to be much more interested in entomology than in herpetology, even though one knows that one has very similar reasons in favor of both possible interests. Similar considerations apply to love.

This is too short a discussion to settle the issues about the relation between love's reasons and love's rationality, but it will have to do for now because our main concern at this point is rather the relation between love's reasons and love's particularity. Regarding reasons for love, the chief conclusion to be drawn from the argument of section 1 is that they must *not* be *teleological* reasons. That is, it is not a reason for *loving* that what concerns us in the beloved is a way or means to some ulterior end. If the beauty of the beloved, for example, is a reason for loving that person or thing, that cannot be because we see the beloved's beauty as a way of satisfying a more general interest in beauty. But that leaves open quite a variety of ways of understanding reasons for love—a larger variety, no doubt, than we will be able to consider here.

We will focus first, and mainly, on reasons that appeal to qualities that the beloved has—as when Romeo loves Juliet for her intelligence, beauty, bravery, and so forth. We may call them *qualitative* reasons for love. In this connection, pretty clearly, we will think first of *desirable* qualities—though, as I shall suggest, they are not the only qualities that can play this part. How should these reasons be understood as operating, given that we are not going to understand them as teleological reasons?

A first thing to be said about this is that if we look at what in practice seems to be involved in having qualitative reasons for loving someone, they don't in fact imply

18. This last point is a brief and rough statement of the view of those philosophers who advocate "satisficing." See especially Slote, *Beyond Optimizing*.

19. The argument of Lamb, "Love and Rationality," seems to me to depend on this assumption, but not to offer any persuasive defense of it.

that the lover has a more general desire for, or interest in, the quality that is involved in the reason. Saying that Romeo loves Juliet, for example, for her wit and bravery does not imply that he is moved by a general liking or desire for those good qualities. He may have no such general liking or desire, even though he does love Juliet for her wit and bravery. He may find these qualities uninteresting or even threatening in most people, but attractive in her. There will probably be reasons for this difference—but one of them may be that he loves her and not them; the explanatory link between love and one's reasons for it is not a one-way street. Our interest in the good qualities of people we love is quite different from our interest in the same qualities in other people; and one sometimes prizes, in a person one loves, qualities to which one is indifferent or hostile in others. So, then, in specifying qualities in the beloved for which one loves the beloved, and which provide reasons for loving the beloved, one is not indicating that the lover has a general interest in, or desire for, those qualities. What *is* one doing? Typically, I think, one is simply specifying, in part, what it is that the lover finds appealing in the beloved in the particular case.

I have two suggestions to offer for developing our understanding of this point. The first is that we can find in love an evaluative judgment, and we can construe these qualitative reasons as reasons for that judgment, and thus as more like reasons for a belief than for an action or a desire.[20] To love something is at least in part to value it. To say, "I love it, but it's absolutely worthless" (or even worse, "I love him, but he's absolutely worthless"), is to utter a paradox. For in the absence of a special explanation, to say sincerely that one regards something as worthless, without qualification, is to show that one does not love it.

Turning to the beloved, as Josef Pieper puts it, the lover could sincerely say, "It is good that you exist."[21] Not that holding this judgment of the beloved's value as a mere opinion is sufficient to constitute love. One can believe that it is good that a certain person or object exists without caring much about it at all, but a lover must be personally glad that the beloved exists. The lover's valuing of the existence of the beloved includes "assenting, consenting, applauding, affirming, praising, glorifying, and hailing," to quote Pieper again.[22] There may be exceptional cases in which a lover wishes, on balance, for the nonexistence of a loved one who is in misery; but such a wish must struggle against a prizing of the beloved's existence that remains even there. But while the celebrating or prizing of the beloved's existence involves more than a belief, it does involve believing there is something importantly good about the beloved's existence.

Applying this point to divine love, we confront Nygren's claim that God's love is "unmotivated" and "indifferent to value." Agape, in Nygren's view, has "no motive outside itself, in the personal worth of men. . . . It is only when all thought of the worthiness of the object is abandoned that we can understand what Agape is."[23] Not

---

20. There is interesting discussion of reasons of this sort in G. Taylor, "Love."
21. Pieper, *About Love*, pp. 19, 27. In chapter 4, section 5, I have had something to say about the sense in which this particular sort of value judgment should be understood.
22. Pieper, *About Love*, p. 19.
23. Nygren, *Agape and Eros*, p. 76f.

that Agape stands in no relation at all to value, but it creates, rather than finds, value in its object. "God does not love that which is already in itself worthy of love, but on the contrary, that which in itself has no worth acquires worth just by becoming the object of God's love."[24] Transposing Nygren's claims into a metaethical mode which may be alien to him, we may say that he seems to hold a pure divine love theory of what the value of finite things consists in.

In chapter 1, section 3, I have given reasons for rejecting such a theory in favor of one that sees the value of finite things, and God's love for them, as grounded at least partly in their imaging God, imperfect and fragmentary though that imaging is. I believe that our experience of value strongly supports such an intrinsic aspect to the grounding of value. Reflection on the nature of love supports the same conclusion. Love seeks and finds things to prize and celebrate in the beloved, and regards them as good. Even divine love would be the richer rather than the poorer for finding such value in the beloved.

This is not to say that the intrinsic value of finite things *deserves* God's love. We may still think the value of divine love incommensurate with any value it finds in its object. It may even be part of the nature of love for an individual thing to contain more than is deserved by the individual's qualities, if I am right in arguing that there must be in such love an attachment to the individual over and above any interest in qualities. Prizing and celebrating the value of the beloved is a central manifestation of love, but it need not and perhaps cannot be the only ground or even the main ground of love.

This is not an argument for everything the theologian of grace may want. It is not an argument for *amazing* grace. I am writing philosophy, and what is established or suggested by philosophical argument is, as such, not likely to be amazing in the relevant sense.[25] But I hope that I am saying nothing to preclude an amazing discovery of grace, and that what I have said contributes to a conception of God and of love that is not incongruous with a grace that may be, nonetheless, amazing.

What values may love find to prize and celebrate in the beloved? If the beloved is a person, there will be the rich complexity of excellences that constitute the value of a person as such, as discussed in chapter 4, section 5. That probably is indeed a large part of what one typically prizes in loving a person, but the qualitative reasons one offers explicitly for such a love are likelier to focus on good qualities that distinguish the beloved from other persons. The reasons we have imagined Romeo as giving for his love of Juliet are of the latter sort. The value that each person possesses *as* a person may nonetheless constitute a more important reason for love. It certainly constitutes a weightier *justification* for love, if I was right in arguing in chapter 4 that the excellence of persons as such has a qualitative superiority over the narrower excellences with respect to which persons can excel each other.

To the extent that love involves believing that there is something wonderful about the beloved, and that it is good that the beloved exists, the instancing of spe-

24. Nygren, *Agape and Eros*, p. 78.
25. Could philosophical argument confirm the thought that our very existence is evidence of an *amazing* divine interest in us? Perhaps; but pursuing such a cosmological argument would carry us far from our present topic.

cific excellences of the beloved can offer reasons for those *beliefs*. This is one place where considerations of rationality impinge on reasons for love, and here we can see why there would be some lapse of rationality in giving 'Because he is a monster of immorality' as a reason for loving someone. For that should be a reason against rather than for believing that he is wonderful or that it is good that he exists.

As reasons for *belief*, Romeo's reasons are universalizable. If he gives Juliet's wit and bravery as reasons for valuing her, he is committed to agreeing that wit and bravery in other people would also be a reason for thinking that they are wonderful, or that it is good that they exist. But there is much more to love than such beliefs, and I think Romeo's reasons do not commit him to loving, in the same way that he loves Juliet, other people who have those admirable qualities.

I promised a second suggestion as to how qualitative reasons for love work; and it is needed at this point. Qualitative reasons for love, such as Romeo's loving Juliet for her beauty, do not just express reasons for *beliefs*. They also express motives for being *glad* that the beloved exists—for *celebrating* the beloved—and for *caring* about the beloved and *wanting* to be *related* to the beloved in various ways. That is something else that needs to be understood: how are Romeo's reasons related to these emotions and desires? My suggestion is that they explain what it is that we like (or, more broadly, that appeals to us) about the beloved, and that what they explain is perhaps more a matter of *how* than of why we love.

It is an erroneous prejudice to suppose that the appeal a particular good has for us must be explained by our interest in a more general good. Commonly, when something appeals to us, or we like it, we are reacting to a particular case, and the immediate and primary object of our valuing is something individual and particular. We see something beautiful, and we react to it, valuing that particular thing. For this reason it would commonly be much less accurate to say that one likes this or that that one presently perceives or experiences or thinks about or knows, *as* an instance of something more general that one likes, than to say that liking this particular thing *is* an instance of one's liking the more general thing. Alternatively, we might say that one's liking the more general thing is simply a generalization over one's liking the particular things, or perhaps a disposition to like the particular things.

Observing birds in the spring, I am thrilled by the brilliant orange of a male Baltimore oriole. I like the bird for its color; the beauty of the color is a reason for my liking both the bird and the experience of seeing it. Does that mean that I like them because I value that color more generally? No; my response to the particular sighting is much more immediate than that. It is true that I like orioles and brilliantly colored birds in general, but that is primarily a generalization over particular occasions on which I see such birds and like them.

I may also have a general disposition to like such sightings, and my liking the brilliant color in general could be explicated partly in terms of such a disposition. This need not be the case; I may not have a very general disposition behind my particular liking. I may like the sight and smell of the first rain I have experienced in months even if I usually dislike the experience of rain; and I see nothing irrational in that. But we should consider the case in which I do have the relevant general disposition.

A general disposition to like seeing brilliantly colored birds may be a *cause* of my liking a particular sighting, but I think hardly a *reason* for liking it. The brilliant color may be such a reason, but the disposition is not. More important, the disposition does not constitute an attitude toward an object more general than the particular birds and sightings; it is rather a disposition to like the particulars. A merely causal disposition to like or prize particulars of a certain sort, we may say, does not "infect" our attitude toward the particulars as a teleological reason for the attitude does. If I value a particular object for a teleological reason, I value it as a way or means to an ulterior end, and that structures my attitude toward the particular; it is part of the content of my attitude toward the particular. But a general disposition that is one of the causes of my valuing a particular object will not in general be part of the content of my attitude toward the particular. There may be a quality of Juliet that connects with a disposition in Romeo to like that quality in a woman and to love a woman with that quality. But the attitude produced by that disposition is a very particular interest in Juliet, a delighting in *her* possession of that quality, and a desire for a relationship with her and no other, rather than for a relationship with whoever best manifests that quality.

These considerations apply to qualitative reasons for love. To say that Romeo loves Juliet for her beauty, wit, and bravery is not to say that his love for her is an expression of a general interest in, and liking for, women that are beautiful, witty, and brave. As we have already noted, he may not have a general liking for such women; but even if he does, it is most plausibly construed as a generalization over, or disposition for, likings of particular women. Qualitative reasons for love are therefore not in general inconsistent with love's particularity.

Thus far we have focused on cases in which good qualities of the beloved are taken as reasons for love. These reasons are particularly significant for the relation between love and value, but it would be a gross oversimplification to think of them as the only type of reasons for love, and we should at least take note of some other types. The most paradoxical, perhaps, are reasons that appeal to *un*desirable qualities of the beloved.

Some forms of helplessness can move us to love though we do not like them. 'Because he suffers so much' expresses a reason one may have for loving someone, even though one wishes he did not suffer at all. Reasons for love can appeal to pity as well as to admiration, as is implied when we are told that Desdemona loved Othello "for the dangers [he] had passed," and that in so loving, "she did pity them."[26]

In a way such cases support my views about love's particularity; for when a person is loved for an undesirable quality, it will normally be clear that this reason for love is not a manifestation of a general desire or liking for the quality. In another way, however, this type of reason for love is problematic as well as puzzling; for in general it seems perverse to like anything bad for its badness. I suspect in fact that when we find something appealing by virtue of an undesirable quality, the appeal of the latter rests on a less obvious interest in something good. There are at least two ways in which this may occur.

26. Shakespeare, *Othello*, act 1, scene 3.

One is that a person's suffering or need can serve as a window, so to speak, through which her value as a person can be seen—a window into her humanity and the preciousness of her life. This point may also help us to understand the otherwise puzzling fact that mere familiarity may serve us as something like a reason for caring about someone. David Hume observes that "*acquaintance*, without any kind of relation, gives rise to love and kindness. When we have contracted a habitude of intimacy with any person; tho' in frequenting his company we have not been able to discover any very valuable quality, of which he is possess'd; yet we cannot forbear preferring him to strangers, of whose superior merit we are fully convinc'd."[27] We would commonly be more saddened by the death of someone to whom we merely say hello every day than by the death of a stranger of whose superior merit, as Hume says, we are fully convinced. But that is reasonable enough. What Hume overlooks is that even though we do not discover any *superiority* over other people in those whose company we frequent, we can hardly fail to discover the very valuable qualities that constitute their personhood, so that their concrete and particular value as persons will be better known to us than that of strangers.

The other way to be noted here in which a person may move one's love through her suffering or need is that through it one may be drawn to the possibility of helping or comforting her, and in this way one may be attracted to an excellent feature of a possible relationship with her. This brings into view another large family of reasons, which we may call *relational* reasons for love. They are important, but often difficult to understand. When asked to give a reason for our love or affection, we often say such things as 'Because she's my daughter', 'Because he's my friend's son', 'Because she took me for walks when I was a child', 'Because we were in combat together', or perhaps, where love is moved by pity, 'Because he needs me'. In these reasons we appeal, not to intrinsic qualities of the loved one, but to ways in which we are (or may be) related to the loved one.

Typically we are appealing to something good (probably even excellent) about the relationships in question—the mutual caring and sharing experienced in combat, good things that one person has done for the other, the structures of meaning that the relationships provide for the parties' lives. As in qualitative reasons for love, however, the focus in the relational reasons is on the particular. It would not be plausible, in most cases, to construe them as manifestations of an interest in objects more general than particular individuals and our particular relationships with them. You do not have to have a general desire or liking for parenthood to have it as a reason for loving someone that she is your daughter, nor does loving someone because you were in combat together depend on a general desire or liking for having had that type of experience. It would seem that even the divine love can have relational reasons, understood in this way, inasmuch as it can prize good features of God's relationships with creatures.

One remaining point about reasons for love is important for the relation between love and value. There is not much place in them for comparison. That you are good-looking is an appropriate reason for loving you—something a lover may

---

27. Hume, *Treatise of Human Nature*, p. 353.

well like about you. That you are better looking than Robert Redford or Julia Roberts is not—unless it's just a way of saying that you are very good-looking indeed. What has Redford or Roberts to do with loving *you*? That Juliet is the best looking woman Romeo knows is suspect as a reason for loving her. Suppose he meets an even better looking woman; will he then have less reason for loving Juliet, even though she has not changed? That *Starry Night* is one of Van Gogh's greatest paintings is certainly a reason for wanting to see it (or to own it, if one could), but not, I think, for loving it. That it projects a certain mystical excitement is a reason for loving it.

One reason that the reasons stated in comparative or superlative terms in these examples are not exactly reasons for love is that, if they do more than put an exclamation point on the lover's noncomparative esteem for the object of love, they appeal to an interest in something more general, and thus fail to connect with love's particularity. How Juliet's beauty compares with that of other women is obviously relevant to Romeo's general interest in beautiful women. For an understanding of his love for her in particular, however, it is more relevant to know what he likes and celebrates that is intrinsic to her—her individual beauty and, perhaps, more precisely the shape of her nose. How beautiful other women are does not have the same relevance. A baby's smile is wonderful, and celebrated as such by a parent's love. It does not matter that billions of babies have smiled as wonderfully before.

Comparative reasons have something unappreciative about them. There is a saying, popular among strenuous optimizers, that "the good is the enemy of the best." But in love the best may be the enemy of the good. Or, to apply the point more plainly to the present context, optimization and maximization are enemies of appreciation; and appreciation is part of the soul of love. This may seem paradoxical to our competitive souls, which sometimes feel most appreciated when we are favorably compared with others. But in truth, being placed on a scale, even at the top of it, is as such quite different from being loved or appreciated for oneself; it is precisely being valued as an instance of the scalar value. In our appreciation of a work of art, likewise, the thought that it is better than other works is an intrusion into our immediate enjoyment of it—or perhaps a lapse from the intensity and adventure of direct encounter into the security of a conceptual control that puts everything "in its place." The comparison with other works may enable us to see things we would otherwise have missed. But the comparison degenerates into a game and loses its connection with the love of art if we are not able to carry our new knowledge back into an uncomparative appreciation of the beauty or other aesthetic value of the work in itself.

Part of what is at stake here is that love requires a certain focus, a certain kind of attention to the beloved. In this, love involves a main feature of the stance that is essential to Martin Buber's conception of an "I-Thou" relationship. According to Buber, "Every actual relationship to another being in the world is exclusive. Its Thou is freed and steps forth to confront us in its uniqueness. It fills the firmament—not as if there were nothing else, but everything else lives in *its* light."[28] Despite the

---

28. Buber, *I and Thou*, p. 126; cf. ibid., p. 59 (*Werke*, vol. 1, pp. 130, 83). I have followed Walter Kaufman's free but vivid rendering, but have kept the older translation of Buber's *Du* as 'Thou', where Kaufmann uses 'You'.

personalistic overtones of 'Thou' (*Du*), Buber is speaking of a type of relationship one can have with a wide range of "beings," specifically including plants and animals and products of culture (*geistige Wesenheiten*: literally, spiritual beings), as well as with human persons and God.[29] The type of attention emphasized in the quoted passage can mark our relationships with a wide range of objects, personal as well as impersonal.

Buber's description of the exclusiveness of this attention seems extreme. The Thou "fills the firmament." Can such a claim be true of love? Must the object of love really be appreciated in a way that blocks everything else out of awareness, and that does not relate it to anything else? Can we recognize the object's shape without relating it spatially to something else? Can we so much as recognize a property of the object without classing it as similar to other possible or (more likely) actual objects? Has its likeness to other things no relevance to our appreciation of it?

The last of these questions bears particularly on my views. For I have claimed both that love's appreciation may focus on an excellence of its object, and that excellence of finite things consists in a resemblance to or imaging of God. Must not God therefore stay in the picture when we love and appreciate finite things? Is it not part of what we consciously appreciate in some religious music (and indeed in Van Gogh's *Starry Night*) that they point beyond themselves to something more divine?

Buber's qualification of his claim is important, therefore. The Thou "fills the firmament—not as if there were nothing else, but everything else lives in *its* light."[30] The "exclusiveness" here is more a matter of focus than of literal (and therefore total) exclusion. Other objects are in view, but only insofar as they illuminate the nature or the meaning of the Thou or the object of love. To ask seriously whether the beloved is more (or less) excellent than some other object is to shift the focus of attention, demoting the beloved from being *the* focus to being at best one of two or more coordinate foci. Such a question is therefore no part of the fullness of appreciation.

These considerations support the claim that ideal love, and hence divine love, is grace, in the sense that it is not grounded in the comparative degree of excellence of its object but finds its reasons in a noncomparative appreciation of the object. God's love should be seen as directed exclusively to things that are good, but not dominated by caring about whether they are the best. And the same should ideally be true of our love, God being the standard of goodness in motivation as in other matters. Even with regard to love for God, to the extent that one can envisage or respond to the divine nature as it is in itself, I think one ought ideally to love it, not for its superiority as such, but simply for the goodness it has in itself independently

---

29. Buber, *I and Thou*, pp. 56–61.

30. Some things Buber says suggest more intransigence, more reluctance to accept such a qualification. In particular, his denial that a Thou, as such, can be an object of *Erfahrung* (experience)— though it can be an object of *Erlebnis* (also naturally rendered as "experience" in English)—seems to me best interpreted as a denial that in knowing a Thou as such we can know it implicitly as related to other objects in ways that satisfy Kant's requirements for *Erfahrung* of an object. (See *I and Thou*, p. 55f.) But I doubt that such an extreme abstraction from causal contexts (for instance) yields a coherent conception of knowing a Thou; and Buber does not adhere consistently to it. (Consider what he says we can see about a tree in contemplating it as a Thou: *I and Thou*, p. 58.)

of any comparisons. That is presumably the way in which God loves the divine nature, not from pride of ownership but simply for its character, and not from an interest, competitive or otherwise, in superiority.

4. Hesed

The central theme of our discussion thus far in the chapter has been the particularity that is a feature of love for practically any sort of object. Love's particularity brings with it some of the characteristics of grace, but particularity, by itself, constitutes at most a thin version of grace. In central cases grace will be a type of love for *persons*, and a fuller appreciation of grace's grounding in the nature of love requires a focus on such a central case.

The case I have in mind is a type of love, and grace, that has a central place in the social and religious world of the Hebrew Bible. It goes there by the name of חֶסֶד (*hesed*). חֶסֶד is not the Hebrew word that is linked by translation traditions, by way of the Greek word χάρις (*charis*), to the English word 'grace'. That historic role belongs to חֵן (*hen*), which, like χάρις in secular Greek, signifies a "favor" that can be quite arbitrary and episodic, as Hesed is not. I believe there is substantial scholarly support, however, for the view that "in many respects . . . the developed Christian meaning of grace is more akin to the Hebrew חסד" than to חֵן.[31] For one thing, חֶסֶד, like χάρις in the New Testament and unlike חֵן, is heavily used to characterize God's love.

Like most words in natural languages, חֶסֶד has a range of uses, but it typically expresses a concept of great ethical interest. It is one of the most famously untranslatable words in the Bible, as it signifies an attitude, and a virtue, that have no precise name in English. The King James Version of the Bible renders חֶסֶד commonly with the much-loved coinage 'lovingkindness', and often with 'mercy' (corresponding to the ἔλεος of the most ancient Greek translation), but these terms miss much of the significance of the original. The Revised Standard Version (RSV) commonly uses 'steadfast love' to translate חֶסֶד, taking it to mean "loyal devotion grounded in love which goes beyond legal obligation and can be depended on to the utmost."[32] The long phrase just quoted (not the shorter 'steadfast love') captures quite well the sense that interests me. Writing as a philosopher rather than a biblical scholar, I will use 'Hesed' as an English word, a term of art that signifies a conception I want to develop here, whether or not my Hebrew exegesis is accurate. There are two sides to the conception.

One is that Hesed is a loyal and dependable devotion. חֶסֶד is aptly translated by 'loyalty' in some contexts (e.g., 1 Samuel 20:15 RSV), and usually signifies a factor in an ongoing relationship. Hesed issues in particular acts of kindness, but they are done out of a *commitment* to a person whom one loves, or with whom one has, at least, a valued relationship. This is the aspect of Hesed that is captured by

---

31. Mitton, "Grace," p. 467.
32. Mitton, "Grace," p. 467.

the translation 'steadfast love'. The ongoing relationship need not be a particularly close one. Hesed is of course especially valued in close relationships, but it may be important in any sort of social relationship. Many of the troubles of contemporary American society can be traced to a lack of the Hesed that should obtain between members of different groups in the society whether or not their relations are close.

Commitment is connected with love's particularity. We may doubt love's interest in any individual object where there is not an attachment to the individual that endures for at least some period of time. Commitment is not the only form of attachment to an individual, but it is the most highly valued (or involved in the most highly valued forms), and rightly so.

In the second place, Hesed "goes beyond legal obligation." חֶסֶד is used particularly often to speak of kindnesses (such as forgiveness) to which the agent is bound by no strict duty. That is why 'mercy' is often an apt translation of חֶסֶד, and why it can be seen as a version of grace. Hesed can be demanded in a friendship (1 Samuel 20:14–17), and one can be severely criticized for failing to show Hesed, especially to a benefactor (Judges 8:35). Nevertheless, Hesed involves doing more than one is strictly obliged to do. This is a way (not the only one) in which Hesed's commitment is open-ended. If one does only one's duty, narrowly construed, one may well have failed to show Hesed. One might conceptualize this in Kantian terms by saying that it is an *imperfect duty* to have and show Hesed—that is, a duty to have it and show it in some way or other, though the particular acts that show it are not individually obligatory. That may fit many contexts, but in others, including some cases of forgiveness, and God's love toward creatures, Hesed goes beyond anything that should be demanded as a duty. It is still seen, however, as a virtue or excellence that it is much better to have than to lack.

These two sides of the conception belong together, for a commitment to a person cannot be very full or dependable if it does not go beyond strict obligation. Community quickly breaks down if we do no more than we are obliged to do. What persons need in their relations with others goes far beyond anything that can or should be spelled out in a system of rules of duty. Commitment to a person as such must be open-ended. This point is connected also with love's particularity. If I am committed only to do my duty to you, my commitment seems to be more to duty than to you. In being committed to the person, and not just to appropriate behavior as such, love takes on the character of Hesed. Moreover, the firmness and open-endedness of Hesed's commitment require a readiness for "mercy," for forgiveness in some contexts, and making allowance for weaknesses. It cannot rest on fine calibration or comparative assessment of its object's merit or excellence.[33]

The type of commitment represented by Hesed is intimately connected with personhood or selfhood. In its ideal form it is extravagantly firm and open-ended, grounded in a noncomparative, unmeasured, but not necessarily uncritical valuing of the person. A person is at a minimum someone to whom it makes sense to be

---

33. I think this is true of the dominant conception of חֶסֶד in the Bible, but here I am developing the inner dynamics of my own conception of Hesed rather than engaging in biblical exegesis. And it must be acknowledged that some biblical appeals to חֶסֶד breathe a spirit of "One good turn deserves another," rather than any profound personal commitment (e.g., Joshua 2:12, Judges 1:24).

committed in that way. Fully achieved selfhood involves being committed to one's own life in that way, and typically depends causally on receiving such a commitment from one's parents or primary caregivers.

This form of love responds appropriately to the kind of value that persons have. Its commitment outruns anything that can be justified quantitatively or comparatively by the facts about a person; it can seem crazy in relation to our finitude and imperfection and sheer contingent oddity. Yet human life, deeply experienced, discloses depths that seem to invite nothing less than such commitment. This expresses the ambiguity (in a certain sense) of our relation to the infinite Good. Our value as persons is a mediation or participation of something immeasurably wonderful; yet we are immeasurably far from the divine perfection. This doubly frustrates any attempt to provide a quantitative measure of our likeness or nearness to the divine goodness; it is elusively imaged in us, rather than present in any precise degree.

The concept of Hesed has its historical origin in a society in which ties of family, relations between patron and client, and obligations of gratitude loomed much larger than they do in ours. Nevertheless, its pattern of dependable commitment that is open-ended in its giving, and forgiving but not always undemanding, represents a virtue that is needed in any society, even if ours has not seen fit to give it a name. Is it a virtue that belongs also to God? The writers of the Hebrew Bible had no doubt that it does, and it is hard to disagree with them if we conceive of God's relation to us as personal at all, for Hesed seems to fit the nature of personhood and of love (including its particularity) so excellently that it is hard to exclude it from the perfection of the divine love.

5. Love's Universality

Historically the idea of grace has reassured, but also frightened. If love, divine as well as human, has a particularity that outruns its reasons, we may fear that it will be arbitrary. If it is not carefully proportioned to the degree of merit of its object, we may fear that it will be unfair. Such concerns have led many to think of "the kingdom of justice," in Albert Camus's words, as "opposed to the kingdom of grace."[34] There is much in the history of theology to feed these fears. An emphasis on grace has sometimes been linked with a doctrine of "election" according to which God has chosen some humans for salvation, by free grace, while (explicitly or implicitly) choosing others for eternal damnation, though all were sinners and the lucky elect *deserved* salvation, and God's love, no more than the miserable reprobate.

These concerns are connected with a fundamental issue in human ethics. About whom are we to care? Must we care about all people? Or is it enough to care about those whom we happen to like, or with whom we have particular social bonds— our families and friends, the members of our tribe or nation or church? Much evidence suggests that human moral consciousness began with the more restricted sort of ethical concern. Almost all developed ethical thought today holds more univer-

34. Camus, *The Rebel*, p. 103.

salist or cosmopolitan principles, but the grounds of the cosmopolitanism are usually not among the better developed parts of the ethical system. It is not surprising
that questions pertaining to boundaries of moral concern, such as those regarding
justice between nations and the moral status of fetuses and nonhuman animals, are
among the most persistently difficult and controversial of ethical issues.

In developing a conception of ideal love, and of divine love, most of us would
probably think it should be universalistic, including love for all persons, and perhaps for all creatures. But can we argue for the universality of divine love without
compromising its character as grace, and the freedom of God in loving? I will try to
show here that we can.

The first point to be made in this argument is that love's particularity does not
need an election in which anyone is shut out. Our competitive souls tempt us to
think otherwise. There have doubtless been many for whom the idea of grace would
have been less reassuring, and who would have felt less loved by God, if they had
not thought of themselves as among "the chosen of the Lord," in a sense that excluded many other people as less favored by God. To suppose that the significance
of God's love for oneself depends on such exclusion of others, however, is to think
of love in precisely the sort of comparative terms that love's particularity rules out.
If God's love for you is a matter of God's attention to and regard for you individually, why should it be enhanced by God's loving someone else less? To be sure, human
lovers have limited capacity for attention, which leads us to compete for their attention. The kind of love that humans can and should have for all God's creatures,
or even for all people, is very thin, and lacking in particularity with regard to most
of its objects; but divine capacities are presumably not limited in such a way that
attention to one creature would diminish the attention God could give to another.

There may nonetheless remain worries about the *grounds* that a doctrine of grace
would or would not allow for the universality of divine love. My conception of love's
particularity seems to exclude one sort of guarantee of fairness or universalism, in
that it implies that love in general, and God's love in particular, must involve motives that are distinguishable from any commitment to general principles. Just as
love for anyone, or anything, in particular must be more than an expression of interest in some value more general than the particular object of love, so love for anyone, or anything, in particular must be more than an expression of commitment to
any general principles. This might lead us to fear that a God of grace, or simply of
love, would not be as fully guided as we should wish by the principles that are commonly seen as the firmest support of fairness, impartiality, and wide horizons of moral
concern.

From the supposition that God has motives distinct from commitment to such
principles, of course, it does not follow that God will act, or love, contrary to them.
Perhaps I can offer grounds for universality of the divine love that are consistent
with my account of it as grace. Such grounds might be sought, first of all, in the
reasons for loving that I allow that God has; but our pickings will be slim here. I
can't say that God has some reason to love all creatures, and no reason not to love
any; for God has some reason not to love any of us, in our sins and imperfections.
It does fit my conception of grace to argue that God has essentially the same kind
of reasons both to love and not to love any one of us, and that God's love is not

grounded in more and less; so there is no reason to expect God to pick and choose. But such reasoning about reasons is not a strong proof of universality, given that love in its particularity goes beyond any reasons the lover has for it.

A more promising line of argument might run as follows. It seems to us intuitively that a more universal love is more *admirable* than a less universal love; loving *every* creature is more admirable, in a being that is capable of it, than loving some and not others. Indeed, the idea of loving every one (in an excellent way) seems to express a pinnacle of excellence in loving. Hence love for every one is plausibly ascribed to God, the maximally admirable being. I am inclined to buy this argument.

This does not imply that we all (or any of us) *deserve* to be loved by God, but rather that loving all is most fitting to God's magnificence. What is magnificent here is particular love for each, not embrace of a general principle under which particulars happen to fall. One can also say on this account that the universality of divine love is grounded in the overflowing abundance of God's love, which is a major part of its magnificence.

A parental analogy may be helpful here. We think parents ought to love *all* their children. We may sometimes say they should love all of them *equally*, but such quantification is not really appropriate. What we hope to avoid is not all differences in love, but the kind of differences that make it impossible to avoid comparing the loves in quantitative terms. The ideal parent is not calibrating love to each child, but loving each with full particularity. There is some sense in which each should be "everything" to the parent, though of course that cannot be literally true. In Buber's terms, each child should sometimes "fill the [parent's] firmament." The parents (if any) whose caring (equally) about their children is just an expression of devotion to an ideal of parenthood are not fully loving the children, and are certainly not ideal parents. But it remains the case that ideal parents would love *all* their children. The ground for this would lie mainly in the "parent heart," rather than in the excellence of the children, though of course the parents would find excellences to prize in the children. If we suppose that all creatures stand to God in something analogous to the relation of children to parents, the inference to the universality of divine love (supposed maximally excellent) is obvious.

This argument favors grounding universal love in the divine nature, and that may give rise to theological concerns about limiting the freedom of God's grace. God's *grace* may be compared with God's *justice*. Theologians have generally agreed that God's justice is universal, exceptionless; but God's grace has often been thought not to be universal. This is understandable. We think humans are obliged to be just in every case without exception, but grace seems more optional, as does love. In fact, we are *unable* to love everyone, except in a fairly thin sense that falls far short of the fullness of love. Should we say then that God's justice is more surely guaranteed by the divine nature than God's grace?

That would suggest or imply that grace is less firmly a part of God's goodness—and of goodness in general—than justice; and I see no compelling reason to accept such a suggestion. Let us agree that there is *no obligation* to love that is laid on God, from outside, so to speak, by the nature or character of creatures. Many theologians and philosophers would add that there is no such obligation, grounded in the nature or situation of creatures, or even in their relation to God, for God to be *just* to them; but let us set that issue aside here and assume, for the sake of argument, that God is obliged to be just. It does not follow that grace is implied any less surely or less universally than justice by God's nature or character, nor that the metaphysical modality of God's grace is any different from that of God's justice. If God has a moral obligation to be just, that is a moral modality quite distinct from the metaphysical necessity that may belong to God's justice—as is shown by the fact that we certainly do have a moral obligation to be just but our justice certainly is not metaphysically necessary. God's grace may therefore have the same metaphysical modality as God's justice even if they differ in moral modality. If so, then love, and indeed grace, are as firmly a part of goodness as justice. That in turn implies that something that is not morally obligatory flows as surely from the nature of goodness as something that is obligatory. I believe that is correct; the fulfillment of obligation is only one branch of goodness, as will be discussed in detail in chapter 10.

I am inclined indeed to hold that the metaphysical modality of God's graciousness is the same as that of any of the other attributes that constitute in fact God's goodness. In chapter 1, section 5, I stated that I am inclined to think that that modality is metaphysical necessity, and that that is compatible with the freedom that should be ascribed to God. That can apply to grace too, as an attribute of God, and to its extending to all actual creatures. It does not follow that particular acts of grace are necessary (as I said in chapter 1 that particular acts manifesting the divine goodness should not be viewed as necessary). There may be a wide variety of acts in each case that would satisfy the divine graciousness. In this respect the divine grace may be freer than the divine justice. That is, the range of acts that would satisfy the divine graciousness in a particular case may typically be wider than the range of acts that would satisfy the divine justice in a particular case. That probably cannot be proved, but we may speculate with some plausibility that it is true.

7

DEVOTION

In chapters 5 and 6 we have evaluated types of love primarily with regard to their suitability for inclusion in *divine* love as a supreme standard of excellence in love. In the present chapter we turn our attention to the articulation of a motivational ideal for *human* beings.

1. The Ethics of Motives

One of the most interesting developments in moral philosophy of the last three decades is the growth of interest in what is sometimes called "agent ethics"—that is, in the branch of ethical theory primarily concerned, not with the kinds of action we ought to perform, but rather with the kinds of persons it would be good to be. I believe that what and whom one loves or cares about, and how, is the most important factor in determining what kind of person one is, ethically speaking. We may refer to the part of agent ethics that deals with this factor as "the ethics of motives." It is still an underdeveloped part of moral philosophy. The lion's share of the attention that has been paid to agent ethics has gone to the theory of virtues and vices— that is, to the ethics of traits of character. These are not unrelated topics. Appropriate motives are essential to virtue. But motives are not the same as traits of character, which are more enduring and more general than many motives. Love for an individual person is an example of a motive that is too particular to be a trait of character (or, hence, a virtue or vice), though one may hope it will be enduring.

A good motive is one that contributes to its possessor's being a good person. What makes a motive good? There are two main approaches to answering this question. One focuses on the instrumental value of the motive, the other on a more intrinsic excellence. I favor the second approach, but I will begin with a short discussion of the first, which I have elsewhere called "motive utilitarianism."[1]

The motive utilitarian evaluates motives by the utility of having them. The better of two motives, on this view, is the one whose consequences are better. The relevant consequences are the consequences of *having* the motive, which include the consequences of acting on the motive (if one does), but may also include much more, since motivational states affect life in other ways besides being acted on.[2] One might expect a utilitarian to think the best of motives is the motive of utility—that is, the desire (or even the determination) to act always in the way that will have the best consequences; but that may not be the motive with the highest *instrumental* value if, as Sidgwick plausibly claims, "Happiness [general as well as individual] is likely to be better attained if the extent to which we set ourselves consciously to aim at it be carefully restricted."[3]

Someone might wish to argue that the motive of utility must be the best motive, because it aims at the best result. In so arguing, one might remain an *act* utilitarian, evaluating *acts* by their utility; but one would have abandoned *motive* utilitarianism. For one would be evaluating the motive of utility, not by the value of its consequences, but rather by the value of the end at which it aims. The latter way of evaluating a motive is a prime example of the more intrinsic, less instrumental sort of evaluation that is the principal alternative to motive utilitarianism. It is an aspect of our very limited control over our lives that the value of the consequences of having a motive can be quite different from the value of the end at which it aims.

There is no doubt that the value we assign to motives is affected by our view of the value of their consequences, and reasonably so. We might not set so high a value on caring about truthfulness, for example, if it were not so important for communication, and hence for human life; and the sociable desire for the company of one's friend would probably seem less desirable if it were not thought likely to contribute to the happiness of both parties. Nevertheless, I do not believe that the ethical goodness of motives can plausibly be seen as resting solely or primarily on the value of their consequences. Certainly the value of motives is not in any simple way a function of their utility. The value of a love of art, for example, cannot be explained very well in terms of its utility. A pure love of art is a good motive in a way that healthful tastes, such as a taste for exercise or a distaste for fatty foods, are not, though the consequences of latter may well be at least as good as those of the former.

The known utility of a motive does not of itself suffice to make the motive a credit to its possessor. Your distaste for fatty foods may speak well for you if it reflects an interest in good health, or a responsiveness to other people's benevolent

---

1. Adams, "Motive Utilitarianism."
2. This is argued in detail in Adams, "Motive Utilitarianism," pp. 470ff.
3. Sidgwick, *Methods of Ethics*, p. 405.

interest in your health. But apart from such connections with other characteristics, it says little or nothing about what kind of person you are, ethically speaking. If it is a matter of taste, a distaste for fatty foods is no better a motive ethically than a distaste for green clothing, despite its greater utility.

I believe that a more plausible way of evaluating motives must depend heavily on less instrumental factors that constitute excellence of the motives.[4] The most obvious of these factors is the value of the end at which the motive aims, but the way in which the motive aims at it is also important. Mere tastes are rarely, if ever, as excellent as loves can be. Loves are more serious, engage more of the self, and involve attending with care to better and worse ways of relating to the object. Still the value of the end is an essential determinant of the excellence of the motive. Good motives seek good ends and not bad ones.

This chapter will explore the possibility of organizing the ethics of motives around an ideal of love for the good as such. On my theistic interpretation of the good, this will be an ideal of devotion or love for God. Theists have commonly embraced such a motivational ideal. It is commended in words as sacred to Judaism as any text can be, which were singled out by Jesus as expressing the first commandment of all:

> Hear, O Israel: the LORD our God, the LORD is one; and you shall love the LORD your God with all your heart, and with all your soul, and with all your might. (Deuteronomy 6:4–5)

The repeated 'all' in these lines presents a decisive question for the interpretation of religious devotion. Is the consuming character of love for God to exclude other appealing motives, or to integrate them into itself? I will come down firmly on the integrative side. This is the view of most theistic thinkers; and even an interpreter of religion as critical of traditional theism as John Dewey found the distinction between religion and morality in the integrative character of religious devotion. "The religious," he wrote, "is 'morality touched with emotion' only when the ends of moral conviction arouse emotions that are not only intense but are actuated and supported by ends so inclusive that they unify the self." And Dewey added that "this comprehensive attitude . . . is much broader than anything indicated by 'moral' in its usual sense."[5]

2. The Fragmentation of Value

Ethical integration is a controversial subject in contemporary philosophy. The idea of "the fragmentation of value,"[6] as Thomas Nagel has called it, has sparked some of the most interesting recent writing in ethics. It presents the picture of a plurality

4. I thus reject motive utilitarianism more decisively than I did when I first discussed it; cf. Adams, "Motive Utilitarianism," p. 481.

5. Dewey, *A Common Faith*, p. 22f.

6. This is the title of chapter 9 of Nagel, *Mortal Questions*. Related ideas are found in Williams, *Moral Luck*, chaps. 1, 2, and 5, and in the discussion of "admirable immorality," in Slote, *Goods and Virtues*, chap. 4.

of evaluative standpoints, each with some claim on our appreciation and concern, which form no ordered system. Among them morality must compete on equal terms with the others, there being no presiding, overarching standpoint from which it can be judged that morality "ought" always to win, according to some participants in the discussion.

At least in a general way, this is an old idea. Over half a century ago, Walter Lippmann characterized "modern man" as one for whom "each ideal is supreme within a sphere of its own. There is no point of reference outside which can determine the relative value of competing ideals." Quoting Lippmann, H. Richard Niebuhr made the apt theological comment, "Polytheism of this sort is no peculiarly modern problem."[7]

Contemporary support for the fragmentation of value is rooted largely in reaction against what might be called "excessive high-mindedness"—that is, against moral and religious ideals that seem to many to leave too little room for interests not obviously and narrowly moral or religious.[8] I am sympathetic with this reaction, but it confronts me with an obvious challenge. Can love for God provide an integrating principle for our motives and values without an oppressive excess of high-mindedness? This is really the central question of the present chapter. In sections 2 and 3 it will be discussed in relation to the challenge posed by the advocates of the fragmentation of value; and in sections 4 to 7, in relation to the similar challenge posed by the particularity of love.

One recent defense of a fragmentation of value that has many points of contact with my concerns is Susan Wolf's essay "Moral Saints."[9] It is an exception to the prevailing neglect of the subject of devotion in contemporary moral philosophy. Wolf criticizes the ideal of "maximal devotion to [the] interests" of morality.[10] It will be simplest to follow her in using the word 'morality' and its cognates in a rather narrow sense, in which maximal devotion to the interests of morality will mean a life maximally "dominated by a commitment to improving the well-being of others or of society as a whole,"[11] to which I think Wolf would let us add a commitment to the *rights* of others without losing the specifically moral focus.

Wolf argues that it can be good *not* to aspire to such devotion. For in a life so dominated by humanitarian concern and endeavor there will not be room for many other human excellences. There will not normally be time and energy to pursue a devoted commitment to excellence in art, for instance, or in athletics or philosophy. And the "moral saint" will not be able to give those other interests the kind of

---

7. Niebuhr, *Radical Monotheism and Western Culture*, p. 31, quoting from Lippmann, *A Preface to Morals*, p. 111.

8. Though we should not overlook the similarity of the problem to that with which Henry Sidgwick concluded his great book: that in case "of a recognized conflict between self-interest and duty, practical reason, being divided against itself, would cease to be a motive on either side" (Sidgwick, *Methods of Ethics*, p. 508).

9. Wolf ("Moral Saints," p. 437 n. 5) acknowledges the influence of Nagel's essay on "The Fragmentation of Value."

10. Wolf, "Moral Saints," p. 435.

11. Wolf, "Moral Saints," p. 420.

priority in her life that they must have if love for them is truly to flower. Wolf argues that we have reason to admire many who have devoted themselves to such nonmoral excellences, and to be glad that they have done so. She does not exactly deny that extremes of humanitarian dedication can be wonderful in their own way; but she claims that we can appropriately choose for ourselves, and hope that our loved ones will choose, ideals that are incompatible with maximal devotion to the interests of morality. In most of this Wolf seems to me to be right.

In agreeing so far with Wolf I am resisting a tendency in much ethical thought, both religious and secular, that I regard as moralistic in a bad sense and overly centered in personal relations. This tendency played a prominent part in ethical conceptions that I formed in my youth, so that it was hard for me to see how it could be ethically good to be interested in beauty or truth, art or philosophy, for their own sake, since such interests were not interests in persons. This implication came to seem to me humanly intolerable, however—the more so the more clearly I recognized, for example, that no serious intellectual enterprise can be pursued with honesty and integrity without caring about the attainment of truth for its own sake. Indeed, it seems that even personal relations can hardly be developed with honesty and integrity if we do not care about truth for its own sake.

Such a narrowly moralistic conception of good motives is not just humanly intolerable; it suggests much too small a conception of the good, and of God, if we conceive of the Good itself as God. I have argued in chapter 5, section 5, that God should be conceived as appreciating the values that are the objects of intellectual and aesthetic interests, as caring about them for their own sake—and even as loving strange things that we do not begin to understand how to care about. Important as it is to be good to people, the divine goodness is not so cozy as to be confined to that, but is rather of fearsome immensity. With an adequately large conception of God's interests, it should be possible to unite devotion to God with an interest in any good thing for its own sake.

Wolf's targets are primarily secular rather than theological. She does not mean to criticize misconceptions of God. Her critique addresses a different error, which I, however, still regard as a religious mistake. There is for many (and not the least admirable) among us a strong temptation to make morality into a substitute for religion, and in so doing to make morality the object of a devotion that is maximal, at least in aspiration, and virtually religious in character. But morality, conceived as narrowly as Wolf conceives of it, is not a suitable object of religious devotion. Maximal devotion to it would not only be oppressive, as Wolf argues. From a religious point of view it would also be idolatry. The conclusion I draw is that an appropriate object for maximal or religious devotion should be larger than morality, though it should also provide a basis for a strong commitment to morality. I think, of course, that it should be God.

Wolf, however, seems to draw the conclusion that we should live without maximal devotion altogether. I have quoted her definition of "the moral point of view." She contrasts it with what she calls "the point of view of individual perfection," which is "the point of view from which we consider what kinds of lives are good lives, and what kinds of persons it would be good for ourselves and others to be." "Each point of view," she says, "takes account of, and, in a sense, subsumes the other."[12] The perfection of each individual is one, but only one, of the goods to be taken into account from the moral point of view; and moral goodness is a very important excellence, but not the only one, to be considered from the point of view of individual perfection. She is prepared to grant that "moral value" is "an important, even the most important, kind of value we attend to in evaluating and improving ourselves and our world"; but she denies that our values should be understood as "a hierarchical system with morality at the top."[13] For she does not think that it is necessarily best, let alone obligatory, to pursue other values only insofar as is morally best. Is there, then, some other evaluative perspective, presiding over the moral and perfectionist points of view, from which we should judge in each case which should receive the precedence? Unable to see how any theory could articulate such a viewpoint, Wolf suggests that "at some point, both in our philosophizing and in our lives, we must be willing to raise normative questions from a perspective that is unattached to any particular well-ordered system of values."[14]

What is disturbing about such an idea of the fragmentation of value is not merely that we may be faced with hard and painful choices about which we are bound to have conflicting feelings. That is just a fact of life, and no plausible theory will deny it. The deeply disturbing feature of the proposed or threatened fragmentation is the suggestion that some such conflicts are between types of value so fundamental and so incommensurable that there is no well-defined point of view from which one can do justice to all the competing values.

3. The Integration of Value

The problem of integration we must face if we are to overcome this fragmentation has both a subjective and an objective side. I begin with the subjective side. Subjectively the problem is about the integration of a person's motives. It is healthy as well as inevitable to have motives that sometimes conflict. We could be immune to inner conflict only by being insensitive to many of the values and concerns that appropriately engage our interest and sympathy. But personal integration is also an important ideal. We rightly want to be able to act out of a consistent and coherent sense of our own character and interests. To have inner conflicts is not necessarily to be at war with oneself; the difference is important, but not easy to explain.

If I am at war with myself, I will sometimes have no better explanation for a decision than to say, "There was a fight in me, and this side won." The two sides in me will look at each other with unsympathetic hostility, and perhaps with a sort of incomprehension. For from the perspective of the motives that favor one side in the conflict, no value can be seen on the other side.

If I am at peace with myself, I may still have conflicting motives, but they will be related in such a way that each, so to speak, can acknowledge the others as good

12. Wolf, "Moral Saints," p. 437.
13. Wolf, "Moral Saints," p. 438.
14. Wolf, "Moral Saints," p. 439.

and as belonging to the same family. I will not have to deplore, with part of my character, another part of my character. Few if any of us, I imagine, have fully attained such inner harmony, but it seems a desirable part of a motivational ideal.

It places certain requirements on the way in which I make decisions and settle any inner conflicts. I need an inclusive perspective; ideally, none of my motives would need to be simply suppressed—though the viability of that ideal doubtless depends on my *not* having certain motives. And if I am not to be just a battleground on which now one side wins and now another, I need a basis for saying what is most important to me. Must this be a perspective that is "attached," in Wolf's terminology, to a "well-ordered system of values"? There certainly need not be any algorithm or set of rules that would predict my preferences and decisions. But my values must form a system at least in the sense that my motives have enough kinship among themselves for me to be at peace with myself in the way I have indicated. The system must have enough order to it that there can be facts about what is most important to me, and a basis of comparison of my different values. And I must be attached enough to the system to have a reasonable constancy over time in the pattern of what I care about, and how much; otherwise I become again a fluctuating battleground, and it will be hard to speak of character or integrity in my case.

My basis for weighing different practical considerations might conceivably be a stable but purely subjective pattern of preferences. But we commonly seek a more objective basis of evaluation. This may indeed be important to the stability of our motivational integration. Excessive reliance on values that we regard as merely subjective may give us too little basis for constancy of purpose, and sap the will to live when the springs of desire run dry.[15] We need not suppose that there is just one decision that would be right for anyone in our situation; but it may be important to see our decisions against a background of objective values and of motives that would be objectively good for us and for others to have. And we want to know what those values and motives would be.

This brings us to the objective side of the problem. Is there an objective criterion of the value of motives to which we can appropriately turn at this point? I argued in section 1 that the *instrumental* value, or utility, of motives does not yield an adequate criterion of the ethical value of motives. The most obvious alternative to utility as a general criterion of the value of motives, I have suggested, is to appeal to the value of their objects, the value of the ends they seek. Our esteem for the most obviously moral motives fits this criterion well. Caring about the rights and interests of other people is a good motive even when it does not have good consequences, because it is a valuing of something good. Conscientiousness is a good motive to the extent that it is rooted in regard for genuine goods,[16] but not to the extent that it is an expression of an irrational superego, or of devotion to a structure of evil such as the Nazi death machine. More controversially, perhaps, a pure love of art, as I have suggested, is a good motive, though not a straightforwardly moral one; and

---

15. This is one of the classic problems of the "aesthetic" life, as described in the works of Kierkegaard, especially *Either/Or*, vol. 1.

16. How conscientiousness is to be rooted in regard for genuine goods is a major subject for discussion in chapters 10 and 11.

the most obvious reason for the value of the motive is the excellence of the art. This
will not be the whole story about the value of motives; as I have already acknowledged, their instrumental value is not totally irrelevant, and such factors as the difference between loves and mere tastes rightly affect our evaluation. Still the value of
the motives' objects seems the best place to start in looking for a perspective on our
motives that is both objective and integrative.

Is there a comprehensive point of view from which we can make sense of valuing motives on the basis of the value of their objects? I think so. It is a point of view
from which we value *goods*—human beings and their health and happiness, but also
more impersonal goods or excellences such as beauty—and perhaps also the good
of nonhuman creatures. And it is a point of view from which we seek not merely a
useful instrument but an *ally*—someone who will value those goods, or some of them,
with us. Whether we count it a "moral" point of view will depend on how broadly
we construe 'moral'; but I doubt that much is at stake in that issue for a theistic
ethics whose loyalties find their ultimate focus in God rather than in morality as
such.[17]

This conception of the evaluative perspective is supported by attitudes that are
connected with the evaluation of motives. We admire good motives, but our attitude toward someone whose "heart is in the right place" is not exhausted by admiration. There is also a sense of social union, or aspiration to social union, with such
a person; our feeling about her is typically a friendly feeling. We view the good motive
as rendering her a friend or ally—or perhaps more accurately, an ally or potential
ally insofar as we too love the good. It coheres with this perspective also that we
regard love for aesthetic goods, for example, as less essential to being a good person
than caring about honest dealing and the good of other persons. Some good alli-

---

17. The issue is clearly important to Nagel. Having proposed the idea of "the fragmentation of
value," in an article of that title, he has more recently argued, in his book *The View from Nowhere*,
that we can reasonably hope that the fragmentation of value can be overcome from a distinctly moral
point of view. He now rejects what he describes as Wolf's belief that "morality cannot be judge in its
own case, and that we should expect that there will sometimes be good reasons for resisting its claims."
His morality would include principles or intuitions limiting its own claims, indicating when it is (morally) permissible to be guided by nonmoral reasons. He argues that morality can limit itself in this way
both because it seems that people in general are likelier to be better off living under a morality that
permits them often to pursue nonmoral ends, and because there is a "threshold, hard to define,"
beyond which "it is unreasonable to expect [the sort of beings we are] to sacrifice themselves," and
the nonmoral ends about which they care deeply, to the end of morality (pp. 200–203; quotes from
p. 202).

I largely agree with these claims of Nagel's. Morality can limit itself as he describes, and principles or judgments about when it is permissible to give precedence to one's nonmoral interests deserve a place in morality. But his argument is limited in two respects that are important for our present
purpose. It is concerned almost wholly with drawing a boundary between the obligatory and the optional; and it is focused on the evaluation of "specific, isolable practical decisions," as Wolf notes about
her earlier paper; whereas she is more concerned with "individual personal ideals," and hence focuses
more widely on the evaluation of character, motivation, and pattern of life (Wolf, "Moral Saints,"
p. 437 n. 5). In accordance with my aims in this chapter, I have focused on the evaluation of motives,
and on the nature of good motives, rather than of obligatory motives. I assume that some motives are
good that are not morally required.

ances depend on shared love for aesthetic goods, but no good alliance is possible without a measure of conscientiousness and benevolence.

In asking, from this point of view, what motives would be good ones for us to have, we are asking what motives would make us allies of those who love the good. These motives will be ways of loving the good. If we add, as I think theists should, that the Good itself is to be identified with God, we are at least close to the conclusion that good motives are forms of love for God, or at least of implicit love for God.

I have sketched a generous point of view, and have doubtless oversimplified in doing so. Those who love goods are not all allies in practice. Sometimes they are rivals for the same good, and sometimes they are devoted to alternative goods that compete for limited resources and opportunities. Thus their very love for goods can put them in conflict with each other. This must be acknowledged; but if we are talking about love for the Good as such, and about good motivation, we must insist on the larger validity of the generous point of view. In caring about the good of my philosophy department I am in competition in various ways with other departments in my university and with philosophy departments at other universities; such competition is not excluded by the generous point of view. But if I do not see those other departments in principle and more fundamentally as allies in the pursuit of philosophy and in the mission of the university, then I have lost perspective and my love for my department is not clearly a good motive and not clearly a manifestation of love for the Good as such. Similarly and more generally, the value of our motives, and their belonging to love for the Good, can be compromised by a failure to appreciate goods and loves that are not part of our own calling; such a failure can be quite evil, or can lead to evil.

4. The Problem of Total Devotion

It is no easy task to flesh out the idea that all good motives are (at least implicitly) forms of love for God. How could a love for art, an aspiration to intellectual honesty, a regard for the well-being of one's neighbor, be forms of love for God? The history of religion gives reason to wonder whether the ideal of a life organized around devotion to God is any less oppressive than that of a maximal devotion to morality, any more compatible with a wide range of values and motives.

The hardest question here is not whether the theistic ideal must denigrate aesthetic and intellectual values, for example, in the name of narrowly moral concerns. Much theistic religion has been narrowly moralistic in that way, but such narrowness is not essential to theism. If God is creator and lover of beauty as well as of people, and the standard of nonmoral as well as moral value, it would seem as possible in principle to relate nonmoral as moral values to love for God.

The really hard question is whether the sort of maximal devotion to God demanded by theism is compatible with love for anything finite at all.[18] If we are to

---

18. I have discussed this question at greater length in Adams, "The Problem of Total Devotion." In parts of this chapter I am borrowing material from that earlier paper, although the ideas expressed here are in some ways different.

love God with *all* our heart and soul and strength, will any room be left in our hearts for the love of anything else (such as our neighbor)? An integrative ideal of theistic devotion will seek room for love of finite goods *within* love for God rather than in competition with it; but how?

This would be no problem, but a verbal sophistry, if 'with all your heart' here were a synonym for 'wholeheartedly' and signified only an unconflicted enthusiasm, as it sometimes does. But religious devotion is more than wholeheartedness or unconflicted enthusiasm. It is supposed to occupy a person's life so fully that nothing is left outside the realm in which it reigns. And so it must, if it is to provide a principle for integrating *all* one's motives. The problem, then, is how a genuine and serious interest in something finite (such as love for one's neighbor) can be a part of one's life that at the same time expresses love for God. Assuming that many such interests in finite things are commendable, how can all good motives be forms of love for God?

One of the more influential approaches to this problem in Western religious history—perhaps the most influential—was proposed by St. Augustine of Hippo, and has often provided a rationale for asceticism in concrete programs of religious devotion. It turns on the subordination of means to end. Augustine distinguishes between *enjoying* something and *using* it. "For to enjoy is to cling with love to some thing for its own sake [*propter se ipsam*]; whereas to use is to apply what is used to the obtaining of that which you love (provided it ought to be loved)."[19] What is used, in other words, is treated as a means to the end of enjoyment. Augustine introduces this distinction in order to make the point that God is to be enjoyed but other things, God's finite creatures, ought only to be used. He explicitly applies this schema to the love of one's neighbor:

> For it is commanded us to love each other; but it is a question whether man is to be loved by man for his own sake or for the sake of something else. For if for his own sake, we enjoy him; if for the sake of something else, we use him. But it seems to me that he is to be loved for the sake of something else. For as for what should be loved for its own sake, the blessed life consists in that. . . . But cursed is he who puts his hope in man.[20]

This is not a successful solution to the problem, because it does not allow for anything that really deserves the name of *love* of one's neighbor, or of any other finite thing. It says that we are to care about our neighbor—about our neighbor's good and our relations with our neighbor—not for her own sake but only as a means to our own enjoyment of God or some other ulterior end that is involved in love for God. But what is really loved must be loved for its own sake, as I argued in chap-

19. Augustine, *De doctrina Christiana*, I, iv, 4.

20. Augustine, *De doctrina Christiana*, I, xxii, 20. There are passages in Augustine's works that suggest a more attractive conception of the relation between neighbor-love and devotion to God; but what I present in the text is, so far as I know, the most clearly articulated and the most influential of his views on this subject. His views are discussed much more fully in Adams, "The Problem of Total Devotion," pp. 171–74.

ter 6, section 1. Where something is regarded only as a means or instrument, we can say that we "value" it, but not that we "love" it. I do not *love* my car, for example, unless it means something to me that transcends its resale value and its usefulness for transportation. Similarly, if I do not care about my neighbor's well-being, or any relationship with him, except because I believe it will help me to enjoy God as I desire, I do not love my neighbor. Nor do I love art or philosophy or any other finite good if I do not love it for its own sake.

A program for the integration of motives need not be theistic to offend in this way against love's particularity. Plato's program for the ascent of Eros to the Beautiful in the *Symposium* offends in the same way, as we also saw in chapter 6, section 1. An extremely duty-oriented version of Wolf's "moral saint," who would not care about anything except as a way or means of fulfilling her duty, would likewise fail to love anything but duty.

The fault, in these ways of trying to integrate all good motives into devotion to a supreme good, lies in their *teleological* structure. That is, it lies in the attempt to integrate motives and values by treating all other goods as mere *means* or *ways* to one supreme Good. It is principally in that way, as I argued in chapter 6, that love's particularity does not allow its objects to be related to more general values. We also saw there, however, that this does not prevent particular objects from being loved in some sense "for" their goodness.

5. Love for the Good as Organizing Principle

There seem to be people who are quite integrated motivationally but who do love particular persons, and other particular goods, for their own sake. This suggests that teleological subordination is not the only possible integrative principle for the organization of motives. There are in fact others. One of the most important is suggested by our discussion of reasons for love in chapter 6, section 3.

I argued there that particular persons and things can be loved for their good qualities, which can provide *reasons* for loving them, and that that does not imply that love's particular objects are being valued as ways or means to a more general goodness. Part of that argument was that in loving, liking, or prizing something for a good quality, one does not necessarily have a more general interest in that quality, and that where one does have a more general interest in the quality, the general interest is often best understood as a mere generalization on one's valuing particular instances of the quality, or sometimes as a disposition to value particular instances. The case in which one has a fairly general disposition to value instances of a good quality is the case that interests me in the present context.

As I argued before, such a disposition does not interfere with love's particularity because it does not "infect" the content of the attitudes it engenders toward particulars in the way that teleological subordination does. In valuing a particular for the sake of an ulterior end, one values the particular as a way or means to that end; the value one sets on the ulterior end, and its more fundamental status, are part of the content of one's attitude toward the particular. In valuing a particular because of a disposition to value things with certain qualities, however, one may perfectly well value the particular as an end in itself; and a valuing of the relevant qualities more generally need not be part of the content of one's attitude toward the particular. In saving money for a down payment on a house, your teleologically structured interest in the money includes (as more important) an interest in an ulterior end (the house) that is distinct from the money. But if Romeo's love for Juliet is partly caused by a disposition to love a woman with the shape of nose she has, it does not follow that an interest in that attribute as it might be possessed by *other* women is any part of his interest in Juliet. The scope of the disposition, in other words, is more general than the scope of the attitudes it is a disposition to acquire.

A good person will have a general disposition to value things that are good (and not to value the badness of anything as such). This does not mean that she will actually love every good thing that crosses her path in life; that would be beyond the physical and psychic resources of mere mortals. But she will have a quite general disposition that will blossom into love for some good things, and liking for others, and at least respect for most good things that catch her attention. These attitudes resulting from her disposition will be valuings of particular goods. She may also have attitudes toward goodness in general, but that is another matter. Her disposition to value good things is not as such an attitude toward goodness in general (though it may be connected with such attitudes), because it is not an attitude at all, but just a disposition.

Not being an attitude toward goodness in general, such a disposition will not constitute love, in the fullest sense, for goodness in general—though someone who has it may well be said, in a looser sense, to "love goodness." Certainly such a disposition would not constitute a very robust love for the transcendent Good itself (if there is such a thing) or for God (if God is the Good itself), precisely because the attitudes it engenders are attitudes toward particular finite goods. A general disposition to value particular good things would go quite a long way, however, toward integrating one's motivational system in an obvious way around the Good. If God is the Good itself, and if finite things are good by resembling or imaging God, then God will be, at least implicitly, the focus around which one's motives are organized, to the extent that one is moved by a disposition to value things that are good.

Because of the particularity of all the full-blown interests that it involves, we may still hesitate to speak of this integration of motives as a form of even implicit devotion to God or to the good. In real life, however, and certainly in a motivational ideal, the disposition to value particular good things is not likely to be unaccompanied by more general valuings and interests. Indeed, the disposition is likely to be sustained by attitudes toward the good as such. Unless one is quite unselfconscious about the structure and patterns of one's motivational system, one can hardly remain content with nothing more general than a disposition to value particular objects of certain types. One will form more general attitudes toward the types, and one will evaluate structural features of one's motivational system, though this will not necessarily make one's attitude toward particulars any less particular. Such general attitudes are important for personal integration, and without them we may not find adequate meaning in our lives as wholes, or in our selfhood, even if our particular pursuits are animated by lively particular interests.

Ideally at any rate, the good person will be *for* the good, or goodness, as such. That will be one of her more general attitudes. It will be distinct from her attitudes toward good particulars, but it will affect them. It will lead her to count qualities as reasons for liking or loving something, for instance, if she judges the qualities to be good. That will not necessarily cause her to love (or even to like) possessors of all such qualities, but it will surely affect her dispositions with regard to liking and loving particulars.

One of the most important ways in which a general attitude of being for the Good, or for goodness, as such, may be expected to affect our motivational dispositions is by way of *higher order preferences*. I take the liberty of using 'preferences' here to signify desires and aversions, wishes, likes and dislikes, and similar attitudes of favor and disfavor, whether or not they involve rejection of an alternative; and by 'higher order preferences' I mean preferences that take other actual or possible preferences of one's own as the object of their concern. The latter preferences, as objects of the higher order preferences, may be known as "first-order preferences." Higher order preferences play an important part in our lives. You may wish that you did not want to smoke, or that you liked healthful vegetables more than rich desserts. You may be glad that you like your job. You may aspire to be a person who cares about other people. You may want, and you may even be committed, to go on loving a certain person.

It is important, for preserving the particularity of first-order preferences, that the content and the teleological structure (if any) of a higher order preference is typically different from that of the first-order preference that is its object. My end in wanting to have altruistic desires may be to be a better person; but if I do have genuinely altruistic desires, *their* end will be the good of other people, not my own improvement. If you want to like healthful vegetables, that higher order preference probably has health as an ulterior end. That is, you value the liking of the vegetables as a means to health. If you actually come to like the vegetables as you wish to do, however, that first-order preference will be a matter of liking the taste of the vegetables for its own sake, and not as a means to anything else. When you liked rich desserts more than the vegetables but wished that you preferred the vegetables, what you wished was not that you valued eating the vegetables as a means to health; that, you already did. What seemed desirable but not immediately within your grasp was a more intrinsic preference for the taste of the vegetables. This is one of those rather frequent cases in which a difference of teleological structure makes it hard to get from a higher order preference to the first-order preference that is its object, since the former depends on motives that cannot exactly be motives of the latter.

It is widely and plausibly thought that a preference is more fully yours if it is the object of a favorable higher order preference of yours. You may be said to "identify" yourself with a desire that you are glad you have, and to "dissociate" yourself, in some measure, from a desire that you wish you did not have. In virtue of such an "identification and withdrawal, accomplished through the formation of a second-order volition," Harry Frankfurt argues, an "unwilling addict," who "hates his addiction and always struggles desperately, although to no avail, against its thrust," can meaningfully claim that "the force moving him to take the drug is a force other than his own," even though it "is in a literal sense his own desire."[21] Similarly a person who feels compassion, and is sometimes effectively moved by it, but who sees it as a weakness, regrets it, and often suppresses it, is not a truly compassionate person.

Consider in this light the case of someone who has a commendable love for art. She cares about excellence in art, and prizes good art for its own sake. I think we must also suppose that she is glad that she cares about art in this way. If she regretted her interest in art, seeing it perhaps as an immoral frivolity, or if it were a matter of indifference to her whether she cared about art or not, though in fact she does, then we could hardly say that she *loves* art. Unaffirmed by a higher order preference, her regard for art would be more like a mere taste than a love.

What would motivate her higher order preference for loving art? If her relation to art is happy, she will be glad that she loves art because of the joy that it gives her. Even if she is a frustrated artist, whose talents unhappily fall short of her dreams, her first-order love of art will have a momentum that carries through to a higher order preference. For any interest that is sufficiently self-involving to count as a love will normally[22] include an interest in the lover's ongoing pursuit of relationship with the object of love, and hence will necessarily include an interest in continuing the interest that is implied in such a pursuit.

These motives intrinsic to the first-order preference are likely, however, not to be the only motives for the higher order preference. For example, our art lover might want to love art because artistic interests are fashionable in her set. That would be a snobbish motive, and might be thought to compromise the worth of her love for art, even if what it motivates is a desire to love art and not just to be thought to love it. One of the better motives she could have for wanting to love art is a desire to be someone who cares about excellence in some form, and who loves good things and not bad ones. That desire could be a highly commendable part of a motivational ideal that she has for herself.

This need not compromise in any way her caring about art for its own sake. For first-order preferences do not in general have the same ends as higher order preferences about them, as I have already pointed out. From the supposition that someone prizes her love of art partly because that love satisfies her motivational ideal that she should care about (some forms of) excellence, it does not follow that she prizes good art even partly because the art satisfies a more general interest in excellence. Indeed her first-order interest in excellence may not be very general, and her motivational ideal need not demand that it should be. She may be content to have little interest in athletics, chess, cooking, or carpentry, and hence little interest in

---

21. Frankfurt, "Freedom of the Will and the Concept of a Person," p. 12f. Because Frankfurt's paper is largely about freedom of the will, it is much more focused than I mean to be here on the relation of desires to action. The "second order volition" of which he speaks is a desire, not merely to have a first-order desire, but to have it control one's action. This feature, more important for Frankfurt's argument than for mine, is possessed by some but not all "higher order preferences" in my sense.

22. There are probably exceptions to this generalization in cases where something like a bereavement has made manifestly impossible the continuation that would otherwise be desired; but the present argument need not ride on these cases. In allowing such exceptions I may be in disagreement with Frankfurt, "The Importance of What We Care About," p. 260.

achieving excellence in those fields, so long as there are enough forms of excellence that she does care about.

Motivational ideals are an important sort of higher order preference, and loves that are a fully integrated part of your life will be consonant with your motivational ideal if you have one. It is plausible to suppose that a desire to be someone who cares about some forms of excellence, and who loves good things and not bad ones, should be part of everyone's motivational ideal. This is a way in which we can reasonably believe that being more or less explicitly *for* the good as such ought to provide an integrative organizing principle for our motivational structures, including our loves.

Indeed we are approaching the point at which it may be reasonable to speak of *love* for the good (or for God) as the organizing principle of such a motivational structure. Suppose you have a strong general disposition to value good things, loving some, liking more of them, respecting still more of them. Suppose in addition you have a conception of goodness and use it in such a way that you may be said to have an attitude of being *for* the good in general—for example, in allowing your conception of goodness to determine, for the most part, what qualities you count as reasons for loving something. Suppose further that your higher order preferences regarding your motives are shaped by a motivational ideal of being someone who is for the good in such ways as we have considered. These suppositions would be sufficient, I think, to warrant us in describing you as someone whose motives (including loves) are integrated around a love of goodness. If we can add that the conception of the good around which your motives are organized in these ways is that of an ideal or standard that transcends the value of the finite goods you experience, then we can even say that your organizing, integrative principle is love for the transcendent Good, and for God if God is that Good.

The explicitness of one's love for God may depend on the degree to which one's conceptualization is theistic. For a motivational ideal, however, that may be less important, religiously as well as ethically, than what can be present in an implicit love for God. If it is love for God, the real God, and not for our idea of God, that is in question, the theistic conceptualization may be less important than how faithfully the finite things we are disposed to love image God.[23]

Is there a place, in the sort of Good-centered integration of motives that I have just sketched, for those most ordinary motives that are not particularly good or bad, though they are perfectly acceptable? Tastes and distastes, especially those that are relatively spontaneous rather than cultivated, are generally to be numbered among these ethically indifferent motives. So are physical drives, such as hunger and thirst and the desire to rest when fatigued. Sexual desires offer richer possibilities of ethical assessment because of their richer involvement of loves and traits of character; but they certainly include a physical drive, and there is a level of sexual craving, attraction, and pleasure to which it seems foolish to ascribe merit or demerit. And there are other desires that are not particularly physical, such as an interest in exciting stories, that seem to be both natural and ethically indifferent.

23. Cf. chapter 8, section 3.

One might try to integrate these motives into love for the good by arguing that the objects desired, in each case, are good, or more generally that the motives aim at pleasure, health, or vitality, which are goods, and indeed excellences, of the most fundamental importance, though not of the highest prestige. And no doubt it is generally true that the objects of these desires are good, though we might have doubts in some cases. But there are at least two weighty arguments against regarding such desires as forms or manifestations of love for the good. For in the first place they often do not carry with them much interest in the comparative excellence of alternative ways of satisfying them. And in the second place they are apt to be much the same in people who do and those who do not in a general way love the good. Virtually everyone, whatever their ethical stance may be, will sometimes have hunger and thirst and desires for rest, some sexual desires, and some tastes in food and entertainment. That we have these at all can hardly be ascribed to our larger loves, ideals, and commitments. They are natural responses to physical and cultural stimulation and environment. As such they are neither good nor bad motives. We get no credit or discredit just for having them, though we may get some for the form that the more complex and variable of them take in us.

To a large extent these ethically indifferent motives can be seen as part of the given material of our lives on which our larger aims must work. At a minimum, they, or our response to them, must be disciplined. We will never accomplish our larger aims if we do not learn to control our impulses, and to keep the satisfaction of physical drives, desires for rest and entertainment, and so on, within a structure that serves our larger aims.

Some moral and religious visions are ascetical in the sense that they seek to minimize the role in our lives of these natural motives that do not originate in our larger ends. They are not just to be controlled, but repressed and, so far as possible, extirpated. This approach seems to me to embody an excessive fear of the threat to self-control that they pose. It is preferable to affirm the natural motives as part of an affirmation of one's natural vitality. This vitality is excellent; indeed, I should say it is a large part of the image of God in us. To honor it in oneself can be a form of love for the good. (To honor it as a gift of God to oneself can be a form of love for God in another way too.) In this way one can have favorable higher order preferences regarding these natural motives, and can thus include them in an integrated motivational pattern organized around love for the good. It is chiefly one's attitudes toward them and one's choices regarding them, and the place one assigns them in one's life, that determine whether they are in fact integrated into such a motivational pattern.

What I have now said about the good, and hence about God, as the focus of an integrated motivational system is possibly the most important and certainly the best grounded solution I can present to the problem of accommodating genuine loves for finite objects within an ideal of devotion to God. It is a solution that holds our attitude toward God and our attitude toward finite goods at a certain distance from each other, however, and we may still aspire to a *closer* integration of the two types of love. In the remaining two sections of this chapter we turn to a couple of possible steps in that direction, but they will be riskier, both theologically and philosophically.

6. Love as Enjoyment

In chapter 5, section 1, I argued that Plato's identification of Eros with *desire* for *future* good overlooks the possibility that it might also be admiration, liking, or other valuing of *present* good. Plato's error suits the strategy of teleological subordination for integrating interests in finite goods into love for the supreme Good. For the clearest way for a quest for one future good to be a vehicle for a quest for another future good is for the former to be valued as a way or means to the latter. It may be worth exploring the possibility that there is a way of valuing *present* good in which valuing one good can serve as a vehicle for valuing another without anything like a teleological subordination that would keep either good from being valued for its own sake.

Specifically, I believe it is possible to *enjoy* one present good *in* enjoying another where both are enjoyed for themselves, neither of them merely as a means or way of enjoying the other. We commonly enjoy other people *in* enjoying something else, for instance in enjoying what we do together. In many such cases we enjoy the other people themselves, but we do not enjoy *only* the person. This is obviously true of shared pleasures. We enjoy the caviar and the music for their own sake too, and might still enjoy them if eaten or heard alone.

How is this relevant to the theological problem of total devotion? Is love for God a valuing of future or of present good? Both, surely. Aspiration, indeed longing, for a better, fuller, closer relationship with God has a central place in theistic piety. Biblical hope *waits* for the Lord, and the Psalmist cries,

> As a hart longs for flowing streams,
> so longs my soul for thee, O God.
> My soul thirsts for God, for the living God.
> When shall I come and behold the face of God? (Psalm 42:12)

At least equally important, however, are attitudes of love for God as a *present* good. The soul of worship is *admiration*, and there is a place in it for *enjoyment* of God. Even St. Augustine, though he generally views love as a quest or longing for infinite satisfaction not yet attained, nonetheless relates the most important kind of love to present rather than future good, inasmuch as he speaks of it as *enjoyment*.

Can we enjoy God *in* enjoying finite things? Suppose one enjoys the sunlight on the leaves and is the more excited because one catches there (as one believes) a glimpse of the beauty of the Creator at work. Is it right to say that this is an experience in which one enjoys God *in* enjoying the light on the leaves? And if so, can it also be right to say that one *loves* God *in* loving the light on the leaves? I think so, but I may need to overcome a suspicion that loving the light and loving God are too accidentally connected for the former to be really integrated into the latter.

The idea of the *glory* of God may be helpful at this point. This term is used at important points in the Bible to signify the manifestation of God's goodness in and through the goodness of created things. It is used in this way against the background of other uses in which the glory of God is conceived as a more direct and more obviously supernatural manifestation of the divine, envisaged (or even perceived) as a radiance of light. In the contexts that presently concern us, however, the imagery of light is metaphorical, and the glory may be manifest in phenomena that can also be viewed as perfectly natural.

A central text of this sort is the hymn of the seraphim in Isaiah's vision, which is used, slightly modified, in the communion liturgies of many Christian churches: "Holy, holy, holy is the LORD of hosts; the whole earth is full of his glory" (Isaiah 6:3).[24] The glory of God of which the whole earth is full is presumably present in ordinary as well as extraordinary phenomena. Perhaps it is in the sunlight on the leaves; at any rate I will take that as an example.

What interests me here is the *structure* of seeing and enjoying the glory of God in such a phenomenon. There are two essential moments in it. One is the moment of enjoying and admiring the created phenomenon, the light on the leaves, for what it is in itself. The other is a moment in which the created good is seen as fragmentary and pointing beyond itself, a moment that we may take as constituting a glimpse of a transcendently good object, a dim awareness of something too wonderful to be contained or carried either by our experience or by the finite objects we are perceiving. I believe there are many experiences, particularly experiences of beauty, that have this bipartite structure. They lend important support to Platonic and theistic belief in a transcendent Good.

I have spoken of two "moments," but I do not mean to imply that they succeed each other in time. In fact, I think they are normally simultaneous. And the connection between them is essential, not accidental, to the second moment. Not that we set *the same value* on the finite and the transcendent good; we recognize that the value of the transcendent good is far higher. But our valuing of the finite good in the first moment is the stuff of which the second moment is made. It is our love, our liking, our admiration and enjoyment of the light on the leaves that suggest to us the greater good. If we do not care for the light on the leaves, for its own sake, the divine glory will not be visible to us in this experience. So if this is an experience of loving God in the mode of admiring (or adoring) and enjoying God, it would seem to be a case in which love for a finite good is an integral part of love for God. Three objections to this way of relating other interests to love for God claim discussion here.

1. There are cases in which it seems odd to say that in enjoying a work we enjoy its creator. Do we enjoy Rembrandt himself in enjoying his paintings? Perhaps not. Rembrandt is gone and has left his works behind for us to enjoy. But God is not like that. On theistic as distinct from deistic conceptions of creation, the Creator has not gone away and left the creatures behind, but remains unceasingly active in them. Shall we compare God then to a dancer, who cannot go away and leave her performance behind? (Or if she leaves a motion picture of her work, there is nothing odd in saying we enjoy her in enjoying the film.) Well, in a theistic as distinct from a pantheistic view, the Creator is more distinct from the creatures than the dancer from the dance; but they are not as separable from God as the paintings are

---

24. A similar conception of the divine glory as manifested in creatures is found also in the New Testament (e.g., 2 Corinthians 3:18).

from the painter. God is neither as wholly immanent in the world as the dancer in the dance, nor as purely transcendent over it as the painter over the paintings. On a theistic view, however, I think there is enough immanence to support speaking of enjoying God in enjoying created goods.

2. We may doubt whether it would be reasonable to expect or hope to enjoy God in *all* our enjoyment of finite goods. Probably on most occasions when we enjoy a hearty breakfast or a funny movie we will notice nothing about the experience or its finite object that points beyond them to a transcendent Good; and we may well doubt that we *ought* to notice anything of the sort. Even if their goodness *is* an imaging of God, it does not seem to be the sort of goodness that reminds us of its relation to the transcendent. Perhaps this is mainly a sign of our blindness, and an ideal religious consciousness would be able to enjoy God in even the humblest goods; but I would not want my argument to rest heavily on that claim.

The objection is not just about the humblest goods. You may think it reasonable to want your lover to concentrate some of the time on you alone, and not to be always enjoying something else in enjoying you. It is sometimes presented as a religious ideal to be consciously thinking about God at every moment,[25] but perhaps that would be too great an intrusion on serious love for any creature. Given our limited capacity for attention, we may need sometimes to focus on a creature we love, without consciously attending to anything else—not even to God; and perhaps that applies to some moments of enjoyment. What theists cannot allow as desirable is an important ongoing interest that one *never* views in relation to God. Indeed, for reasons indicated in section 5, having *any* very integrated ethical perspective requires that one's important interests *sometimes* be viewed in relation to that perspective. But it is much less plausible to demand that every moment include conscious attention to the larger perspective, or to God. So perhaps we should not expect *all* our enjoyment of finite goods to include enjoyment of God in the conscious way I have sketched earlier; it does not follow that such enjoyment of God, in many cases, is not one of the threads that should weave our interests into an integrated pattern that constitutes a love for God.

3. Some may think my proposal assigns too high a place to the enjoyment of finite goods. There are forms of the mystical quest in which the goal is to experience and enjoy God directly, rather than in any created object. The desire for such unmediated enjoyment of God has often been seen as a touchstone of love for God, or at least of the purest love for God. This has sometimes contributed to regarding the love and enjoyment of finite things as religiously suspect, at best a distraction, at worst idolatry, since on this view they cannot mediate the enjoyment of God to which we should aspire.

In fact there are at least two types of theistic piety. One is the mystical quest that seeks to go beyond creatures and know and love God directly. The other type meets God mainly *in* creatures. The view being developed in this book is commit-

---

25. If one really holds a theistic view, that will be part of the framework of every moment of one's consciousness, as the belief that we live on the more or less spherical surface of a planet is for most of us. The ideal mentioned here asks something more: that God should be, at every moment, an object of explicit attention.

ted to the validity of this second way of piety. But I do not wish to take up toward the other way a stance as polemical as both ways have often taken toward each other. It is not necessary to deny the validity of either way.

The second way, which meets and loves God in creatures, finds a classic expression in the First Epistle of John in the New Testament, which declares that "he who does not love his brother, whom he has seen, cannot love God, whom he has not seen" (4:20). We might be tempted to read this as meaning that loving one's brother is practice for loving God—as if by jumping over the low bar of loving the visible we might gain enough strength and skill to clear the high bar of loving the invisible. But that gives an inept sense. The relation between loving the visible and loving the invisible is surely not that of easier and harder tests of the same ability. The intended sense, I believe, is that it is *in* loving each other that we know, and are able to love, God. As the Epistle says, "Love is from God, and everyone who loves is begotten from God and knows God. He who does not love does not know God, for God is love. . . . No one has ever seen God. If we love each other, God dwells in us and his love is completed in us."[26]

It is very much an implication of this text that the glory of God, and specifically God's love, can be known and enjoyed *in* a human love that images the divine love, however imperfectly. The emphasis of the text, though, does not fall on *enjoying* God's love, but rather on *sharing* it. That brings us to another, perhaps more fundamental relation between love for God and other loves.

7. Love as Alliance

The aspect of love for God to which we now turn our attention has this in common with enjoying God, that it is a matter not merely of *desiring* a certain relationship with God but of *having* one. It is not a part of religious aspiration but of its consummation. The best of interpersonal loves involve *friendship*—not just the *desire* to be friends (though that is also involved) but actually *being* friends. Theists have often thought of religious life in terms of friendship with God.[27]

Friends are allies. They share goals and projects. One way in which that happens is that you may embrace a goal just because it is your friend's goal, without caring about it for its own sake. In that case your sharing the goal obviously manifests your love for your friend. That might suggest that the most perfect friendships would be characterized by this kind of sharing of projects.

In fact that seems not to be the case. The friendships we regard as most perfect are characterized by a more profound alliance, a fuller sharing of interests, in which shared goals are valued for their own sake by both parties. When we speak of "shared interests," we normally mean being interested in the same things for their own sake; we do not mean just being interested in the friend's interests for the sake of the friend.

---

26. 1 John 4:7–8, 12. Cf. the Gospel according to John, 1:18, thought by many scholars to come from the same circle, though not the same author, as the Epistle.
27. For Christianity, John 15:12–16 is a classic text on this point.

If I love bird-watching and my wife has never cared about it, she might go birding with me and even "cultivate an interest" in the activity, for the sake of our relationship, or to encourage me to do something I enjoy; but so long as those are her only motives in the matter, we do not yet "share an interest" in birds. That will occur only if she too becomes interested in birds for their own sake.[28] (Of course, we don't need to share all our interests. What matters is that we share some that are important enough.)

Alliance with God is a major theme of the Bible. It is part of the idea of *covenant*. The original reference of 'covenant' is to a variety of treaties and agreements, but in its fullest development a covenant is also an alliance.[29] Jeremiah's prophecy of a new covenant is particularly rich in suggestions for our subject: "This is the covenant which I will make with the house of Israel after those days, says the LORD: I will put my law within them, and I will write it upon their hearts; and I will be their God, and they shall be my people" (Jeremiah 31:33). Two features of this famous prophecy should be noted here. The first is that the new covenant is to constitute an alliance, a social union: "I will be their God, and they shall be my people." The second is that this alliance is to be perfected by God's law, God's Torah, God's guidance being written inwardly on the people's hearts, so that their own deepest impulses and values will guide them in accordance with God's will. Surely the internalization intended is motivational as well as cognitive. The people are not only to know, but also to want, what God wants; and I think it is natural to suppose that they are to want it for its own sake, that they are to "love kindness" (i.e., Hesed [חסד]), for example, as another prophet declares (Micah 6:8).[30]

Here the motivational internalization of God's will is seen as constituting the best sort of alliance or social union with God. And social or personal union at its best is certainly one of the highest forms of love. This indicates a way in which loving, for its own sake, what God loves for its own sake can constitute an important part of loving God.

Here, once again, my account must face the question whether it relies on a connection that is too accidental to relate us to God in the relevant way. Suppose what I love just *happens* to be the same as what God loves; surely that is not enough to constitute a social union between me and God, or to make me one who loves God. Alliance with God cannot be a mere accident; but it is not, in religious conceptions of it, and there is no need to conceive of it as an accident. In the Bible, covenants between God and humans are initiated by God. In Jeremiah's new covenant it is God who is to write the divine guidance on human hearts—no accidental connection that!

Now, however, it may be objected that if a social union is to be part of our love for God, and not just of God's love for us, it is not enough for God to contribute to it in a nonaccidental way; we must do so too. Those who emphasize God's initia-

28. Cf. Raz, *The Morality of Freedom*, p. 33.
29. The biblical terms ברית and διαθήκη, which are generally translated by 'covenant' in English, are often rendered by cognates of 'alliance' in French and Italian; and this gives an illuminating sense in many contexts.
30. On Hesed, see chapter 6, section 4.

tive and causal efficacy, or inspiration, in the matter may think of our contribution in terms of *submission* to God's direction. The importance of this conception in Islamic ideals of religious piety is well known; we find a Christian version of it in Anders Nygren's statement that "man's love for God signifies that man, moved by [the] Divine love, gratefully wills to belong wholly to God." This combines the thesis that "love towards God . . . is the *free*—and in that sense spontaneous—surrender of the heart to God" with Nygren's view that "God is not the end, the ultimate object, but the starting-point and permanent basis of neighborly love. He is not its *causa finalis*, but its *causa efficiens*."[31] On the other hand, if one is inclined theologically to place more emphasis on human spontaneity, and to see the inscription of God's concerns in human hearts as arising largely from people's attention to what they see of God, that would also fit my present argument. The theological issue between these two approaches need not be decided here.

I have been discussing this form of love for God in terms of alliance of *theists* with God, but I do *not* mean to imply that only theists should be regarded (by theists) as allied with God. As I have said before, I am as interested here in implicit as in explicit love for God; and whether we share God's loves depends much more on what we love (for its own sake) than on whether we conceptualize it theologically. Nor is the sharing of God's loves by nontheists merely accidental, if God is the Good itself as I suppose. In a theistic perspective, nontheists and theists are equally creatures of God, and their good impulses come equally from God. The loves and concerns of nontheists as well as theists may be inspired by their attention to goods that in my view are images of God. And theists as well as nontheists may be moved by manifestations of the glory of God much more often than they think of them in consciously theological terms. So we can think of a sort of implicit alliance with God as helping to constitute an implicit love for God. Doubtless alliance with God can be more fully developed if it is theologically explicit, but theological explicitness does not guarantee the authenticity of such alliance. The latter point connects with a main theme of chapter 8.

31. Nygren, *Agape and Eros*, pp. 213, 94, 216.

8

IDOLATRY

In chapter 7 I proposed a motivational ideal organized around love for the good—and I identify the Good itself with God. Love for any good object or any type of good can be part of a motivational pattern or structure that constitutes love for the good, and at least implicitly for God. But not all devotion to good things is good. It is possible to care to excess even about things that it is good to care about. It is good to love one's work, if the work is constructive activity that one is able to do well. But the consuming concentration on work of the so-called workaholic is not a good thing. It is or can be good to love one's country, most of us think; but excesses of nationalistic passion have been among the ugliest and most harmful motives of our century. Provided one's beliefs about right and wrong are reasonably enlightened, it is good to be committed to do what one thinks is right. But an excessive concern about the rightness of one's own behavior can make one a self-righteous prig.

There is clearly an objectionable excess of some sort in these cases, but it would be hasty to assume that the fault in them is simply a matter of desires that are too strong. Perhaps some other distortion is involved. We need a more careful anatomy of good motives gone bad. That is the task of the present chapter.

This subject can be treated in theistic ethics under the heading of idolatry. In its original sense 'idolatry' means worshiping an image of a deity, and we shall see in the end that this sense is not irrelevant to our inquiry. Here, however, 'idolatry' is used primarily in an extended sense, to signify giving to anything finite a worship, a devotion, a trust, or any other response that belongs only to God. This extended sense has been very influential in modern theology; a typical formulation is Paul Tillich's: "Idolatry is the elevation of a preliminary concern to ultimacy. Something essentially conditioned is taken as unconditional, something essentially partial is boosted into universality, and something essentially finite is given infinite significance (the best example is the contemporary idolatry of religious nationalism)."[1]

The first thing I want to do here is to dwell briefly on Tillich's contrast of partiality and universality. H. Richard Niebuhr identifies monotheistic devotion with "universal loyalty," by which he means loyalty to God as "the principle of being itself," and at the same time "loyalty to each particular existent in the community of being and to the universal community." This loyalty to existents as such is connected with an Augustinian affirmation of "the value of whatever is."[2] The crucial point in monotheism, for Niebuhr, is the relating of all being and all value to a single source. To the extent that our loyalties are confined within limits that exclude some bearers of value, we fall short of genuine, or, as Niebuhr calls it, "radical," monotheism. Loyalties to finite objects may fitly be styled "idolatrous" if they are so all-absorbing as to be incompatible with monotheism.[3] From this we may infer that love for any finite object, or realm of objects, is idolatrous if it is so exclusive as to keep us from caring about other instances or types of good. A social group, for instance, is an idol for those who care about people only if they belong to it.

There is certainly something right about the ideal of universal loyalty. In chapter 6, section 5, I argued that God should be conceived as loving all created beings. A human person, likewise, who loves the good, and is an ally of God, should be, in principle, *for* what is good in every context. If I do not at least deplore injustice wherever it occurs in the world, I do not really love justice. And if I love art, but hold athletic excellence in contempt, my love of the good is at best incomplete. If some finite and partial good is the only good I am for, surely I have made an idol of it. The universal character of true love for the good forms a background to much of what is said in this chapter.

At the same time the ideal of universal loyalty is attended with obvious problems. To care, or even know, in particular about all the goods and evils in the world exceeds the capacities of any human being. And if we are to care effectively about anything in particular, we will have to care more, in some ways, about some goods than about other comparable goods that are known to us. That is why I add the qualification 'in principle' to the claim that one who loves the Good should be *for* every good. A full discussion of these issues about universality and particularity in human love, however, would carry us away from the main concerns of this chapter. My main ideas for dealing with them will be developed in chapter 13, on vocation.

---

1. Tillich, *Systematic Theology*, vol. 1, p. 13.
2. Niebuhr, *Radical Monotheism and Western Culture*, p. 33f.
3. The terminology of "idolatry" does not in fact figure prominently in Niebuhr's account, but his contrast of monotheism with its alternatives clearly reflects the concerns that give rise to discussions of idolatry.

Here I shall explore three approaches to the nature of idolatry (in the extended sense of 'idolatry' that I have indicated). They will certainly not exhaust the subject, and it may be that not everything worth saying about disproportionate motivation can be said in terms of idolatry. But I think we can get in this way considerable light on the structure of a possible theory for this area of ethics.

1. Priorities

The ideal of religious devotion to God is often characterized in terms of loving God more than anything else. Correlatively, idolatry is identified with preferring anything to God. As a widely used Christian hymn puts it,

> Jesus calls us from the worship
>   Of the vain world's golden store,
> From each idol that would keep us,
>   Saying, "Christian, love me more."[4]

There is undoubtedly something right about this. It will be part of any ideal of theistic devotion that one should not love anything more than God. But the concept of loving something more than God is problematic.

If we think of love for God as a system of motives, feelings, and dispositions connected with one's *idea* of God, then it may be fairly clear in some cases that a person loves some finite thing more than God. Theists will view this as a religious deficiency, but it is not clear that it must result from an excessive or idolatrous love for the finite object. The deficiency might lie primarily in one's ideas or beliefs about God. Atheists will normally have no explicit love for God, and may therefore love other things more without loving them excessively. And theists may have ideas of God too stunted or distorted to provide an adequate focus for their loves.

Deficiencies of these types do not enter the picture if we are thinking of an "implicit" love for God—love for the Good itself, which is identical with God—but love not necessarily connected with an idea of God, or even of a transcendent Good. Now it is not so clear, however, what it would be to love some good thing more than God—that is, more than the Good itself. For, as I argued in chapter 7, love for any good thing can be part of a sort of love for the good as such, and hence at least implicitly for God. And if it is a part of one's love for God, how could it exceed one's love for God? The answer, of course, is that an idolatrous love for a finite good is one that is bloated in such a way that it no longer fits within love for God or the good as a part of it, but competes with it. But then it seems that a comparison of strengths between one's love for the finite good and one's love for God is not very serviceable as a criterion of idolatry; for it is only after the two loves have become competitors that the comparison first acquires its point, and the possibility of yielding the answer that one loves something else more than God. The criterion we

4. Cecil Frances Alexander (1852), quoted from *The Hymnal*, no. 233.

need is one that will tell us when love for a finite good has ceased to form part of love for the good or for God and begun to compete with it.

One attempt at a criterion, which I think is rather popular, puts the idea of priorities, of putting the idol first versus putting God first, in terms of preferences regarding courses of action. If one is prepared to abandon, disobey, or slight God in order to please another person, or in order to pursue some other end, then one has made an idol of that person or end. Nontheists interested in adapting the concept of idolatry might say analogously that any love or interest is idolatrous to the extent that it leads us, or is apt to lead us, to do what we know is morally wrong. This is not altogether misguided, but I will argue that being preferred to God or duty in this way is neither necessary nor, without qualification, sufficient for a motive to be idolatrous.

That it is not *necessary* for idolatry can be seen, I think, by reflecting on the "knight of infinite resignation" in Kierkegaard's *Fear and Trembling*. Kierkegaard virtually defined religiousness in terms of absoluteness of devotion to the religious object. He sought a way in which religious passion could be made infinite, and idolatry excluded. One of his earliest attempts at this is the strategy of infinite resignation. The knight of infinite resignation has "concentrate[d] the whole substance of his life and the meaning of actuality into one single desire,"[5] for a particular beloved person, and then has renounced her for the sake of God. But he keeps the concentrated passion for the human beloved ever "young"[6] in his heart, for that is what makes his resignation "infinite" and thus makes it a relation to God.

Contrary to Kierkegaard's intention, I believe this outward renunciation of the beloved does not abolish but shelters the "knight's" idolatry of her—shelters it from the vicissitudes and ordinariness of real relationships—so that it can retain exaggerated proportions. It still crowds out interests in other finite things and defines the possibility (or rather impossibility) of happiness for him.[7] Religiously, however, the most offensive feature of this pattern is that the knight's passion for his "princess" serves to define, by its continuing intensity, the meaning of his life and specifically the religious character of his devotion to God. Martin Buber's comment on Kierkegaard's similar interpretation of his own sacrifice of his engagement with Regine Olsen is a telling thrust, in my opinion. "God as Regine's successful rival? Is that still God?" asks Buber.[8] What we see here is an idolatry that can remain in the organization of the heart even when God is voluntarily preferred to the idol.[9]

I claim also that having a motive that leads one to act contrary to one's loyalty to God or one's known duty, and in that sense to prefer some other object to God or duty, is not *sufficient* to constitute idolatry. Such a motive is not necessarily idolatrous, though the action is wrong. One's motive in acting wrongly need not be a particularly strong one, let alone excessively strong. This is obvious in many cases

---

5. Kierkegaard, *Fear and Trembling*, p. 43.
6. Kierkegaard, *Fear and Trembling*, p. 44.
7. Kierkegaard, *Fear and Trembling*, p. 50.
8. Buber, *Between Man and Man*, p. 57. I have adopted the Danish spelling of Regine's name.
9. I have discussed the treatment of resignation in *Fear and Trembling* more extensively in Adams, "The Knight of Faith," p. 389f. I am drawing some material here from that paper.

of weakness of will. When one goes on reading a newspaper article that one does not care very much about, for instance, though one knows it will make one (wrongly) late for an appointment, it is implausible to suppose that the article or its content is the object of an idolatry.

Even when our motive in acting wrongly is a very strong one, the misdeed does not necessarily show the motive to be excessively strong. Almost any strong motive can tempt us in some contexts to do wrong, and we can succumb to temptation; but we should not therefore wish our motives to be mostly weak. This point can be illustrated by the case on which Michael Slote relies most heavily in his argument that there is such a thing as admirable immorality.

It is an example that has been discussed rather widely in the literature on the fragmentation of value, the case of "a familiar but somewhat fictionalized Gauguin," as Slote puts it. Gauguin abandoned his wife and children to go to Tahiti and paint, producing the works so many of us admire. We are to suppose that he cared about his moral obligation to his family, and was deeply pained, indeed "full of remorse," over the economic destitution he was causing them and the betrayal of which he was guilty, but that the motivational force of these moral feelings was "overcome" by his passionate devotion to painting.[10]

Slote holds three theses that lead him to speak of this case as a case of admirable immorality. (1) Gauguin's desertion of his family was morally wrong, "even repelling." (2) "Single-minded devotion to aesthetic goals or ideals" is admirable and "a virtue in an artist." But (3) "artistic single-mindedness" is "inconceivable apart from a tendency to wrongdoing," and therefore is morally objectionable.[11]

I agree with the first thesis; Gauguin's action cannot be justified morally. But there is a short answer to Slote's argument: (2) and (3) are inconsistent; why should we admire a passion so idolatrous as to be inseparable from a tendency to wrongdoing? As one of Slote's critics has put it, "We admire traits, such as artistic passion, patriotism, and parental devotion on the assumption that they are not excessive."[12] For our present purpose, however, that is too short an answer. We want to understand the difference between an admirable artistic passion and one that is so excessive as to be idolatrous. Granting ourselves a wider fictional license than Slote has assumed, we may imagine several Gauguins.

Gauguin (A) manages to pursue his art while remaining with his family. Many would describe his devotion to art as "single-minded," but he tries to keep it in some sort of balance not merely with the claims of his family and friends but also with his love for them. He often lays aside his painting to do what would be better for them, or for his relationship with them, instead of what would be better for his art. As art demands, however, he jealously guards a very large share of his time and energy for painting. And sometimes, perhaps even fairly often, he goes on painting when he knows it is his moral duty to attend to something else instead. On such occasions he does wrong. But his artistic passion may nonetheless be almost wholly admirable. An intensity of love that exposes one to temptations to wrongdoing to which one

10. Slote, *Goods and Virtues*, pp. 79–81.
11. Slote, *Goods and Virtues*, pp. 83, 80, 92.
12. Flanagan, "Admirable Immorality and Admirable Imperfection," p. 43.

sometimes succumbs is not thereby shown to be immoral or idolatrous. The increased risk of wrongdoing (which I would hesitate to call "a tendency to wrongdoing") is regrettable, but it does not show the intense love to be morally objectionable. What kind of life could one lead without having interests in one's work, one's family, one's economic situation, one's political causes that are strong enough to tempt one at times to do something immoral? A human being so innocuous as to lack all such motives would probably not be very admirable even from a moral point of view.

Other Gauguins leave their families to paint in Tahiti. Gauguin (B)'s passion for art was so irresistible that he was *unable* to stand against the temptation to desert his family. Or perhaps we should say, a little more cautiously, that though not literally irresistible, it was so *obsessive* as to make it virtually certain, in the circumstances, that he would abandon his family. Gauguin (B) may perhaps be Slote's Gauguin, who is "*driven* by the passion."[13] Such an obsession can plausibly be counted as idolatry, unless perhaps it is too pathological; but why should we admire it?

Gauguin (C) is not obsessed, but is freely resolved to let *nothing* stand in the way of his art. He has not just abandoned his family; he never attends to any duty, human need, or friendship at any cost to his painting. Such a resolution is an evil and ugly idolatry; it is not admirable at all. And the resolution is so comprehensive, and so large a part of Gauguin (C)'s motivational pattern, that I doubt that the love of art that inspires it can be sufficiently disentangled from the resolution to claim any admiration for itself.

Gauguin (D) stands somewhere between Gauguins (A) and (C). He does not just occasionally succumb to temptation, for he abandons his wife and children and he "stands by" that decision, and regards it as "justified" in some nonmoral sense.[14] He is unwilling to make the sacrifice of his art that would be involved in staying with his family. But he is not comprehensively resolved to let nothing interfere with his art. Like Gauguin (A) he often lays aside his painting to be helpful or friendly to another person, though he sometimes fails to do that when he should. This Gauguin (D) is another candidate for the role of Slote's Gauguin. He is the most complex of these characters, and the hardest to assess for our present purposes. His persistent unwillingness to sacrifice his art to his duty to his family seems idolatrous, but it is a much smaller part of his motivational pattern than Gauguin (C)'s more comprehensive immoral resolution. It is therefore less clear that we cannot make a distinction and say that his love of art is admirable in itself, though a persistent part of the behavior it inspires is idolatrous.

A different position between Gauguins (A) and (C) is occupied by Gauguin (E). Like (A), he pursues his art without leaving his family. Unlike (A), however, it cannot be said of him that he tries to balance the claims of his art against the claims of other people, or that he "often" is attentive to other people at cost to his art. Indeed, when he genuinely has a choice, and when it would not involve an immorality as gross as abandoning his family to misery, he is *usually*, or almost always, unwilling

13. Slote, *Goods and Virtues*, p. 82.
14. Slote's terms; see his *Goods and Virtues*, pp. 84, 86.

to make any sacrifice of his art for the benefit of others. But, unlike (C), he has made no immoral resolution to that effect; it is just the pattern of his behavior. Here, if anywhere, we can speak of "a tendency to wrongdoing"; and a motive that is "inconceivable apart from" it will not be admirable. What is not so clear is whether Gauguin (E)'s passion for painting is indeed conceptually inseparable from the immoral tendency. We might try to separate it by noting that it is not necessarily more intense than Gauguin (A)'s admirable passion. It could just be that (E) cares less about other people, or is generally less disposed to attend to their rights and interests at cost to his own projects. This hypothesis would be confirmed if we found that before taking up art, while he divided his time and energy among several hobbies and business projects, (E) was no more attentive to other people than he is now. In this case, Gauguin (E) seems simply selfish, rather than idolatrous.

For completeness, we should also mention Gauguin (F), who remains with his family, but at the cost of giving up his painting. Nonetheless, his love of art burns as passionately as ever. After many years, he is still miserable over his sacrifice. He cannot enjoy life with his family, and is full of resentment toward them, although he is extremely conscientious in his behavior. This Gauguin's continuing passion for art is idolatrous in my opinion, like the love of the knight of infinite resignation for his princess, though he voluntarily prefers his duty to it.

These reflections confirm that being one's motive in particular choices contrary to God and morality is neither necessary nor sufficient for a love or interest to be idolatrous. As we have seen, people sometimes have a good motive of appropriate strength as their primary motive in doing something wrong (though there is normally something wrong with their total motivational pattern in such a case); and one may have, and even nourish, an idolatrous passion while voluntarily and conscientiously frustrating it. On the other hand, I think we can say that a passion, love, or commitment to any finite good is idolatrous if it is so absorbing as to be *incompatible* with doing usually what one morally and religiously ought to do, or with living virtuously in one's various relationships, as in the case of Gauguins (B) and (C), and perhaps (D) and (E). This is one way in which love for a finite good can be so bloated as to be a competitor, rather than a part, of love for the good or for God.

2. Need and Detachment

Another way is involved in the case of Gauguin (F) and the knight of infinite resignation. Their idolatry does not prevent them from doing what they know is morally or religiously right. In the realm of voluntary action they are able to give up the object of their idolatry. But their lives revolve, so to speak, around the place where it isn't. They are not able to be happy without it. There is even some suggestion that they feel they would betray the meaning of their lives if they were to be happy without the idol.

These are cases of excessive or inappropriate *need* for a finite object. This sort of idolatry is found, not in loving another human being very much, but in feeling that life is meaningless without him; not in the most intense enjoyment of philosophy, but in feeling that one would not be oneself if one could not do philosophy;

not in liking other people and wanting to be their friend, but in feeling that one is or would be worthless if rejected by them. One sees it in a widowed person who, after several years, is still unable or unwilling to resume a normal social life, and cannot even be really engaged in conversation on any subject except the loss of his or her spouse.

One of the most extreme cases is that of people who kill themselves over the loss of a lover, being literally unwilling to live without their beloved. This motive is clearer if, like Romeo and Juliet, they believe the loved one dead. In the suicide of a jilted or unrequited lover, which I suppose is more frequent, the motivational waters are muddied by the likelihood that the act is vindictive or in some way an attempt to gain or reclaim the other person's affections. The Romantic spirit has seen in the suicide of Romeo and Juliet the embodiment of an ideal of love—an admirable idolatry, if not an admirable immorality. I do not admire it. Whether Shakespeare personally admired it, I do not know; but the language of his play reflects a moral and religious culture that disapproved of it. When Juliet calls Romeo "the god of my idolatry," the conflict with Christian ethics is obvious; and when Romeo calls himself "fortune's fool," the phrase evokes the Stoic commonplace that caring too much about external goods is folly because it puts one at the mercy of fortune.[15] Even in a thoroughly modern cultural setting, if we knew people who had done in real life what Romeo and Juliet do, I think most of us would not admire their feeling that life was not worth living without the other person. We would consider it exaggerated and foolish, though we would feel sorry for them.[16]

There is a reason that my discussion of this type of idolatry has focused on responses to actual or contemplated loss of the loved object. A person whose life may plausibly be said to revolve around her job or her marriage, while she has them, is not necessarily idolatrous. We cannot pursue, concretely, every possible interest; and some concentration of energy on particular projects and relationships is necessary for an effective and healthy organization of life. A pattern of activity and attention that has an obvious chief concrete center in a tightly knit system of projects and relationships may still be a part of love for the good, or for God, and is even consistent with a "universal loyalty" that is in principle *for* the good wherever it is found. But it can hardly be a part of love for the good as such if one maintains, or is disposed to maintain, this organization of life around a particular project or relationship when it can no longer be pursued in a way that realizes the goods that one prizes in it.

This is not to say that one who loves the good, or God, will pursue particular projects and relationships only *as ways* of loving the good. She can and should care about them for their own sake, and need not be indifferent to their replacement by alternatives that would equally be ways of loving the good. For this reason, love for the good as such is quite compatible with real and intense grief over the loss of a loved object. It is when the grief dominates life for too long a time, or does not coexist with a will to live through it, that we may speak of idolatry. And even then it is only

15. Shakespeare, *Romeo and Juliet*, act 2, scene 2, and act 3, scene 1. I owe this interpretation to Professor D. W. Robertson, Jr.
16. As Shakespeare's Chorus does in *Romeo and Juliet*, prologue, line 7.

fair to be cautious of doing so in any particular case; for losses can trigger depressions that have such organic roots as not necessarily to manifest an excessive attachment.

The love of God, or of the good, is not a competitor of particular attachments within a wide, normal range of intensities. Neither does it appear here primarily as a project that other projects are made to serve. It is manifested in a disposition to love and pursue particular goods. And it is part of this disposition that one will tend to find other particular goods to pursue when the pursuit of one that one loves is definitively blocked.

It is noteworthy that excessive need, as a form of idolatry, typically involves an inability to value oneself appropriately. One feels that without the idol one's life is or would be meaningless or not worth living. Love of the good, on the other hand, carries with it a positive valuation of one's own life so long as it contains possibilities of loving and pursuing goods. Religiously we can say that if one loves God, explicitly or implicitly, one can find meaning in being oneself and loving God in that way, whatever may happen to the finite objects of one's loves, though one will not be invulnerable to the pain of grief. And that will limit the desperateness of one's need for the particular finite objects. Again I must add, of course, that the failure of self-valuation is not reliable proof of idolatry, because depression can block or interfere with this manifestation of love for God.

Here is a basis, I think, for a response to Bernard Williams's theory of "ground projects." He seems to think it a normal and very acceptable feature of human life that a person will have "a nexus of projects, related to his conditions of life," that play a "ground role" in the sense that "the loss of all or most of them . . . would remove meaning" from his life—that if they were frustrated or lost, "he might as well have died." This is what I am calling an idolatry of excessive need. And Williams at least comes close to saying that a person cannot reasonably be required to give up his ground projects for the sake of impartial morality. "There can come a point," he says, "at which it is quite unreasonable for a man to give up, in the name of the impartial good ordering of the world of moral agents, something which is a condition of his having any interest in being around in that world at all."[17]

But surely it is possible to care passionately about particular goods and projects and still to feel that they do not exhaust the value of one's life. The meaning of one's life is open-ended, one may feel, because one confronts an immeasurable ocean of actual and potential good. One cannot attend to more than a little bit of it at once, and one does well to care passionately about that little bit. But at the same time one can be for the good in principle and everywhere. And the actual or possible loss, or even the sacrifice, of particular goods that one loves can be faced, not without pain, but with the expectation that while there is life, there will be goods to be loved, and meaning to be found in loving them. Surely we have reason to desire this disposition both for ourselves and for our associates, and hence to want not to have "ground projects" in Williams's sense.

17. Williams, "Persons, Character, and Morality," pp. 12–14.

In effect I am proposing an ideal of *detachment*. Various sorts of detachment have been advocated by religious and philosophical traditions as diverse as Buddhism, Epicureanism, Stoicism, and ascetical Christianity. From what I have already said it should be evident that I do not share the suspicion of passionate attachment as such that is at least sometimes found in all the traditions I have just mentioned. But I believe they are right in holding that some kind of detachment from particular finite objects deserves a place in our motivational ideal, as necessary for spiritual freedom and for the right sort of orientation toward what is truly good.

While I have criticized Kierkegaard's conception of "infinite resignation" as a way of escaping idolatry, I believe his repeated wrestling with ideals of detachment is particularly interesting, and deserves notice here. At least in parts of his work, such as the *Concluding Unscientific Postscript* and the description of the "knight of faith" in *Fear and Trembling*, he tries to articulate an ideal of detachment that is compatible with a hearty interest in finite goods. Devotion to "the absolute *telos*," or God, cannot take the form of simply excluding interests in finite things, or "relative ends," as Kierkegaard calls them; for it is impossible for human beings to live without relative ends, as he argues. "The task," therefore, is one of "striving to reach the maximum of maintaining simultaneously a relationship to the absolute *telos* and to relative ends, . . . by making the relationship to the absolute *telos* absolute, and the relationship to the relative ends relative." Kierkegaard notes that "it is not an easy thing" to do this; and his attempts to explain how it is to be done attain only an uneven success.[18]

At one point in the *Postscript* he offers the following vignette of the detached attitude in life that he favors:

> Let the world give him everything, it is possible that he will see fit to accept it. But he says: "Oh, well," and this "Oh, well" means the absolute respect for the absolute *telos*. If the world takes everything from him, he suffers, no doubt; but he says again: "Oh, well"—and this "Oh, well" means the absolute respect for the absolute *telos*.[19]

This clearly strikes the wrong note. One who says, "Oh, well," does not care *enough* about some of the finite goods one might lose (a spouse or child, for example). Two pages later, however, Kierkegaard does better:

> An adult may very well whole-heartedly share in the play of children, and may even be responsible for really bringing life into the game; but he does not play as a child. One who understands it as his task to exercise himself in making the absolute distinction sustains just such a relationship to the finite.[20]

This may still not be absolutely the right note, but it does capture something of the ideal of a detachment in which one cares "whole-heartedly" but not desperately about finite goods.

18. Kierkegaard, *Concluding Unscientific Postscript*, p. 364f.
19. Kierkegaard, *Concluding Unscientific Postscript*, p. 368.
20. Kierkegaard, *Concluding Unscientific Postscript*, p. 370.

3. Misidentification

Something similar to the idolatry of exaggerated need can happen with exaggerated hopes.[21] It is possible to organize a life, not around a good that one already enjoys, or once enjoyed, but around some as yet unattained summit from which one expects the equivalent of heaven on earth. Such a pinnacle of fantasy may be sought in the realm of professional success or material possessions or personal intimacy or sexual experience. In any of these cases it can embitter or destroy the real but limited goods that can be attained in these and other areas.

This is the form of idolatry that St. Augustine most feared. He viewed human life as a quest for infinite satisfaction, fueled by a torrent of desire that cannot rest in anything less. This vision, which animates Augustine's famous narrative of his own life, is the very center of his apologetics, his case for monotheistic religion. Countless readers have found in it a persuasive picture of their own need and aspiration. And the great danger that attends this quest, as Augustine sees it, is that we shall seek our infinite satisfaction, not in the invisible supreme Good, but in visible creatures that are by no means equipped to provide it. Experience testifies to the reality of such a danger.

An exaggerated deference to human authority, opinion, or taste can also be a form of idolatry. A life may find its organizing principle in fashion or respectability, or in satisfying the real or imagined expectations of parents, employers, or colleagues. The idols need not be people one loves, or even likes. They may be feared or envied, or simply people on whom one is dependent.

The idolatry of authority could be based on an exaggerated need for the love or approval of the persons deferred to; but there are other possibilities. One's parents may be dead, the favor of one's peers unattainable, but still one feels one must conform to their wishes and tastes. Perhaps, in some irrational and deeply neurotic way, one is trying nonetheless to win their approval. But often, I think, it is more plausible as well as simpler to suppose that one has allowed the desires and opinions of others to define the good, or at any rate the goods one is to pursue, and one is trying to conform because it seems to one the best way to live. And this may be a main motive even where one has a real possibility of pleasing the other people.

Respectability and fashionableness are counterfeit goods, for the most part, and so are many other forms of conformity to other people's ideals and expectations. And a life organized around counterfeit goods has been deflected from the pursuit of true good. There is a point here that is very important for distinguishing between this sort of idolatry and the ordinary and inevitable social rootage of our interests and our view of the good. Our interests are always inspired to some extent by the interests and beliefs of others; the influence of parents in this matter is especially profound. But the development of our interests is normally shaped also by our own more or less autonomous sensitivity to real goods that are involved either in the

---

21. It can happen also with exaggerated fears. I will not discuss this form of idolatry here, partly because it would be distracting to try to deal at this point with the difficult and religiously important issue of how much it is appropriate to fear death.

particular interests or in a more comprehensive form of life that we aspire to live; and this is very important to the possibility of love for the good being seen as the organizing principle of one's life. There is an idolatry of authority when one is mainly responding, not to real goods as one apprehends them, but to other people's desires and opinions.

In idolatries of excessive hope and excessive deference to authority there is something like a cognitive error, which is particularly obvious in the case of illusory hopes. Theologically, I am tempted to say that in these cases there is a *misidentification* of God, or the supreme Good. The object of fantasy is assigned the role of the Good itself; or the views and feelings of other people are allowed to define what is good, as only divine views and feelings could properly do. This is an exaggeration, of course. Few people would make such a misidentification explicitly, or at the level of theory. And even implicitly it is probably rare for anyone to go more than a certain distance in that direction. It is quite possible, however, to go far enough for the label of "idolatry" to be apt, and for the distortion of one's life to be grave.

The possibility of misidentifying God or the Good itself may be approached in another way by considering perversions of religion and morality. One reason for focusing on *implicit* love in developing a motivational ideal is that explicit devotion to God or the good is a good motive only to the extent that one's conception of God or the good is at least roughly accurate in relevant respects. It is at best morally ambiguous, and can be downright evil, to be explicitly devoted to a God whom one conceives as a cruel and arbitrary tyrant, to a racist or sexist vision of human excellence, or to a justice that one identifies with the institutions of an oppressive society. Many of the worst episodes of human history—episodes of persecution, torture, and murder motivated by religious and ethical commitments—can be traced to such misconceptions. Other forms of moral badness may cohabit with professed religion or morality through a view of God or morality that simply fails to be connected with certain areas of life.

Where errors of these sorts are gross enough, it may make sense in theistic ethics to say that someone has misidentified as God a (fictitious) being that is not qualified for the role of the supreme Good. Perhaps this is still an exaggeration; for I suspect it is wisest, in the semantics of theism, to hold that the same actual being, if God exists, is the extension of quite diverse concepts of God. But there is another sort of misidentification that is literally possible. It happens when one fails to distinguish devotion to God or the good from devotion to one's own religion or one's own idea of God or the good. This distinction is not easy to make; for one cannot be explicitly devoted to God or the good except under an idea of one's own. But the difference between God and our religious ideas and practices is great, and has been emphasized by many prophets and teachers of the theistic faiths. Tillich makes the point very clearly:

> Holiness cannot become actual except through holy "objects." But holy objects are not holy in and of themselves. They are holy only by negating themselves in pointing to the divine of which they are the mediums. If they establish themselves as holy, they become demonic. . . . This happens continually in the actual

life of most religions. The representations of man's ultimate concern—holy objects—tend to become his ultimate concern. They are transformed into idols. Holiness provokes idolatry.[22]

Here we approach the original sense of 'idolatry'. Of course ideas of God are not "graven images"; but, as theologians have often pointed out, they share some of the relevant characteristics of physical idols. They serve to represent the divine, and they can be the focus or even the object of devotion. They also share the fundamental religious inadequacy of graven images: God is immeasurably greater than they can clearly represent. This is an appropriate context for speaking of the *transcendence* of the Good over our conceptions of it. To treat religious or ethical ideas in a way that fails to respect the transcendence of God, or of the Good itself, is an important form of idolatry.

How shall we avoid it, given that we cannot be intentionally related to God or the good except by way of our ideas of them? The answer I propose rests on our ability to reexamine critically any of our values and beliefs. Though we can hardly be consciously guided by what is really good as distinct from what we think is good, we can recognize that we may be mistaken. In that recognition we take seriously the transcendence of the Good and its reality that is independent of what we think about it. Devotion to a transcendent Good or God is therefore expressed in an openness to revision of our ethical and religious ideas and beliefs. Rigidity in this area, on the other hand, can be a symptom of idolatrous failure to distinguish our beliefs from their transcendent object, of taking "something essentially conditioned . . . as unconditional," as Tillich puts it.[23]

Grave practical problems confront us at this point. The value of explicit devotion to the good, or to God, depends on what we believe about God, or about the good, as I have already remarked. Anyone who has a serious, explicit moral or religious commitment will have, and ought to have, some convictions that are extremely resistant to change. We will not easily doubt that killing people is generally wrong; and the religious commitments of Jews, Christians, and Muslims are not easily separable from their respective beliefs that God is revealed in the Torah, in Jesus, or in the Quran. But even such central beliefs always present possibilities of reinterpretation. Contemporary debate makes clear that it is not hard to doubt parts of the boundaries of the concept of murder. And christologies and doctrines of revelation can be revised in various ways. Moreover, I do not think it is wise to try to draw up a list of unrevisable beliefs in one's morality or religion. One holds various beliefs—some more, some less firmly, some very firmly indeed. It is as a whole that a system of ethical or religious beliefs must be held open to revision, and as a whole that it permanently confronts the challenge that it is distinct from, and inadequate in relation to, the Good or the God that it represents.[24]

---

22. Tillich, *Systematic Theology*, vol. 1, p. 216.
23. Tillich, *Systematic Theology*, vol. 1, p. 13.
24. Cf. Quine, "Two Dogmas of Empiricism," p. 42f. There is an obvious analogy here with Quine's view of the relation between beliefs and experience; but I am thinking of the relation of a set of beliefs to an intended object that transcends experience.

There is a two-sidedness in the nature of theistic faith. On the one hand, it involves commitment. Its commitment is primarily to God, but that cannot be real in any human life without some commitment to beliefs and practices that have a good measure of quite human intellectual definiteness. And commitment involves a certain tenacity, decisiveness, and abandon in adhering to these beliefs and practices—a refusal to "hedge one's bet" on them in the light of the possibility that they may be wrong—a refusal to abandon the practices if they cost too much or to treat the beliefs, in most ways, as "merely probable."[25]

On the other hand, theistic faith involves, or should involve, the consciousness of its own fallibility and imperfection. The ideal practical expression of this confidence is not indecisiveness or halfheartedness in one's concrete religious commitments but self-critical openness, without rigidity or defensiveness, in relation to internal and external challenges to one's commitments; and an expectation that one will change, a hope that one will grow, in one's view of God. Similar reasons could be given for a two-sided stance of commitment and self-critical openness in nontheistic faith in the good.

The self-critical side of this stance is in tension with the ideal of an integrated motivation and system of values. People who are sensitive to real goods and evils will continually encounter situations, and have feelings, that do not fit neatly into the system of values they bring to them. A morally ideal life cannot be found in a static integrated system but can only be approached in a continual effort of reintegration, combining old and new elements. One must be able to disturb an existing integration in order to accommodate new insights or convictions. For it is only so that one can give effect to a recognition that what one has already achieved never corresponds adequately to the Good itself. A somewhat disorderly, unintegrated system, or nonsystem, of values is not the ideal; but it would be better than fanaticism. People have done dreadful things in the name of great goods—goods of religion or political idealism or even morality—because their systems of values have been unified in such a way as to leave them deaf to the cries of a value that did not fit in their system.

In some ethical thought such an open and critical stance as I am advocating is associated with autonomy. What I have in mind does involve a good measure of thinking and feeling for oneself, and is incompatible with excessive deference to other people's authority, but it is not exactly autonomy. Not in the Kantian sense, for it involves a responsiveness to one's feelings as much as to reasoned argument. And in an ordinary sense a commitment might be quite autonomous and still be idolatrous in something like the way I am trying to rule out. A person might be committed to a certain way of life out of sheer self-will, thinking it good because it pleases him, or because he likes the image of himself it presents. He might know that that is the basis of his commitment, and might still be so determined to adhere to his choice that he is unwilling to reconsider it in any important respect, or to pay any attention to moral feelings that may be bruised by it. Such inflexibility would show that

---

25. This point is discussed much more fully in chapter 16. See also Adams, *The Virtue of Faith*, pp. 42–47.

he is not devoted to the good as such, or to God, but to his own way of life. This is a narcissistic idolatry; it might be said that his own will, or his own way of life as his own, is the idol.

One thing that is missing in such a case can be seen as a kind of heteronomy or theonomy—the aspiration to relate one's life to a standard of good that transcends all one's desires, feelings, beliefs, and commitments, though one cannot be related to it except through them. I will not say that without such an aspiration one cannot even implicitly love the Good. But without it one lacks an important defense against rigid commitments that constitute a sort of idolatrous alternative to love of the Good.[26]

26. Some theological issues connected with idolatry that are not discussed here are explored in Adams, "Idolatry and the Invisibility of God," from which much of the material of section 3 is drawn.

9

SYMBOLIC VALUE

In the last two chapters, in articulating a motivational ideal of devotion to God, I have emphasized the possibility and importance of *implicit* love for God. It is obvious, however, that religious teaching has placed great value on explicit profession of religious belief, and on its explicit expression in ritual and other religiously symbolic behavior. To a modern mentality it may be perplexing that such matters should be thought ethically important. We may be able to remove some of that perplexity, and at the same time enrich our moral conceptual system, if we attend to the more general question of the ethical value and importance of symbolic expression.

1. Martyrdom

Let us begin with a puzzle about martyrdom. 'Martyr' is a Greek word for witness [μάρτυς], lightly anglicized. An act of martyrdom is an act of testifying to, or standing for, something that one believes. It is distinguished from other sorts of testimony by the fact that the martyr pays a substantial price for her action. The word 'martyr' brings first to mind cases in which the price was death, but I shall not confine my attention to such cases. The costliness of the action, it should be added, is due in some way to other people's opposition to the martyr's cause. Someone who impoverishes himself to build a monument to a hero universally admired is not a martyr.

Martyrdom is praised by many religious traditions and demanded, in certain situations, by some. The ancient Christian Church was uncompromising in its insistence that Christians must not deny their faith, and must not offer a pagan sacrifice, under any threat or duress whatever. Yet it is not obvious what was the good of martyrdom, in many cases, or what harm would have been done by conforming outwardly to the pagan demand, while retaining the Christian faith in one's heart. For the Church demanded a willingness to bear witness that was not conditional on the likelihood that the consequences would be good. The blood of the martyrs may have been the seed of the Church, but the obligation of confessing the faith was not seen as conditional on historical fruitfulness. Without entering into the question whether it was right to regard such a stance as obligatory, we can probably agree that the martyrs command our intuitive admiration. And what I am interested in elucidating is a rationale, presumably not consequentialist, that might lie behind our admiration.

What reason can be offered for being willing to pay the price of martyrdom for no obvious good result? Why wouldn't it be better to stand up for one's beliefs only when the consequences are likely to be good? One possible response to these questions would be an appeal to religious authority. Christians, it may be said, are forbidden to deny Christ, or to worship anyone but God, and therefore must not conform to demands such as the Roman Empire periodically addressed to them. It is hard to rest in this answer, however. For we can hardly help asking why God would want you to be a martyr if it would do no good. And if there is no good reason for God to command martyrdom under such circumstances, that will undermine the plausibility of the belief that it is commanded.

Moreover, the problem can be duplicated in a secular context, in which the appeal to religious authority is not available. Martyrdom over a political issue can seem admirable, if not imperative, to many people, of a wide variety of religious and secular persuasions. The following incident comes from the life of a theologian, but I think our feelings about it will not depend on the religious faith of the protagonist. The story is about Dietrich Bonhoeffer, well known as a leader of resistance to Hitler in the Protestant church in Germany, who was put to death by the Nazis at the end of the Second World War. His friend and biographer Eberhard Bethge records that on the afternoon of 17 June 1940, while he was sitting with Bonhoeffer in an outdoor café at a German seaside resort, the café's loudspeaker, with a sudden fanfare, broadcast the news that France had surrendered.

> The people round about at the tables could hardly contain themselves; they jumped up, and some even climbed on the chairs. With outstretched arm they sang "*Deutschland, Deutschland über alles*" and the Horst-Wessel song. We had stood up too. Bonhoeffer raised his arm in the regulation Hitler salute, while I stood there dazed. "Raise your arm! Are you crazy?" he whispered to me, and later: "We shall have to run risks for very different things now, but not for that salute!"[1]

1. Bethge, *Dietrich Bonhoeffer*, p. 585.

On Bethge's interpretation, which certainly seems to be confirmed by later events, Bonhoeffer had not gone over to Nazism, or even lost his nerve. Rather he was in the early stages of a change of strategy and personal response, from public protest in the 1930s to conspiracy within the German government during the war—conspiracy that actually involved Bonhoeffer's employment in the German military intelligence service. The epithet 'martyr' is widely, but only very loosely, applied to Bonhoeffer.[2] His public opposition in the thirties certainly involved some degree of martyrdom. He suffered for it. But he was not killed or even imprisoned for *that*. What he died for was heroic enough, but it was precisely not martyrdom. He was executed for his part in a conspiracy to kill Hitler. That activity was not testimony; it was not publicly acknowledged but secret. It involved much necessary, and in my opinion commendable, deception.

I admire Bonhoeffer, and I would not presume to say that he *ought* to have chosen a different course on the occasion described; but I would *like* his life story better if it did not contain that Hitler salute. On first reading about the incident I shared his friend's apparent shock at Bonhoeffer's action. And even on reflection I do not think it would have been "crazy" to have refrained from the salute, even if it would have involved some sort of martyrdom. This is indeed the first point that I want to use the story to make. Even if we think that Bonhoeffer's path of secret and ultimately conspiratorial opposition was defensible, and maybe heroic, I imagine that most of us, perhaps all of us, will feel that it would also have been admirable to have refused to give the Hitler salute. And this reaction clearly needs no appeal to religious authority to sustain it. It is grounded rather in a conviction, widely shared by people of many religious and nonreligious orientations, that Nazism was a great evil. But it does not rest on a belief, which I do not hold, that an act of silent protest, in Bonhoeffer's situation, would be likely to have had good consequences. So I face the question, what is admirable about a costly and probably ineffective act of protest.

Some may think that this way of putting the question overlooks the effects of the action on the agent. Could the reason for refusing to offer a salute to Hitler, or a pinch of incense to the genius of the emperor, be that offering it would be harmful to your own moral or spiritual life? I grant that it would be harmful, if you see the act as one of religious disloyalty, or abandonment of your moral ideals. But why should you see the act in that way? This is just another version of the original question, what religious or moral value there is in the act of martyrdom.

Our quest for a better answer to this question may begin with the central idea in the concept of martyrdom, the idea of *testimony*. The main thing that is ethically required of testimony, we may think, is *truthfulness*.[3] But we are not likely to find an adequate explanation of the value of martyrdom in the general value of truthfulness. Most of the lies and deceptions that Bonhoeffer was obliged to practice in his conspiratorial activity, for example, are much easier to accept, morally, than the Nazi

---

2. I do *not* mean to suggest that he deserves less honor than those to whom the epithet strictly applies.

3. That truthfulness is worth prizing for its own sake I have argued in chapter 6, section 2. St. Augustine was not altogether off the mark in treating martyrdom as a prime case for the ethics of truthfulness: Augustine, "On Lying," 13; "To Consentius: Against Lying," 3.

salute. And if we would admire at all the quixotic truthfulness of someone who would not use forged identity papers to escape from the Nazis because it would involve lying, we would certainly admire that much less than a refusal to give the Nazi salute. This indicates that the value we see in martyrdom is something more than the value of truthfulness.

In particular, the content of one's testimony matters, as well as its truthfulness. Being truthful about one's name and address does not matter in the same way as expressing what one believes about a great moral or religious issue. And I think that is because in the latter case one is testifying, not just *about* something, but *for* or *against* something. The issue in martyrdom is not just one of truthfulness, but also, and more important, of what one is for and against. Expressing one's loyalty to Christ in verbal or symbolic behavior is an important way of being for Christ. Refusing to engage in behavior expressive of loyalty to Nazism is an important way of being against Nazism. And it is a major part of virtue to be for the good and against the bad. This I believe to be the main connection between martyrdom and virtue, and the main source of the value of martyrdom.

2. The Moral Value of Symbolism

We take it for granted that an action can be good or bad because of what it *causes*, or is meant to cause. I claim that an action can also be good or bad because of what it *symbolizes* or stands for. That is the main idea of this chapter, and it deserves some development.

When we think of an alternative to valuing an action for its consequences, we think naturally of regarding the action as *intrinsically* valuable. And no doubt symbolic value could be contrasted as intrinsic with merely instrumental value. But there is another way in which the label 'intrinsic' is not very apt for the sort of symbolic value that most interests me. For in the ancient contrast of *nomos* and *physis*, convention and nature, we associate the intrinsic with the natural; but the symbolism involved in martyrdom is conventional rather than natural.

Theories of signification and communication have long noted that there are natural signs, which are causally rather than conventionally connected with what they signify. And a natural sign is sometimes regarded as a symbol of what it signifies. "The midnight oil," for example, is (or was) a natural symbol of diligence in study. It required no convention to establish this connection, because diligence naturally caused students to burn oil in their lamps late at night.

Natural signs or symbols, like conventional symbols, can be used both to communicate information and to mislead or deceive. For instance, you could leave a light burning on your desk, to give a misleading impression of diligence, when you go to a movie. Many of us customarily leave some lights on in our homes in the evening, whether we are at home or not, to give potential burglars the idea that someone is there. If we are there, what we suggest is true; if we are out, we are trying to deceive.

We may frown on such deception if it causes undeserved harm, or if it amounts to pretending to a virtue that one does not possess. But we do not regard it as lying, and even people who would have qualms about lying to potential burglars normally have no compunctions about leaving the lights on. There is no false testimony in misleading natural signs—for the simple reason that there is no *testimony* at all in them. For testimony (like lying) requires *commitment* of a sort that is (logically) possible only within a conventional system of mutually understood intentions, such as a language. It is the conventions that determine that an action is testimony, and what it attests. Lying is a kind of violation of the conventions. And martyrdom, as I have said, is first of all testimony. No doubt we could have conventions by which natural signs would be used to attest what they naturally signify. But that is not the usual case.

This may seem to intensify the problem about martyrdom. We are being asked to value an action, not only apart from the value of its consequences, but also on the basis of a meaning that does not belong to it naturally, but only in relation to certain conventions. This objection can be overcome, however. What is positively or negatively valued is not raising one's arm or making certain sounds as such; it is expressing commitment or loyalty to a belief or cause. Such expression, I have argued, is good or bad insofar as it is a way of being for or against something good or bad. Expressing love of the good, and opposition to the bad, is naturally and intrinsically good, though the form it takes is variable and conventional.

This is not to say there is a form it could take without any conventions at all. Indeed, it is only by virtue of our systems of conventional symbolism that we are able to be "for" or "against" most goods and evils. A dog can desire food, and perhaps can love its mistress. A dog can also be mean or gentle. But if we said that the dog loves gentleness or hates meanness, all we could mean is that it tends to like gentle actions and tends to dislike harsh ones. There is no way that the dog could be in favor of gentleness in general or opposed to meanness in general. How is it that we can be for or against such goods and evils in a way that dogs cannot? Clearly it is by virtue of our ability to make use of conventional symbolism to express explicitly, to others or to ourselves, our allegiance or opposition.

And while it is certainly possible to be for or against a good or evil without expressing that openly, it is not easy. If you express explicitly, sincerely, and openly, to your friends at least, your Christian faith or your hatred of Nazism, you take a stance. You are for Christianity; or you are against Nazism. Now suppose that, under the pressure of persecution, and perhaps justifiably, you suppress all outward expression of your loyalties. After a while you yourself may begin to wonder how much reality there is in your opposition to Nazism. Are you actually opposed to it, or do you only wish you could be?[4] These considerations make clear, I think, the importance of symbolic expression for morality, if moral goodness consists largely in being for the good and against the bad.[5]

4. These problems emerge vividly, in a fictional representation of life under fascism, in Silone, *Bread and Wine.*
5. The assumption expressed in this clause deserves emphasis. Some who have heard this argument have asked if it does not depend on the assumption that there is a God, or at least a transcendent Good, to be an object of symbolic affirmation. I think not, though my theory as a whole is clearly committed to that assumption. The argument depends, not on an assumption about the nature of the good one is for, but on the assumption that it is morally good to be for the good (whether or not one's being for it is effectual). The argument, however, probably does depend on the assumption that moral goodness has a more than merely instrumental value.

Ethical theory has paid little attention to the value that can belong to actions by virtue of their expressing symbolically an allegiance to the good or an opposition to the bad. The value of consequences, by contrast, is a dominant consideration in most ethical theories. If it is not exclusively the consequences of the actions themselves, as in act utilitarianism, then it may be the consequences of adopting certain rules, as in rule utilitarianism or (with somewhat different tests applied to the consequences) in Rawls's theory of justice. Theories of virtue, alternatively, may focus on the consequences of dispositions or traits of character. The tendency to evaluate the way a person lives in terms of its consequences is pervasive in contemporary ethical theory.

The value of consequences is certainly important for ethics, but we may well wonder why the symbolic value of actions has been neglected. If we take it for granted that the value of what we cause, or at least of what we intentionally cause, is important to the moral quality of our lives, why should we not assume that the value of what we stand for symbolically is also important to the moral quality of our lives? We sometimes speak of that quality, after all, in terms of the "meaning" of our lives— and there is no reason to suppose that conventional symbolism is irrelevant to meanings!

One reason for the focus on consequences, no doubt, is that ethical theorists have been concerned to show that ethical thinking is *rational*, and an argument from the value of consequences to a prima facie value of the means of attaining them is viewed as the clearest paradigm of practical rationality. There are also reasons for symbolic action, however. I have tried to indicate the most important, which is that symbolic action is a way of being for what one loves and against what one hates. Wanting to find significant ways of being for what one loves and against what one hates is an important part of loving and hating. One therefore has an important reason for giving symbolic expression to one's loyalties. Symbolic action expressing love for the Good and hatred of evils is therefore prima facie rational for those who love the Good.

This may be viewed, however, as a self-regarding reason; and that may be a further cause of the neglect of symbolic value in moral theory. Morality is thought to be concerned with our lives as they impinge on the interests of other people; and the expressive significance of my action as a part of my life does not impinge on your life as clearly, heavily, or inescapably as some of the consequences of my action may. It is for reasons of this sort that the "clean hands" motive for refusing to employ evil means to good ends is often thought to be selfish. And "clean hands," though hardly a matter of conventional symbolism, are a matter of expressing one's loyalties and convictions clearly in one's life.

This objection is not altogether to be dismissed. It would be selfish to give the symbolic, or more broadly the expressive, value of one's life an invariable precedence over the value of consequences. Some aspects of the task of weighing these two types of consideration against each other will be considered in the next section. But the argument that would dismiss all appeal to symbolic value as at best irrelevant to the concerns of morality rests on a misconception of the interests that it is morality's business to protect. If our interest in each other were merely competitive and exploitative, we would view each other only as potential obstacles or instruments, and would not care, at bottom, about the intrinsic quality of each other's lives, but only about their consequences. But those are surely not the only interests for which morality should care. In a morally more desirable system of relationships we care about each other as partners and friends, and therefore have interests in the intrinsic quality of each other's lives. In particular, it matters to us what other people are for and against, as that profoundly affects the possibilities of alliance and social union with them. A morally good person, from this point of view, is not just a useful person but an ally of the good and of those who love the good. And such a person will have reason to perform acts that symbolically express love for the good, and hatred of evils.

This point applies with special emphasis to theistic ethics. An omnipotent deity can hardly have a *merely* instrumental interest in any creature. The causal consequences of our actions God could secure without our aid, if God were willing as well as able to intervene in the course of nature. What even omnipotence most obviously cannot obtain without our voluntary choice is our voluntary expression of allegiance to God or to the good. This is a reason for thinking the intrinsic and expressive value of human actions more fundamental in relation to divine omnipotence than their extrinsic and instrumental value.

3. Eschatology and Ethics

It is not only symbolic action, of course, that expresses our loves and loyalties. Loving the good gives us plenty of reason to care about the consequences of our actions, and striving to produce good consequences can be an expression of such love. Indeed, if the obtaining of good consequences of significant magnitude, or the prevention of bad ones, is a realistic possibility, it commonly will and should seem more important to love for the good than a purely symbolic expression. The expressive value of a symbolic act can be undermined if its expected consequences are too costly to the concerns it is supposed to attest.

Whether it would be good to perform an act whose value is mainly symbolic, such as an act of martyrdom, may therefore depend on what other possibilities of action are available in the situation. If Bonhoeffer had a unique opportunity, by pretending to be a Nazi, to assure the success of a conspiracy to overthrow the Nazi regime, then I think it would be irresponsible for him to refuse to give the Hitler salute, despite its moral distastefulness. On the other hand, if there was no realistic hope of successful resistance, conspiratorial or otherwise, to Nazism within Germany, then the symbolic protest of refusing to salute might have been the best available way of being against Nazism. Probably Bonhoeffer's actual situation lay somewhere between those extremes, though closer than he could believe to the more pessimistic one.

This illustrates a more general point which is of great importance for the relation of religion to ethics. What it is reasonable or good, or even makes sense, to do depends on our possibilities of action, and thus on our situation in the world. What that situation is, is a largely empirical question; and its details are subject to political, economic, medical, and other sorts of analysis and prediction. Comprehensively, however, and very often in detail, it is subject to great uncertainty. The future is largely unknown to us; and so, arguably, are the metaphysical grounds of our existence. These mysteries are a main topic of speculation, faith, and meditation in all religious traditions. And it is very largely because it affects our view of our situation in the world that religion affects ethics.

One way in which this works can be seen in a dispute within contemporary Christian ethics. In the middle of our century the "Christian realism" of Reinhold Niebuhr, with its endorsement of participation in political conflict and its acceptance of some violence as a necessary evil, was the moral theory with the greatest influence, not only on American Christian ethics, but probably also on American public life. Some of the most interesting recent work in Christian ethics has criticized Niebuhr sharply from the point of view of what is often called the "Anabaptist" tradition of Christian pacifism. In a notably systematic presentation of that position, James McClendon has located a major part of his disagreement with Niebuhr in the area of *eschatology*;[6] and that poses the issue I wish to examine.

In theological parlance, 'eschatology' signifies the doctrine of "last things"—death and resurrection, the return of Christ, final judgment, heaven and hell. Beliefs on these subjects have been an obvious part of Christian views of our situation in the world, and have played a correspondingly important part in Christian ethics. In my opinion (though not McClendon's) the main point of disagreement between him and Niebuhr in this area is in what has been called "*realized* eschatology."[7]

This term might seem contradictory. How can a claim about what has already been realized be part of a doctrine of last things? The phrase is used in fact to express the claim that part of what has been expected in an earlier eschatology has already happened. It might be clearer and more accurate to speak here of a theology of history rather than an eschatology. In another way, however, the title 'eschatology' remains appropriate, particularly for ethics. For while we are dealing with a view of history that embraces the past and the present as well as the future (and that has always been at least implicitly true where eschatology is spoken of), there remains, at least for ethics, a special interest in the future. We need and strive to form some opinion about what we can expect or what we should hope for, though for realized eschatology and for ethics the accent may fall on the nearer future. This is true of both Niebuhr and McClendon.

McClendon's pacifism is rooted in his conviction that Christians as such are called to live the life of the Kingdom of God in the midst of this present age, and that the extent to which the Kingdom has already come is sufficient for that attempt to make sense. Accordingly, he criticizes "Niebuhr's rejection of the efficacy of the Holy Spirit to make Christians Christ-like, his downplay of the new birth as

6. McClendon, *Systematic Theology*, vol. 1, p. 320. McClendon claims that Niebuhr lacks an eschatology in the sense that his vision of sin and grace in human history "form[s] a seamless whole without recourse to any future consummation." It should be noted that McClendon prefers, with some reason, to name his tradition "baptist."

7. Ironically, the idea of a future consummation does not play a very fully articulated role in McClendon's own ethics, so far as I can see. See my review of McClendon's book, from which I have drawn some material for the present discussion.

a real transformation of human life," and "an overemphasis [on sin] that makes
of Niebuhr's ethic a strategy for (discriminately) sinful living in an (indiscriminately)
sinful world, rather than a strategy for transformed life in a world become new in
Christ Jesus." "Niebuhr," he charges, "is too grimly 'realistic' in his assessment of
the revolutionary possibilities of Christian community; his realism overlooks the
new life in Christ."[8]

I agree with McClendon that Niebuhr seriously underrated the possibilities of
a real spiritual transformation of human life, here and now. But I think history might
support Niebuhr in responding that McClendon's view of "the revolutionary possibilities of Christian community" goes too far in the opposite direction. It is one of
the lessons of Christian history, as Niebuhr saw it, that the Christian commitment
of even the best of Christian communities is itself a standing temptation to spiritual pride, and that all such communities fall from time to time into very harmful
sins and errors. This may lead one to doubt that the contrast between church and
world can bear the moral weight that McClendon wishes to lay upon it.[9] And if,
with Niebuhr, one finds it less plausible to think that God's grace is at work pre-
eminently in sanctifying a revolutionary Christian community, one may also, with
Niebuhr, find it more plausible to seek God's grace in a fairly rough-and-tumble
participation in the secular life of one's society.

I incline more to Niebuhr's side in this dispute, but I am not trying to settle it
here. My aim is rather to show how differences in what we might broadly think of
as eschatology inevitably and appropriately affect views in ethics. This applies to
secular as well as theological ethics, though the eschatological assumptions may be
less explicit in secular ethics. The dispute between McClendon and Niebuhr finds
a clear parallel, indeed, in contemporary moral philosophy.

McClendon's counterparts are those who would devise their ethical theory primarily for an ideal society. Rawls's theory of justice, for example, is offered to us as
a "strict compliance" theory, assuming general conformity to the principles of justice. How it is just to respond to widespread injustice, or to other practical obstacles
to the implementation of ideal principles, is left to be worked out later.[10] This seems
reasonable if we take a fairly optimistic view of our chances of approximating full
compliance with the ideal of justice. Those who take a more Niebuhrian view of
human sinfulness, however, might expect more guidance from a theory that devoted
less attention to ideal conditions of rational agreement, and more to the acceptance
and limitation of conflict.

Derek Parfit may be in the same eschatological boat with Rawls. Parfit says that
when "deciding what we believe" in moral theory, "we should first consider our Ideal
Act Theory," which says "what we should all try to do, simply on the assumptions
that we all try, and all succeed." Such a theory is "ideal" rather than "practical,"
Parfit agrees, because it is a fact that "we are often uncertain what the effects of our

8. McClendon, *Systematic Theology*, vol. 1, pp. 320, 161.
9. McClendon, *Systematic Theology*, vol. 1, e.g., pp. 17f., 234.
10. Rawls, *A Theory of Justice*, p. 8f. and §39. Rawls acknowledges that the issues thus post-
poned are "the most pressing and urgent matters" (p. 9), but believes they will be best illuminated by
the ideal theory. I am more skeptical of that.

acts will be," and "some of us will act wrongly."[11] Nevertheless, he regards it as a devastating criticism of a moral theory if successful implementation of its Ideal Act Theory would have worse consequences than the successful implementation of some other Ideal Act Theory.[12] Why should this be a decisive test for an ethical theory? We may well be skeptical of Parfit's test if we take a Niebuhrian view of the possibilities of human virtue and moral agreement. The beauty of an unattainable ideal may rightly inspire us when we are thinking about the intrinsic value of an act or a practice. But when we are evaluating an act or a practice on the basis of something so extrinsic as consequences, it would seem to be only the actual or probable consequences that matter, not the consequences that would obtain in an ideal state that will never be realized. If our eschatology is sunnier, on the other hand, at least as regards the nearer future, and if we suppose that reflection on these matters, and on the benefits of a certain ideal practice, might actually lead to sufficiently general conformity with the practice to achieve a good measure of the benefits, then Parfit's test may begin to look more relevant and more reasonable.

Search for a secular counterpart to Niebuhr might begin with act utilitarians (or "utilitarians," for short). They do not rely on a supposed possibility of any group approximating strict or general compliance with an ideal code.[13] For the utilitarian agent is supposed to do what will probably have the best results, given the *actual* probabilities regarding the behavior of others. If the others are virtuous, the utilitarian takes that into account. If the others are vicious, utilitarian principles apply in exactly the same way, though the best obtainable results may not be so happy.

In another respect, however, utilitarianism is not so Niebuhrian, and may be charged with needing an excessively optimistic eschatology. For utilitarianism is an ethics for people who think they can plan the future. This is not to say that the utilitarian must be able to shape the future to her heart's desire; her lot may be harder than that. But she must have a measure of control over the future; and utilitarianism holds each of us responsible, in principle, for the *whole* future. Two conditions must be satisfied if utilitarian reasoning is to be useful in a situation. One is that we must be able with reasonable reliability to estimate the conditional probability of alternative possible consequences of alternative courses of action. The other condition is that we must have possibilities of action that have a significant chance of substantially improving the outcome as we see it. In many, perhaps most, contexts of choice it is a serious question whether these conditions are satisfied.[14]

11. Parfit, *Reasons and Persons*, p. 99f. To the practical difficulties I would add that we are often mistaken about such matters.

12. Parfit, *Reasons and Persons*, p. 103.

13. This point is made in Sowden, Review of Parfit, *Reasons and Persons*, p. 526.

14. I have not resisted the temptation to take a potshot at utilitarianism. My larger argument in this chapter is not, however, a refutation of utilitarianism. The focus of my argument is on the ethical importance of what we stand for, as distinct from what we cause or try to cause; and I have not tried to prove that symbolic value cannot be accommodated as a special sort of "utility" in a broadly utilitarian calculus. I do not, in fact, think that such a calculus provides a very natural context for symbolic value; in some of the most interesting symbolic actions, the agent throws such calculations to the winds and simply affirms her values symbolically, and may be quite right in doing so; but that is not the main burden of my argument here. An important recent attempt to incorporate "symbolic

This is a question that obviously confronted Bonhoeffer in the situation I described earlier. I suspect that in fact neither condition was satisfied for him—that is, that he did not have a significant chance of improving the outcome, and his best estimates of his chances were not reliable. There is a gaping hole in most modern ethical theories, and not just in utilitarianism, at this point. They have nothing to say to us in a situation of helplessness. This has not always been true of ethical theory. Most religions have much advice for the helpless, though some contemporary religious ethics is more exclusively activist. In philosophical ethics, Stoicism is famous for its views about how to cope with outward helplessness.

One reason for the difference may be that many modern theories construe the task of ethics too narrowly, as guidance for *action*. Ethics is not only about how to act well, but more broadly about how to *live* well. And whether we like it or not, helplessness is a large part of life. Human life both begins and ends in helplessness. Between infancy and death, moreover, we may find ourselves in the grip of a disease or a dictatorship to which we may be able to adapt but which we cannot conquer. Even if our individual situation is more fortunate, we will find ourselves relatively helpless spectators of most of the events in the world about which we should care somewhat, and many of those about which we should care most, if we are good people. Dealing well with our helplessness is therefore an important part of living well. An ethical theory that has nothing to say about this abandons us in what is literally the hour of our greatest need.

A central part of living well is being for the good and against evils. We face the question, how we can be for and against goods and evils that we are relatively powerless to accomplish or prevent. One of the most obvious answers is that we can give more reality to our being for the goods and against the evils by expressing our loyalties symbolically in action. For this reason acts of martyrdom represent a particularly important possibility of living well for people who find themselves in situations of comparative helplessness—oppressed peoples, persecuted minorities, and inmates of concentration camps, for example. For the same reason sickbeds are rightly surrounded by acts of mainly symbolic value—though the degree of costliness and the context of conflict that would make them a martyrdom is normally lacking here. When our friends are ill, most of us are not able to do much about their health. But we can still be *for* them, and that is important to all of us. Sending cards and flowers are ways of being for a sick person symbolically. They may also have the good consequence of cheering up the patient, but that will be because he is glad that his friends are for him. The symbolic value of the deed is primary in such a case.

---

utility" in a calculus of utilities is in Nozick, *The Nature of Rationality*, esp. pp. 26–35, 48–49; but I am not sure how similar Nozick's conception of symbolic utility is to my conception of symbolic value. Freudian symbolism plays a prominent part in his account (pp. 26–27, 32) that I think it could not play in mine. Conversely, a value derived from symbolizing a deity or an ethical principle, which is central to my account, does not cohere neatly with the emphasis on (causally evaluated) outcomes and actions in his stipulation that "the symbolic utility of an action *A* is determined by *A*'s having symbolic connections to outcomes (and perhaps to other actions) that themselves have the standard kind of utility" (p. 48)—where the standard kind of utility "is measured in situations that are wholly causal" (p. 48 n). Nozick's account and mine agree, however, that symbolic value or symbolic utility need not itself be *causally instrumental* in producing any kind of good (Nozick, p. 48).

This line of thought might seem to lead to the conclusion that Bonhoeffer *ought* to have refrained from the Hitler salute in the incident I described, if I am right in suspecting that his real political situation was one of powerlessness. But this inference should be resisted. Martyrdom is a way of being for the Good, and against evils, even when one is helpless, but it is rarely the only way. Pursuing a conspiratorial struggle against an evil regime is also a way of being against it, even when the struggle is hopeless, and even if one knows it is hopeless. I am skeptical of any general rule about *how* to be for the good in such a situation; it seems to me rather to be a matter of vocation.

Something similar can be true where one is not helpless. The attainment of a good result, where that is possible, is often of greater moral urgency than the clarity of one's testimony. But I think it is not always morally required to follow (if one can) a path of political power in which one could do good but at the cost of having to make compromises that would leave one's life symbolically ambiguous as a testimony to one's ideals and principles. One may have to choose, in biblical terms, between being a prophet and being a king. Such a choice, again, can be seen in terms of vocation, which is the subject of chapter 13.

4. Worship

These considerations about eschatology (in a loose and extended sense) and the place of symbolic value in ethics apply to both secular and religious ethics. There are reasons, however, why symbolic action is especially important for religious ethics. One is that there is a tendency for religion to see human life in a framework that emphasizes or even magnifies the place of helplessness in human life, and that consequently enlarges the need for symbolic action. This can be illustrated from the best loved sacred text of theistic Hinduism, the Bhagavad Gita. A rich and many-stranded poem, rather than the consistent development of a philosophical theory, the Gita presents multiple possibilities of interpretation. But one can hardly deny the centrality of the idea that one ought to engage in action (*karma*) while in some sense renouncing its "fruits." The fruits are the consequences the action will naturally have, both in one's present life, by empirical causal laws, and in future incarnations, by the retributive laws associated with the Indian conception of karma. The fruits will certainly follow, except insofar as one is able, through mysticism, to break out of the whole system of karma; but one's action should not be for the sake of the fruits. Underlying this idea, I believe, is a mystical intuition of a true Good, unattainable by karma, beside which all possible fruits of karma pale into insignificance.

Why, then, engage in action at all? This is one of the first questions the Gita considers, and it gives the answer that it is simply impossible to refrain from action. "For no one remains inactive even for a moment. The states of all existence make everyone act in spite of himself" (III, 5). If this is not to be a bondage, one needs a way of acting that is an alternative to acting for the sake of the fruits. Perhaps not the only alternative, but one that is repeatedly proposed in the Gita, is to offer one's actions as a *sacrifice*. "It is true, this world is enslaved by activity, but the exception is work for the sake of sacrifice. Therefore, ... free from attachment, act for that purpose" (III, 9). "Whatever you do, or eat, or sacrifice, or offer, whatever you do in self-restraint, do as an offering to me," says Krishna (IX, 21).[15]

Sacrifice, in the literal sense, is of course a ritual action. Its significance is highly symbolic, and largely conventional. The Gita records a primitive view of sacrifice as instrumentally efficacious (III, 10–16), but emphasizes a different view, in line with the renunciation of the fruits of action. To treat all one's actions as sacrifice, as recommended by the Gita, is in effect to adopt a convention giving them symbolic significance as expressions of one's devotion to God.[16] In this way symbolic value is invoked to fill the place of the instrumental value that has been disparaged.

The devaluation of the consequences of ordinary action in at least a main strand of the Gita may seem extreme from Western points of view; but Western religion has a counterpart in the idea that the most important goods cannot be controlled by our action, but depend on God's grace. Where this idea is stressed it naturally produces an emphasis on the symbolic value of action. The Heidelberg Catechism, for example, asks,

> Since then we are redeemed from our misery, by grace through Christ, without any merit of our own, why must we do good works?

and answers,

> Because Christ, having redeemed us by His blood, renews us also by His Holy Spirit after his own image, so that with our whole life we may show ourselves thankful to God for His beneficence, and that He may be glorified through us . . .

To be sure, the Catechism goes on, with debatable consistency, to add a consequential bonus, adducing as "further" motives for good works

> that we ourselves may be assured of our faith by its fruits, and by our godly walk may win our neighbors to Christ.[17]

But the symbolic value of Christian behavior, as an expression of gratitude to God, is clearly given precedence over its instrumental value. The parallel with the Bhagavad Gita, both in the question and in the answer, is striking, especially given the distance that in many ways separates the two religious traditions.[18]

---

15. Bolle, trans., *The Bhagavadgita*, pp. 39, 41, 109. I have also been helped by the renderings and commentary of Zaehner, trans., *The Bhagavad-Gita*.

16. The convention may of course have been divinely instituted. In the interpretation of Zaehner, trans., *The Bhagavad-Gita*, p. 394, doing one's caste duty counts as an offering to Krishna because Krishna is the author of the system. Here the value of obedience is seen as mainly expressive.

17. *Heidelberg Catechism*, qu. 86; I have adopted a few emendations of the translation.

18. To sacrifice and thanksgiving, as categories for the ascription of symbolic religious value to behavior, may be added witness or testimony. Karl Barth, the most eminent twentieth-century protagonist of the tradition represented by the Heidelberg Catechism, claimed that "the essence of [Chris-

Both of these texts illustrate the centrality of *worship* in theistic ethics. The whole ethical life is clearly assimilated to worship when its value is interpreted in terms of sacrifice or the expression of gratitude to God. The importance of symbolism to religion is nowhere more evident than in the phenomenon of worship; for the significance and value of actions as worship depends heavily, if not entirely, on the conventional significance of symbols.

Something of ethical importance can be done in worship that we cannot accomplish except symbolically. We may or may not think that the Bhagavad Gita and the Heidelberg Catechism underrate the instrumental value of ordinary human activity. But we can hardly deny that our ability to do good, and even to conceive of good and care about it, is limited. Our nonsymbolic activity, perforce, is a little of this and a little of that. Getting ourselves dressed in the morning, driving or riding or walking to work, and then home again to dinner, we try, on the way and in between, to do some good, to love people and be kind to them, to enjoy and perhaps create some beauty. But none of this is very perfect, even when we succeed; and all of it is very fragmentary. One who loves the good should be *for* the good wherever it occurs or is at stake. But we do not even know about most of the good and opportunities for good in the world, and we cannot do very much about most of what we do know. We can care effectively only about fragments that are accessible to us. Intensively, moreover, as well as extensively, we cannot engage the whole of goodness nonsymbolically. I have an inkling of a goodness too wonderful for us to comprehend, but concretely I must devote myself to getting the text I am writing a little clearer and more cogently argued than the last draft.

Symbolically we can do better. Symbolically I can be for the Good as such, and not just for the bits and pieces of it that I can concretely promote or embody. I can be for the good as such by articulating or accepting some conception of a comprehensive and perfect or transcendent Good and expressing my loyalty to it symbolically. There is no way that I can do it without symbols. It is for this reason, I believe, that when religious thinkers have sought alternatives to the instrumental value of actions, they have tended to focus on symbolic rather than on more intrinsic values. My actions can have a more intrinsic goodness insofar as they imitate or image God, on my theistic view. But the relation to the transcendent Good is never as clear in the imitation as it can be in the symbolism. Hence the symbolism provides something for which there is no adequate substitute.

Theists find this value of symbolism supremely in worship. Limited as the extent of my love and beneficence and political influence must be, I can still *pray* "for all sorts and conditions of" people.[19] Qualitatively limited as I must be in

---

tians'] vocation is that God makes them His witnesses" (Barth, *Church Dogmatics*, vol. 4, part 3, second half, p. 575). The meaning of life, or a large part of it, can be found in expressing the truth about God.

19. At this point I have more than once encountered the objection that intercessory prayer is meant to be efficacious. I grant that one who prays typically hopes to influence the course of events by influencing God. But it is important to distinguish prayer from magic. Even if God responds to it, prayer is communication with God, not placing one's hands on the levers of the universe. They remain in God's hands. In central cases of intercessory prayer one's action is not based on calculations

the goodness of my life and even in my conception of the good, I can still name and praise a transcendent Good. And fragmented as my concerns are in dealing with various finite goods, I can integrate my love for the good in explicit adoration of the one God.

Grave moral and religious temptations attend this symbolic integration. It must not be allowed to become a *substitute* for such nonsymbolic goodness as is possible for us, fragmentary and imperfect as the latter must be. The biblical prophets sternly and rightly denied the value of merely symbolic worship in lives that included no concrete imitation of the divine justice.[20] In most situations symbolic expression by itself does not constitute love for the good—or for anything. But a genuine love for the good can find in symbolic expression an integration and completion that would otherwise be impossible. It is perhaps because there is a real need in this area that reformers who have wanted to do away with traditional religious beliefs have sometimes tried to introduce symbolic rituals that would be a functional equivalent of traditional worship.

If what I have said about helplessness is right, it is not surprising that the need for worship is felt especially in connection with death. In Jewish liturgy, for example, the prayer that is most strongly associated with mourning and commemorating the dead, the Kaddish, has hardly anything to say about death or mourning, but is mainly devoted to praise of God. The first sentence sets the theme: "Magnified and hallowed be his great name in the world which he has created according to his will."[21] Precisely because there is nothing we can do about a death that has occurred, we want to affirm the meaning of life in the face of it by expressing symbolically our allegiance to the supreme Good. However little we can do, if we can do anything at all we can worship. As Isaac Watts put it,

> I'll praise my Maker while I've breath,
> And when my voice is lost in death,
>   Praise shall employ my nobler powers:
> My days of praise shall ne'er be past,
> While life and thought and being last,
>   Or immortality endures.[22]

---

of expected utility or of probable results. For example, if one starts observing which formulations in prayer "work" in terms of results, and using those that do, one is crossing the line from prayer to magic. In praying, no doubt, one may be *trying* to obtain what one asks, but the attempt proceeds solely by *symbolizing* that one is *for* what one asks. The symbolic value of the prayer is more fundamental than any instrumental value it may have.

20. Amos 5:21–24; Isaiah 1:10–17, 58:1–9; Micah 6:6–8; Jeremiah 6:20.
21. Pool, *The Kaddish*, p. xiif.; Luban, *The Kaddish*, p. 20f.
22. Isaac Watts, quoted from *Congregational Praise*, p. 8.

III

THE GOOD
AND THE RIGHT

10

OBLIGATION

One of the standard topics of ethical theory is the relation between the right and the good. Some see them as distinct and coequal categories of evaluation. Others would subordinate the good to the right, or the right to the good. A few may prefer to think about ethics in terms of the good alone, with no very distinct role for the right. As the structure of this book suggests, I believe the good provides the proper framework for thinking about the right, and not the other way around; but I do think the right, and categories closely related to it, have a distinctive and important role in ethics.

Although the right is traditionally contrasted with the good in this way, the word 'right' will have a secondary role in our discussion of the topic. That reflects one of the differences between the right and the good. The good has a conceptual priority over its opposite that the right does not have. Badness is to be understood in relation to the good (as I argued in chapter 4, section 1). Even those who disagree with me about that will not claim to understand goodness in terms of badness; they will think badness only coordinate with goodness. But right is to be understood in relation to wrong. The role of the contrast between right and wrong is determined largely, as I shall argue, by the appropriate reactions to wrong. And in relation to wrong, the word 'right' is ambiguous. It can have a weak sense, in which a right action is one that is *not wrong* to do, or a strong sense in which a right action (or perhaps more often *the* right action) is one that is *wrong not* to do. For that reason it is commonly clearer to speak of an action as *permissible*, in the former case, or *obligatory*, in the latter case, rather than using the ambiguous word 'right'. I will generally speak of the part of ethics that we take up at this point as the realm of "moral obligation" (or simply of "obligation") though judgments belonging to it may be expressed using 'wrong', 'right', 'ought', 'permissible', and a variety of other normative terms.

Though I speak of the topic as *moral* obligation, I take it to include religious obligation, if that is distinct from *strictly* moral obligation. Its relation to social (for example, institutional) obligation is an important topic of this chapter. I do not believe that anything like the same sort of obligation has a place in other areas of value, such as the aesthetic.

The obligatory, we may say, is what we *have* to do. Part of what we mean in saying this is that doing something that would otherwise be good *instead* of something obligatory would normally be grounds for serious moral criticism. There are things that would be good to do that we don't have to do. I think there are even things it would be best to do (indeed, morally best to do) that we don't have to do; actions that are better than we have to do are *supererogatory*. It is controversial whether any action is supererogatory in this sense, but supererogation is at least conceptually possible. Someone who says something would be morally best but one isn't morally *required* to do it may be making a substantive ethical mistake, but surely need not be manifesting a deficiency of linguistic understanding or an aberration of linguistic usage. This is one way in which the concept of the obligatory marks off a potentially smaller territory than that of the good.

This is not to say there is no essential relation between the right and the good or (perhaps more obviously) between the wrong and the bad. Behavior may be bad in some way (slothful or cowardly, perhaps, or aesthetically crude) without violating any obligation or moral requirement, but what is wrong, I think, must always be bad. Wrong action as such opposes the good in one of the ways that constitute badness. That is because anything we can plausibly regard as moral obligation must be grounded in a relation to something of real value; this is a point that will engage much of our attention in our discussion of obligation.

The badness that belongs thus to a wrong action will usually dominate our evaluation of it, but a bad action may still be good in some ways as well as bad in this one (and perhaps in others too). The possibility of actions being good in some ways and bad in others was rejected with some vehemence by Immanuel Kant, who declared that "it is of great consequence to ethics in general . . . to preclude, so far as possible, anything morally intermediate . . . in actions."[1] This sort of "rigorism," as Kant called it,[2] may be natural in a system in which, as has been interestingly

---

1. Kant, *Religion within the Boundaries of Mere Reason*, p. 47 (Ak VI,22). In the context Kant rejects even more emphatically the possibility of persons having characters that are partly good and partly bad. This is not the place to discuss whether that rejection is consistent with his views, developed in the same book, about "the battle of the good against the evil principle for dominion over the human being" (ibid., p. 77/Ak VI,58).
2. Kant, *Religion within the Boundaries of Mere Reason*, p. 48 (Ak VI,22).

argued,[3] nothing is good independently of its relation to morally ordered will. In a framework such as mine, however, in which the goodness of finite things consists in fragmentary and multidimensional resemblance to a supreme Good, it is to be expected that actions (and other things) will sometimes be partly good and partly bad. In particular, as I argued in the first section of chapter 8, a motive does not cease to be good simply because it is sometimes part of the inspiration of a wrong action. An action so inspired, though unambiguously wrong, may be good in a way, as expressing a good motive, as well as bad in another and normally more decisive way.

The most important difference between the right, or obligation, and the good, in my opinion, is that right and wrong, as matters of obligation, must be understood in relation to a *social* context, broadly understood, but that is not true of all the types of good with which we are concerned. The beauty of a scene or the badness of a pain can be understood in abstraction from any social setting. Something similar seems true even of the excellence of courage. If a human being alone, facing a tiger, shows courage, that courage may be noble and excellent independently of any system of social relations. Even if we imagine the person to have lived alone in the jungle so long as to have ceased long since to think about social relations, we can still view the courage as noble. Perhaps it is not exactly a *moral virtue* apart from any role in social life, but it is still an excellence.

If I have an obligation, on the other hand, I believe it can only be in a personal relationship or in a social system of relationships. If an action is wrong, likewise, there must be a person or persons, distinct from the agent, who may appropriately have an adverse reaction to it. For the meaning of the obligation family of ethical terms is tied to such reactions to the wrong. My main project in this chapter is to argue that facts of obligation are constituted by broadly social requirements. In chapter 11 I will argue further that those that have full moral validity are aptly understood as constituted by divine commands, and thus by requirements arising in a social system in which God is the leading participant.

1. Sanctions and the Semantics of Obligation

We do not call anything wrong, unless we mean to imply that a person ought to be punished in some way or other for doing it, if not by law, by the opinion of his fellow-creatures, if not by opinion, by the reproaches of his own conscience. . . . It is part of the notion of Duty in every one of its forms that a person may rightfully be compelled to fulfil it. . . . There are other things . . . which we wish that people should do, which we like or admire them for doing, perhaps dislike or despise them for not doing, but yet admit that they are not bound to do; it is not a case of moral obligation; we do not blame them, that is, we do not think that they are proper objects of punishment.[4]

3. See, e.g., Korsgaard, *Creating the Kingdom of Ends*, chaps. 8–9.
4. Mill, *Utilitarianism*, chap. 5, paragraph 14. Similar claims about the meaning of moral obligation terms are argued at length in Gibbard, "Moral Concepts: Substance and Sentiment," though

These words of John Stuart Mill seem to me substantially correct, expressing, as they purport to, a truth of *meaning*. It is the starting point of my argument.

In this discussion I will presuppose the account of the relation between the semantics and the metaphysics of morals that I presented in chapter 1. Specifically, I will assume the same view of the relation between the meaning of 'right' and 'wrong' and the properties of rightness and wrongness that I advocated regarding the relation between the meaning of 'good' and the property of goodness. The nature of moral obligation is not given by the meanings of the words, such as 'right', 'wrong', 'obligation', and 'ought', that are used to express it. What we understand if we understand what those words mean in the relevant contexts is rather a complex role that moral obligation plays in a scheme of things. The scheme of things includes straightforwardly empirical features such as human actions, feelings, and utterances; but obligation is not the only distinctively ethical feature of the system. Relations to other distinctively ethical features, such as rights and guilt, are also involved in defining the role of obligation. Most important, an adequate account of the role of obligation properties will be permeated with notions of value, and my account of the right will presuppose the account I have given of the good.

As in the case of goodness, the semantics of obligation leaves metaphysical questions open, regarding the reality and nature of obligation. We can understand the role of obligation and still ask, 'Is there really something that is suited to fill this role? And if so, what is the best candidate?' The best candidate, I will argue, is to be understood, roughly, in terms of social relations and, ultimately, in terms of divine commands; but first I want to focus on what we can learn from the semantics of obligation.

As with the meaning of 'good' in chapter 1, we are concerned here with the meaning of obligation terms in some but not all contexts. The same role, and hence the same property, may be represented by different words, and words that are often used for it do not always represent it. We can use 'right' and 'wrong' to express agreement and disagreement, for example, without any implication that an obligation is involved. A great deal of philosophical discussion of the nature of obligation has centered on the meaning of 'ought'; but 'ought' is a very general term of recommendation, and can be used to give various kinds of advice which may have little to do with obligation. 'Ought' would not normally signify an obligation in 'I think you ought to take the better-paying job', for example, or in 'Visitors to Oxford ought to take a walk in the Meadows if the weather is nice'.

Some will say that in the examples I have just given, 'ought' is not used in its "moral sense," and that is why they are irrelevant to the nature of moral obligation. It might be questioned whether it is necessary or wise to distinguish *senses* of 'ought' here, but that is not the main point at issue. If the suggestion is that whether an 'ought' statement makes a claim about obligation depends on whether the advice or judgment is given from a moral point of view, that seems to me a mistake. There are certainly obligations that are not moral obligations—some legal obligations and

---

Gibbard means to embed the claims in a larger theory that is at bottom noncognitivist and antirealist, and hence very different from mine.

financial obligations, for instance, are not moral obligations. Conversely, the use of 'ought' from a moral point of view does not guarantee that an obligation is signified. This is particularly obvious in the case of many explicitly or implicitly hypothetical imperatives. If I ask what you think would be morally best for me to do in a given situation, and you say you think I "ought" to do thus and so, it may be clear from the context that you are not ascribing an obligation to me but only saying what you think would be best. Hypothetical imperatives are not the only examples of this point, however. One who says, 'The religious leaders of the world ought to launch an appeal to protect the physical environment in which humanity must live', would not normally be taken as saying that the leaders have an obligation to do this, but only that it would be a good idea, though the judgment seems to be made from a moral point of view. The use of 'ought' in these cases expresses a moral opinion, but does not carry the implication of moral *requirement*.

What must be true, on broadly semantical grounds, of anything that is to count as moral requirement or moral obligation? One main point, surely, is that we should *care* about complying with it.[5] There are more and less important obligations, of course, and it is appropriate to care less about the less important ones. Caring too much about them can constitute a neurotic scrupulosity. But anything that really is a moral obligation should be treated with a certain seriousness. If we shrug it off with a 'Who cares about that?' we are not really treating it as a moral obligation. It is part of the semantically indicated role of moral obligation that it is something one should take seriously and care about. Likewise, it is important that it be something one can be motivated to comply with; a related point, which will be important in section 3, is that the nature of obligation should be such as to ground *reasons* for compliance.

Part of taking moral obligation seriously is our response to violations of it—that is, to wrong actions, in the relevant sense of 'wrong'. If an act is morally wrong, then in the absence of sufficient excuse,[6] it is appropriate for the agent to be blamed, by others and by himself. An agent fully responsible for a wrong act is to blame. "To say that he would *be to blame*," Allan Gibbard suggests, "is to say that it would be rational for him to feel guilty and for others to resent him."[7] In incorporating such views into my scheme of things, I will treat 'appropriate' and 'rational' as expressing kinds of goodness, and probably of excellence. It is likely that we will have beliefs about the goodness and badness of such sanctions as feelings of guilt and resentment in various contexts, and such beliefs may in some ways constrain the judgments we can consistently make about moral obligation.

Gibbard understands blame in terms of *feelings* of guilt and resentment. I agree that such feelings are importantly typical of blame, but blaming need not be emotional. Blame can also be constituted by behavior such as reproaching, punishing,

---

5. On this point, cf. Adams, "Motive Utilitarianism," pp. 477–79.
6. A particularly interesting sort of excuse is the erroneous belief that the act was right. Thinking that leads to such an error can claim our respect, and when it does, we are rightly reluctant to blame the conscientious agent (especially if the error is not too disastrous). If she later recognizes that the act was wrong, however, it may be appropriate for her then to feel some guilt for the act.
7. Gibbard, *Wise Choice, Apt Feelings*, p. 45. Cf. Gibbard, "Moral Concepts," p. 201f.

and (in the case of self-blame) apologizing. Such behavior is emphasized in Mill's statement of the point that concerns us here (which I quoted). Of course, the behavior must be sincere if it is to be real blame. What is essential to the role of wrongness is that blame in some form is appropriate when an agent is fully responsible for a wrong action.

It is part of the roles of moral obligation and wrongness that fulfillment of obligation and opposition to wrong actions should be publicly inculcated. Not only is it appropriate to have the attitudes I have indicated toward them; it is also good to try to teach or train people to have those attitudes toward them. Typically it is appropriate, if need be, to apply some social pressure in the process of inculcation.

These constraints on the nature of moral obligation seem to me to be built into the meaning of the discourse of moral obligation, and thus broadly analytic; but they are ignored or rejected in some influential ethical theories. Utilitarians have sometimes tried to sever the link between obligation and sanctions, on grounds indicated by Henry Sidgwick's statement that "in distributing our praise of human qualities, on utilitarian principles, we have to consider primarily not the usefulness of the quality, but the usefulness of the praise"[8]—a consideration which obviously applies to blame as well as praise, and to acts as well as qualities. Sidgwick infers that if a nonoptimific act (one that does not lead to the best result) proceeded from a generally optimific disposition, it may be wrong to blame the agent, because the disposition ought to be encouraged. Similarly utilitarians who hold that acts that fail, by a small margin, to maximize utility are wrong sometimes deny that we should be blamed, or even feel guilty, for voluntarily performing such acts, on the ground that if we cared seriously about small increments of utility, worrying over them or suffering reproach from ourselves or others in such matters, more happiness would be lost than gained thereby. As is well known, Sidgwick also held the related view that the expression of moral opinion and sentiment in general should be governed by the utility rather than the truth of the proposed utterance, or at least that one's views should not be made known unless their disclosure would be optimific, and that utilitarians might well think that certain of their views about what it would be right and wrong to do should for this reason be kept secret or esoteric.[9] This conflicts with the constraint that one who regards something as a moral obligation should think it should be publicly inculcated, except perhaps in extraordinary circumstances.

These conclusions do seem to follow from the principle of evaluating every action on the basis of its utility, but we may wonder what utilitarians of this persuasion are adding when they say of actions acknowledged to be nonoptimific that they are therefore wrong. They seem not to be talking about what I think we normally speak of as "moral obligation." A consideration that one ought not to worry about, or incur some degree of reproach for disregarding, falls thereby in the category of the morally optional rather than the morally required. Sidgwick's utilitarian claims about what one morally "ought" to do lose nothing to which he is consistently entitled, so far as I can see, if they are interpreted simply as claims about what it is *morally best* to do. Obligation plays no part in his theory, on this reading.

8. Sidgwick, *Methods of Ethics*, p. 428.
9. Sidgwick, *Methods of Ethics*, p. 490.

This argument turns on an ethical or normative feature of the role of obligation. It is by cutting the link between right and wrong and what *ought* to be praised
and blamed, not what will in fact be praised and blamed, that Sidgwick (in my
opinion) loses contact with moral obligation. It is not a misunderstanding of the
conceptually mandated role to maintain, as he also does, that an action can be a
breach of moral duty even though it would not in fact be punished, censured, or
disliked by one's fellow creatures. In this he is criticizing one of the cruder forms of
social theory of the nature of obligation, the view that "when we say that a man
'ought' to do anything, or that it is his 'duty' to do it, we mean he is bound under
penalties to do it; the particular penalty considered being the pain that will accrue
to him directly or indirectly from the dislike of his fellow-creatures."[10] Nevertheless, I do believe, and will argue, that some of the pressures other persons (especially
God) bring to bear on us play a part in constituting our moral obligations.

Derek Parfit offers an interesting argument in defense of a consequentialist who
accepts (more than Parfit himself does) Sidgwick's suggestion that the utilitarian or
consequentialist doctrine ought not to be publicly inculcated. Parfit calls a theory
"self-effacing" if it implies that one ought to try to bring it about that it is not believed. He notes that on some views, "a moral theory cannot be self-effacing," but
"must fulfil what Rawls calls 'the publicity condition'; it must be a theory that everyone ought to accept, and publicly acknowledge to each other." Parfit claims, however, that this view is tenable only for those who "regard morality as a social product." He thinks that "if a moral theory can be quite straightforwardly *true*, it is clear
that, if it is self-effacing, this does not show that it cannot be true."[11] Thus he seems
to imply that requiring moral theories to satisfy the publicity condition commits
one to some sort of subjectivism or antirealism. But that is surely wrong.

The publicity condition does connect morality with society; for it says that a
moral theory, as such, must be meant to be publicly adopted. By their very meaning, it may be argued, claims about moral obligation have implications about how
certain social practices ought to be related to the types of behavior discussed in the
claims. Part of what is meant by saying that a certain type of conduct is morally
wrong is that it ought in general to be publicly discouraged as wrong. This is not to
say that the opinion that it is *occasionally* right, in special circumstances, to lie about
moral principles is logically inadmissible. To affirm a principle of conduct, however, while denying that it ought *in general* to be inculcated, if it is applicable to
people in general, is not to affirm it as a principle of moral obligation. In this respect claims about moral obligation differ, no doubt, from scientific and mathematical claims. A proposition of nuclear physics or molecular biology can be objectively
true even if the danger of abuse is so great that it ought not to be divulged. But that
is because the rightness or wrongness of publicizing them is extraneous to the content of scientific statements. If the publicity condition is not extraneous to the content of moral claims, it is hard to see how this compromises their objectivity, since
it has not been shown that it cannot be "straightforwardly true" that a type of con-

10. Sidgwick, *Methods of Ethics*, p. 29.
11. Parfit, *Reasons and Persons*, p. 43.

duct ought to be publicly discouraged as wrong. To make this point, of course, is not yet to say anything about how objective a matter moral obligation will turn out to be on the theory I shall adopt.

Close kin to the views that would collapse the notion of the morally obligatory into that of the morally best are those that would collapse it into the notion of what we have most reason (from a moral point of view) to do. We may see an example of this when considerations that Thomas Nagel has been characterizing as impersonal or agent-neutral *reasons* for action become "*demands* of impersonal morality"[12] without any argument (that I have detected) for the transition—a transition that leads, I think, to some of his most excruciating problems. Nagel goes on to make, with some care, a distinction between the required and the merely acceptable; but it is between the "rationally required" and the "rationally acceptable," and the rationally required is simply what it would be irrational not to do.[13] There is nothing in this that represents the full force of moral requirement or obligation, for there is a large difference between doing something irrational and doing something morally wrong. To the extent that I have done something morally wrong, I have something to feel guilty about. To the extent that I have done something irrational, I have merely something to feel silly about—and the latter is much less serious than the former.

I anticipate the reply that if what one has done is irrational for *moral* reasons, then it is morally wrong as well as irrational; but that does not follow, so far as I can see. Suppose the preponderance of moral reasons favors your not walking on the lawn, but also favors your not worrying very much about it and not feeling guilty if you do it—perhaps because it would be better, on balance, for all concerned if we do not worry much about such things. Suppose, in other words, that it would be (mildly) irrational for moral reasons for you to walk on the grass, but also irrational for moral reasons for you to feel guilty about doing so. Suppose it would also be morally irrational for us to try to make people feel that they *must* not walk on the grass. In that case, I submit, we should conclude that walking on the lawn does not violate an obligation and is not morally wrong, though it is (mildly) irrational on moral grounds. The concept of moral obligation is not there just to tell us about balances of moral reasons, but rather to express something more urgent—though of course I grant that the word 'ought' can be used just to assert a preponderance of reasons (and not necessarily moral reasons).

2. Guilt

Obligation is one of the sterner, not the mellower, parts of ethics. I have argued that the role, and therefore the nature, of moral obligation cannot be understood apart from its relation to guilt. If I voluntarily fail to do what I am morally obliged to do, I am guilty. I may appropriately be blamed by others for my omission, and ought normally to reproach myself for it, in some degree. Perhaps I may incur some

12. Nagel, *The View from Nowhere*, p. 189; emphasis mine.
13. Nagel, *The View from Nowhere*, p. 200.

just punishment for it. The presence of obligation in a moral system divides actions into three classes which can be distinguished precisely in terms of guilt. If an action is *morally wrong*, one is guilty if one does it. An action that is *morally optional* (morally permitted but not required) can be either done or omitted without guilt. But if an action is *morally required*, or obligatory, one is guilty if one omits it. (I assume in each case that one is fully responsible.) Examining the nature of guilt will help us understand how moral obligation depends for its role on a broadly social system of relationships.

The word 'guilt' is not properly the name of a feeling, but of an objective moral condition which may rightly be recognized by others even if it is not recognized by the guilty person. However, feelings of guilt, and other reactions to guilt, may reasonably be taken as a source of understanding of the objective fact of guilt to which they point. We do not have the concept of guilt merely to signify in a general way the state of having done something wrong. Such an abstract conception of guilt fails to make intelligible, for example, the fact that guilt can be expiated, discharged, or forgiven. It also results in a rather tight and empty circle in understanding, inasmuch as a major part of what distinguishes wrongness (as a member of the obligation family of properties) from other sorts of badness is precisely its connection with guilt.

It is true that one is not guilty, however unfortunate the outcome, for anything that was not in some way wrong. But there are two other typical features of wrong action that are responsible for much of the human significance of guilt. One is harm that one has caused by one's (wrong) action. It is wrong to drive carelessly, for example, and no less wrong when one is lucky than when an accident results. But the burden of guilt one incurs is surely heavier when one's carelessness causes the death of another person than when no damage is done. Many moralists are uncomfortable with this fact; but even if we were to define 'guilt' one-sidedly as meaning only the state of having done something wrong, the other, more complicated fact of having caused great harm through one's wrongdoing remains, and is a fact that we care about in a special way which is reflected in our actual, intuitive use of the word 'guilt'. Harm caused to other people is not a feature of all guilt, however. One can be guilty for a violation of other people's rights that in fact harmed no one.

A more pervasive feature of guilt is alienation from other people, or (at a minimum) a strain on one's relations with others. If I am guilty, I am out of harmony with other people. Typically there is someone who is, or might well be, understandably angry at me. This feature is central to the role of guilt in human life. It is connected with such practices as punishing and apologizing. And it makes intelligible the fact that guilt can be (at least largely) removed by forgiveness.

Suppose I have done something that has offended a friend, resulting in estrangement. I think I was wrong to do it; I feel guilty. But if there is a reconciliation and my friend forgives me, I will feel released from the guilt. Indeed, I will *be* released from the guilt. The view that in such a case the guilt consists largely in an alienation produced by the wrong act is supported by the fact that the ending of the alienation ends the guilt.

This should not surprise us if we reflect on the way in which we acquired the concept, and the sense, of guilt. In our first experience of guilt its principal significance was an action or attitude of ours that ruptured or strained our relationship with a parent. There did not have to be a failure of benevolence or a violation of a rule; perhaps we were even too young to understand rules. It was enough that something we did or expressed offended the parent, and seemed to threaten the relationship. This is the original context in which the obligation family of moral concepts and sentiments arise. We do not begin with a set of moral principles but with a relationship, actual in part and in part desired, which is immensely valued for its own sake. Everything that attacks or opposes that relationship seems to us bad.

Of course this starkly simple mentality is premoral. We do not really have the concepts of moral obligation and guilt until we can make some sort of distinction, among the things we do that strain relationships, between those in which we are at fault or wrong and those in which we are innocent or right (not to mention those in which we are partly wrong and partly right). In grasping such a distinction we must learn to make some critical judgments about the moral validity of the demands that people make on us. Nevertheless, I believe it is not childish, but perceptive and correct, to persist in regarding obligations as a species of social requirement, and guilt as consisting largely in alienation from those who have (appropriately) required of us what we did not do.

This is a controversial position. It is widely agreed that learning about guilt begins in the way that I have indicated, and that the value we place on good relationships, not only with parents but also with peers, is crucial to moral development. But some moralists hold that in the highest stages of the moral life (perhaps not reached by many adults) the center of moral motivation is transplanted from the messy soil of concrete relationships to the pure realm of moral principles; and a corresponding development is envisaged for the sense of guilt.

It is certainly possible to come to value—even to love—an ethical principle for its own sake, and this provides a motive for conforming to it; but this way of relating to ethical principles has more to do with ideals than with obligations. To love truthfulness is one thing; to feel that one *has* to tell the truth is something else. Similarly, failing to act on a principle one loves seems, as such, more an occasion of shame than of guilt.[14] Suppose I have done something that is simply contrary to some principle that I believe in. It is not that I have done significant harm to anyone, or alien-

---

14. Cf. the suggestion that it is because of a rooting of moral motivation in a desire to express one's moral identity "that Kant speaks of the failure to act on the moral law as giving rise to shame and not to feelings of guilt," in Rawls, *A Theory of Justice*, p. 256. I am not sure whether Rawls's own conception of the sense of moral guilt and its development is irreconcilable with mine. He says the only "feelings of guilt in the strict sense" are feelings of "principle guilt," belonging to a developed stage of morality and based on one's valuing moral principles, seeing them as expressing one's nature as a rational agent in a society of free and equal members (ibid., p. 474f.). That sounds rather like what he thought Kant reasonably interpreted as shame rather than guilt. Perhaps, however, Rawls means only that autonomous valuing of moral principles one has violated is necessary, but not sufficient, for genuine feelings of moral guilt; for elsewhere he seems to think that the sense of guilt involves apprehension of the "resentment and indignation" that others may appropriately feel at one's action (ibid., pp. 446, 483). I am indebted to Paul Weithman for helping me to see the possibility of this reading of Rawls, and the questionableness of the interpretation of Rawls that appeared in Adams, "Divine Commands and the Social Nature of Obligation," p. 268f.

ated myself from anyone. The situation does not call for apologies or reactions to anticipated or possible or appropriate anger, because there is no one (let's suppose not even God) who might be understandably angry with me about it. I think it is neither natural nor appropriate for me to feel *guilty* in such a situation. Maybe someone is entitled to think less of me for the deed. Perhaps I will see less value in my own life on account of it. I may in this way be alienated from myself, though not from anyone else. But these are reasons for feeling ashamed or degraded, rather than for feeling guilty.[15]

It is significant that insofar as my reaction arises from my personally valuing a principle, it may not matter very much whether the principle is moral or aesthetic or intellectual. I could be degraded in my own eyes by doing something I regard as aesthetically or intellectually unworthy of me. But we would not normally speak of aesthetic "guilt." Guilt is not necessarily worse than degradation, but they are different. And a main point of difference between them is that, in typical cases, guilt involves alienation from someone else who required or expected of us what we were obligated to do and have not done, or who has been harmed by what we have done and might reasonably have required us not to do it. This is not to deny, of course, that shame commonly accompanies guilt, and feelings of shame are often part of our complex reaction to things of which we judge ourselves to be guilty.

3. Social Requirement

The role that our moral discourse marks out for obligation obviously has other features besides its relation to guilt. One of them is that obligations constitute reasons for doing that which one is obliged to do, and reasons for refraining from doing that which it would be wrong to do. This does not distinguish obligation from other ethical properties and relations, but it is an essential point about the role of obligation. Even if it were discovered (as of course it will not be) that there is a certain pain produced in the agent by all and only right actions, and a certain sensory pleasure yielded by all and only wrong actions, it would be absurd to say that rightness and wrongness *are* the properties of producing that pain and pleasure, respectively. For those properties would give us no reason whatever to do what would produce the pain, nor to avoid what would produce the pleasure. One problem about the nature of obligation is to understand how it grounds reasons for action.

This will not be much of a problem if we assume that one is obliged only to do things that one expects to have good results. Then the goodness of the results provides a reason, and one's desires for such good consequences a motive, for doing what one is obliged to do. Unfortunately, those who (like me) are not consequen-

---

15. It is along these lines that I would reply to Samuel Clarke's attempt to understand the sanction of moral obligation in terms of one's being "self-condemned" if one acts contrary to "the judgment or conscience of [one's] own mind, concerning the reasonableness and fitness of the thing, that [one's] actions should be conformed to such or such a rule or law" (Raphael, ed., *The British Moralists*, vol. 1, p. 202). Clarke's account is not adequate, in my opinion, to distinguish the sanction of guilt from that of shame, nor wrongness from other moral defects.

tialists cannot assume that obligations will always be so happily attuned to the value of expected results. We think we may be obliged to tell the truth and to keep promises, for example, when we do not expect the consequences to be good, and when we have no idea what the consequences will be. What would motivate us to do such a thing?

Even nonconsequentialist moralists may not be satisfied with the reply that the conscientious agent has good enough reason for her action simply in the fact that it is right. This seems too abstract. John Rawls (certainly no consequentialist) writes, "The doctrine of the purely conscientious act is irrational. This doctrine holds . . . that the highest moral motive is the desire to do what is right and just simply because it is right and just, no other description being appropriate. . . . But on this interpretation the sense of right lacks any apparent reason; it resembles a preference for tea rather than coffee."[16] If we are to see the fact of having an obligation as itself a reason for action, we need a richer, less abstract understanding of the nature of obligation, in which we might find something to motivate us.

According to social theories of the nature of obligation, having an obligation to do something consists in being required (in a certain way, under certain circumstances or conditions), by another person or a group of persons, to do it. This opens more than one possibility for understanding obligations as reasons for action. One reason or motive for complying with a social requirement, of course, is that we fear punishment or retaliation for noncompliance. This is undoubtedly a real factor, which helps to keep morality (and other benign, and not so benign, social institutions) afloat. But here we are primarily interested in what *other* motives there may be for compliance.

The alternative explanation that I wish to pursue is that *valuing one's social bonds* gives one, under certain conditions, a reason to do what is required of one by one's associates or one's community (and thus to fulfill obligations, understood as social requirements). The reason I have in mind is not one that arises from a desire to obtain or maintain a certain kind of relationship, though such a desire can obviously be a motive for complying with social requirements. The reason I have in mind is rather that I value the relationship which I see myself as actually having, and my complying is an *expression* of my valuing and respecting the relationship. This is a motivational pattern in which I act primarily *out of* a valuing of the relationship, rather than with the obtaining or maintaining of the relationship as an *end*.[17]

A *morally valid* obligation obviously will not be constituted by just any demand sponsored by a system of social relationships that one in fact values. Some such demands have no moral force, and some social systems are downright evil. A genu-

16. Rawls, *A Theory of Justice*, p. 477f. This passage is quoted, with approval, in Wallace, *Virtues and Vices*, p. 116. What I have said thus far about consequentialist and nonconsequentialist reasons for fulfilling an obligation largely follows Wallace's (much fuller) line of argument. The treatment of conscientiousness in Wallace's book (pp. 110–18) provided a major impetus for the development of my main line of thought in this section, though his views are much more Aristotelian than mine.

17. Motives that we act "out of" are interestingly and persuasively distinguished from teleological motives in Stocker, "Values and Purposes."

inely moral conception of obligation must have resources for moral criticism of social systems and their demands. I do believe, however, that there is a *premoral* conception of obligation in which we can see social facts as constituting obligations independently of our moral evaluation of those facts. This is a controversial belief, but important to the explanatory force of social theories (and divine command theories) of the nature of obligation.

It will be particularly important if we believe (as I think is plausible) that the actions of commanding, demanding, and requiring cannot be understood or identified apart from their tendency to create obligations. For if the obligations so created had to be fully moral obligations, there would be an obvious circle in trying to explain the nature of moral obligation in terms of commands, demands, or requirements of society or of God.[18] A premoral conception of obligation, on the other hand, identifies a kind of sociological fact, closely connected with such linguistic (and social) events as commanding, which can be used in explaining the nature of moral facts of obligation. Or so I claim.

That we have such premoral conceptions of commanding and obligation seems to me evident from such facts as the following. I can use the concepts of commanding, obeying, and disobeying to describe goings-on in social systems that I regard as morally questionable or worse. It would not normally occur to me to put shudder quotes around 'command' in such a context. We can imagine a morally underdeveloped society in which people speak of the chief, for example, as issuing commands, and of themselves as having obligations arising from the chief's commands, without ever raising a question about the moral validity of these commands and obligations. Even if we asked them whether they have a "real" obligation to obey the chief's commands, and whether it would "really" be wrong to disobey them, we may suppose, they would hardly know what to make of our questions; they would not see them as a subject for intelligent discussion. In this case they would not have a genuinely *moral* conception of obligation; yet they would have concepts of command and obligation that serve them effectively in describing their social system and living within it, and that we too could use as anthropologists in describing their system. In fact, I believe the concept of command that I would use in that way is the same that I actually use in describing things that happen in social systems of which I disapprove. To be sure, we who do have a conception and practice of moral critique of our social systems may want to append such qualifiers as 'institutional' or 'official' to the terms 'obligation' and 'duty' when we are speaking of social obligations that we do not morally endorse; but I think the fact remains that much of our understanding of social and linguistic systems depends on our grasp of premoral conceptions of obligation.

To say that a conception of obligation is premoral is of course not to say that it is totally nonnormative. Even the most premoral or amoral conception of obligation can only characterize a social system in which most of the participants regard the indicated obligations as providing substantial reasons for complying with them.

---

18. This problem is posed in Wolterstorff, *Divine Discourse*, chap. 6. Wolterstorff, however, holds the view I am opposing here, that the (speech) acts in question are to be understood in terms of *moral* obligation.

A conception of *moral* obligation, however, will insist on *better* reasons for complying. That is, it will impose a certain kind of critique of reasons for complying. I will next try to show that a system of *human* social requirements can go some distance toward meeting this requirement although, in the end, I believe the moral pressure not to make an idol of any human society pushes us toward a *transcendent* source of the moral demand. Several aspects of the relational situation are important to the quality of our reasons for complying with social requirements, and are relevant to the possibility of such requirements constituting moral obligation.

1. Morally good reasons will not arise from just any social bond that one in fact values, but only from one that is rightly valued—that is, from one that is really good. How much reason one has to comply with the demands of other people will depend in no small part on the value of one's relationship with them. And a social requirement that is to constitute a moral obligation must arise in a relationship or system of relationships that is good or valuable.

If the relationship is with a community, the individual's attitude toward the community and her participation in it make a difference to the value of the relationship. The relation may arise through the individual's action—commonly through a history of acts of loyalty and caring within the relationship; occasionally through the action, beloved of social contract theorists, of voluntarily joining the community or consenting explicitly to its institutions and principles. But the community's attitude toward the individual is at least as important. Does the community value the individual? Is its attitude toward her supportive and respectful?

It is well known that these questions have in fact a great influence on moral motivation. An individual who feels neglected, despised, abused by the community will be alienated, and will be much less inclined to comply conscientiously with society's demands. In the end I am not prepared to say that the alienated person should be totally exempt from blame for immoral or "antisocial" behavior; but on a social theory of the nature of obligation such behavior must sometimes be seen, not mainly as a falling away from impersonal standards of right action, but as part of a conflict with society in which society was the first offender.

Where community prevails, rather than alienation, the sense of belonging is not to be sharply distinguished from the inclination to comply with the reasonable requirements of the community. A "community" is a group of people who live their lives to some extent—possibly a very limited extent—in common. To see myself as "belonging" to a community is to see the institution or other members of the group as "having something to say about" how I live and act—perhaps not about every department of my life, and only to a reasonable extent about any department of it, but it is part of the terms of the relationship that their demands on certain subjects are expected to have some weight with me. And valuing such a relationship—loving it or respecting it—implies some willingness to submit to reasonable demands of the community. One is willing to comply, not as a means of satisfying a desire *to* belong, but as an expression of one's sense that one *does* belong, and one's endorsement of that relationship.

2. Our reasons for complying with demands may also be affected by our evaluation of the personal characteristics of those who make them. One may have more reason to comply with demands made by an individual or group that one admires

than by one that one holds in lower esteem.[19] This is not true of every sort of demand. What other people demand of us for their own needs and well-being we have as much reason to give to unimpressive as to impressive people. Where what people ask is not for their own well-being, however, I think we normally have more reason to comply with the requests and demands of the knowledgeable, wise, or saintly.

3. How much reason one has to comply with a demand depends not only on the excellence of its source and of the relationship or system of relationships in which the demand arises, but also on how good the demand is. This involves the question whether the action that is demanded would be good, and whether the sanctions implied in the demand are appropriate. It also involves evaluation of the relational history of the demand itself. Does the making of the demand affect the relational situation for the better or for the worse? And what is the wider social significance of the demand? Is it an expression of a project or social movement that is good or bad? A social requirement that is to constitute a moral obligation should be a good one in these and other ways.

It is particularly important that the demand, and the social system of which it forms part, should be good in ways that fall under the heading of *fairness*. Procedurally this means, for instance, that the making and any enforcement of demands should be consistent, and that requirements should be applied on the basis of what are sincerely and reasonably believed to be facts. Substantively it means that a system of requirements should respect the interests of all persons in a way that is good. For our present purpose that very general formulation is preferable to one that incorporates some one of the many controversial views on the question, what ways of respecting everyone's interests are good.

One might be tempted to object that in helping itself to values—values of relationships, of actions, of personal characteristics, and of requirements—a theory of the nature of obligation becomes viciously circular. But this objection would be mistaken. A theory of the nature of obligation is not a theory of the nature of value. Obligation and value have different roles in an ethical system, as I have been emphasizing; and a theory of the nature of one is not automatically a theory of the nature of the other. One could try to explain the nature of the good in terms of obligation; and then of course it would be viciously circular to invoke the goodness of relationships or demands in explaining the nature of obligation. But that is not the approach that is being followed here. I have in fact already sketched a theory of the nature of the good that does not presuppose anything about obligation. The goodness of actions, relationships, personal characteristics, and demands that is invoked in the present discussion of the nature of obligation can be assumed to be faithful imaging of God, as explained in chapter 1.

4. An opposite and more tempting objection would be that if we have the values of actions and demands, we do not need the actual social requirements to explain the nature of moral obligation. This would also be a mistake. If we are thinking about the nature of obligation, and about the reasons we have to comply with

---

19. Cf. Rawls, *A Theory of Justice*, p. 465: It is favorable to "the development of the morality of authority" that the parents "be worthy objects of [the child's] admiration."

possible demands, it matters that the demand is actually made. It is a question here of what good demands other persons do in fact make of me, not just of what good demands they could make. The demand need not take the form of an explicit command or legislation; it may be an expectation more subtly communicated; but the demand must actually be made.

It is much more fashionable in ethical theory to treat moral reasons and moral obligations as depending on judgments about what an ideal community or authority *would* demand under certain counterfactual conditions. However, I am very skeptical of all these conditional accounts, for two reasons. First (the metaphysical reason), I doubt that the relevant counterfactuals are true, partly because they seem to be about free responses that are never actually made.[20] In the second place (the more distinctively moral or motivational reason), I do not think I care very much about whether these counterfactual conditionals are true. This is not to deny that I care about some things that are closely connected with them; it is just to say that the counterfactuals themselves are motivationally weak. By contrast, actual demands made on us in relationships that we value are undeniably real and motivationally strong. Most actual conscientiousness rests at least partly on people's sense of such demands.

The actual making of the demand is important, not only to the strength, but also to the character, of the motive. Not every good reason for doing something makes it intelligible that I should feel that I *have* to do it. This is one of the ways in which having even the best of reasons for doing something does not as such amount to having an obligation to do it. But the perception that something is demanded of me by other people, in a relationship that I value, does help to make it intelligible that I should feel that I have to do it.

The social requirement theory has important advantages in relation to the two major features of the role of moral obligation that I have discussed thus far: its connection with guilt, which is a main ground of the distinctiveness of obligation, and the reason-giving force of obligations. There are other tests that it passes with flying colors.

One of these has to do with the answers it will give to questions about what is in fact obligatory. The types of action that we confidently believe to be right and wrong are an important determinant of the role of moral obligation. It would be unreasonable to expect a theory of the nature of obligation to yield results that agree perfectly with pretheoretical opinion. One of the purposes such a theory may serve is to give guidance in revising our particular ethical opinions. And of course pretheoretical opinion does not agree perfectly with itself; that is, it is far from unanimous. But a theory could be rejected out of hand if most of the obligations it assigned us were to perform actions that have always been regarded by most people as wrong. There is a limit to how far pretheoretical opinion can be revised without changing the subject entirely. This feature of the role of moral obligation presents no difficulty for the sort of social theory of the nature of obligation that I have been

---

20. For grounds for doubting the truth of such counterfactuals about free responses see Adams, "Middle Knowledge and the Problem of Evil."

developing. For the actions that are actually required, and well required, by society will obviously be actions that are regarded by most people as obligatory.

Given that the role of moral obligation is partly determined by the obligations we actually believe in, it seems also to be part of the role of moral obligation to be *recognized*. Rightness should therefore turn out to be a property that not only belongs to the most important types of action that are thought to be right, but also plays a part (perhaps a causal part) in their coming to be recognized as right; and similarly for wrongness. These properties should not be connected in a merely fortuitous way with our classification of actions as right and wrong. A social requirement theory takes care of this beautifully. For on any plausible moral sociology, actual social requirements play a large role in our coming to hold beliefs about moral obligation; and I think it is also plausible to suppose that our belief formation is sensitive to the values of relationships and demands that should play a part in a social requirement theory.

Such a theory is on weaker ground, however, when we come to *objectivity* as a feature of the role of moral obligation. So far as we have a conception of these matters, we conceive of moral rightness and wrongness as properties that actions have, and of moral obligations as features of people's situations, that are mostly independent of our beliefs. This objectivity that belongs to the role of moral obligation is responsible for the initial implausibility of emotivist and other noncognitivist or antirealist theories about the nature of obligation. It is expressed in such convictions as the following: What the Nazis did to the Jews was wrong whether or not the Nazis thought so, and it would have been all the more horribly wrong if they had managed to persuade the Jews that it was not wrong. I cannot get rid of a moral obligation by persuading myself and others that I do not have it; all I can do in that way is live a lie.

On the other hand I may wrongly think I have an obligation that I do not have. In the past it was widely held that my believing, even misguidedly, that I have an obligation morally obliges me to fulfill it. To many of us today, however, it seems that if a person who takes too narrow a view of her own rights rebels against a falsely assumed burden of obligations, the moral gain in throwing off some of the shackles of servility may be more important than the damage to her conscientiousness. We also would not be inclined to censure Huckleberrry Finn for acting contrary to his erring conscience in not turning in a runaway slave. In short, we do not think people are under any valid obligation to perform duties they mistakenly believe they have, except insofar as we respect the erring views.

The question that arises at this point for a social theory of the nature of moral obligation is whether it is too subjectivist. Does it make it too easy for a society to get rid of its obligations by changing its demands? The theory can give some reassurances. It is completely objectivist in relation to any individual. I cannot change what society requires of me by changing my beliefs about it. And on the view of the nature of the good that I am presupposing here, even a whole society cannot make an action or a demand good just by changing its beliefs or its demands. But on the social theory of the nature of obligation, as developed thus far, society would be able to eliminate obligations by just not making certain demands; and that seems out of keeping with the role of moral obligation.

And this is not just a disturbing possibility. Moral reformers have taught us that there have been situations in which none of the existing human communities demanded as much as they should have, and things that were morally required were not actually demanded by any community, or perhaps even by any human individual, in the situation. In this way actual human social requirements fail to cover the whole territory of moral obligation.

Where demands are made, moreover, they sometimes conflict, both as between different social groups and within a single society. Which demands constitute the genuine moral obligations? 'Those that are good, and arise in good relationships,' may be our first answer. Often, however, both sets of demands and relationships will manifest some degree of goodness, but a flawed goodness. Even if one set is clearly better than the other, it may not be good enough to settle such an issue with the force of obligation.

These are all reasons for thinking, as most moralists have, that actual human social requirements are simply not good enough to constitute the basis of moral obligation. I have already briefly indicated my reasons for not taking refuge in counterfactual conditionals about what *would* be required by an ideal society or ideal observer. I have not exhaustively canvassed the possibilities for dealing with the problems exclusively in terms of actual social requirements in combination with moral values of relationships, demands, actions, and so forth. If we are theists, however, it is not necessary, and seems to me somewhat unnatural, to confine ourselves to that apparatus, since a more powerful theistic adaptation of the social requirement theory is obviously available. It will be the subject of chapter 11.

11

DIVINE COMMANDS

1. Placing the Theory in Its Context

A divine command theory of the nature of moral obligation can be seen as an idealized version of the social requirement theory. Our relationship with God is in a broad sense an interpersonal and hence a social relationship. And talk about divine commands plainly applies to God an analogy drawn from human institutions. A possible history of the conception of moral obligation begins with social practices of promising and of commanding and obeying, and associated roles of authority. In these practices there is necessarily a place for some sort of conception of obligation, though it is not likely to have been at first a fully moral conception. Initially no need may have been felt to distinguish between what is required by human authorities and what is truly, objectively, or morally required. Experiences of abusive authority and conflicting social demands naturally give rise, however, to a search for a source and standard of moral obligation that is superior to human authorities. Belief in superior personal powers or gods suggests the obvious hypothesis as to the nature of such a superior standard. This history is an imaginative construction, not based on anthropological research; but I suspect that it approximates the actual history of the conception of moral obligation in more than one society.

More important, I believe that a theory according to which moral obligation is constituted by divine commands remains tenable, and is the best theory on the subject

249

for theists, inheriting most of the advantages, and escaping the salient defects, of a social theory of the nature of moral obligation. In section 2 I will sketch what I take to be the main reasons for thinking that divine commands are (at least for theists) the best candidates for the role of broadly social facts that would constitute moral (and of course religious) obligation. Theories of this general type are sometimes stated in terms of God's "will" rather than God's "commands," and in section 3 I will explain why I prefer the formulation in terms of commands. The remainder of the chapter will be devoted to other issues connected with this theory: in section 4, the question what it is for God to command something, and one thing rather than another; and in section 5, the popular objection that the theory is opposed to a kind of "autonomy" that we ought to have in moral matters. Our darkest fear about divine command morality, the fear that God might command, or be thought to command, something evil, will be confronted in chapter 12.

We should be clear, first of all, about some things that are *not* claimed in the divine command theory that I espouse. Two restrictions, in particular, will be noted here. One is that when I say that an action's being morally obligatory consists in its being commanded by God, and that an action's being wrong consists in its being contrary to a divine command, I assume that the character and commands of God satisfy certain conditions. More precisely, I assume that they are consistent with the divine nature having properties that make God an ideal candidate, and the salient candidate, for the semantically indicated role of the supreme and definitive Good, as discussed in chapter 1. It is only the commands of a definitively good God, who, for example, is not cruel but loving, that are a good candidate for the role of defining moral obligation. This point and its implications will be developed further in section 2 of this chapter and in section 2 of chapter 12.

The other restriction to be noted here is adumbrated in chapter 10. It is that the divine command theory, as I conceive of it, is a theory of the nature of obligation only, and not of moral properties in general. In particular, it is not a theory of the nature of the good, but presupposes a theory of the good. The first restriction, noted in the previous paragraph, is one of the points at which this is important; for in articulating the necessary conditions on the characteristics of a God whose commands are to constitute the standard of moral obligation, and in developing the related reasons for accepting divine commands as such a standard, I make full use of the account of the nature of the good that I have given in part I.[1]

---

1. Although the divine command theory that I presented in my first essay on the subject differs in important ways from that presented here, it largely agrees on this point, stating that value concepts may be presupposed "in giving reasons for . . . attitudes toward God's commands. . . . Divine command theorists, including the modified divine command theorist, need not maintain that *all* value concepts, or even all moral concepts, must be understood in terms of God's commands" (Adams, "A Modified Divine Command Theory of Ethical Wrongness," p. 109). This restriction of the scope of the divine command theory to the obligation portion of ethics is (in my opinion) not sufficiently observed in Chandler, "Divine Command Theories and the Appeal to Love," which criticizes my earlier theory precisely with regard to the viability of the restriction that I impose in terms of God's character. Chandler (p. 231) states that a divine command theory "asserts that ethical facts consist in facts about the will or commands of God"; and this broad conception of the theory seems to me to be presupposed in his arguments, though 'ethical facts' includes facts about the good that I have never claimed to understand in terms of divine commands.

This restriction of the scope of the divine command theory to the realm of obligation may be contrary to the expectations of some readers. Much of the discussion of divine command theories in analytical philosophy of religion has assumed that they would be intended to explain the nature of all values. On this point, however, my approach is not untraditional; the pattern of a divine command theory of the nature of obligation presupposing an independent conception of the good was familiar in the seventeenth century, during the heyday of divine command metaethics.

A clear example of this is found in John Locke's *Essay Concerning Human Understanding* (1690).[2] He holds that

> Good and Evil . . . are nothing but Pleasure or Pain, or that which occasions, or procures Pleasure or Pain to us. *Morally Good and Evil* then, is only the Conformity or Disagreement of our voluntary Actions to some Law, whereby Good or Evil is drawn on us, from the Will and Power of the Law-maker. (II,xxviii,5)

The most important such law is the divine law commanded by God.

> This is the only true touchstone of *moral Rectitude*; and by comparing them to this Law, it is, that men judge of the most considerable *Moral Good* or *Evil* of their Actions; that is, whether as *Duties, or Sins*, they are like to procure them happiness, or misery, from the hands of the ALMIGHTY. (II,xxviii,8)

Here the nature of nonmoral good and evil (as pleasure and pain) is understood independently of God's commands, and is used to explain the nature of the obligation imposed by divine commands.

A similar theoretical structure may be discerned in the writings of Richard Cumberland and Samuel Pufendorf, who define natural good as "that which preserves, or enlarges and perfects, the Faculties of any one thing, or of several"[3] or as consisting "in that aptitude by which a thing is capable of benefitting, preserving, or perfecting another thing,"[4] and then assume facts of good and evil in explaining obligation in terms of divine commands.[5]

---

2. The following two quotations are from the *Essay*. The view of Locke's early *Essays on the Law of Nature* may be different.

3. Cumberland, *A Treatise of the Laws of Nature*, p. 165.

4. Pufendorf, *On the Law of Nature and of Nations*, I,iv,4, in Pufendorf, *Political Writings*.

5. The presupposition of an independent theory of the good in a divine command account of obligation is also foreshadowed in Francisco Suárez's discussion of natural law, when he declares, "This will, prohibition, or precept of God is not the whole reason for the good or evil involved in the observance or transgression of the law of nature. On the contrary, it necessarily presupposes the existence of a certain honorableness [*honestas*] or shamefulness in the actions themselves, and joins to them a special obligation of divine law (Suárez, *On Laws and God the Lawgiver*, II,vi,11). Suárez, however, is less thoroughly a divine command theorist of the nature of obligation than Cumberland, Pufendorf, and Locke. Regarding all of these thinkers, I have found the discussion of the relation of divine command theories to natural law theories in the seventeenth century in Schneewind, *The Invention of Autonomy*, very illuminating.

To be sure, the good presupposed by moral obligation according to Cumberland, Pufendorf, and Locke is not the excellent, as in my theory, but only what is good *for* someone. I think all three of them rely much too heavily on reward and punishment in explaining the nature of moral obligation, though Cumberland and Pufendorf struggle to reduce this reliance. But their dependence on ideas of reward and punishment serves to underline the point that their divine command theories are theories of obligation only and not of all values; for the idea that something might be made noninstrumentally good or bad by a promise of reward or a threat of punishment has no plausibility, and I doubt that it has been endorsed by any serious philosopher.

2. Divine Commands and the Role of Obligation

Since my theory incorporates these restrictions, I will rely freely on the account of the nature of the good that I have presented in part I, and on assumptions about the character of God, in arguing, in the present section, that a divine command theory agrees very well with the features of the role conceptually assigned to moral obligation, as we have noted them in chapter 10. I will develop this argument with regard to several features, beginning with the reason-giving force required by the role. What I have to say about that is parallel to the discussion in chapter 10 of the sorts of reasons we should expect for complying with moral requirements.

Writers on divine commands have often stressed hope of reward and especially fear of punishment as a motive or reason for compliance. This was noted in section 1 with regard to major seventeenth-century authors; and there can be no doubt that this motive has been showcased in much theistic ethics. I can hardly claim that this is wholly wrongheaded, inasmuch as my underlying social theory of obligation, developed in chapter 10, makes the possibility of someone being offended, and the appropriateness of sanctions, in the event of nonfulfillment, a central feature of the nature of obligation. It remains true, however, that the fear of punishment is not the best of motives, either morally or religiously; and emphasis on it can lead to the suspicion that the obligations under discussion do not fully fill the emotional and motivational role that we expect of *moral* obligations. There are better motives for compliance with divine commands, grounded in subtler aspects of a complex structure of requirements and sanctions.

1. I would particularly stress reasons for compliance that arise from a social bond or relationship with God. As in the case of human social bonds, the force of these reasons depends on the value of the relationship, which theistic devotion will rate very high indeed. If God is our creator, if God loves us, if God gives us all the good that we enjoy, those are clearly reasons to prize God's friendship. Further reasons may be found in more particular religious beliefs about covenants God has made with us for our good, or other things God has done to save us or bring us to the greatest good. Such beliefs are obviously subject to test by the problem of evil, but that is too large an additional topic to be adequately discussed here.

Many reasons of the sort I have just suggested can be characterized as reasons of gratitude. Gratitude is instanced by Pufendorf as a source of reasons for regarding the command of another as giving rise to obligation,[6] and I should perhaps indicate here my response to two objections that J. B. Schneewind has recently proposed against this point in Pufendorf's theory.[7] "One is that the appropriateness of repaying benefits with gratitude must itself be . . . imposed by God, which raises the question of its justifiability." On my views, the appropriateness of gratitude is an excellence, a form of the excellence of prizing excellent relationships and of acknowledging the good deeds of others; and like excellence in general, it does not depend on God's commands. (I grant that Pufendorf's very austere conception of natural goodness may not allow him this treatment of the appropriateness as an excellence.) Schneewind's other objection is "that gratitude is only an imperfect duty and hence may not be exacted" with the strictness with which Pufendorf would exact obedience to God's commands. In my account, however (whatever may be true of Pufendorf's), gratitude is not what is being exacted but is rather a motive for complying with God's commands. Perhaps gratitude to God is religiously required, but my present argument does not depend on that.

2. I have noted that it contributes importantly to our reasons for complying with demands if the personal characteristics of the demander are excellent or admirable in relevant respects. This desideratum is spectacularly overfulfilled in the case of divine commands. God is supremely knowledgeable and wise—indeed, omniscient. On the view advocated here, indeed, God is the Good itself, supremely beautiful and rich in nonmoral as well as moral perfection.[8]

The motivational relevance of this point did not escape the great sociologist Émile Durkheim in his attempt to parody theistic ethics to get a conception of society as the source of moral obligation. "The good," he wrote, "is society . . . insofar as it is a reality richer than our own, to which we cannot attach ourselves without a resulting enrichment of our nature."[9] The religious root of this idea is obvious. Durkheim is right in thinking that the richness, for us, of the being from which requirements proceed is an important reason for compliance; but I think human society is not good enough for the role in which he casts it. The majesty of moral requirement is much better sustained by a source in a transcendent Good than in any human society.

It might be thought that if God is the constitutive standard of excellence as I have claimed, the ascription of excellence to God will be trivial and without content, merely saying that God is like God. This does not follow, for the claim that God is the standard is not inscribed as the first line on a blank slate of ethical theory. It is made, rather, against the background of many substantive beliefs about what properties are excellences that must be reflected somehow in the character of any being that is the standard of excellence.

6. Pufendorf, *On the Law of Nature and of Nations*, I,vi,12.

7. Schneewind, *The Invention of Autonomy*, p. 136.

8. Cf. Cumberland, *A Treatise of the Laws of Nature*, p. 13: the "*Authority*" of the "*Laws of God*" (which for Cumberland include "the *Conclusions of Reason* in *moral* Matters") arises in part from the "essential *Perfections*" of "their *first Author* or efficient Cause."

9. Durkheim, *L'éducation morale*, p. 110.

One important excellence is justice. It clearly matters to the persuasive power of God's character, as a source of moral requirement, that the divine will is just.[10] Here, if my theory of obligation is not to be circular, I must be using a "thin theory" of justice, so to speak, which does not presuppose moral obligation as such.[11] Without going beyond such a thin theory I can say, for example, that God judges in accordance with the facts, and cares about each person's interests in a way that is good—and that it will be important to resist those inferences from the course of history that have often led to the belief that the rich enjoy more of God's favor than the poor.

Not that it is enough for a divine command theory of obligation to avoid triviality and circularity in characterizing the justice of God. It must also avoid contradiction. The latter threat is vividly presented in Schneewind's account of Leibniz's objection to Pufendorf's divine command theory. Leibniz argues that

> the voluntarist [i.e., the divine command theorist] can make no sense of the fact that God is praised because he is just. Leibniz is not making the point that linguistic philosophers of our century, believing they follow G. E. Moore, would have in mind. He is not simply claiming that voluntarism mistakenly makes the sentence "God is just" vacuous. His point is rather that we can think that God is just even though he has no superior over him. We think, that is, that someone can be just or law-abiding without the existence of a superior imposing law on him and sanctioning him. But the voluntarist thinks justice requires such a superior. Voluntarism is therefore mistaken about the concept of justice.[12]

My response to this objection turns on the relation of justice to obligation or duty. It depends on what I have called a "thin theory" of justice. Leibniz takes Pufendorf to suppose that "duty and acts prescribed by justice coincide."[13] And certainly philosophers sometimes speak of justice in a sense in which it essentially includes discharging one's obligations and doing one's duty. But that is not the sense in which it seems to me important to say that God is just. God is not praised as dutiful or law-abiding. The justice for which God is praised belongs in the first instance to the ethics of excellence or virtue rather than to that of obligation. It chiefly involves responding well to the various claims and interests involved in a situation (and we have, as I have said, a lot of substantive beliefs about what it is to respond well). Responding well is an excellence, and God is praised as the supreme and definitive standard of it, as of excellence in general. It does not essentially involve being

10. The importance of God's justice for the grounding of a divine command theory is rightly emphasized in MacIntyre, "Which God Ought We to Obey and Why?" It was wrongly neglected in some of my previous papers on divine command metaethics.

11. The terminology of a "thin theory" comes from Rawls, *A Theory of Justice*, though I am making a most un-Rawlsian use of it.

12. Schneewind, *The Invention of Autonomy*, p. 252. The argument under discussion is found in Leibniz, *Political Writings*, pp. 70ff. If this were a historical essay, I would want to discuss the primary source; but Schneewind's formulation, while it seems to me faithful to Leibniz's intent, puts more clearly and vividly the point that concerns us here.

13. Leibniz, *Political Writings*, p. 70.

under obligation, and can therefore belong to God even if God is not subject to obligation in the same sense as we are. God's justice, so understood, grounds obligation, rather than being grounded in it. God's commands, that is, spring from God's way of relating to creatures and their interests; and it is partly because the latter is taken to be an ideal candidate for the role of definitive exemplar of the relevant sort of excellence, that God's commands can plausibly be taken as constituting moral obligation.

3. The goodness of the command is particularly important to our reason for obeying a divine command. It is crucial (and plausible on the assumption that God is the supreme Good) that God's commands spring from a design and purpose that is good, and that the behavior that God commands is not bad, but good, either intrinsically or by serving a pattern of life that is very good. It matters to the plausibility of a divine command theory, for example, that we do not believe that God demands cruelty.

The goodness that I have thus ascribed to God's commands, to God's personal characteristics, and to God's relationship to us is the goodness whose nature I discussed in previous chapters—a goodness of which God is the standard, but which we can recognize to a significant extent. The order of presentation is significant here; it reflects the restrictions on the force and scope of a divine command theory that I stated in section 1. A theory of the good for which God is the constitutive standard of excellence need not presuppose moral obligation, but my theory of moral obligation does presuppose my theory of the good. It is only a God who is supremely excellent in being, in commanding, and more generally in relating to us, whose commands can plausibly be regarded as constituting moral obligation.

4. Given the importance I have ascribed to goodness, we might wonder if it matters whether commands are really issued by God. It may be suspected that all the work in my theory is being done by the supposed goodness of God and God's commands—that really nothing would be lost if we just said that our overriding, fully moral obligation is constituted by what *would* be commanded by a supremely good God, whether there is one or not.[14] My reasons for thinking that that is not an adequate substitute for actual divine commands parallel my reasons for not being satisfied with an ideal, nonactual human authority as a source of moral obligation.

First of all, I do not believe in the counterfactuals. I do not believe that there is a unique set of commands that would be issued by any supremely good God.[15] Some commands, surely, could not issue from a perfectly good being; but there are some things that such a deity might command and might not command. This is most obvious, perhaps, where religious ceremonies are concerned. Many people believe they are under divine commands to perform certain rituals. Few of them would claim

---

14. This type of objection is emphasized in Chandler, "Divine Command Theories and the Appeal to Love."

15. Nor, likewise, do I believe that, apart from an actual divine act of prohibiting, there is a unique set of prohibitions that it would be consonant with the nature of a supremely good God (and thus appropriate) to sanction with the adverse reactions characteristic of moral prohibition.

that any supremely good God must have commanded everyone, or someone, to perform those particular rituals. Something similar may be true of more controversial cases. It is not obvious to me, for example, that there is not a diversity of principles regarding euthanasia that could have been commanded by a supremely good God; perhaps different weightings of the importance of preventing suffering as compared with other values at stake would be possible for such a deity. I may still think I have grounds, in my own and other people's moral sensibilities, and in whatever evidence I take myself to have of God's dealings with humanity, to believe that God has in fact issued certain commands on the subject. And since commands must be communicated in order to be commands, those who are subject to the commands would presumably have had different feelings, perceptions, or evidence on the subject if God's commands had been different; but that does not imply that a perfectly good God could not have commanded differently.[16]

In the second place, even aside from any doubts about whether these counterfactuals about good Gods are true, it seems to me that they are motivationally weak. They do not have anything like the motivational or reason-generating power of the belief that something actually is demanded of me by an unsurpassably wonderful being who created me and loves me. The latter belief is therefore one that ethical theory cannot easily afford to exchange for the belief that such and such *would* have been demanded of me by a supremely good God.

Besides their reason-giving force, there are several other ways in which divine commands are well suited to the role of constitutive standard of moral obligation.

1. A main advantage of a divine command theory of the nature of moral obligation is that it satisfies the demand for the *objectivity* of moral requirement. Being commanded and forbidden by God are properties that actions have independently of whether we think they do, or want them to. Divine commands are more unqualifiedly objective than human social requirements, inasmuch as their factuality is independent of socially established as well as individual opinions and preferences.

2. I noted in chapter 10 that we rightly expect a theory of the nature of right and wrong to yield a large measure of agreement with our *pretheoretical beliefs* about what actions are right and wrong. Divine commands do not have the same connection as human social requirements with pretheoretical moral opinion, and therefore do not have the same guarantee of agreement with it. But there is another way in which divine command theorists can be reasonably assured of sufficient agreement with pretheoretical views. For our existing moral beliefs are bound in practice, and I think ought in principle, to be a constraint on our beliefs about what God commands. We simply will not and should not accept a theological ethics that ascribes to God a set of commands that is *too much* at variance with the ethical outlook that we bring to our theological thinking.

I do not mean to reject the possibility of a conversion in which one's whole ethical outlook is revolutionized, and reorganized around a new center. That should be possible even in a secular approach to ethics, and all the more in a religious one. But if we are to retain our grip on ethics as a subject of discourse, we can hardly

---

16. The issues of this paragraph are discussed more fully in Adams, "Moral Arguments for Theistic Belief," p. 148f.

hold open the possibility of anything too closely approaching a revolution in which, so to speak, good and evil would trade places. (Much more that bears on his will be said in chapter 12, section 3.)

3. A divine command theory easily satisfies the principle that facts of moral obligation should *play a part in our coming to recognize* actions as right and wrong. For it is part of the notion of a divine command, as of any command, that it is communicated (as we will see more fully in sections 3 and 4). A God who issues commands must act in such a way as to make it more likely that those to whom the commands are revealed will come to think right what is divinely commanded and wrong what is divinely forbidden. God may do this in creating our faculties, in providentially governing human history, in inspiring prophets, and perhaps in other ways.

4. In chapter 10 I stressed the connection of moral obligation with the possibility of *guilt*, and the connection of guilt with rupture or straining of valued relationships. It is obvious that in theistic traditions guilt has been powerfully connected with rupture or straining of our relationship with God. A divine command theory of the nature of obligation facilitates the understanding of moral guilt as involving offense against a person. It also enriches the possibilities for dealing with guilt by helping us to understand guilt as something that can be removed, at least in one significant dimension, by divine forgiveness.

This is a significant advantage of a divine command theory, but it needs to be seen in a more complex context. Concretely, in typical cases, in theistic perspective, the problem of guilt has at least four dimensions. The most important for theists, the transcendent dimension of guilt, is damage to one's relationship with God. It is this that is most obviously and directly repaired by the repentance and forgiveness that constitute reconciliation with God. A second dimension is damage to relationships with human persons one has wronged; if this is to be repaired, it must be by reconciliation with *them*, and this is not always possible, nor always morally advisable to attempt (in "this life," at any rate).

In the third and fourth dimensions, it is the offender personally that is ruined, rather than a social relationship. And here we may distinguish, a bit artificially perhaps, between corruption and defilement. Corruption and defilement are as deeply connected with the good as with the right. By themselves, apart from their relation to an offended person, they do not constitute guilt, in my view, but they are certainly felt to be connected with it in serious cases.

Guilty action typically proceeds from a morally (and perhaps religiously) *corrupt* disposition. This calls for a sort of regeneration or healing, which may in some measure be inseparable from reconciliation with God and other people. It involves repentance, but may also involve much more; and religious traditions have much to say (and to do) about it.

In guilt one may also feel a *defilement*, from which one wishes to be cleansed.[17] This is a problem about the excellence or worth of one's life.[18] It is in principle dis-

---

17. Cf. Swinburne, *Responsibility and Atonement*, p. 74.

18. Cf. Otto, *The Idea of the Holy*, p. 55. Otto's vivid account of the sense of sin as a negative valuation of the self is illuminating and relevant at this point, though I do not mean to endorse it in every detail.

tinct from the problem of corruption, for the defilement most closely connected with guilt could remain even if the corrupt disposition were healed. Guilt is rooted in the past, but one's past remains a part of one's life. If one has done wrong, there is still that evil in one's life. If it is significant enough, it raises the question how, as a religiously or morally serious person, one can continue to affirm one's own life as a worthwhile project.

Religious language about being "cleansed" from sin, or about the sinner being "justified" by being "counted" as "righteous" by God, serves mainly, in my opinion, to address this problem of defilement. This problem is not primarily social, but the religious solutions on offer have a fundamentally social and relational aspect. God offers renewed love; God offers rituals of expiation; Christ dies for us.[19] In ways such as these God invites us to participate in a larger story, and a relationship, that has, from its divine participant, sufficient value to swallow up the negative value of our sin.

That such a relationship is indeed the source or ground of the greatest value in our lives is a nontrivial assumption of typical religious solutions of the problem of moral defilement. More than any other of the "great dead philosophers" of the modern period, Immanuel Kant took this problem seriously, as a problem about one's moral worthiness. It was difficult for him to accept any solution to the problem, in my opinion, because he was committed to finding the chief value of one's life in the goodness of one's individual will, rather than in a larger, relational whole deriving most of its worth from a much better being to whom one is related.[20]

3. Divine Command and Divine Will

If we are to understand moral obligation in terms of divine commands, we must suppose that God has issued the relevant commands. Commands are speech acts, and this suggests difficult questions about the application of the concept of commanding to God, as we shall see in section 4. One might be tempted to escape these difficulties right at the outset by replacing the concept of God's commands with that of God's will. The two concepts often seem interchangeable in theistic ethics, and believers may think of their ethical reflection as an attempt to "discern the will of God." And God's will, unlike God's commands, seems to exist and have its content independently of what God does to communicate it. Theories similar to mine have sometimes used the concept of divine will rather than that of divine command in explaining the primary ground of obligation. Mark C. Murphy has recently presented an illuminating and uncommonly well-developed argument for preferring the divine will formulation,[21] which puts additional pressure on me to explain why I still adhere to the divine command formulation.

19. If God uses ritual and historic events to enhance the meaning of our lives, the enhancement is typically effected, I suspect, by the *symbolic* value of the events; cf. chapter 9.

20. I have discussed this topic more fully in my introduction to Kant, *Religion within the Boundaries of Mere Reason*.

21. Murphy, "Divine Command, Divine Will, and Moral Obligation." Cf. also P. Quinn, "Divine Command Theory," which cites Murphy's paper.

One reason is that a shift of attention to the concept of divine will can hardly dispense the student of religious ethics from the task of trying to understand a concept that plays such an important role as that of divine commands does in the ethics of most theistic traditions. But that is not yet a very deep explanation, and may not carry very much theoretical weight. Reasons that dig deeper are more complex and require a fuller discussion.

1. The most obvious problem for divine will theories of obligation is that according to most theologies, not everything wrong or forbidden by God is in every way contrary to God's will. It has commonly been taken as following from God's omnipotence and providence that nothing happens that is totally contrary to God's will, though deeds are in fact done that are wrong and contrary to God's commands. Many theologians have distinguished between God's *antecedent will* and God's *consequent will*. God's antecedent will is God's preference regarding a particular issue considered rather narrowly in itself, other things being equal. God's consequent will is God's preference regarding the matter, all things considered. It has commonly been held that nothing happens contrary to God's consequent will, though many things happen contrary to God's antecedent will. On the typical view, to be sure, God's consequent will is partly permissive; some things are permitted by God that are not fully caused, or even intended, by God.

Clearly, the ground of our obligations is not to be found in God's merely *permissive will*, or more broadly in God's consequent will, inasmuch as all the wrongdoing that actually occurs is not contrary to them. An identification of the ground of obligation with God's antecedent will confronts the difficulty that we are sometimes morally obliged to make the best of a bad situation by doing something that it seems a good God would not have preferred antecedently, other things being equal. With what divine will, then, can we identify the ground of ethical obligation? The usual response has been to say that the divine will by which we are ethically bound is God's *revealed will*. And what is God's revealed will? Either it is substantially the same as God's commands; or, if it includes something else, perhaps advice or "counsels," the commands will be the most stringently binding part of it. Either way it will be God's commands that will ground obligation as such.

Murphy's paper has convinced me, however, that partisans of a divine will theory of obligation may be able to escape this argument. The key point for their escape would be that the concept of antecedent will involves a certain abstraction. God's antecedent will is what God prefers relative to a subset abstracted from the complete actual circumstances of the event. There are degrees of abstraction, and God's antecedent will that determines obligation, on Murphy's view, will be among the least abstract in the circumstances assumed in it. Murphy suggests that it will be one "which takes into account all relevant circumstances other than the actual choice."[22] That may do the trick for him; so I will not lay much weight on this argument.

---

22. Murphy, "Divine Command, Divine Will, and Moral Obligation," p. 20. Murphy states his account of obligation in terms of "antecedent intention" instead of "antecedent will." The appeal to intention is part of a commendable effort to avoid allowing mere divine *wishes* to constitute obligations. I am uneasy about the conception of a divine "intention" regarding what *we* should do (which we may frustrate), even if it is an "antecedent" intention; but I pass over this issue here.

2. The seriousness of the difference between divine will and divine command formulations of a theory of obligation obviously lies in what we say about the cases (if any are possible) in which there is a divergence between what God wills in the relevant way and what God commands. If God commands something that God does not (in the relevant way) want us to do, are we obliged to do it? If God (in the relevant way) wants us to do something but does not command us to do it, are we obliged to do it?

It is not easy to answer the first question either way, but I think the case it poses should not be taken as a relevant possibility in theistic ethical theory. Some theistic thinkers have thought it might even be actual—that God may, for example, have commanded Abraham to kill his son Isaac as a sacrifice without (in the relevant sense) wanting him to do it.[23] Murphy seems to think that in such a case one's obligation would be to do what God wants rather than what God commands,[24] but I think that is far from obvious for theists. Religiously, after all, obedience to God is in large part a matter of *respect* for God; and interhuman examples suggest that respect would follow commands in preference to unexpressed desires. The wait staff in a restaurant show me benevolence, perhaps, but scant respect, if they bring me what they think I want instead of what I actually ordered.

The issue is further complicated by the consideration that any reason for believing that God does not (in the relevant sense) want us to do something will virtually always be a reason, of approximately equal strength, for believing that God has not commanded us to do it. This is related to the even more fundamental point that, as Murphy puts it, "there is something troubling about the idea of God's commanding us to do something that He wills that we not do."[25] Troubling indeed: the inconsistency seems grounds for doubt that either the volition or the command involved in it could be serious enough to consitute an obligation. I therefore believe that neither a divine command nor a divine will theory of obligation should build on the supposition of such a possibility. Having said this, I may owe an explanation of how I would understand such a story as that of Abraham and Isaac; at this point I will just issue a promissory note, which will be elaborately paid off in chapter 12.

3. The opposite sort of divergence between divine will and divine command, in which God wants us to do something but does not command us to do it, is an important possibility for theistic ethics. It is on this point chiefly that I think the divine command account is to be preferred. The important possibility for theistic ethics here is the possibility of supererogation. It should be possible for God to decide not to require us to do everything that God would prefer that we do, thus leaving some of the preferred actions supererogatory rather than required. It is controversial within theistic religious traditions whether God in fact has left anything supererogatory; but I think it is no virtue in a theistic metaethics to rule out supererogation as impossible by the very nature of obligation.

23. A recent example of this interpretation of the biblical story is cited in Murphy, "Divine Command, Divine Will, and Moral Obligation," p. 9.
24. A similar opinion on this point may be suggested in Ezekiel 20:25–26, which I will quote in a related context in chapter 12, section 2.
25. Murphy, "Divine Command, Divine Will, and Moral Obligation," p. 23 n. 17.

This is connected with the distinctiveness of obligation. As I argued in chapter 10, to say that an action is obligatory is to say more than that it is the best thing to do. It is to say that one in some sense *has* to do it, and that various sanctions against not doing it are appropriate. For many reasons, we often do not want people to be *obliged* to do what we want them to *do*. So far as I can see, God can have such reasons too, so that we should not expect God to want God's wanting someone to do something to impose, automatically, an obligation to do it.

Once we are clear that there is a difference in principle between its being best that we should do something and our being obliged to do it, and a related difference between wanting someone to do something and wanting her or him to be obliged to do it, I think it should be clear that if any divine volition is suited to issue directly in an obligation that we should do something, it would be a volition that we should be obliged to do it rather than a volition that we should do it. Otherwise God will have no opportunity to take into account possible reasons for wanting something to be done *without* wanting it to be obligatory. For this reason divine will theorists might prefer the alternative of taking the existence of the obligation, rather than the doing of the deed, as the object of the divine volition that is to ground obligation.[26]

This alternative would share with divine command theories the advantage of leaving it open to God to allow for supererogation. It leaves us faced, however, with the question why God would ever leave the obligatory uncommanded. Given the strong connection, for which I have argued, between obligation and the appropriateness of social pressure, why would God ever want something to be obligatory but not command it? Perhaps, of course, in view of a mix of advantages and disadvantages, God would have an antecedent but not a consequent volition that the action be obligatory, and would not command it; but in that case the action would presumably not be obligatory, since what God wills antecedently but not consequently does not happen—certainly not insofar as it depends on God. So it seems implausible to think of divine volitions regarding obligations as grounding obligations without God issuing the relevant commands.

4. The main benefit that I can see in replacing divine commands with divine will in a theory of obligation would be avoiding the problems that attend the requirement that commands must be revealed or communicated in order to exist as commands. This benefit would depend on the assumption that the relevant divine will can be what it is, and impose obligation, without being revealed. But this yields an unattractive picture of divine-human relations, one in which the wish of God's heart imposes binding obligations without even being communicated, much less issuing in a command. Games in which one party incurs guilt for failing to guess the unexpressed wishes of the other party are not nice games. They are no nicer if God is thought of as a party to them.

It is implausible to suppose that uncommunicated volitions impose obligations. This is not a point about the knowability of moral facts in general, and I do not

---

26. This alternative is considered and rejected in Murphy, "Divine Command, Divine Will, and Moral Obligation," pp. 10–16. The argument I propose here is not one of those discussed there.

mean to derive it simply or directly from the principle that 'ought' implies 'can', though that principle may be hovering in the background.[27] It is rather a point about how obligations can be grounded in interpersonal relations, broadly understood. We are considering views on which moral obligation is understood in terms of what God *requires* of us. But requiring is something people *do* in relation to each other. It essentially involves communicative *acts*. The will of a legislator imposes no obligation without being communicated, as Francisco Suárez, for example, acknowledges, although he is one who uses the terminology of divine *will* in explaining the "special" or "preceptive" obligation of divine law.[28]

5. Murphy seems to favor the view that a divine volition can ground obligation without being communicated in a divine command, but he is unwilling to rest his position heavily on the assumption that it is true. Even if "moral obligation . . . must depend on divine command," he holds, "all that would follow is that the expression of God's will is at least a *validating condition* of obligation." The *grounds*, or "cause, or source," could still be in the divine will, and that is what Murphy mainly wants to affirm.[29] I am more than willing to affirm it too, in an important sense, inasmuch as divine commands, as voluntary acts, must necessarily have their grounds or cause or source in the divine will. More than that, the divine commander will surely be conceived as willing rationally, coherently, harmoniously. We will therefore suppose that the commands of such a deity are grounded in volitions that the commanded acts be obligatory, and that they be done. What I mean to insist on is just that the divine will must be communicated in order to impose obligations. As long as that is true, I don't see why we should not interpret obligation in terms of divine commands; I also don't see why we should not regard the commands as at least *part* of the grounds of the obligations.

4. What Is a Divine Command?

A divine command theory of the nature of obligation requires a strong answer to the question, What it is for something (and indeed for one thing rather than another) to be commanded by God?[30] According to such a theory, God's commands are the standard, conformity to which constitutes the ethical validity of human social requirements, and the correctness of one against another when they disagree; and God's commands may go beyond human standards, revealing new ethical obligations not previously known. If divine commands are to fill these roles, there must be a fact of the matter about what God commands. It must be an objective fact, independent in some ways of human social requirements; and it must be richly

27. Murphy ("Divine Command, Divine Will, and Moral Obligation," p. 8) seems to assume that principle would be the reason for requiring communication for voluntary grounding of an obligation.

28. Suárez, *On Laws and God the Lawgiver*, II,vi,24.

29. Murphy, "Divine Command, Divine Will, and Moral Obligation," p. 8f.; emphases mine.

30. What is said here supersedes, on some points, positions taken in Adams, "The Concept of a Divine Command," from which, however, I draw extensively in this section.

determinate, containing answers (whether we can prove them or not) to ethical issues on which humans disagree. A divine command theorist is confronted, therefore, with the question, What would constitute such a fact?

This is a difficult question. Its difficulties are connected with the fact that commands are a form of communication, a type of speech act. A command does not
exist or have any force unless it is issued—that is, unless it is in some way communicated. The concept of a command of God falls under the wider concept of God's
speaking, or the word of God. God is no ordinary participant in any linguistic community. This suggests the question whether God literally speaks, or is literally, or in
the primary sense, the author of discourse, as Nicholas Wolterstorff persuasively
argues in his recent book *Divine Discourse*, or whether the concepts of speaking and
commanding apply to God only in an analogical or metaphorical sense. This question will receive no precise answer here. Either the literal sense or a strong enough
analogy could sustain a divine command theory. A merely metaphorical use of 'command' might give the theory too little content, but I believe our investigation will
support a reasonably strong analogy.

In order to exist, a command must be issued. It must be communicated to those
who are subject to it. How does God do this? How are God's commands revealed?
Many people, on hearing of a divine command theory of obligation, assume that it
must ground obligation in scriptural injunctions, and perhaps even that it presupposes a rather "fundamentalist" interpretation of religious scriptures. This assumption is quite mistaken. A divine command theory of the *nature* of ethical obligation
does imply that God somehow communicates commands to humans, but it is consistent with a wide variety of hypotheses about how the commands are revealed and
how they can be known by us. This variety is rightly stressed in the recent book *The
God Who Commands* by Richard Mouw:

> My own commitment [says Mouw], in dealing with issues of religious authority,
> is to the kind of *sola scriptura* emphasis that was a prominent feature of the
> Protestant Reformation, and is still dear to the hearts of many conservative
> Protestants. But I want in no way to imply that a belief in the moral relevance of
> divine commands is the exclusive property of people who spell out the issues of
> authority in a strong bibliocentric manner. For example, some Christians . . .
> understand "natural law" in such a way that when someone makes moral
> decisions with reference to natural law that person is obeying divine commands.
> Others hold that submission to the *magisterium* of a specific ecclesiastical body
> counts as obedience to divine directives. Others assume that individual Chris-
> tians . . . can receive specific and extrabiblical commands from God, such as
> "Quit smoking!" . . . Still others hold that the will of God can be discerned by
> examining our natural inclinations or by heeding the dictates of conscience.[31]

It is important to my project to insist on a range of possibilities at least as wide
as Mouw suggests for the communication or revelation of divine commands. For
the ethical obligations whose nature I propose to analyze in terms of divine com-

---

31. Mouw, *The God Who Commands*, p. 8.

mands are not just those of some particular sort of Christians, or even of adherents of all the theistic religions, but those of human beings in general. For this purpose it is important to understand divine commands as cognitively accessible to human beings quite generally, and hence in a wide variety of ways. "Natural law" is a historically obvious possibility, though it is not a favorite conception of mine. I do think our "inclinations" and "conscience," among the possibilities mentioned by Mouw, can be vehicles for the revelation of divine commands, though I do not mean to rule out scriptures and other vehicles historically tied to particular religious traditions, as I will discuss in the final section of chapter 15.

Reasoning will play an important part in our cognitive access to divine commands, on my view at any rate. It is crucial to the prospects for a divine command theory as part of a coherent philosophical or theological ethics that human claims about what God has commanded are subject to rational assessment and criticism. If a divine command theory is embedded in a theory of the good, and presupposes it, as I propose, we must expect this assessment to involve judgments about the compatibility of purported commands with the goodness of God—that is, with the character of a deity who is to serve as the supreme standard of goodness. We may inquire both about the goodness of what is commanded and about the appropriateness of sanctions or adverse reactions against what is forbidden. These considerations will constrain our judgments of obligation—though it may be less natural to speak of them as "constraining" God's commands, since those commands spring from God's character, which is the standard of goodness in this matter.

One way in which it is plausible to suppose that divine commands are revealed is through human social requirements, and that is particularly important in the context of the present discussion. A divine command theorist should want to say that a divine prohibition of murder, for example, has been made known very widely to the human race. And the dissemination of such prohibitions has surely taken place largely through human systems of social requirement. Even scriptural commandments may be related to such systems, if we think of them (as many interpreters do) as expressing, on their human side, systems of ethical requirement accepted and backed and transmitted by religious communities. Theologians who think of them that way may want to say that social processes involved in the formation of the biblical text were vehicles of divine revelation.

God can speak through a solitary prophetic voice, of course, as well as through the requirements collectively embraced and enforced by a community. The prophet's outcry still constitutes a demand, however—a demand made or backed by the prophet—and a demand that is social in a broad sense, though an individual is unlikely to be able to articulate as comprehensive a system of requirements as a community can. What distinguishes the prophet's relation to social requirement is that the divine command may not be received by the prophet as required by any human community, but only as imposed by God.

These reflections suggest that some theists might well suppose that God's commands are promulgated largely, though not exclusively, through human social requirements. On this view, the divine ethical requirements will not form an entirely separate system, parallel and superior to human systems of social requirement. Rather, human moral systems will be imperfect expressions of divine commands; and the question of their relation to God's commanding will be whether and how far they are authorized or backed by God's authority, not whether or how they agree with an eternal divine commandment laid up in the heavens.

This takes us back to our fundamental questions. What constitutes God's authorizing of a requirement or, more broadly, God's issuing of a command? What determines or defines the content of a divine command? In my opinion, a satisfactory account of these matters will have three main points. (1) A divine command will always involve a *sign*, as we may call it, that is intentionally caused by God. (2) In causing the sign God must intend to issue a command, and *what* is commanded is what God intends to command thereby. (3) The sign must be such that the intended audience could understand it as conveying the intended command. I will discuss these points in turn, the first much more briefly than the others.

1. The sign may be any of the possible vehicles of revelation discussed previously, or others: a scriptural text, the utterance of a prophet or some other historical event, the requirements of some human community, or features of an individual's consciousness. Since one way in which a command differs from a mere wish is in being a voluntary action, God must *do* something to issue a command; and what God must do is at least in part to produce a sign that is cognitively accessible to some "audience," since a command is an act of communication.

Most questions about *how* God causes the sign can be left open here—for instance, whether God causes it by a special divine intervention or as part of a vast train of consequences of an initial act of creation.[32] One family of issues of which we should be aware concerns the (probably typical) case in which our proximate signs of God's commands are words or deeds of other people, or requirements imposed by them. How are we to think of the freedom of human action and its relation to divine causality in these cases? Is there a mixture of divine and human causality here, and may the resulting sign be only an imperfect expression of the divine command? Can a definite divine command have been given if it has never been perfectly expressed to us? Perhaps so; human commands can be imperfectly expressed—ungrammatical, or even somewhat inarticulate, or burdened with useless information and emotional "static"—and still be quite definitely given, if the intended audience could reasonably be expected to understand them. Or may human words convey divine commands, not because God has caused those words, but because the human author has been authorized or deputized to speak on God's behalf?[33] If so, how has God given a sign authorizing the deputies? And has God set limits to their authority, and if so by what signs? Such questions arise in theologies of divine discourse, and different theologies give different answers to them. What we must recognize, at the level of generality of our present discussion, is that a divine command theory of the nature of obligation may be committed to there being correct answers to some such questions.

---

32. Persuasive reasons favoring the first of these alternatives are given, in the context of a much fuller discussion of the causal issues of this paragraph, in Wolterstorff, *Divine Discourse*, chap. 7.

33. The case for such "deputized discourse" as an important way in which God may speak is interestingly argued in Wolterstorff, *Divine Discourse*, pp. 42–51.

2. Arguably, *we* sometimes say things we did not mean to say. God can hardly be thought of as making such mistakes, however. Moreover, there is probably no sign, in religious scriptures or anywhere else, of such obvious and uncontroversial revelatory import that we could reasonably say that it *must* be a divine command to do thus and so, regardless of whatever intentions God did or did not have regarding it. So I think God's intentions must enter into the determination of the character and content of a divine act as a command. This is not to say that God is a transcendent Humpty-Dumpty who can give any arbitrary meaning at all to any sign at all. There are constraints from the side of the audience, or the context of communication, even when God is the communicator; but that is part of my third point, and is not yet our main concern.

For the present our focus is on the intention God must have in commanding. It is the intention to command a certain action. It thus presupposes a practice of commanding, and whatever institutional setting that practice requires. Linguistic and other social practices can create types of action which cannot be understood apart from the practice. Home runs, for example, can exist only in the context of a game whose rules provide for events of a certain type to constitute a home run, and assign a certain significance to such events, a significance that cannot be fully understood apart from the aims that are essential to wholehearted participation in the game. Similarly, commands cannot be understood as such without some relation to a practice of commanding, the institutional setting in which it has its home, and the typical personal dispositions and social pressures that give the practice its point. If God intends to command us to act in a certain way, God must know of a practice (presumably a human practice) of commanding and intend to do something in relation to us that is at least analogous to what humans do in issuing commands to other humans. In other words, the divine intention borrows its content from the human practice of commanding. This does not ground a serious objection to a divine command theory. A practice of commanding exists in virtually all human communities, and I think we need not worry about what obligation would be (if it would exist at all) for persons who do not live in communities in which they use language to *require* things of each other.[34]

One central feature of the human practice of commanding is that persons to whom commands are issued have some obligation to obey them. If their relationships to the commander are not such as to sustain obligations, the command is not valid; perhaps it is not "really" a command. This feature of the practice is surely part of what is taken into the content of God's intentions in commanding. That

34. Murphy claims it is a major objection to grounding obligation in divine commands, as distinct from divine will, that "it makes God's capacity to obligate dependent on the existence of *certain highly specific* forms of community that are conventional *and for the most part do not exist at all*" ("Divine Command, Divine Will, and Moral Obligation," p. 7; my emphases). He has suggested a highly specific, and fictitious, form of theocentric community in which God's commanding would be readily intelligible; but it seems to me intelligible enough by analogy with practices that exist in practically all human communities. It is therefore not necessary to press the question, which could also be raised, whether a purely fictitious human practice could not serve as a model for understanding divine commands. It is essential, of course, on my account, that the signs by which God commands are not fictitious.

might be thought to create a problem of circularity for the theory that the nature of obligation is to be understood in terms of divine commands. The solution to this problem is that the kind of obligation whose nature is to be understood in terms of divine commands is fully valid moral (and religious) obligation, whereas the obligation that is presupposed as involved in the practice of commanding is a premoral social or institutional obligation that may or may not have full moral validity (as I argued in chapter 10, section 3).

It is a related feature of the practice of commanding that the commander also undertakes obligations—for instance, to accept certain types of behavior as obedience to the command. Does God in commanding undertake (and intend to undertake) such obligations? I think the answer must be yes. Again we are talking here about premoral obligations, in the first instance, but we may ask whether they are not also fully valid moral obligations, having been intended and authorized by God's own command. Here I think the answer must be more qualified. In really issuing a command, God not only authorizes people to insist that they have obeyed if they have acted in certain ways; it would also be contrary to divine justice, and hence to the divine nature, for God not to recognize such obedience. The premoral obligation that God undertakes in issuing the command is thus validated by the same source that constitutes our moral obligations, but God's relation to it remains fundamentally different from our relation to moral obligation. Our moral obligations are imposed, through commands, by a will distinct from our own, if a divine command theory of obligation is correct; but that is not true of any "obligations" God may have.[35]

3. We can trace a path of argument from our second main topic in this discussion, the intention of the commander, to the third, the understanding of the audience. Philosophers who wish to avoid dependence on an understanding of complex social practices in understanding the meaning of speech acts such as commanding, and the intentions of those who perform them, may be tempted by a more individualistic account of such notions, in which they would be reduced to psychological terms. An influential account of this sort is Paul Grice's analysis of the notion of a speaker's meaning in terms of the speaker's intention "to produce some effect in an audience by means of the recognition of this intention," so that "to ask what [the speaker] meant is to ask for a specification of the intended effect." In commanding, Grice suggests, one utters something with the intention of impelling an audience to do something, and to have as a reason for doing it their recognition of this intention in one's utterance.[36] The application of this account to the case of God's commanding might seem initially to be simpler and

---

35. My discussion of this topic is inspired by (and a response to) Wolterstorff, *Divine Discourse*, ch. 6. My affirmation of God's having moral obligations is more qualified (at least explicitly) than Wolterstorff's, but the view I adopt here has considerable similarity to the view Wolterstorff suggests that would ground God's moral obligations in requirements of God's character (ibid., pp. 110–13). I allow somewhat more room here for speaking of God's obligations than I did in Adams, "A Modified Divine Command Theory of Ethical Wrongness," p. 115; but I still affirm the central point made there, that God "is not subject to a moral law not of his own making."

36. Grice, "Meaning," pp. 219–21.

more straightforward than the account that I have proposed, but I think it is actually more fraught with difficulty.

The great problem with it is the implication that in commanding people to do anything, God must intend to be understood by those people as commanding them to do that. To this we may add the widely accepted thesis that, as Grice puts it, "one cannot have intentions to achieve results which one sees no chance of achieving."[37] The latter thesis will limit God's intentions more narrowly than ours, because God knows more. Suppose in particular that God has perfect and certain knowledge of the future, as has commonly been believed. Then if any people do not in fact recognize a given text or sign *s* as conveying a command from God to perform action *a*, God must always have known with certainty that they would not so recognize it. It follows that God cannot have intended to obtain that recognition from them, and hence, on the view now before us, that God cannot have used *s* to command those people to do *a*. In short, the view seems to have the consequence that divine commands cannot be unrecognized or misunderstood by those to whom they are addressed. This is a serious disadvantage of the view, for several reasons.

One is that if we are interested, as I am, in the possibility of understanding the nature of ethical obligation quite generally in terms of divine commands, we will hope to understand the concept of a divine command in such a way that ethical imperatives to which nontheists see themselves as subject might be understood, at least in some cases, as commands of God addressed to them. But if God's commands must be intended by God to be recognized by their addressees as commands of God, and if God knows with certainty that the nontheist will not recognize anything as coming from God, it follows that God does not address any command to the nontheist. This is perhaps the least of our problems. For we can relax the requirement of intended recognition of the speaker without drawing all the teeth of the theory. We can suppose it is enough for God's commanding if God intends the addressee to recognize a requirement as extremely authoritative and as having imperative force. And that recognition can be present in nontheists as well as theists.

Problems about the possibility of conflicting interpretations of divine commands cannot be dismissed so easily. Such conflicts are a central part of the history of theistic religions; and it is a central presupposition of normal forms of the debate that there is a possibility of one interpretation of a divine command being correct against another where both interpretations have some basis in signs recognized in a shared tradition. But if there is actually disagreement about the meaning of a supposed divine command, and if God (being omniscient) knew there would be, then there is no meaning that God can have intended the supposed command to be recognized by all the parties to the dispute as having, on the disputed point. And hence, on Grice's theory, God cannot have addressed the same command on that point to all the parties. A theory of divine commands that so radically undercuts the possibility of correctness in a disputed interpretation is very unsatisfying.

Even apart from disagreements, the possibility of imperfect understanding is very important to the role of the idea of divine commands in theistic religious tra-

---

37. Grice, *Studies in the Way of Words*, p. 98.

ditions. A great deal of study, discussion, and reflection makes sense only in rela-tion to the belief that it is possible to come to a fuller understanding of God's com-mands than one now has. This belief is threatened if God's commands cannot mean anything that God did not know would be recognized by all their addressees.

These problems should be of concern even to theologians who would abandon the doctrine of complete divine foreknowledge; for they, in general, will still ascribe to God enough knowledge for God to be certain in advance that there would be much of the misunderstanding implied by religious accounts of the vicissitudes of revelation and interpretation. Fortunately (from my point of view), it is not plau-sible in any event to hold that speakers cannot mean, or command, more than they expect all or most of their audience to understand. For instance, I would not want to be deemed to have meant, and said, in my undergraduate lectures on Kant's *Critique of Pure Reason*, only what I thought it epistemically possible that virtually everyone in the class would understand. On some topics, with most audiences, a lower standard of communicative success than that is reasonable. I *want* everyone to understand exactly what I mean; but I cannot exactly *intend* it, because I know it is virtually certain that some will not understand. Conversely, I may think that I now understand better than I ever did before, and better than most other readers have, what Kant meant by a certain passage of the *Critique*. I believe, controver-sially no doubt, that such interpretive beliefs can in principle be objectively correct. And I think their correctness is to be understood in terms of what Kant intended to *say*, not in terms of any hopelessly unrealistic intentions he may have had about being *understood*.

It does not follow, of course, that what one can reasonably expect one's audi-ence to understand by certain signs imposes no constraint at all on what one can mean (or command) by those signs. Under normal circumstances, for instance, one could neither command nor intend to command a subordinate to load a truck by saying, in English, "Bring me a cup of coffee." And that is because one could not intend to issue such a command in English without knowing enough about com-manding and about English to know that no one (in normal circumstances) could understand "Bring me a cup of coffee" as a command to load a truck. Using signs that one knows no one could understand as a command to do *a* does not count as commanding anyone to do *a*. So if an omniscient being issues commands, it must be by signs that *could* be understood by the intended audience, or a significant part of it, as the intended commands. It is not necessary that the signs *will* be so under-stood, or that the commander must believe that they will; that would burden us with the problems of Grice's analysis after all. Rather, the signs must be such that they would be likely to be understood in the intended sense if the intended audi-ence had a good attitude toward the commander and the relevant situation, and did a good job of interpreting the signs.

This point is connected with the social and normative role of commands. One who issues a command intends to bring it about that those who are subject to it will be blameworthy if they do not conform to it—that it will be appropriate (good in the relevant way) to blame them in that case. But it would obviously be unfair (and thus not good in the relevant way) to blame people for failure to conform to a com-mand they could not understand, unless their inability to understand is due to something bad about their attitude or response. Hence the commander must intend the command to be understandable in the indicated sense—which implies that if the commander has the knowledge and powers of God, the command must actually be understandable.

This affects not only what divine commands can have been issued, but also who can be subject to them. For people differ in their ability to understand any sign as a particular divine command. This is most obvious where the signs are particular prophecies, scriptures, or historic events. God cannot have intended such signs to be understood by people who would never know of them, and would never receive signs of similar meaning deriving from them. Only people whom God expected to know of the relevant signs, and to be able to understand them in the intended sense, can be subject to divine commands conveyed by those signs, as part of their intended audience.

Principles of moral obligation constituted by divine commands are not time-less truths, because the commands are given by signs that occur in time. People who are not in the region of space-time in which a sign can be known are not subject to a command given by it. Of course, if the signs by which some divine commands are given are moral impulses and sensibilities common to practically all adult human beings since some (not too recent) point in the evolution of our species, all of us can fairly be counted as subject to those commands. But the conception of a divine command allows for divine commands with historically more restricted audiences. That is a historically important and ethically interesting possibility which will be discussed further in chapters 12, 13, and 15.

5. Autonomy

One of the commonest objections against theories that give divine commands a major role in morality is that they sin against autonomy. Autonomy is one of the favorite themes of modern ethical thought, though what is meant by 'autonomy' is by no means always the same. The idea suggested by the etymology of the word (*autos* = self, *nomos* = law) is that as a human moral agent one is, or should be, a (moral) law unto oneself—that one should find the moral law within oneself. On the face of it, this does seem contrary to the idea of God's commands constituting the moral law for us human agents. The latter seems to posit a heteronomy (*heteros* = other, *nomos* = law) inasmuch as it places the source of the moral law for us in the command of *another*. Autonomy is commonly seen as characteristic of moral maturity; conversely, a morality of divine commands is often censured as immature, or even "infantile."[38]

'Autonomy' has so many senses in ethical discussion, and there are so many forms of divine command theory, that there is no uniquely right answer to the question whether a divine command theory is incompatible with autonomy. It would hardly

---

38. Nowell-Smith, "Morality: Religious and Secular," has as its "central thesis" that "religious morality is infantile" insofar as it "consists in obedience to commands" (pp. 95, 97). This is one of the texts addressed in the very helpful discussion of the charge of immaturity in chap. 1 of Mouw, *The God Who Commands*.

be possible, therefore, to present a single defense of all divine command theory as such against the charge of heteronomy. Some forms of theological ethics do seem to me immature, and I would not want to defend them. What I propose to do is rather to explain in what senses the divine command theory that I do want to defend is and is not compatible with autonomy.

There are at least two senses in which it is not.

1. There are some moral theories—Kant's being the most famous example—in which the autonomy of the moral agent is treated as constituting the nature of the moral law. According to Kant, the moral law is essentially a law that we give ourselves, because it is constituted and shaped by the nature and structure of practical reason, which is each agent's own practical reason although it is the same in all of us. This Kantian theory is an alternative to divine command theories of the nature of obligation, and is clearly inconsistent with them. This is not to say that every important feature of Kant's ethical theory is inconsistent with divine command theories. Divine command theorists may find many points of substantive agreement with Kant (as most moralists will), and could in principle adopt one or more of his famous formulations of the content of the moral law. As divine command theorists, however, they will not agree with his account of what constitutes moral obligation. That is not exactly an objection to divine command theories, any more than it is to Kant. I have acknowledged from the outset that there are many alternatives to my theory, some of them very impressive; and I have not undertaken to refute them all.

2. The idea of autonomy has been used in expounding views of the nature of obligation, as we have just noted. It is also used in expounding ideals of character. 'Autonomy', we may say, is often presented as a name of a virtue. That is the way of thinking of autonomy with which we will be most concerned here.

An extreme form of it is the ideal of autonomy as what we may call *total inner-directedness*. A person who is autonomous in this extreme sense will rely exclusively on her own reasoning and/or feelings in adopting moral principles, values, and priorities. Her moral judgments will not be totally insulated from what is going on outside her, for she will have to learn the facts of her situation in order to apply her moral principles to them. But what the rest of the world is to contribute to her moral thinking is just the nonmoral material for it. The distinctively moral content is all to come from within herself.

This is certainly an ideal of autonomy which is inconsistent with my divine command theory, and with any social theory of the nature of obligation; but I see no compelling reason to accept it. I admire a large measure of independent-mindedness, but I think the morality that any one of us could have invented from scratch would have been a pretty inferior product, and anything we could invent for ourselves would not have quite the force of obligation. We learn morality from others, and I don't think we ever wholly outgrow the need to do so. I have argued, further, that the pressure of other persons' demands remains a large part of the pressure of moral obligation. Refusal ever to be swayed (selectively, of course) by the moral stance of others whom one respects, and by the pressure of their demands, as a *moral* pressure by which one's own conception of one's moral obligations *may* need to be corrected, strikes me as an unattractive rather than an admirable independence.

On the other hand, there are several traits that might be characterized as forms of autonomy which I do admire and can accept as part of an ideal of virtue consistent with my divine command theory. Four of them will be discussed here.

1. The most elemental is *responsibility*. Most of us might not be likely to think of it as a form of autonomy, but it is invoked in some attacks on divine command morality as heteronomous. Graeme de Graaff writes:

> There is no room in morality for commands, whether they are the father's, the schoolmaster's, or the priest's. There is still no room for them when they are God's commands. A moral agent is only in very special circumstances permitted to shelter behind the excuse, 'I was ordered to do it.' In morality we are responsible for our own actions and responsible even for those actions which are responses to commands.[39]

In one way de Graaff is attacking a "straw man," so far as theological ethics is concerned. Who proposes to use 'God ordered me to do it' as an *excuse*? Who will really say, 'I know it was wrong, but God ordered me to do it'? What divine command theory will license us to say such a thing? Nothing that God commands is wrong, and no divine command theorist will say otherwise.

Those who take moral obligation to be constituted by divine commands need not (and generally do not) deny that they are responsible for what they do in response to those commands. On the contrary, they hold themselves responsible to obey God's commands, and thus to do their duty. Very likely they also hold themselves responsible to interpret God's commands correctly, and to discern what those commands imply in the situation in which they find themselves. It is unfair to accuse them of abdicating their moral responsibility, even if you think they have quite wrongheaded views about the nature of obligation. People who hold themselves accountable for doing their duty do not abdicate their moral responsibility simply by holding erroneous metaethical views about the nature of duty.[40]

But perhaps what I have just said reflects a one-sided interpretation of the charge of abdicating responsibility. Perhaps the claim is that divine command moralists narrow the scope of their responsibility by holding themselves responsible only to obey orders. The first responsibility which a child receives from its parents is normally responsibility to follow very simple and direct instructions: for example, not to go in the street under any circumstances. As the child matures, it is ready to receive more responsibility. We speak of someone receiving or accepting *more* responsibility in proportion as fulfilling the responsibility involves making decisions that are more than just decisions to obey (and probably in proportion as the decisions are more complex in other ways too).

Divine command moralities differ widely in how much responsibility of this sort they assign us. Some try to prescribe as much as possible of the detail of life in

39. de Graaff, "God and Morality," p. 34.
40. Cf. Outka, "Religious and Moral Duty," p. 234: "Autonomy is positively insisted on [by Kierkegaard] in the sense that the agent must freely yield to God's sovereignty and assent to his command."

unambiguous commands that people are taught by their religious community; in that way they do narrow the scope of ethical responsibility. But I do not advocate such a morality. Many divine theories assign us a much wider responsibility.

If we accept "You shall not commit murder" as a divine command, for instance, we may still be left with responsibility for interpreting the command. What properly counts as murder? Many cases will be obvious, and our responsibility there will be to obey. Who really thinks we should have more discretion than that, when the question is whether we should poison our rich uncles? But what about turning off the respirator of someone who is expected, with virtual certainty, never to awaken from a coma? There a divine command theorist (like most other people) may have more to decide than whether to obey; and the responsibility is heavy. There is also in principle the more fundamental responsibility of deciding whether murder is really forbidden, though we may trust that it will not be a hard decision for any of us. Theological and secular ethical theories may provide different ways of thinking about that question, but they do not necessarily assign us different degrees of responsibility for deciding it.

2. The case of children being given "more responsibility" as they get older is closely related to another form of autonomy that we may call *moral competence*. The morally competent person is able, and willing, to make moral judgments about particular cases, based on her own principles, perceptions, and feelings. She may draw her principles, consciously, from religious scriptures or from community norms and traditions, but she applies them herself. A moral community can hardly function effectively without a considerable measure of such competence on the part of a considerable portion of its members. Even if its moral code is exceptionally detailed, cases will arise in which judgment is required to apply the code, and the community will be dependent on members who are willing to accept the responsibility for making such judgments, and who do it well. With a less rigid, more creative form of moral life that I and many others would admire more, there will be even more need for judgment. On any plausible account of moral virtue, moral competence of this sort will be a major part of it. The main point to be made about it here is that adherents of a divine command morality also need moral competence, and that a divine command theory can provide as large a scope as any other metaethical theory for competence in the application of moral principles or, more broadly, in the recognition of right and wrong in particular cases.

3. We take a decisive step further in autonomy if we take up and hold the sort of *critical* (and self-critical) *stance* that I advocated at the end of chapter 8 as a remedy for idolatry, subjecting to critical scrutiny any ethical ideas that we have or meet. This is in no way contrary to a divine command conception of obligation, or to loyalty toward God. Indeed, it may be demanded by loyalty toward God, if God is truly a transcendent Good. For God is distinct from any ideas we may have about God, and more perfect than they can be. One's loyalty toward God may therefore be manifested in one's critical examination of all claims and beliefs about what God has commanded, and hence about what is right and wrong. Indeed, it may be manifested in critical scrutiny of the claim that God issues commands at all. As I argued in chapter 8, theories about God, mine or anyone else's, are not to be confused with God. There are certainly forms of religious belief and life that have not encouraged

such a critical stance, but I see no reason that a divine command morality should not encourage it.

4. The value we set on autonomy may also have to do with how we *care* about moral issues. In pressing his charge that a morality of divine commands is infantile, P. H. Nowell-Smith quotes a horrible example from a well-known devotional book: "I give no almes [only] to satisfie the hunger of my Brother, but to fulfill and accomplish the Will and Command of my God; I draw not my purse for his sake that demands it, but his that enjoyned it."[41] One who serves goods that he cares about is more autonomous, in an important way, and more admirable, than one who obeys commands or rules without caring about any goods but those of obedience as such. It is better to avoid lies because one loves truthfulness, to deal fairly because one values fairness and the people with whom one deals, and to give to charity because one cares about people's needs, than to do those things just because one has been commanded, even by God, to do them.

It does not follow, however, that the introduction of divine commands in ethics debases our motivation in well-doing. The problem, if there is one, is not peculiar to divine command theories. There surely is such a thing as moral obligation or duty. But one who has too formal and abstract a concern for doing his duty (whatever the nature of duty may be)—a concern too detached from caring about other goods—lacks the sort of autonomy that concerns us here, and is less admirable for lacking it. The grounding of moral obligation in divine commands that I propose does not favor such an abstract concern for duty. On the contrary, it explicitly seeks the reasons for accepting a controlling role for God's commands in true goods about which one is invited to care independently of the commands. Apart from such an embedding of the morality of obligation in its relation to goods that we may reasonably be expected to love, it will be hard to have any attractive conception of it.

In the context of a divine command theory, the autonomy involved in loving the various goods to which obligations are related may be brought under the heading of "theonomy." The thinker most associated with the idea of theonomy is Paul Tillich, who explains: "Autonomy asserts that man . . . is his own law. Heteronomy asserts that man . . . must be subjected to a law, strange and superior to him. Theonomy asserts that the superior law is, at the same time, the innermost law of man himself, rooted in the divine ground which is man's own ground."[42] What I mean to employ here is not Tillich's complete and richly individual theory of theonomy, but just the idea of a merging of divine authority and autonomous valuing in moral motivation. Respect for divine authority motivates, largely because it coheres with, orga-

---

41. Browne, *Religio Medici*, p. 90 (II,2); quoted in Nowell-Smith, "Morality: Religious and Secular," p. 104. The bracketed, somewhat softening "only" is not in the manuscripts and earliest editions of Browne's work, but was added in the last editions published during his lifetime. In the context, Browne seems concerned to distinguish supernatural from natural charity, and also to disparage instinctive as contrasted with conscientious charity. Nontheistic as well as theistic moralists can of course be led astray by the latter concern.

42. Tillich, *The Protestant Era*, p. 56f. The history of the term 'theonomy' did not begin with Tillich; cf. Mouw, *The God Who Commands*, p. 18.

nizes, supports, and is supported by goods that we care about for their own sakes. These are goods that God too must be conceived as caring about for their own sakes. In loving them we enter into God's love for them. In this way theonomy is a form of the alliance with God that I discussed in chapter 7, section 7.

The connection with the argument of chapter 7 is important. One reason that divine command theories of obligation have appealed to many theists is that such theories have seemed especially congruous with the religious demand that God be the object of our highest allegiance. If our supreme commitment in life is to doing what is right just because it is right, and if what is right is right just because God wills or commands it, then surely our highest allegiance is to God. But my divine command theory seems not to have this advantage, for I emphasize reasons for obeying God that are grounded in other goods that we are to value for their own sake and independently (to some extent) of our beliefs about God's commands. I am therefore not proposing a commitment to obeying God's commands *just* because they are God's commands, but also for other reasons.

As I argued in section 2, our evaluation of God's character, and especially of the content of purportedly divine commands, is important to our reasons for obeying. This has implications for the motivational ideal of devotion to God that I advocate. I cannot consistently conceive of it as unquestioning commitment to an individual being, independent of one's evaluation of that being's character and demands. The devotion to God that I favor must be understood as based on the divine perfection in such a way as to be profoundly shaped by one's own moral sensibilities.

Whether one should object on religious grounds to this consequence of my divine command theory is a question about the ideal of devotion to God. One version of such an ideal demands a teleological subordination of other values to obedience to God. On this view, obedience to whatever God may command ought to be the only thing one values for its own sake; any other good is to be valued only as a means to obedience to God. This does imply that God's commands should be obeyed *just* because they are God's commands. This view is liable to serious objection, however. In chapter 7 (with preparatory argument in chapter 6), I argued that a conception of devotion to God in terms of a teleological subordination of other values does not allow the devout really to love anything other than God; for instance, it does not allow them really to love their neighbor, as commanded in Judaism and Christianity. For this reason I proposed an alternative conception of the ideal of total devotion to God, in which love for God is an organizing principle into which one integrates genuine love for other goods that one is to prize for their own sake, as God does. This conception of theistic devotion coheres with the form of commitment to obedience to God that I propose in this chapter.

It might be thought that traditional theistic piety demands obedience to God's commands *just* because they are God's commands, but that is not clearly correct. Both in Exodus and in Deuteronomy the Bible prefaces the Ten Commandments with the statement "I am the LORD your God, who brought you out of the land of Egypt, out of the house of bondage" (Exodus 20:2; Deuteronomy 5:6). This is surely meant as a reason for obedience grounded in the value of the relationship between YHWH and Israel established by YHWH's redemptive action—and thus an example of one of the types of reason for obedience to which my account appeals.[43] A similar thought can be found in a more contemporary source noted for emphasis on the sovereignty of God: Karl Barth asks what is the basis of God's claim on our obedience, and answers that "God calls us and orders us and claims us by being gracious to us in Jesus Christ."[44]

43. For emphatic development of this line of thought in a rabbinic work of the fourth century C.E., see Levenson, *The Death and Resurrection of the Beloved Son*, p. 168f.

44. Barth, *Church Dogmatics*, vol. 2, part 2, p. 560. Barth is emphatic that "by deciding for God [one] has definitely decided not to be obedient to power as power" (p. 553). In fairness I should also note that two reasons to which I appeal, God's all-sufficiency for our good, and "that God is the essence of the good, the eternal good itself," are rejected by Barth as grounds of God's claim on us (though he accepts them as attributes of God) (pp. 554–56). If I read him right, however, Barth's objection to these two reasons is not that they compromise one's devotion to God, but that they do not give priority to God's initiative as the appeal to grace does. Obviously Barth's objection to them has not persuaded me.

12

ABRAHAM'S DILEMMA

1. The Dilemma Stated

A convincing defense of a divine command theory of the nature of obligation must address our darkest fear about God's commands—the fear that God may command something evil. Certainly some of the things that God has been *thought* to require have been evil. Rivers of blood have been shed in obedience to supposed divine commands. Can we accept a divine command theory without assuming a potential obligation to perform such horrible deeds?

One case dominates discussion of this issue, the biblical story of the sacrifice of Isaac or, as it is more accurately called in Jewish tradition, the binding (עקדה, *akedah*) of Isaac (Genesis 22:1–19). This has long been a central narrative for Jewish and Christian traditions and (with some variation) for Muslims also. Its salience for our present purpose owes much to one of the classics of modern religious thought, Søren Kierkegaard's *Fear and Trembling*, in which ethical issues about the story are raised with exceptional sharpness and made the focus of a profound examination of the relation between religion and ethics. This is not the place to discuss Kierkegaard's work in detail,[1] but the questions I will pose are certainly influenced by him. The

---

1. *Fear and Trembling* is discussed more fully in Adams, "The Knight of Faith."

thought that the history of child sacrifice poses an ethical problem for religion is of course much older than Kierkegaard. The Epicurean philosopher-poet Lucretius, a contemporary of Cicero and Julius Caesar, writing in the first half of the first century B.C.E., proposes Agamemnon's sacrifice of his daughter Iphigenia as a horrible example, concluding with the pungent comment, *tantum religio potuit suadere malorum* ["How great the evils that religion has been able to inspire!"].[2]

The evil of child sacrifice is not tightly tied to belief in divine commands. It is likely that the immolation of children has often been initiated by human agents seeking to express religious devotion or to obtain divine assistance in a crisis (e.g., 2 Kings 3:26–27), without the presupposition of a specific divine command. But the story of the binding of Isaac does begin with a command from God, and Kierkegaard has made reflection on that aspect of the story inescapable.

A brief summary of the story will suffice here (though it will not bear comparison with the matchless narrative of Genesis 22, or with Kierkegaard's brilliant retellings). God speaks to Abraham, commanding him to sacrifice his beloved son Isaac as a whole burnt offering on a mountain that God will show him, and Abraham sets about to comply. At the climax of the story Abraham binds Isaac on the altar and takes the knife to kill him, but is stopped by the voice of an angel declaring that the willingness he has evidenced to make such a sacrifice at God's behest is enough. Instructed by the angel not to kill his son, Abraham finds and sacrifices a ram instead. The angel declares that God will bless Abraham's descendents because he has not withheld his son.

Did Abraham do the right thing? Before the order to sacrifice Isaac was countermanded, was it right or wrong for Abraham to kill his son, or to intend to do so? That is more or less the question (or one of them) that Kierkegaard poses for us. It is a question about which Kierkegaard's Abraham agonizes, and in that respect he is a modern, nineteenth-century Abraham. Kierkegaard does not distinguish him from the biblical Abraham (though he emphasizes his contemporary relevance), but the thought that Abraham might be doing something *wrong* in killing (or planning to kill) Isaac as a sacrifice is one of which there is absolutely no trace in Genesis 22. Certainly the biblical Abraham sees something *in some way bad*, even horrifying, about killing his son. Thoughts, or at least feelings, of that character are present (though not very explicit) in the atmosphere of the narrative. The biblical Abraham is not such a monster as to lack them. I have emphasized the distinction between the wrong and the merely bad, between the obligation family of concepts and the value family of concepts; and the thought that is missing from Genesis 22 is precisely the thought that it is, or might be, morally wrong for Abraham to slay Isaac on the altar.

Its absence from the Genesis narrative probably reflects a cultural background in which child sacrifice was a generally accepted practice and disapproval of this manifestation of a parent's generous piety toward a deity was not part of the religious repertoire. It is strongly disapproved in later biblical texts, and in postbiblical Judaism and Christianity. The prophet Jeremiah clearly views the practice as for-

2. Lucretius, *De rerum natura*, Book 1, line 101.

bidden by God, and wrong, when he represents YHWH their God as condemning the people of Judah, saying, "They have built the high place of Topheth . . . to burn their sons and their daughters in the fire; which I did not command, nor did it come into my mind" (Jeremiah 7:31).[3] Yet it is commanded, arguably, in one of the oldest texts of biblical law: "The first-born of your sons you shall give to me. You shall do likewise with your oxen and with your sheep: seven days it shall be with its mother; on the eighth day you shall give it to me" (Exodus 22:29–30).[4]

In the biblical text that has come down to us, edited undoubtedly by opponents of the practice, child sacrifice is usually represented as a pagan practice, idolatrous as well as cruel; and we know that human children were routinely sacrificed to other gods by Israel's neighbors. But the Bible does retain at least one record of a completed human sacrifice to YHWH, Jephthah's sacrifice of his daughter (Judges 11:30–40). And the book of Judges contains no suggestion that anyone disapproved of Jephthah's killing his daughter, though he regretted the vow that obliged him to do so. The story evidently comes from a culture in which a father's sacrificing his child to YHWH was a recognized part of the religious repertoire.[5]

If we think of the biblical Abraham as belonging to such a culture, it may occur to us to ask whether my divine command theory implies that it would not have been wrong for him to kill his son as a sacrifice. Why would that be implied? It would of course be implied if God really commanded him to do it. For reasons that will appear more fully later, however, I agree in fact with Jeremiah that the true God never commanded any such thing—never even thought of doing so, as Jeremiah put it. The thought that concerns us here is rather that the biblical Abraham would not have received any sign that he (with his cultural background) could reasonably be expected to have interpreted as a command of God explicitly or implicitly forbidding the sacrifice of his child—from which it would follow, by my lights, that he was not morally forbidden to do it. That is a sort of historical relativity that is indeed possible on my account of the nature of obligation, though I doubt that we can know enough about the biblical or historical Abraham and his cultural situation to know what signs he had received or how he would have been likely to interpret them. In any event I would emphasize that no such historical relativity is in-

3. Cf. Jeremiah 19:1–9, 32:35. For repudiation of the practice by Jeremiah's younger contemporary Ezekiel, see Ezekiel 20:25–26, which I will discuss later. I follow Levenson, *The Death and Resurrection of the Beloved Son*, p. 42, in attributing these statements, or their substance, to the historic Jeremiah and Ezekiel; but I claim no expertise in the often disputed attribution and dating of texts from the prophetic books.

4. Verses 28–29 in the Hebrew. I have changed the RSV's "its dam," which suggests a distinction between animals and humans, to "its mother," which renders quite literally the undiscriminating Hebrew אמו. It should also be noted that "its" and "his" are indistinguishable in Hebrew, which has no neuter gender.

5. For persuasive argument on this point, and on the interpretation of the texts cited in this paragraph and the preceding one, see Levenson, *The Death and Resurrection of the Beloved Son*, chap. 1. I am much indebted to Levenson's fascinating discussion of child sacrifice and the binding of Isaac in the Bible and postbiblical traditions. At least two kings of Judah, Ahaz and Manasseh, each burned a son as an offering (2 Kings 16:3; 21:6) and, as the Bible, in condemning them, does not mention pagan deities as receiving these sacrifices, we may conjecture that they were offered to YHWH.

volved in my account of good and evil. There is nothing in my metaethics to keep me from saying that child sacrifice was and is a hideous evil in the life of any individual or culture that has practiced it, despite any religious virtues that they may have exemplified in the practice.

The Abraham of whom I wish mainly to speak here is not the biblical Abraham, however. He is not exactly Kierkegaard's Abraham either, but he is modern enough to share the latter's agony over the thought that it is ethically wrong to sacrifice his son. He holds all three of the following beliefs—or rather, he finds them all initially plausible, overwhelmingly so, in his situation, though he recognizes their mutual inconsistency.

(1) If God commands me to do something, it is not morally wrong for me to do it.

(2) God commands me to kill my son.

(3) It is morally wrong for me to kill my son.

These three propositions constitute what I call *Abraham's Dilemma*. They are an inconsistent triad. Taken together, they are mutually contradictory; (1) implies that if (2) then not (3). But formal consistency can be restored by denying any one of the three. Which one should Abraham (or I) deny? In section 2 I will consider, and reject, two approaches in which proposition (1) would be abandoned. Then in section 3 I will discuss which of the two other propositions must be rejected.

2. Can It Be Wrong to Obey God?

The most popular basis for rejecting proposition (1) would probably be the view that what is morally wrong is eternally and necessarily wrong, and would therefore still be wrong, and certainly not obligatory, even if God commanded it (and never forbade it). This view is flatly inconsistent with my divine command theory of the nature of obligation; for if moral wrongness consists in being forbidden by God, something that is never forbidden by God cannot be wrong. The interesting question here for me is not whether I should reject this view, as I obviously must, but how far I can satisfy intuitions that may lie behind it.

That what is wrong is eternally and necessarily wrong, I do not believe. As indicated in chapter 11, section 2, I think there are points on which it is contingent what a perfectly good God would or would not determine to be wrong. That is not to say that I think such a deity could ordain child sacrifice. The divine nature may be such that it is impossible for God to want such a thing. Whether that is so is connected with a more general issue of the modal status of God's moral properties, and the discussion of that issue in chapter 1, section 5, will not be repeated here. I would not claim, however, to have offered a *proof* that God absolutely could not command something evil. So I had better face the question, What if God did command something evil? Suppose child sacrifice is evil but God really did command it; would it still be wrong to do it? Would it then be wrong *not* to do it?

I mean these as counterfactual conditional questions; I am not seriously entertaining the hypothesis that God really commanded something evil. It is interesting, however, that the prophet Ezekiel seems to accept such a hypothesis. Recounting the divine punishment of Israel's idolatry and other sins, he represents YHWH as saying, "Moreover I gave them statutes that were not good and ordinances by which they could not have life; and I defiled them through their very gifts in making them offer by fire all their first-born, that I might horrify them" (Ezekiel 20:25–26). The implication seems to be that these horrible sacrifices were offered to YHWH, not just to other gods, and under commands that YHWH gave to punish the people. Some of the questions that most concern me here are not addressed by Ezekiel. He does not discuss whether the command of child sacrifice was "given" by God only in the sense that God *caused* it to be believed, or whether it was also *authorized* by God and thus imposed a really valid (though horrible) obligation. Nor does he discuss whether it was *wrong* for the people to sacrifice their children in obedience to these commands. What is clear is that he thinks it was *bad* (defiling, horrifying) for them to do so.

I cannot consistently say that it would be *wrong* to obey such commands if they were really authorized by God. Nor can I say that it would be (unqualifiedly) *bad* to obey them if they truly reflected God's character. For under those conditions (which may be impossible) obedience would not have the properties that I think are in fact wrongness and (unqualified) badness. It does not follow, however, that I must say it would be wrong or bad to *dis*obey the commands under those conditions; and that is the point I want to emphasize here. It brings with it a clarification of my divine command theory.

In proposing that moral obligation is constituted by divine commands, I have not yet said much about the question under what conditions they do this. But I have indicated that there are some necessary conditions to be satisfied, and the reasons I have given for accepting divine commands as the definitive standard of moral obligation suggest some plausible conditions. Specifically, I have argued that the goodness of God, the goodness of God's relationship with us, and the goodness of God's commands themselves, all are important in accrediting God's commands for their role in constituting obligation. A deity that was what we would intuitively call *cruel* would not be a good candidate for the role of supreme Good, and the cruel commands of such a being would not be a good candidate for the standard of moral right and wrong. I would not say it would be wrong to disobey such commands of such a being.

That being so, I should probably identify moral wrongness, not simply with the property of being contrary to commands of God, but rather with the property of being contrary to commands of a certain kind of God. Perhaps I should say specifically: contrary to commands of a *loving* God, though probably a more precisely satisfactory formula could be devised. We could dispense with this qualification if (as I suspect) the requisite sort of lovingness follows necessarily from the divine nature; but since I do not claim to have proved that it does, nor even to have worked out in detail how it might follow from the divine nature, I will let the qualification stand.

If there were no loving God, then (on an adequately qualified version of my view) no acts (either of obedience or of disobedience) would have the property that

I identify with moral wrongness. In that situation some other property (which on my view *is not* moral wrongness, but only similar to it) might be a good enough candidate, and the best available, for the semantically indicated role of moral wrongness;[6] I do not think disobedience to cruel commands of cruel quasi-gods would have that property. We will surely approve of the decision of the Purka clan described in the following anthropological report:

> There is a tradition that the men of Purka clan were once faced by their clan-gods' demand for human sacrifice, but rather than comply with this gruesome demand they rushed to the nearest river, and threw the sacred whisk symbolizing the female clan-deity into the water, and hence have performed the sacrificial rites only with the symbol of the male god who accepts the sacrifice of a goat and a cow.[7]

Believers in *moral dilemmas*, who think it can be fully and unqualifiedly wrong, for certain reasons, to perform a certain action, and also fully and unqualifiedly wrong, for other reasons, not to perform it, might offer a different reason for rejecting proposition (1). The proposition holds:

(1) If God commands me to do something, it is not morally wrong for me to do it.

The reason I gave above for believing that (1) follows from my divine command theory is that if wrongness is the property of being contrary to God's commands, then nothing can be wrong unless it is contrary to God's commands. In so arguing I left a loophole, however, for the suggestion that doing something God commanded me to do might still be contrary to a divine command, and thus wrong, if God gave me contradictory commands. Thus, if God commanded Abraham never, under any circumstances, to kill an innocent child, but also commanded him specifically to kill his (innocent) son Isaac, then, it might be argued, it would be wrong for Abraham to kill Isaac, because that would be contrary to God's general command, yet also wrong for him not to kill Isaac, because that would be contrary to God's specific command. Some readers have taken this to be the situation of Kierkegaard's Abraham. I don't, because I take Kierkegaard to represent the general command against killing the innocent as "suspended" by God in Abraham's case; but the hypothesis of such a strong moral dilemma arising from conflicting divine commands is certainly worth considering on its own merits.

Moral philosophers generally agree that it is possible for prima facie obligations to conflict. That is, there can be generally valid moral grounds for thinking an action obligatory, and other generally valid moral grounds for thinking it wrong. For instance, it is generally wrong for me use your property without your permission, and it is also wrong for me to allow a child to drown when I could have saved his

---

6. Here I presuppppose the account of the relation between the semantics and the metaphysics of value presented in chapter 1, section 1, and adapted to the semantics and metaphysics of obligation at the beginning of chapter 10, section 1.

7. von Fürer-Haimendorf, *Morals and Merit*, p. 146; quoted in Little and Twiss, "Basic Terms in the Study of Religious Ethics," p. 73.

life by throwing him a life preserver (yours, in the imagined case). This is not a hard dilemma, however. I am morally obliged to throw your life preserver to the child (if it's the only one available), and it is not wrong, all things considered, for me to do so. I may owe you a sort of apology (not a very abject one) for doing it, but that is the only part of a "guilt" reaction that can rightly be expected of me; and no one should blame me for it.

Some dilemmas are much more agonizing than this, of course, affording no "obvious right answer" to the question, What should I do? One may think it was morally necessary to do something, but feel it was a horrible thing to do (or "to have to do"), and that it would be indecent to justify oneself with any sense of complacency to those who may have suffered from it. Some philosophers think it is best to deal with such cases by saying there is sometimes no available action which it is not *wrong, all things considered* to perform, and that full, genuine guilt is then inevitable.

I favor the opposite opinion, according to which all available alternatives may indeed be *bad* in important ways, but there must always be at least one that is not *wrong*. This view is strongly supported by a conception of moral obligation, and of the corresponding possibility of moral wrongness, as constituted by demands of a deity or other persons or a society. For such requirements cannot plausibly be taken as constituting moral obligation unless they are reasonable, and it cannot be reasonable to require something contradictory or impossible.

In an illuminating defense of a view of Abraham's predicament as a dilemma that has only wrong answers, Philip Quinn says, "One crucial assumption for my argument is that the moral realm is not the only source of ultimate values whose realization might be promoted by human actions. The tendency to moralize the whole of our lives is to be resisted."[8] I agree that life should not be wholly moralized; but if God is the ultimate ground of all values (as I think Quinn agrees), it will hardly be a mistake to *theologize* the whole of our lives. And theologizing the whole of our lives, as I have argued in chapter 7, should be strongly integrative. Commenting on Quinn's paper, Linda Zagzebski asks, "Though it is not unreasonable to say that God's goodness includes more than the moral, isn't it unreasonable to say that any one part or aspect of God's goodness can be in conflict with any other?"[9] I suppose even God can be pulled in opposite directions by competing reasons, but could the divine goodness be so conflicted as to be unwilling to treat any alternative as permissible under the circumstances?

These arguments are not likely to settle the issue about moral dilemmas, but I think even if there were situations in which every possible action would be contrary, all things considered, to divine commands, Abraham's Dilemma would not be likely to be among them. The most plausible cases for inescapable violation of God's commands would be cases in which divine commands that are quite general (say a command to respect certain rights, and a command to prevent certain sorts of disasters) come into conflict and God has not said how to deal with the conflict. But Abraham is said to have been commanded quite specifically to sacrifice Isaac, and such a par-

---

8. P. Quinn, "Moral Obligation, Religious Demand, and Practical Conflict," p. 203.
9. Zagzebski, Review of Audi and Wainwright, p. 108. I am indebted to Zagzebski for very helpful discussion of these issues about dilemmas and divine commands.

ticular command seems to imply a suspension of any contrary commands from the same source. A command so specific that does not carry permission to do what is commanded might be thought to show the commander to be so lacking in consistency as to be unfit for the exalted role of defining moral obligation.

3. What Should We Believe about God's Commands?

Let us therefore set aside the possibility of solving Abraham's Dilemma by rejecting proposition (1). There are two other propositions in the inconsistent triad:

(2) God commands me to kill my son.

(3) It is morally wrong for me to kill my son.

These are the propositions that most strongly distinguish the Abraham of this dilemma from the Abraham of Genesis 22, who neither doubts (2) nor so much as entertains (3). Which of them should our Abraham reject?

Immanuel Kant voted solidly to reject (2), declaring that "Abraham should have replied to this supposedly divine voice: 'That I ought not to kill my good son is quite certain. But that you, this apparition, are God—of that I am not certain, and never can be, not even if this voice rings down to me from (visible) heaven.'"[10] It is not easy to reject Kant's verdict, and no easier if we follow Kierkegaard's insistent advice to imagine one of our own contemporaries confronted with Abraham's Dilemma. I have often asked my students, "What would you think if you asked your neighbor why he was building a large stone table in his backyard, and he said, 'I'm building an altar, because God has commanded me to sacrifice my son as a whole burnt offering. Won't you come to the ceremony tomorrow morning?'" All agree that the neighbor should be committed to a mental hospital.

I believe Kant's response is substantially correct. The problem, as he recognizes, has an epistemological dimension. Among purported revelations, which of them are authentic and really come from God? Hardly any religion supposes that all of them do. The conception of God as the Good proposed in the present book suggests an ethical criterion. This theological conception is not offered as a way of discovering goodness for the first time, but as an account of the nature of a goodness with which we are assumed to have some acquaintance. Holding such a conception, we must test purported messages from God for their coherence with ethical judgments formed in the best ways available to us. Our practice of ethical judgment may well be shaped, and may well have been shaped already, by religious influences; but at each step a vision of the Good, and of God as the Good, must be controlling, and must be preferred, if need be, to inferences from nonmoral phenomena supposedly caused by God. The example before us evokes especially strong intuitive support for the

10. Kant, *The Conflict of the Faculties*, p. 283n (Ak VII,63). Similar statements can be found in Kant's *Religion within the Boundaries of Mere Reason*, pp. 100f., 179f. (Ak, VI,87, 186f.).

Kantian preference for inference from 'ought' to 'is' as opposed to inference from 'is' to 'ought' in moral theology.

Even in applying an ethical criterion, however, we should not reject proposition (2) too easily. The profound resonance that the story of the binding of Isaac has sustained in several religious traditions demands that we take seriously, at least for a bit longer, the possibility of rejecting proposition (3) instead. Religion would be not only safer than it is, but also less interesting and less rich as a resource for moral and spiritual growth, if it did not hold the potentiality for profound challenges to current moral opinion. Religion's connection with the transcendent would be threatened if it could not demand costly sacrifices for distinctly religious reasons, or if one's acts of faith and devotion could not be allowed to be costly in any way to anyone besides oneself. If we believe in divine commands at all, we should not want to hold that they can never be surprising. The command addressed to Abraham in Genesis 22 is not to be rejected simply because it challenges prevailing values, or because it demands too much of Abraham and his family, or because it gives purely religious expression precedence over the worldly good of Abraham's son.

We are not likely to believe that it is never right to sacrifice for any cause the well-being of those for whom we care and are responsible. Most will defend, in some circumstances, the willingness of nations to sacrifice their sons in warfare. Genesis 22 has been viewed, sometimes with bitterness, as a precedent for that willingness.[11] Those who most strongly disapprove of all such sacrifices to Mars commonly do approve of standing up for one's political convictions in some cases where that is likely to result in hardship for one's family. Where the political cause is sufficiently good and important, I imagine that few of us would disapprove of persisting in one's loyalty to it even at some risk to the lives of one's family.

To say that such sacrifices may be justified for a political but never for a purely religious cause is not to offer an argument against religion, but simply to reject it. The history of martyrdom is full of people who have been honored (rightly, I think) for expressing their religious convictions, and refusing to renounce them, even when their martyrdom would obviously result in great suffering for their families as well as for themselves.

The annals of Jewish martyrdom offer particularly poignant and self-conscious parallels to the sacrifice (as many saw it) of Isaac. This is richly documented, with reference to the persecutions in Germany connected with the first Crusade in 1096, in Shalom Spiegel's fascinating study of the resonance of the *akedah* in medieval Judaism, *The Last Trial*. Confronted with the sole alternatives of death and forced conversion to Christianity, hundreds of Jews chose to die as sacrifices, more or less ritually cutting each other's throats. The following story is told of a Rabbi Samuel and his son Yehiel, also a rabbi, who in those dire circumstances, "offered his throat for slaughter by his father. Whereupon the father recited the appropriate blessing for the slaughter of cattle and fowl, and the son responded with 'Amen.' And all

---

11. For an eloquently bitter example, see the poem of Wilfred Owen relating Abraham's action to the First World War, quoted in Judah Goldin's introduction to Spiegel, *The Last Trial*, pp. xvi–xvii n. 12.

those who were standing around them responded in a loud voice, 'Hear, O Israel, the Lord our God, the Lord is One.'"[12] And the father cut his son's throat, having first inspected the sword and found it to be flawless for ritual purposes.[13] The chronicler exclaims, "How extraordinary was the stamina of the son who *unbound* let himself be slaughtered,"[14] thus invoking the memory of Isaac, who was said in Jewish tradition to have asked to be bound lest fear cause him to do something that would spoil the sacrifice.[15]

Most of us, I imagine, will admire the father and son in this story, and will not blame them—whether or not what they did is exactly what our own conscience would tell us to do in like circumstances. If they claimed that God told them to do what they did, I would not say that no such command could come from God. Why does their action seem to deserve such respect?

Probably the most important factor affecting our response is that Samuel and Yehiel are facing a desperate situation, engulfed in an evil not of their own making. None of their options is a happy one. Death at the hands of their persecutors would be a cruel fate. Betraying their sacred convictions would be worse. Death is not chosen gratuitously in this context, but for a compelling reason that anyone who has any sympathy for their religion can understand. By treating the death of Yehiel ritually as a sacrifice they can at least confirm, dramatize, and possibly enhance its religious meaning.

It is significant that the alternative to death is their own repudiation of a religious loyalty. Few alternatives would so convincingly justify the choice of death. The Jewish martyrs may be compared at this point with the mass suicide at Jonestown, which probably does not command the respect of most of us in the same way. The Jonestown believers faced events that would very likely have destroyed the communal institutions in which they were living, but would not have forced them to abjure their faith. Preferring death to apostasy is something we understand, and are rightly reluctant to blame. Rightly or wrongly, we are much less inclined to admire, and much more inclined to blame, someone for preferring death to living on without a particular physical or social setting for one's religion—though we can certainly understand that the latter might be a grievous loss.

In the particular comparison before us, our judgment is likely to be affected also by our general respect for Judaism and the contrasting suspicion in which we are likely to hold the "cult" that organized Jonestown. That is an appropriate *type* of influence on our judgment, whether or not our judgment about Jonestown in particular is fair. "Religious judgment," as we might call it, is not to be sharply distinguished in these matters from moral judgment, and probably already has a lot of moral judgment in it. I'd rather not rely too heavily on this line of argument, however, as this is not the place for comprehensive assessment of the comparative merits of different religions.

12. Medieval source quoted in Spiegel, *The Last Trial*, p. 22.
13. Spiegel, *The Last Trial*, p. 23.
14. Medieval source quoted in Spiegel, *The Last Trial*, p. 22.
15. Spiegel, *The Last Trial*, p. 147.

Another salient feature of the story of Samuel and Yehiel is that the son is a willing victim. Indeed, he is the first to propose the sacrifice. This certainly pulls some of the teeth from any charge that his rights are violated by his father, and makes it much easier for us to approve of what they did. This is not a feature of all of the reports of Jews sacrificing each other to escape persecution in this period. There are reports of "babes and sucklings" being killed in this way too,[16] and it is doubtless harder for us to approve of that. I do not know whether the infants, if not sacrificed, would have been killed by the persecutors, or baptized and brought up as Christians. On anything like the latter assumption, if the story were played out in a culture similar to our own today, we would think the children's rights were violated by sacrificing them. I am not inclined to judge harshly what was done, heroically in a way, and in desperate circumstances, in the eleventh century, in a cultural context in which there was conflict about which religion was the right one, but general agreement that it was worse to die in the wrong religion than to die young. For our own thinking about Abraham's Dilemma, however, the issue of consent is one that cannot simply be dismissed. That is why I have preferred to focus on the case of the adult, and willing, Yehiel as one in which it might not have been wrong for a father to sacrifice his son.

Do our reflections on this example show us a way in which it might be right to solve Abraham's Dilemma by abandoning the claim (3) that it was morally wrong for Abraham to kill his son, in order to retain the claim (2) that God commanded him to do it? I think not. Of the factors that inclined us to approve of the sacrifice of Yehiel, the one that most easily carries over to Abraham is our general respect for their religion; Abraham is after all the "father of faith" to several distinguished traditions. But this is not enough to settle the issue, for deservedly respected religious figures can certainly make grave errors of judgment; and we are particularly likely to be unable to agree entirely with them across a long interval of centuries.

The issue of consent is quite problematic in the case of Abraham and Isaac. Genesis 22 leaves it an open question whether Isaac consented; it certainly does not present him as volunteering to be sacrificed. Though calling him a boy (נער), on the other hand, it does represent him as old enough to carry the wood for the burnt offering (presumably quite a lot of wood); traditional exegesis has inferred that he could not have been physically compelled against his will, though that hardly assures fulfillment of a high standard of fully voluntary consent.

Consent was not a significant feature of the ancient practice of child sacrifice. The usual age of the children sacrificed was probably from birth to about four years; certainly that was the case at Carthage, a Phoenician colony which has left us the most extensive evidence of the practice that we have from any Mediterranean site.[17] More important still, for our understanding of the practice, the sacrifice was con-

---

16. Spiegel, *The Last Trial*, p. 19.

17. Levenson, *The Death and Resurrection of the Beloved Son*, pp. 20ff. The Carthaginians, like the Phoenicians, spoke and wrote a language so close to Hebrew that one could think of them as dialects of the same language. In fairness I should note that in the story of Jephthah, his daughter, apparently an adolescent, does consent, though not with the enthusiasm that the rabbis would later ascribe to Isaac (Judges 11:34–40).

ceived as a maximally precious gift from the *parents* to the deity; and that is surely the meaning of the "offering" and the "not withholding" in Genesis 22:2, 16. In this conception the status of the child is much too close for our comfort to that of being the parents' *property*. There is not sufficient "moral distance," as Ronald Green puts it,[18] between parent and child for the question of the child's *rights* against the parent to arise. That does not justify *us*, however, in failing to raise that question.

That killing Isaac (especially without his consent) would violate his rights, even if it was his father who did it, is one of the ways in which we are likeliest to think it would be wrong for Abraham to sacrifice Isaac. This point has not been stressed, so far as I know, in Jewish and Christian religious critiques of child sacrifice; but the development of such critiques, particularly in Judaism, is associated with a greater moral distance between parents and children. It is perhaps more than coincidence that the books of Jeremiah and Ezekiel, which (as we have seen) reject child sacrifice, also both repudiate the proverb "The fathers have eaten sour grapes and the children's teeth are set on edge," which they interpret as expressing traditional acceptance of the punishment of children for their parents' sins. "As I live, says the Lord GOD, this proverb shall no more be used by you in Israel. Behold all souls are mine; the soul of the father as well as the soul of the son is mine: the soul that sins shall die" (Ezekiel 18:2–4; cf. Jeremiah 31:29–30). Here, and in virtually all of the later Jewish and Christian traditions, the children stand before God on their own account. When they are seen in that light, their sacrificial death can no longer be seen primarily as their parents' gift. Thus the original meaning of child sacrifice, the meaning it has in Genesis 22, is undermined by a more adequate vision of the moral and religious significance of the children's lives.

This recognition of moral distance between children and their parents is reflected in postbiblical Judaism and Christianity in the prevalence of interpretations that see Isaac as a willing victim.[19] The rabbis typically describe him as thirty-seven years old at the time of the trial, and thus fully competent to give his assent. His willingness is so accentuated that in some expansions of the story in midrash Isaac has become its principal hero. There are even midrashim in which Isaac expresses his willingness to be slaughtered *before* God gives the command for it.[20]

The sacrifice of a volunteer certainly seems less offensive morally than the sacrifice of an unconsenting victim. But this is not a full or convincing resolution of Abraham's Dilemma. We want to know whether one should believe that God really commanded the sacrifice; and thinking of the sacrifice as suicidal rather than homicidal is hardly enough to remove the objection to regarding the command as genuinely issued by God.

Willing or unwilling, the intended death of Isaac lacks what I think is the most important feature that makes the self-offering of Yehiel understandable and admi-

18. Green, "Abraham, Isaac, and the Jewish Tradition," p. 7f.

19. This connection of ideas is asserted, with reference to Hellenistic Judaism, in Levenson, *The Death and Resurrection of the Beloved Son*, p. 191f.

20. Green, "Abraham, Isaac, and the Jewish Tradition," p. 9. The emphasis on Isaac's willingness is abundantly documented in Levenson, *The Death and Resurrection of the Beloved Son*, pp. 187–92, and especially in Spiegel, *The Last Trial*.

rable as an act of religious faithfulness and heroism. It is not a response to an independently existing crisis, or to a train of evil already in progress. If Isaac has to choose between death and the renunciation of a precious religious loyalty, nothing but the demand for sacrifice itself forces that on him, nor does anything else force the sacrifice on his father Abraham. For Kierkegaard this is indeed a distinctive characteristic of Abraham's deed; it is what distinguishes him, as a knight of faith, from "tragic heroes" whose sacrifices meet generally intelligible needs.[21] It is "'temporally' pointless," as Gene Outka puts it.[22]

It does not even have the kind of religious point that the sacrifice of Yehiel has. Why would God command such a horrifying deed with no extrinsic point to it? Why would God see the sacrifice as desirable? Without a satisfying answer to this question it will be hard to be justified in believing that the demand for sacrifice comes from God. Under the circumstances, it would seem that any positive value attaching to Isaac's death must be internal to the action of Abraham—and perhaps of Isaac, if he is a willing victim. It must be a symbolic or at least an expressive value, dependent on the *meaning* of the act. But what good meaning would the act have?

A positively valued meaning stressed by many interpretations of the story is found in the *obedience* of Abraham and Isaac. One can understand that a good God might value obedience to (good) commands, and might prize it the more when it overcomes a serious temptation to disobey. But why would God want to be obeyed in such a horrible way? It is not as if the world contains so few occasions for the heroic performance of duty that God would need to create a crisis by commanding an otherwise pointless killing.

The primary meaning envisaged in the ancient practice of child sacrifice was undoubtedly that of expressing devotion by making an especially costly and precious gift to the deity. We can understand thinking that such devotion is a great good, but this meaning is undercut by ethical reflections that we can hardly reject. I have already pointed out that seeing the child as having rights even against his parents undermines views of child sacrifice that focus on the parents' gift. But even the interpretation of a voluntary offering of one's own death as a precious gift can be undermined by reflection on what the offering or demanding of such a gift says about the recipient.

The meaning of a gift depends not only on its costliness to the giver but also on the desires or values of the recipient. How would you like to receive for your birthday a brightly wrapped box with a card on it announcing "the costliest and most precious gift I could find," and open it to discover the severed head of either the giver or the giver's child? What could be more horrible? Who would have thought you'd want that? Should we say, "It's the thought behind the gift that counts"? That's the conventional way to set aside the consideration of the recipient's desires and values, but it seems obscene here. The thought behind this gift could only be read as insulting—as I said, who would have thought you'd want that? For the "thought" that conventionally validates the gift has to include at least the hope that you will

---

21. Kierkegaard, *Fear and Trembling*, pp. 57–59.
22. Outka, "Religious and Moral Duty," p. 215.

like the gift, and who but a monster would like such a gift as this? By the same token, it seems hardly honoring to God to suppose that God would like, and therefore welcome or command, the otherwise pointless killing of a person. (This is not, of course, to say that God would not welcome someone's making a self-offering of a death that could not be avoided anyway, or that could not honorably be avoided, as in the case of Yehiel.) The original supposedly positive meaning of child sacrifice depends (for us, at any rate) on avoiding not only the question of the child's rights but also the question of what the sacrifice presupposes about the deity's attitude toward the child.

Kierkegaard suggests a different religious point for the intended sacrifice of Isaac. If God's demands coincide too neatly with those of universal morality, he fears, one will not have a sufficiently individual and personal relationship with God. The "teleological suspension of the ethical" for Abraham meets this religious need, as Kierkegaard sees it.[23] There is much to be said for the idea of individual vocations from God, and for allowing them to put some pressure on other ethical considerations, as I will argue in chapter 13. I will also argue there, however, that such vocations can generally be conceived in terms of goods that God has given us to love. Surely there are plenty of ways for God to give individual vocations without commanding a gruesome and otherwise pointless sacrifice.

I conclude that in any cultural context in which it is possible to worry about Abraham's Dilemma it will hardly be credible that a good God has commanded the sort of sacrifice that is envisaged there. To this conclusion it may be objected that an omnipotent deity would have the power to cause a sign that we could not credibly fail to interpret as a genuine command from God to offer otherwise unnecessary human sacrifices.[24] I am not sure this is true; Kant's remark that I have quoted about a voice ringing from the sky suggests that he thought it is not. But suppose it is true; how should we respond if God confronted us with such a sign? Should we obey, trusting that God will see to it that obedience works out for the best, even if we do not see how?[25] Or should we change deities, like the men of the Purka clan described earlier?

I have already indicated my approval of the decision made in the Purka clan, but I would need to imagine the unimaginable in order to rule out the other alternative. Much would depend on whether we could see the author of the command as the supreme Good. If we could, then perhaps trusting obedience might seem the right course. A situation in which I would find it reasonable to believe that a good God had given such an abhorrent command seems to me so unimaginable, however, that I think it is at best a waste of spiritual energy to try to decide what one should do in that case. If we hold anything like a typical Jewish or Christian theology, God's giving such a command is not to be expected. I doubt that a theology should try to prepare conditionally for such a radical shake-up of its own convictions as the acceptance of such a command would entail. It does not honor God to

---

23. Kierkegaard, *Fear and Trembling*, pp. 68–81.

24. A similar objection to the Kantian position is pressed in P. Quinn, "Religious Obedience and Moral Autonomy," p. 275.

25. Cf. P. Quinn, "Religious Obedience and Moral Autonomy," p. 276.

prepare oneself mentally for receiving such a command. Consider an analogy: it would hardly be an expression of confidence in your spouse to ponder in any but the most abstractly theoretical way the question what you should do if your spouse demanded your cooperation in a serious crime. So long as it is possible for us at all to dismiss them, I think it is the part of religious as well as moral wisdom to dismiss all thoughts of our actually being commanded by God to practice something as horrible as human sacrifice. The question whether God commands such a thing should stay off our epistemological agenda as long as it possibly can, which I expect will be forever.

13

VOCATION

Is there some task in the universe that is *mine* in a morally valid way? Are there ethical concerns that have my name on them, so to speak? The idea that there is such a thing is a very important idea, and one that it might be difficult to live without. There are so many goods in the world that I could promote, and so many needs in the world that I could try to meet. There is a danger that I will be either fragmented, going too many different ways; or crushed, seeing my obligations as unlimited; or immobilized by the clamor of competing claims. An idea of what is *my* task in the universe, and what things are *my* things to care for, may both impel me and free me to devote my attention to those things.

But what makes a task mine? How does an ethical concern get my name written on it? In some cases there is no special problem about this. Those are the cases in which application of accepted general ethical principles to the empirical non-normative facts of my situation tells me that I am morally obliged to do a certain thing. The cases in which I am most likely to be morally fragmented, crushed, or immobilized, however, are those in which this procedure fails to write my name legibly on any particular task. Is there, then, some other, more individual way, less dependent on general ethical principles, in which a task might become mine and be recognized as mine? In a theistic ethical theory an affirmative answer to this question may be offered in terms of *vocation*. That is the central idea of this chapter.

292

It has roots in moral experience, as the following example may help us to see. On 7 July 1939 a young German theologian boarded a ship in New York, hoping to reach home before war broke out in Europe. He had arrived in the United States only about a month before, invited by American friends and admirers who wished to provide him with a refuge from Nazism. Deeply opposed to the Nazi regime, he had wanted at least a temporary escape. He was personally threatened, his possibilities of ecclesiastical and theological work were disappearing, and all his options in Germany were morally painful. But within days of landing in New York he was feeling very uneasy about the idea of staying in America. He described himself as "homesick," and found it "almost unbearable" not to know what was happening to his friends and associates at home. His diary speaks of "the whole weight of self-reproach because of a wrong decision" that "comes back and almost chokes one," and records the resolution, "If trouble comes now, I shall go right back to Germany. I cannot stay out here alone; I am quite clear about this, for after all, over there is where I live." Within a few more days he had committed himself to an early return. He himself had "further thoughts" about the decision, asking himself, "Is it not irresponsible, having regard to so many other people, simply to say No to one's own future and to that of many others?" His American sponsors were surprised, perplexed, and disappointed. To one of them he explained, "I have made a mistake in coming to America. I must live through this difficult period of our national history with the Christian people of Germany. I will have no right to participate in the reconstruction of Christian life in Germany after the war if I do not share the trials of this time with my people." On the ship bound for Europe, he wrote, "Since I have been on board, the inward disharmony about the future has ceased, and I can think without any reproaches about the shortened time in America."[1]

In this incident from the life of Dietrich Bonhoeffer, familiar to students of recent Christian theology, we have a vivid example of a decision in connection with which it is natural to speak of "vocation." Bonhoeffer's reflections suggest that his decision was rooted in a sense of *belonging* in Germany, in his *caring* about certain people and projects and wanting to *participate* in a certain social process. In the end what he did seems to have been what he most *wanted* to do, in the circumstances. Clearly, however, his deliberation was not just about what he really wanted to do, let alone what would be best for him personally or make him happiest. On the other hand, it was not just a matter of drawing consequences from general principles of obligation, either. Few would think that such principles implied a moral obligation for Bonhoeffer either to remain in America or to return to Germany. And if they did, the implication was at any rate not a clear one, as he himself seems to have agreed. Yet he obviously believed there was a possibility of going *wrong* in some important sense.

Theological ideas about vocation contributed to the way he thought about this possibility. But I think the sense of such a possibility is one that is likely to be present

---

1. Bethge, *Dietrich Bonhoeffer*, pp. 554–59, 565; cf. pp. 540–44. Bethge's biography, massively documented and the work of an intimate associate, makes it possible to use Bonhoeffer as an example with some hope that one is dealing with reality.

even to nontheists in the experience of comparable choices. The theological idea of vocation is an interpretation of a moral phenomenon that it does not create out of nothing. If a nontheistic view provides no satisfactory interpretation of the phenomenon, that is a disadvantage of the view. But I shall not pursue that polemical line of argument here; I will be fully occupied with my own interpretation.

1. Singular Judgments in Ethics

In relation to the larger structure of ethical theory, our topic is in part an issue about the place of singular judgments in ethics. A singular judgment or proposition is one whose content is determined by the identity of one or more individual persons or objects to which it refers. Singular judgments are typically expressed with the aid of proper names or demonstrative or indexical expressions. 'John F. Kennedy was assassinated', 'That's a tall woman', and 'I'm tired' are all most naturally interpreted as expressing singular propositions or judgments. It is a disputed question in metaphysics whether singularity goes all the way down, or whether all individual identities could in principle be constructed from qualitative or general facts, so that we could do without the singular form of judgment if only we knew enough. I have argued elsewhere that singularity is in principle irreducible,[2] but that metaphysical issue need not be settled here. It is perfectly clear that we do not know enough to do without singular judgments, whether or not we could dispense with them if we knew infinitely more.

There are singular ethical judgments—for instance, such judgments as would normally be expressed by the following sentences: 'It is morally permissible for me to break this promise in the present circumstances' (which is triply singular in form), 'Mary's anger seems fully justified in this situation', and 'You don't have sufficient reason to blame him so harshly'. Such judgments are obviously essential to the practical function of ethical thought, which depends on its application to particular persons in particular situations. It is often claimed, nonetheless, that ethical judgments must be in principle *universalizable*—that if anything is right (or wrong, or good, or bad) for me in this situation, it must be so also for anyone sufficiently similar in any situation sufficiently similar.

Influential as it is, this universalizability thesis seems to me doubtful. For instance, there are cases in which people want to say something of the following form: '*I have to* do this [and they mean they *ethically* or *morally* have to do it]—but I am not prescribing a law for anyone else'. I take this to imply, 'I am not saying that anyone else similarly situated would be under the same obligation'. Sometimes people who feel called or obliged to do something heroic or difficult or controversial will say this about the action that they propose for themselves. Some pacifists, for example, say it about their own pacifism. Such claims are appealing. I would be reluctant to say that they cannot be right. Yet they do seem inconsistent with the universalizability principle.

---

2. Adams, "Primitive Thisness and Primitive Identity."

One way of dealing with this problem is through a theory of vocation. If we conceive of the strongly individual obligations in cases like these as vocations, and conceive of a vocation in these cases as a command of God addressed to a particular individual,[3] then strongly individual obligations can be reconciled with the universalizability principle, or at least with a restricted form of it. For the obligations of a person who has received a vocation from God will be the same as the obligations of any other person whose situation is sufficiently similar. Of course, only those who have received the same vocation from God will be in a sufficiently similar situation. Similarity (even exact similarity) of *mundane* situation will not be sufficient. With respect to mundane situations (which do not include God's commands), moral facts may not be universalizable.

Since many philosophers will be at least initially disinclined to admit this as an addition to the ways in which one's name may get written on a task or concern, let us review the major alternatives before proceeding (in section 2) to a fuller development of the idea of vocation. In many minds the leading alternative will be an ethical system in which all singular judgments of obligation are to be derived from principles of obligation that are perfectly general, in combination with singular judgments about the nonmoral facts of the situation. The general principles of obligation in such a system might be either consequentialist or nonconsequentialist. Consequentialism will be reserved for a fuller treatment at the end of the present section, as I suspect it will be the leading rival of the idea of vocation. For now let us assume that the general principles of obligation are nonconsequentialist.

Nonconsequentialist principles of obligation sometimes imply an answer to the question what we should do in a particular situation, but not always. Such principles, on typical nonconsequentialist views, do not try to dictate our whole lives, but leave some things morally optional, and leave room for supererogation. By the same token, they will not write our name on a task or concern in every situation in which we may want to look for one with our name on it. For instance, as already remarked, it does not seem plausible to suppose that general principles of this sort, combined with nonmoral facts, would tell Bonhoeffer what to do in the situation described previously.

In any event, it seems unlikely that we would be able, practically speaking, to make sufficient application of general principles for moral purposes without relying on some singular judgments of distinctly ethical content. There are a wide variety of cases in which we think we are entitled to moral judgments, about the particular case, which we cannot justify on the basis of general ethical principles plus the nonmoral facts of the situation. I will mention two examples.

1. It might be wondered how firmly someone's statements and other acts have committed her to act in a certain way. If she has not made any explicit promise, it may be hard to be confident of any general principle that we might use to decide the issue. In fact, when trying to decide whether such a principle is correct, we com-

---

3. This is not a final formulation of my conception of an individual vocation. I also do not mean to exclude the possibility of extending the idea of vocation to provide for vocations of communities as well as individuals, but I will not have much to say here about that possibility.

monly consult our intuitions about particular cases that do and do not fall under it. So if one is trying to decide how committed someone is in a given case, it may be much closer to the truth to say that one's singular judgment about the particular case will be part of one's evidence for any general ethical principles one accepts as relevant to it, than to suppose that one could provide a grounding in terms of general ethical principles and singular nonmoral judgments for one's singular moral judgment about the case.

2. We might ask what would be equitable compensation for a certain loss—for instance, the destruction of an object of great sentimental value. No doubt there are some general ethical principles that we can formulate about equitable compensation. But they are not likely to be nearly fine-grained enough to do the job. Therefore, one of the things that is characteristic of judgments of equity is that in order to make them one has to have a certain *sense* of equity. And what that boils down to is that one has to be able to judge directly about a particular case, what, roughly speaking, would be an equitable compensation in this case. This will be a singular judgment with ethical content.

These examples support the thesis that some of the most fundamental judgments we are able to make about particular cases in ethics are at once singular judgments and moral judgments. But no moral judgment is invoked in these examples that is not *universalizable*, in the sense of applying to any sufficiently similar person in any sufficiently similar situation. It is easy to accept the following claims about the respective cases: (1) If somebody else had behaved in a sufficiently similar way, she would be committed if and only if this person would be committed. (2) If two losses are sufficiently similar, whatever compensation is equitable for the one is equitable for the other. In considering how much is enough to commit a person, or to satisfy equity, we may be unable to answer without making some singular judgment of the form 'This is enough in these circumstances'; but any such judgment may well imply that anything sufficiently similar is enough in sufficiently similar circumstances.

The question addressed in both examples is about the *appropriateness* of a certain response in a particular situation. This is an important type of ethical question. Indeed, it is central to some approaches to ethics.[4] I have been treating questions of appropriateness as questions of goodness, indeed of excellence. The question here is a question of the goodness of fit of an action with a situation, a question of how excellently the action responds to the situation. The issue that arises for me at this point is whether considerations of such goodness of fit (in combination with general principles of obligation) suffice to write our names on whatever tasks they should be written on.

I think they do not. Consider again the example of Bonhoeffer's decision described previously. I don't think the issue facing him either was or should have been

---

4. Consider, for instance, the identification of virtue with "an ability to recognize requirements which situations impose on one's behaviour" in McDowell, "Virtue and Reason," p. 333; or the characterization of "the primary task of religious morality" as "an intention to relate to all things in a manner appropriate to their relations to God" in Gustafson, *Ethics from a Theocentric Perspective*, vol. 1, p. 158.

settled by Bonhoeffer on the basis of goodness or badness of fit between action and situation. Returning to Germany was certainly the more heroic decision, but also led to forced choices between morally obnoxious alternatives. Staying in America offered the surer possibilities for fruitful activity, but would also separate him from most of his present friends and colleagues and tasks (doomed as those tasks might be). Each course of action was supported by strong enough reasons to fit the situation very well. Perhaps the more heroic action is the more excellent, but it is not moral wisdom to prefer always the more heroic alternative. In an essay he was working on at this time, Bonhoeffer himself wrote, "To hold out to the last may be commanded, to flee may be allowed, perhaps even demanded. . . . God does not call everyone to martyrdom."[5] The concept of his vocation or "calling" is explicit here; he was capable of putting it also in terms of his "destiny."[6] If Bonhoeffer thought it inappropriate to remain in America, that was not because it did not fit his situation, but because it did not fit his vocation. The concept of vocation gives form to an ethical deliberation that can continue beyond the point at which it is recognized that either course of action can be justified as fitting the situation.

One might try to avoid the category of vocation and stay within the categories of excellent response by taking every noticeable relevant fact about oneself and turning it into a feature of the "situation." But this is far too likely to short-circuit the deliberative process. The question, Which is the right course of action *for me*? becomes Which course of action would be appropriate for any person in my situation, with my history, relationships, feelings, etc.? As long as nothing like the concept of vocation enters into it, the latter question too quickly, easily—and often correctly—gets the answer that such a person could appropriately go either way.

Moreover, it would distort Bonhoeffer's deliberation to try to make excellence of response the framework for it. He certainly cared about the excellence of his own response. But the organizing motif of his deliberation was more outward-looking than that. The deliberation was highly self-referential, and appropriately so; but Bonhoeffer's question is not 'How can I turn in the best performance?' It is closer to 'What are my responsibilities?'—though the responsibilities in question are not evident to an external view. Explicitly, of course, it is 'What is God calling me to do?' or 'Where do I belong?'

It remains to consider, as I promised, a *consequentialist* alternative to vocation in the assignment of moral tasks to individuals. The consequentialist approach will see my name as inscribed on precisely those tasks which are such that my attempting them, under actual conditions, will have, or is likeliest to have, the best results, all things considered. This is a "direct" consequentialism that applies the test of utility to particular actions. The consequentialist derives singular judgments about what ought to be done in a particular situation from equally singular judgments about what is likely to result from alternative possible actions in that situation, together with judgments about the comparative value of those possible results. Some of the

5. Bethge, *Dietrich Bonhoeffer*, p. 564.
6. Bethge, *Dietrich Bonhoeffer*, p. 559: "We cannot separate ourselves from our destiny" (with regard to his return to Germany).

latter are likely to be singular judgments of value; whether their singularity can be eliminated need not concern us here. We also need not worry here about those objections to consequentialism that charge that it is apt to direct us to do things that seem intuitively to be wrong, for we need only consider a limited consequentialism that tells us to undertake precisely the most optimific of those enterprises that are permitted by correct principles of obligation. Plausible discernment of a vocation, after all, will be similarly constrained by principles of obligation.

Consequentialist deliberation and deliberation guided by a concept of vocation are apt to have something else in common too, for doing good will be central to any plausible vocation. They will differ, however, in the ways that they focus on goods to be achieved. To accept and pursue a vocation is in large part to have a *personal project*, or a set of personal projects, to which one is committed. If the vocation is to have moral or religious validity, of course, the personal project must be a good one. It may be a piece of research to be accomplished, an organization to be served and developed, a child's life to be protected and fostered. Having the project will typically involve loving something to some extent. It will at any rate involve caring about something in particular, as one does in loving, and not just as a way of doing the most good. Such projects seem to be important parts of both the happiest human lives, and those that we admire most.

It has been charged against consequentialism that it would deprive us of such projects.[7] The target of this charge is precisely consequentialist deliberation, the form of moral decision making in which one's aim is to do *whatever* will have the best consequences. The complaint is that such deliberation, and the motivation involved in it, leave too little room for commitment to particular projects. This objection may be made at a rather theoretical level: if we are always guided by the global aim of maximizing utility, it seems to follow that we pursue particular projects chiefly or only as ways of maximizing utility, and not for their own sake, or not enough so. At a more practical level, it may be observed that projects we may care about typically compete for resources with other worthy enterprises. We will hardly be effectively committed to our own particular projects if we worry too much or too often whether what is best for them is best for the world as a whole.

Another, related danger of consequentialist deliberation highlights one of the advantages of personal projects and a conception of vocation. Accomplishing anything very good commonly requires willpower, determination, and persistence in the face of discouragement. On the way to such a goal one is likely to encounter painful situations in which it will seem, and perhaps even be, reasonable to believe that some other investment of one's energies would probably yield better results. One who is committed to consequentialism (about particular actions) will find it harder to brush that thought aside and go on with the project than someone who is committed to the project in a way that goes beyond consequentialist calculations. But if we are not prepared to brush such thoughts aside, will we ever accomplish anything difficult?

---

7. Bernard Williams is an important sponsor of this charge. See Smart and Williams, *Utilitarianism: For and Against*, pp. 110–18. For another influential version of the charge, see Wolf, "Moral Saints."

The consequentialist, of course, will be quick to answer that what I have just said will be taken into account in good consequentialist deliberation. The importance of persistence and the likelihood of overreacting to disappointments will be weighed heavily in the scales, and the apparent advantages of giving up in a discouraging situation will be discounted accordingly. In theory, I grant that this calculation might yield a good answer, if executed correctly; but I doubt that commitment to consequentialism will provide enough strength against temptations to abandon projects. In practice, consequentialist deliberation seems all too likely to lead to more of easy good, and less of difficult good, than a less rigorously consequentialist commitment to particular projects would produce.

Another major objection to consequentialism is that, in directing us to do *whatever*, or whatever of otherwise permissible actions, will have the best results, it imposes on us heavier burdens than we can bear. It invites me to approach each decision as if I were a god, and indeed the only god,[8] albeit a god with sadly limited resources. My choice, or whatever feature of myself I am evaluating from a consequentialist perspective, is to be viewed as the last piece in a cosmic jigsaw puzzle, responsible for shaping the history of the whole world. Others are enjoined to assume a similar responsibility, but I am not to regard them as responsible in a way that relieves me of any responsibility. For me their actual choices and characters, and the conditional probabilities of their possible future choices and characters, are to be simply data for rational calculation and manipulation.

Consequentialism assigns to each of us a responsibility to which both our cognitive and our executive capacities are disastrously unequal. This is particularly obvious in a case like Bonhoeffer's. His opportunities were severely constricted by forces both out of his control and hostile, and there was really no telling what victories or catastrophes might lie ahead on the path he actually chose. He was painfully aware of this; yet despite his efforts to base his major decisions on brutally realistic assessments of his situation, I think events suggest that he persistently underestimated the power of evil in the Nazi regime. And I know of no way in which we might reasonably expect to be wiser than Bonhoeffer, or be assured of not making such mistakes. Hence Bonhoeffer's decision to return to Germany looks more rather than less rational when he gives a frankly nonconsequentialist reason for it, saying, "Not as if we were essential, as if we were needed (by God?), but simply because that is where our life is, and because we abandon, destroy, our life if we are not back in the fight."[9]

In view of our inescapable limitations, we need responsibilities much more limited than that of optimizing the future history of the world. Unmanageable responsibilities are not morally empowering. Much moral energy can be wasted in guilty imagination of duties we know we are not going to perform. The concept of vocation speaks to our need. A vocation is more limited and more specific than responsibility for the whole future of the world. It may be very difficult, but it is always a path that we may actually follow; a sense that it is given to us as a real possibility,

8. Cf. Meilaender, "*Eritis sicut Deus.*"
9. Bethge, *Dietrich Bonhoeffer*, p. 560.

and one that engages enough of our love to motivate us to follow it, is an important mark of a vocation.

The consequentialist alternative to vocation that I have been criticizing is, as I said at the outset, a direct consequentialism that applies the test of utility to particular actions. I am not attacking every form of consequentialism. Indeed, most of my argument harmonizes well with an indirect consequentialism in which the test of utility is applied to practices of deliberation and the fundamental aims and commitments that frame them. I have suggested that we are likely to do more good if we try to discern and follow a true vocation than if we directly aim at doing the most good. That could be an indirect consequentialist justification for deliberation in terms of vocation. That does not bother me, for it does not follow that the indirect consequentialist has no need of a conception of vocation. On the contrary, an indirect consequentialist justification for deliberation in terms of vocation is a reason for trying to find an acceptable conception of vocation. Those who believe that vocations have in fact been given by God may not think they need a consequentialist justification for their validity, but can cheerfully grant that the indirect consequentialist justification is there.

What would tend to render the concept of vocation superfluous would be the identification of one's true vocation with the course of life in which one would do the most good. But that identification does not follow from indirect consequentialism about practices of deliberation; for the most optimific practice of deliberation does not necessarily lead to the most optimific individual lives—though it must lead to individual lives that, on average (so to speak), are quite optimific by comparison with alternative possibilities. The thesis that we are likely to do more good if we try to discern and follow our true vocations than if we directly aim at doing the most good is consistent with the claim that our true vocations are not necessarily the courses of life in which we would individually do the most good; for if there is a possible course of life for me that would be more optimific than my true vocation, it may be quite unlikely that I would actually discern and follow that course if I made optimizing my aim.

2. A Conception of Vocation

'Vocation' is one of the words that people are most apt to use, in English today, when they wish to speak of a task that is theirs in a way that relates to them personally and not just to their situation. But if we mean, as I do, to use 'vocation' in this way, we must distance ourselves from the everyday usage in which one's "vocation" is simply one's work, the type of gainful employment in which one is engaged, and "vocational education" is training for such employment. 'Vocation' is a Latinate synonym of 'calling', but the word is ordinarily used now to talk about jobs, with little if any thought of anyone "calling" us into them. I do take the idea of being called (by God) quite seriously as part of my conception of vocation, and I do not mean to identify a vocation with a job or line of work.

A vocation, in my sense, is something more comprehensive than a job or type of employment. In principle the whole of one's life can be seen as falling within the scope of one's vocation; it is a matter of who and what one is called to be. One's work will typically fall within the scope of one's vocation, but so will one's personal relationships. Particular spousal or parental relationships, for instance, can be part of one's vocation. So also can unpaid political activity, and volunteer work. We can distinguish also between cases in which one's work is a central feature that contributes much to defining the shape of one's vocation, and cases in which the center of one's vocation lies somewhere else though it requires one to have a job and to "do a good job." Surely there are many who have the center of their vocation in their family life, and who take jobs mainly to help support themselves and their families economically. Having a job, they will normally be called to perform its duties honestly and well; but which job it is may not matter much to their vocation, and it may fit their vocation very well to quit the job on short notice to take another that pays fifty cents an hour more. A useful concept of vocation must *not* be understood in such a way that "serious commitment to vocation means that one lives to work."[10]

The identification of vocation with job or work may once have been motivated by the desire of ensuring that everyone could have a vocation and easily recognize it.[11] I agree that vocation is not just for an elite. As I conceive of it, everyone has a vocation. But I do not think we should expect a vocation to be easily recognized. We all have plain duties that are not hard to discern, but we do not need the concept of vocation to deal with *them*. It will be part of our vocation, broadly understood, to do our plain duties; but the concept of vocation earns its keep in harder cases, where plain duties conflict (and thus become less plain), or at least fail to identify the path we should take. To discern one's vocation is, in large part, to recognize who and what one ought to be, and that takes time. It requires some depth of understanding of who one is and what one's possibilities are, and perhaps some listening for the voice of God; it is not easy.

A vocation is a call from God, a command, or perhaps an invitation, addressed to a particular individual, to act and live in a certain way. How do we receive such a vocation? Few of us hear voices in the night, and fewer still would be wise to trust them. If each of us has a vocation, it must usually come in some other way. The identification of vocation with one's job, or more broadly with tasks that society may happen to have thrust upon one, is a tempting but misleading solution. I think we can do better by understanding vocations primarily in terms of love for the good.

10. Meilaender, *Friendship*, p. 87. Meilaender is characterizing a traditional Protestant conception of vocation, and is rightly critical of the implication expressed in these words. A main part of his remedy is to make vocation less central in life, whereas I prefer to break the identification of vocation with work. He would also break the popularly accepted strong linkage between vocation and self-fulfillment (a linkage which he rightly notes was not intended by the Protestant reformers); my account leads in a different direction because of the way its emphasis on loving goods connects with the account of a person's good I have given in chapter 3.

11. The claim is often made that Luther and other Protestant reformers encouraged this identification so that all Christians might see in their daily lives the level of religious significance that had been seen in the monastic life, to which the word 'vocation' had usually referred in the Middle Ages; and I take this to be largely true. It should be noted, however, that family relationships were not always omitted from early Protestantism's conception of vocation, as they are from our everyday sense of 'vocation'. On this history cf. Barth, *Church Dogmatics*, vol. 3, part 4, pp. 600–602; Marshall, *A Kind of Life Imposed on Man*; and C. Taylor, *Sources of the Self*, chap. 13.

Each of us, I would say, is called to love the good (and thus to love God, if my theistic account of the good is correct). This is our most comprehensive task for the whole of our life. What writes our name on more specific tasks? My suggestion is that vocation is primarily a matter of *what goods are given to us to love*, and thus of *our part in God's all-embracing and perfect love*. This will not be the whole story about vocation, but I think it is the best leitmotif for the subject; it is obviously congenial to the approach to ethics developed in this book. It exploits the idea of a relation between finite and infinite goods as a framework for thinking about which tasks and responsibilities are ours.

I argued in chapter 6 for a conception of God's love as at once particular and universal. The divine love extends to every creature God has made, but it does not lose sight of the individual in a sum or average of utility. As any authentic love must, it prizes all its objects individually for their own sakes. In a famous image God may be likened to a shepherd who is willing to leave ninety-nine sheep in the desert and search until he finds any one sheep that is lost (Luke 15:1–7).

Our love cannot be all-embracing and fully personal at once, as God's is; and on a theistic view, it need not be. It is not up to us to create or develop a love that will be only as perfect as it is in us. The role of our love is rather to participate in a love that exists in its perfection, prior to us, in God. We are to imitate it, manifest and mediate it to others. Our vocation will call for our love to participate in both the universality and the particularity of the divine love, though not in the same way.

We can be, in principle, *for* whatever is good anywhere, and we can *respect* all persons and all sorts of good, and we are called to act on that respect in various contexts. If the concept of vocation is not to discredit itself as a cloak for selfishness, we must not forget to think of our vocation as a participation in an all-embracing love for what is good. If we are not in some way *for* distant and alien goods as well as those near and dear to us, if our focus on the people and projects that are our special concern turns to hostility toward competing goods, or stinginess toward needy strangers, we cannot rightly think of ourselves as taking a part in *God's* love.

For this reason a vocation is more than any particular project or set of particular projects. As a part in God's all-embracing love it demands a measure of openness to duties and needs that have little to do with our own focused concerns, a reluctance to turn our backs on people who may need us in particular, or who may need a fair share of help from us, though we would otherwise have little interest in them. Attending to such needs and duties can be part of our vocation even where our motivation to do it is (quite appropriately) thinner than what we would ordinarily call "love."

At the same time, however, if we are to participate in the character of the divine love as *love*, we must also love some persons, and some kinds of good, in a way that we cannot, as human beings, love all. If we were to participate only in the universality of God's love we would not need the concept of vocation. It is the goods that are offered to us to love in a more particular way that chiefly delineate our individual vocations. We need to know how to give these goods the kind of focused attention that is necessary for loving them genuinely and effectively, reserving for them an adequate (though not all-consuming or idolatrous) measure of our time and energy and resources that we will shelter from all but the most urgent of other claims on them.

If I am right in thinking of loving goods as the primary structure of vocations, our vocations will not have the structure of a list of things we have been told to do. Rather they will be shaped largely by *projects* that we make our own. 'Project' is used here in a broad sense, widely popular with philosophers, in which a project need not (though it may) aim at an "end product." Living a certain kind of life, being a certain kind of person, loving a particular person—likewise the flourishing of the other person—all can be projects in this sense. Projects are characterized by some level of ongoing personal commitment. In emphasizing them I do not mean to deny that one may rightly feel it a part of one's individual vocation that one "must" or "can't" perform a certain action, where what is at issue is not exactly commitment to an ongoing project. But even in such a case it is reasonable to be more confident of a judgment that at least coheres with a sense of who one is called to be that is largely shaped by projects given and accepted.

Vocations, thus conceived, answer to our need for responsibilities proportioned to our capacities. For a theistic conception of vocation there is a single project for the world, God's project, that is prior to any of our projects; and each of us is to take a part in it. We are responsible only for our part; there are outcomes that are other people's responsibility, or God's, in a way that limits our responsibility.

Though I have characterized vocation as structured by projects one is called to love, it must also be emphasized that a vocation is something more than a personal project or "avocation." I love to watch birds, and expanding my "life list" of species of birds that I have seen is a project of mine; but it remains a merely personal project. Even though it expresses a measure of love for certain goods, and can be seen as playing a part in fulfilling my general vocation to love the good, I would never say that I have a vocation to watch birds. It's something I feel perfectly free not to do if I don't feel like it, and my interest in birding has nothing like the moral weight of a vocational consideration to throw into the scales when a difficult decision is to be made. That I might find interesting and beautiful "life birds" in a certain place is a perfectly good reason to consider when I'm thinking about where to vacation, but not when I face a morally important decision. If I have a specific vocation to be engaged in a certain project—if that is part of what defines the shape of my vocation—that does carry a lot of weight in important decisions, and I am not perfectly free to neglect it whenever I don't feel like attending to it.

My vocation claims me, and it defines my responsibilities. For that reason the topic of vocation belongs at least loosely to the obligation department of ethical theory, and not just to the study of the good. A call from God involves something like the pressure of a divine requirement. These considerations suggest that vocations should be conceived as *commands* of God addressed to particular individuals. I think that has been the usual conception in Protestant thought, and it was my assumption until some years ago, when I was brought up short by a question after a talk I had given on vocation. I was asked if a vocation could not be an *invitation* from God in some cases, rather than a command. Reflection has led me to agree with that suggestion, and it is reflected in my account of vocations as structured by goods that are *offered* to us to love.

A vocation to life in a religious order was the example that I think was fore-most in my questioner's mind, and it is a good example of a vocation that is likely to begin, at least, as an invitation rather than a command. A vocation to marriage is a similar example. In both cases one is drawn, we hope, by seeing a real opportunity given to one to love certain goods, and persons, in a certain form of life. In both cases it is generally thought that the decision to take up the opportunity should be very free, and it may be doubted whether someone who sees no acceptable alterna-tive to it is ready for such a decision; in that way the vocation is viewed as an invi-tation rather than a command. But it is still much more than an avocation or merely personal project. As an invitation to play a part in God's love, it offers something like a commission with which one will be entrusted and not merely an opportunity to do as one likes. In both the cases mentioned, the invitation once accepted leads to commitments, obligations, and responsibilities. One may have a *duty* to persist in it. I suppose there are vocations in which one has no duty to persist in the project beyond a limited period of time; but even there, if it is really a specific vocation, I think it will be an invitation to take up a certain project with a certain seriousness, commitment, and sense of responsibility for the time one is engaged in it. The moral weight it can bring to the scales of decision will depend on the seriousness and re-sponsibility to which one is invited.

This is not to deny that vocation can take the form of a command. A task or project may be presented as ours in a way that has imperative force. If some of us feel that we would not be doing our part, small as it may be, in the universe if we did not do philosophy, that may be a valid awareness of a quite individual duty, a vocation that is a command. Likewise, one may be right to feel that a particular political cause is "laid on one's heart" in a way that *demands* that one make it one's own; and that may be a vocation in the form of a command.

3. Actuality and Goodness

If we are to think of the main lines of a vocation in terms of goods that are offered to us to love, we must attend both to the goodness and to the actual offering or giving. The theme of actuality has a particularly prominent place in much thought about vocation. I will argue that it deserves such a place, but must be tempered by attention to the theme of goodness.

Theistic thinking about vocation commonly relies on beliefs about God's ac-tivity in creating and providentially governing the world, as that activity affects an individual's situation in the world. It is inferred that features of my actual situation are to be regarded as given me by God, and as defining responsibilities, concerns, and projects that are assigned to me as a vocation. Two aspects of actuality are com-monly seized on by this inference. In the first place, what is perceived as "natural" is ascribed to God's creative purpose, and what is seen as "unnatural" is regarded as contrary to the divine gift. In the second place, the demands of existing social insti-tutions, "my station and its duties," are ascribed to divine providence, and seen as ethically authorized thereby. I shall first explore some of the advantages of these ways of thinking—advantages that may not be obvious to modern mentalities. Then I shall note some of their (to us) rather obvious dangers, and try to articulate a way of embracing the advantages while doing battle with the dangers, if not avoiding them altogether. These ideas have been so closely connected with the concept of vocation that without sorting them out we cannot be confident of having a tenable account of vocation.

In real ethical reflection and choice about one's life, one can hardly escape taking *actuality* as a guide to some extent. Possibility, even the possibility of good, is so vast and illimitable that we will be hopelessly adrift if we do not in some way accept actuality as defining in part who we are to be and what we are to do; we may hope we can accept it gratefully.[12] The concept of vocation is strongly connected with actuality. As an offer or assignment of a role that is specially one's own, vocation is a call to be, among other things, oneself, and therefore to value something that is actual in oneself as object of the divine love.[13] Thinking about our vocation in terms of goods that are offered to us to love also directs our attention to the actual, both in respect of the love and of the offering.

The merely possible can hardly be loved in the same way as the actual—partly, I think, because the merely possible is not individual in the same way as the actual.[14] Love normally involves an attachment to something actual, and a special interest in caring for it. So if one's vocation is always to participate in the divine love, it will typically involve caring in a special way about something actual.

Even among actual goods, some are offered to me to love in a way that others are not. This difference, this offering, is surely manifested in something actual. If I can care effectively about a particular good, that will be due to actual features of my situation and my capacities. If a particular good draws or claims me, it will be through actual features of my motivation and consciousness.

A certain respect for the actual is particularly important to what might be called *the contingent in ethics*. A good example of this is the right that most of us think that parents have to be allowed to live with their own children and bring them up. This is not an inalienable right. It can be forfeited through abuse or incompetence. But in normal circumstances it cannot be overridden merely by the consideration that better parents could be found for the child.

There is a certain air of contingency about parental rights. It is not hard to see that they are important to relationships and ways of living that we rightly value, and that arrangements respecting them are therefore good. But it is also not impossible to imagine alternative arrangements that from an abstract point of view may seem as good or better. Parental rights are often not respected in fictitious utopias. And even if we thought we could show that no other alternative would be as good as their recognition, that would hardly explain or articulate the sense of wrong we are apt to feel if these rights are disregarded. Other creatures outwardly similar to

12. This is a leading idea in Kierkegaard, *The Sickness unto Death*, pp. 29–42. Kierkegaard also argues that to be too tightly bound to the actual, and unable to pursue possibilities, is equally a deformity of spirit.

13. This is also one of the themes of Kierkegaard's *Sickness unto Death*. It is a theme that will be taken up more fully in section 4.

14. See Adams, "Actualism and Thisness."

us might differ from us in this respect, we may think, but these rights are part of what defines who *we* are in an ethical sense.

The conception of vocation gives me a way of accounting for such rights that "saves the appearances" both of their contingency and of their objective validity, and that gives due significance to the *actuality* of the goods that they protect. Parents' relationships with their children have been given them by God, as a part of their vocation, through the divine activity in creating us and through the providential ordering of the history of human society. The moral force of such rights can be seen as backed by the respect due to divine gifts.[15] This is consistent with supposing that if we came upon creatures, otherwise like us, who lived with evident satisfaction in different arrangements for bringing up children, we might be persuaded that they had received different gifts, and a different vocation, from God.

In ways such as this, actual goods invite our love and claim our respect as merely possible goods cannot, but there is a powerful objection against ethical appeals to actuality, or against inferences from 'is' to 'ought' (as I pointed out in chapter 2, section 4). It is a main task of ethical judgments to discriminate, among the things that are or may be actual, those that are or would be good. It follows that actuality by itself cannot be an adequate ethical criterion. From 'Whatever is, is right', in its most banally straightforward interpretation (which I would not ascribe to any important philosopher), it seems to follow that whatever will be, will be right—from which in turn we may infer that it does not matter ethically what we do, for whatever we do, it will be right.

One way of trying to drive a wedge between 'Whatever is, is right' and 'Whatever will be, will be right' is to take the former as a reason for opposing change. This interpretation of the appeal to actuality is historically common, and that gives rise to a serious objection to the appeal, an objection that is not just theoretical but practical and even political. The appeal to respect for actuality, it may be charged, is a piece of ideology in the Marxian sense, constructed to defend a social status quo. In all its forms, including ideas of the natural and religious ideas of vocation and providence, it has throughout history been used for that purpose. Sexist social structures are perpetuated by ideas about what is normatively natural for men and women, and systems of class and caste have been supported by appeals to divine providence or to the supposed natures of the persons involved.

I agree with much in this objection. If we are to retain a role in ethics for the appeal to the actual, as I think we must, we need to find a better interpretation than that which takes it as a reason for opposing change. On my preferred interpretation it will operate not autonomously, but as a subordinate consideration in relation to judgments of value. It is a basis for choosing among *goods*. If there actually exists something intrinsically good—a human life or form of life, perhaps, a personal relationship or system of relationships—it may appropriately claim or rightly engage our respect or love in a way that a merely possible good could not; and this may

15. My use of this idea is inspired by its application to a case in some ways similar and in some ways different (the case of our right to keep parts of our bodies even if, in this age of transplants, someone else could make better use of them) in Read, *The Right Medicine*.

provide a reason for preferring it to imaginable alternatives that might in some sense be better. I say only that it *may* provide such a reason; I do not mean to be formulating a universal rule that actual goods are always to be preferred to merely possible ones. Actuality is only a factor that may, in the way I have sketched, enter into one's evaluative and ethical discernment. It is in this way, I think, that the actuality of forms of parent-child relationship can contribute to grounding our sense that there are rights in these matters that must be respected. But they can do this only on the assumption that what is thus respected and protected is good. The actuality of a social arrangement or practice is of no avail to defend it against a charge that it is unjust, or otherwise bad. Even if an actual form of life is good enough to deserve a measure of affection and loyalty, we may be called to change it radically or abandon it if that is necessary in order to correct an injustice or to pursue a newer project that claims our love.

Two pitfalls are especially to be avoided here: an inappropriate reliance on concepts of nature and the natural in identifying one's vocation, and identification of one's vocation with the social situation or role in which one happens to find oneself. My critique turns first to the idea of the "natural." Certain more or less prevalent institutions, patterns, or aims of human social life are asserted to be natural. In theistic contexts the inference is then drawn that they express God's purpose in creation, and should therefore be honored and maintained. What is perceived as "natural" is ascribed to God's creative purpose, and what is seen as "unnatural" is regarded as contrary to the divine gift. Ideas of this sort are obviously in tension with the truth (stressed in chapter 2, section 1) that saintliness can seem as "unnatural" as wickedness; but they have been a persistent feature of Christian theological ethics—though sometimes they have been expressed less in terms of the natural than of divine "orders" or "mandates" in creation.[16]

An explanation and justification of rights to a prominent role in bringing up one's children, for example, might rely on the claim (which I avoided in my account of them) that it is part of our "nature" to have them. This use of the concept of the natural confronts a notorious difficulty. How, except by a miracle, could any action, or anything that is or could be actual in the natural world, be contrary to nature? Suppose we adopted a system in which these rights were not respected; how would that be shown to be unnatural? It would be no miracle. By doing it we would show, insofar as we are part of the natural world, that we are naturally able to do it. How then would it be contrary to nature? If, as moderns, we have abandoned Aristotelian conceptions of natural teleology, it will not be easy for us to answer this question. *Our* biology will not help us here, for the ultimate aim of the main teleology it recognizes, the propagation of one's genes, is not plausible as a controlling aim for ethics.[17]

The contrast of natural and unnatural appears in a different light, of course, if it is combined with the traditional Christian idea of a historic Fall of humanity from a state of "original righteousness." In that view it is the original unfallen state that is truly natural, and present actual human life is unnatural in various ways, and also

---

16. Brunner, *The Divine Imperative*; Bonhoeffer, *Ethics*.

17. The argument for this conclusion is convincingly developed in FitzPatrick, *Functional Teleology, Biology, and Ethics*.

wrong in those ways. This account is no easier than Aristotelian teleology to combine with our evolutionary biology, but the crucial point in the present context is
epistemological. This way of distinguishing between natural and unnatural will not
provide us with a useful criterion for identifying our vocation, because our only
plausible way of judging what an unfallen state would have been like is by way of
prior judgments about what ways of life for human beings would be good ones (or
perhaps about how God has commanded us to live, if we believe that has been revealed to us more directly).

These are among the reasons why attempts that have been made, for example,
to establish that one or another actual sexual practice is contrary to nature no longer
seem plausible to many of us. There is a certain arbitrariness, indeed, to historic
arguments of this sort. Persistent sexual abstinence clearly frustrates our biological
end of reproduction more than bisexuality does; yet it is the latter rather than the
former that has historically been regarded as unnatural. I make this argument, of
course, by comparing large patterns of life in relation to the biological end, whereas
traditional arguments have focused on teleological claims about particular acts. But
that is just the point: it seems arbitrary to prefer one focus to the other. There certainly are forms of sexual behavior that enhance human life, and others that harm
it; but the concept of the natural is not likely to help us in making the distinction.

Ethical use of the concept of the "unnatural" may seem more plausible to some
of us in another area, as we may use it in expressing our objection to certain ways of
prolonging the lives of terminally ill patients. This argument also involves a certain
arbitrariness, however. None of us will object to prolonging the lives of diabetics by
injections of insulin, though the injections are just as artificial as respirators and
intravenous feeding tubes. The difference that controls our judgment is obvious.
Insulin injections typically enable diabetics to live lives that are worth living, but
we doubt that heroic treatments do that for the terminally ill. Our real (and right)
objection to many of the latter treatments is that they aren't worth it; they don't
accomplish enough for the goods of human life to outweigh their experiential and
economic costs. There remains, I believe, a morally important difference between
not using a respirator and giving a lethal injection; but I think the distinction between killing and letting die can be defended without admitting the "unnatural" as
an ethical category.

It is also important not to identify one's vocation with one's present social role.
The concept of vocation must not be treated as a way of endowing existing social
arrangements with the aura of the sacred. This happened in important strands of
early modern thought. The presumed role of divine providence in placing people
where they were was allowed to be the principal sign of God's call to particular tasks,
and people were advised to remain in the vocations thus identified as their own.
This way of thinking about vocation had obvious conservative implications. It did
not encourage social and economic mobility (though it did not effectively stop it),
and it urged most people to leave politics to the few who were seen as having it as
part of their vocations.[18]

---

18. See Marshall, *A Kind of Life Imposed on Man*, with much documentation, with particular
reference to English thought. Cf. Bonhoeffer, *Letters and Papers from Prison*, p. 6.

The mistake in such thinking is failing to distinguish clearly between the situation *in* which we are called and to which we must respond in our vocation, and the projects *to* which we are called. One's actual circumstances condition and in various ways influence and limit one's vocation. The vocation, however, is not the circumstances, but what one is called to do in them. A disabling illness may restrict possibilities for action to a very narrow compass, and some wish to speak of such an illness as itself a vocation for those who have it. That is a metonymy that may (or may not) be inspiring and harmless in a pastoral context but is misleading in ethical theory. The vocation is to love the good in those ways that remain possible in the illness.

If we find ourselves in an existing social arrangement, and especially if we cannot readily get out of it, it will presumably be part of our vocation to deal with that fact; but it does not follow that it is part of our vocation, or should be a project of ours, to remain in that arrangement or to sustain it. A prisoner in Auschwitz, for example, is presumably called to do whatever she can in that terrible situation to maintain her selfhood and dignity, and to love her fellow prisoners; but it would be obscene to suggest that she is called to make being imprisoned in Auschwitz a project of hers. Auschwitz is an extreme example, of course, but whatever we think about divine providence, we must recognize that existing social arrangements are always (also) the product of a human history that includes a great deal of injustice. That being so, the fact that we have inherited social arrangements assigning different duties to persons on the basis of their sex and ancestry, for example, does not justify equating those arrangements with the voice of God or allowing them to define our vocations.

For such reasons, the *goodness* of what is given us to love is even more important than the actuality of it, for thinking ethically about our vocations. We are to love only goods (including persons) and to adopt only good projects. If we are considering whether we should treat a particular project as central to our vocation, we must consider whether we have an actual possibility of pursuing it fruitfully, but also and even more important, whether it is good enough. We are not dispensed from critical reflection on the latter question, the question of value, just because we are already involved in the project, or other people urge it on us, or tradition demands it of us. The fact that other people assign us a role in sustaining a social arrangement does not make it part of a valid vocation if the arrangement is not worth sustaining—or if the role does not connect in certain ways with who we are, but that is part of the topic to which we now turn.

4. Vocation and Selfhood

I have described vocation, in passing, as a matter of "who one is called to be." This aspect of the subject deserves a fuller development, which may aptly begin with some reflections on Kierkegaard. Selfhood was (famously) one of his major preoccupations. It is strongly connected with the idea of a purely individual command of God in his *Fear and Trembling*, where the very point of the command to sacrifice Isaac is seen in the personalization of Abraham's relation with God by his receiving a divine command that cannot be universalized or derived from ethical principles that apply to everyone.[19] The case of Abraham, as presented in *Fear and Trembling*, is not a particularly plausible model of vocation, for reasons I have discussed at length in chapter 12. Kierkegaard has left us, however, a more plausible and equally interesting case of vocation in the story of his own broken engagement, which is widely thought to motivate many of the concerns of *Fear and Trembling*.

Having fallen in love with, and courted, Regine Olsen, a woman much younger than himself, Kierkegaard proposed marriage and was accepted. "But inwardly," he wrote several years later, "the next day [after becoming engaged to Regine] I saw that I had made a false step."[20] Having decided that it was a mistake, he set about to break the engagement; and when Regine would not agree to a termination, he felt obliged to end the relationship in what appears to have been a particularly harsh or even cruel way.

What were Kierkegaard's reasons for breaking the engagement? In the account from which I have quoted he mentions penitence about his past life, and the thought that his melancholy would prevent marital happiness. There was also an explicitly religious dimension. "But there was a divine protest, that is how I understood it. The wedding. I had to hide such a tremendous amount from her, had to base the whole thing upon something untrue."[21] In this document, however, the divine protest is not unambiguously a vocation in the sense that concerns us. It could be just a moral scruple derived from a supposed need to conceal from Regine certain facts (not identified in Kierkegaard's papers) and a general principle requiring openness in marriage.

The idea of vocation comes into the story much more clearly if we succumb to the practically irresistible temptation to interpret as substantially autobiographical the story of the broken engagement in "Quidam's Diary" in Kierkegaard's pseudonymous work, *Stages on Life's Way*. Like Kierkegaard, Quidam worries about being unable to satisfy the requirements of marriage with respect to openness.[22] And like Regine, Quidam's fiancée fights to keep the engagement from being broken. A third character in *Stages on Life's Way* renders the following verdict on this struggle: "If she had conquered he would have been lost. Even though her light-heartedness (which after all is a security which steadily depreciates) had been capable of making him a happy husband, this is not what he ought to be."[23]

The last clause is the key: "This is not what he ought to be." The suggestion is being made that Quidam, and I think Kierkegaard, has a certain vocation. There is something that he ought to be which is incompatible with fulfilling the role of a happy, and correspondingly a satisfying, husband; and therefore he ought not to be married.

What is it that he ought to be? Why is it incompatible with a happy marriage? The answer suggested at the beginning of the diary, where Quidam starts to wrestle with the question, "whether I was capable of giving my life such an expression as

19. Kierkegaard, *Fear and Trembling*, pp. 68–81.
20. Kierkegaard, *Journals*, p. 70.
21. Kierkegaard, *Journals*, p. 71f.
22. Kierkegaard, *Stages on Life's Way*, p. 342. 'Quidam' is Latin for 'Someone'.
23. Kierkegaard, *Stages on Life's Way*, p. 390.

marriage requires," is that he is called to be a soldier on a certain kind of frontier, which involves a certain kind of spiritual struggle whose intensity is not likely to make for conjugal bliss.

> Ought a soldier of the advance guard to be married? Dare a soldier on the frontier (spiritually understood) take a wife, a soldier on duty at the extremest outpost, who is fighting day and night, not exactly against Turks and Scythians, but against the robber bands of an innate melancholy, a soldier of the outpost who, even though he does not fight day and night, though for a considerable period he has peace, yet never can know at what instant the war will begin again, since he cannot even dare to call this quiet a truce?[24]

Certain judgments about Kierkegaard's case seem to me plausible.

1. The view I am taking Kierkegaard to have had about his vocation seems to me at least partly, and importantly, right. Not, I think, in all parts of it. It is hard to swallow the idea that anyone is called by God to be unhappy or melancholy. But Kierkegaard's actual achievement makes it humanly and religiously credible that he was called to struggle in a peculiarly introverted way on a certain spiritual frontier; and it is also quite plausible that this particular sort of struggle would have been incompatible with a good sort of marriage. I do not mean to suggest that all sorts of spiritual struggle are incompatible with a good marriage—quite the contrary. But it is hard to imagine "the Kierkegaard we know and love" as a happy and satisfying husband, and that is surely connected with the kind of struggle in which he was engaged, or with the (highly introverted) manner in which he felt called to struggle.

2. I also think that it was very likely right for him to break his engagement. His judgment in thinking that he ought to do that, both for Regine's sake and for the sake of his vocation, was probably sound. This certainly does not mean that I think he was blameless, either in proposing marriage in the first place, without having taken stock of all this, or in the harsh and probably indefensible *manner* of his breaking the engagement. But on the central issues as to what Kierkegaard's vocation was, and whether in view of that it was right for him to break his engagement, I am inclined largely to agree with him—or at least to think that his position commands respect and that there is not a sufficient basis for disagreeing with him. This is a point to which we will return in section 5.

Vocation is intimately related to selfhood in this example. It is significant that the crucial statement in the verdict on Quidam is not "This is not what he ought to *do*," but "This is not what he ought to *be*." Kierkegaard sees the vocation first and foremost as a vocation to be a certain kind of person—and, in the closest connection with that, to pursue certain projects which, in his view, are partially constitutive of selfhood. Wrestling in a certain intense and introverted way with certain kinds of spiritual issues was such a project for Kierkegaard. A vocation connected in this way with selfhood could not in his view be attached solely or even primarily to "my station and its duties." In fact he saw his vocation leading him out of the social roles that society would impose on him.

24. Kierkegaard, *Stages on Life's Way*, p. 188.

On this view Kierkegaard's selfhood has a normative constituent. A fact about what he, Søren Kierkegaard, *ought* to be is part of what *makes him* who he is. This is not a metaphysical thesis. It is not being claimed that Kierkegaard's vocation is one of his essential properties, which are metaphysically necessary for his identity in the strictest sense. The concept of selfhood at work here is more ethical than metaphysical. Kierkegaard's selfhood, in the sense in which it is spoken of here, and in which he usually speaks of it, is constituted by those facts about him that make questions about his identity in the metaphysical sense humanly and morally interesting. His vocation is part of what makes him who he is in the sense that it is part of what gives his existence, his life, a unity that is humanly and morally significant. It is part of what matters about his being himself.

Viewed in this light, my self is not just who I actually am, but who I am to become. Of course it is connected with who I already am, but it may also be different enough to surprise even me. The call to become and to be oneself will plausibly be a part of each person's vocation, the self in each case being different. This is a peculiarly fundamental part of our vocation. It cannot be taken from us by any misfortune that leaves us able to deliberate intelligently at all; in hard circumstances it may be virtually our whole vocation. It is probably the main vocation of children; and we never outgrow it, for we have never finished becoming ourselves. And this is not a merely personal project; it is to be our project, but is also a responsibility. Or so at least it appears in theistic perspective, in which there is a Creator who cares about one's becoming oneself, and to whom one can be responsible for it.

As this presupposes, being a self in the relevant, morally charged sense is not automatic, or just genetic. We learn to be a self by acquiring, and learning to value, the ongoing, self-referential projects of being a person of a certain kind and living a life of a certain kind. And we learn this by being *taught* to value and pursue such projects. The society in which we grow up *demands* that we become a self in these ways. Other cultures demand a somewhat differently shaped self, but all demand development of some sort of self. This is not an offense against children, because there is little or no chance of their enjoying good lives unless some form of selfhood is demanded of them. It also happens, fairly often (at least in our culture), that as a person matures, she comes to object to some aspect of the shape of selfhood she was taught to value and pursue. It doesn't fit *her*, or it is simply *bad*—or so, at any rate, she comes to believe. Both the social teaching and demand and the protest that rises in the individual can be, and I think commonly are, signs by which God communicates an individual's vocation to be a certain sort of self—ways in which goods defining a certain self-project are offered to the individual to love.

The obvious centrality of the self to any conception of an individual vocation gives rise naturally to the question whether we could not adequately account for the phenomenon in terms of internal properties of the self without appeal to God's commands or any other form of divine calling. Two such accounts will be considered here. In the first it is claimed that one gives oneself a vocation by choosing a project and committing oneself to it. Kierkegaard's emphasis on the importance of choice could sometimes be read as suggesting this idea, as when he has Quidam explain why he cannot give up his reserve by saying, "I have employed fifteen years to form a life view for myself and to attain proficiency in it. It is a life view which stirred my enthusiasm and was entirely in accord with my nature, and so I cannot suddenly be made over."[25] Should we think that Quidam (or Kierkegaard) has given himself a vocation by forming a life view for himself?

It must be granted that on any ethically tolerable view of vocation it will be possible at least to delimit one's vocation by undertaking commitments to other people. In thinking about what sort of person I ought to be and what projects I ought to have, at any given time, I surely must take into account the commitments I have made to other people, if they are counting on me to fulfill them. But Quidam's vocation (and Kierkegaard's) is too solitary to have arisen in this way.

In any event, the view that I can give myself a vocation just by choosing it or committing myself to it is hard to accept. Suppose I were to set myself to become gregarious, or to become introspective—forming for myself a view of life built around that, and trying determinedly to adhere to it. Could I in that way make that part of my vocation? I think not. I might be totally unsuited to the project; but even if it fit me well and I succeeded in it, my choosing it does not give it the moral weight of a vocation, does not make it a responsibility of mine, does not make it part of what I *ought* to be.

According to a second reductionistic account my vocation may be seen as constituted by my moral feelings and intuitions, particularly including my feelings and intuitions about my vocation—conjoined, of course, with other facts about my situation. Suppose you believe yourself called to take a demanding and low-paid job in a nonprofit social service agency. Being asked, "Why do you think you are called to do that?" you might say that you feel a concern for the needs to be served. Perhaps you would say, "God has laid this concern on my heart"; but someone might try to grant you the vocation as a personal humanitarian imperative, while avoiding the theological interpretation, by grounding the imperative in psychological facts about your concern. On this reductionist account the concern you feel is not just the ground for your belief in the imperative, but the ground of its existence. The key premise in the account will be that there is a general imperative to act on certain kinds of concerns if one feels them in certain types of situations. So if you did not feel this concern, you would not have a vocation to take the social service job. But given that you do feel the concern, and that there is a general imperative to act on such feelings in such a situation, it is your duty and vocation to take the job.

I cannot wholly disagree with this account. If a vocation is a command or invitation from God, it cannot exist without being communicated by God to the person to whom it is addressed. In that sense it must be revealed to the addressee. As I argued in chapter 11, section 4, such communication requires signs that are intended by God to convey the command (or invitation) and that can be understood by the addressee as conveying it. I should think that a valid vocation would commonly have a sense of vocation among the signs by which it is communicated and, in being communicated, also constituted.

If a sense of vocation partially constitutes a valid vocation, however, that is not because of a general ethical imperative to act on one's feelings, but because the feel-

25. Kierkegaard, *Stages on Life's Way*, p. 342.

ing in this case (though quite possibly not in all cases) is intended by God to communicate a vocation. The subjectivistic reduction of the notion of vocation casts our feelings in a different role from that which they are rightly assigned in concrete thinking about a vocation. One who says, "This concern has been laid on my heart" as a reason for believing in a vocation would normally regard the feeling of concern as something like a perception of a claim on her, which is not created by her concern but communicated to her by it. She would not think, "This is a fact about me which gives rise to a vocation in view of a general principle about acting on certain types of felt concern." Furthermore, she need not (and I hope she would not) believe in the very dubious general imperative 'Act on this type of feeling of concern in this type of situation.' A theory of vocation is quite a different thing from a subjectivistic ethics that obliges you to act on certain kinds of feelings. Who I am normatively, as Kierkegaard would surely agree, is not just a matter of how I feel, but something I try to use my feelings to discern.

5. Vocation and Conflicting Values

We will have at best a very truncated conception of vocation if we do not confront the fact that vocations can conflict with other values and, in a sense, with other obligations. This fact is crucial to an understanding of the factor of *moral weight* that I have argued is essential to vocation. In speaking of moral weight one presupposes that different and in some ways conflicting values are being weighed against each other. And if what has moral weight is an obligation, the idea of casting it into the scales presupposes that in advance of the weighing it is only a prima facie obligation, an obligation by which one is bound *other things being equal*, but which may be outweighed by other values or obligations. In advance of the weighing, likewise, other obligations weighed against it will in general only be prima facie obligations too.

If one has received a direct and unambiguous command from God to perform a particular action in a particular actual situation, that vocation will presumably impose an overriding and not merely a prima facie obligation. But we may expect such commands to be rare; and if there are conflicting values and obligations in the situation, they will need to be taken into account in thinking critically about the interpretation of any signs that might be taken as communicating such a command. The more normal case, surely, will be one in which the signs that communicate a vocation delineate a shape of life, presenting goods to be loved, projects to be made one's own, and thus give rise to prima facie obligations, with moral weight that must be cast into the scales of decision.

Where conflicting values affect a decision, one's vocation must of course be tested as well as weighed. The belief that one has been called, or individually commanded (or even just invited) by God, to do something is not one to be accepted uncritically, even if it is supported by strong feelings. It is subject to various tests: the test of conformity with other ethical and religious beliefs that one accepts, the test of congruence with other facts that are known about oneself and about the world, and the tests of living it out: Is the sense of vocation strengthened or weakened by prayer?

Does it survive tribulation? Is acting on it fruitful? The value of the actual results will be a more important test in some contexts than in others. If I felt a strong sense of vocation to paint, but my paintings all turned out to be worse than mediocre, you might well suspect that my sense of vocation was not in touch with the relevant reality. But the frustration of his efforts does not lead me to think that Bonhoeffer's sense of vocation to oppose Nazism was not in touch with moral and spiritual reality. I do not mean to give the impression that a sense of vocation should be easily overthrown by negative results on some of these tests. For one of the things that is important about a sense of vocation is that it is something that can give one guidance, and on which one can act with some firmness, in the face of discouragement and in the face of some negative results.

The moral weight of a vocation means, among other things, that it can be right to pursue a vocation when it impinges painfully on the interests, or even the rights, of other people. In pursuing a vocation one is *apt* to come into collision with the interests of other people. It is not just something that may happen; rather, it is in the nature of the case. Vocations would be unlikely to collide with other human interests only if they were morally weightless or simply derived from calculations about the rights and interests of other people; but in that case we would have little use for the concept of vocation. The potentiality for conflict is enhanced if, as I urge, we conceive of vocations as quite likely to lead us to depart from established social expectations rather than to fulfill them. Experience suggests that this potentiality is fairly frequently actualized. Kierkegaard's breaking of his engagement, described in section 4, provides a vivid example in which I have argued that it is plausible to think he was right to follow his sense of vocation at the cost of breaking a weighty prima facie obligation and causing some pain (though less, in the end, than his vanity imagined) to another person.

Let us think about some other examples. If you pursue a vocation to take a low-paid social service job, it may be that this action will cause considerable distress, and perhaps even some hardship, to your family. Perhaps they will be opposed to it, and you will have to consider whether, in this situation, it is right to follow your sense of vocation against the wishes, and to some extent the interests, of people to whom you are closely bound. A more extreme case is that of the fictionalized Gauguin whom I discussed in chapter 8, section 1, who left his family to go to Tahiti to paint. He was motivated by something that Michael Slote has characterized as an overwhelming passion for painting,[26] but that I would like to think about in the present context as something like a strong sense of vocation to paint—though not necessarily as something that Gauguin conceptualized theologically. We can ask, 'Can Gauguin have been right in leaving his family to follow a vocation to paint?'

A final example is closer to home. Many of us feel a vocation, or something like a vocation, to do philosophical research. But it is a very demanding activity. It demands a lot of time and a lot of emotional and other concentration and energy. There are almost always other good and useful things that we could do that would benefit other people—things like spending more time with our students or with

26. Slote, *Goods and Virtues*, chap. 4.

our families, or answering a higher proportion of our mail. These activities have a larger immediate payoff for the well-being of others than our philosophical research, and maybe their benefit to others will still be larger in the long run. Should we go ahead and do the research anyway? Well, I do. But is that right?

Gauguin's leaving his family probably lies beyond the limit of what it could be right to do in pursuit of the kind of vocation that might be involved there. That case illustrates the point that even if one has, or has had thus far, an ongoing vocation to love and pursue a certain project, it can be idolatrous, and terribly so, to refuse to set the project aside to attend to a more urgent duty or need. In the other cases I have just mentioned, however, I am inclined to think that it may well be right, and in some such cases would be right, to pursue one's vocation anyway, at some cost to other people. What basis might or should this judgment have? One could try to base it on consequentialist grounds, arguing in the case of the social worker, for example, that you could probably do enough good in the low-paid job to outweigh the economic and emotional costs to your family. In the case of philosophical research, one could try to argue that one will ultimately do more good for the world by producing one's great essay than one would do by spending more time with one's students or answering one's mail or whatever else one might do instead. I do not find the consequentialist justifications very satisfying—partly because their truth seems at best so uncertain, and also because relying heavily on them seems in many cases immodest, to put it mildly.

In the case of philosophical research, one could try to argue on the basis of ordinary nonconsequentialist commitments to other people. I have accepted a job, one of whose official duties is that I should be engaged in philosophical research. However, I do not find this account of the matter terribly compelling because I imagine that many of us would satisfy adequately the obligations of this sort that we have if we did less research than we actually do and than we feel called to do. It seems to me more plausible to hold that the vocation one believes one has is itself a ground of the rightness of the actions that it requires.

There is an alternative justification to be considered. One has only prima facie obligations to keep one's promises, answer one's mail, and in general to do things that are good for other people. Being prima facie obligations, they can be overridden in various ways. Clearly they can be overridden by stronger obligations. But it has been claimed that they can also be overridden by "justifiable self-preference." In order for ethics to be tolerable for us human beings, on this view, it should contain the provision that it is permissible to pursue one's own interests under reasonable conditions, including conditions in which one is pursuing one's own interests in preference to fulfilling a prima facie obligation such as promoting the good of others or keeping a promise, when one's own interest is sufficiently important to one in proportion to the weight of the prima facie obligation. Only a sufficiently heavy prima facie obligation can oblige one to set one's own interests aside. It is a feature of the theory of self-preference I have in mind that how important an interest is to one—how much weight it has to set aside a prima facie obligation—is not a normative but a purely psychological question. How much one cares about it is all that counts. Pushpin is as good as poetry, as far as justifiable self-preference is concerned.

On this view, it might be claimed, Kierkegaard is justified in breaking his engagement, the social worker is justified in taking the low-paid job, and we are justified (at least much of the time) in pursuing our philosophical research, because we want to do these things. They are necessary in order to pursue interests that we care very much about. Of course we have to weigh those interests of ours in proportion to the interests of other people that are involved; but we may at least often conclude that the prima facie obligations with which they conflict are not weighty enough to oblige us to go against our own interests.

Having a vocation plays no essential role in this pattern of justification; it is not seen as justifying one in doing anything that one would not be justified in doing if one just wanted badly enough to do it. I think that is implausible. Intuitively it seems to me that a divine vocation, or even a subjective but plausible sense of vocation, or of something like vocation, does have more force than a mere strong desire has to override a prima facie obligation. For example, I think that on balance it was wrong for Gauguin to leave his family and go to Tahiti. But I would at least think better of him, on the whole, supposing him to have done this out of something like a sense of vocation to paint, than I would if I thought he had done it merely out of an intense desire. Similarly, it seems to me that a sense of vocation does have more force than a mere desire would have to justify doing philosophical research, at the expense of other worthy projects; that seems to me to be true even though I think that philosophizing is a noble end even as the object of a mere desire. No doubt more than one account might be offered of what gives a sense of vocation more justifying force than mere desires, however intense, can have. But theists will surely think that having a vocation (either a command or an invitation) from God to do something would indeed be a strong justification for doing it.

14

POLITICS AND THE GOOD

The inclusion here of a complete framework for political philosophy, as a part of ethics, would unduly expand an already large book. I shall not try even to sketch a theory of justice, for example, or of political legitimacy. It is incumbent on me, nevertheless, to say something about the role to be assigned to the good in political ethics; for many will at least initially be inclined to suspect that the prominence and foundational role of the good in my ethical theory threatens to subvert aspirations (which I share) for a broadly liberal political order. These suspicions, which may be aggravated by the religious character of my theory of the good, must be addressed.

According to a much-cited essay by Ronald Dworkin, "liberalism takes, as its constitutive political morality," a conception of equality that "supposes that political decisions must be, so far as possible, independent of any particular conception of the good life, or of what gives value to life."[1] According to Charles Larmore, like-

---

1. Dworkin, "Liberalism," p. 64. This conception of liberalism seems to me no longer advocated in Dworkin's more recent work, *Life's Dominion*. On the topic introduced in this paragraph I have been much helped by the discussion and critique of antiperfectionism in Raz, *The Morality of Freedom*, chaps. 5–6. My argument in this chapter also has a number of points of contact with Hurka, *Perfectionism*, chaps. 11–13, although I have significant disagreements with Hurka's "Aristotelian perfectionism." One difference that affects my argument, and that will be discussed in section 1, is that my views do not have the broadly consequentialist structure of Hurka's.

wise, "Political liberalism has been the doctrine that . . . the state should be neutral. The state should not seek to promote any particular conception of the good life because of its presumed intrinsic superiority—that is, because it is supposedly a *truer* conception."[2] The best known and most influential attempt to limit the role of conceptions of the good in a liberal polity is doubtless the thesis of John Rawls that in a liberal political conception of justice "the concept of right is prior to that of the good."[3] Rawls has also stated that in political liberalism the government cannot act "to advance human excellence," though he qualifies this by allowing that it may encourage those "political virtues" that "characterize the ideal of a good citizen of a democratic state."[4] These three accounts of liberalism may not exactly coincide. I mention them here in summary form just to give an initial idea of an issue that I will be addressing.[5] There are other forms of liberalism that do not raise this issue.

Various reasons have been offered for renunciation of appeals to the good in politics. I will mention those that seem to me most important. It is generally and rightly assumed that in a free society there will almost surely be persons and groups holding quite diverse conceptions of the good. In saying this I do not mean to express skepticism about the possibility of rational discussion of conceptions of the good; but philosophical experience does not suggest that such discussion, freely pursued, is likely to settle all important disagreements. Liberals wish especially to avoid interfering with the freedom of individuals to pursue their own conceptions of the good, and wish also to avoid government action that systematically disadvantages any group that holds a conception of the good that is not favored by the government or by a majority of the population. The priority of right is suggested as a way of avoiding these evils. (I leave aside, for the moment, the worry that free discussion is as unlikely to issue in general agreement about the right as about the good.) Among types of good, moreover, an emphasis on excellence is particularly feared as possibly subversive of political and economic equality.

In previous chapters of this book I have taken positions that are in tension with some or all of the proposed restrictions on appeals to the good. The most obvious is that I have given an account of the concept of the good as prior to that of right, at least for purposes of general ethical theory. Another point of tension is the treatment of well-being or welfare, an inevitable topic of political thought. I have ar-

---

2. Larmore, *Patterns of Moral Complexity*, p. 43. So far as Larmore endorses the doctrine, however, "it does not require that the state be neutral with respect to all conceptions of the good life, but only with respect to those actually disputed in the society" (ibid., p. 67; cf. p. 47). In fact, Larmore's argument for neutrality of the state, appealing to a sort of discourse ethics, seems to me more relevant to neutrality on controversial issues as such (including issues about obligation or the right) than on issues about the good as such. Cf. Greenawalt, *Private Consciences and Public Reasons*, p. 79: "Those who advocate neutrality between controversial ideas of the good life mean to cover neutrality between controversial moral claims about personal ethics, even when those claims concern matters of personal obligation."

3. Rawls, *A Theory of Justice*, p. 31; cf. Rawls, *Political Liberalism*, pp. 174–76.

4. Rawls, *Political Liberalism*, pp. 179, 194f.

5. Another version of liberal neutrality is central to the argument of Ackerman, *Social Justice in the Liberal State*; and others are discussed in Barry, *Political Argument*, pp. 66ff., and *Justice as Impartiality*.

gued in chapter 3 that an adequate account of well-being cannot be given purely in terms of the satisfaction of wants and desires, but must appeal to considerations of excellence—precisely the sort of conception of good most likely to be viewed by many liberals as politically pernicious.

I will have occasion to contend on particular issues with some of the authors whose work on these topics I most admire, but I will not give a comprehensive exposition or critique of any theory other than my own. I also will not try to discuss every type of political theory with which some of my views may conflict. As elsewhere in this book, I will concentrate on development and defense of my own views. I will argue that considerations of excellence have a legitimate place in political ethics, and that they can be used to give solid grounding to the rights that most concern liberals. In this I will be disagreeing at a number of points with some exponents of liberalism, but there are also important points of agreement. Many of the agreements and disagreements will go unmentioned here, as there is not space for a full and balanced account of the authors discussed. The views of Rawls, for example, on the role of the good in politics are of such great (and increasing) subtlety that it would take a very long digression to do them justice.

1. Perfectionism and Equality

There are many relations in which principles of right and wrong in political matters could stand to considerations of excellence, in a theory that admits the latter as grounds for political action. One theory on this subject that has come in for increasing discussion is what Rawls, who opposes it, calls "perfectionism," the doctrine that one of the chief aims of a society in arranging its political institutions should be "to maximize the achievement of human excellence in art, science, and culture."[6] It is essential to an understanding of most of what I have to say in this chapter that my position is *not* a form of perfectionism. 'Perfectionism' would indeed be an odd name for my position, inasmuch as I deny (in chapter 2, section 1) that perfect virtue is a possibility for human beings. More substantively, I am not committed to the maximizing aim in terms of which Rawls characterizes perfectionism. Still less do I favor the consequentialist structure of the perfectionism recently proposed, in illuminating detail, by Thomas Hurka.[7]

I am committed to a divine command account of the metaphysics of right and wrong in political matters as in the rest of ethics, and divine command theories are widely associated with nonconsequentialist principles of obligation. There is no logical necessity to that association, however. Some divine command theorists played a part in developing utilitarianism.[8] As, on my view, the divine commands are issued by a deity who cares about excellence, and as I believe that we must often be guided, in judging what God has commanded, by our beliefs about God's concern

---

6. Rawls, *A Theory of Justice*, p. 325.
7. Hurka, *Perfectionism*.
8. Cf. Schneewind, *The Invention of Autonomy*, pp. 101–17, 406–11.

for what is good, I may fairly be asked why I should not suppose that God's commands have a consequentialist structure that enjoins us to maximize the sum of excellence in the world.

In fact positions I have already taken tell strongly against such a supposition. Most decisive, perhaps, in this regard is the thesis of chapter 10, section 1, connecting obligation with sanctions against wrongdoing. In view of that connection I must think of God's decisions in commanding as guided less directly by the question, What actions would it be good for people to perform? than by the question, What behavior would it be good to oppose with sanctions of punishment, anger, or feelings of guilt? This perspective is unlikely to issue in a thoroughgoing consequentialism, because it seems unlikely that it will be optimific to have the relevant sanctions against all and only nonoptimific behavior. If it incorporates the sort of account of evil I have suggested in chapter 4, moreover, it will be a perspective from which it will seem much more appropriate to direct such sanctions against behavior that violates an existing excellent being than against behavior that merely fails to be excellent, even if a larger sum of excellence is apt to be lost by the latter than by the former. Anger, for example, is obviously a more appropriate response to an attack on something good than to the mere absence of value. These points affect much of what I will have to say, particularly about rights, in this chapter.

It is not my view that the regard that God has, and that we should have, for excellence is a desire to maximize the sum of excellence existing. As expounded in chapters 6 and 7, ideal love for the good is primarily love for particular excellent beings, considered one at a time. It is concerned to respect existing excellent beings, and especially to avoid violating them. It is also concerned to enhance the excellence enjoyed by actual persons (for reasons indicated in chapter 3), but for their sake rather than for the sake of an abstract quantity or degree of excellence. Ideal love for the good seeks *alliance* with and among rational creatures, and therefore cares at least as much about their being *for* the good, and *for* each other, as about their *causing* good. Divine commands springing from such love should not be expected to form a consequentialist system, of a perfectionist or any other sort. Consequentialism is still less to be expected if the commander is an omnipotent deity who, having at the deepest level no need for instruments, may be assumed to care for each creature for its own sake, and not merely as a means.

Rawls's rejection of perfectionism evidently has as a main motive a widely shared fear of inegalitarian implications of perfectionism. It is incumbent on me here to explain why I believe the admission of considerations of excellence as grounds for political action, and even for fundamental constitutional decisions, does not imply support for objectionably inegalitarian treatment of individuals or groups.[9] My own rejection of perfectionism is a step in that direction, but I will not pretend that it disposes of all fears of this sort.

---

9. The more extensive argument for this conclusion in Hurka, *Perfectionism*, chaps. 12–13, is illuminating. So is the (sometimes disturbing) discussion in Nagel, *Equality and Partiality*, chap. 12.

It must be granted that a state's pursuit of excellence is likely to be more advantageous to some of its citizens than to others, because of differences in their tastes and situations. But such consequences need not be unfair or objectionably inegalitarian. Any state action at all is likely to be more advantageous to some citizens than to others; that is a main reason there will always be conflicts in politics. Rawls acknowledges that the kind of constitutional regime he advocates will have effects that are much more favorable to some ways of life than to others, and will lead to the dwindling or even the disappearance of some ways of life that are inherently worthy alternatives. He calls this a "loss," and must surely admit that it will be painful, perhaps even tragic, for some individual members of society. He rightly insists that this does not show that it is unfair to adopt political arrangements that have such consequences, especially since any political system would have similar consequences.[10] By the same token, the fact that appeals to excellence in politics will be more advantageous to some than to others does not show that there is anything unfair about them. Of course, we must always be alert to the possibility that the differential impact of public policies is unjust in particular cases. If, for example, it deprives some of a minimally decent economic standard of living, there will be a powerful argument that something must be done to avoid or rectify that.

The risk of unfairness increases, of course, when governments (or other institutions) apply tests of excellence to individual persons or (more commonly and more appropriately) to their performances. I argued in chapter 4, section 5, that the most important type of excellence possessed by persons is one with respect to which we cannot be compared as more and less excellent. There are excellences of talent and performance, however, with respect to which persons do differ and can be compared, and these differences are often important to the pursuit of excellence—as well as to other pursuits. If the state supports a symphony orchestra, it will want to employ the most excellent conductor it can. Assessing the excellence of candidates presents ample opportunity for unfairness but not, I think, an inevitability of unfairness. In any event, similar opportunities for unfairness will abound even in a state governed wholly by want-regarding considerations, if it seeks to employ persons who will most effectively satisfy citizens' wants. Whether or not excellence, as such, is among its aims, a government will need to be guided by principles of fair competition in filling positions. What principles are fair and correct in this area is a subject of burning controversy in our society, but I do not think the doctrines developed in this book have particularly dangerous implications regarding it.

Excellences compete with each other for realization; we cannot maximize the realization of all of them. Freedom and equality may plausibly be viewed as excellences of societies; they compete with each other and with other excellences to some extent. Maximum equality, in particular, seems unlikely to be realized in a liberal society, because one of the most central values of the latter is freedom for individuals and groups to pursue their own projects and their own conceptions of the good, and this free pursuit is unlikely to leave everyone equally successful or equally

---

10. Rawls, *Political Liberalism*, pp. 193–99. Rawls is adapting similar points made in Larmore, *Patterns of Moral Complexity*, pp. 42–47.

advantaged, even if the state takes steps to prevent or even out wide disparities in wealth. For reasons partly expressed in section 2, I do not think maximum equality is worth purchasing at the cost of liberal freedoms; so the question I think most worth asking is not about the compatibility of the pursuit of excellence with *maximum* equality, but rather with a more moderate equality to which liberals may reasonably aspire.

The principal question here is whether the pursuit of excellence requires, or must claim to justify, wide disparities in wealth, or a social class system, or even inequalities before the law. There is one historically prominent type of political appeal to alleged excellence of persons that is obviously obnoxious in these respects, but is also so blatantly spurious that no plausible theory of excellence will support it. This is the appeal implicit in the etymological meaning of 'aristocracy' (rule by the best). The claim is that a certain class of people, typically identified by their genealogy, are more excellent than others, and therefore deserve political, economic, and social privileges not available to others. This is such an utterly implausible claim that it is hard not to suspect some sort of bad faith behind it. The members of privileged classes have always been distinguished from other individuals by their political, economic, and social power, rather than by any degree of excellence that others could not have attained if they had comparable opportunities. No reasonable principle of fair competition will allow membership in such a class to be counted in favor of a candidate for a position or opportunity in a state-supported enterprise. Even if considerations of excellence are given a reasonable place in politics, arguments for aristocracy, in the indicated sense, will still be implausible.

To be sure, people's motivation and capacity for pursuing excellences are affected by family background, "since so much education and culture is transmitted informally through the family," as Thomas Nagel points out. But I think we should resist his further inference that "a society which supports creative achievement and encourages maximum levels of excellence will have to accept and exploit stratification and hierarchy."[11] Families that transmit cultural values do not require a hierarchy of classes, and need not produce social stratification. Parents who teach their children to care about good art can also teach them that it's bad to look down on other people.

A more cautious, but still objectionable, inegalitarian argument would not ascribe to particular individuals or families any inherent superiority in excellence, and would not claim for them any personal right to their positions of privilege. It would simply justify the existence of wide disparities in wealth and other forms of social privilege, claiming that excellence will be pursued more effectively if some people have vastly larger means than others to pursue it. ("Somebody needs to belong to the privileged class; so why not me?") This may be the type of argument that Rawls most wishes to forestall by rejecting perfectionism; he considers, "for example," an argument in which it would be "maintained that in themselves the achievements of

---

11. Nagel, *Equality and Partiality*, p. 132. I believe that Nagel's views on the subject under discussion are less widely divergent from mine, and more egalitarian, than suggested by the unhappy statement just quoted.

the Greeks in philosophy, science, and art justified the ancient practice of slavery (assuming that this practice was necessary for these achievements)."[12]

Here again I think the objectionable argument is apt to rest on a sort of bad faith. It may be true that those ancient achievements would not have occurred, in their historical circumstances, without slavery; but, if so, that is largely because the achievement of excellence was *not* an important enough goal of the society as a whole. It would be naive to suppose that the wealth and leisure of the privileged classes in ancient Greece went mainly to the creation of the sort of excellence we rightly admire; most of it no doubt was consumed in humdrum self-indulgence. For a society that really cares enough about the pursuit of excellence, it will virtually always be more efficient, as well as fairer, to give direct public support to a variety of excellence-pursuing enterprises, with fair competition for positions in them, rather than to accept wide disparities of personal wealth and privilege in the pious hope that the privileged will use their advantages for excellence.[13]

It may be claimed that there are some particular excellences that require inequality. Nagel suggests that we may, for the sake of excellence, want a few people to live lives of great luxury ("haute cuisine, haute couture, and exquisite houses") that could not be possible for most people. He may be right in thinking that many people want this, deriving "pleasure . . . from knowing and hearing about lives of luxury and taste led by others";[14] but I don't think this furnishes a powerful argument from excellence for preserving vast economic inequalities. As I have already pointed out, we cannot have all human excellences in a single society. So even if Nagel has identified excellences that could not exist in an egalitarian society, it may still be worth giving them up for the sake of goods characteristic of greater equality. I do not know how one would show that more or higher excellences are possible in a society that has vast disparities of wealth than in one that does not have them. I am also skeptical about Nagel's examples. *Must* haute cuisine and haute couture be so expensive as to require great wealth? Or is it just that our present economy leads to their being priced that way? *Must* the most exquisite buildings be used only by a privileged few? (Probably most of the most spectacular buildings have some public use.) More broadly, *must* an economically egalitarian society be aesthetically impoverished?

2. Civil Liberties

Civil liberties are among the concerns that are dearest to liberal political philosophers. I believe, and will argue, that considerations of excellence are essential to the best understanding and defense of civil liberties. It does not follow, of course—nor do I believe—that such a defense, or any other, should be officially adopted by the state. What I think does follow is that persons do well to allow themselves to be swayed by considerations of excellence in adopting a stance on this fundamental political issue.

---

12. Rawls, *A Theory of Justice*, p. 325.
13. I take myself to be in agreement with Nagel, *Equality and Partiality*, p. 136, on this point.
14. Nagel, *Equality and Partiality*, p. 138.

Liberties, in this context, are a species of rights. Rights, in the broadest sense, are more or less enduring principles of right and wrong that confer on persons or societies of persons (the right-holders) claims, permissions, powers, or immunities.[15] The liberties that concern us will typically be clusters or packages of permissions to do things, claims against others not to interfere with our doing them, and possibly immunities that prevent others from depriving us of these permissions and claims.[16]

There are purely moral rights, determining what individuals are *morally* permitted or empowered or (for the sake of other individuals) *morally* obligated or not empowered to do. There are purely legal or institutional rights, determined by what public laws and courts, and the rules and authorities of other institutions, require, permit, and make possible, whether they should or not. The existence or nonexistence of rights of the latter sort is a merely social and not a fully moral fact, as I have argued in chapter 10, section 3, that the existence of purely institutional obligations is.

There are also rights that governments and other institutions ought, morally, to grant, whether they do in fact or not. These rights are sometimes classified as "natural," though they won't be here. They are of a mixed character, partly moral and partly legal or institutional. Persons are often said to "have" them, even in states where they are not legally recognized or protected; and that is clearly a moral thesis. On the other hand, they are not purely moral rights; the claim that we have them is not normally a claim about how individuals ought to treat each other, independently of legal and institutional arrangements. It is primarily a thesis about what legal and institutional arrangements there ought to be. It is with theses of this mixed moral and institutional character that we shall be principally concerned in the present discussion of rights.

Civil liberties are a species of rights that there is weighty reason to establish and protect. They deserve very strong protection, though they will normally be subject to qualifications or limits that I will not in general try to define here. For instance, freedom of religion obviously should not include a right to kill a person as part of a sacrificial ceremony.

Some freedoms are not *important* enough to be numbered among the civil liberties. At the present time I am permitted legally (and no doubt morally) to drive either north or south on College Street between Elm and Chapel in New Haven; in the broadest sense I have a right to do that. But that is not one of my civil liberties; there is no strong moral reason for maintaining it. Not long ago I was not permitted to drive north on that stretch of College Street; it was a one-way street, southbound. So far as I can see, there is no compelling moral ground for preferring one of these arrangements to the other. This is not to deny that a more general freedom of movement is an important civil liberty. If a pattern of one-way streets were being used to prevent me from ever leaving a certain part of town, that would be violating

15. This enumeration of types of right, but not all of my terminology, derives from the well-known classification of Hohfeld, *Fundamental Legal Conceptions*. Hohfeld's distinctions are accorded fundamental importance, for instance, in Thomson, *The Realm of Rights*, pp. 39–90.

16. Here I largely follow Thomson, *The Realm of Rights*, pp. 281–85.

a right that I surely ought to have, and that is important enough to count as a civil liberty in the relevant sense.

Of what sort are the weighty reasons to establish and protect civil liberties? Much discussion emphasizes the value of persons' being able to satisfy their desires. That is certainly not irrelevant, but it can hardly be the whole story. Continuing with an example pertaining to freedom of movement, suppose I want to cross a large river but can't, because the people around me, through sheer laziness, are unwilling to do anything about building a bridge that I am unable to build unaided. I may well be exasperated at their uncooperativeness, and may even have reason to think that they have violated some right of mine—if, for example, we all agreed to build the bridge, and I have done my part, but they have failed to perform. But even if they have broken a contract with me, they have not thereby infringed my civil liberties. That would happen in the much more offensive case in which the bridge exists but an armed guard of my neighbors prevents me, by threat of violence, from cross-ing—refusing me a passport, so to speak, because they do not like my complexion or my opinions, or simply because they do not want me to get to the other side. In this second case there is not just a frustration of my desire to get across the river, as in the first case; there is also a violation or threatened violation of my person. To focus here only on the question whether my desires regarding my physical location are satisfied is to miss the main point, which is that I am outraged by a hostile, co-ercive relationship. I think this is characteristic of our interest in individual free-dom in general. What fuels the passion for liberty is not so much a concern for the satisfaction of desire as a revulsion for certain kinds of coercion.[17]

This point is very important for issues about the "enforcement of morality" by the criminal law. Liberals commonly hold (rightly, in my opinion) that badness or even moral wrongness of conduct is not sufficient to justify attaching criminal pen-alties to it, and that it is generally wrong to criminalize conduct that does not ex-pose persons other than the agent to harms or risks that they have not voluntarily accepted. Why would it be wrong to criminalize it? Not just because it is good for people to be able to do what they want. Some of the conduct we ought not to treat as a crime is genuinely deplorable. Few of us would accept it as a good reason for a public or private action that it would help people who want to do such things to do them. Much more important is the evil of coercion.

The evil that concerns us most is to be understood here, along lines developed in chapter 4, as violation of something sacred, or at least of a great good, and typi-cally of a person. Where there is not a sufficiently compelling reason for it, such violation is one of the types of conduct at which it is most obviously appropriate to be angry, and hence one of the types most plausibly regarded as divinely prohib-ited. Most criminal punishment for serious offenses, including imprisonment as well

---

17. Coercion, as I understand it in this chapter, involves a manifestation or threat of serious hostility. In the cases of particular concern here, it involves a threat of seriously adverse consequences. I agree with Joseph Raz that "coercion by threats . . . is the form of coercion relevant to political theory"; and his definition of this type of coercion seems likely to pick out approximately those cases that I have in mind, though it would require adaptation to my theoretical framework (Raz, *The Morality of Freedom*, p. 149).

as corporal punishments, does violate persons. The bending or attempted bending of people's wills by the threat of such punishment is also violative. Coercion by the criminal law is therefore usually a great evil, even when it is justified.[18] Exceptions confirm the point. Many of us find it relatively easy to approve of "paternalistic" laws prohibiting acts that tend, uncontroversially, to harm only the agent, such as driving or riding in a car without a seat belt—so long as the penalties attached to the conduct are only modest fines, which do not seem to violate persons.

For this reason we may hold quite different attitudes to criminalization and to other governmental attempts to discourage conduct regarded as bad. Most of us do not regard smoking tobacco as intrinsically evil, but it certainly is harmful, primarily but not exclusively to the smoker. I believe it would be wrong to subject the possession and use of tobacco (where it does not foul the air for others) to serious criminal penalties, because of the evils of coercion and punishment. Other government action to discourage smoking or make it more difficult, without coercion, perhaps by raising taxes on tobacco products, seems entirely appropriate.

Polygamy[19] is regarded by most in our society as morally objectionable, but it is no longer prosecuted as a crime in some jurisdictions, so long as no spouse is deceived and no one tries to be *legally* married to more than one individual. That is as it should be, for legal coercion and punishment would be an offensive violation of persons in such a case, if all the participants are acting voluntarily, and especially if they are acting on reasons of religion. At the same time, it also seems appropriate for society to refuse to extend legal recognition, and its associated benefits, to polygamous marriages, on the ground that such family structures are inherently unfair to the women involved in them, and should therefore be discouraged.

There is no strong movement for legal recognition of polygamous marriages in our society, but there is one for legal recognition of marriages between persons of the same sex. If one thinks, as I do, that enduring same-sex unions should be legally recognized but polygamous unions should not, what reason can one give? An essential part of the reason I would give is that same-sex unions can and often do realize most of the personal benefits and moral excellences to which traditional heterosexual marriages aspire, without any such structural unfairness as is involved in polygamy.

Some rights are more important than others. Some liberties are more important than others.[20] No rights or liberties are more important to liberals than those comprised under the heading of freedom of conscience, including freedom of expression, especially but not exclusively on political subjects, and freedom of religion, the freedom to adopt and practice any religion or none. There is an increasing tendency to associate with these, as of comparable importance, freedom of intimate association. Contrasting with these are economic freedoms, which are an important part of a typical liberal social order but which few liberals think should be as inviolable as freedom of conscience.

18. This point is much more richly appreciated in Hart, *Law, Liberty, and Morality*, than in many treatments of the subject.

19. Here, as normally, this means what is more precisely called *polygyny*, the marriage of one man to two or more women.

20. Cf. Rawls, *Political Liberalism*, pp. 291–99.

This difference is important to my argument. I am not just asking why we should have a right of freedom of conscience. Any plausible view of these matters must let us have resources to vindicate this right. But beyond that I am asking why freedom of conscience should be given (as I believe it should) a strong priority over economic freedoms and most other political considerations. It follows, of course, that the priority of freedom of conscience cannot be simply derived from a general right to freedom of all sorts;[21] what is our reason for thinking that this freedom should be specially inviolable?

The main reason, I think, is that legally recognized and assured freedom of conscience protects interests of greater importance to the intrinsic excellence of human life than the interests protected by economic freedoms. This reason for special protection for freedom of conscience expresses a judgment of comparative value that I think is not very controversial in our society. Still it is a judgment of objective value— a judgment not based wholly on the desires or preferences of the persons involved. Some liberals have wished to avoid all reliance on such judgments in constitutional matters, but I do not see a satisfactory alternative to them in distinguishing, as we must, the most important from less important freedoms. The restriction of movement involved in having one-way streets can be inconvenient and even extremely frustrating, but it would be silly to regard one-way streets as a serious infringement of liberty. And that is not because most people care less about driving than about speaking out for unpopular political causes, as Dworkin has pointed out.[22] I think we should tolerate more governmental interference in economic behavior than in religion, sexuality, and the expression of our thoughts and feelings; but I do not suppose less interest and desire are invested in economic behavior than in other activities.

The distinguishing mark of the freedoms that most deserve protection is that they are most closely connected with our personhood and the significance of our lives, so that it is more plausible to say that something sacred has been violated if coercion denies them to us. This is not to say that every individual exercise of the protected freedoms is excellent; some such acts are doubtless very bad. My claim is rather that the greatest values in human life depend on people being able, and allowed, to make their own decisions in these matters, so that an interference with *freedom* to make such choices is apt to be a violation of something sacred, whether the actual choice will be a good one or not. It is a familiar point about civil liberties that we do not give them much protection if we respect them only where we judge the choices actually made to be good.

It is equally important, I think, that we will not give adequate protection to civil liberties if we respect them only where they are exercised from a point of view

---

21. On this point I agree with Dworkin, *Taking Rights Seriously*, pp. 271–78. He proposes there, however, to derive the status of freedom of conscience from a general "right to equal treatment" (ibid., p. 273). That seems to me unlikely to give freedom of conscience a secure enough priority over economic concerns. We are only too well aware of powerful forces in the twentieth century that have thought it necessary and right to deny freedom of conscience in many cases in order to ensure more equal treatment of citizens in the economic realm.

22. Dworkin, "Liberalism," p. 61; cf. Dworkin, *Taking Rights Seriously*, pp. 270–72.

that we recognize as *reasonable*; for in matters of conscience, and especially of religion, there is widespread disagreement, not just about what is true, but even about what is reasonable. There are obviously kinds of unreasonableness that no society can tolerate, even if they are presented as an exercise of conscience; but the bounds of the reasonable are narrower, I think, than the realm of human possibility that claims our special respect. There are, after all, forms of "madness" that are important expressions of the grandeur of the human spirit. My argument for liberty of conscience, therefore, does not depend on the possibility of reasonable disagreement,[23] although I grant that reasonable disagreement is possible regarding a large proportion of religious and ethical issues. My argument focuses rather on the violation of the sacred that I claim is involved in the coercion of even an erring conscience.

An alternative to my approach would be to try to discriminate on utilitarian grounds between the freedoms deserving more and less stringent protection. That is the strategy suggested by the professedly utilitarian rationale of John Stuart Mill's famous essay *On Liberty*. Mill's renunciation of nonutilitarian considerations in this context is required by his general position in moral philosophy, but suits ill with his specific aims regarding liberty. I doubt that the stringent and sweeping protection for individual liberty that Mill advocates can be convincingly defended on utilitarian grounds. Certainly the utilitarian argument he offers is not adequate to the whole task.

Intuitively, moreover, certain liberties seem—at least to me—to have a claim to respect and protection that is intrinsic and largely independent of any utilitarian calculation. Indeed, part of the point of enshrining our most prized freedoms in the Constitution is to shield them, not only from the meddlesome or paternalistic intrusions on which Mill focuses, but also from (possibly utilitarian) fears of the risks they may pose for other major aspects of the public good. Perhaps we could give a utilitarian argument for so defending them, but the spirit in which they are defended is not utilitarian, and they would not be so jealously guarded as they are if their defenders did not see something at stake in them that transcends utilitarian calculations. What is at stake in the freedoms of religion and expression and intimate relations is something that touches the core of personhood, and to abridge these freedoms is to do violence to persons in their spiritual and social being. That is the most urgent reason for the special protection accorded them.

My argument here has important points of contact with an argument Rawls gives for "the priority of liberty" in his *Theory of Justice*. Thinking of the correct principles of justice as those to which persons would agree in an "original position" of idealized knowledge of general truths and ignorance of their own particular char-

---

23. As some liberals do in defending one form or another of neutrality of the state in relation to religious and "comprehensive" moral views. See Nagel, *Equality and Partiality*, pp. 159–62; Rawls, *Political Liberalism*, pp. 48–66; Barry, *Justice as Impartiality*, pp. 168–88. It should be noted that for Rawls (*Political Liberalism*, p. 62) the concept of the reasonable is primarily political and only partly epistemological, and in some contexts largely signifies a disposition to play fair and to reciprocate tolerance. I do not mean to deny that a lack of that disposition is one of the factors that can make it morally difficult or impossible to tolerate someone's position.

acteristics and situations, he emphasizes that in arriving at such agreement the parties in the original position "must assume that they may have moral, religious, or philosophical interests which they cannot put in jeopardy unless there is no alternative. One might say that they regard themselves as having moral or religious obligations which they must keep themselves free to honor."[24] What leads the parties to give to equal basic liberties a largely indefeasible priority over other considerations of justice? "The strength of religious and moral obligations as men interpret them seems to require" it, "at least when applied to freedom of conscience."[25]

In this formulation the special protection of freedom of conscience is required, not merely by desires or preferences that persons in the original position would have there or would anticipate having in real life (as some aspects of Rawls's theory might lead us to expect him to hold), but by "the strength of religious and moral obligations." Rawls adds the qualification "as men interpret them," and states that "from the standpoint of [his conception of] justice as fairness, these obligations are self-imposed; they are not bonds laid down by this conception of justice."[26] Certainly his conception of justice does not commit him on particular issues of religious ethics, such as whether it is wrong to labor on the sabbath day. But I doubt that he can in this way free his argument from a more general commitment to the objective importance and value of acting on moral and religious convictions.

Suppose the parties in the original position do not actually hold the belief in the objective importance of conscience. The reflection that in real life they may hold it, and may find the demands of conscience imperious, may still move them in the original position to afford constitutional protection to their freedom to act on the belief. On the other hand, we may ask why the reflection that in real life they may find their economic ambitions *more* imperious (as some people do) should not lead them to compromise the priority of freedom of conscience in their legislation.

In the face of this sort of challenge H. L. A. Hart has suggested that the priority of freedom of religion (though perhaps not of all Rawls's basic liberties) could be defended in the original position in terms of which possible constraints would be "worse for" persons suffering them.

> It might be said that any rational person who understood what it is to have a religious faith and to wish [to] practise it would agree that for any such person to be prevented by law from practising his religion must be worse than for a relatively poor man to be prevented from gaining a great advance in material goods through the surrender of a religious liberty which meant little or nothing to him.[27]

I agree with Hart's judgment of which is worse, but I do not think it can plausibly be defended in terms of strength of desires and preferences; that desire for material

---

24. Rawls, *A Theory of Justice*, p. 206.
25. Rawls, *A Theory of Justice*, p. 208.
26. Rawls, *A Theory of Justice*, p. 206.
27. Hart, "Rawls on Liberty and Its Priority," p. 252. The bracketed word corrects an evident misprint.

gain can be as intense as religious desires is precisely the point of talking about wealth as an object of idolatry. What Hart invites us to recognize must rather be that it is *objectively* worse to be prevented from practicing one's religion, because of the *objective* importance of religious issues in human life.

Rawls's strongest objection to compromising the liberty of conscience is similar: in *A Theory of Justice* he insists that "the persons in the original position . . . cannot take chances with their liberty"; for "to gamble in this way would show that one did not take one's religious or moral convictions seriously."[28] The clear implication is that the parties in the original position will avoid the compromise or gamble because they do take religious and moral convictions seriously. And if they must take them seriously to decide on the priority of liberty, it is not clear how Rawls can defend the priority of liberty without taking them seriously himself (as he surely does). This seriousness must amount to a belief in the *objective* importance and value of religious and moral convictions, since the position Rawls is developing is intended not just for himself but for rational people generally.

Perhaps Rawls's "political constructivism"[29] would lead him to respond at this point that freedom of conscience should be respected, not because of a special *value* of conscience, but because one should want to live with others on terms that all "reasonable" persons could accept, and even reasonable persons cannot accept constraint against a reasonable conscience. This argument presupposes that it is indeed "reasonable" to set a specially high value on conscience, but Rawls might claim that that does not commit him to the claim that conscience objectively possesses this value. Still his liberal scheme as a whole requires him also to say that it is *not* reasonable to set such a high value on economic freedoms; and at this point his identification with the assignment of a higher objective value to freedom of conscience seems very close.

In his more recent work, *Political Liberalism*, Rawls echoes and broadens Hart's suggestion that a priority for liberty of conscience is required by an understanding of the nature of religious and moral conscience. If the parties in the original position were to compromise or risk the liberty of conscience of the persons they represent, Rawls says, "they would show that they . . . did not know what a religious, philosophical, or moral conviction was."[30] As with Hart's argument, this cannot mean merely that understanding the nature of morality and religion would show them how much their real-world counterparts might care about such convictions; for they might care as much about wealth. The understanding that demands a special guarantee for liberty of conscience must be an understanding that enters into the self-understanding of religious, philosophical, and moral conviction so far as to affirm the objective value and importance of conscience.

I will not take the time here for a detailed discussion of the several other arguments that Rawls offers for the priority of the basic liberties, and specifically for a strong guarantee of freedom of conscience. None, perhaps, are as powerful as the

---

28. Rawls, *A Theory of Justice*, p. 207.
29. Rawls, *Political Liberalism*, lecture 3.
30. Rawls, *Political Liberalism*, p. 311; cf. p. 312.

argument I have been discussing. The most persuasive, I think, are those in *Political Liberalism* that are based on the idea that freedom of conscience is necessary "for the adequate development and full exercise of the two powers of moral personality over a complete life,"[31] the two powers being "a capacity for a sense of justice and for a conception of the good."[32] I would agree that any abridgment of freedom of conscience throws an obstacle in the way of the development and exercise of these moral capacities. This is one way of explaining that freedom's importance and value for human life. But what is it about the moral capacities that grounds a privilege for the freedom connected with them? I do not see any way in which this type of argument for strong protection of freedom of conscience can be freed from reliance on belief in the objective value or importance of the moral capacities.

Rawls's arguments also seem to me to presuppose the objective value of a sort of *autonomy* in their evident implication that "the adequate development and full exercise" of the moral powers would be autonomous; for a more authoritarian ideal might imply that the moral powers would develop better with less freedom. Rawls argues that a "conception of the person" in which the two moral powers are central and highly valued is required by a "conception of social cooperation" at which political liberalism aims.[33] So far as I can see, however, to value the relevant sort of social cooperation is already implicitly to value the relevant sort of autonomy; for history plainly shows that forms of social cooperation are possible that involve far less liberty.

I shall not try to determine here how far, or whether, this dependence on belief in the objective value or importance of conscience is inconsistent with Rawls's intentions for his argument for the status of liberty of conscience. In any event, it is not a deficiency in the argument, in my opinion. Conscience does demand a special respect, and that is because of what conscience is and the value that it has objectively. My main aim in discussing this aspect of Rawls's thought is to make the positive point that appeal to the objective value and importance of certain sorts of excellence is important to the grounding of the priority of liberty of conscience.

3. Church, State, and Culture

The grounding I have proposed is not the only excellence-based grounding that can be considered for the strong protection liberals typically advocate for civil liberties. One that is importantly different from mine has been proposed by Joseph Raz. It will be instructive to examine the difference, which is reflected in Raz's claim that "the importance of the liberal rights is in their service to the public good," and specifically "to the promotion and protection of a certain public culture."[34]

31. Rawls, *Political Liberalism*. The formulation is from p. 293; the arguments regarding freedom of conscience are in pp. 310–24.

32. Rawls, *Political Liberalism*, p. 19.

33. Rawls, *Political Liberalism*, pp. 299–304.

34. Raz, *The Morality of Freedom*, p. 256.

Taken by itself, that claim might suggest that Raz advocates a communitarian rather than an individualistic basis for liberal rights; but he is not so easily placed on that spectrum. The character of the public culture he proposes to promote is shaped by the requirements of an ideal of personal autonomy. This is largely an ideal of individual life, but in a way that will shortly come to our attention it is also "in part a social ideal."[35] And in any event, according to Raz, individual ideals require particular cultural contexts for their realization.

In chapter 11, section 5, I indicated my support for an ideal of individual autonomy that includes the traits of responsibility, moral competence, a critical stance, and caring about important goods for their own sake. I imagine that all of those traits would be included in Raz's ideal of autonomy, though he does not emphasize all of them. His ideal of autonomy includes more than mine, however. It is "an ideal of self-creation," and it is essential to it that it can be realized only in a personal history of choice among "an adequate range of options," which Raz conceives as individually worthy but mutually incompatible alternatives.[36] The conditions that autonomy requires for its existence, according to Raz, are three: "appropriate mental abilities, an adequate range of options, and independence," which consists in freedom from coercion and manipulation.[37] Raz's main reason for defending the liberal rights is that they are important for assuring these necessary conditions of autonomy.

My principal disagreement with Raz has to do with the "adequate range of options," which is not a requirement of my ideal of autonomy. I do agree that there are characteristic excellences, and great ones, of lives that are autonomous in Raz's sense; and I personally much prefer living in a society that provides the sort of range of choices that he favors. But my conception of autonomy is meant to be a possible ingredient in a wider range of religious, moral, and social ideals than Raz's; and I am not convinced that a type of culture that provides the range of options Raz demands is objectively superior to all those that do not. Raz acknowledges that autonomy, in his sense, is "inconsistent with various alternative forms of valuable lives."[38] On the other hand, he also assumes, without argument, that a culture that "does not support autonomy" will be "inferior" to a liberal culture that does.[39] Why should he not rather suppose that the excellences that may be realized in such diverse cultures are incommensurable with each other, as he thinks that alternative goods often are?[40]

35. Raz, *The Morality of Freedom*, pp. 246, 265, 378. In defending liberties for the sake of an ideal of personal autonomy, Raz's argument is similar to J. S. Mill's argument for liberty, which was the subject of a brief comment in section 2. But Raz's argument, though it has a teleological aspect, is not designed, as Mill's is, to find its home in a utilitarian or consequentialist ethical theory (see Raz, *The Morality of Freedom*, chap. 11).

36. Raz, *The Morality of Freedom*, pp. 370, 372, 395–99.

37. Raz, *The Morality of Freedom*, pp. 372, 377f. There is something to be said for advocating freedom from manipulation as well as from coercion, but, in the interest of brevity, I will not take up the complex topic of manipulation here.

38. Raz, *The Morality of Freedom*, p. 395.

39. Raz, *The Morality of Freedom*, p. 423.

40. Raz, *The Morality of Freedom*, pp. 321–66, 395–99.

Reflection on what is known about morally and religiously homogeneous cultures should make us hesitant, I think, to rank them all as objectively inferior to pluralistic cultures. Anthropologists tell us how in preliterate societies religion is so inextricably interwoven with other aspects of the culture that even to speak of religion as a separate category is to import an alien conception from our life into the understanding of theirs. Students of religion are charmed, and sometimes inspired, by the way in which religion has permeated everyday life through total cultural acceptance in many times and places, even in more complex and developed traditions such as those of Christianity. And we see that this permeation was made possible by the shared religious commitment of a complete society, and is not possible, in the same way, in a pluralistic society. By contrast, it is a well-known feature of "secularized" societies that social practices and realms of interaction are isolated from each other—the worlds of work from those of religion and family, for example. This facilitates our working together in a pluralistic society, but it also has the consequence that we find it difficult to view many areas of our common life in the framework of as richly detailed and as comprehensively integrated an ethical outlook as may be applied to all of life in a more homogeneous culture.

So there is something to be said for a morally and religiously homogeneous society. I am personally addicted to a pluralistic society with rather fluid boundaries between the diverse traditions in it. I agree with Raz that such a society has great attractions in what it makes possible, both in the awareness of human potentialities and achievements and in the development of what Raz calls personal autonomy. And even if we wanted to, most of us will not be able to avoid living in a society that is more or less of this type. Nevertheless, I think that something of great value may be lost thereby. We cannot reasonably hope to enjoy in a pluralistic society *all* the advantages of a more homogeneous society. "There is no social world without loss," as Rawls puts it.[41] Some social arrangements seem to have few advantages, but all have disadvantages.

I do not believe that what is lost in establishing a pluralistic society is more important than what is gained,[42] but I also do not want to rest my argument for civil liberties on the view, to which Raz seems committed, that what is lost is less important. I am not convinced of any objective rank ordering in the matter, and I do not think any rank order is likely to command as wide an assent as we should want in the foundations of a constitutional argument. I think the badness of coercing, or trying to coerce, a person's conscience provides a much stronger and more intuitive foundation for the argument.

The badness of coercion also plays a part in Raz's argument. One of the necessary conditions of autonomy, as he sees it, is the freedom from coercion and manipulation that he calls independence. Society's not coercing individuals in their choice among significant and worthwhile options is not just a *means*, causally understood, to autonomy; it is part of what *constitutes* autonomy, in Raz's view. For this

---

41. Ascribing the idea to Isaiah Berlin; Rawls, *Political Liberalism*, p. 197.

42. I have argued elsewhere that "a pluralistic society is not a less favorable environment than a religiously homogeneous society" for the kind of spiritual pilgrimage to which I think Christians, at least, should aspire; see Adams, "Religious Ethics in a Pluralistic Society," p. 110f.

reason, he says, "autonomy is in part a social ideal. It designates one aspect of the proper relations between people."[43] This is a perceptive remark. Coercion is not only a violation of an individual person; it also constitutes a bad relationship between the persons involved, and we ought to care about the excellence of our personal and institutional relationships. That is a further reason for the state to abstain rigorously from coercing persons' consciences.

That is not, however, the reason that is emphasized in my defense of civil liberties. Raz's argument at this point has a teleological structure. Noncoerciveness is an important feature of both the "autonomy" and the "public culture" to which Raz aspires. In order to achieve these aspirations the state should be noncoercive in relation to the choices of its citizens (so long as they do not seriously harm others). This is not a bad argument, but I want an argument that will appeal more strongly to people who may not fully share Raz's ideals of public culture and individual choice. I want to argue that it would be wrong to suppress or abridge liberty of conscience in order to achieve a morally and religiously homogeneous culture, even if you believe that a more homogenous culture would be better on the whole than a pluralistic one. I therefore want an argument for upholding freedom of conscience even if it is not conducive to the form of public culture that you think the very best. This will not be a teleologically structured argument, but will rather appeal to what is sometimes called an "agent-centered constraint." That is, it will not be an argument for aiming at a certain result, but rather for not doing acts of a certain kind. What it seeks to protect is not a goal to be achieved, but a value that must be respected, given that it exists. The argument is that infringing the liberty of conscience is a violation of the sacred inasmuch as it violates persons, and what is most important to their excellence, and that something of this character is appropriately prohibited under almost any circumstances, even to achieve a great good.

It is interesting that Raz gives an argument that seems to be of just this sort in a different but related context. He holds that the state ought to refrain from coercive intervention to discourage morally objectionable behavior unless the behavior is harmful to someone other than the agent. Why? Because "the means used, coercive interference, violates the autonomy of its victim."[44] Here is a means that ought not to be used even to prevent a decidedly nonideal state of affairs. Raz himself may feel no need for this more peremptory type of justification for the protection of the more highly valued civil liberties; but I think in fact it is important, as those most tempted to compromise civil liberties are likely to have social ideals rather different from Raz's, but may still recognize that the coercion of a person's conscience is a horrible thing for the state to do.[45]

It is important that the type of argument I have proposed for the defense of liberty of conscience can be seen as a very strong argument from many *religious* points

---

43. Raz, *The Morality of Freedom*, p. 378.

44. Raz, *The Morality of Freedom*, p. 418. Raz thinks manipulation should be restrained by the same principles as coercion (ibid., p. 420).

45. A desire for a similarly peremptory argument for liberty of conscience seems to be reflected in Rawls, *Political Liberalism*, pp. 309–12.

of view.[46] It is far too often taken for granted, in discussions of this topic, that religious toleration, and religious liberty for all, can be no more than a second best for serious religious believers, on the assumption that they must wish that state authority would suppress all competing faiths and compel everyone to adhere to *their* favored religion. Obviously religion has all too often motivated such intolerance. Religious persecution may be the single most demoralizing aspect of the history of our civilization. Undoubtedly such persecution has commonly been seen by its perpetrators as justified in the interest of maintaining the values of a religiously homogeneous society. But there are also central aspects of the main religious traditions that lead to condemnation of persecution, and that is what my argument is meant to pick up. To the extent that these traditions stress, as in general they do, that the main thing of real worth in religious observance is sincere and willing adherence, devotion, loyalty, worship, and service, they cannot see value in coerced religious conformity.[47] They must rather view attempts to coerce persons to adhere to a religion as a violation of the sacred, an assault on faculties, functions, and processes of the greatest religious importance.

It is possible, no doubt, that some religious persons will reason that even though coerced adherence to a religion is of no value in itself, it may be justified as leading in the long run to advantages for the one true religion (theirs). To this it is possible to respond, in most religious traditions, that it is wrong to do evil that good may come, *especially* in matters of religion. The symbolic value of action is paramount in religion, as perhaps nowhere else. In theistic perspective one may say that God can take care of God's own cause. It is by no means honoring to God to suggest that God's cause is served by the most blatant violation of the most sacred capacities of human persons.

What I have just sketched is a religious debate that can take place in most religious traditions, and has taken place in several. It is a debate in which I think the cause of freedom of conscience can prevail—though it would of course be presumptuous for me to pretend to adjudicate the debate in any tradition but my own. Liberty of conscience is, among other things, a religious idea, and the sacredness of persons' consciences, to which my argument appeals, is a religious idea.[48] Historically, indeed, liberty of conscience owes much to the religious sense of the sacredness of

---

46. It is similar, for instance, to the argument of the Second Vatican Council's "Declaration on Religious Freedom," which "declares that the right to religious freedom has its foundation in the very dignity of the human person," and in the solemnity of the obligation to seek and follow religious truth (Abbott, ed., *The Documents of Vatican II*, p. 679; cf. p. 675). See also Murray, *Religious Liberty*, pp. 230–42.

47. Cf. Locke, *Epistola de Tolerantia*, pp. 68–69: "True and saving religion consists in the inward faith of the mind, without which nothing has any value with God; and such is the nature of human understanding, that it cannot be compelled by any outward force." (I have emended Gough's translation at one place.) Likewise the Second Vatican Council's "Declaration on Religious Freedom" (chap. 2, section 10) states: "The act of faith is of its very nature a free act. . . . It is therefore completely in accord with the nature of faith that in matters religious every manner of coercion on the part of men should be excluded" (Abbott, ed., *The Documents of Vatican II*, p. 689f.). A similar point can be made about coerced conformity to *moral* ideals; cf. Hart, *Law, Liberty, and Morality*, p. 57.

48. Cf. the comment of Franklin Littell in Abbott, ed., *The Documents of Vatican II*, p. 698: "The case for religious freedom does not begin with politics but with religion."

conscience, and to the growing belief, in contexts of religious disagreement, that it is more important, in religious as well as secular perspective, to secure the religious freedom of all than to try to impose one's own religion on the whole society.[49]

In arguing for liberty of conscience as a matter of refraining from violating something sacred, I have cast the issue of civil liberty as a religious issue. And so it is, in the broad sense of 'religious' in which Ronald Dworkin has held that "a belief in the objective and intrinsic importance of human life has a distinctly religious content."[50] Those who wish to preserve religious neutrality on constitutional questions may wish to avoid the term 'religious' here. What cannot be avoided, I think, are decisions regarding at least a functional equivalent of the sacred. We face the question whether anything in human life (and if so, what) has a sufficiently exalted, profound, and important value to lay a fairly peremptory claim on us to a much higher level of legal protection than, for example, property rights. A constitutional order cannot be neutral on that question. I have argued that it is inescapably a question of the good, and my theory is one which (with many religious outlooks) does not make a sharp distinction between religious and moral questions of the good.[51]

That the reason I have urged for protecting freedom of conscience is at most *broadly* religious must be emphasized. One need not believe in God or adhere to any traditional religion to hold conscience sacred in the relevant sense. Adherents of a wide variety of outlooks, some of them quite secular by ordinary standards, can agree that conscience claims and deserves respect of a higher order than most other interests do, and that we owe such respect to other people's consciences as well as our own.

According such priority to freedom of conscience may face opposition from some religious traditions or from those who are suspicious of moral and religious earnestness. We face the question whether special constitutional protection for freedom of conscience itself involves an invidious religious discrimination or an "establishment of religion." To this I think we must reply that the state cannot maintain neutrality on all religious issues, except in a narrower sense of 'religious'. The question how strongly freedom of conscience should be protected is a broadly religious issue on which one can hardly avoid taking a stand in framing a constitution for a democratic society. Strong protection of such freedom is doubtless a benefit to the morally and spiritually serious for which those who are less serious may at times have to bear some cost. On the other hand, according lower priority to freedom of conscience might well lead to the more serious suffering a particularly odious sort of assault on their integrity.

This is not to deny that there are ways in which the state should be neutral on religious issues. For one thing, the liberty of conscience should certainly include the freedom to express views denying its value, and the value of any of the principles

---

49. Cf. Rawls, *Political Liberalism*, pp. xxiii–xxvi; Raz, *The Morality of Freedom*, p. 251f.

50. Dworkin, *Life's Dominion*, p. 163.

51. I will not offer here a general view of the place of religion in public life. I have said something on the subject in Adams, "Religion after Babel" and "Religious Ethics in a Pluralistic Society." The detailed and moderate treatment of it in Greenawalt, *Private Consciences and Public Reasons*, seems to me particularly illuminating and generally plausible.

that have been proposed as supporting it. In addition, I will shortly argue that there is good reason to exclude any governmental establishment of religion, if 'religion' is understood in a narrow enough sense.

These points bear on the advisability of using a broad sense of 'religious' in constitutional argument in an American context, as Ronald Dworkin does in *Life's Dominion*. The First Amendment to the Constitution of the United States contains two clauses dealing with religion, one prohibiting an "establishment of religion" and the other assuring the "free exercise" of religion. I leave it to experts in jurisprudence to debate whether 'religion' should be understood in the same sense in the two clauses;[52] but if it should, and if the no establishment clause requires government neutrality on whatever issues are religious in the sense of that clause, then my argument to this point implies that it must be a narrow sense, for there is no chance of a government remaining neutral on all issues that are religious in Dworkin's broad sense. This is not at all to deny that a strong constitutional protection of freedom of conscience ought to extend to the issues that Dworkin considers broadly religious, and I certainly do not deny that it is intellectually illuminating to think of them as fundamentally religious. The point is rather that strong constitutional protection of liberty of conscience ought to extend to a wider range of issues than those on which government can remain strictly neutral.

In what sense, then, can and should a state avoid any establishment of religion? It is no accident that this question is often discussed in terms of "separation of church and state," as the need for avoiding establishment is strongly connected with religious institutions and traditions. What are the evils prevented by prohibiting an establishment of religion? In large part, of course, support for the no establishment clause is inspired by the fear that a government that supports an established church will persecute people who belong to other religious groups, or to none, as has happened only too often. To this extent the no establishment clause serves the ends of the free exercise clause, and I agree with the moral priority which that order of things assigns to the latter. As a leading legal scholar has put it, "The most basic defense of separation of church and state is that it is conducive to religious liberty; religious liberty is considered *more fundamental* than nonestablishment of religion."[53]

The evils to be avoided may be subtler than persecution. Even where there is no actual religious persecution, individuals can be grievously wronged by acts that symbolically identify the state, or subinstitutions of it, with a particular religious institution or tradition (or with an antireligious one, as has happened in some Marxist states). The crucial underlying issue here is the relation between religious identity and civic identity. Membership in a religious institution, or adherence to a religious tradition, commonly plays a large part in a person's sense of "who she is"; and thus we speak of "religious identity." Something similar can happen with adherence to an ideology such as Marxism that is secular, and not religious in a narrow sense. Coercing a person to give up something that is a part of her "identity" in this sense is certainly a violation of the person, but pressures that stop short of coercion and

52. Cf. Greenawalt, "Religion as a Concept in Constitutional Law."
53. Greenawalt, *Private Consciences and Public Reasons*, p. 67.

violation can still be harmful and highly offensive. The latter is true of actions that require a person to choose between her religious identity and her civic identity.

The issue of school-sponsored prayer in American public schools furnishes an obvious example. It is important to the issue that public schools in the United States are strongly connected with civic identity. They are perceived by children and adults as places where children are initiated into being American. Students from abroad who do not intend to become Americans are also welcomed (we hope) in such schools, but physical or symbolic exclusion from the school community would be for most children a stinging denial of their developing civic identity as Americans. That is exactly what will happen if the school sponsors prayers that any of the children perceive as incompatible with their religious (or nonreligious) identity. If such children participate in the prayers, they do violence to their own religious identity. If they opt out of the prayers, they separate themselves symbolically (and perhaps physically, for the duration of the prayers) from the community of the school which sponsors the prayers. Prayer is heavily charged with symbolic significance; that's much of the point of it. There is no way that an American public school that sponsors prayers can fail to make participation in the prayers symbolic of the civic identity that the school is helping its pupils to develop.

What's so bad, one might ask, about a symbolic opting out of an aspect of civic identity? Why shouldn't children learn early to resist certain aspects of their society's culture? Perhaps they should, but forcing people to opt out of civic identity in order to preserve their religious identity is extremely threatening and quite sinister, because both types of identity are so important to who we are, and because civic identity is so important to what we can expect of each other. We are only too familiar with the ways in which fusion of civic and religious identities has led in various times and places to persecution, and even genocide, directed against those who were denied full participation in the civic identity because of their religious identity.

As this suggests, I believe the forms of governmental establishment or sponsorship of religion (or of any personal identity–constituting ideology) that should be strenuously avoided are those that tend to conflate civic identity symbolically with a religious or ideological identity. Just which governmental acts should be avoided for this reason must be left to discernment of the significance, including especially the symbolic significance, that the acts would have in their actual or likely cultural context. The "wall of separation" between church and state currently maintained by the courts of the United States may include more extensive prohibitions than could be justified in detail by the sort of argument I have offered, but I suspect it serves pretty well to protect the goods that should be protected by it. It is probably safer to have more separation than we absolutely need.

If the no establishment clause thus gets a less peremptory justification, and a more contextually variable interpretation, than the free exercise clause, that is as it should be. The latter enshrines essential rights; the former is less universally necessary. It would be empirically ridiculous to claim that there cannot be a comparatively free and just society with an established church—though an established church can also be a disaster both for human rights and for religion. A just appreciation of the values at stake will also suggest that the state should take more pains to avoid disadvantaging any religious body than to avoid advantaging any. For religious communities are so important to the practice of most religions that placing undue burdens on religious organizations threatens to impair the value of freedom of religious conscience to individuals who possess it.[54]

It is important for my present argument that the reasons I have given for separating church and state do not demand complete neutrality of the government on all issues about excellence, or even on all issues that can be seen as broadly religious. This is good because, as I have argued, such neutrality is not possible for any state, and not all the neutrality that may be possible would be good. If the government is affiliated with, say the Presbyterian Church, and you are a Roman Catholic, a Baptist, a Muslim, or an atheist—or if the administration of your public school sponsors a prayer service for the student body during school hours and you are an atheist—you may reasonably feel that the state is saying symbolically that your religious identity does not fit with your civic identity. But you cannot reasonably draw such an inference if the government (without coercing you to act contrary to your belief) merely acts on a belief about the good, or a broadly religious conviction about the value of human life, which you do not share. That is because particular beliefs of that sort do not typically define personal identities in the same way as comprehensive ideologies and religious institutions and traditions do. Even if your contrary belief on the particular moral issue happens to be important to your personal moral or religious identity, it will not be plausible to say that the government's acting on such a belief makes it part of the civic identity of citizens of the state.[55] Of course it will be important for the government, and public figures, to abstain from symbolic acts that would needlessly effect such an inclusion of a belief in civic identity. Labeling of opposing views as "un-American," for example, offends not only against the civility of public discourse, but also against the equal right to civic identity, in much the same way that an establishment of religion might.

4. State Action to Protect and Promote the Good

Thus far I have argued that, because of the type of evil represented by coercion, the state should generally not treat conduct as criminal if it does not tend to cause harm, except to the agent, even if it is in some other way bad. I have argued for much stronger protection for liberty of conscience; my argument, appealing to the objective importance of certain aspects of human excellence, would probably justify similar protection for some other civil liberties. And I have argued that the state should avoid, so far as possible, acts that tend to define civic identity in ways that exclude the moral or religious identity of any citizen or group of citizens. This seems to leave plenty of room for the state to pursue the good in ways not ruled out by these arguments. Are there any other principles that should limit such pursuit?

Some liberals have wished to divide goods into two classes, one suitable for pursuit by the state, and one appropriate only for pursuit by individuals and volun-

---

tary associations, and none of the state's business. The distinction may be made on the basis of one class of goods being allegedly of a more "public" character, the other of a more "private" character. Or the goods eligible for promotion by the state may be those that are considered to be more or less common to the various views of the good that might be favored by different members of the society, because they are "things that it is rational to want whatever else one wants."[56]

I doubt the validity of any partition of goods in general into two such classes, based on the nature of the good in question. It is surely right for the state to promote some goods that are primarily for the benefit of individuals, and thus not exactly "public"; I will give examples shortly. And it seems (to me, at least) perfectly appropriate in many contexts for the state, or suborganizations of it, to pursue goods, such as literary excellence, that it may well not be "rational to want whatever else one wants." Subject to the restrictions implied by the arguments of sections 2 and 3, we must rely on a judgment that is sensitive to contextual factors as well as the nature of the goods in determining what goods it is wise for the state to protect and promote and when and how.

There remain general considerations, however, to which our judgment may refer. Three will be mentioned here.

1. There are important goods that are not likely to be pursued effectively and fairly if they are not pursued by the state. This may be because the magnitude of the efforts involved exceeds the capacities of individuals and private associations. Alternatively, it may be because of "free rider" problems which tempt individuals not to do their fair share unless the powers of the state are engaged. Where this consideration obtains, it is a strong (not always decisive) reason for the state to protect or promote the good in question.

2. When a good can be pursued effectively and fairly by individuals and private organizations, on the other hand, it will usually be best for the state to leave it to them to do so, for two main reasons. One is that decentralized processes of decision making, such as a free market, are commonly more efficient and more sensitive to a vast array of factors that deserve to be taken into account. The other reason is that a great part of the meaning and value of human life lies in individuals' pursuit of goods according to their own belief and motivation, and in their pursuit of the good in voluntary association with others. The value of the pursuit depends heavily on its sincere, self-motivated, voluntary character; and for that reason excellence is served by individuals and private associations acting with independence as much as they effectively can.[57]

3. If a political order is to be free rather than oppressive, the actions of the state must in general enjoy a large measure of public support. Unanimity is rarely obtainable, however; and strong support may in some ways be harder to obtain in a free political order than in one that restricts freedom of conscience. A free society is likely to be pluralistic with regard to religious, moral, and political convictions, a

56. Rawls, *A Theory of Justice*, p. 253; cf. pp. 62, 92. This is part of Rawls's characterization of "primary goods." He understands them somewhat differently in *Political Liberalism*.
57. The value and limitations of this argument are interestingly discussed in Hurka, *Perfectionism*, pp. 152–56.

considerable variety of which will usually be strongly represented in the society, making it more difficult to achieve agreement on many issues. This is a fact that must be reckoned with, and it will sometimes be inadvisable, or even impossible, for the state to pursue a good because it is too controversial, or simply not supported by enough of the population. It is not evident, however, that this is a more serious problem for the state's pursuit of excellence than for its pursuit of justice, as it does not seem to be systematically more difficult to obtain consensus about the one than about the other.[58] Consider the following sample questions, one about fairness and one about excellence:

(1) Would it be fair to have a more steeply graduated federal income tax in the United States than we have now?

(2) Was Marcel Duchamp a greater artist than Pablo Picasso?

Does anyone seriously think it would be easier to obtain general agreement among interested Americans about (1) than about (2)?

I propose now to illustrate the appropriateness, importance, and character of state action to protect and promote the good by discussion of questions arising in two areas concerned primarily with goods for individuals (welfare and education) and two areas concerned primarily with more "public" goods (the natural and cultural environments).

4.1 Welfare

There is a wide and largely cross-cultural consensus that the state has some degree of responsibility for assuring at least a minimum level of economic or physical well-being for its citizens. The good to be assured here is primarily individual rather than collective. It is controversial how much the state's responsibility should be, but there seems little prospect of accomplishing enough in this realm without considerable governmental action.

The aim is sometimes conceived in terms of assuring a minimum monetary income, which is a minimum level of all-purpose economic means to achieve whatever ends the individual may choose to pursue. However, this is rarely the only way in which the state's responsibility is conceived or discharged. The state, and its citizens, tend to be particularly concerned to assure certain specific goods—notably food, housing, and health care. Governmental action to sustain welfare in the United States includes specific programs to provide all three of these types of good (food stamps, public housing projects, and Medicaid, for example), and the resources committed to these programs are not made available to achieve other goods or ends for the same beneficiaries. It is not the aim of these policies to provide individuals with a basic level of effective freedom to pursue whatever ends they have; it is rather to provide them with specific goods that the public deems

---

58. Cf. Hurka, *Perfectionism*, p. 163. I grant, however, that inaction is less likely to be an appropriate response to controversy where justice is at stake than where excellence is.

particularly important (notably, physical survival and health). Is there good reason for public policy to have this aim?

I believe there is. Let us focus first on food and health care, the case of housing being interesting but less obvious. Among finite goods, the excellence of normal human life is one of those that claim our highest respect. The killing or maiming of a human person is a violation of something sacred, as I argued in chapter 4. So is it, though in lesser degree, if a society (or, arguably, humanity) allows one of its members to die or suffer serious impairment of health for lack of food or medical care that the society could well have provided. Like liberty of conscience, the rights to food and health care are rights that the state is obligated to assure out of respect for the central values of human life.

It is harder to argue that homelessness, in itself, is a violation of something sacred. Uncounted generations of our remote, but already human, ancestors doubtless lived without artificial shelter, and that was no disgrace. In a modern society, however, housing is important not only as protection from the elements (a consideration more important in Minnesota than in California), but also as a setting without which it is difficult or impossible to obtain privacy and to maintain stable employment and social relations. In short, it is a virtually necessary condition of many of the most basic excellences of normal modern life, and that is why the state should be concerned to assure this benefit to its inhabitants.

Where the values at stake are less important, the mere frustration of a desire, no matter how keenly felt, is not so grave an evil as lack of housing or health care;[59] and the state need not be so concerned to prevent frustration of desires as such. There probably are people who would choose unlimited access to whiskey in preference to housing, but the government does not have such a compelling reason to provide them with whiskey as it has to provide them with the housing that they value less. The reason is that the goods that the housing makes possible are (pretty uncontroversially) better and more important than any that large quantities of whiskey make possible. For this reason it is a disgrace to a prosperous country if many of its inhabitants have to sleep in the streets because they lack housing, but it is not similarly a disgrace if many of them cannot afford as much whiskey as they would like.

This is not to deny that the state should be concerned to assure all its people fair and sufficient opportunities to obtain means for the pursuit of their legitimate ends. In assuring fair distribution of economic resources, as such, the state should not in general be concerned to evaluate the comparative excellence of individuals' pursuits, so long as they do not violate the rights of others. Where public concerns fall primarily under the heading of fairness, it is generally reasonable to consider persons' interests as defined by their own aims, the ends that they have chosen. But concerns of *welfare* are different. They are about what is *good for* persons, and that cannot be understood in terms of their preferences, as I argued in chapter 3. For the state, I believe, the concerns of welfare do not belong primarily under the heading of fairness, but under those of humanity and solidarity. A citizen now destitute who enjoyed during most of his life a larger than average share of society's economic

59. On not overvaluing the satisfaction of desire, see also chapters 3 and 4.

resources, and foolishly squandered them on pursuits in which his fellow citizens see little worth, may be thought to have no claim of fairness to public assistance. Even so, it would be shameful for a prosperous society to leave him to die in the street rather than admit him to a hospital.

Of the reasons for not utterly abandoning such an improvident, those of humanity, pertaining to the value of human life, have been discussed previously. It remains to discuss the claims of *solidarity*, which is a main characteristic of a good society. There is anxiety in our society about a perceived weakening of the bonds and supports of community, and those most anxious about it often trace the problem to an undermining of social and cultural authority. I believe, however, that bonds of community are likeliest to be repaired, not by authoritarian measures, which are apt to foment strife, but rather by actions that express solidarity. A person who is abandoned by her society will have relatively little reason to respect its authorities (as I argued in chapter 10, section 3), and that is a point that solidarity addresses. It says to each member of society, not just "We will treat you fairly," but "You are one of us, and we will not abandon you if we can possibly avoid it." It involves the virtue of Hesed, its firmness of commitment to persons, and its readiness to make allowances for personal weaknesses and faults (see chapter 6, section 4).

There are many dimensions to solidarity, and this is not the place to discuss all of them. Solidarity certainly involves a receptiveness to others' reasonable requests for cooperation in the pursuit of their ends, but its strongest commitment is not to such cooperation. The autonomy of all would be badly compromised if all were committed never to let each other's projects fail. Solidarity's commitment not to abandon people cannot therefore be a commitment to all their aims, whatever they may be. It is rather a commitment to the most basic aspects of their good, as assessed by those whose actions are to express solidarity. And that is the province of well-being or welfare.

When public action to assure welfare is grounded in humanity and solidarity, it will be guided largely by public perception of what the recipients most urgently need for their good. In that respect it could be called paternalistic, but it does not raise the issue most often discussed under the heading of paternalism. For I do not mean to suggest that it is appropriate for the state to *coerce* the needy for their own supposed good, as has often been done. That is objectionable; but taking one's own conception of another person's good as one's guide in choosing what assistance to offer is quite different from taking it as grounds for coercing the other person, and the former does not entail the latter.[60]

4.2 Education

Among the benefits that a state is now seen as obligated to make available to all its people (at least up to a certain age), if resources are adequate, is education. There are many morally acceptable ways of organizing education, differing, for example,

---

60. The moral importance of the difference between coercive and noncoercive ways of promoting excellence is rightly stressed in Hurka, *Perfectionism*, pp. 158–60.

in the extent to which schools are organized and administered privately or by the state. Even with regard to private schools, however, it is generally agreed that the state has the responsibility and the right to set and enforce certain standards.

In discharging its educational responsibilities the state must inevitably be guided by views about what it would be *good* for students to learn. These cannot generally be the students' own views, as their views will not be well developed until far along in the educational process. The views of the students' parents may be well developed, and parents are entitled to a role in shaping the education of their children; but few of us think it appropriate for the state to abdicate all responsibility for decisions about the educational needs of children.

Many of these decisions can be based on judgments about what students need to learn in order to become good citizens or to participate effectively in the economy and thus be in a position to carry out other projects. Some such judgments may be controversial in detail, but few will deny that the state has a legitimate interest in these considerations, and a right and responsibility to base educational decisions on judgments about them. An education shaped by no aims but these would be impoverished, however. Much education is rightly aimed at enhancing students' capacity for well-being by developing abilities to enjoy things that are excellent. That is obviously an aim of education in literature, music, and the arts. Who would think that those planning English classes in public high schools should not be influenced by judgments of literary excellence in choosing books to be assigned? But a similar concern for excellence can and should affect the whole curriculum.

I think here of my Latin teacher, F. Niles Bacon, and of my last mathematics teacher, Fred Watson, in the public high school I attended—piety impels me to mention their names because, of the many wonderful teachers I had in the course of my education, they are the ones who meant the very most to me. That is because of the way in which they imparted to me an appreciation of the beauties and other intrinsic excellences of language, mathematics, and rigorous reasoning, an appreciation on which my mind has fed for over forty years now. And that is certainly one of the things they fully intended to do for me and for other students. To claim that, as servants of the state, they had no business having such an aim, because the state should be as neutral as possible on questions of excellence, would be carrying liberalism to the point of madness.

Most of the time, I believe, it is possible for state institutions, with good judgment, to aim at excellence in education without impinging in questionable ways on anyone's rights or interests. Some conflicts do arise in this area, however; and the relation of public education to religion, in particular, is a prominent constitutional issue in the United States. I have already enunciated the principles that I think most important here: that the state should avoid coercive pressure on any student's conscience, and should avoid actions whose symbolic force causes students' civic identity (or school identity) to exclude, or to be conflated with, the religious identity of any of them. These principles properly prevent public schools from sponsoring religious ceremonies or religious indoctrination.

The shoe may pinch tighter for liberals in the controversy about how the theory of evolution should be treated in biology classes in public schools. I take it that large parts (at least) of a broadly Darwinian theory of the evolution of biological species have the status of well-confirmed scientific theory. The theory has, in my terms, important intellectual excellences. Science educators have commonly wanted to teach the theory to elementary and secondary students in quite assertive terms, and sometimes in terms that some families have seen as disparaging to their religious beliefs. This has given rise to movements demanding that students studying the subject in public schools should be presented with a theistic alternative theory (called "creation science" in some versions) alongside the Darwinian theory. These demands, in turn, have been vehemently opposed—often, I think, from a belief that it would be outrageous for a school to expose students to something so unenlightened in a question of science.

This poses a difficult problem for educators who are convinced of the soundness of the Darwinian approach. On the one hand, it would surely corrupt the educational process to compel teachers to tell students something they believe to be false about the merits of an alternative view. On the other hand, there is a real danger here of excluding the religious identities of some students from the identity of a good student as defined by the school, and of exerting some degree of coercive pressure against their religious conscience.

The first point I want to make about this problem is that the inclination of many liberals to insist on teaching the Darwinian theory alone and without qualification must rest on considerations of epistemological *value* rather than of personal *freedom*—truth and confirmation being grounds of value in this context. To argue that children will be *freer* if the state makes them learn true science than if their parents make them learn pseudoscience (even if the children now think they'd rather learn what their parents want them to) smacks of ideas of "positive freedom" that liberals usually prefer to avoid. But if the issue is one of value rather than freedom, we must ask whether there is any good basis for privileging one side in the dispute against the other.

At this point we see a way in which contingencies of controversy in a society may affect what it is appropriate for public educators to do by way of promoting intellectual excellence. The intellectual value of the Darwinian theory is good enough reason to teach it in the public schools—at least as long as it is not a subject of religious or quasi-religious controversy. When the controversy has arisen, however, public institutions need a way of treating the convictions of all parties with respect. If the state takes the position that the methods and results of modern natural science are uniquely rational and therefore should be privileged above religious thought, this treats the central convictions of some citizens with a contempt that threatens to exacerbate social conflict, and to offend against the religious identities of some students in much the same way that school-sponsored prayer does.

There is probably no ideal solution to this problem; and I have some diffidence in writing of possible solutions, because I am no expert in biology or in science education. An elaborate classroom presentation of "creation science" seems hardly justified. On the other hand, I have the impression that the earlier stages of science education in America tend to be more authoritarian and dogmatic than excellence would demand. A less authoritarian approach, viewing science as (among other things) a historically contingent cultural enterprise, might deal better with the problem, presenting in undogmatic terms what most biologists think is well confirmed about evolution, and why, and minimizing pressure on students to give up religiously grounded objections they may have against Darwinian theories. Some forms of creationism may receive, more easily than others, a respectful explicit discussion in such a context.[61] Ideally there would be no expression of contempt for any of the views in the discussion.[62]

4.3 The Natural Environment

The problems of protecting and preserving our natural environment are too large and complex to be dealt with mainly by private action. If states do not act to protect important values, serious, and in some cases irreparable, damage will be done. Indeed, terrible damage has already been done. The case for state action is compelling.

The goods to be protected by the state in this realm are not private or individual goods. There is truly private enjoyment of environmental goods, made possible by private landholdings, for instance; but it should not be a main concern of public environmental policy to protect that for its own sake. One of the main reasons for state protection of the natural environment is that many environmental goods are of such a nature that they cannot be enjoyed by anyone unless they are enjoyed by a whole population of people. This is obviously true of clean air and clean water. It is doubtless to defend these essentially public goods, as by policies controlling pollution and "greenhouse gases" and protecting the ozone layer, that state action in the environmental realm is most urgently needed.

They do not present the most interesting case, however, for study of the relation of the good to human life in general and to politics in particular. For the environmental goods just mentioned can be understood in terms of what is good for human beings, and it is primarily human good that the state is protecting in protecting them. But that is not clearly true of all environmental goods. In particular, it is not clearly true of the preservation of biological species.

Writers on environmental ethics disagree about the proper grounds for their shared commitment to preventing wholesale extinctions of species. It is clear that such extinctions constitute a loss of resources that could be valuable to humans, and some argue that that is reason enough for the protection of species.[63] Others think it important to appeal to a "widely shared intuition that nonhuman species possess intrinsic value."[64] The latter view seems to me correct. Even if a just calculation of the human benefits of biological diversity would justify state intervention to protect the diversity, that is surely not the whole motivation, and probably not the main motivation, of those who urge such intervention. There is not likely to be effective

---

61. Cf. Greenawalt, *Private Consciences and Public Reasons*, p. 208 n. 20.
62. The issue of evolution is not unique in its difficulty for the schools. Greenawalt argues plausibly that it may be impossible for schools to maintain effective neutrality among conflicting views of the value of a gay sexual lifestyle. Even if schools "avoid the subject altogether, . . . the implicit message may be that gays are deviants whose lifestyle is unhealthy and wrong" (*Private Consciences and Public Reasons*, p. 80).
63. This view is defended in Norton, "On the Inherent Danger of Undervaluing Species."
64. Callicott, "On the Intrinsic Value of Nonhuman Species," p. 140.

state action to prevent the extinction of species unless it is largely grounded in a belief in the intrinsic value of the species. And I believe they do possess such value. Biological diversity is part of the beauty of the world, and diverse species, and their interrelations, manifest diverse excellences of life. As I argued in chapter 4, section 4, there is something appalling, a sort of violation of the sacred, in knowingly causing the extinction of a biological kind.

The excellence of biological species is sometimes assimilated to aesthetic value,[65] and I agree that extinction of a species and destruction of a great work of art are horrible in roughly the same way (as I argued in chapter 4, section 4). But properly aesthetic value has a tighter connection with values of human experience than I think the excellence of natural kinds does (which is not to say that the excellence of a work of art resides solely in the eye or mind of the beholder).

At this point a conception of the good as transcending the human has a distinct advantage over purely humanistic conceptions that insist on tracing all value to human preferences and the goods of human life. The latter sort of view is hard-pressed to account for the values of nature and the kind of respect many of us intuitively think we owe them. This is not to say that only a theistic view like mine can account for such values, but the question of the intrinsic value of natural objects and natural kinds is at any rate a broadly religious question.

It can be viewed as a nonsectarian question, however, as it does not of itself define personal religious identities; and in any event the state can hardly avoid taking a stand on it, either actively or by default. I believe it is appropriate for the state to use its powers to prevent our being collectively responsible for the violation of great excellences that is involved in causing the extinction of biological kinds. It is no violation of the rights of citizens for the state to act on such a consideration. Indeed, it may be a morally important right of citizens to be able to seek public action on such a consideration, if that is the only way they can effectively avoid their society's collectively destroying something of great value that ought to be respected.

The issue of preserving biological species deserves comparison at this point with that of abortion. I believe that legal prohibition of abortions, and governmental attempts to make it impossible for women to obtain them, violate rights that women should be assured, although I grant that abortions may violate values of human life that partake of the sacred.[66] The issues differ in two crucial respects, however. One is that each abortion is caused by the concerted action of a few individuals, whereas extinctions of species are generally caused by the uncoordinated actions of many. We are collectively responsible for extinctions in a way in which we are not collectively responsible for abortions. The other and more important difference is that prohibition or prevention of abortion impinges on the lives of women at a particularly intimate level and interferes radically with their control of the form of their own lives and personal relationships, whereas the action of the state in protecting biological kinds need not impinge on any class of persons in as personally violative

---

65. For instance, in the careful argument of Sober, "Philosophical Problems for Environmentalism."

66. See chapter 4, sections 4 and 6.

a way.[67] (Abortion is another case in which the difference between coercion or compulsion and assistance is crucial; the state does not offend against the rights of women if, out of regard for the value of human life, it encourages them to bear children they have conceived, by increasing public financial aid to dependent children.)

The typical costs of environmental protection are of two sorts. There are merely economic costs, which should be distributed as fairly as possible. They do not in general violate anything that deserves such strong protection as to exclude action to preserve environmental values. (The economic issues may be much more urgent in developing economies, but it is not my intention to treat every aspect of environmental ethics in this illustrative discussion.) Sometimes there are also inescapable cultural costs of environmental action. The way of life of some groups of loggers or fishermen may have to disappear sooner rather than later if certain species are to be preserved. These costs impinge on higher values than the merely economic, but I think they are not higher than the values of the natural environment. They are quite comparable excellences that can be thrown into the scales together for political deliberation.

4.4 The Cultural Environment

I have just alluded to cultural values that may rightly be taken into account in public deliberations. The promotion or preservation of cultural values is frequently an object of action by the state. Some of the values are aesthetic, as when the state provides support for the arts. Some are values of sociability, as when urban planning structures space to facilitate certain kinds of interaction. Some, such as the values of historic preservation and museums of natural history, may be less easily labeled. An interesting case is that of the values of human achievement which inspire a political society to support immense projects such as that of landing a human being on the moon. Excellence will rarely be the only consideration in these matters. Instrumental values are usually a factor, and the symbolism of national and local identity is apt to be important too, but I believe that in most cases intrinsic excellences are among the values intentionally promoted, and rightly so.

Questions can be raised about the wisdom or the appropriateness of each of these public endeavors. Some may be simply too expensive. Others might be better left to private action. But few of us would wish the state to abandon them all. State action seems particularly appropriate when private action would probably not be effective, or when any benefits must be enjoyed by a whole population if they are enjoyed by anyone. Both of these reasons apply, for instance, to preserving the scenic values (aesthetic excellences) of a townscape or agricultural landscape through zoning regulations. (The value of the agricultural landscape is perhaps of mixed natural and cultural character, but nothing hangs on that for our discussion.)

---

67. The juxtaposition of the issues of abortion and environmental preservation is not novel. Cf. Rawls, *Political Liberalism*, p. 246. The views Rawls expresses there about what the state may and may not rightly do in the two cases are similar to mine. His attempt to ground the difference of treatment of the cases in the claim that "the status of the natural world and our proper relation to it is not a constitutional essential or a basic question of justice," as he thinks the issues involved in abortion are, seems to me inadequately defended.

It remains the main point to be made on this topic that the excellence of what is to be promoted or preserved is a legitimate consideration for the cultural policy of a state. We rightly want our neighborhoods, shopping districts, and rural land-scapes to be beautiful rather than ugly; we also want good rather than mediocre art and music to be available to us; and we take action accordingly. People's tastes and priorities differ, of course. The government of a free society will be responsive to the preferences of citizens in such matters, and will rightly be reluctant or even unable to override very strongly backed objections to state support of cultural projects that may otherwise seem excellent. What I want to insist is simply that it is no good objection at all to state support of a cultural project that the reasons for it appeal essentially to considerations of excellence.

IV

THE EPISTEMOLOGY
OF VALUE

15

REVELATION OF THE GOOD

1. The Metaphysics and the Epistemology of Value

A distinction was introduced in chapter 1 between the semantics and the metaphysics of value. The semantics of value has to do with the meaning of evaluative terms, whereas the metaphysics of value has to do with the nature of value or with what there is in reality corresponding to our evaluative assertions if they are true. To these branches of higher order ethical theory we can add the epistemology of value, which deals with the nature and grounds of evaluative beliefs[1] (and of evaluative knowledge, if there is any).[2]

We have already had occasion to treat some epistemological topics, especially in chapter 2, sections 3 and 4, and chapter 12, section 3, but systematic treatment of the epistemology of value has been reserved for the end of the book. This place-

---

1. For convenience, in this chapter, where not otherwise indicated, 'evaluative beliefs' will be taken to signify beliefs about right and wrong as well as about good and bad, and beliefs about non-moral as well as moral values—and likewise for other phrases formed with 'evaluative'.

2. I am obviously committed to the thesis that there are true evaluative beliefs. Whether any of them constitute knowledge is a question in the epistemology of value which I will not try to answer here. In agreement with ordinary language, I will speak casually of evaluative knowledge, but I think nothing important in this book depends on that classification.

ment reflects the fact that the framework for ethics developed here is not dominated by epistemological theses. We would choose a different order if we expected epistemology to provide us with a few sharply delineated types of evidence or grounds on which all justified evaluative beliefs must be based. In that case we should presumably begin by articulating and establishing those epistemological principles in order to be sure that everything else we say is properly grounded in them, especially if we suspect that many of the evaluative beliefs on which we would otherwise rely may not be grounded in the epistemologically privileged way. I believe, however, that epistemology is not well fitted to serve us in that way, in this or in most other areas.

As will be explained in section 2, my epistemology of value advises us to rely on a complex practice of forming evaluative beliefs in ways that we had mostly learned before we ever studied moral philosophy, though they can and should be refined and improved by philosophical reflection. I do not see any set of epistemological principles that can usefully serve as a screen or test that everything else must pass before being admitted for discussion in ethical theory. The formation of a wide variety of evaluative beliefs, many of them quite confident beliefs, must precede any useful reflections on the epistemology of value, as also on its semantics and metaphysics.

The metaphysics, epistemology, and semantics of value are closely related subjects. The shape of their interrelationship will differ in different metaethical theories. My epistemology of value has a largely semantical part, as will appear in section 2. A full development of Richard Boyd's naturalistic metaphysics of value (as I expounded it in chapter 2, section 2) would include his epistemology of value, since he holds that the properties that constitute value are to be identified in terms of their causal role in the formation of human beliefs about value. Boyd would presumably develop the metaphysics and the epistemology of value simultaneously. It makes sense, however, to develop the metaphysics first, and the epistemology afterward, when the standard of value is seen as transcendent and its identification is less tightly tied to our doxastic (belief-forming) mechanisms—especially if our primary interest is in the metaphysics.

This order of proceeding has some advantages insofar as our metaphysics of value has implications, or provides resources, for our epistemology of value. I will try to exploit such advantages in sections 3 and 4 of the present chapter. Section 2, however, presents a metaphysically spare account of how in general we form and reasonably hold evaluative beliefs. Section 3 takes up the possibility of accounting for widely held evaluative beliefs theologically, in terms of "general revelation." Section 4 continues the discussion of the idea of revelation, with reference to its potential contribution to understanding the relation between an infinite Good and the contingencies of human history. In this connection it will discuss the space that the ethical framework developed here provides for the "special" revelations claimed by different historic religious traditions, and for a measure of historical and cultural relativism.

The remainder of this first section of the chapter will address the following problem. It is widely believed that the adoption of religious theories about ethics will only add to the disturbing epistemological difficulties of ethical theory. If ethical truths are to be viewed as facts about God, won't the epistemological problems of theology be added to those of ethics? It is hard enough to know what is good and right; won't it be all the harder—perhaps even impossible—if we must first know that God exists, and what God is like, and what God has commanded? For all such knowledge of God is attended with deep epistemological difficulty, as philosophical theologians generally acknowledge, and often insist.

In response to this objection I will argue that the theistic framework for ethics that I favor burdens substantive ethical thinking with no epistemological problems that it does not already have. This is not to deny that my theory carries with it some issues about its own justification; that is true of any theory in the metaphysics of value. The crucial point is that my theory does not make those issues about itself into epistemological problems for ethics, because it does not require us to know anything about God, as such, before we can have knowledge, or adequately grounded belief, in ethics. Here we must remember that the account I have given of the *semantics* of the most general predicates of value is not specifically theological. I have not said that 'good' *means* the same as 'resembles (or faithfully images) God', for instance. What is determined by the meaning of 'good', I have claimed, is a *role* that must be filled by anything that is to be the nature of the good. What is the best candidate for this role is a question for the metaphysics, not the semantics, of morals. I have proposed a theistic hypothesis as to the best candidate. But one does not have to hold the correct hypothesis—or indeed any hypothesis at all—about the nature of goodness in order to understand the meaning of 'good' and to be a competent user of the word.

One also does not need any belief, let alone a correct one, about the nature of goodness in order to know much about what is good. On this epistemological point ethics is similar to the case of natural kinds, which I used as a model in developing my views on the semantics of value. There are many facts about water that have been known to virtually everyone throughout human history: that water is a liquid; that some substances dissolve in it; that it is needed for the growth of most, at least, of the plants that interest us; that humans drink it but cannot breathe it; and so forth. These facts have been known by people who held widely differing theories, or none at all, about the nature of water. And they were known for millennia before anyone could even have formulated the theory that most of believe to be true about the nature of water, that it is H_2O. Historically, no doubt, religious beliefs and concepts are much older than the concepts and theories of modern chemistry, and have influenced the development of ethical concepts. But many ethical beliefs are shared by people of widely varying religious beliefs, or none at all; and nothing in my theory bars me from ascribing shared ethical knowledge to those people.

Another parallel case can be drawn from the history of philosophical theology. Leibniz held a theological theory of the ontological status of the objects of logic and mathematics. He held that the way in which numbers and possibilities, for example, are eternally and necessarily there in reality, so that our thoughts can correspond with them, is that they exist in the divine understanding—that is, they are necessarily and eternally thought by God. This is a theory that has much to be said for it, but that is not our present concern.[3] Leibniz faced the objection that if the truths of

---

3. See Adams, *Leibniz: Determinist, Theist, Idealist*, chap. 7.

logic and mathematics are about thoughts in God's mind, it is impossible for an atheist to know them, which is manifestly false. He responded as follows:

> For in my opinion it is the divine understanding that makes the reality of the
> eternal Truths. . . . Every reality must be founded in something existent. It is
> true that an Atheist can be a Geometer. But if there were no God, there would
> be no object of Geometry. And without God, not only would there be nothing
> existent, but there would also be nothing possible. That does not make it
> impossible, however, for those who do not see the connection of all things with
> each other and with God, to understand certain sciences, without knowing their
> ultimate source, which is in God.[4]

In other words, one can know a lot of mathematics without a metaphysical understanding of what there is in reality for our mathematical thought to correspond to. Similarly, one can form sound beliefs in ethics without entering into theological or other metaphysical theories about what there is in reality for correct ethical beliefs to correspond to.

Indeed, I can go farther in this direction, and say that on my views in the semantics of morals, a considerable range of beliefs about what is good and what is wrong in detail must be prior in principle to sound theorizing about the nature of goodness and the nature of wrongness. This is not to deny that a child might be taught, very early in her moral education, some such principle as 'What's wrong is what God has told us not to do.' But the grounds for accepting a theory of the nature of goodness or wrongness will presuppose an understanding of the role to be filled by the nature; and in my account a lot of particular beliefs about what is good or what is wrong enter into the determination of that role.

This is a case in which "the order of knowing is not the same as the order of being," as a Scholastic philosopher might say. In the order of being, on my theory, the divine nature and the divine commands are prior, or at least foundational, in relation to mundane goodness and wrongness. In the order of knowing, however, one needs quite a range of beliefs about mundane goodness and wrongness in order to have a basis for my theory or any other about the nature of goodness and wrongness. Speaking of "the order of knowing" will be misleading, to be sure, if it suggests that the inferential path between these types of belief is a one-way street. Beliefs about the nature of goodness can rightly provide a basis for criticism and revision of lower order evaluative beliefs. The point on which I wish to insist is only that theories in the metaphysics of value must presuppose some evaluative beliefs of a lower order.

2. Evaluative Doxastic Practices

How do we—and how should we—form those presupposed evaluative beliefs of a lower order? I believe that such beliefs are typically a product of highly developed skills and habits that virtually all of us have acquired and have compelling reason to

---

4. Leibniz, *Theodicy*, section 184.

trust. Following William P. Alston, I will use the term 'doxastic practice' to refer to a suitably integrated set of such skills and habits, a system of ways of forming and holding beliefs, learned in a social context.[5] Alston speaks of distinguishable doxastic practices of sense perception, introspection, memory, rational intuition, and deductive and inductive reasoning as ways we have learned of forming beliefs. To this list we can add an evaluative doxastic practice, or perhaps several of them.

Alston speaks of a doxastic practice as "the exercise of a system or constellation of belief-forming habits or mechanisms, each realizing a function that yields beliefs with a certain kind of content from inputs of a certain type."[6] This is a helpful formulation, but I want to distance myself from one suggestion that it might be thought to carry. The terms 'mechanism' and 'function' might seem to connote a procedure of mathematical precision and determinateness, and that is no part of the conception of evaluative doxastic practices that I mean to embrace. I assume that evaluative doxastic practices rely heavily on tendencies and skills of generalizing, responding to resemblances, and innovating which cannot be reduced to any algorithm. I doubt that Alston assumes otherwise, but I may view doxastic practices as more fluid than he does.

A particularly helpful feature of Alston's formulation is its focus on "inputs" and outputs, the outputs being beliefs. The inputs may also be beliefs; in that case we may say that the mechanism or process is *inferential*. It is of great importance, however, that not all the inputs are beliefs; where they are not, we may say that the mechanism or process is *noninferential*.[7] Deductive inference is an obvious example of an inferential doxastic mechanism. Sense perception affords equally obvious examples of noninferential doxastic processes, in which we have learned to derive beliefs, not from other beliefs, but from our sensations. If we judge that Bill Clinton is on the TV now, or if we judge more cautiously that it looks like Bill Clinton on the TV screen now, in either case we have formed a belief on the basis of a sensation, exercising a skill that we have learned, of recognizing Clinton, or his image, on the basis of a visual sensation. We can agree about that, I believe, without agreeing on any developed theory of the nature of sense perception.

Evaluative doxastic practices involve both inferential and noninferential doxastic processes. Learning properly to form evaluative beliefs involves learning a complex network of implications among beliefs, and thus acquiring a tendency, for example, that would be apt to lead one from the belief that lying is wrong to the belief that it is good to teach children not to lie. But our evaluative competence is childish indeed if it does not go beyond the ability to accept evaluative beliefs that we have been taught and draw correct inferences from them. A mature and autonomous

---

5. Alston, *Perceiving God*, esp. chap. 4. Alston traces aspects of the idea to the work of Ludwig Wittgenstein and Thomas Reid. What I will say about doxastic practices agrees largely, but not entirely, with Alston's views, but I will not try to delineate here, in any systematic way, the areas of agreement and disagreement. Alston develops some aspects of the epistemology of doxastic practices much more fully than I will.

6. Alston, *Perceiving God*, p. 155.

7. 'Inferential' and 'noninferential' are my terms, not Alston's. He speaks of doxastic practices (not mechanisms) as "transformational" if all their inputs are beliefs, and as "generational" if some of their inputs are not beliefs. See Alston, *Perceiving God*, p. 157.

evaluative competence is responsive to a wide range of inputs that are not beliefs. These include feelings, emotions, inclinations, and desires. Just as something about a sensation helps us to recognize President Clinton or an image of him, so something about our own emotions may help us to recognize that something is good or bad. It is not that we form a belief about the emotion that we then use as evidence for the evaluative belief. The doxastic process takes the emotion itself as an input, rather than a belief about the emotion. We may not be able to characterize the emotion adequately except in terms of the evaluative belief, perhaps as a feeling that something would be wonderful or horrible.

To be sure (as Alston emphasizes),[8] any well-developed doxastic practice will include higher order processes of reflecting critically on one's own exercise of the practice. As part of one's self-critical reflection one may well form beliefs about the emotions and inclinations by which one has been influenced in forming evaluative beliefs. One's original evaluative belief may be tested by these higher order beliefs, but could probably not have been derived from them if it had not first been shaped by the original emotion or inclination. The higher order beliefs, moreover, are likely themselves to include evaluative beliefs (perhaps about the "appropriateness" of one's emotions), and to have been formed by noninferential processes (involving emotional "sensitivity," for example) as well as by inferential processes.

Some will think that reliance on feelings, emotions, inclinations, and desires as inputs discredits the claims of evaluative doxastic practices to objectivity, and thus undermines realism about values; for those states of mind are widely regarded as "subjective." In another way, however, this suspicion is at variance with common sense, which treats "good judgment" in evaluative issues as an objective matter, and assumes that it often depends on a sort of emotional sensitivity. No one will deny that there is more variability from person to person in the outputs of most evaluative doxastic practices than in those of sense perceptual doxastic practice. To that extent we must suppose that the former are less reliable than we generally take the latter to be—as we might well expect if the evaluative practices are tracing fragmentary resemblances to a transcendent Good. It does not follow that the evaluative practices are not worth relying on, or should not be given a metaphysically realistic interpretation. We rely on a wide range of medical diagnostic procedures, after all, and are realists about them, even though we are sure that some of them are much less reliable than others, and more subjective because of the ways in which they rely on noninferential doxastic processes in physicians.[9]

Traditional ways of speaking of evaluative doxastic processes in terms of "vision," "intuition," and a "moral sense" can be seen as supported by the important part played by noninferential doxastic processes that take feelings, emotions, inclinations, and desires as inputs. 'Intuition' is the most popular of these terms in present-day moral philosophy. 'Vision' may have more resonance in the Platonic tradition, and is suitable to the idea of imaging a transcendent Good, as vision is

---

8. Alston, *Perceiving God*, p. 158f.
9. This is not, of course, meant to be taken as a refutation of moral antirealism. It is part of a sketch of my own view.

the most adapted of our senses to the perception of very distant objects—though 'intuition' also carries in its Latin etymology the metaphor of seeing or looking. 'Moral sense' may be the most apt of these terms in relation to the actual character of most of the inputs of evaluative doxastic processes.

In using any of these terms it is important to avoid an implication they are sometimes thought to carry, that evaluative judgments are immediate data of something like sense perception. The formation of evaluative beliefs is almost always more complex than that, and inferential doxastic processes, with beliefs as inputs, may feed into it at the same time as noninferential doxastic processes with emotions and desires as inputs. At the same time, indeed, still other noninferential doxastic practices, with sense perceptions—for instance, of a person's face—as inputs, may feed into it. The giving of reasons plays a more central role in most evaluative doxastic practices than in sense perception. The reasons, however, are not just computed but weighed, and the weighing depends on "sensitivities" that involve feelings and inclinations as inputs.

Virtually all developed doxastic practices depend in various ways on beliefs that we already have when we exercise the practice. This is obvious where inferential doxastic processes are concerned, since they take beliefs as inputs from which the output beliefs are inferred. Our doxastic practices also depend, however, on "background beliefs," as Alston calls them, which condition our doxastic processes without exactly serving as premises for an inference. In forming perceptual beliefs, for example, with sensations as inputs, it is doubtless important that we believe that we have sense organs that are functioning normally, important also that we have lots of beliefs about the kinds of physical objects that may be perceived. These background beliefs are not premises from which our first-order perceptual belief is inferred, though they may serve as premises when we come to reflect critically on the process by which the first-order belief was formed. Background beliefs that are important in evaluative doxastic practices may include beliefs about one's own evaluative competence, one's "judgment," or one's "sensibility," and beliefs about the kinds of things being evaluated, as well as a large array of existing evaluative beliefs.

In relying on a doxastic practice one is thus relying not only on the beliefs that are now being formed in the practice but also on the many beliefs that function as inputs or background beliefs in the practice. How did we come by these beliefs? We formed some of them, of course, in our own earlier exercise of the practice; but others were taught to us as part of our initiation in the practice.

This brings us to another fundamental point about doxastic practices, which is that they are *social* practices. We, individually, invented virtually none of the doxastic practices that we use (unless the practices are individuated very narrowly indeed). The most fundamental doxastic practices, including a rich array of evaluative ones, were taught to us in childhood by our parents and other elders. And even those we have acquired later in life, in studying philosophy or textual criticism, for example, or in learning to use a microscope, were in virtually every case learned directly or indirectly from other people who practiced them before we did. As I will explain shortly, this is definitely not to say that doxastic practices are merely imitative; individual variations are often what interests us most in the exercise of them. But the practices, or the most complex of them, were developed not by individuals but by societies, and arguably respond to reality with a richness and subtlety that would be beyond the capacity of any human individual to invent "from scratch."

The teaching of a fundamental doxastic practice to children is at the same time the teaching of a linguistic practice, with its semantics, and also the teaching of some beliefs. In some cases the teacher will be most conscious of the linguistic instruction. One may think one is teaching a child the names of geometrical shapes, for example; and one is doing that. But at the same time one is teaching her to recognize those shapes by sight and touch; that is, one is teaching her noninferential doxastic processes, with sensations as inputs, for forming beliefs about shapes. At the same time also one is expressing, and trying to impart to the child, some of one's own beliefs about the shapes of certain objects.

Evaluative practices are more complex, and will be mastered by children at a later age, than sense perceptual practices. That is due to several factors. One is that the semantics of value (if I am right about it) assigns to values a complex role that children must learn from a wide variety of discourse. Another factor is that evaluative doxastic practice relies on inputs from emotional faculties and experiences that are absent or immature in young children whose visual and auditory acuity may be as good as it will ever be. The learning of evaluative linguistic and doxastic practices begins with children acquiring from their elders a number of particular evaluative beliefs about what is good and bad, right and wrong, naughty, and so forth. These beliefs are only partly understood, or partly developed, at first, because the child understands so little of the role of values, and therefore has so limited an ability to generalize reliably in his use of value concepts. However, some evaluative doxastic processes, such as that connected with 'tastes good' and 'tastes bad', being tightly tied to inputs of which young children are fully capable, may be quite developed in children at a very early age.

That learning evaluative linguistic and doxastic practices involves acquiring a number of evaluative beliefs should not surprise us, if I am right in claiming (as I did in chapter 1, section 2) that the role that the semantics of our evaluative language assigns to values is partly determined by the things that we regard as good. It may be that no *single* received opinion ascribing value to something is analytically true by virtue of the meaning of value predicates, but we could not abandon *all* received opinions on the subject without "changing the subject" of our supposedly evaluative discourse. In learning evaluative linguistic practices, therefore, we must acquire a stock of beliefs that can serve as inputs and background beliefs in evaluative doxastic practices, even though each of them is individually subject to criticism, revision, and possible replacement.

Having stressed the close connection between doxastic and linguistic practices, I must also emphasize that this does not imply a conventionalist view in the epistemology of value. The linguistic correctness of an utterance, which is determined by convention, must be distinguished from the truth of a belief, which is not in general determined by convention. This applies also to evaluative language and belief. A claim that a certain person is morally corrupt but in no way bad would pretty surely be linguistically incorrect because inconsistent with the conventions governing the use of 'morally corrupt' and 'bad'. But a claim that infanticide is not generally wrong as a method of population control can be debated as to its truth, having been admitted as linguistically in order, even though it contravenes a belief that most of us would count among those that collectively contribute to determining the role that is semantically assigned to moral wrongness. We just couldn't entertain too many such outrageous beliefs at once.

As these reflections indicate, it is important for moral realism that evaluative doxastic practices are not merely imitative, and do not require an uncritical adherence to socially received opinion. What one learns in learning such a practice is how to form one's *own* evaluative beliefs. Beliefs that one has acquired from others control the practice as internalized, and thus as one's own beliefs, rather than as other people's beliefs—though a certain respect for the views of others is likely also to be a part of the practice. One learns to rely, in forming one's evaluative beliefs, on one's own experiences and one's own feelings, emotions, desires, and inclinations. The results include, as we all know, a great deal of disagreement in evaluative beliefs. One has not really mastered the practice until one has learned how to conduct an evaluative disagreement, to hold up (rationally) one's end of an evaluative dispute, and also to criticize one's own views.

It is part of evaluative doxastic practice that an individual can criticize, or give reasons for rejecting, any received evaluative opinion. This is an expression of the "critical stance" that is part of the general intentional framework in which we use evaluative terms (at least where morality and excellence are concerned)—a point that was important to my argument for a transcendent Good in chapter 2, section 4. I am not defending a social conformist epistemology. The concept of a doxastic practice is not to be understood as a weapon for enforcing acceptance of received opinions, or a holistic "take it or leave it" attitude toward a socially established moral outlook. The social nature of doxastic practices does imply that in forming beliefs at all we must have at least an implicit and general trust, not only in our own cognitive capacities and skills, but also in those of our society; but it does not imply that we cannot or should not maintain a critical stance toward socially prevalent beliefs, one (or even several) at a time.

The implicit and general trust in one's society that is involved in relying on a doxastic practice at all must be distinguished from the explicit reliance on social or traditional *authority* that may or may not be *part* of the practice. Reflective interpretation of authoritative or canonical texts has been part of a large proportion of evaluative doxastic practices. The texts may be as different as the Talmud and the ethical writings of Kant, and the degree and conceptualization of commitment to the text varies widely. I believe that where there is sufficient wisdom in the text, and sensitivity and imaginativeness in the interpretation, such use of a more or less authoritative text can be, and often has been, a good and broadly reliable evaluative doxastic process; but I am *not* claiming that it must be part of every good and broadly reliable evaluative doxastic practice. Likewise, the fact that we cannot think evaluatively without relying on a large, and largely shared, stock of evaluative beliefs does not imply that our practice must single out certain beliefs or sources as specially authoritative, or even that it must use the concept of authority at all.

Moreover, a good evaluative doxastic practice need not involve a well-defined *tradition*.[10] For that reason I will not make a big issue here of the individuation of doxastic practices—whether, for example, there are many evaluative doxastic practices or only one. Many people in modern societies belong to more than one moral or religious tradition, and treat them eclectically in their own evaluative doxastic practice. This poses dangers of inconsistency; but consistency is not the only virtue in such a practice, and may be in tension with the virtue of comprehensive sensitivity. The central aim of evaluative doxastic practice, on my view, is vision of the good. In relation to the transcendent Good, such vision is always fragmentary and perspectival, which suggests that one may attain a more adequate vision by drawing on several traditions, which may not always be consistent—though one is then faced with a task of integration. Evaluative doxastic practices share with traditions the property of being socially established and transmitted, but differ from them in other ways. The difference is particularly marked if the tradition is intellectually structured as a theory (or as an argument),[11] because of the crucial role that noninferential doxastic processes, taking feelings and desires as inputs, play in evaluative doxastic practices.

We all do engage in evaluative doxastic practices of the sort I have described; but are we justified in relying on them as we do? I do not know of any conclusive proof that such practices are reliable, in the sense of yielding true beliefs; but the same is true of other fundamental doxastic practices, such as induction and sense perception. Nonetheless, it seems to me unthinkable that we should abandon most of our evaluative practices. That is partly because we are probably surer, intuitively as we say, of some of our evaluative beliefs than we are of any argument that might be used to dislodge them. It is also because reliance on evaluative beliefs and evaluative doxastic practices is such a pervasive feature of our thinking (as I argued in chapter 2, section 3). We prefer interpretations that ascribe *better* thought processes to a speaker, and explanations that seem to us *better* (perhaps because they seem simpler or more satisfying aesthetically); and in both of these cases we surely rely on evaluative doxastic practices that are at least partly noninferential. And we often form successful expectations about other people's moral opinions on the basis of our own beliefs about what is fair and good. In these ways evaluative doxastic practices are part of a comprehensive system of belief formation that "works"—that serves us well in making our way in the world (though that itself is no doubt an evaluative judgment), and that is in various ways confirmed by experience (though not conclusively,

10. In this paragraph I may be disagreeing with Alasdair MacIntyre, and perhaps more strongly with some of those who have made theological use of his work. He states, "We, whoever we are, can only begin enquiry from the vantage point afforded by our relationship to some specific social and intellectual past through which we have affiliated ourselves to some particular tradition of enquiry, extending the history of that enquiry into the present: as Aristotelian, as Augustinian, as Thomist, as post-Enlightenment liberal, or as something else" (MacIntyre, *Whose Justice? Which Rationality?* p. 401f.). His position is subtle and carefully nuanced, however; and I have preferred simply to state my own position in the text, avoiding the long digression that would be required to establish whether and to what extent I disagree with him.

11. Cf. MacIntyre, *After Virtue*, p. 207: "A living tradition . . . is an historically extended, socially embodied argument, and an argument precisely in part about the goods which constitute that tradition."

as regards any evaluative judgment, or perhaps any particular judgment at all). This is (a sketch of) as good a justification as I think we can reasonably demand for evaluative doxastic practice; but I grant that it is not as good a justification as we have probably desired. It leaves room—and arguably a need—for a sort of faith, which will be the topic of chapter 16.

3. General Revelation

To rely on evaluative doxastic practice is to treat it as reliable. To hold that it is reliable, under a metaphysically realistic interpretation of the practice, is to claim that there is a tendency (which need not be infallible) for beliefs formed in it to be true, or to approximate the truth. This suggests there should be some causal or explanatory connection between the mechanisms or processes of the practice and the truth of the beliefs formed in it. Versions of realism in the metaphysics of value will be more plausible if they offer us some account of such a connection. Boyd's naturalism obviously passes this test, since it identifies values with clusters of natural properties with which human processes of evaluative thinking are leading us (causally) to identify them. My theistic theory can pass the test too, by invoking God's causality to explain the connection between those evaluative doxastic practices that it endorses and the facts of Godlikeness and divine commands in terms of which it understands the nature of value and obligation. What is offered in each of these cases, of course, is not a detailed or empirically confirmed explanation, but a sketch of a type of explanation that is postulated—plausibly enough in relation to the principles of the respective theories.

For this reason our knowledge, or justified approximately true belief, about the most important sorts of value and obligation will be regarded in my theory as *revealed* to us by God. Two points justify this classification. (1) According to my theory the objects of this knowledge or belief are facts whose nature is constituted ultimately by facts about God, whether we recognize their theological character or not. (2) The reliability of the processes by which we form and accept the relevant beliefs is due in general to God's action intended to lead us to the relevant truths. These two points, the theological character of the subject matter and the divine activity in making it known, are the most essential in the concept of revelation.

Beyond the reasons just given for using the concept of revelation in my theory of the good as well as of the right, revelation is centrally involved in facts of obligation and vocation, in the account given in chapters 11 and 13, because those facts are understood in terms of divine commands or invitations, which essentially involve communication in which God makes known to some extent something that God does to constitute the command or invitation. Facts of goodness or value, on my account, are facts of Godlikeness which do not require communicative acts to constitute them. The revelation of them, accordingly, does not necessarily require any analogue of a speech act, such as commanding or inviting. It can be conceived as a simple disclosing or showing. But I still suppose that revelation, divine action explaining reliable belief formation, is required with regard to the good as well as the right.

The concept of revelation, understood as explained here, must be applied first of all to the ordinary evaluative doxastic practices of a wide variety of human cultures, characterized by great diversity of religious belief and practice. On my account of the semantics of morals the natures of goodness, of wrongness, and so forth must fit certain roles indicated by our use of the corresponding evaluative terminology. These roles are determined in part by prevailing evaluative beliefs and evaluative doxastic practices. These beliefs and practices may be mistaken in various ways and are individually subject to correction. Some of them must be mistaken, since they do not all agree with each other; and we might be a bit off the mark in our thinking in all of them. But there must in general be something right about these beliefs and practices, if there is any nature of goodness or obligation at all. We must have been able, very often, to recognize the good and the right. On my views in the metaphysics of morals it follows that we must have been able, very often, to recognize what are in fact certain relations to God.

This is not to say that we must have recognized their theological character. I cannot regard the recognition of moral truths as an exclusive possession of theists, let alone of a particular religious tradition. For I am theorizing about the nature of a goodness, a badness, and so forth that are spoken of by adherents of many religious traditions and of none; and the evaluative beliefs of all those people are therefore relevant to determining the roles that the natures must fill. Theists of many religious or philosophical backgrounds, however, might accept a theological theory in the metaphysics of value; and if they do, they can then recognize evaluative truths as facts about relations to God, and can thus draw explicit inferences about God from the grounds of evaluative belief that are available to secular as well as religious ethical theories.

Thus I am committed on a major point of theological controversy. Some theologians have maintained that God is revealed, or even known at all, only through the historic revelation of a particular religious tradition. I must disagree with them. My theological treatment of the metaphysics of value cannot be combined with just any theory of revelation, and specifically cannot be combined with such an exclusivist theory. Rather, I require a theory of what has sometimes been called *general revelation*. To affirm a general revelation is to affirm that, by divine action, certain facts about God have been made cognitively accessible in some way to human beings in general. The concept of general revelation is introduced by way of contrast with that of *special revelation*, which applies to the sort of revelation that is supposed to establish a particular historic religious tradition, or contribute to its development. The generality of general revelation means that it can be received by adherents of any religious tradition or of none. A large proportion of evaluative doxastic practices are saturated with religious concepts, and with different ones in different traditions. That is one of the ways in which socially established evaluative doxastic practices differ from each other. I believe nonetheless there is enough overlap among the different received evaluative beliefs and practices for us to be talking about the same thing, and for us to have received some general revelation in this realm.

God's action in general revelation might in principle be part of God's action in creating the world, providentially ordering it so that human beings will develop roughly reliable ways of forming beliefs about the relevant matters. In that case what is generally revealed would presumably be accessible through the exercise of our natural faculties alone. But general revelation might equally well require some divine intervention or grace of illumination on each occasion, provided the grace is given frequently and widely enough to be considered "general." And in that case there might be something supernatural in the formation of some of the relevant beliefs. In any case, a plausible theistic epistemology of value must incorporate ordinary evaluative doxastic practices, accepting them as vehicles of general revelation, though certainly not as infallible. In this way a theistic epistemology of value is not cut off from any of the rational resources of ordinary evaluative thought.

The idea of general revelation is easily confused with that of *natural theology*, but they are distinct. The key point about natural theology is that it is supposed to be *natural*, to be composed of theses that human beings could establish by their unaided natural capacities for knowing and reasoning about the natural environment in which they at all times find themselves. The natural is contrasted with the supernatural, and nature with grace. These contrasts do not have a major structural role in my framework for ethics.

Neither does another contrast that may be suggested by talk about the "natural" in these matters, the contrast between nature and convention. In the light of any anthropological views that are now plausible, a reliance on human ethical consciousness will not fit well with the tradition of disparaging convention or culture in favor of nature. For it seems clear that every human ethical consciousness of which we have any knowledge has been profoundly shaped by a culture and by processes of social change. That was emphasized in the account of evaluative doxastic practices given in section 2. There is no evidence of an ethical outlook that is "natural" in the sense of being one that we would have if we had been raised without any social influence at all—no evidence indeed that we would have any moral awareness at all if we had survived such an upbringing. So if a theistic ethical theory is to assume a fairly general recognition of ethical truths, it must suppose that God is revealed through social process, culture, and convention, as well as through any static or permanent human nature that can be distinguished from them.

As I have indicated in chapter 13, section 3, I doubt the usefulness of 'natural' and 'unnatural' as terms of ethical theory, and (like many other moderns) I doubt the ethical relevance of any teleology that can be discovered simply by the scientific study of nature. This has led me also to avoid the terminology of "natural law." Some might be tempted to identify my theory of obligation as a form of natural law theory. Mine is a divine command theory, and one which envisages many of God's commands as given to human beings quite generally, and treats them as accessible to ethical reasoning. These are features that have belonged to some classical versions of natural law theory (though not all of the latter have been divine command theories).[12] Thinking it wiser, however, in ethical theory not to depend heavily on concepts of nature and the natural, I have preferred to articulate in terms of "general revelation" those features of my view that I share with some forms of natural law theory.

It is important for the epistemology of a theological ethics to avoid undue reliance on concepts of the natural. Any interesting theology will be, at least in part,

12. See Schneewind, *The Invention of Autonomy*, chaps. 2–7.

a reading, an interpretation, of experience, life, the world—an attempt to make sense of them. It will be an interpretation of actuality, and attentive to actuality. In chapter 13, section 3, I have tried to show that theological interpretation of actuality—in terms of gift and vocation, for example—can be of service to ethics. But what sort of reasoning is to guide theology's interpretation of actuality?

There is a temptation to be guided primarily by causal explanatory reasoning. Such reasoning certainly has a place in theology, but it must not be allowed too dominant a role in theological ethics. If it is our sole or principal guide, we may well make inferences about providence and divine purposes that lead all too easily to some version of 'Whatever is, is right'. In an ethically tenable theological reading of actuality, causal reasoning must yield priority to a vision of the Good, and therein to an ethical sensibility shaped by an evaluative doxastic practice as described in section 2. It is unlikely, in any event, that, without the guidance of a vision of the Good, we will be able to make inferences that are both plausible and ethically interesting from natural facts to divine purposes; for, apart from an ethical vision, it is too difficult to answer the question whether any appearance that we are able, and to some extent motivated, to accomplish a particular result should not be regarded as an invitation from God to do so, and evidence of a divine purpose that we should do so.

In terms that I used to make a similar point in chapter 2, section 4, theological ethics must not simply reason from 'is' to 'ought', trying to read divine purposes in the facts of nature and history, and drawing ethical implications from the purposes so inferred. Rather, it must reason primarily from 'ought' to 'is', from moral conviction and vision to what we should believe about God's purposes.[13] It must be willing to take evaluative beliefs as starting points and not just as conclusions in its reasoning. In so doing it will rely on some form (probably a theologically informed form) of evaluative doxastic practice. The inference from 'ought' to 'is' is particularly important for theism because the idea of God is certainly the idea of a reality, but is obviously a dangerous idea for ethics if it is not shaped at least largely by a moral vision. Perhaps it should even be said that if we are not prepared to let our vision of value control in some ways our vision of reality, then we had better not be theists.

4. Special Revelation, Experience, and Change in Ethics

In emphasizing the importance of general revelation for my views, as I have done in section 3, I do not mean to disparage the claims of special revelation or to deny them a role in ethics. Recall that special revelation is revelation that is tied to a par-

13. I am taking sides here on a live theological issue. A dispute about it can be traced in the fascinating interchanges between the theologian brothers Reinhold and H. Richard Niebuhr, chronicled in Fox, *Reinhold Niebuhr*, esp. pp. 132–35, 144–47, 153f.—with Reinhold beginning with ethical convictions and viewing God as a transcendent ideal, and Richard much more concerned to infer divine purposes from nature and history. H. Richard Niebuhr's influential student James Gustafson has adopted the 'is' to 'ought' inferential stance in his monumental *Ethics from a Theocentric Perspective*. I have developed my views on this theological issue more fully, in the context of a critique of Gustafson, in Adams, "Platonism and Naturalism." It is also a recurrent theme of the present work; in addition to chapter 2, see the beginning of chapter 5 and the third section of chapter 12.

ticular historic religious tradition. It is seen (by the eyes of faith in the relevant traditions) in the Torah of Israel, the oracles of Amos, the words and deeds of Jesus of Nazareth, the text of the Quran, for example. What can plausibly be regarded as generally revealed in ethics is fairly limited. The beliefs that are shared widely enough to enter into the semantical determination of the roles to be filled by the natures of goodness, wrongness, and so forth are not sufficient to constitute a complete ethical outlook for any person. For adherents of any particular religious tradition, the beliefs and practices constitutive of that tradition will play a large part in completing their ethical outlook. They will also affect their evaluative doxastic practice and color their view of the moral beliefs they share with those outside their tradition. Such differences of ethical outlook, commonly associated with different religious traditions, have been a persistent feature of human history, and there is much reason to expect them to continue to be so.

These differences are widely regarded as undermining the truth claims of special revelation. How much trust can we place in special revelation if the various purported instances of it contradict each other? This is a reasonable question, and it will not receive a complete answer here. We will be concerned only with the *ethical* deliverances of special revelation, and even that is too large a subject for a really complete treatment in the present context. I acknowledge that some purported deliverances of special revelation do flatly contradict each other, but I think it will be worth exploring ways in which many divergent revelations may not be directly contradictory, but simply different. Such possibilities are suggested by the idea of a transcendent Good ever imperfectly imaged in the contingencies of human history.

Reflection on the relation between history and the Good may begin with the observation that ethics is in large measure an empirical subject. It has often been believed that ethical principles must all be truths of reason, known independently of experience. This is partly because it has been commonly supposed that they must be necessary truths (if truths at all). On my view, of course, principles of moral obligation, being grounded in divine commands, will not be necessary truths; but principles of value may be, and I am inclined to think they are (as explained in chapter 1, section 5). But even if principles of value are necessary truths, it does not follow that our knowledge of them is a priori rather than empirical. It is one of the virtues of recent philosophical work on modality to distinguish clearly between necessity as a metaphysical status and apriority as an epistemological status.

It is not difficult to see how fundamental facts of value would be empirical, on my account of the nature of goodness. The goodness of finite things is a sort of resemblance or imaging of God, the supreme Good. As such it is a rather holistic property. That is not to say that finite things are only good or only bad. They resemble God, and thus are good, in some ways and not in others. But their whole character, or a large part of it, is relevant to the resemblance. We can single out a number of properties in abstraction as tending to count for goodness in their possessors, but only a poor fragment of evaluative doxastic practice can be based on such abstract principles. In order to judge adequately many of the most interesting sorts of value, one must see things whole. One must experience them. It is not normally enough to imagine them, because imagination is much poorer than reality in ways that profoundly affect the values of things. The imagination of a great novelist may show us something interesting about the values of things, but it will normally be something prefigured in moral realities empirically known to the novelist. One of the most important sorts of thing we learn through the collective experience of human history is the possibility and value of various forms of social life; "the possibility of a reasonably harmonious and stable pluralist society,"[14] for example, is an important moral discovery.

Major possibilities of historic, or "special," revelation of the good can be understood in terms of the largely empirical character of our knowledge of value. We may say that the good (indeed, the Good itself) is specially revealed in historic events that manifest possibilities of goodness that we could not otherwise have known. Claims of this sort may plausibly be made about the lives of important and innovative religious personalities, such as Jesus of Nazareth, Francis of Assisi, or Mohandas Gandhi. They may also be made about forms of life that are characteristic of particular religious communities, involving such features as liturgical traditions, observance of commandments, and various ways of being guided by scriptures and traditions; the sense that a real goodness is revealed in such forms of life is surely one of the commonest (and best) reasons for adhering to them. Such claims of historic revelation of goodness need not be inconsistent with each other. Finite things can resemble God in different ways, and the values revealed in different religious traditions may for the most part be simply different, but all genuinely good in their own way—which is not, of course, to say that there will be nothing to criticize in them.[15]

If forms of goodness, ways of imaging God, are specially revealed in this way, by becoming actual at particular points in human history, they must still be recognized as good in order to be known. This recognition will be a form of vision of the good. It must depend on our sense of value, and thus on our evaluative doxastic practices. What is revealed was not already implicit in the doxastic practice, and need not have been; for doxastic practices are ways in which we have learned to recognize quite novel truths, as well as to conserve and revise old ones. But the revelation is received against a background of existing evaluative beliefs, which may be revised, but not entirely discarded, in the process. And so it must be. The part of a revelation of value that could be grasped in a moral vacuum (by any means short of the creation of an ethical mind out of nothing) would be primitive indeed. The vision of the good, grounded in evaluative doxastic practices, has the same essential role here that it has in relation to general revelation. We depend on it to "test the spirits," or the purported revelations, to be as sure as we can be that they really are good, which is the most important test of their being from and of God, the supreme Good.

---

14. Rawls, *Political Liberalism*, p. xxv. I doubt that Rawls would disagree with what I am saying about the case, though he is more explicit about discovery of possibility than about discovery of value.

15. Here, of course, I am adapting the concept of special revelation to play a part in a *philosophical* account. I am not saying anything about the part it may play in defining what is *authoritatively* received in a particular tradition—though what I say here may have implications, welcome or unwelcome, for the latter enterprise.

What one might develop along these lines would by no means be a complete account of special revelation, but only an account of special revelation of *value*. We will turn next to divine commands and special revelation of *obligations*; but besides these ethical matters, there are important claims of special revelation about such matters as God's nature and God's plans for our salvation. These latter claims go beyond the scope of this book, though our sense of value is certainly relevant to them too.

There is room for special revelation in my account of obligation even more obviously than in my account of value. I take moral obligations to be constituted by commands of God, which in turn are constituted in part by signs which must be events or facts empirically accessible to those persons who are addressed by the commands. It is already part of my account that different commands may have been addressed by God in this way to different people at different times and places, and in different historical and cultural contexts. If an event that has central importance in a particular historic religious tradition is interpreted there as communicating a command of God to adherents of that tradition, it is treated, in effect, as a special revelation, and it may be quite reasonable so to regard it. And God may well have issued different commands to different religious communities.

Of course, if you think God has commanded you to do something, and I think it is evil, I will not think God really commanded you to do it. That is another story, and we must deal with the issue it raises. An account of revelation in ethics that avoids the hard cases will not be credible. We do not need to look for conflicts *between* religious traditions to find a hard case. One of the typical problems for a theology of revelation for a particular tradition is that confrontations of morally divergent cultures can be internal as well as external to a religious tradition. Present-day Jews and Christians meet alien cultures in their own sacred scriptures; from this confrontation arise important issues for contemporary theology.

Consider as an example the treatment of slavery in the New Testament. Onesimus, a runaway slave newly converted to Christianity, was sent back to his Christian master by St. Paul, bearing a letter (Philemon), to be sure, in which Paul broadly hinted that it would be good for the master to grant Onesimus his freedom. Was Paul right to do this? Would Onesimus have wronged his master in not returning? Or should the condemnation of slavery almost universally shared by Christians today issue in disapproval of Paul's action, and in the conclusion that the master would have wronged Onesimus by not freeing him?

On some points relevant to this example my views will not warrant any relativization of moral judgment to cultures. This is particularly true about issues of what is good and bad. What is good, on my view, is what faithfully images God; and what God is like in the relevant respects is not different in different times and places. The inherently evil, I have suggested, is what opposes the good or violates an image of God; and this will obviously be no more variable than what is good. Slavery, we now believe, is evil, a violation of persons; we see in it an aspect of moral horror. If we are right about this, slavery is horrible, and an evil institution, even in societies where no one believes so.

With regard to issues of right and wrong and duty, however, my views may allow for more relativization. I have allowed that God may not have issued to all people the same commands that we have received. Indeed, if[16] no one in a society has any thought that a practice such as slavery is wrong, there is some reason to suppose that they have not received a divine command against it, since receiving a command implies a real possibility of being aware of it. And this would be reason for me to say that they were not violating a moral duty, even though the practice was an evil. Of course the fact (if it is a fact) that no one thought slavery wrong does not conclusively show that they had not received, and closed their hearts against, plenty of signs that they could reasonably be expected to have interpreted as moral prohibitions of slavery. Perhaps the sheer badness of slavery must have been such a sign; but if not, perhaps we cannot be assured a priori that every society practicing slavery must have received a divine command against it.

It is also possible in principle that other people should have received commands from God that do not apply to us; and we might have theological reasons to believe this had happened, as Christians have generally believed about some of God's commandments to Israel. In ascribing divine authorship to commands, however, we will be constrained by our beliefs about good and evil, and about God's character and purposes. And in this way our ethical convictions can be in tension with some views of scriptural interpretation and authority. Modern Jews and Christians may well find it hard to believe, for example, that God really commanded Joshua to practice genocide against the Canaanites, no matter what is written in the Bible.

Returning to the question of slavery, we find in the New Testament no clear indication of belief in a divine commandment requiring opposition to slavery or forbidding participation in the practice.[17] There is in St. Paul's writings at least a hint of the idea that in an ideal system of social relationships there would be no place for slavery (Galatians 3:29). But there is also a matter-of-fact acceptance of slavery as part of the actual form of human society (1 Corinthians 7:20ff.). And in parts of the New Testament there are actually injunctions to slaves to be obedient to their masters.[18]

I imagine that this advice was probably corrupted by ideology in the Marxian sense, or by fears of disrupting the status quo. But at the same time it may well have been wise advice. One way of viewing the matter is as a question of vocation (cf. 1 Corinthians 7:20ff.). If we ask what path or paths in life may have been offered to the slaves among the first Christians as a way of participating in God's love, the path of acceptance and obedient service generally counseled in the New Testament is certainly an obvious candidate. Given the circumstances of the time, it may indeed have been part of the only sort of vocation a Christian could realistically see as offered to most of them.

---

16. This 'if' is big, as regards the ancient world, for we are in no position to know anything so sweeping about a society remote in space or time from our own.

17. The view that it was wrong to own slaves seems to have been almost (but not quite) unheard of in the Mediterranean world of New Testament times; for documentation see Bartchy, *Mallon Chresai*, pp. 54f., 63–67, 174f.

18. Colossians 3:22–25; Ephesians 6:5–8; 1 Timothy 6:1–2; Titus 2:9–10—all passages in the Pauline literature but now commonly believed not to have been written by Paul; also 1 Peter 2:18ff.

This is not to say that Christians today should suppose that they can view slavery in the same ethical light as St. Paul or other first-century Christians. That is surely not possible. What the concepts of divine commands and divine vocations help to make possible is an attitude that does not judge earlier generations as if they shared our history and our culture, and that sees them as responding, not perfectly, but with real perceptiveness and real faithfulness, to a divine guidance really given to them and leading them toward a real good.

It is reasonable to have an analogous attitude toward ourselves. We must assume that our ethical outlook will seem defective in some ways to later generations, and that some of their criticisms of us will be right. It has been common for more than a century to speak of "progressive revelation," expressing the hypothesis that God has made use of the development of human thought and culture to communicate a better and better understanding of religious and ethical truth. The adjective 'progressive' may have gone somewhat out of fashion in this context, and for good reason. We have less confidence in progress than our recent predecessors did, and we may well hesitate to buy the implication that later is better. Later will certainly be different, but it may not be silly to fear that the ethical outlook of our successors will be in some ways inferior to our own.

Still there is something in the idea of progressive revelation that I think I must affirm, and that is the view that the development of human thought and culture, particularly in ethics, is a vehicle of revelation, or at any rate of divine guidance. Serious commitment to our own moral beliefs does not require us to suppose that they are superior to what went before, any more than it requires us to suppose that they are superior to what will come after. At the same time, if we are to have an ethical life at all, we must suppose that there is some validity to our moral views. In theological terms, we must believe that the goodness and commands of God are reflected to a significant extent in our ethical consciousness. And if that belief is correct we have presumably benefited from divine guidance, since our evaluative doxastic practices and our ethical outlook are to a considerable extent products of historic development.

It is on this basis that I would answer an objection raised against religious ethics by Bernard Williams, who says, "If ethical understanding is going to develop, and if religion is going to understand its own development in relation to that, it seems inevitable that it must come to understand itself as a human construction; if it does, it must in the end collapse."[19] This objection is theologically naive, though I am sure Williams is not alone in it. It overlooks the possibility that religion will regard its development as a joint product of human construction and divine guidance. And this is not merely a possibility, but almost a commonplace of recent theology.

I have been concentrating on encounters between earlier and later ethical cultures within a single religious tradition, because that is the sort of encounter that has thus far occasioned the richest theological reflection. But I see no reason in principle that theists should not look for ethical understanding and manifestations of

19. Williams, *Ethics and the Limits of Philosophy*, p. 33.

divine guidance in religious traditions different from their own in substantially the same way as they can in earlier stages of their own tradition. In neither case am I suggesting that they abandon their own ethical outlook, or suppose that what they believe is true only "for them." What I am suggesting is rather that a theistic outlook can appropriately include the idea that God may have guided different people in different directions.

16

MORAL FAITH

The topic of this chapter is an important and unjustly neglected idea, which once had much more currency in the intellectual community than it has today—namely, the idea that morality has a need, or something approaching a need, for a kind of faith. It might be thought that a theistic theory of the nature of the good and the right would introduce into morality a need for faith. I will argue, however, that morality has such a need in any case, with or without theism.

The most influential exponent of the idea of moral faith is Immanuel Kant. The idea figures in Kant's development of moral grounds for belief in the existence of God. I will have some things to say here about religious developments of moral faith, but I will have much more to say about more narrowly moral objects of faith. The emphasis will fall on those aspects of the idea of moral faith that I think likely to command the widest agreement, though I do not expect even them to be uncontroversial.

Various points about what the word 'faith' means, in this context, will emerge gradually in the course of this exploration. As a starting point, however, we may say in a very provisional way that faith is, or involves, believing something that a rational person might be seriously tempted to doubt, or even not to believe. Talk about faith is normally concerned with problems that arise from rational possibilities of doubting or disbelieving something that seems important to believe. Indeed, the type of faith I have in view here involves the believer's awareness of such possibilities. It includes doubt, and a certain sensitivity to opposing reasons, as well as a certain resistance to them. In this way the virtue of faith involves holding to a mean between vices of credulity and incredulity.

1. Faith in Morality

So *are* there things that it is morally important to believe, but that there is a rational possibility of doubting or not believing? We might put this by saying that our next task is to identify some articles of moral faith; but that way of putting it sounds like a proposal to draw up a moral "creed," and that would suggest far too much precision of doctrinal formulation. At this point we encounter one of the factors that can make issues of faith uncomfortable for philosophers. As a philosopher I have no desire to escape accountability for the accuracy and the logical implications of anything I say. At the same time I do not believe that any form of words is itself a suitable object of faith. To take a verbal formulation as an object of faith seems to me to be a sort of idolatry, though doubtless it is a form of idolatry that is common enough in religious communities. Faith ought to be a stance in relation to something larger. Moral faith is a stance in relation to goodness and duty, and in relation to possibilities of human action, thought, and feeling and their larger context in human life and in the universe. We can hardly talk about such a stance without articulating its content verbally; but the adequacy of any verbal formulation, as an articulation of the stance, can always be questioned.

The first and most obvious object of moral faith is morality itself, or one's own morality, the morality to which one adheres. The latter will include some form or forms of evaluative doxastic practice in which one participates, as explained in chapter 15, section 2. What I mean by speaking of morality as an object of faith can perhaps best be indicated by evoking an experience that many people have had at some point in their education. It might happen in a course in moral philosophy in which the question 'Why be moral?' is asked, and is answered with a variety of philosophical performances that the student finds fairly impressive but not entirely satisfying. Or the course might focus on questions about the meaning of moral terms, and the student may become puzzled as to what it is that we can be doing when we say that it would be wrong to do this or that. Perhaps the student actually accepts philosophical answers to these questions, but remains uncomfortable about the extent to which the answers still seem debatable. Other doubts might be stirred in an anthropology course that leaves a student wondering whether moral opinions about such issues as the rightness or wrongness of headhunting aren't simply relative to different cultural systems and their expectations. An encounter with Marxian thought, or with some related form of the "hermeneutics of suspicion," might lead the student to doubt whether any moral belief can be anything nobler than an intellectual tool or weapon for the service of the self-interest of the believer or of some group to which the believer belongs. These are among the ways in which a rational person might be seriously tempted to doubt the validity of morality in general, or of the morality that she herself nonetheless professes.

I don't mean to suggest at all that faith must be unreasoned, much less that it must be irrational. Reasons can doubtless be given for philosophical answers to all of these questions. Perhaps one could even rationally justify a morally comforting answer to all of them. I hope so. But would the reasoning prove the case "beyond a reasonable doubt," as you should demand of the prosecutor if you are a juror in a criminal trial? That I wouldn't expect. It is rare indeed to reach such a standard of proof on fundamental philosophical issues. The questions I have raised about the validity of morality are all serious questions that are unlikely to be permanently cleared off the philosophical agenda.

One reason for this is that in responding to such fundamental philosophical issues it is often impossible to avoid a kind of circularity. If we are asked, for instance, to justify the belief that there is "something to" ethics, that it is not a massive socially induced delusion, we will not be able to answer without some essential reliance on our ethical doxastic practice. But that practice is a main part of what is being called into question.[1] Of course it does not follow that we should not rely on the practice; indeed, I think we should. But a certain level of rational discomfort with the situation seems to me appropriate.

And as regards our own particular morality, the one we adhere to ourselves, we can hardly be conscious, in a sensitive and nondefensive way, of what is going on around us in our pluralistic cultural situation without knowing that there are intelligent, generally reasonable, and in many ways admirable people who disagree with us on smaller and larger issues about ethics. Our ethical beliefs must be held together with the knowledge that there is a sense in which "we could be wrong."[2] Not that there is a sense in which cruelty, for example, could really be a virtue, despite appearances; but that many ways of looking at these matters are available to reasonable people, and others could be right against us.

How, then, is it possible to have moral convictions? For surely it is essential to a moral life to hold some strong beliefs about good and evil, right and wrong. Given the exposure of moral beliefs to possibilities of rational doubt, it appears that moral convictions will have to be faith, in the sense that I have thus far loosely defined. This is one way in which morality has a need for faith.

2. Faith in Moral Ends

Thus far I have spoken of morality itself, or its validity, as an object of faith. Perhaps many people will not have experienced more than merely theoretical doubts on that very general and in some ways abstract subject. I turn now to some other, more concrete topics of moral importance on which I think virtually all of us have,

---

1. The type of circularity I have in mind is that discussed in Alston, "Epistemic Circularity." I am much indebted to that paper, but I am more inclined than I think Alston is to emphasize how much is conceded to the skeptic at this point.

2. The possibility expressed here is an epistemic one; and it is a possibility from one's own point of view, an invitation to doubts of one's own, though it may be grounded partly in one's awareness of other people's views.

or have had, or will have doubts that are more personally troubling, perhaps even soul-wrenching. They have to do with the value and the attainability of what we might call "moral ends."

It is in this area principally that Kant saw morality as having a need for faith. He argued that moral commitment must set itself a certain end for whose attainment it aspires or hopes; that this end is only to a very limited extent within our power; that therefore the possibility of the result for which the moral agent must hope depends on there being what I would call a moral order in the universe; and that such an order cannot reasonably be supposed to exist except through the action of a God, in whom we are therefore rationally obliged to believe, if we seriously aim at the end that morality sets as the comprehensive goal of our striving.[3] It is not part of my present project to develop or evaluate Kant's argument as such, and I will not try to determine here how strongly such considerations as these may support belief in the existence of God, though that is a question that interests me very much. Issues about a moral order in the universe certainly lurk in the background of some of the doubts we may have about moral ends, but they may not always emerge.

One place to begin thinking about faith in moral ends is with the question whether human life is worth living—or rather with particular instances of that general question—for example, whether your life is worth living. It is certainly *humanly* important to believe that one's own life is worth living. I won't try to argue that it is *morally* important, or important for morality, though I suspect that it generally is. But at least it is morally important, in typical cases, to believe that other people's lives are worth living. If your friends are going through hard times, they may or may not be tempted to despair. Either way it is likely to be important to them to have your support as a person who believes in them and in the value of their lives. Harsh circumstances may try your faith that their life is worth living, which makes it seem natural to speak of "faith" in this context. Having that faith might be essential to being a good friend, and not having it might be letting the other person down in a particularly hurtful way. Thus having faith that another person's life is worth living might be important to moral virtue, since being a good friend is a part of moral virtue.

What does it take to have faith that a friend's life, or one's own, is worth living? It is closely connected with caring about the person's good, the friend's or one's own. There is more than one way to care about a person's good. There is a way that is merely pity, in the sense in which pity is rightly despised. It is caring only that the person should be spared the suffering of pain. It is natural, of course, to want to avoid pain; but a view that sees nothing to value in a person's life except the avoidance of pain offers no support for meaningful living.

Caring more constructively about a person's good involves taking that person's life as a project that one prizes. If it is your good, the project belongs to you in a way that it does not belong to me, and it is yours rather than mine to determine the

3. Kant, *Critique of Practical Reason*, chap. 2 of the "Dialectic"; and *Religion within the Boundaries of Mere Reason*, the first edition preface. Cf. Adams, "Moral Arguments for Theistic Belief."

shape of the project; perhaps I will think of it as your vocation, and as God's project too. In any event, if I care about your good, I add myself as a sponsor of the project. And this I can hardly do without believing that your life is worth living. To have faith that a person's life is worth living will sometimes be manifested in clinging stubbornly to that person's life as a project to which one is committed, refusing to give up hope for her. It will involve a certain resistance to reasons for doubting the value of that person's life.

Few judgments are more dangerous morally than the judgment that another person's life is not worth living, or not worth living any more. Such judgments can tempt us literally to murder. I grant there are cases, for instance of irreversibly comatose persons, in which it is morally necessary to make such a judgment. But I think it is almost always the part of moral wisdom to cling as stubbornly as one can to the belief that the other person's life is worth living, at least as long as the other person wants to go on living it, and often even when the other person is tempted to despair.

I have been discussing cases of friendship, but I do not mean to suggest that those are the only cases in which it is morally important to believe that other people's lives are worth living. It is also important to believe that distant lives, such as those that are lost to famine in Somalia, or to genocide in Bosnia, are worth living, or would be if they could be preserved. We may be more tempted not to value lives that are very different from our own, but surely some moral defect would be involved in not believing that those distant lives are worth living.

Other instances of a need for faith in moral ends may be sought in connection with the question whether the *moral* life is worth living. This is actually a family of questions, one of which is whether a morally good life is better *for* the person who lives it than an immoral or amoral or morally misguided life. Philosophical opinion is divided on the question whether it is *morally* important to believe that the moral life is better *for oneself*, some philosophers holding that moral commitment should be entirely independent of questions of self-interest, while others think it would be deeply immoral not to believe that doing a bad action would be bad for oneself.

Be that as it may, it is hard to deny the moral importance of believing that the moral life will be good, or is apt to be good, *for other people*. For it is part of moral virtue to care both about the other person's good and about the other person's virtue. Morality requires that we encourage each other to live morally. But how could we do that in good conscience if we thought living morally would be bad for the other person? Are we to encourage others to act morally so that we, or the less scrupulous, may take advantage of them, or so that we may all lose out together? Those are not morally attractive propositions; but if, on the other hand, we cease to encourage each other to act morally, we have abandoned morality as a social enterprise. So it seems that if we do not believe that living morally is at least normally good for a person, there will be a conflict in the very soul of our morality that threatens to tear it apart. But while few doubt that it is generally advantageous to have the rudiments of honesty and neighborliness, it is notoriously easier to doubt that some of the finer fruits of morality are good *for* their possessors, when all the consequences they may have are taken into account.

Another question about the value of the moral life is whether it is better for the *world*, or at least not bad for the world, and not too irrelevant to be worth living. As H. Richard Niebuhr put it, those "who are loyal to justice" trust "that devotion to justice will not result in futility."[4] This trust or faith or belief is severely tested, by both the failures and the unforeseen consequences of moral efforts. Yet it does seem important for morality to believe that living morally is good for the world, or if not, then to believe that the moral life is of such intrinsic value that it is worth living for its own sake, whatever does or does not result from it. For how else can we care about morality as morality itself requires?

In these questions I have assumed that we *can* at least live moral lives. But that too can be doubted. Who emerges unscathed from a morally rigorous examination of conscience? And where conscience discovers no fault, a hermeneutics of suspicion may suggest that our deepest motives, hidden from our own eyes, are too self-seeking to give any moral satisfaction. Indeed, we all have real moral faults, and doubtless we all will continue to have real moral faults; but it is crucial for morality that we believe that moral effort can be successful enough to be worth making. For one cannot live morally without intending to do so, and one cannot exactly intend to do what one believes is totally impossible. Religious traditions have tried to deal with this problem with doctrines of grace. Moral philosophers, with the notable exception of Kant,[5] have paid less attention to the problem; but it seems that morality does have need for faith that a moral life is possible enough for us to be worth trying.

I will mention one more item of faith in a moral end. We might call it faith in *the common good*. More precisely, it is a matter of believing that the good of different persons is not so irreconcilably competitive as to make it incoherent to have the good of *all* persons as an end. It is of course necessary to have enough moral realism to see that the interests of some people must sometimes be balanced against the interests of others. Without that, one could hardly have anything we would recognize as a sense of justice. But if we can manage to view the problems of fairness and conflicting interests within the framework of a conception of human good that is predominantly cooperative, or if we can at least avoid viewing the good of different persons as irreconcilably conflicting goals, then we may still be able to take a stance that is fundamentally *for* everyone and *against* no one. And such a stance is what morality requires if it is to be more than a parochial or tribal loyalty.

What we must resist most strongly here is an ultracompetitive view of the pursuit of human good as a sort of zero-sum game, in which every good that anyone enjoys must be taken away from someone else. With such a view it would be impossible to include the good of *all* persons among one's ends. We are perhaps unlikely to see the pursuit of human good as a zero-sum game among individuals; but I suspect we are all too prone to see it as something close to a zero-sum game among nations or groups, and in that we are closer than we like to imagine to genocide and kindred crimes against humanity.

---

4. Niebuhr, *Faith on Earth*, p. 59.
5. Kant, *Religion within the Boundaries of Mere Reason.*

Much of the temptation to doubt or abandon our beliefs in moral ends arises from the fact that these beliefs are concerned not only with ideals but also with the relation of ideals to actuality, the possibility of finding sufficient value in the lives of such finite, needy, suffering, ignorant, motivationally complex, and even guilty creatures as we are. It is sometimes hard to believe that actuality is as supportive of moral ideals as these beliefs imply that it is. This is an aspect of the problem of evil that confronts all moral persons, nontheists as well as theists. Encounters with evil can shake our faith in moral ends, very much as they can shake faith in the existence, power, and goodness of God. Perhaps there is some good, purely philosophical answer to all the doubts about moral ends. But even if there is one, it is unlikely to *silence* the doubts, just as no theodicy is likely to *dispose* of the theological forms of the problem of evil. In both cases a need for faith remains.

This is of course the point at which Kant connected morality with religious belief. It may indeed be easier to retain one's faith in moral ends, at least in some cases, if one believes in some sort of moral order in the world—a life after death and a God or a karma that guarantees the sure reward of virtue, or at least an order that assures the virtuous life of being likely to contribute to a greater good, perhaps through "intelligence as a force in social action," to borrow a phrase from John Dewey's version of moral faith.[6] Moreover, the impulse to integrate one's moral faith with the rest of one's view of reality is healthy. Perhaps an attempt at such integration is rationally or morally demanded of us. And the attempt is obviously apt to involve a special interest in views that support belief in the possibility of moral ends. There may be here a reason, strong or weak, for thinking we have a moral need to believe in some cosmic order, as an ultimate object of moral faith. For the present, however, I am content to have argued just that we have a moral need to believe in more particular possibilities of moral ends, as proximate objects of moral faith.

Two objections to this argument may be considered here. One of them might appeal to things that John Dewey says in developing the version of moral faith to which I have referred. He argues that in trying "to prove that ideals are real not just as ideals but as antecedently existing actualities," philosophers and theologians "have failed to see that in converting moral realities into matters of intellectual assent they have evinced lack of *moral* faith."[7] He is concerned that believing the ideal is already actual, apart from our efforts, can lead to moral laziness. His argument might suggest that the object of moral faith should be simply the ideal, and not the relation of the actual to it. But this is not borne out by the full development of Dewey's own position. He already departs, more perhaps than he realizes, from a narrow conception of moral faith as faith in the ideal alone, when he says that "all endeavor for the better is moved by faith in what is possible, not by adherence to the actual."[8]

That endeavor for the better is moved by faith in what is possible is a nice formulation, one that I think Kant, for example, would approve. Faith in a moral end

---

6. Dewey, *A Common Faith*, p. 79. Cf. Baier, "Secular Faith," where the faith morality needs is seen as a form of "faith in the human community and its evolving procedures"—as "faith in a community of just persons" (p. 293f.).

7. Dewey, *A Common Faith*, p. 21.

8. Dewey, *A Common Faith*, p. 23.

is generally faith in a *possibility* of good. But we must ask what is meant by 'possible' in this context. Surely faith in the possibility of the ends of morality, the possibility of moral good, is not just belief that moral good is imaginable, or that it is logically possible or consistent. It is faith in a stronger possibility, an actual attainability, of moral good. And, as Kant saw clearly, faith in a strong possibility of this sort involves some sort of faith in what is actual. It involves faith, or at least a living hope, that actual causal circumstances are not so adverse, all things considered, as to preclude realization of the moral ends.

Another possible objection to my argument about faith in moral ends is that the beliefs I demand are more high-flown than morality needs. It may be suggested that our beliefs about actuality will provide sufficient support for morality as long as we believe that we're doing pretty well within the moral system, that honesty is the best policy, that laws will be enforced against us, that immoral behavior will elicit attitudes and responses that we won't like from other people, and so forth. My main answer to this objection is that such low-flown beliefs may sustain minimal moral compliance, but won't sustain moral *virtue*. My concern is with moral faith as a part of moral virtue. The attitudes of mind that morality demands are surely not limited to those involved in minimal moral compliance. Morality could hardly exist, indeed, if all or most people had no more than the attitudes of minimal moral compliance. There must be many people who have more virtue than that, for the morality of the merely compliant is largely responsive to the more deeply rooted morality of others. True virtue requires resources that will sustain it when society is supporting evil rather than good, and when there is considerable reason to doubt that honesty is the best *policy* from a self-interested point of view. Thus virtue requires more moral faith than mere compliance may.

3. The Cognitive Aspect of Moral Faith

It is time to attend to a misgiving that some philosophers are likely to have about this line of thought. Is it really correct to speak of *believing* in these contexts, or is something less cognitive demanded in moral faith? For example, does one really *believe* that a person's life is worth living? I have argued that this "belief" is closely connected with *caring* about that person's good, clinging stubbornly to the person's life as a project, and the like. Should faith that a person's life is worth living just be *identified* with such caring?

The issue thus raised could be viewed as a general one about cognitivism and noncognitivism regarding ethics and values, but I want to narrow the focus as much as possible in this context. I have committed myself in previous chapters to views about the meaning of ethical terms and the relation of value judgments to truth, but I want to set those issues aside in order to concentrate on some of the concrete features of moral faith that incline me to speak of "belief" here. One reason for this narrow or concrete focus is that philosophical experience suggests that no theory on those metaethical issues is likely to attain a very high degree of certainty. Moral faith is therefore a stance we will have to take, if we are reasonable, in the face of the recognition that any metaethical theory we may hold *could* rather easily be mistaken.

So it would be good to have an understanding of the stance that does not presuppose very much metaethics, though doubtless anything we say about moral faith may have implications for more general theories in the field.

I think both will and feeling are involved in moral faith, as will be discussed in sections 4 and 5. But I do not think that moral faith is *merely* will and feeling, or that believing another person's life is worth living is *merely* caring about that life. Moral faith is not sheer exercise of willpower, or expression of emotion, or both together. Any characterization of it as merely self-assertion, self-expression, or self-consciousness does violence to an intention central to moral faith, an intention of respecting something more commanding, and at least in some cases more external to the self, than mere personal preference and feeling.

This is the most important reason for speaking of moral faith as a sort of "belief," and it is connected with the possibility of error. It is characteristic of the sort of faith I am discussing to acknowledge a sort of possibility that one could be mistaken in it—typically, a possibility that one could be mistaken and never know it. To deny that possibility, particularly where another person's life is concerned, would be to adopt a stance altogether too egocentric. I may believe that another person's life is still worth living, though she no longer believes it, in her terminal illness. But I must recognize that I could be tragically mistaken, mistaken in a way characteristic of false *beliefs*. That is, I must recognize that in some sense it *could* be that her life is not worth going on with. Faith confronts a temptation to doubt precisely because such possibilities of error must be recognized, and in a way respected.

To this argument it may be objected that emotions too can be mistaken, or inappropriately related to reality, as when one is angry at someone who has done nothing wrong or harmful or offensive.[9] The possibility of inappropriate anger, however, may be best understood on the assumption that the angry person is implicitly committed to a belief that the target of anger has done something objectionable. It is far from clear that we can understand how an *emotion* of faith in the value of life can be inappropriately related to reality if we cannot understand how faith can be, or involve, a false *belief* that life is worth living. In any event, the possibility of an objectively appropriate or inappropriate relation to reality is precisely the aspect of moral belief most subject to metaethical doubts, and also the aspect that seems to me most important to the nonegocentric character of moral faith. So long as we must acknowledge this possibility in our faith, it is hard for me to see what would be gained by eliminating belief from our conception of faith.

Connected with the possibility of error is the giving of reasons for and against beliefs. We do give and entertain reasons for and against items of moral faith, and moral beliefs in general. And the structure of giving and entertaining reasons for them is at least very similar to the structure of reasoning about other sorts of belief. In thinking about items of moral faith one uses logic, one aims at consistency and at coherence with one's beliefs on other subjects, and one is responsive to one's sense

---

9. I am indebted to Michael Otsuka and the editors of the *Journal of Philosophy* for calling my attention to objections of this sort.

of "plausibility," as we sometimes put it. All of that is grounds for classifying moral faith as a sort of belief.

Particular interest attaches to the question of the responsiveness or unresponsiveness of moral faith to the evidence of *experience*. Faith in morality itself, or in the validity of one's own morality, is not, I think, strictly empirical. This is not to deny that empirical evidence is relevant to it at all. The empirical dependence of many particular evaluative beliefs is not at issue here, but I believe in fact there is a sort of empirical confirmation of the soundness of moral thinking in general, derived from the way it "works" for us.[10] This confirmation is far from rigorous, however, and in any event the validity of a morality is not apt to be tightly enough tied to particular experiences for any question of a direct empirical proof or refutation to arise. That is not the case, however, with what I have called faith in moral ends. Our faith in the value of particular human lives, in the value and the possibility of a moral life, and in the possibility of a common good, can be put under strain by particular experiences. Indeed, adverse experience is precisely what gives rise, as I have argued, to a problem of evil for moral faith.

There is thus a considerable empirical element in faith in moral ends. But I do not believe that science, or social science, could devise a definitive empirical test of the truth of faith in any moral end. One reason for this is a certain vagueness or indefiniteness of content. A form of words, as I have argued, is not an appropriate object of moral faith; and a faith in some sense the same can persist through considerable revision of its verbal formulation. Because objects of faith are not precise formulations, but have vaguer contours that permit reformulation in the face of adverse experience, we cannot identify experiences that are unequivocally predicted or excluded by such items of faith as that so-and-so's life is worth living. Hence faith is not normally subject to definitive proof or refutation by any specifiable finite set of experiences. And from the perspective of moral faith, this is as it should be, for moral faith is *supposed* to be resistant to adverse evidence.

Empiricists may take offense at this feature of faith. A familiar attack on some forms of theistic faith comes to mind here. Antony Flew asked, "Just what would have to happen not merely (morally and wrongly) to tempt but also (logically and rightly) to entitle us to say 'God does not love us' or even 'God does not exist'?" He charged that if theistic formulations are continually revised to avoid definitive refutation by experience, then theism will suffer "death by a thousand qualifications."[11] I think logical positivists often greatly underestimated the amount of empirical content in religious beliefs; but Flew shows some real insight into the nature of faith. Faith as such is indeed resistant to adverse experience, and is apt to revise itself before simply accepting refutation. Flew is right that faith is in danger of evacuating itself of content if its resistance to refutation is undiscriminating or absolutely unconditional. Nonetheless, I believe that resistance to adverse experience, and to refutation in general, is an appropriate feature of faith; and I will argue this with specific reference to moral faith.

10. See chapter 15, sections 2 and 4.
11. Flew, "Theology and Falsification," pp. 99, 107.

It is interesting to note a passage in which Kant seems to agree, declaring that "in knowing [*Wissen*] one still listens to counter-reasons, but not in believing [*Glauben*, that is, in moral faith], because this turns not on objective grounds but on the moral interest of the subject."[12] Kant's comment about "moral interest" directs us to an important consideration here. Our interest in items of faith is importantly different from our interest in scientific hypotheses. One of the reasons why we want scientific hypotheses to be precisely formulated is that we welcome their conclusive falsification (at least if they are not too central to our conception of things). Conclusive falsification of a hypothesis is *progress* in science. But falsification of an item of faith is *not* progress—at least not from the perspective within which it is an item of faith. To think that falsification of the belief in morality itself, or of the belief that a moral life is worth living, might be pure progress is already to hold an amoral view, a morally bad view. The falsification might be progress toward knowing the truth, but that sort of progress is not, and ought not to be, the only thing that concerns us here. A loss of moral faith would be the loss of something precious.

To this it may obviously be objected that if the moral faith is false, then the loss of it would be the loss of something not so precious after all. This objection is not as good as it looks at first. One weakness in it is that when we consider what we would lose in giving up a belief as falsified, we have to consider the value the belief has if it is true as well as if it is false. For if we were sure that whenever we are seriously tempted to abandon a belief as falsified, it really is false, then all sincere resistance to such temptation would already have collapsed. But when we resist refutation of an item of moral faith, we may, and should, be thinking of the danger of being misled into giving it up while it is true. From a moral point of view that would be a worse mistake to make than the mistake of clinging to moral faith while it is false. Even if an item of moral faith is false, moreover, we are not likely in abandoning it to attain anything corresponding to the moral value of believing it if it is true. Either way there is of course the value of believing the truth; but there is an additional moral value in moral faith, or made possible by moral faith, if it is true, which would not be replicated in acceptance of a morally emptier truth. In view of this important asymmetry, I think it would be foolish to say that there is the same kind of value in refutation as in confirmation of moral faith, whereas it is quite reasonable to say that there is the same kind of value in falsification as in verification of a scientific hypothesis.

It is worth noting that the balance of potential payoffs is much more equal when it is a question of revising moral faith, rather than abandoning it. For if revision of moral faith leads to truth, or to a closer approximation to truth, it will presumably not be a morally empty truth, but a view that is morally more adequate. If a revision of moral faith is correct, the revised faith will presumably have *more* moral value than the unrevised had. Thus we can hope that revision of moral faith will be progress from a moral point of view. This is a further reason for thinking it is good for moral faith to combine a variable, revisable form with a vaguer but more enduring core,

---

12. Kant, *Logic*, p. 80. I am indebted to Houston Smit for calling this passage to my attention. Kant goes farther than I would in declaring that faith does not even *listen* to counterreasons.

so that self-critical growth and development may be combined with constancy of commitment.

Items of faith are not hypotheses to be tested by experience, though we may well want their *formulations* to be tested by experience. Items of faith may in fact be tested by experience, but we are not trying to refute them. We are trying to live by them. In science we commonly have reason to frame hypotheses in such a way that they are liable to conclusive refutation by experience. But if we have reason to have faith in something, we have reason to conceive of the object of faith in such a way that our faith can change and develop without being abandoned as it is tested by experience. This does not mean that moral faith is wholly unempirical, let alone noncognitive, but that it involves a different way of accommodating thought to experience, a way that is reasonable in some cases, given the diversity of human interests at stake in morality and in science.

Maybe this suggests too stark a contrast between morality and science. Perhaps in science too a variable, revisable form, consisting of hypotheses up for refutation, is to be distinguished from a core that is more resistant to change, and that is an appropriate object of commitment or (dare we say it?) faith. Notoriously, the reliability of induction, and more broadly of empirical scientific methods, has been doubted by reasonable persons; and it may not be possible to set the doubts to rest in a completely satisfying way. Yet a refutation of the reliability of induction would not be scientific *progress* in the same way that a refutation of the meteorite explanation of the extinction of dinosaurs might be. Indeed, it is hard to see how we could make progress in empirical science at all if we abandoned induction. So perhaps there is a place, or even a need, for *faith* in the highest level beliefs of science. That is a suggestion[13] that is not at all unwelcome to me; but I will not pursue it here, as I wish to keep my focus on *moral* faith.

4. The Volitional Aspect of Moral Faith

Probably all belief involves the will. Part of believing a proposition is in general being disposed to act on the assumption that it is true. That is also part of *faith*, but faith involves the will more deeply than that. To have faith is always to be *for* what one has faith in. It is perfectly consistent to say you *believe* that Clinton will win but you're still planning to vote for Bush; but a genuine Bush supporter could hardly have *faith* that Clinton will win. *Moral* faith involves being *for* something in a special way. Like religious faith, it involves *commitment*.

There is doubtless moral and religious belief that does not amount to faith and does not involve commitment. That can occur, perhaps most easily in a relatively homogeneous society, if one simply accepts what one has been taught of ethics and religion in much the same way that one accepts what one has been taught about the past, but without caring much about it or making much effort to live by it. Here

---

13. For which I am indebted to Marc Lange, though it would be presumptuous of me to commit him to its correctness.

the ethical and religious beliefs seem more like something that has happened to the person than like a stance he has taken. That does not relieve him of responsibility for them; but it does mean that he is not *committed* to them, and we would certainly not speak of them as *faith*. We also would not think such beliefs a credit to the person, even if we agreed with them.

Another way in which one could hold an ethical or religious belief without commitment is *tentatively*. And this is sometimes appropriate. To hold as merely probable a theological opinion about the virgin birth of Jesus, or a moral opinion about whether a fetus has rights, may show commendable humility and restraint. One is not exactly committed to such a belief, and it is not an instance of faith. One who holds all her moral beliefs in this way, however, is not a moral person. '*Probably* it's wrong to torture innocent children' and '*Probably* the moral law is binding on us' are hardly recognizable as expressions of a moral stance. Neither is '*Probably* we are entitled to treat a Hitler as wrong or evil, and not just as someone who has a different point of view'. And while a thoroughly moral person might indeed say, '*Probably* Uncle Al's life is still worth living', it would not be an expression of faith.

Kierkegaard was a pioneer in exploring the aspect of faith that we touch here. It has long been recognized that there is something incongruous in holding an article of faith as merely probable. Classical accounts of Christian faith expressed this by speaking of a *certainty* of faith, or of a "sure confidence," or a "feeling of full assurance," as Calvin puts it.[14] Kierkegaard is as emphatic as Calvin that an opinion held as merely probable cannot constitute faith, but he does not speak of faith in terms of feelings of assurance. On the contrary, the faith that interests him is one that coexists with an acute awareness of the "risk" that it is wrong. "If I wish to preserve myself in faith," says Kierkegaard, using a memorable image, "I must constantly be intent upon holding fast the objective uncertainty, so as to remain out upon the deep, over seventy thousand fathoms of water, still preserving my faith."[15] This is a type of faith that will typically coexist with doubt.

We may not agree with everything Kierkegaard says about the desirability of uncertainty. In section 5 I will have something to say about the importance of something like confidence for the moral life, and I would say much the same about the religious life. For most people in the modern world, however, a confidence amounting to subjective certainty seems neither possible nor desirable. Whatever our ethical or religious commitment, and whatever our confidence in it, it must be held together with the knowledge that there is a sense in which "we could be wrong," as I have already noted. On this issue about the nature of faith—moral as well as religious faith—Kierkegaard seems likelier than Calvin to speak to our condition.

How, then, can we be *committed* to an ethical or religious outlook and way of life? Kierkegaard sees commitment in terms of decisiveness, and while in some ways his view is probably too voluntaristic, I think his emphasis on decisiveness is more importantly right than wrong. The attitude of the will, broadly understood, is cru-

14. Calvin, *Institutes*, vol. 1, p. 560f. (III,ii,15).
15. Kierkegaard, *Concluding Unscientific Postscript*, p. 182.

cial to commitment. The possibility that one is wrong may be recognized, but at certain points it must be disregarded in one's decisions and actions and way of life, and one's "bets" must not be "hedged." This is the heart of Kierkegaard's account of faith.

While tentativeness seems quite appropriate in some ethical and theological opinions, a moral life, like a religious life, requires a core of commitment, and in relation to that core we are not prepared to accept attitudes toward probability and doubt that seem perfectly appropriate, or even praiseworthy, in relation to most other topics. It is not morally acceptable to "hedge one's bet" on morality. Factoring into one's financial decisions whatever chance of error one sees in one's forecasts of economic trends is prudent, and usually commendable. But if I factor into my practical deliberations a "10 percent chance that morality is a delusion," or a "25 percent chance that my efforts to lead a moral life are just a waste of energy and opportunity," or a "30 to 50 percent chance that my children will be better off if they subordinate morality to self-interest," then I have stepped outside the moral life.

"A wise man . . . proportions his belief to the evidence," claimed David Hume.[16] A moral person, however, will have a degree of commitment to some central ethical beliefs that is more than proportionate to the strength of the evidence or arguments supporting them. In that sense morality requires a faith that goes beyond what we can establish by reasoning. It does not follow that the beliefs to which a moral person is committed cannot all be favored by reason, in preference to alternatives. It is just that reason's support for them is not likely to be as solid as morality's.

Closely related to the central role of commitment in faith is the phenomenon of *struggles* of faith, or striving for faith. That we strive for faith is connected with an important point that I think American pragmatist philosophers got right, that our cognitive project is one of developing a system of beliefs that can be integrated not only with experience but also with the living of a moral life, and more broadly a good life. The striving often takes the form of *clinging* to faith. This phenomenon is familiar to most religious believers, and I think it has a place in moral as well as religious faith. A moral person has reason to cling to moral faith, with some tenacity, when it is tried by doubts.

In such clinging there is a desire to hold a particular belief, which is certainly not just a desire to believe whatever is true. It is easy for us to have a bad conscience about this, for we tend to think that both the reliability and the honesty of a belief are apt to be corrupted if one is influenced, in holding it, by the desire to hold it. It is often claimed also that one cannot be aware of being influenced by such a desire without that awareness undermining the belief that is recognized as influenced by it; but I think this undermining need not occur, and often does not, in cases of clinging to faith. Why is that? And must the belief be seen as corrupted by the desire?

Well, why would belief be undermined or corrupted by such awareness? If impartial desire to believe whatever is true is likelier to lead to true belief than the desire to cling to one's present belief, then the influence of the latter sort of desire may well corrupt the reliability of one's belief formation process. And if one sees

---

16. Hume, *An Enquiry Concerning Human Understanding*, p. 73 (section X, part I).

the reliability of one's thinking as reduced in this way, that may undermine one's confidence and one's sincerity in believing. But *is* the impartial desire more likely to lead to truth than the desire that strives for faith? It will be, where one has fairly reliable truth-finding faculties that are independent of one's desires (or independent of all but the impartial desire to believe whatever is true).

In ethics, however, I do not think we have truth-finding faculties independent of our desires. Whatever may be the nature of ethical truth, it is not plausible to suppose that those whose hearts are in the wrong place are as likely to find it as those whose hearts are in the right place. If I hold moral convictions, I will not suppose that my ability to grasp their truth is independent of the way in which their content moves my feelings and my will; and to be moved in the relevant way is in part to want to hold the convictions; it is not independent of volitional commitment to them. To suppose that our thinking in such matters would be more reliable if we did not care which conclusion we come to, so long as it is the correct one, is to propose an implausibly coldhearted conception of what would constitute reliable thinking in ethics.

The matter is more complex than that, however, and I will surely not be able to exhaust its complexity here. For not every desire to hold a particular ethical belief seems to be an appropriate motive. Suppose, for instance, that one wants to believe that a certain course of action is right because one stands to profit from it financially. Clinging to the belief from that motive, though humanly understandable, does not seem admirable, and we would not want to dignify it with the title of "moral faith." And the desire to profit financially from a course of action does seem unlikely to contribute to the reliability of any moral judgment concerning the action. Such a motive for an ethical belief seems as suspect epistemologically, and morally, as a financially motivated desire to believe that tobacco smoke does not cause cancer, or to believe that our current energy policies are not leading to catastrophic global warming.

In other cases we may face more delicate questions about the appropriateness of desire as a motive for belief. Suppose I hold an opinion one way or the other about the rightness or wrongness of a law permitting women, unconditionally, to have an abortion on demand. Believing my position right seems to give me a reason to want to continue to hold it. Moreover, assuming this desire is grounded in feelings about relevant matters, such as fetuses and women's lives, there is no reason in this case to suppose that my judgment would be more reliable if I were not moved to want to retain my belief. So is it appropriate for me to *cling* to my belief on this issue in the face of any misgivings that may arise? That seems very doubtful, and its doubtfulness is connected with the distinction I made earlier between revising and abandoning moral faith. A humane and reasonable moral faith will include the belief that we all could be more enlightened ethically than we are, and will therefore demand an openness, as unprejudiced as we can manage, to certain revisions of our ethical opinions.

But which revisions are those? Are some of our moral judgments items of moral faith, to which we should cling, whereas others are mere moral opinions, to which we should try not to be attached? Or ought we to be as open as possible to revision of any of our beliefs about particular ethical issues? Must we try to give an unprejudiced hearing to the golden-tongued prophet of a movement that seeks to persuade us that we have been wrong in condemning slavery or genocide, for example? Surely not; there are some moral judgments that it would be a betrayal of morality, or of humanity, to think seriously about abandoning. I have no formula for determining which moral issues we ought to regard as issues of faith, and which as mere matters of opinion, or for determining how strong and unyielding a degree of commitment is appropriate on a given issue of moral faith. But if it seems to us that giving up a particular moral conviction would amount to an abandonment of other human beings, or of a significant part of the moral meaning of our own lives, those are certainly reasons for regarding the matter as an issue of faith.

The line between moral faith and moral opinion may fall in different places for different people with different histories. For many students utilitarianism may be an opinion that can be adopted and abandoned with little struggle. For John Stuart Mill it was something more—a commitment that he shared with other people and that structured his life's projects, a faith that he strove to reshape rather than abandon in the light of objections and his own experience.

A question that is regularly and rightly addressed to me in view of these claims is whether moral faith is still a virtue when it is faith in the wrong cause. I believe it can be, though not if the cause is too indefensible. The possibility of virtues being manifested in the service of the wrong cause is crucial for the morality of conflict. Conflict is dehumanized when we lose the sense that our enemies can be admirable in opposing us, even though we think them wrong. It is a sort of self-righteousness to think that nothing matters by comparison with being on the right side. Epic poets and professional politicians have known that respecting one's enemies is commonly of at least comparable importance. Recognizing and admiring in one's antagonist such virtues as courage, loyalty, and faith is a major ingredient of that respect.

Like courage, like loyalty, faith is a dangerous virtue. We may rightly refuse to call them virtues at all where they are part of a pattern of moral depravity. But if we refuse them the title of virtue wherever they are implicated in understandable moral error and contribute to guilt or disaster, we deny appropriate recognition to the frail and fragmentary character of our grasp of moral and other truth.

5. The Emotional Aspect of Moral Faith

There remains an important aspect of faith about which I shall say only a little here. A voluntary decision to commit yourself to a proposition does not, by itself, amount to faith. Even the decision plus a bunch of good reasons for your decision still are not sufficient for a sincere belief, let alone a conviction.

Faith as I conceive of it moves in a space bounded on the one side by subjective certainty (which Calvin ascribed to faith, but I do not) and on the other side by the subjectively incredible. Within that space it is often hard to tell, subjectively, how far one's faith is supported by one's sense of what is more plausible, and how far by willpower. But both, I think, are normally involved.

It is also not easy to specify what more is required beyond willpower. One is tempted to say that what you believe must *seem true* to you, or at least must not *seem false*. Seeming true or seeming false in this context is largely a matter of *feeling*, and as a first approximation we might try to identify the requisite feeling as at least a minimal degree of *confidence* in the view that you hold.[17]

This is not adequate as it stands, however. If you are depressed, you may doubt that your life is worth living. It may not *feel* worth living; it may *seem* to you that it is not worth living. In such a case we can hardly say that you have *confidence* that your life is worth living. Yet in precisely this sort of case it is very likely both possible and right for you to cling to *faith* that your life is worth living.

Is it sheer willpower if you do cling to it? Surely not. Willpower cannot give you a belief in a hypothesis that is not "live" for you, as William James put it.[18] Probably no amount of willpower could give you the belief that 2 + 2 = 5, or even that you will never die. Nor, I imagine, could sheer willpower give you the belief that the number of bald eagles that laid eggs in 1993 was even rather than odd. If you succeed, against emotional appearances, in clinging to the faith that your life is worth living, the clinging must feel different from trying to believe one of those patently false or humanly undecidable propositions. Perhaps you feel some level of trust in some reasons for clinging to faith, or perhaps giving up faith "feels wrong" to you.

But 'confidence' is hardly the right word here.[19] It suggests a state of feeling that is much less troubled than faith has often to endure. In some ways I prefer the word 'courage', provided I can make clear that I do not mean courage as a mainly voluntary virtue. I mean courage in a sense in which it is felt more than chosen, the sense in which it might be a direct product of being "encouraged." In Greek it would be θάρσος (*tharsos*) rather than ἀνδρεία (*andreia*); in German it would be *Mut* rather than *Tapferkeit*.[20] The courage of which I would speak is not sheer willpower or voluntary determination, but an inner force which carries one forward, and is *felt* as sustaining determination. We may hope that such emotions are responsive to reality. They must be, if we are to have much chance of living a life both good and grounded in reality. In a sense indicated by my argument (not to mention other senses) "the just shall live by faith."[21]

17. For interesting discussion of the importance of confidence in an ethical outlook and life, see Williams, *Ethics and the Limits of Philosophy*, pp. 170–71. Williams sees it, however, as "basically a social phenomenon," one which exists in individuals, but only in a much less adequate form if it is not shared by their society as a whole. My focus on faith under trial leads me to be more interested in aspects of belief that can exist in individuals without being shared by a whole society.

18. W. James, *The Will to Believe*, pp. 2–3.

19. Here I would like to unsay something I said in *The Virtue of Faith* (p. 46): "Peace, joy, gratitude, and the freedom to love are supposed to flow from a confidently held conviction that God is good." This is not only too simple; it is a "Pollyanna" sentiment.

20. Cf. Tillich, *The Courage to Be*, pp. 5–6, a text that inspired the theme of this paragraph.

21. Romans 1:17; cf. Habakkuk 2:4.

BIBLIOGRAPHY

This bibliography mentions only works cited in this book. Page references in the text and notes are to a reprint or English translation if one is listed in the bibliography. I have usually quoted from a published English translation, but I have sometimes emended the translation and have sometimes given my own translation— normally without noting the fact, as this is not a work of historical scholarship.

Abbott, Walter M., ed. *The Documents of Vatican II*. New York: Herder and Herder/Association Press, 1966.

Ackerman, Bruce A. *Social Justice in the Liberal State*. New Haven, Conn.: Yale University Press, 1980.

Ackrill, J. L. "Aristotle on 'Good' and the Categories." Reprinted in Barnes et al., eds., *Articles on Aristotle*, vol. 2, pp. 17–24.

Adams, Robert Merrihew. "Actualism and Thisness." *Synthese* 49 (1981): 3–41.

———. "The Concept of a Divine Command." In Phillips, ed., *Religion and Morality*, pp. 59–80.

———. "Divine Command Metaethics Modified Again." *Journal of Religious Ethics* 7 (1979): 66–79. Reprinted as chap. 9 of Adams, *The Virtue of Faith*.

———. "Divine Commands and the Social Nature of Obligation." *Faith and Philosophy* 4 (1987): 262–75.

———. "Divine Necessity." *Journal of Philosophy* 80 (1983): 741–52. Reprinted as chap. 14 of Adams, *The Virtue of Faith*.

————. "Existence, Self-Interest, and the Problem of Evil." *Noûs* 13 (1979): 53–65. Reprinted, with major corrections, as chap. 5 of Adams, *The Virtue of Faith.*

————. "Has It Been Proved That All Real Existence Is Contingent?" *American Philosophical Quarterly* 8 (1971): 284–91. Reprinted as chap. 13 of Adams, *The Virtue of Faith.*

————. "Idolatry and the Invisibility of God." In Biderman and Scharfstein, eds., *Interpretation in Religion*, pp. 39–52.

————. "Involuntary Sins." *Philosophical Review* 94 (1985): 3–31.

————. "The Knight of Faith." *Faith and Philosophy* 7 (1990): 383–95.

————. *Leibniz: Determinist, Theist, Idealist.* New York: Oxford University Press, 1994.

————. "Middle Knowledge and the Problem of Evil." *American Philosophical Quarterly* 14 (1977): 109–17. Reprinted as chap. 6 of Adams, *The Virtue of Faith.*

————. "A Modified Divine Command Theory of Ethical Wrongness." In Outka and Reeder, eds., *Religion and Morality*, pp. 318–47. Reprinted as chap. 7 of Adams, *The Virtue of Faith.*

————. "Moral Arguments for Theistic Belief." In Delaney, ed., *Rationality and Religious Belief,* pp. 116–40. Reprinted as chap. 10 of Adams, *The Virtue of Faith.*

————. "Motive Utilitarianism." *Journal of Philosophy* 73 (1976): 467–81.

————. "Must God Create the Best?" *Philosophical Review* 81 (1972): 317–32. Reprinted as chap. 4 of Adams, *The Virtue of Faith.*

————. "Platonism and Naturalism: Options for a Theocentric Ethics." In Runzo, ed., *Ethics, Religion, and the Good Society*, pp. 22–42.

————. "Primitive Thisness and Primitive Identity." *Journal of Philosophy* 76 (1979): 5–26.

————. "The Problem of Total Devotion." In Audi and Wainwright, eds., *Rationality, Religious Belief, and Moral Commitment*, pp. 169–94.

————. "Pure Love." *Journal of Religious Ethics* 8 (1980): 83–99.

————. "Religion after Babel." In Sharma, ed., *God, Truth, and Reality*, pp. 62–71.

————. "Religious Ethics in a Pluralistic Society." In Outka and Reeder, eds., *Prospects for a Common Morality*, pp. 93–113.

————. Review of McClendon, *Systematic Theology*, vol. 1. In *Faith and Philosophy* 7 (1990): 117–23.

————. "Saints." *Journal of Philosophy* 81 (1984): 392–401. Reprinted as chap. 11 of Adams, *The Virtue of Faith.*

————. "Self-Love and the Vices of Self-Preference." *Faith and Philosophy* 15 (1998): 500–13.

————. *The Virtue of Faith and Other Essays in Philosophical Theology.* New York: Oxford University Press, 1987.

Alston, William P. *Divine Nature and Human Language.* Ithaca, N.Y.: Cornell University Press, 1989.

————. "Epistemic Circularity." *Philosophy and Phenomenological Research* 47 (1986–87): 1–30.

————. *Perceiving God: The Epistemology of Religious Experience.* Ithaca, N.Y.: Cornell University Press, 1991.

Anderson, Elizabeth. *Value in Ethics and Economics.* Cambridge, Mass.: Harvard University Press, 1993.

Anselm. *Monologion.* In St. Anselm, *Basic Writings.* Trans. S. N. Deane. 2nd ed. La Salle, Ill.: Open Court, 1962.

————. *Proslogion.* Presented, with related texts, English translations, and commentary, by M. J. Charlesworth. Oxford: Clarendon Press, 1965.

Aquinas, Thomas. *Summa Theologiae.* Many editions and translations. Cited by standard divisions.

Arens, W. *The Man-Eating Myth: Anthropology and Anthropophagy.* New York: Oxford University Press, 1979.

Aristotle. *Metaphysics*. Many editions and translations. Cited by standard reference system.

———. *Nicomachean Ethics*. Many editions and translations. Cited by standard reference system.

———. *Physics*. Many editions and translations. Cited by standard reference system.

Audi, Robert, and William J. Wainwright, eds. *Rationality, Religious Belief, and Moral Commitment*. Ithaca, N.Y.: Cornell University Press, 1986.

Augustine (Aurelius Augustinus). *De doctrina Christiana*. In *Corpus scriptorum ecclesiasticorum latinorum*, vol. 80. Ed. William M. Green. Vienna: Hoelder-Pichler-Tempsky, 1963. English translation by D. W. Robertson, Jr., *On Christian Doctrine*. New York: Liberal Arts Press, 1958.

———. "On Lying." Trans. H. Browne in Schaff, ed., *Nicene and Post-Nicene Fathers*, vol. 3, pp. 455–77.

———. "To Consentius: Against Lying." Trans. H. Browne in Schaff, ed., *Nicene and Post-Nicene Fathers*, vol. 3, pp. 479–500.

Baier, Annette. *Postures of the Mind: Essays on Mind and Morals*. Minneapolis: University of Minnesota Press, 1985.

———. "Secular Faith." *Canadian Journal of Philosophy* 10 (1980): 131–48. Reprinted in Baier, *Postures of the Mind*, pp. 292–308.

Barnes, Jonathan, et al., eds. *Articles on Aristotle*. 4 vols. London: Duckworth, 1975–79.

Barry, Brian. *Justice as Impartiality* (*A Treatise on Social Justice*, vol. 2). Oxford: Clarendon Press, 1995.

———. *Political Argument*. London: Routledge and Kegan Paul, 1965.

Bartchy, S. Scott. ΜΑΛΛΟΝ ΧΡΗΣΑΙ [*Mallon Chresai*]: *First-Century Slavery and the Interpretation of 1 Corinthians 7:21*. Missoula Mont.: Society of Biblical Literature, 1973.

Barth, Karl. *Church Dogmatics*. 4 vols. in many part-volumes. Trans. G. W. Bromiley et al. Edinburgh: T. and T. Clark, 1936–69.

Bethge, Eberhard. *Dietrich Bonhoeffer*. New York: Harper and Row, 1977.

Biderman, Shlomo, and Ben Ami Scharfstein, eds. *Interpretation in Religion*. Leiden: E. J. Brill, 1992.

Blum, Lawrence. *Friendship, Altruism, and Morality*. London: Routledge and Kegan Paul, 1980.

Bolle, Kees W., trans. *The Bhagavadgita: A New Translation*. Berkeley: University of California Press, 1979.

Bonhoeffer, Dietrich. *Ethics*. Ed. Eberhard Bethge; trans. Neville Horton Smith. New York: Macmillan, 1961.

———. *Letters and Papers from Prison*. Enlarged edition. Ed. Eberhard Bethge. New York: Macmillan, 1972.

Boyd, Richard. "How to Be a Moral Realist." In Sayre-McCord, ed., *Essays on Moral Realism*, pp. 181–228.

Brandt, Richard. *A Theory of the Good and the Right*. Oxford: Clarendon Press, 1979.

Brink, David O. *Moral Realism and the Foundations of Ethics*. Cambridge: Cambridge University Press, 1989.

Brown, Deborah. "The Right Method of Boy-Loving." In Lamb, ed., *Love Analyzed*, pp. 49–63.

Browne, Sir Thomas. *Religio Medici*. Ed. Jean-Jacques Denonain. Cambridge: Cambridge University Press, 1953.

Brunner, Emil. *The Divine Imperative*. Trans. Olive Wyon. Philadelphia: Westminster Press, 1947.

Buber, Martin. *Between Man and Man*. Trans. Ronald Gregor Smith and Maurice Friedman. New York: Macmillan, 1965.

———. *I and Thou*. Trans. Walter Kaufmann. New York: Scribner's, 1970.

———. *Werke*. Vol. 1, *Schriften zur Philosophie*. Munich and Heidelberg: Kösel-Verlag and Verlag Lambert Schneider, 1962.

Butler, Joseph. *Fifteeen Sermons Preached at the Rolls Chapel.* Ed. T. A. Roberts. London: SPCK, 1970.

Buttrick, G. A., et al., eds. *The Interpreter's Dictionary of the Bible.* New York: Abingdon Press, 1962.

Callicott, J. Baird. "On the Intrinsic Value of Nonhuman Species." In Norton, ed., *The Preservation of Species,* pp. 138–72.

Calvin, John. *Institutes of the Christian Religion.* 2 vols. Ed. John T. McNeill; trans. Ford Lewis Battles. Philadelphia: Westminster Press, 1960.

Camus, Albert. *The Rebel.* Revised translation by Anthony Bower. New York: Vintage Books, 1957.

Catullus. *Selections from Catullus.* Ed. Michael Macmillan. London: Oxford University Press, 1921.

Chandler, John. "Divine Command Theories and the Appeal to Love." *American Philosophical Quarterly* 22 (1985): 231–39.

Congregational Praise. London: Independent Press, 1951.

Cooper, John. "Aristotle on Friendship." In Rorty, ed., *Essays on Aristotle's Ethics,* pp. 301–40.

Copp, David. "Explanation and Justification in Ethics." *Ethics* 100 (1990): 237–58.

Copp, David, and David Zimmerman, eds. *Morality, Reason, and Truth: New Essays on the Foundations of Ethics.* Totowa, N.J.: Rowman and Allanheld, 1984.

Cumberland, Richard. *A Treatise of the Laws of Nature* [*De legibus naturae*]. Trans. John Maxwell. London, 1727. Facsimile reprint, New York: Garland Publishing, 1978.

Daniels, Norman, ed. *Reading Rawls.* New York: Basic Books, 1975.

Darwall, Stephen, Allan Gibbard, and Peter Railton. "Toward *Fin de siècle* Ethics: Some Trends." *Philosophical Review* 101 (1992): 115–89.

de Graaff, Graeme. "God and Morality." In Ramsey, ed., *Christian Ethics and Contemporary Philosophy,* pp. 31–52.

Delaney, C. F., ed. *Rationality and Religious Belief.* Notre Dame and London: University of Notre Dame Press, 1979.

Dewey, John. *A Common Faith.* New Haven, Conn.: Yale University Press, 1960.

Douglas, Mary. *Implicit Meanings: Essays in Anthropology.* London: Routledge and Kegan Paul, 1975.

———. *Purity and Danger: An Analysis of Concepts of Pollution and Taboo.* London: Routledge and Kegan Paul, 1969.

Durkheim, Émile. *L'éducation morale.* Paris: Félix Alcan, 1925.

Dworkin, Ronald. "Liberalism." In Stuart Hampshire, ed., *Public and Private Morality.* Cambridge: Cambridge University Press, 1978. Reprinted in Sandel, ed., *Liberalism and Its Critics,* pp. 60–79.

———. *Life's Dominion: An Argument about Abortion, Euthanasia, and Individual Freedom.* New York: Alfred A. Knopf, 1993.

———. *Taking Rights Seriously.* Cambridge, Mass.: Harvard University Press, 1977.

Feinberg, Joel. *Offense to Others.* Vol. 2 of *The Moral Limits of the Criminal Law.* New York: Oxford University Press, 1985.

Field, Hartry. *Science without Numbers: A Defense of Nominalism.* Princeton, N.J.: Princeton University Press, 1980.

FitzPatrick, William. *Functional Teleology, Biology, and Ethics.* Ann Arbor, Mich.: UMI Dissertation Services, 1995.

Flanagan, Owen. "Admirable Immorality and Admirable Imperfection." *Journal of Philosophy* 83 (1986): 41–60.

Flew, Antony. "Theology and Falsification." In Flew and MacIntyre, eds., *New Essays in Philosophical Theology,* pp. 96–99, 106–8.

Flew, Antony, and Alasdair MacIntyre, eds. *New Essays in Philosophical Theology.* New York: Macmillan, 1964.

Foot, Philippa. "Utilitarianism and the Virtues." *Proceedings and Addresses of the American Philosophical Association* 57 (November 1983): 273–83. Expanded reprint in *Mind* 94 (1985): 196–209.

Fox, Richard Wightman. *Reinhold Niebuhr: A Biography.* San Francisco: Harper and Row, 1987.

Frankfurt, Harry. "Freedom of the Will and the Concept of a Person." *Journal of Philosophy* 68 (1971): 5–20.

———. "The Importance of What We Care About." *Synthese* 53 (1982): 257–72.

Gauthier, René Antoine, and Jean Yves Jolif. *L'Éthique à Nicomaque.* 2nd ed. Vol. 2, pt. 1. Louvain: Publications Universitaires, 1970.

Gibbard, Allan. "Moral Concepts: Substance and Sentiment." *Philosophical Perspectives* 6 (1992): 199–221.

———. *Wise Choices, Apt Feelings: A Theory of Normative Judgment.* Cambridge, Mass.: Harvard University Press, 1990.

Goodman, Nelson. *Problems and Projects.* Indianapolis: Bobbs-Merrill, 1972.

Green, Ronald M. "Abraham, Isaac, and the Jewish Tradition: An Ethical Reappraisal." *Journal of Religious Ethics* 10 (1982): 1–21.

Greenawalt, Kent. *Private Consciences and Public Reasons.* New York: Oxford University Press, 1995.

———. "Religion as a Concept in Constitutional Law." *California Law Review* 72 (1984): 753–81.

———. *Religious Convictions and Political Choice.* New York: Oxford University Press, 1988.

Grice, Paul. "Meaning." *Philosophical Review* 66 (1957). Reprinted in Grice, *Studies in the Way of Words*, pp. 213–23.

———. *Studies in the Way of Words.* Cambridge, Mass.: Harvard University Press, 1989.

Griffin, James. *Well-Being: Its Meaning, Measurement, and Moral Importance.* Oxford: Clarendon Press, 1986.

Gustafson, James. *Ethics from a Theocentric Perspective.* 2 vols. Chicago: University of Chicago Press, 1981, 1984.

Hallie, Philip P. *Horror and the Paradox of Cruelty.* Middletown, Conn.: Center for Advanced Studies, Wesleyan University, 1969.

Harman, Gilbert. "Is There a Single True Morality?" In Copp and Zimmerman, eds., *Morality, Reason, and Truth*, pp. 27–48.

———. "Moral Explanations of Natural Facts: Can Moral Claims Be Tested against Moral Reality?" *Southern Journal of Philosophy* 24, supplement (1986): 57–68.

———. *The Nature of Morality: An Introduction to Ethics.* New York: Oxford University Press, 1977.

Hart, H. L. A. *Law, Liberty, and Morality.* Stanford, Calif.: Stanford University Press, 1963.

———. "Rawls on Liberty and Its Priority." *University of Chicago Law Review* 40 (1973): 534–55. Reprinted in Daniels, ed., *Reading Rawls*, pp. 230–52.

The Heidelberg Catechism, in German, Latin and English: With an Historical Introduction. Prepared and published by the German Reformed Church in the U.S.A. New York: Charles Scribner, 1863.

Henson, Richard. "Utilitarianism and the Wrongness of Killing." *Philosophical Review* 80 (1971): 320–37.

Hohfeld, Wesley Newcomb. *Fundamental Legal Conceptions.* Ed. Walter Wheeler Cook. New Haven, Conn.: Yale University Press, 1919.

Hume, David. *An Enquiry Concerning Human Understanding.* Indianapolis: Hackett, 1977.

———. *A Treatise of Human Nature.* Ed. L. A. Selby-Bigge. Oxford: Clarendon Press, 1888.

Hurka, Thomas. *Perfectionism.* New York: Oxford University Press, 1993.

The Hymnal. Philadelphia: Presbyterian Board of Christian Education, 1939.

James, Henry. *The Portrait of a Lady*. New York: Norton, 1975.

James, William. *The Will to Believe and Other Essays in Popular Philosophy*. New York: Longmans, Green and Co., 1897.

Kant, Immanuel. *The Conflict of the Faculties* (1798). Trans. Mary J. Gregor and Robert Anchor, in Kant, *Religion and Rational Theology*, pp. 233–327.

———. *Critique of Practical Reason*. Several editions and translations.

———. *Critique of Pure Reason*. Trans. and ed. Paul Guyer and Allen W. Wood. Cambridge: Cambridge University Press, 1998. Cited by pages of the first (A) and second (B) German editions.

———. *Logik*. Ed. Gottlob Benjamin Jäsche (1800), various modern reprints. English translation by Robert Hartman and Wolfgang Schwarz, *Logic*. Indianapolis: Bobbs-Merrill, 1974.

———. *Religion and Rational Theology*. Trans. and ed. Allen W. Wood and George di Giovanni. Cambridge: Cambridge University Press, 1996.

———. *Religion within the Boundaries of Mere Reason: and Other Writings*. Trans. and ed. Allen W. Wood and George di Giovanni, with introduction by Robert Merrihew Adams. Cambridge: Cambridge University Press, 1998.

Kierkegaard, Søren, *Concluding Unscientific Postscript*. Trans. David F. Swenson and Walter Lowrie. Princeton, N.J.: Princeton University Press, 1941.

———. *Either/Or*. Vol. 2. Ed. and trans. Howard V. Hong and Edna H. Hong. Princeton, N.J.: Princeton University Press, 1987.

———. *Fear and Trembling* and *Repetition*. Ed. and trans. Howard V. Hong and Edna H. Hong. Princeton, N.J.: Princeton University Press, 1983.

———. *The Journals of Kierkegaard*. Trans. and ed. Alexander Dru. New York: Harper Torchbooks, 1959.

———. *The Sickness unto Death*. Ed. and trans. Howard V. Hong and Edna H. Hong. Princeton, N.J.: Princeton University Press, 1980.

———. *Stages on Life's Way*. Trans. Walter Lowrie. New York: Schocken Books, 1967.

Korsgaard, Christine M. *Creating the Kingdom of Ends*. Cambridge: Cambridge University Press, 1996.

Kraut, Richard. "Desire and the Human Good." *Proceedings and Addresses of the American Philosophical Association* 68, no. 2 (1994): 39–54.

Lamb, Roger E. "Love and Rationality." In Lamb, ed., *Love Analyzed*, pp. 23–47.

———, ed. *Love Analyzed*. Boulder, Colo.: Westview Press, 1997.

Larmore, Charles. *Patterns of Moral Complexity*. Cambridge: Cambridge University Press, 1987.

Lear, Jonathan. "Ethics, Mathematics and Relativism." *Mind* 92 (1983): 38–60. Reprinted in Sayre-McCord, ed., *Essays on Moral Realism*, pp. 76–94.

Leibniz, Gottfried Wilhelm. *Discourse on Metaphysics*. Many editions and translations. Cited by section number.

———. *The Political Writings of Leibniz*. Trans. and ed. Patrick Riley. Cambridge: Cambridge University Press, 1972.

———. *Theodicy*. Several editions. English translation by E. M. Huggard. La Salle, Ill.: Open Court, 1985. Cited by section number.

Levenson, Jon D. *The Death and Resurrection of the Beloved Son: The Transformation of Child Sacrifice in Judaism and Christianity*. New Haven, Conn.: Yale University Press, 1993.

Lippmann, Walter. *A Preface to Morals*. New York: Macmillan, 1929.

Little, David, and Sumner B. Twiss, Jr. "Basic Terms in the Study of Religious Ethics." In Outka and Reeder, eds. *Religion and Morality*, pp. 35–77.

Locke, John. *Epistola de Tolerantia/Letter on Toleration* (1689). Ed. Raymond Klibansky; trans. J. W. Gough. Oxford: Clarendon Press, 1968.

————. *An Essay Concerning Human Understanding*. Ed. Peter H. Nidditch. Oxford: Clarendon Press, 1975. Cited by standard divisions.

Luban, Marvin. *The Kaddish: Man's Reply to the Problem of Evil*. New York: Yeshiva University, 1962.

Lucretius (Titus Lucretius Carus). *De rerum natura*. Ed. Cyril Bailey. Oxford: Clarendon Press, n.d.

MacIntyre, Alasdair. *After Virtue: A Study in Moral Theory*. Notre Dame, Ind.: University of Notre Dame Press, 1981.

————. "Which God Ought We to Obey and Why?" *Faith and Philosophy* 3 (1986): 359–71.

————. *Whose Justice? Which Rationality?* Notre Dame Ind.: University of Notre Dame Press, 1988.

Mackie, J. L. *Ethics: Inventing Right and Wrong*. Harmondsworth, England: Penguin Books, 1977.

Malament, David. Review of Field, *Science without Numbers*. *Journal of Philosophy* 79 (1982): 523–34.

Marshall, Paul. *A Kind of Life Imposed on Man: Vocation and Social Order from Tyndale to Locke*. Toronto: University of Toronto Press, 1996.

McClendon, James Wm., Jr. *Systematic Theology*. Vol. 1, *Ethics*. Nashville: Abingdon Press, 1986.

McDowell, John. "Virtue and Reason." *The Monist* 62 (1979): 331–50.

Meilaender, Gilbert. "*Eritis sicut Deus*: Moral Theory and the Sin of Pride." *Faith and Philosophy* 3 (1986): 397–415.

————. *Friendship: A Study in Theological Ethics*. Notre Dame, Ind.: University of Notre Dame Press, 1981.

Mill, John Stuart. *On Liberty*. Many editions. Cited by standard divisions.

————. *Utilitarianism*. Many editions. Cited by standard divisions.

Mitton, C. L. "Grace." In Buttrick et al., eds., *The Interpreter's Dictionary of the Bible*, vol. 2, pp. 463–68.

Moore, G. E. *Principia Ethica*. Rev. ed. Ed. Thomas Baldwin. Cambridge: Cambridge University Press, 1993.

Mouw, Richard J. *The God Who Commands*. Notre Dame, Ind.: University of Notre Dame Press, 1990.

Murdoch, Iris. *Metaphysics as a Guide to Morals*. London: Penguin Books, 1992.

————. *The Sovereignty of Good*. New York: Schocken Books, 1971.

Murphy, Mark. "Divine Command, Divine Will, and Moral Obligation." *Faith and Philosophy* 15 (1998): 3–27.

Murray, John Courtney. *Religious Liberty: Catholic Struggles with Pluralism*. Ed. J. Leon Hooper. Louisville, Ky.: Westminster/John Knox Press, 1993.

Nagel, Thomas. *Equality and Partiality*. New York: Oxford University Press, 1991.

————. *Mortal Questions*. Cambridge: Cambridge University Press, 1979.

————. *The View from Nowhere*. New York: Oxford University Press, 1986.

Narveson, Jan. "Moral Problems of Population." *The Monist* 57 (1973): 62–86.

Niebuhr, H. Richard. *Faith on Earth: An Inquiry into the Structure of Human Faith*. Ed. Richard R. Niebuhr. New Haven, Conn.: Yale University Press, 1989.

————. *Radical Monotheism and Western Culture*. New York: Harper Torchbooks, 1970.

Nietzsche, Friedrich. *Thus Spoke Zarathustra*. In *The Portable Nietzsche*. Ed. and trans. Walter Kaufmann. New York: Viking Press, 1954.

Norton, Bryan G. "On the Inherent Danger of Undervaluing Species." In Norton, ed., *The Preservation of Species*, pp. 110–37.

————, ed. *The Preservation of Species: The Value of Biological Diversity*. Princeton, N.J.: Princeton University Press, 1986.

Nowell-Smith, P. H. "Morality: Religious and Secular." *Rationalist Annual* (1961). Reprinted in Ramsey, ed., *Christian Ethics and Contemporary Philosophy*, pp. 95–112.

Nozick, Robert. *Anarchy, State, and Utopia*. Oxford: Basil Blackwell, 1974.

———. *The Nature of Rationality*. Princeton, N.J.: Princeton University Press, 1993.

Nussbaum, Martha C. *Love's Knowledge: Essays on Philosophy and Literature*. New York: Oxford University Press, 1990.

Nygren, Anders. *Agape and Eros*. Chicago: University of Chicago Press, 1982.

Otto, Rudolf. *The Idea of the Holy*. 2nd ed. Trans. John W. Harvey. London: Oxford University Press, 1950.

Outka, Gene. "Religious and Moral Duty: Notes on *Fear and Trembling*." In Outka and Reeder, eds., *Religion and Morality*, pp. 204–54.

Outka, Gene, and John P. Reeder, Jr., eds. *Prospects for a Common Morality*. Princeton, N.J.: Princeton University Press, 1993.

———. *Religion and Morality: A Collection of Essays*. Garden City, N.Y.: Doubleday Anchor, 1973.

Owen, G. E. L. "Logic and Metaphysics in Some Earlier Works of Aristotle." Reprinted in Barnes et al., eds., *Articles on Aristotle*, vol. 3, pp. 13–32.

Parfit, Derek. *Reasons and Persons*. Oxford: Clarendon Press, 1984.

Patterson, Richard. *Image and Reality in Plato's Metaphysics*. Indianapolis: Hackett, 1985.

Phillips, D. Z., ed. *Religion and Morality*. London: Macmillan, 1996.

Pieper, Josef. *About Love*. Chicago: Franciscan Herald Press, 1974.

Plato. *Phaedo*. Many editions and translations. Cited by standard reference system.

———. *Republic*. Many editions and translations. Cited by standard reference system.

———. *Symposium*. Many editions and translations. Cited by standard reference system.

Pool, David De Sola. *The Kaddish*. New York: Union of Sephardic Congregations, 1964.

Pufendorf, Samuel. *Political Writings*. Ed. Craig L. Carr; trans. Michael J. Seidler. New York: Oxford University Press, 1994.

Putnam, Hilary. *Mind, Language, and Reality: Philosophical Papers*. Vol. 2. Cambridge: Cambridge University Press, 1975.

Quine, Willard Van Orman. *From a Logical Point of View*. 2nd ed., revised. Cambridge, Mass.: Harvard University Press, 1963.

———. "Two Dogmas of Empiricism." First published in *The Philosophical Review* 60 (1951). Revised version in Quine, *From a Logical Point of View*, pp. 20–46.

Quinn, Philip L. "Divine Command Theory." Forthcoming in Hugh La Follette, ed., *A Guide to Ethical Theory*.

———. "Moral Obligation, Religious Demand, and Practical Conflict." In Audi and Wainwright, eds., *Rationality, Religious Belief, and Moral Commitment*, pp. 195–212.

———. "Religious Obedience and Moral Autonomy." *Religious Studies* 11 (1975): 265–81.

Quinn, Warren. *Morality and Action*. Cambridge: Cambridge University Press, 1993.

Railton, Peter. "Naturalism and Prescriptivity." *Social Philosophy and Policy* 7 (1989): 151–74.

Ramsey, Ian T., ed. *Christian Ethics and Contemporary Philosophy*. London: SCM Press, 1966.

Raphael, D. D., ed. *The British Moralists, 1650–1800*. 2 vols. Oxford: Clarendon Press, 1969.

Rawls, John. *Political Liberalism*. New York: Columbia University Press, 1993.

———. *A Theory of Justice*. Cambridge, Mass.: Harvard University Press, 1971.

Raz, Joseph. *The Morality of Freedom*. Oxford: Clarendon Press, 1986.

Read, James. *The Right Medicine: Philosophical Investigations into the Moral Wrongness of Killing Patients*. Ann Arbor, Mich.: University Microfilms, 1988.

Rorty, Amélie O., ed. *Essays on Aristotle's Ethics*. Berkeley: University of California Press, 1980.

———. *The Identities of Persons*. Berkeley: University of California Press, 1976.

Runzo, Joseph, ed. *Ethics, Religion, and the Good Society: New Directions in a Pluralistic World*. Louisville, Ky.: Westminster/John Knox Press, 1992.

Sandel, Michael, ed. *Liberalism and Its Critics*. New York: New York University Press, 1984.

Sayre-McCord, Geoffrey. "Moral Theory and Explanatory Impotence." In Sayre-McCord, ed., *Essays on Moral Realism*, pp. 256–81.

———, ed. *Essays on Moral Realism*. Ithaca, N.Y.: Cornell University Press, 1988.

Schaff, Philip, ed. *A Select Library of the Nicene and Post-Nicene Fathers of the Christian Church*. Vol. 3. Grand Rapids, Mich.: Eerdmans, 1956.

Scheffler, Samuel. *The Rejection of Consequentialism*. Rev. ed. Oxford: Clarendon Press, 1994.

Scheler, Max. *Wesen und Formen der Sympathie*. In Scheler's *Gesammelte Werke*. Vol. 7. Ed. Manfred S. Frings. Bern and Munich: Francke Verlag, 1973. English translation by Peter Heath, *The Nature of Sympathy*. Hamden, Conn.: Archon Books, 1970.

Schneewind, J. B. *The Invention of Autonomy: A History of Modern Moral Philosophy*. Cambridge: Cambridge University Press, 1998.

———. *Sidgwick's Ethics and Victorian Moral Philosophy*. Oxford: Clarendon Press, 1977.

Shakespeare, William. *Othello*. Many editions. Cited by standard divisions.

———. *Romeo and Juliet*. Many editions. Cited by standard divisions.

Shapiro, Stewart. "Conservativeness and Incompleteness." *Journal of Philosophy* 80 (1983): 521–31.

Sharma, Arvind, ed. *God, Truth, and Reality: Essays in Honour of John Hick*. London: Macmillan, 1993.

Shaver, Robert. "Sidgwick's False Friends." *Ethics* 107 (1997): 314–20.

Sidgwick, Henry. *The Methods of Ethics*. 7th ed. New York: Dover, 1966.

Silone, Ignazio. *Bread and Wine* (*Vino e pane*). Trans. Eric Mosbacher. London: Dent, 1986.

Slote, Michael. *Beyond Optimizing: A Study of Rational Choice*. Cambridge, Mass.: Harvard University Press, 1989.

———. *Goods and Virtues*. Oxford: Clarendon Press, 1983.

———. "The Rationality of Aesthetic Value Judgments." *Journal of Philosophy* 68 (1971): 821–39.

Smart, J. J. C., and Bernard Williams. *Utilitarianism: For and Against*. Cambridge: Cambridge University Press, 1973.

Sober, Elliott. "Philosophical Problems for Environmentalism." In Norton, ed., *The Preservation of Species*, pp. 173–94.

Sowden, Lanning. Review of Parfit, *Reasons and Persons*. In *Philosophical Quarterly* 36 (1986): 514–35.

Spiegel, Shalom. *The Last Trial: On the Legends and Lore of the Command to Abraham to Offer Isaac as a Sacrifice: The Akedah*. Trans. Judah Goldin. Woodstock, Vt.: Jewish Lights, 1993.

Stocker, Michael. "Desiring the Bad: An Essay in Moral Psychology." *Journal of Philosophy* 76 (1979): 738–53.

———. "Values and Purposes: The Limits of Teleology and the Ends of Friendship." *Journal of Philosophy* 78 (1981): 747–65.

Stout, Jeffrey. *Ethics after Babel*. Boston: Beacon Press, 1988.

Sturgeon, Nicholas L. "Harman on Moral Explanations of Natural Facts. *Southern Journal of Philosophy* 24, supplement (1986): 69–78.

———. "Moral Explanations." In Copp and Zimmerman, eds., *Morality, Reason, and Truth*. Cited from the reprint in Sayre-McCord, ed., *Essays on Moral Realism*, pp. 229–55.

Suárez, Francisco. *On Laws and God the Lawgiver* (*De legibus, ac Deo legislatore*). Cited by standard divisions from the portions in Suárez, *Selections*.

———. *Selections from Three Works*. Ed. James Brown Scott. Vol. 1, Latin texts. Vol. 2, English translations by Gwladys L. Williams, Ammi Brown, John Waldron, and Henry Davis. Oxford: Clarendon Press, 1944.

Swinburne, Richard. *Responsibility and Atonement*. Oxford: Clarendon Press, 1989.

Taurek, John. "Should the Numbers Count?" *Philosophy and Public Affairs* 6 (1977): 293–316.

Taylor, Charles. *Sources of the Self: The Making of the Modern Identity*. Cambridge, Mass.: Harvard University Press, 1989.

Taylor, Gabriele. "Love." *Proceedings of the Aristotelian Society* 76 (1975–76): 147–64.

Thomson, Judith Jarvis. *The Realm of Rights*. Cambridge, Mass.: Harvard University Press, 1990.

Tillich, Paul. *The Courage to Be*. New Haven, Conn.: Yale University Press, 1952.

———. *The Protestant Era*. Abridged edition. Trans. James Luther Adams. Chicago: University of Chicago Press, 1960.

———. *Systematic Theology*. Vol. 1. Chicago: University of Chicago Press, 1951.

Vlastos, Gregory. "The Individual as Object of Love in Plato." In Vlastos, *Platonic Studies*, pp. 3–42.

———. *Platonic Studies*. Princeton, N.J.: Princeton University Press, 1973.

von Fürer-Haimendorf, Christoph. *Morals and Merit: A Study of Values and Social Controls in South Asian Societies*. London: Weidenfeld and Nicolson, 1967.

Wallace, James D. "Excellences and Merit." *Philosophical Review* 83 (1974): 182–99.

———. *Virtues and Vices*. Ithaca, N.Y.: Cornell University Press, 1978.

Wiggins, David. "Truth, Invention, and the Meaning of Life." In *Proceedings of the British Academy* 62 (1976). Reprinted in Sayre-McCord, ed., *Essays on Moral Realism*, pp. 127–65.

Williams, Bernard. *Ethics and the Limits of Philosophy*. Cambridge, Mass.: Harvard University Press, 1985.

———. *Moral Luck*. Cambridge: Cambridge University Press, 1981.

———. "Persons, Character, and Morality." In Rorty ed., *The Identities of Persons*. Reprinted as chap. 1 of Williams, *Moral Luck*.

Wolf, Susan. "Moral Saints." *Journal of Philosophy* 79 (1982): 419–39.

Wolterstorff, Nicholas. *Divine Discourse: Philosophical Reflections on the Claim That God Speaks*. Cambridge: Cambridge University Press, 1995.

Zaehner, R. C., trans. *The Bhagavad-Gita*. Oxford: Clarendon Press, 1969.

Zagzebski, Linda. Review of Audi and Wainwright, eds., *Rationality, Religious Belief, and Moral Commitment*. In *Faith and Philosophy* 6 (1989): 103–10.

Zimmerman, David. "Moral Realism and Explanatory Necessity." In Copp and Zimmerman, eds., *Morality, Reason, and Truth*, pp. 79–103.

INDEX